Museum, Archive, and Library Security

Lawrence J. Fennelly

BUTTERWORTHS
Boston • London

Library of Congress Cataloging in Publication Data

Fennelly, Lawrence J., 1940-
     Museum, archive, and library security.
     Bibliography: p.
     1. Museums—Security measures. 2. Archives—Security measures. 3. Libraries—Security measures.
I. Title.
AMI48.F46 1983   069.5'4   82-14741
ISBN 0-409-95058-0

Published by Butterworth Publishers
10 Tower Office Park
Woburn, MA 01801

10 9 8 7 6 5 4 3 2 1

Printed in the United States of America

To the important people in my life....
my wife *Annmarie*....my children,
Alison-Margaret, Larry, Billy and *Stephen*.

Contributors

Stephen J. Allen, Public Relations Consultant, Stephen J. Allen and Associates, Boston, Mass.

Donna Carlson, Administrative Assistant, Art Dealers Association of America, Inc., New York, NY

C.G. Coates, Director of Security, National Museum of Canada, Ottawa, Ontario, Canada

Saul L. Chafin, Harvard Union Police Department, Cambridge, Mass.

Keith Forbes, Director of Security, Los Angeles County Museum of Art, Los Angeles, CA

Osborne Frazier, Director of Security, National Board of Education, Newark, NJ

Alain Goffier, Head of Security, The Louvre Museum, Paris, France

John E. Hunter, Museum Curator, National Park Service, Lincoln, Neb.

Albert S. Janjigian, Vice President, Aritech Corporation, Framingham, Mass.

Byron M. Johnson, Division of Building Research, National Research Council of Canada, Ottawa, Ontario, Canada

Herman Kreugle, Vice President, Visual Methods, Inc., Westwood, NJ

Steven Keller, Chicago, Ill.

John B. Lawton, Fine Arts Insurance Consultant, Huntington Block Insurance, West Hartford, CT

J. Laurie Paulhus, Security Director (Retired), National Art Gallery, Ottawa, Ontario, Canada

Leonard Poteshman, Sgt. Retired, Los Angeles County Sheriffs Dept., Art Theft/Fraud Unit, Los Angeles, CA

Renata Rutledge, Institute of Museum Services, Washington, DC

Charles Schnabolk, Institute for Museum Security, New York, NY

Lou Tyska (Past President of the American Society for Industrial Security), Director of Security, Revlon, Inc., New York, NY

Hans Urbanski, Erste Allgemeine Versickerunys Aktiengesellschaft, Vienna, Austria

Timothy G. Walch, National Historical Publications and Records Commissions, Washington, DC

Stephen U. Weldon, Superintendent, Winterthur Museum, Winterthur, Del.

Joseph Wylie, Northeast Director of Sales, Wachanhut Corp., Boston, Mass.

Contents

Foreword xi

Preface and Acknowledgements xv

I. Introduction 1
1. Introduction to Museum Security 3
2. The Many Facets of a Museum Security Director's Job 17

II. Risk Management 31
3. The Insurance of Objects of Art 33
4. Insuring Works of Art 49
    Appendix 4.1 Fine Arts Insurance 58

III. Managing Museum Security 65
5. Museum and Gallery Security Management Techniques 67
6. Common Sense Security for Museum Libraries 93
7. Fundamentals of Public Relations Communications 111
8. Crisis Public Relations Communication 131

IV. Fire Prevention and Emergency Planning 163
9. Building Security and Fire Safety 165

10. Fire Protection Systems and Fire Prevention Techniques 177
     Appendix 10.1 Fire Training Program 233
11. Museum Disaster Planning 235
     Appendix 11.1 Emergency Procedures for Libraries 271
     Appendix 11.2 Salvage of Water-Damaged Library Material ... 277

V.   **Security Methods for Museums, Art Facilities,
     and Libraries** 281
12. Security Theory for a Large Museum 283
13. Intrusion Detection Systems for Residences, Libraries, Small
     Museums, and Art Galleries 297
     Appendix 13.1 Specifications for a Fully-Zoned Ultrasonic
     Intrusion Alarm System 315
     Appendix 13.2 Application Guidelines for Exterior Intrusion
     Detectors 321
     Appendix 13.3 Application Guidelines for Interior Intrusion
     Detectors 324
     Appendix 13.4 Terms and Definitions for Intrustion Alarm
     Systems 327
14. Designing Security Alarm Systems for Libraries, Museums,
     and Art Facilities 341
15. Standards for the Design, Installation, Testing, and Maintenance
     of Interior Intrustion Detection/Alarm Systems 373
16. Museum Television Security 427
     Appendix 16.1 Glossary of CCTV Terms and References 486
17. Physical Security Standards 495
18. The Security Survey 505
     Appendix 18.1 Perimeter Protection 519
     Appendix 18.2 Lighting and Security 523
     Appendix 18.3 Locks and Key Control 529
     Appendix 18.4 Files, Safes, and Vaults 538
     Appendix 18.5 Intrusion Alarms 550
     Appendix 18.6 Security Surveys for Libraries 552
19. Security Inspection and Evaluation 557
20. Transportation of Cultural Art Objects 579

VI. **The Security Force** 589
21. The Guard Force 591
22. Job Descriptions for Security Supervisors and Security
     Officers 619

23. Developing Policies and Procedures 635
Appendix 23.1 Post Orders 667
24. The Museum Guard Pocket Manual 679
25. Guidelines for Guard Training 699
26. Motivating Security Personnel 713
27. Vicarious Liability of Security Administrators for the
Actions of Their Guards 727

VII. Art Theft and Investigation 739
28. Interpol Symposium on Thefts of Works of Art and
Cultural Property 741
29. Reporting Stolen Works of Art 767
30. Art Theft Investigation 779

Bibliography 807
Index 877

FOREWORD

This book meets an urgent need. Experienced professional practitioners from throughout the world have here, for the first time, shared their skills in a series of practically-oriented studies which address the immediate concerns of all those entrusted with the protection of precious objects and the documentation of mankind's heritage.

This book comes at a moment when new museums, libraries, corporate data centers, and archives are being planned and when older repositories require renovated security systems to prevent loss, vandalism, plagiarism, espionage, as well as ever more sophisticated methods of computer-theft and the illicit traffic in antiquities and art objects.

The editor of these studies has for over a decade supervised the protection at Harvard University of extraordinarily diverse collections — ranging from delicate fossils, the oldest map, and the famous "Glass Flowers" to "moon rocks," secret diplomatic documents, and dangerous samples of genetic engineering produced by experimental manipulation of DNA molecules.

The Institutes which contain these various collections are as diverse as their contents. Thus, Mr. Fennelly's work has required the design, installation, and management of security systems in historic halls, which are themselves architectural treasures, in modified old buildings which through generations had been constantly adapted and re-adapted for many different functions, as well as in modern structures carefully designed to simultaneously facilitate instruction, research, safe-storage, and displays.

The people served by Mr. Fennelly's security measures include Nobel laureates, technicians, students, tourists, school-children, and scholars from every nation — as well as those kings whose 4000 year-old archives are being preserved intact here and, we hope, those untold future generations who will learn from them.

In the course of his Harvard responsibilities, the editor has consulted extensively with security officials from other institutions throughout the world, and eminent specialists in electronic surveillance, insurance, training of guards, and all aspects of the protection of collections. Experience gained in compiling his previous book on *Crime Prevention & Loss Prevention* has enabled Mr. Fennelly to select contributors and topics for this book with an eye to what will prove most useful.

In some ways protection of collections is as old as mankind itself: In the Genesis account of the Forbidden Fruit, a sophisticated psychological "silent alarm" system seems to have incriminated Adam and Eve by a detectable change in their behavior. Long before writing, the enormous fortifications at pre-pottery Neolithic Jericho indicate that, despite the sweltering heat at our Globe's lowest spot, fear of unwanted intrusion required the laborious construction of a security system 6000 years ago.

The very letters you are reading on this page seem to be the result of early efforts to protect precious objects! Writing seems to have started separately but at about the same time (3500 B.C.) in both Egypt and Mesopotamia — as security systems.

From the banks of the Nile, the earliest hieroglyphs we can decipher seem to be 'badges,' official symbols such as crowns or animal totems which later usage confirms as the designations of rank and regions. Adorning knife handles and ceremonial objects (such as knob-like mace-heads and cosmetic palettes), those badges are sometimes combined with battle scenes which probably depict specific incidents during the reigns of rulers who we know only by their symbols such as King 'Scorpion.' Still today those badges proclaim that the objects they ornament belonged in one way or another to the collection of each badge owner.

From the Tigris and Euphrates plain, the earliest messages we can understand clearly are lists of objects: schematically rendered as pictographs of tripod-stands, vases, livestock, or sleds used before the introduction of wheels. Each object-type is followed by strokes which obviously stand for numbers. These inventories of temple collections may themselves have derived from even earlier systems of 3-dimensional tokens. From as late as 1500 B.C., on the outside of a hollow clay tablet (excavated by Harvard at the site of Nuzi) were listed the quantity of sheep which belonged to each of three different herders, while inside rattled the appropriate number of pebbles.

Even long after writing systems had fully developed, seals continued to be used to control documents, packages, and doorways by inspiring fear that unauthorized access could be detected. A uniquely clever seal forgery (also from 1500 B.C. Nuzi) has been recently found to demonstrate that in antiquity custodians of collections could have profited from prophylactic skills similar to the expertise assembled by Mr. Fennelly in this book.

It is devoutly to be hoped that these studies mark the beginning of a new era of international cooperation among those responsible for preserving humanity's cultural legacy.

Dr. Carney E. S. Gavin
Curator, The Harvard Semitic Museum

Dr. Carney E. S. Gavin is;
— Associate Director and Curator of the Harvard Semitic Museum
— Chairman, Harvard University Museums Council's Committee on Decessioning and Committee on Photographic Rights and Reproduction Policy
— Director, UNESCO-sponsored International F.O.C.U.S. Project
— Senior Consultant for the planning of the Museums of Bahrain,
— Honorary Member, Friends of Old Damascus

Preface and Acknowledgements

Over the past several years I have often wondered about the lack of readily available information on security for museums, art galleries, and libraries. There are certainly many of these institutions throughout the world, and many have a security director. Surely there is a need to protect rare and cherished art treasures and cultural objects. Why so few books? I believe that the simple reason for this is that the subject is so large and complex that it discourages would-be authors from writing.

Museum, Archive, and Library Security is a contributed book which attempts to address all of the security related problems that are likely to arise. Thus, I gathered material covering such important topics as insuring works of art, security management, fire prevention, emergency planning, security methods, policy and procedures for the guard force, training, and investigation. Since these concerns are international in scope, I invited experts from many countries to share their expertise. It was my intention to produce a practical, comprehensive reference that would assist security directors, curators, archivists, and librarians in the protection of their rarities and works of art.

Although the emphasis is on museum security, most of the information here can easily be applied to galleries, libraries, and residences and corporations which display valuable objects.

I will be forever grateful to the many professionals for their cooperation, assistance, friendship, and especially for their confidence in me in undertaking this project.

My sincere thanks to all the contributors who made this book possible. Without their help, guidance and involvement it would not have been possible to complete.

A special thanks to Saul Chafin, Jack Morse, and George Walsh whose continuous support does not go unnoticed; to Dave Priestly who read much of this material; and to Lee Kirkwood and Tom Kissane CPP who stimulated my interest in the art world.

My deep appreciation and thanks to the following for their guidance and assistance when we were in the early stages of development: Robert Burke, Dave Liston, E.B. Brown, Donna Carlson, Donald Mason, John Hunter, Chuck Coates, Alan Gore, Steve Keller, Keith Forbes, Dave Bailey, Kevin Fennelly, David Muir, Alan Erickson, Lou Tyska CPP, Cliff Crane, John Maloney, and a special thanks to the staff at the Milton Library.

To the secretarial staff who aided me in completing this book — Susan Tilly, Vickie Fox, Jo-Ann Jordan, Claire O'Callaghan, Carol Blute and Marie Mooney — thank you very much.

L.J.F.
1982

I. INTRODUCTION

1. Introduction To Museum Security

John E. Hunter

My purpose here is to introduce you to the security programs of the National Park Service. Before doing so, I think we should agree on just what we mean when we use the term "security" or refer to "museum security" in particular.

To most people, security usually means only protection against theft and possibly vandalism. Certainly prevention or detection of theft and vandalism is very important and becoming increasingly so. But security does not refer only to theft and vandalism. A good security program is concerned with *all* risks. Museums and other park facilities are threatened by burglary, vandalism, robbery, bombings, bomb threats, arson, accidental explosion, earthquake, flood, tornado, fire, and other similar events. Our staffs and visitors are threatened by these same events as well as assault, robbery, rape, and other crimes against persons.

Thus, we see that security is supposed to be concerned with all risks. Since we are concerned mainly with museum security, how may we define it? I think that museum security is *a mechanism that provides for the protection of col-*

This chapter was originally a speech given at the Basic Curatorial Methods Course, Mather Training Center, November 17–21, 1980. The following article is considered a U.S. Government work, and no copyright for this information is asserted by the author or this publication. Published with the permission of the National Park Service, U. S. Department of the Interior.

lections, equipment, information, personnel, and physical facilities and that prevents influences that are undesirable, unauthorized, or detrimental to the goals or the well-being of the museum. I shall discuss the following aspects of Park Service museum security:

- The Service's regulations and policies on the protection of property, particularly museum property.
- The Service's physical security program, particularly as it applies to the protection of museum collections.
- Some of the resources you can depend upon for assistance in improving the security of your own park museum.

REGULATIONS AND POLICIES
OF THE NATIONAL PARK SERVICE

The Service's security and crime prevention programs have their basis in the various statutes requiring federal agencies to properly manage and protect their buildings and other property. The most pertinent statute is Title 40 of the United States Code entitled "Public Buildings, Property, and Works." Paragraph 486(c) of Title 40 requires the head of each executive agency to issue such orders and directives as may be necessary to carry out the government's property management regulations.

This and other statutes have been translated into the *Code of Federal Regulations.* The most pertinent part of the code is contained in Title 41, which is "Federal Property Management Regulations." Part 101, Subpart 20.5, is entitled "Physical Protection"; it prescribes policies and methods for the physical protection of buildings and grounds operated by GSA and other federal executive agencies. Other CFR parts that govern our security program include the Department of the Interior's property management regulations in Part 114 of CFR 41.

The Department of the Interior has supplemented CFR 41. Chapter 1 of Part 444 of the *Departmental Manual* "provides guidelines on that part of the Departmental security program related to measures designed to safeguard personnel; prevent unauthorized access to Federal real and personal property and records and safeguard against espionage, sabotage, vandalism, and theft." Part 306 of the *Departmental Manual* provides further guidance, in this case for the protection of automatic data processing equipment and information.

In addition to these codes and regulations, our security program is governed by the NPS *Management Policies.* The *Policies* are the park's primary reference source in the day-to-day conduct of the security program. Chapter 5 of the *Policies* requires the Park Service to "protect for optimum preservation all historic objects entrusted to its care." In this same chapter, under the section entitled "Security Measures for Cultural Properties," we read: "In the management and maintenance of its cultural resources, the National Park Service shall employ the most effective concepts, techniques, and equipment to protect them against fire, theft, and other threats without compromising their integrity."

This same section goes on to require security surveys for parks, security systems where needed, compliance with fire codes, and the use of fire detection and suppression systems where warranted. Chapter 7, "Use of the Parks," gives further policies for crime prevention, physical security, and structural fire prevention.

The newest and best source of guidance and instruction regarding Park Service museum security is NPS-28, the new *Cultural Resources Management Guidelines*. In NPS-28 we find, for the first time, a description of the acceptable forms of protection for historic structures and museums. We also find the first strong statement of a heretofore largely ignored Park Service policy, namely: if a cultural resource, such as a furnished historic house, cannot be protected in any other way, then changing its public use to avoid threatening situations must be considered. Later I will talk more about NPS-28 when discussing potential protective measures for museums.

The last source of instruction on security matters that you should know about is the NPS publication *Manual for Museums*. Chapters 4 and 12 and Appendix G of the *Manual* contain many helpful suggestions that can be followed by park museum staffs. Similar, but not as detailed, information may be found also in Paragraph I of the NPS *Museum Handbook,* primarily in Appendix G.

THE PHYSICAL SECURITY PROGRAM

The Service's Physical Security Program was developed in response to a steady increase in the number of burglaries, larcenies, and acts of vandalism that have occurred within the Park System over the last few years. The traditional approach to law enforcement — apprehension of the person who has committed a criminal act — appeared no longer capable of dealing effectively with crimes against property. It became obvious that a new approach to combating these crimes was needed if we were to adequately protect the cultural, natural, and fiscal resources entrusted to our care.

In January 1974 the staff position of Physical Security Specialist was created within the Division of Protection in the Washington Office. The person assigned to this position, Captain Weston P. Kreis of the U.S. Park Police, developed goals and objectives for the new Physical Security Program.

Program Goal: Protect and preserve National Park Service and concessioner property with special emphasis upon historic structures, objects and sites.

Program Objectives: 1. Reduce the number of opportunities available to persons to commit acts of vandalism, larceny, robbery, burglary, and arson.
                                         2. Deter or detect the illegal intruder.
                                         3. Detect the presence of fire and smoke in buildings.

Later in 1974 the Washington Office directed each regional office and service center to appoint a Physical Security Coordinator to assist the Physical Security Specialist in realizing these goals and objectives. In most regional offices, the Regional Law Enforcement Specialist was given the assignment as a collateral duty. In a few regions, such as mine, other staff members received the assignment. This situation continues today. Unfortunately, because of funding constraints and personnel ceilings, no region has a full time Physical Security Coordinator.

Our Physical Security Program has been based and implemented on one primary concept, that of *crime prevention*. The currently accepted definition of crime prevention is: "The anticipation, the recognition, and the appraisal of a crime risk and the initiation of activities to remove or reduce it."

Operating on the basis of this fundamental concept, the Physical Security Program seeks to remove or reduce crimes against our property by reducing the opportunities for criminal activity in all units of the Park System.

This approach to physical security is based on another concept or equation: MEANS + MOTIVE + OPPORTUNITY = CRIME. In the Park Service, we are in no position to influence the motives of potential criminals or to eliminate their skills. However, we are in a position to affect dramatically the opportunities that exist for criminal activity. And opportunity reduction has proven to be a highly effective means of reducing property losses from vandalism and burglary. Obviously, because opportunity reduction is one way to remove or reduce the chances of a crime occurring, it must be instituted before the fact, not after it; hence, it becomes one form of crime *prevention*.

The thrust of the Physical Security Program over the past six years has been along four main lines: employee training, standards development, preventive planning, and correction of existing problems.

Employee Training

Our training efforts are intended to make employees aware of the extent and causes of our crime and security problems and to give them the skills needed to combat these problems. Five Service-wide security courses have been held, the first in 1975 at Mammoth Cave National Park and the others at the Federal Law Enforcement Training Center in Glynco, Georgia. About 150 Service employees have taken this one-week course. Our law enforcement rangers receive about eight hours of physical security instruction during their initial, eleven-week introductory training course and several hours during their annual one-week refresher training courses. Several of the Regional Physical Coordinators have sponsored one-week courses for employees in their respective Regions, including one developed mainly for park concessioners.

Several of the Regional Coordinators and some law enforcement Rangers have attended the National Crime Prevention Institute in Louisville, Kentucky. We participate to varying degrees in the activities of the American Society for Industrial Security and the National Burglar and Fire Alarm Association. Some of us have attended the Art Security Institutes offered by the University of Delaware and the University of Minnesota.

Standards Development

As far as standards development is concerned, the Park Service has adopted the standards published by Underwriters Laboratories and the National Fire Protection Association. We also have adopted the standards being produced by the Law Enforcement Standards Laboratory and the Fire Research Center of the National Bureau of Standards. These performance standards deal with such matters as intrusion and fire detection devices, door and window assemblies, locking devices, and equipment for law enforcement personnel and patrol vehicles. By utilizing these free, scientific sources of information, we are better prepared to adopt and employ cost-effective security and fire protection measures.

In addition to following standards developed by others, we have developed certain standards in-house. The Division of Museum Services here at Harpers Ferry has promulgated standards for the design and construction of museum exhibits. These standards — when followed — ensure that the safety and security of objects on exhibit will receive a high priority during the design phase of an exhibits project. Standards for the protection of historic structures in accordance with the general requirements found in the *Management Policies* have now been published in the new *CRM Guidelines*. We are hopeful that these standards will form the basis for the uniform application of cost-effective protective measures for furnished historic structures and, to some extent, for visitor center museums.

I have been involved with developing performance standards for the various types of intrusion detection and alarm systems we often use in our buildings. At the moment, these standards are in the form of a draft document entitled "Design Criteria for High-Security Interior Intrusion Alarm Systems." This document has been used on a trial basis several times to guide in the design of intrusion detection systems for park visitor centers. It is about to be used in an historic structure for the first time. Eventually, I hope to work the bugs out of this document and submit it for Service-wide adoption. Once this has been done, I anticipate developing similar design criteria for fire detection systems.

Preventive Planning

The third of the four elements of the Park Service Physical Security Program is preventive planning. This element consists of two parts. The first is an effort to "design out" security problems during the planning stages of a project. The second involves writing and implementing a Crime Prevention and Physical Security Plan for each park and office in the System.

The first part, that of designing out problems, requires the cooperation of architects, engineers, exhibit designers, historic preservation specialists, interpreters, maintenance personnel, curators, and others who are involved in various ways during the planning process. Designing out potential problems takes place whether the plans are for a new exhibit in an existing visitor center, for a new visitor center with new exhibits, for the refurnishing or restoration of an historic house, or for an historic structure that is to be used adaptively for offices, quarters, or other park functions. In the initial stages of the planning process, requirements are established for the level of security that will be needed, based on the nature and value of the structure and its contents. At all subsequent stages, the plans are reviewed by people such as myself to ensure that these requirements will, in fact, be met in the finished product.

For example, if I am reviewing the plans for a new visitor center that will include an exhibit room and space for a museum collection storage, I will examine the plans and specifications for the building as if I were a burglar trying to gain access. I will look at door and window hardware, glazing, lighting, roof construction, routes for access to openings and to the roof, check for places in which to hide, and try to determine if an intrusion detection system will be required to compensate for any weaknesses inherent in the design when the design itself cannot be changed. If potential problems are found during this review, I will prepare written comments and suggestions for corrective action for submission to the designer. Generally, my Regional Director will indicate to the Denver Service Center or to the Harpers Ferry Center that the problems will have to be corrected before the plan can be approved. On occasion, however, round-table meetings of the professionals within the regional office will conclude that the correction of some problems will not be cost effective or that they can be dealt with just as effectively after construction is completed.

My experience has been that few architects and exhibit designers, even those who have worked for the Park Service for many years, appreciate the necessity for good security in a museum or furnished historic house. This is one area in which our Physical Security Program has met with only mixed success. However, I am optimistic that continued rejection of plans by those of us in the regional offices and future strict adherence to the security standards now in NPS-28 will eventually result in museum and exhibit plans that have no security problems inherent in their designs.

The second part of preventive planning is a relatively new one: the development of Crime Prevention and Physical Security Plans for each unit and office of the Park System. This program element was instituted in January 1979 by memorandum from the Washington Office. Portions of two paragraphs from this memorandum will explain why we have these new Plans.

> The National Park Service began a physical security program in 1974. Since then we have provided crime prevention instruction to employees; appointed physical security coordinators in the Washington office, regional offices, Denver Service Center and Harpers Ferry Center; and developed informational materials for visitor use. Statistical evidence for the past several years reveals a progressive increase in the number of larcenies and burglaries committed. This has led us to conclude that many of our park areas have done little, if anything, to prevent this type of criminal activity. We believe that sufficient time has elapsed in which to analyze potential crime risks and provide initial preventive planning. The traditional request for additional personnel may be legitimate in certain circumstances, but it must be recognized that other options are available for the reduction of crime in our parks.
>
> Effective with the receipt of this memorandum, each region and park shall develop a crime prevention program as provided for in the Management Policies. Each program shall, as a minimum, include the following:
> 1. A security survey to determine vulnerability to criminal activity.
> 2. Preventive measures to reduce or eliminate vulnerability.

Over 95 percent of the parks and offices in the System now have the plans required by the Washington Office. While each park's plan is written to deal with its own peculiar crime prevention and security problems, all the plans have certain common features. Among them are:

1. The leadership and participation of management in the development and operation of the security program.
2. Regular security surveys by qualified personnel and a provision for corrective actions to be taken in response to the results of the surveys.
3. The orientation and training of all employees (permanent, temporary, seasonal, and volunteers) in security awareness, with emphasis on proper attitudes and defining each employee's security responsibilities.
4. An appropriate level of security for all park property, including collections, capital equipment, supplies, buildings, money, firearms, and historic sites, monuments, and ruins.
5. An appropriate level of security for all concessioner property.
6. Security and protection of all visitors and employees against such

crimes as robbery, assault, rape, and thefts from cars and camp sites.
7. Dissemination of crime prevention information to all visitors via posters, handouts, and messages in interpretive presentations if appropriate.
8. An annual review and analysis of the park's crime and security problems followed by implementation of appropriate preventive measures and necessary changes to the park's Plan.
9. Appointment of a collateral duty Physical Security Coordinator in each park and office to work with his counterpart in the Regional Office.

It is too early to tell whether having Crime Prevention and Physical Security Plans for each park will reduce crime and improve security. But even if the future reduction of incidents is not dramatic, at least the effort of preparing and implementing the plans makes everyone involved think about his role in solving the park's problems and has heightened security awareness at all levels. If we can maintain this sense of personal responsibility, I think the plans will prove to be the best part of our overall program.

Correction of Existing Problems

Correcting security problems in existing facilities is the fourth element of our Physical Security Program. This work generally is carried out by the park staffs with guidance from the Regional Physical Security Coordinator, usually in the form of a Physical Security Survey Report. These reports are prepared following intensive surveys of park facilities and interiews with key people on the park's staff. Survey reports may recommend changes in operating procedures, improved key control, replacement or augmentation of inadequate door and window hardware, installation of security glazing or lighting, installation of intrusion or fire detection systems, structural modifications to a building, addition of locks to exhibit cases, increased surveillance of exhibit areas during public hours, or creation of an emergency operating plan for protection of park resources in case of a disaster.

When I prepare a survey report, I explain the problems found and how they can lead to losses, offer one or more potential solutions to each problem, and then present a package of solutions that complement each other and that I consider to be the most cost effective approach to improving the overall security posture. Insofar as possible, I provide information about the cost of implementing each alternative solution or package of solutions so that the Superintendent can select one that will best fit his budget. I may also include copies of useful journal articles and copies of product literature or catalogs from manufacturers of security products that I believe could be used beneficially by the park.

My report goes directly to the park Superintendent, with copies to the Regional Director and to the Physical Security Specialist in Washington. The Superintendent is urged to implement as many of the corrective actions as he can within his own manpower and money resources. If additional manpower or money is required or if construction or renovation will be required, the Superintendent is urged to program for these resources or for the work at the earliest possible moment and to give these requirements a high priority in allocating funds within his annual budget. Occasionally, when a particularly acute problem is found, we are able to reallocate funds within the Regional Office or get a supplemental appropriation from Washington.

When conducting a security survey, some of the Physical Security Coordinators also will conduct a fire prevention survey. However, fire prevention generally is the responsibility of the Regional Safety Officer. Therefore, when fire hazards are encountered, they will be reported to the Safety Officer, who will institute corrective measures. If a fire detection system is needed, the Physical Security Coordinator and the Safety Officer may work together to plan the system, particularly if an intrusion detection system is to be installed at the same time. We find that fire protection in our facilities generally is not a problem, except in recently acquired structures, because fire prevention has been a strong, ongoing program of the Park Service for many years. However, fire detection systems in our buildings have not been common. We are currently emphasizing the need for good fire detection and hope to see systems in most buildings within a few years.

One of the most recent efforts of the Physical Security Program has been to encourage once again the complete cataloging of park museum collections on the principle that cataloged objects are less likely to be stolen and more likely to be recovered because a full description will be available to law enforcement agencies. Parks are encouraged to photograph their collections, or at least the more valuable or sensitive objects, and quite a few have done so. We also encourage the regular updating of the dollar values placed on individual objects in a collection so that Superintendents and other managers will be aware of the value of the property they are reponsible for protecting and preserving. This effort has met with very limited success owing to the unfamiliarity of many park staffs with the current market values of the objects in their collections and the difficulties and expense inherent in professional appraisals.

In this discussion of correcting existing security problems — the fourth element of the Service's security program — I have touched upon several ways to improve museum security. There are literally hundreds more we could discuss if space permitted. Since it does not, I want to outline ten *major* types of actions that can be taken in most park museums.

1. One person on the park staff should be given the responsibility for the security of the museum and its contents, as well as for putting into opera-

tion any protective measures deemed necessary. The individual selected for this duty should be thoroughly familiar with the museum and its collection. His responsibilities should include periodic, methodic checks of all rooms in the museum to detect any losses, to note evidence of any carefully planned "thefts in the making," to note any hazards to collections (such as leaking pipes or fire hazards), to observe the state of housekeeping, and to ensure that security devices are functioning. In many parks, these duties may be assumed by the park's Physical Security Coordinator. In others, such duties may more logically belong to the person in charge of the collection.

2.   Employee training sessions should include some time devoted to museum security. All employees should be reached by this training. Training should emphasize the need for alertness on the part of all personnel to guard against theft and vandalism. It should inform personnel of precisely what steps they may take when confronted by an incident, including not only reporting procedures, but also recommended conduct for the staff member who might interrupt a theft or other crime in progress. Prompt reporting of missing objects should be emphasized; personnel should also be encouraged to report unusual incidents, disturbances, or suspicious conduct.

3.   You should identify irreplaceable or particularly sensitive and attractive objects in the collection, especially those on exhibit. Carefully analyze the nature and effectiveness of the protection currently given such objects. Keep in mind that a locked glass exhibit case is not necessarily a good form of protection. Many museum thefts have occurred because someone simply broke out the glass. Sensitive objects often require additional protection, such as burglary-resistant glazing or an alarm on the case or perhaps storage in a safe rather than in a conventional storage cabinet. To provide additional protection at times of high risk, such as when the museum is very crowded or when special activities are taking place, consider altering normal personnel schedules and duty stations or assigning more personnel to attendant duty in the museum.

4.   Review the museum's opening and closing procedures. Closing procedures should include inspection of *all* areas for persons hiding in the building and for fire hazards. Opening procedures should include a thorough inspection of all exhibits and storerooms to check for possible unauthorized entry and for thefts during the night.

5.   Review your park's lock and key control system. Are adequate procedures in effect for checking keys in and out from a single responsible staff member? Have policies been established governing who has need for keeping keys permanently, overnight, or only during working hours? Distribution of keys to personnel having no need to enter an area after hours only increases the chances of a loss occurring because of lost or stolen keys. Laxity in key records invites unauthorized possession and duplication of keys and weakens security.

6. Carefully inspect the effectiveness of protection for your storage areas. Are they equipped with adequate locks? Are there policies governing the time when these doors may be unlocked and when they must be locked? Are there policies controlling who has access to these areas and under what conditions? Are these policies enforced?

7. Review your protection for museum property records. Are they safe from fire? Are they safe from theft or, if not, are duplicates of *all of them* kept elsewhere? Catalog and accession records should not be accessible to visitors, researchers, or non-museum employees except under your supervision. Thefts of an object and its associated records are extremely difficult to prove and to trace.

8. Consider providing cloakroom facilities for checking visitors' packs, briefcases, packages, and sharp objects (such as umbrellas) before they enter the museum or the historic house. Many museums and libraries that permit visitors to bring packages and briefcases into their facilities will inspect them on the way out. Some museums require visitors to check everything, even purses, when they enter. Such checking is especially useful when the facility is large or spread out or when many objects on exhibit are not behind glass, as is the case in furnished houses.

9. Consider the need for some type of intrusion detection system to either alert protection forces to an after-hours intrusion or to alert visitor center staff to an act of theft during public hours. Some systems will do both. An alarm system can be an appropriate and cost-effective means of supplementing existing physical and structural security measures. You must also consider the need for a fire detection system. A burglar might make off with one or two items; a fire can totally destroy your entire collection. When considerating alarm systems, it is vital that you remember that such systems offer no protection in and of themselves. They serve only as extensions of the eyes and ears of the staff: if there is no one to respond to an alarm, its ringing is of no value.

10. Consider including protection of the museum collection, or at least the most important objects, in the park's plan for handling fires, natural disasters, and other such emergencies. When a collection includes irreplaceable, extremely valuable, or unique objects, park personnel should be thoroughly trained to act promptly and properly in an emergency that threatens these objects and should be prepared to remove them from the museum after seeing to the safety of visitors and other staff.

All crime prevention and law enforcement authorities agree that security can never be guaranteed in any institution. That holds for museums as well. We must live with this reality and act accordingly. We must not lose sight of the fact that the museum collections of the National Park Service consitute a major cultural resource of this nation. These collections also are government property. They must be protected to the very best of our abilities.

RESOURCES

In developing a security program for your park and for your museum, rely on the people, the programs, and the resources existing for your benefit both inside the Service and out. Seek help from your park's protection staff when you do a security survey of the museum. Your park and regional Physical Security Coordinators are available to assist with a survey and to recommend corrective actions. Use these specialists; they are there to serve you.

There are also many security consultants outside the Service who can be brought in to develop a park museum security program. Some of them specialize in museum security, but most are generalists. Their services usually are expensive, but, if you have a particularly knotty problem that your park and regional office specialists cannot solve, hiring an outside consultant may be worthwhile.

Security directors of nearby private-sector museums can also be excellent sources of assistance. They usually have a great deal of experience, often in law enforcement, before coming into the museum world. Many maintain membership in various security and law enforcement organizations and can draw upon other members' experiences in solving problems. Among the organizations that can be tapped through museum security directors are:

- The Museum Association Security Committee of the American Association of Museums.
- The International Committee for Museum Security of the International Council of Museums.
- The American Society for Industrial Security which has a Museum Library, and Archive Security Committee.
- The International Association of Chiefs of Police.
- The National Burglar and Fire Alarm Association.

Finally, avail yourself of the many training opportunities that are open, both inside the Service and out. As I indicated earlier, the Park Service offers an annual one-week security course. Similar courses are offered from time to time by the regional offices. You can attend the courses at the National Crime Prevention Institute and at local colleges and universities, such as the University of Delaware and the University of Minnesota. The American Association of Museums and the American Association for State and Local History sponsor museum security seminars on an occasional basis as do state and regional museum associations and arts councils. Your Regional Curator can let you know what may be available in your region. If you are a member of museum or historical organizations — as you should be — you will be notified of seminars and workshops automatically.

In conclusion, let me remind you that the primary purpose of a park museum is the care and preservation of its collection for the present and future benefit of the people. This purpose sometimes is forgotten in the contemporary emphasis on the interpretation of collections and on the provision of a variety of visitor services. But we must remember that, without preservation and protection of the collection, there may be nothing to interpret and nothing to visit. All other programs and activities of the museum, no matter how desirable they may be, must remain secondary to the main obligation of the museum to protect its collections and other resources.

The state of museum security in the Park Service today is a reflection of how much concern Superintendents and park curators have for their responsibilities. Good security depends, ultimately, upon a determination of what measures management considers to be the most effective and upon a commitment to invest manpower and money in those measures. This commitment must be made even if it means diverting manpower and money away from other programs. It is up to you, as curators of park collections, to demonstrate to management the necessity of their making that commitment. In addition, you must personally do all that you can to improve security within the scope of your own personal area of responsibility and operation. The ethics of the museum profession demand no less of you.

2. The Many Facets of a Museum Security Director's Job

Renata Rutledge

What do Catherine the Great's snuff box, Professor Freud's cap, and George Washington's false teeth have in common? Mighty little, one would say, except that each one of these objects has been stolen from their respective museums in recent times. Their disappearance is representative of the widespread and diversified thievery that plagues museums, here and abroad. For instance, about 18,000 works of art are said to have been stolen in 1978 in the United States alone.[1]

It is safe to assume that the cultural property of museums, which have been in existence since antiquity, has been in peril of theft from the very start. Therefore, art theft itself is hardly a new phenomenon, but its alarming increase these last few years has caused great concern in the museum community. As a consequence, being in charge of the security and safety of an art museum has become a job of considerable importance and one that requires a wide variety of skills and talents.

A chief of museum security with a streak of the romantic in his soul (and there must be some of those) may well be imagined paraphrasing that famous poem by Browning and quote, in talking of the job at his museum: "How do I SERVE thee? Let me count the ways. . . ." And the ways will indeed be countless, complex, and extremely demanding. A quick rundown will show that the chief has to be an organizer, a firm disciplinarian, legal expert, diplomat and psychologist, technician with an understanding of electronics, computers, and all sorts of devices, a sleuth, a fire fighter, and effective public figure, a good administrator, and — last but not least — a lover of art (to a certain degree) and a person of endless energy and resourcefulness. In the UNESCO handbook on "The Guarding of Cultural Property" by William A. Bostick the job of the Chief Museum Security Officer is defined in these terms:

1. He should have extensive military or police training in security at both the working and the management level and be capable of planning and executing an overall museum security programme.
2. He should have taken some formal training in police work at the college level.
3. He should be legally deputized or have the necessary training to be deputized, which will qualify him to make an arrest and carry a gun.
4. He should have the personality and qualifications to act either diplomatically or firmly as the occasion requires.
5. He must have good powers of communication — both verbal and written.
6. He should report first to the business administration head of the museum and not to the building superintendent. His second superior should be the museum director.
7. His recommendations on security should be given considerable weight and only overridden by this immediate superior or by the director, preferably in writing. This is especially important in the installation of leading loan exhibitions.
8. He should have good relations with the personnel he supervises and those to whom he reports. He should get along well with members of the curatorial staff, as he must on occasion ask them to give precedence to security precaution over aesthetic considerations.[2]

Within this framework, certain priorities will have to be established. The first line of "defense" will be twofold: (a) a team of quality security personnel and (b) the implementation of a sound training program. The human element, the selection of the staff, and the training program will have to be approached with the specific institution in mind, because each museum, according to its type and the age and layout of its "plant" as well as the nature of its collection, presents specific and unique security problems. It is up to the chief of security to analyze these carefully and adapt a modus operandi accordingly. To implement concepts of an effective security set-up will of course require high-quality personnel. To attract desirable employees, weed out the potential weak links in the chain of command and establish not only paramilitary discipline but also mutual trust and proper motivation — these are some of the prime concerns of the security chief.

PROTECTING ASSETS

One of the many reasons that the duties of security have multiplied can be traced to the fact that the scope of cultural institutions has moved beyond the primary function of displaying works of art. Museums now play a significant role in education, research, and conservation and have in many cases become community centers with wide-ranging activities, serving a large and diversified public. This diversity of purpose and access necessitates the development of a highly individualized, far from standard type of security system that has to be designed for the unique character and functions of the museum.

Basically, the concept of guarding an institution full of highly valued, irreplacable objects that is open to the public presents its guardians with an ambiguous role. How does one act as a gracious host to millions while also maintaining the stance of an ever-alert "watchdog"? The role requires just the right mixture of tact and firmness. The key to the role is the establishment of very definite guidelines that will set the tone and create an atmosphere that will make the visit to the museum a pleasant experience. How friendly should a guard be? How responsive to a visitor seeking information (a ploy used by museum thieves)? How does one teach the staff to develop that "sixth sense" needed to spot potential troublemakers? It is the head of security who has to find a way to strike the delicate balance between being host and guardian.

An interesting new concept in surveillance has been established at the Georges Pompidou Centre of Art and Culture in Paris. Aside from the traditional guards, security is supplemented by a battery of hostesses who are not only bilingual guides but also, while conducting visitors about, serve to aid in the surveillance of the premises. This is an experiment that should be of interest to our museums, with their extensive corps of volunteers whose services could be utilized in a similar fashion. A security chief's job demands great ability in leadership and training of the personnel under his or her command.

Theoretically, technological advances have made the possibility of a high degree of security a reality. But all devices will only be fully effective when under the supervision of security officers who have complete knowledge and control of them. This is particularly true of any nighttime patrol. A classic example of the lack of integration of guard security and mechanical security is the case of the theft of the "Star of India" at the Museum of Natural History in New York. The security staff had simply never been told of the existence of a contact alarm attached to the case — and therefore had not turned it on.

The choice of the second requirement, protective devices and alarms, depends entirely on individual circumstances. The selection of appropriate equipment is preceded by a careful analysis of the location's physical layout, surroundings, types of exhibits, extent and training of its security force, interaction of the staff, fire protection, and the nature and speed of responses and counteraction available. A reliable combination of technical protection is of course an absolute requirement in small museums that may not have any nighttime patrol. As Shakespeare put it: "Take heed, have open eyes, for thieves do foot by night," an apt warning since most major museum thefts take place at night.

Contrary to other institutions, such as banks, factories, and storage areas, the importance of the aesthetic aspect of a museum also becomes a factor. Unaesthetic and obtrusive devices that upset the design scheme of galleries and exhibits are obviously out of place in an environment dedicated to the advancement of culture and to the best of man's and nature's creations.

To aggravate the problem further, there is the fundamental paradox of protecting priceless treasures without violating the free and relatively unrestricted environment that is so vital to a museum. If banks, in spite of their extreme vulnerability, are conscious of the extent of compromise necessary to provide a pleasant environment for their customers, while at the same time discouraging crime, how much more significant is this challenge in a museum or library, devoted to creating an aesthetic or unobtrusive setting for the enjoyment of beauty or intensive study? What then must be done to meet all these complex challenges? It would indeed be presumptious of me, like bringing owls to Athens, to talk to you, experts in the field who have much to contribute, about surveillance equipment and alarm systems. However, aside from the pure technology, the fundamental means of meeting the challenge must include the following considerations:

1. The quality of security personnel and its proper training, as well as its most efficient utilization and allocation.
2. The emphasis of security awareness of the professional staff of the institution and its strict adherence to security regulations; annual security reviews.
3. Clear identification of the institution's assets and their location — in other words, a precise inventory.
4. Evaluation as security risks of every new installation and exhibit design, integrating security concepts with architectural and display features.
5. Development of a crisis or disaster management plan that deals with such matters as crowd control, power failures, and other emergencies.
6. A comprehensive fire control program.
7. Libraries and archives require the additional precaution of careful

identificaion of readers, limited access to rare material, keeping logs of those who have access, and close control of material borrowed from the institution.

THE SECURITY DIRECTOR'S TASKS

It is up to the security director to develop esprit de corps as well as a sense of pride in the importance of the work the staff is involved in. A review of one of the most sophisticated and extensive training programs, that of Smithsonian Institution, reveals the breadth of the subjects covered. It ranges from the basic functions to understanding of the organizational structure; assistance to the public in giving information, assuring personal safety and handling special situations (VIPs, handicapped, special groups). Basic museum security branches out to include property and key control as well as access control; employee screening, communications, alarms, and manning posts as well as night supervision. Emergencies have to be dealt with and guidelines and procedures established for fire, accident, evacuation, reponse to crime, and natural disasters. Administrative duties include writing reports, scheduling, logistic control, weapons control, and maintenance. The supervisory role is examined in terms of leadership, motivation, performance rating, and union/labor relations. The roster of these subjects makes it clear that the chief of security must tackle many problems that extend beyond a daily, clockwork routine. Although theft and vandalism loom large in the life of a museum, one of the most feared dangers is that of fire. The enormous values involved here of objects that are irreplacable and may be irreparably damaged in a fire make the subject of fire prevention a primary concern of the security chief. He will have to be familiar with all the best and the newest in equipment available in the market and learn to evaluate and choose the most appropriate type. Once it is installed, he has to see to it that it is tested on a regular basis.

Preparedness for all kinds of other disasters has to be carefully mapped out by evolving operation procedures that will include drills for the whole museum staff, a knowledge of crowd control, and, given the tenor of our times, techniques to counteract terrorism.

It is obvious that the security director must maintain a close working relationship with the local police and fire departments. Routine inspection tours and testing of equipment are essential as a precaution, and local authorities should be apprised of such events as major loan exhibits and receptions at the museum. It is the director's function to encourage the entire staff to take an active interest in all security matters, although he may have to anticipate a certain degree of resistance or indifference, a complaint voiced by many security directors.

In spite of all the efforts and understanding that a security director may expend on his personnel, the ability to spot those who are troubled or just plain larcenous or vulnerable to outside pressures may not suffice to avoid one of the most painful and unpleasant aspects of the job: dealing with the danger from within, internal theft. When it happens, and it does with greater frequency in recent times, the director's skills as a sleuth, diplomat, and psychologist all may have to come into play. Internal thefts occur quite regularly now, in both small and major museums throughout the land. Neither such mammoths as Smithsonian (with its superbly trained personnel) nor the prestigious Metropolitan Museum and the Chicago Art Institute have been spared. And that's just the tip of the iceberg. For obvious reasons, museums are hesitant to admit to internal larceny.

Many a security administrator must have sleepless nights weighing the matter of whom he can trust and how far up in the museum hierarchy he may reach in establishing stringent rules of access and control, affecting the museum as a whole! No standard procedure, used throughout the museum community, exists at present, but most security directors strive for some kind of pass system and strict access control to make it easier for security to carry out its duty.

The Legal Aspects

A serious hindrance in assuring reliability and stability of personnel is the limitation set by law regarding meaningful background check and references of potential employees. Smaller institutions in particular cannot afford, on their limited budgets, to make thorough investigations and must largely depend on the "buddy" system of the network of security personnel to deal with the delicate question of an applicant's records via word-of-mouth recommendation.

A good grasp of certain laws applies not only to hiring and firing practices, but also to carrying out the chief's function as a law-enforcement officer vis-à-vis the public. He must be aware of all laws relating to the rights of individuals. A litigation-conscious citizenry will very quickly resort to legal action if there is any question of false accusation. Therefore, the chief must know all about criminal codes, the extent of guard authority, the Miranda law, search and seizure, and rules of evidence. In some museums where guards are armed, laws in regard to the use of weapons, weapons qualification, and instruction will have to be considered.

Modern Technology

Fortunately, modern technology for protection has made tremendous strides, so that beyond the reliance on the fallible human element, there is now a whole spectrum of computer science, electronics, and mechanical devices to aid in the safeguarding of the assets of a museum. The control center of a museum can be likened to its nerve center where every aspect of security, fire precaution, climate control, and conservation can be put under a guard's surveillance. Security chiefs, such as E. B. Brown of the Kimbell Art Museum at Ft. Worth, Texas, sometimes design their own console with built-in features that have become models of protective efficiency and effectiveness. Mr. Brown, an "apostle" of museum security, along with many others, is part of a network of professionals that meets and communicates on a regular basis to discuss and solve mutual problems. Because of their magnitude, national and international conferences have become more frequent and colleges offer seminars on the subject. Such organizations as UNESCO's International Committee on Museum Security (ICOMS) and the American Society for Industrial Security (ASIS) have contributed, through their literature, meetings, and communications, to making information more accessible to beleaguered security officers and assure the profession of a constant exchange of new concepts.

Yet the technical advances also point up still another headache associated with the profession. There is a great need to find a way to evaluate the many options. Little or no comprehensive objective test data are available at present to aid security directors in making the right choice of "hardware."

The conscientious security director will find himself confronted by such questions as what are the particular hazards of this display? what is its value? its vulnerability? how big a crowd will it attract and what will the traffic pattern be like? where should guards be stationed to supplement mechanical devices? These are some of the determining factors that will govern his choice.

Keeping up to date with the onslaught of a steady stream of new systems, new products, as security has entered the field of big business, makes heavy demands on the busy schedule of the director's days. Besides evaluating the new gimmicks in terms of the facility, there will be pressure from sales people and, once a selection has been made, an intricate sales and service contract will have to be scrutinized closely. It is essential that the director make sure to get not only the best product, but also the best possible service contract (a vital element in dealing with highly sophisticated equipment). No need to stress that, in times like these, security chiefs will have to go to battle to receive their slice of the ever-shrinking, inflation-ridden budget "pie." Ah, money! There's hardly a single, hard-pressed security director who will not tell a woeful tale of how long security has been relegated to being the museum "stepchild." In an interview that appeared in *Stolen Art Alert*, Allen Gore, director of security at the Metropolitan Museum of Art, has this to say — and we quote him at length, because it is so much to the point:

> For so long, the security department has been treated as a stepchild in the family. The security office was in the basement, while other administrative offices were upstairs. Quite often no more thought was given to security departments or their guards and supervisors than that they were to wear uniforms and act as scarecrows.
>
> Security is more complex and should be intricately involved in the management of the museum from its input into special exhibition areas for pedestrian control to fire safety. Security should play a strong role in museum life, and it should be at the ground floor level, when decision-making takes place and budget is put together.[3]

His concise statement is borne out by what is a common denominator in the many talks we had with security chiefs: a persistent complaint that too many museum administrations take a "locking the stable, after the horse is stolen" stance in dealing with security. The awareness for better security only emerges when the worst has happened. The classic example is that of an embattled security director at a West Coast art museum who is now, after years of pleading, getting the kind of system he had asked for for years. A security survey made the board and the administration see the light. But why this sudden responsiveness? Because of a major (and predictable) theft of one of the museum's prized paintings.

MUSEUM THEFT

The increase of museum theft can be traced to several causes. The tremendous expansion of the museum-going public at a time of shrinking support money has contributed to making the job of guarding museums much more difficult. There are now close to 5,000 museums in the United States that reported 350 million visitors in 1979, a figure which represents a 16 percent increase of attendance over the preceding five years. Art and history museums, the two types that display the greatest amount of art objects and are therefore most vulnerable to theft, reported a 36 percent or 125 million share of the total attendance.[4]

Just quoting a few further attendance figures, mostly at art exhibits, will demonstrate the massive crowds that are attracted to the special events, known as "blockbusters," in the last few years. Most recently the *New York Times* estimated that "a crowd twenty-five times the size of Napoleon's army had marched through three and a half miles of the Picasso exhibition's display of 1,000 paintings, sculptures, drawings and prints." Summing up the Picasso show's statistics, it seems that between 1.2 and 1.5 million people are believed to have seen the exhibit. Among other recent exhibits of blockbuster dimensions is of course the King Tutankhamen exhibit, which reportedly packed in 6 million people nationwide, while the Splendors of Dresden were viewed by 1.5 million in Washington alone. To dramatize these figures further, it has been established that museums attract *seven times* the crowds that attend the three major-league sports events (baseball, basketball, and football) *combined*!

Controlling such crowds, safeguarding them as well as the exhibit, is a job on the scale of a major military operation, with which the *Times* writer actually compared it. It requires organizational skills which must take into consideration every last detail, must take in every possible emergency, and puts a tremendous strain on a museum's facilities and staff. That all these operations, and only a few have been cited here, really came off without any major mishap and ran smoothly is very much due to highly sophisticated security techniques and excellent planning in our museums, and are a great credit to members of the security profession.

So here we have vast crowds drawn to museums with all the ensuing publicity. It is happening at a time of a never-before-experienced inflation in the value of art objects. This increase has, in some instances, grown fifteen-fold and the soaring prices at art auctions, galleries, and museum purchases frequently make headlines on the front pages of newspapers and are hyped by the media. Such pervasive publicity certainly tantalizes the art thief and contributes to the dramatic rise of art crime. Art thievery has attained global proportions and seems to be well supported by an international network of shady art dealers and criminal organizations of an as yet unknown magnitude.

In his highly informative book *The Double Market* (Hampshire, England: Saxon House, 1975) Keith Middlemas gives a lively account of the brisk trade in stolen art between countries and continents that does not differ too much from a description of legitimate world-wide commerce. It is so well entrenched that it seems almost hopeless ever to bring it under control.

Even trends in art theft have become apparent: with the soaring price of gold, gold objects and coin collections became prime targets. Generally, as thieves became more sophisticated and more wary of risks, it was often found that small artifacts were much "in demand." This may force security staffs to reevaluate alarm systems (for small cases in particular), examine certain areas that had previously been considered of minor importance, drawing minimum traffic. The necessity of rethinking previous designs for protection will call upon the security director's ingenuity and flexibility, as he is facing the challenge of changing patterns of behavior on the part of the public (and thieves in particular).

Now that the ugly specter of art theft has been raised, still another facet of the director's job emerges. Confronted with a loss, the director of security will have to conduct the first steps of the investigation; be prepared to face the media and a battery of inquisitive reporters; deal with the insurance people and the possibility of ransom; deal with the local police and, if the object is suspected to have been taken across state lines (which is usually the case) and is of considerable value, with the FBI and Interpol.

Several factors contribute to this upsurge of theft of cultural property:

1.   Cultural objects, and especially art objects, are enjoying an un-precedented boom, with the demand outstripping the supply, making art thievery a lucrative if risky profession. Rumors and speculation by the FBI indicate that organized crime now plays a part in these thefts, many of them committed on a "made to order" basis.

2.   The "art boom" has received a great deal of attention from the media. Record art sales, auctions, and purchases as well as thefts are mak-ing headlines almost on a daily basis. Publicity of this kind is not always harmful, as it sometimes alerts dealers to watch out for stolen articles, but on the whole the experts agree that too many recent stories, as the article in the *New York Times Magazine* that discussed security systems in great detail, may inspire more burglaries and therefore can do a lot of harm.

3.   "Blockbuster" exhibits, as mentioned before, not only draw huge crowds but also attract attention to the high value of the collections on display, an obvious incentive for burglary.

4.   There are novel motivations for theft and vandalism. Aside from per-sonal greed or the desire of an individual to acquire a particular ob-ject, some of these crimes are committed for ransom, for personal publicity, or as an expression of political protest. Even the specter of terrorism is not beyond the realm of possibility. A strategy for such an eventuality must be planned beforehand by museums as well as community officials.

CONSERVATION

Greater awareness of the importance of conservation also affects the security staff. Climate control and proper lighting are given a lot more attention, and it is not unusual that in smaller museums, with their limited budgets, the securi-ty force is charged with checking instruments and other paraphernalia of climate and light control. This adds another aspect to the security chief's chores, re-quiring the need to become knowledgeable of the characteristics of a wide vari-ety of materials and possess an understanding of the conditions necessary for their preservation. As if all these requirements are not sufficient to keep him occupied twenty-four hours a day, there is still another side to the so-called museum explosion that very much concerns the security force and adds another responsibility to a director's chores.

MUSEUM EXPANSION

Greater attendance, along with the expansion of collections, has lead to a widespread trend of building addition, reconstruction, and renovation. Although nearly half of the nation's museums have been founded since 1960, many of our venerable institutions are showing their age and have facilities that have become inadequate. The needs of the 1980s could hardly have been anticipated at the time many of our museums were built. Furthermore, conflicts of preservation versus security are not unusual in these older buildings. They become particularly problematic in historical buildings, where architectural integrity is to be maintained. But regardless of these sentiments, building projects abound.

Times of construction and renovation, with all their movement, displacement, traffic, and "invasion" of outsiders, are particularly trying for the security staff. Controlling the operation becomes a responsibility that has proved at times to be overwhelming, as witnessed by several major thefts that have occurred during building projects and were directly linked to them. It is often all too easy for workmen, who have been engaged in repairs and are therefore known to the guards, having access to all parts of the building, to be tempted to take advantage of the situation. Maybe one of the most celebrated cases of this kind was the theft of the *Mona Lisa* from the Louvre. It was taken in 1911 by Vincenzo Perugia, who had worked as a painter and decorator at the museum and therefore encountered no difficulty in removing the painting. In recent times, the celebrated Cézanne theft at the Chicago Art Institute was traced to a packer and framer, employed by the museum, who walked out with the "goods" during a period of redecorating and reinstallation.

New installations spell headaches for the director. Here again, there may be a whole new "ballgame" in the offing, when collections on loan (often arriving even at odd times of the night) have to be unpacked, moved about, and installed in such a way as to create an absolutely safe environment for them. Sometimes, the lender will spell out very specific conditions under which the exhibit must be displayed, thus necessitating a reassessment of existing systems.

One security director who is highly sensitive to the hazards of construction programs is Gerard Shirar, chief of security at the Boston Museum of Fine Arts, which is undergoing some major structural changes. It includes the addition of the new West Wing. In discussing the project, Mr. Shirar stresses several points. First of all, he participated in all phases of the planning of the new wing from the very start, so that the security system was treated as an integral component of the design for the wing. He also wrote all the specifications for the system. Once the plans were finalized, bonds were required to be posted by the competitive bidders to whom the plans were submitted. Furthermore, a whole series of stipulations were set up for the prime contractor regarding access control and constant surveillance of the traffic in and around the construction site. These rules were strictly enforced. Thus Mr. Shirar's role in the project was three-fold: his input in the planning of the security system, utilizing innovative concepts of control; his supervision of the construction itself, as it affected security; and the supervision and coordination with curatorial staff in the carefully phased clearing of certain areas that were affected by the new addition.

The new West Wing, now finished, was erected without any incidents and the smooth operation was, no doubt, due to all the well thought out preparation. The wing remained completely self-contained until the final days, when the connecting doors were opened. Access from the connecting roof is barred by a high fence, and scaffolding and ladders, simple and obvious means of entry that have sometimes been overlooked during construction "fever," were also rendered inaccessible.

This again is an example of the wide range of activity and the extent of the responsibility of a security director. It is important to keep in mind that a museum's security record plays a vital role in the very existence of the institution, when one considers the question of donors and loans. In order to attract donors or establish a lively exchange of exhibits, the security record for effective protection comes under close scrutiny. Special exhibits involve the director in the problems of art in transit, when packing and unpacking and seeing that the objects are safely loaded and unloaded become part of his domain.

Needless to say, insurance premiums certainly are to a large extent determined on the basis of a museum's clean safety record. When cost cutting is on everybody's mind, insurance costs are certainly an important item.

Now that all the challenges, headaches, and problems have been explored, why, one may ask, would anyone want to undertake the job of a security director in a museum? With all the pragmatism attached to the profession, a fair share of idealism should enter the makeup of the person who does this kind of work. Along with the headaches, there are also the rewards of the job. Certainly a person with a sense of beauty and a love of history will take pride in being charged with the protection of our cultural heritage. This would make the job meaningful, and so would the knowledge that one is making sure that future generations will be able to enjoy our patrimony. Museums have become a significant factor in our educational system and their functions have become vital in opening new vistas to our young people. There must be satisfaction in contributing to such an endeavor. Much progress has been made in encouraging and stimulating the arts in this quarter of the century. President Kennedy, looking at the importance of the arts in the long view of history, put it this way:

> The life of the arts, far from being an interruption, a distraction, in the life of a nation, is very close to the center of the nation's purpose — and is a test of the quality of a nation's civilization.

NOTES

1. Pranay Gupte, "The Big Business of Art Theft," *Portfolio* 1 (April/May 1979): 66.
2. William A. Bostick, *The Guarding of Cultural Property* (Paris: UNESCO, 1977), p. 20.
3. Allen Gore, in *Stolen Art Alert* 1 (November 1980).
4. *Museum Universe Survey & Museum Program Survey*: 1979 report conducted by the National Center for Educational Statistics.

II. RISK MANAGEMENT

3. The Insurance of Objects of Art

Hans Urbanski

It is perhaps a consolation to observe that a time like ours, which is described as being extremely materialistic, concedes to art, which can be taken as the epitome of materially inexpressible values, an ever more important role.

Perhaps it is in this sense also a consolation to observe how even those who, in disregard of the law, seek their livelihood in the field of crime, turn more and more to the appropriation of works of art, but obviously for the reason that their disposal seems possible in ever-wider strata of society; indeed, the desire for their acquisition is in many ways comparable to the passion of the diseased. There is no consolation in this context, however, for insurers, whose loss rates naturally rise in a correspondingly steep curve, nor is there much comfort for the citizen of a country which, proud of its laboriously built up treasure of art, feels the loss or destruction of prized works as a burning wound.

And so it is a timely undertaking to research the roots of that dangerous rank-growing marsh plant of our civilization, crime in the field of art, and

This chapter was originally a lecture given to the Austrian Insurance Technical Association on 29 January 1975 and printed as a special impression from Volume 3 of *Die Versicherungsrundschau,* magazine of the Association, for March 1975. Translation: J. I. Hamilton (7/7/75). It is reproduced here by permission of the author.

especially to shed light within the narrow framework of insurance on the known dangers surrounding objets d'art, and to point out the possibilities of preventing loss and seek forms of cover which meet insurance requirements.

THE PHENOMENON OF ART

In order to approach the problem one must endeavor to approach the remarkable phenomenon of art. It is often attempted to define the work of art more or less as the product of a creative act which expresses a particular idea of its author either through the originality of its form, its material, or its color: certainly a very vague definition, but others are little better. It is strange only that the concept of beauty does not appear in it or in most definitions, whereas the popular idea simply equates art and beauty.

I personally would include the concept of fascination as a factor in the definition of a work of art in the full knowledge that this does not constitute any particularly tangible greatness either, but rather points to the mystical unconscious. But it is precisely this which seems to me to be necessary for the explanation of the essence of art and above all its powerful effect on the great host of artistic laymen. In the far, far back moment in time when art was born, it was certainly not the sense of aesthetic beauty which guided the hand of the cave dweller in depicting the mammoth and the elk in red earth on the wall of his cave; no doubt it was rather the conjuring up of some supernatural power which might bring and preserve success in the hunt and, with it, life. From there through the Egyptian tumulus reliefs, which came to life to serve the gods, through the countless statues of gods and figurines of household gods, through the ruins of gigantic dwelling places of the deities, all art has been for age upon age nothing more than the superstitious redemption from fear of the disfavor of envious powers and the ardent beseeching of fate.

Relatively late, only in about the Periclean age, where, once freed from the Persian foe, the Grecian people shook off the other secret fears of dim and dank antiquity, art appears "in quiet simplicity and noble greatness," to borrow Winckelmann's words, freed at last from the fetters of cult, a wonderful symbol of, above all, the freedom of man.

Similarly the West felt, after the almost exclusive linking of art to the Christian church, the liberating springtime of the Renaissance, which, with the slogan consciously formulated in the last century of "art for art's sake," essentially defines even our present-day attitude to art. But never, even in those ages in which, like ours, people feel fully free, with a right to indulge in the strangest extremes in the field of creative art, never was the connection with primeval fears and wishes, even with a certain belief in hopes and superstition — in short, with a certain rationally indefinable fascination — quite supplanted.

Any frightful product of pop art which is presented as art annoys us, not as would an oversalted soup or a badly cut suit, but as blasphemous behavior toward a place of cult worship. Indeed, it seems almost as if we would like now, after the periods of "liberated art," which set harmony and beauty as goals in place of the exorcism of demons, to draw art back closer to its magic-irrational beginning. "When we beautify something we do it for the public, for ourselves the truth suffices," as a modern artist puts it, and I would like to add "the truth and the magic." Then the reason why the Venus of Willendorf, the Corsican rock pillars, and the stone pillars of the mysterious sun temple of Stonehenge have such a startling similarity with many good and true products of modern art is explained. This remarkable phenomenon of time, this new fascination of art, together with people's enormously improved circumstances and the pleasure of decorating one's home with works of art and opportunities of doing so, has called forth the boom in the art market which puts any gold rush, and successful stock-exchange speculation, in the shade for increase in value. In a materialistic society money is also a yardstick of sentiment, and the prices achieved in the last few years for works of art which, paradoxically, as good as remained unchanged under the effect of the worsened economic situation, are a proof of the fascination which the work of art exercises for whatever reason on our civilization.

THE VALUE OF ART AND ART THEFT

It is therefore not to be wondered at if the work of art, originally always a cult object, has been since earliest times the object of theft or destruction in order to deprive the enemy of the source of supernatural aid. Certainly soldiers in later times had primarily purely material aims in view, but even if one looks at the catalogue of the Burgundian booty which fell into the hands of the Swiss after the battle of Grandson, there is hardly a piece which derived its value purely from the material or from the perfection of its craftmanship. Rather was there in the main highly dubious, but for one reason or another revered, relics in the most magnificent mountings, precious stones which were good for this or that grief or illness, gold altars, illuminated prayer books, talismans, and amulets. If one could have asked these plain-thinking Swiss in the depths of their souls, the elimination of this magic was to them more important than the disappointingly small material gain.

Somewhat more systematic and already with an eye for true artistic value, the Swedes then plundered half of Germany. At last Napoleon set the record. I myself possess a six-volume work with the grand title *Le musee Napoleon,* which lists the works of art acquired by him.

Those individuals or associations of individuals, or, more commonly, gangs which in this sphere make life so unpleasant for us insurers find themselves in such distinguished company. Their activity is remarkable!

Thus, for example, there occurred on the same day, 11 November 1974, thefts of a collection of Utrillos, Picassos, etc., worth 4 million francs in Grasse, France; pictures to the value of 5 million francs from a rich American in Paris; objets d'art worth 1 million francs from the Chateau Thoiry; and a collection of ivory statuettes of incalculable value from an antique dealer in the center of Paris.

In France "only," 1,261 important pictures were stolen in 1970, 1,824 in 1971, 2,712 in 1972, 3,700 in 1973, and in 1974 well over 4,000.

In 1973 there were art thefts from 127 chateaux; 245 churches were broken into; and 53 museums and 69 big art dealers suffered burglaries.

I draw here on French observations because there the danger threatening works of art is, I believe, the most clearly recognized and the most promising protective measures are being elaborated — and also because insurance is setting itself on new paths.

The Mona Lisa

And so the most spectacular art insurance ever entered into has just concluded with the happy return of the *Mona Lisa*, undamaged, thank God, to the Louvre. It was insured, as it obviously has no market price, for an agreed value of 200 million francs, i.e., about 900 million shillings. The premium charged was 5 per mille, i.e., 1 million francs. A special floating container with temperature control was produced for it, of such a weight, however, that one man cannot move it. To avoid attention the picture was transported on an ordinary airliner, but without other passengers than the Director of the Louvre, a laboratory and installation team, police, and an insurance representative. For the flight over Soviet territory all military airports were put on alert. During the exhibition the *Mona Lisa* had to be guarded by a team of sixteen watchmen in addition to the normal museum security staff. A special exit into a strongroom had to be open permanently in case of emergency. War and political crimes — for example, piracy — were excluded from the insurance. The question of reduction in value in the event of damage is always a difficult one, and in this case was dealt with on the basis that in the event of a reduction in value of up to 20 percent a lump sum would be paid out, but if the reduction in value were greater a previously appointed arbitration court of five noted experts would decide on the matter.

The policy was written with the "Nordstern" of Paris as leader, which is rightly the crowning achievement of their manager there, Mr. Schmit, who is quite an outstanding expert and indeed today's leading art insurer. Half the world participated in the cover by way of coinsurance and reinsurance.

It is, in general, not too often that state property is insured, and in the Louvre the *Mona Lisa* is still uninsured. But at the beginning of the century it was the object of one of the first really large art thefts. It disappeared for a full two years and was finally discovered undamaged in the possession of an Italian worker, today one would say a guest worker, for whose national pride it was intolerable that this Italian work of art should be in French ownership.

Perhaps this incident was the reason that insurance on the picture was taken out. At the time it was held as an unshakable criminological proposition that all works of art were, for a thief, absolutely unconvertible into cash and there was hardly any stealing of widely known works of art apart from thefts committed for such strange motives.

The Ghent Altar

A second, no less sensational, theft of a hardly less famous painting revealed another way of realizing cash from a stolen work of art, namely blackmail, with the threat of destroying it. On the morning of 10 April 1934, the verger of the cathedral of Saint Bavon in Ghent discovered that the left leaf of the most famous so-called Ghent altar which was kept there, was missing. This folding altar, by Hubert van Eyck, who ranks as the father of northern European painting, already had an eventful history behind it. Kaiser Josef did not like the representations of Adam and Eve in extremely natural state and had banished them to the loft. In the turmoil of the revolution the altar was further dismantled and finally some leaves were sold. The purchaser was the King of Prussia, and these pictures were the showpiece of his Berlin gallery. Being a folding altar, both sides of the leaves are painted, and in order to show both sides they were cut in two. In 1919 Germany was obliged to return the pictures as reparation for the burning down of the Louvain library and so the Ghent altar was for the first time put fully together again.

But on 10 April 1934, the lower left leaf depicting the "Francs Juges" on the inside and John the Baptist on the outside, was taken. All investigations were in vain. Then the bishop received a letter containing a left-luggage ticket from Brussels Nord Station and saying that the Saint John was deposited there as proof that the writer had the other leaf, which would be returned on payment of 1 million francs. The Saint John was indeed found in the left-luggage depository. Endeavors were made to discover the letter writer, to set traps for him, but all in vain. After several months there was a church assembly at which a respected member of the church council became ill. The man requested a doctor, then a priest, then a lawyer, and explained that he wanted to say where the missing leaf was. Before the priest arrived the man had passed on. Copies of the blackmail letters were found on him, but to date there has been no trace of the missing leaf, which was finally replaced by a copy made from old photographs of the original. Here arose the delicate problem of how far restoration or reconstruction can go without being mere counterfeiting and so that the replacement could not be considered a counterfeit one of the Francs Juges has the facial features of King Albert and another those of Leopold III.

But the adventure of the Ghent altar was not yet at an end. To save it from the German invasion the Belgians removed it to the Chateau de Pau in the Pyrenees. The German art commissioner, Count Metternich, deserved much credit for preservation, but when he went to assure himself of the altar's condition, it had disappeared. The French commandant told him that a truck had come and taken it away on a "direct order of the Führer." Then strangely enough my own career as an art insurer became involved with the Ghent altar. In fact it was while I was busy for weeks on end, in the closed-down salt mine above Altausee, with the recording and valuing of the Rothschild collection for insurance of the transit to America, that the Ghent altar was found right there in a special cache.

Problem of Art Insurance

These weeks when I hardly saw daylight were among the most interesting of my life. They brought before my eyes in graphic form the whole spectrum of the problems of art insurance and awoke in me a never-waning interest in them. Every morning it was like a renewed fairy tale when I found myself, after a long walk through absolutely black dark galleries, in an enormous realm of salt divided up by wooden planking in which, while I was there, were still piled up a large part of the treasures of the Kunsthistorisches Museum, works of art from almost every part of formerly occupied Europe and the greater part of the most important Viennese collections, Rothschild, Figdor, Bondy, Guttmann, etc. They still bore the old catalogue numbers, but on the chests the stampmark "Führermuseum Linz" could already be read. I had pushed under my very nose the three main questions which crop up again and again in any art insurance.

Identity

The first is the question of identity. The seemingly simple questions, is this picture really this, is that chair really that, already raise a big problem. In spite of the most painstaking Nazi precision some objets d'art had ended up in confusion. These were put in a "room of unknown owners" and the owners themselves, or previously brought in experts, or former house servants, etc., were invited to view these objects and then bring proof of ownership. In practice this was successful only in the fewest cases. The Baroness

Rothschild, for example, was almost arrested because she claimed some paintings as hers which had not belonged to her, whereas she failed to recognize an Ostade and several other pictures which were later shown to be her property. In most cases there were no photographs at all, and when there were they were so bad that they could hardly serve as proofs. Descriptions in catalogues were as good as useless.

I would therefore refer here to one basic principle which must be of quite decisive significance for the insured and makes loss settlement enormously easier for the insurer, namely the requirement of a good photographic record of each insured objet d'art. The solution rate for thefts of specifically major works of art is fortunately still pretty high, although the thieves have lately been trying to wipe out their trail by overpainting of pictures and sending them abroad. But almost always their recovery is due to the immediate distribution of photographs through Interpol and the magazines of the antique trade, which of course can only be done where good original photographs are available.

In Austria, where, thank God, the work of international gangs has still not been detected, local gangs concentrating on thefts from churches have unfortunately had a lot of success. Dependent churches without a permanent priest are of course the favorite target and can hardly be secured by means of normal protective measures. Here photography has successfully proved itself the only countermeasure. By a general system of photographic documentation the sale of stolen church property has been made so difficult that, as the police assure me, the number of break-ins into churches is declining again.

The highest European councils have concerned themselves with this problem, and the Council of Europe in Strasburg discussed for its part a proposal that the data of all important works of art in Europe should be stored in a computerized data bank so as to be able to pass on electronically to the police, customs, etc., the description of the object in case of theft. If this utopian plan has no chance of being put into effect, something similar is planned in France on a voluntary basis, and according to the opinion of experts there it could even be set up, together with the suggested creation of a police unit specializing in art thefts. I have seen the letter of the Minister of the Interior, Mr. Poniatowski, which promises these efforts his energetic support.

Authenticity

When a work of art has once been clearly identified the second stage is to prove its genuineness. With rising art prices, a forgery industry of enormous size has of course developed, particularly in the field of painting. Thus, for example, in a work on Utrillo, 600 known forgeries were identified besides 400 certified works of the master. As this form of damage is only rarely of any consequence to insurance, I will pass over it.

Valuation

The third problem is valuation. I believe I have already been able to show from the outset what an emotionally subjective aura surrounds the work of art. Possession, long gazing at it in different lights and in one's own individual atmosphere, enhances daily for the loving owner his understanding of the work, and daily it becomes for him more valuable. The thought of the artist, caught in a random creative moment, lives ever more with the owner of the work, and if he has to sell it, this is for him like taking leave from a great experience.

So, unconsciously, an even greater discrepancy arises between the individual subjective value of the objet d'art and its modest trade quotation. In Austria a work can generally only be insured for its real worth. Even if the object is insured for more, the insured may only claim its real worth in the event of loss, for our legislation rests on the standpoint that insurance may not lead to enrichment, and a payment over market value would represent enrichment.

In the Anglo-Saxon countries and also in France things are different. There one can insure for a so-called "agreed value," that is, a sum agreed to beforehand between insured and insurer which must be paid in the event of loss. Thus, the way is open to a determination of value which, understandably in this domain, is purely subjective. With us the fear is always present that if the chance of insuring above market value is given, this could present a temptation to fraud. The same was feared of replacement-value insurance in fire, but these fears were never fulfilled either in the sphere of industrial insurance or in the household business, where one can insure certain items for replacement value. I therefore hold the view that the valuation of a work of art, which is in any case very problematical by reason of its individual character and its literal irreplaceability, must to some extent take account of the above-mentioned subjective factor, that is, the value which the article has for the owner. Just as in other branches of insurance there is a valuation clause, according to which the insurer cannot in fact be obliged to make an overpayment beyond the actual value, but any disagreement in the event of the loss can be avoided by establishing beforehand the bases of indemnification, so a somewhat subjective valuation of a work of art which is not capricious and is considered viable by an expert can also be made on which insurer and insured can agree at the outset according to the local legal norms.

Austria has another special feature: there are many fine houses, many beautifully appointed castles and country mansions with valuable objets d'art which in most cases are not, or are not desired to be, in the form of a collection in contrast to France, where every second beautiful interior figures as a collection. Thus, in this country almost all objets d'art in private hands are not in practice insured as collections under the latter's more stringent provisions but snuggle together in the comfortable bed of household insurance, which was designed for quite different purposes, under the coverlet of the low, cozy premium rate of about 1.5 per mille, the one essential feature differentiating it from the all-risks insurance common in the West being that only losses from fire, burglary, or water damage, but not damage of other kinds, are covered. Indeed, this form of insurance has the disadvantage for the insured that where there is an overall sum insured, the loss arising from the destruction of an individual item is very difficult to adduce in figures, and where there are high values and a large claim, there is also in most cases underinsurance. It is therefore proposed in France to endeavor to introduce a clause into household insurance not only on new cases, but by way of enactment into existing policies as well, whereby a photograph of the object must be supplied when making a claim for the loss of a single item valued at more than 10,000 francs. It is hoped on the one hand to facilitate the identification of the object (so important for its recovery) and on the other hand to bring home to the insured what values he possesses, what sum insured should be selected, and which objects should be scheduled.

A particular worry is the art property in our castles. It must be viewed as extreme severity on the part of the legislature that basically the castle's inventory is subject to property tax in the same way as the share portfolio of the businessman held for purely commercial reasons. While in the one case there is a fully unproductive accumulation of assets, which is nonetheless burdened with maintenance costs, difficult to realize and in many cases preserved only out of traditional-ethical motives, in the other case are yield-bearing, easily convertible securities which are not weighed down with sentimental value. If in over forty years' practice I have never experienced a single case where an authority required information from us on sums insured, which of course we would never have supplied, there exists for the insured, by reason of the lack of insurance secrecy on the lines of bank secrecy, the fear that sums insured could at some time be used against him. This is certainly not the case, but as the Inland Revenue, when it claims property tax on these objects, can only calculate it in fact on the market value, the above-mentioned method of a mixed objective-subjective valuation gives the opportunity of explaining such a discrepancy to the Exchequer. A matter of great concern, as much for the owners as for insurers, is presented by the castles in that they are mostly in exposed, lonely places and because of their size the installation of security systems appears very costly or possible only with difficulty. In France and Italy risks of this kind are often insured only where there is a modern security system. The soft spot of Austrian insurance for insuring works of art — one must almost reproach oneself with being to some extent easygoing in this field — has not yet resulted here in any state of emergency in insurance. I do not feel that we insurers and the owners of notable objets d'art should let things go so far that international gangs are actually attracted to our country through the lack of security precautions and then, having learned from our losses, we insurers have to demand stringent conditions and high premiums for the maintenance of insurance protection. Spurred on by the international wave of burglaries, the technology of security has developed enormously in the last few years, and I would like at this point to appeal urgently to all owners of works of art to reflect on this problem and to consult with their insurance companies as well as with police units expressly set up in this connection.

The two largest art thefts in Austria so far, the theft of the painting from the Shlägl Foundation and the arms collection from Suthner castle in Kirchstetten, were both made from almost completely unsecured buildings.

ART THEFT FOR POLITICAL AND FINANCIAL BLACKMAIL

The theft of the leaf from the Ghent altar for blackmail purposes found all too abundant imitation in the following decades. What at one time seemed protected by being internationally known was now a particularly tempting object for blackmail. Austria was the first to feel the effect when seven famous Cézannes, among them the *Joueurs aux Cartes* from the Louvre, were stolen in Provence. As the exhibition had been previously shown in Vienna at the Belvedere, it was insured in Austria under the lead of the Union-Wiener Städtische. Exceedingly skillful negotiations succeeded in the finding of all seven Cézannes in an abandoned car at the end of a dark street in Marseilles, after the discreet payment of 5,800,00 shillings. The thieves were extremely nervous and had threatened the destruction of the pictures, as happened in fact with a Renoir in a similar case in France.

Even more modern is the art theft for the purpose of political, not financial, blackmail. This was the case in the (so far) greatest of all art thefts when nineteen paintings worth about 400 million shillings were stolen on 2 May 1974 from the Irish country house of the South African diamond millionaire Sir Afred Beit. As price for their return, food supplies for the starving population of the Congo to the value of £8,000,000 and the release of four Irish terrorists were demanded.

Such crimes for political motives present a quite special threat in that those committing them, for the most part stirred by passion, react in a completely unforeseeable manner and do not come from the "crowd," i.e., the criminal fraternity, which in other cases is most often the best source of information, whereas here one can find out nothing. It is almost an even worse situation if political passion concentrates on the damaging of a famous work of art, as happened in Cambridge in May 1974 to the *Three Kings* painting by Titian, which was disfigured by three paint strokes causing £30,000 worth of damage.

Motives for Blackmail

Thefts for blackmailing motives stay within limits which must be adjusted to the ability of the victim to pay, or the amount of his insurance. More recently it has been noticed that this ransom game seems already to be becoming too stale for the altogether routine-minded criminal world of today and that the total conversion into cash of the stolen object is now the aim. Clearly exceedingly well informed as to the difficulty of effectively disguising the identity of a work of art and the inevitable shortcomings of Interpol, thieves are sending stolen pictures from country to country through a visibly superbly functioning system of illicit disposal. They are slightly altered by overpainting and made suitable for hanging by faked pedigrees so that two well-known Renaissance pictures stolen from Italian museums were solemnly presented in German museums as new acquisitions and stolen French pictures were resold in the most official auctions in small American towns. Such disposal is understandably only possible with a system of receivers functioning on an international level. All states are aware that in combating the criminals attention is devoted far more to the person committing the theft than to the receiver. In Austria in particular the receiver enjoys the full leniency of the court until his guilt can be unambiguously proved, which is most often extremely difficult, and he has, as ever, more than enough time to wipe out his trail. It must be generally emphasized how the antique dealers, jewelers, etc., concerned, cooperate in solving art thefts and contribute in a most essential way, through the publication of the description or the photograph of the object, to its recovery.

But in the end, there must be collectors today in the Western world who in an unscrupulous enthusiasm order this or that object from criminal consortia. Of course they can only look at them, once they have them, with the public kept out — alone, as it were, in the cellar at midnight. This can provide no purely aesthetic pleasure, but here the consciousness of power and an echo of the distant demonic-magical origin of art must, at least subconsciously, be at work and the, in this way, co-guilty possessor of the stolen work of art seeks unconsciously to be able to banish with this possession the dark forces of magic. Here, as in other spheres, moments from the dawn of man became strangely enmeshed with phenomena of an overdeveloped civilization.

And so there are a whole series of world-famous works of art about which it was originally accepted that they could only be stolen purely for blackmail purposes but which to this day have not reappeared although many years have gone by since the crime: *La Lectrice* by Renoir, which was stolen from an American museum, the *Madonna* by Pisano from the National Gallery in London, the *Triptich* by Fra Lippo from a gallery in Chiasso, *The Life of Christ* from the Eglise Saint Nicolas in Paris, the *Saint Michael* from Moulins Cathedral, the relic with the stone from the grave of Christ from the Church at Villers, the Gothic cup from the Chateau d'Attre in Belgium, and many, many more generally well-known works of art have been gone from sight for years.

Finally, sport, which can exercise such a fascination on the young generation, seems also to want to enroll among the possible motives for art thefts. That is to say, when the 80-kilogram bronze statue *La Source* by Maillol disappears of an evening from its pedestal in the Tuileries gardens, a place which is frequented to about the same extent as the gardens around the Marie-Therese monument, to be found again next morning "naked and freezing" leaning against a wall near a police station, then this art theft is certainly to be regarded only as a sporting test of daring. One may hope, however, that our youthful sport enthusiasts will use other provided fields of activity and leave art property in peace.

INSURANCE AND THE INTERNATIONAL EXCHANGE OF EXHIBITIONS

The reproach is made against insurance that its costs hinder the international exchange of exhibitions. This is unfortunately correct — not as a reproach but as a fact. Insurance expenses often come to more than 50 percent of the total costs. As an inspired disciple of art I racked my brains for a very long time for a remedy. The increase in crime on an international level did not favor my efforts. The problem was aired throughout the world. Premiums generally fall when a wide-ranging portfolio can be achieved. This way was tried in America, where there is a host of private galleries which are insured throughout and contain very high values. In Europe where there are mainly state galleries which are not insured throughout, the spread of risk is accordingly just not there. Gigantic sums insured come up for insurance for a short period only at exhibitions in premises which are often not very well adapted and thoroghly unsafe against fire. Exhibition insurance is generally from nail to nail, which means that all risks of loading, transit, unloading, exhibition, and return transit are covered.

Insurers must always consider two things: (1) What is the probable loss amount I must work on? (2) What can happen in the worst most improbable catastrophe? The estimation of point (1) will vary enormously according to the works exhibited and their presentation. Point (2) will always coincide for the careful insurer with the sum insured, for there are unfortunately examples of this being so, as in the case of the Crystal Palace fire in Munich, where the whole exhibition fell victim to the fire. The premium will also have to be composed of two parts, namely the consideration for the probable loss payment on the one hand and, on the other, an amount by way of provision for catastrophe, which, unfortunately and against all probability, always strikes again.

The total premium volume for art insurance in Austria is uncommonly small and offers no spread of risk. We are therefore thrown back onto the heavy use of reinsurance precisely in this sphere. The international reinsurer, influenced more by the ever-worsening claims incidence internationally than by the still-tolerable Austrian claims figures, will naturally charge the premium which seems to him appropriate according to his international experience. Not familiar with local data he will, moreover, not accept the optimistic-seeming assertions of the Austrian insurer, but out of prudence will always base his calculations on the full sum insured as the possible loss figure. Thus it lies to only a small extent in the hands of the Austrian insurer to promote the putting on of exhibitions in Austria by charging moderate premiums.

A lot of moves have also been made abroad toward reducing exhibition premiums. Thus in England a government guarantee can be issued to private owners of exhibition articles for exhibitions of general cultural interest. Oddly enough this measure has done little damage to the insurance market, as private owners declined the government guarantee and preferred an insurance policy. It is strange to see how in several countries insurance comes back into favor in spite of all castigation if threatened with the specter of nationalization.

A second move consisted in museums and private owners agreeing to insure only 80 percent of the value in order to achieve at least a 20 percent reduction. Private owners, who in any case lend their treasures only reluctantly, were for the most part not agreeable.

Exhibition insurance is and remains a problem. I do not believe we would have gotten the interesting Chinese exhibition to Vienna if the insurance problem had become a political one. The state undertook here, as is well known, a cash guarantee of over 1 billion shillings.

If I may be permitted to make a proposal, it is as follows. The first part of the premium about which I was speaking, that is to say the probability premium, must always be charged because it goes back in practice, after deduction of a certain administration coefficient, to the claimants. The second premium coefficient, as mentioned earlier, is perhaps set too high by the international reinsurance market out of understandable anxiety. The occurrence of a catastrophe is conceivable but very unlikely. If now the state would give for this extreme possibility a guarantee for the difference between the estimated probable loss and the sum insured, there would exist a much smaller need for reinsurance.

International nervousness would become less of a factor and very significant premium savings could be achieved. If one could convince the competent authorities that this guarantee would be called upon only in the most unlikely event, most probably never, and can as good as certainly never fully come into play, and that the otherwise supported exhibition activity would essentially be promoted in a more, indeed probably the most, inexpensive way, then this proposal must fall on receptive ears with the competent authorities. At the same time there would have to be particular cooperation with the police authorities on the insurance of exhibition articles, as happens in general on the security systems, in which international experience at the disposal of insurers can play an important role. This kind of loss prevention will always be the best argument for the lowering of premiums.

CONCLUSION

Works of art, testimonies to the deepest spiritual aspiration of bygone ages and our own, may all be seen as memorials, and this year of memorial protection should essentially be construed as a year in which we particularly make their preservation our business.

If it is lately the task of insurance to reimburse the value of a work of art in the event of its being destroyed or damaged, it is also the natural ally of the police and all other forces of law and order in our country. Where state bodies are often inhibited in the extent of their action by unavoidable formalism and extraneous obstacles, insurers can draw on practical experience and seize those initiatives which the present situation demands.

International involvement, particularly in the reinsurance sphere, will yield enlightenment on those perils which in the main operate earlier in big countries than they do here, but which almost all eventually arrive here if also in the main, thank God, in attenuated form.

And so I venture to put forward my own personal views and suggestions as follows:

The value of works of art is the only value which has not fallen in recent times and, for top quality, is still rising. This shows that works of art will continue to be sought after out of purely material considerations of property investment or for the other psychological motives mentioned at the outset. This will fan the criminal activity prevalent in this sphere, which has taken frightening proportions in Italy, France, and England and from which it is unlikely that Austria will be spared. It is therefore in our interest to protect and preserve our artistic heritage. The owners of irreplaceable art treasures must facilitate their identification above all by means of photographic documentation. Insurers must accordingly teach their outside staff that valuable objets d'art in private ownership can no longer be hidden away in the overall sums insured under household insurance and the apartment houses where they reside cannot remain without burglary protections. Police and insurers maintain routine cooperation for recommending to insureds the best and cheapest security system for the individual case. Cooperation with the police for the suppression of the network of receivers remains to be intensified. The great auction houses, Sotheby's and Christie's, have seen their way to enlist the aid of the catalogues of the works of art stolen throughout the world set up by Interpol, often with the assistance of insurers, before they accept an article for auction. In many countries an antique dealer can buy a work of art from a private owner only if the vendor can to some extent prove his identity and his ownership of the work.

In Austria there is even a trade paper for antique dealers and jewelers giving the description and, unfortunately only rarely, a photograph of stolen objects. The interval between the theft and its discovery and the all too often insufficient description detract, however, from its full effectiveness.

In one town in Germany the antique dealers even resorted to self-help and set up an interesting warning system. If for any reason a suspicious person appears in a shop wanting to sell something without leaving it for viewing, the shopkeeper rings up three specific colleagues, who ring up a further three colleagues, so that all dealers participating are warned in a snowball operation within the shortest possible time.

The main interest of the international criminal community seems to concentrate on pictures, whereas in Austria the field is dominated by small gothic or baroque sculptures stolen from churches. After pictures come antique silver, old carpets, and Gobelin tapestries as favorites, but there was a loss in England in 1973 where china worth more than £40,000 was stolen from a private house and a first edition of Shakespeare worth more than £10,000 disappeared from the University Library in Manchester. Then old clocks and jade and ivory carvings follow in order of popularity. Engravings, lace, and glassware, which for centuries were among the most sought-after articles, arouse little interest.

In comparison with the problems of motor insurance, industrial and fire insurance, etc., which touch the vital nerve of the insurance market, the insurance of objets d'art, which will always be a very small percentage share of the market, may seem to be of very minor importance.

A branch of business like insurance, which is entirely dependent on popular confidence, should always remain conscious of its psychological roots, and in this sense protection and preservation of our art property are a specially important factor. The loss of a work of art which is dear to the hearts of the people arouses storms of grief and anger, and its discovery, delight and exultation.

If we therefore endeavor, in this year devoted to the high aim of preserving our dearest treasures, to serve this aim effectively with new thoughts and ideas, this will, I feel, be reckoned by people at large as a credit to the insurance industry and we shall be able to say with true inner satisfaction that over and above the duties of our commercial and technical tasks we have been able to contribute something to the preservation of the most beautiful and valuable of our possessions.

4. Insuring Works Of Art

John B. Lawton

The importance of good security for the protection of fine arts of any nature can not be overemphasized. In these disturbed economic times of inflated values, particularly of fine arts — to say nothing of crime, fires, vandalism, etc. — which plague our society nowadays, security of the best possible kind is a must. Equally important is the proper insurance of fine arts whether for museums, dealers, historical societies, libraries, or corporate and private collectors. All have a tremendous stake in such property, which runs into many millions of dollars in value. Along with this dollar value there is also an intrinsic value that is inestimable, and it follows that the best in security and insurance protection is mandatory if the owners of such property, as well as the public who view it in ever-increasing numbers, are going to be able to continue enjoying its very existence.

Other chapters of this book treat extensively the intricate and technical details of numerous and complex security systems and those best suited for one's particular needs. This chapter, however, is devoted to fine-arts insurance, not as an underwriter's guide but rather as a guide for collectors of all kinds in what to look for in obtaining the broadest fine-arts insurance available at the most reasonable cost. As a matter of fact, proper security and fine-art insurance are practically inseparable, for it would be difficult to find an underwriter who would not first want to know what sort of security system your premises had in force before he would be willing to consider writing your insurance. Hence the adage that you should first put your money into safety and security and then become concerned with proper insurance.

Fine Arts are considered within the insurance industry as "floating" property; that is to say, it is not restricted to one stationary location but may be covered wherever it may be, including while in transit and at various locations. As such it is written as Inland Marine Insurance, the latter having had its origins in Ocean Marine Insurance, the oldest known form of insurance in the world. It is generally written as "All Risk" Insurance, which more precisely means "All Risk of physical loss or damage from any external cause" subject only to the exclusions named in the policy. In other words, all losses from any external causes are covered except those specifically excluded in the policy. Such exclusions are generally wear and tear, gradual deterioration, moths, vermin, inherent vice, damage due to any repair, restoration, or retouching process, mail shipments unless by registered first-class mail, war risk, and loss by nuclear radiation or radioactive contamination. These are the customary and standard exclusions, and anything beyond them makes for a more restrictive policy than is desirable. For example, a policy that excludes theft or breakage of fragile articles or vandalism might be purchased at slightly less cost, but for the type of property involved this is certainly not to be recommended.

THE INSURANCE POLICY

At the conclusion of this chapter is included a copy of what is believed to be about the broadest form of fine-arts insurance policy available in the market today, and it is worthy of some serious study by those who are charged with obtaining fine-arts insurance protection. It contains in one single policy what in years past took a multiplicity of policies to accomplish, and on a simplified basis that eliminates a great deal of clerical detail. Granted, this form is designed for museums, but the same broad coverage in somewhat different format is available for dealers and corporate or private collectors. It consists of four parts, namely, Permanent Collection, Temporary Loans, Legal Liability, and International Transportation and Exhibition. The various sections are optional and may be purchased to cover all of them or any combination that is needed.The last section, entitled "General Conditions," includes, along with much of what is known as "boiler plate" clauses, typical of most insurance policies, the term of the policy, the coverage provided, what the policy does not insure, and what is probably one of the most important features of the policy — the Valuation Clause, which determines in the event of loss the basis on which the claim will be paid.

It is not the intent of this chapter to review the policy form paragraph by paragraph but rather simply to highlight those features that make it particularly suitable to fine-arts insurance buyers who are looking for the broadest coverage at a cost that comes within budgetary limitations. Taking the various sections in their same order the following points are particularly worthy of comment.

Permanent Collection

Paragraph 1 of this section clearly defines what property is covered as part of the permanent collection. It is all inclusive in that it covers four different interests including long-term loans, which is considered a part of the permanent collection. It is also important to note that this section is written on a blanket basis which eliminates the need for endless schedules of items insured. The latter is an outmoded, extremely cumbersome manner of writing such insurance.

Paragraph 2, however, is the key to determining the amount of insurance that will apply to the permanent collection. It is also the determining factor on cost, which is usually a flat annual premium that is subject to renegotiation on each anniversary date of the policy. The total overall value of the permanent collection has, of course, a bearing on the premium charge but cost of insuring this 100 percent to value would, in most cases, be prohibitive. The solution to this problem, and to bring the cost within budgetary capabilities, is to determine what is known as a "PML" — Probable Maximum Loss — or, in other words, the value amount in any one area of the museum that might reasonably be expected to be subject to one severe loss. This might be a series of adjacent galleries, a storage area, etc., where there is a concentration of values. While some of the smaller museums might have a greater concentration in rather confined areas and would need a proportionately higher loss limit on their premises, most museums cover a wide area, sometimes on several floors or even several buildings, and these and similar physical characteristics enter into establishing a PML and a reasonable loss limit on the permanent collection. This is not to say that a major catastrophe might possibly destroy the whole museum, but the caliber of most museum construction, the security and protection and the extreme precautions taken, make such a happening quite remote. In any event, once the PML is established, which may vary from perhaps 10 to 50 percent or more of the total values, this then would be the limit of liability to set forth in Paragraph 2 (a) on which the premium charge is predicated.

Another important part of this section is Paragraph 4 (Deductible), which would apply to each separate occurence of loss. Usually this is an amount of $1,000 for which a sizable credit in the annual premium is allowed. This effects a substantial savings in premium. Such a deductible may be for higher amounts at higher credits but is dependent on a given museum's financial resources, although the greater part of the savings comes within the first $1,000 of the deductible and is then on a gradually decreasing scale.

It should be noted that such deductibles under Paragraph 4 do not apply to property described in Paragraph 1 (b) and (c).

Temporary Loans

Incoming and outgoing loans represent a major activity of most museums these days. With such activity, insurance is essential, for in most cases lenders will insist on adequate insurance being carried by the borrower before being willing to lend the art works. Furthermore, borrowers assume responsibility for such property and could ill afford to be without adequate insurance protection. Otherwise they would not be able to borrow the property in question.

In Paragraph 1 of this section it is important to note that the coverage is on a "wall to wall" basis, or "nail to nail," as it is known in some countries. This simply means the property is covered from the time it leaves its normal repository on the owner's premises until returned thereto, or to another point designated by the owner, including while in transit and while on exhibiton or otherwise at any location within the United States and Canada during the period of the loan. Limits of liability under this section are not the determining factor for premium purposes but should be adequate under Paragraph 2 to take care of the anticipated maximum exposure, or loan, whether incoming or outgoing.

Paragraph 3 (Records and Reports) is the provision that predicates the premium charged based upon what total values, either incoming or outgoing, are at risk of the Insured, including what is in due course of transit, as of the last day of each preceding month. All such loan activity involves Loan Agreements that should be executed between the lender and the borrower prior to the actual loan. It is on the basis of the values stipulated in these agreements that such monthly reports are completed, and the premium charge is computed each month at the rate indicated therein. This puts it on a "pay as you go" basis by the month, and if there is nothing at risk on the last day of the month then there is no charge — and vice versa.

Suffice it to say, however, that this method of handling loan activity simplifies the clerical detail considerably as compared to some past — and even present — practices of reporting values outstanding on a daily or weekly basis, individual transits, individual locations during the period of the loan, fragiles and non-fragiles, or other details. Granted, some values may cease to be at risk during the latter part of a given month and not be included in the report as of the last day of the month. On the other hand, some values may become at risk toward the end of the month and be reported for the full month. Overall, however, these average out for both the insured and the company, to the point that the premium charge is equitable for both parties.

Legal Liability

When borrowing property of others the owners sometimes insist on carrying their own insurance on the loaned property during the period of the loan, and in the event of loss the owners would be reimbursed by their own insurance. The borrower, however, is still legally liable for such property, particularly if there is any degree of negligence on the part of the borrower. In either event the owners' insurance company who paid the claim is legally entitled to subrogate (in the absence of a waiver of subrogation under the owner's policy, which is difficult to obtain in many cases) against the borrower's insurance, or in the absence of insurance, against the borrowers themselves for the amount of the claim paid to the owner.

It is here that the Legal Liability section comes into play. This section protects the borrower against any such action. Generally speaking this coverage is a fringe benefit which can be included for a reasonable amount without a premium charge. When an owner chooses to maintain his own insurance, however, it is still wise for the borrower at least to attempt to obtain waiver of subrogation under the owner's insurance during the period of the loan.

International Transportation and Exhibition

One of the unique features of this policy is this section, which covers the art works worldwide, including while in round trip overseas transit via vessels or aircraft and while at overseas locations wherever they may be while on exhibition or otherwise. There was a time, and still is among some companies, when a number of separate policies are required to take care of such foreign exposures, particularly overseas transits. Under this policy form, however, such operations are covered on the same "wall to wall" basis as domestic loans and only one report per month of such activity is required.

Overseas loans, both incoming and outgoing, are very prevalent these days, whether individual art works on loan or traveling exhibitions of unbelievably high values such as the so-called "blockbusters" that reach into many millions of dollars in value but which could not travel without adequate insurance being provided. An outstanding example of this activity was the Picasso Exhibition at the Museum of Modern Art in New York in 1980, the largest incoming exhibition ever to reach the United States. Its total value of several hundred million dollars was not only the highest valued exhibition ever to travel, but the number of items comprising the exhibition was the largest, over seven hundred, and required innumerable air flights each way, many from France but from many other sources as well. It took the expertise of many individuals and concerns to handle an exhibition of this magnitude. A major task was the arranging and handling of the insurance requirements for the exhibition. The United States Government Indemnity Act was also an important factor, without which the problems would have been ever greater, but of course the total values went far beyond the limits of the Indemnity Act provisions and necessitated a great deal of commercial insurance. It is a good example of what can be accomplished by an insurance broker knowledgeable in the insurance of fine arts, together with astute underwriters, equally knowledgeable in the same field, when called upon to go to extremes of providing the necessary coverage under difficult circumstances.

But enough of the details of the policy form. It is enough to say it is designed to treat all facets of fine-arts insurance for a given musuem, and, as mentioned before, the same broad and comprehensive coverage is available for dealers, corporate and private collectors, and others whatever the source of its purchase may be. The policy represents many years of experience in the handling of such insurance for principal museums, dealers, and collectors throughout the country. Many revisions of the policy were made over the years, from very restrictive forms of protection to what it provides today.

NEED FOR FINE ART INSURANCE VERSUS COSTS

As mentioned early on in this chapter, security and insurance are essential to, and inseparable from, art works of every nature. The utopia of 100 percent freedom from loss of art work is, unfortunately, an unobtainable goal. Attempted thefts, fires, vandalism, and similar acts will undoubtedly always be with us, but excellent security goes a long way in minimizing such occurrences. Nevertheless, proper insurance protects the owner of such property when such acts do occur, even in the failure of safeguards against them. It protects not only the owner's investment in the property but also enables him to have funds available to replace the lost or damaged property with suitable substitutes.

Then, too, there are losses beyond the realm of security that are unforeseeable or uncontrollable in which insurance plays such an important role. Granted, many should be controllable but are not. The fire at the Museum of Modern Art in 1958 should have been controllable but was not. It started through the carelessness of a contractor doing renovations. The flooding of the Corning Museum of Glass in 1972 was a result of hurricane Agnes and resulted in five or six feet of mud and water in the museum — an act of God that was neither foreseeable in the area nor controllable but nevertheless resulted in over $2 million in damages. The theft of three Cézannes worth $3 million from the Art Institute of Chicago in 1978 was the result of dishonesty on the part of an employee in the Shipping Department. They were recovered months later, but only after considerable effort was expended in accomplishing their safe return. Then, too, there are damages in transit that can and do occur; there are simple accidents in handling for which there is often no logical reason. But, unfortunately, such things do happen despite the best of precautions and should be protected against by proper insurance — and not the kind that excludes some and covers others but insurance that covers all such happenings including the catastrophic losses that one hopes will never happen but can and sometimes do.

Much has been written and discussed concerning the cost of fine-arts insurance, some of it well informed and some of it pure conjecture. The truth of the matter is that it actually is one of the less expensive forms of insurance, at least from the standpoint of rates. Granted, if total values run into the millions of dollars the premiums can be very significant, but, proportionately, not nearly so much as other forms of coverage such as automobile, homeowners, or various types of commercial insurance lines. Surveys have been conducted that allege rates on fine arts that are too high in relation to the losses that have been incurred, but this is really not quite so. It is true that insurance companies have had some very profitable years in writing fine-arts insurance but they also have had some losers. Besides, they are constantly assuming tremendous liabilities that have sometimes resulted in losses that run into millions of dollars. To be able to assume such liabilities and pay such losses it is essential for them to have a number of profitable years in which to build up sufficient reserves to pay the catastrophic losses that are inevitable every few years, to say nothing of the continual run-of-the-mill losses that go on every year. The surveys of the loss experience in this field are not a true indication of the proper level of rates, as their statistics are not accurate enough to reveal the actual picture. In fact, some well-publicized surveys have either ignored or have not had a response from some of the sources that have had the most severe losses. This, by itself, distorts the whole picture. The fact remains that while insurance costs can be, and are, an important item in any museum's or collector's budget, the insurance companies must make a reasonable profit over the years in this or any other class of insurance, for otherwise the market as we know it today could very readily tend to evaporate.

Except for private collections, fine-arts insurance is what is known as an uncontrolled class of insurance business, that is to say, it is not regulated by state rating authorities as is the case with automobile, fire insurance on your home, or various types of casualty insurance. While private collections are regulated, they are minimally rated, but for museums, dealers, and others the individual underwiter is free to establish whatever rate or rates he feels are justified, be they high, low, or in the middle, depending on the underwriting facts of a given risk that are presented to him. In reaching his decisions he will take into consideration a number of important factors such as construction of the building or buildings involved, their security against the perils of fire and burglary, the total values involved, the personnel and management of the institution, etc., so it is advisable to be patient with the numerous questions that are asked either in person or by application as they can be of material benefit to you. Once satisfied that these factors are favorable he will then determine the fire contents rate that is specifically published by the individual states on all buildings, whether they be private dwellings, museums, commercial buildings, or whatever. To this rate he will add an "all risk" loading for perils other than fire, and this total rate applied to the amount of insurance determines the premium charge. There are, however, a number of devices that may be utilized at the underwriter's discretion such as deductibles, loss limits based on an estimated PML, etc., that he may use to reduce substantially the premium charge, or monthly rates if the coverage is so written.

Those charged with the task of obtaining proper insurance on works of art, whether they be the Registrar, the Business Manager of a museum, or a private collector himself, have a serious responsibility. Actually, there are three parties sharing this responsibility, the owner of the property or his representative, his or their broker, and the company quoting on or writing the insurance. Of these three parties a knowledgeable broker who is well versed in fine-arts insurance is the owner's best ally, for he will work on behalf of the owner in obtaining the best possible coverage while at the same time endeavoring to keep the cost within reasonable bounds, whether for a museum, dealer, or private collector. In the case of museums the person charged with obtaining such insurance will undoubtedly have to answer to a higher authority such as the Board of Trustees, and it is advisable for him to seek out several proposals from different sources if only as a matter of comparison both as to policy form itself as well as the cost − and it is useful also to keep in mind the fact that the least expensive insurance is not necessarily the best, and, in fact, may have many pitfalls.

Under these circumstances and considering the objects at risk and the values involved, some time and study of this subject and the policy form that is a part of this chapter could save some regrets later on in the event of the loss of valuable art works. At least with proper insurance being in force there is recompense available. If it is a damaged object there is coverage provided for restoration costs and even for depreciation in value, if any, resulting from the damage, both of which can be very substantial. If there is a total loss of an object or objects, then funds are available for reimbursement to the extent of the current market value of the objects lost or destroyed. In either event the owner's investment in the property is fully protected and funds are available for necessary repairs and restoration, depreciation in value, or replacement with other works satisfactory to the owner. Some owners may never have a loss if they are extremely fortunate, but if they do their investment in the right kind of insurance will not only provide a great deal of peace of mind but will also prove to be an advantageous investment in itself.

Appendix 4.1

Fine Arts Insurance

MUSEUM COLLECTION

AND

TEMPORARY LOANS

The insurance companies signatory hereto
(hereinafter called the Company)
each only for itself and not one for another
by this joint policy of insurance
do insure

(hereinafter referred to as the Insured)

For the percentage underwritten for each and every loss covered hereunder as
set forth under their respective names.

HUNTINGTON T. BLOCK INSURANCE
2101 L STREET, N.W.
WASHINGTON, D.C. 20037
TELEPHONE: (202) 223-0673
TOLL FREE: (800) 424-8830

INDEX

PARAGRAPH   PAGE

Museum Collection

1. Property Insured 1
2. Limits of Liability 1
3. Premium 1
4. Deductible 1

Temporary Loan Collection

1. Property Insured and Coverage 1
2. Limits of Liability 1
3. Records and Reports 1

Legal Liability

1. Coverage 1
2. Non-assumption of Liability 2
3. Limit of Liability 2

International Transportation and Exhibition

1. Coverage 2
2. Limit of Liability 2
3. Basic Ocean Marine Clause (reference to) 2
4. Premium and Reports 2

General Conditions

 1. For account of whom it may concern 3
 2. Loss Payable 3
 3. Policy Term 3
 4. Perils Insured Against 3
 5. Perils Excluded 3
 6. Valuation of Property 3
 7. Packing Provision 3
 8. Pairs and Sets Clause 3
 9. National and International Expositions 4
10. Other Insurance Clause 4
11. Misrepresentation and Fraud Clause 4
12. Notice of Loss 4
13. Examination Under Oath 4
14. Settlement of Claims 4
15. Loss Buy Back Clause 4
16. No Benefit To Bailee Clause 4
17. Subrogation Clause 4
18. Sue and Labor Clause 4
19. Suit Against Company 4
20. Collection From Others 5
21. Appraisal Clause 5
22. Cancellation Clause 5
23. Changes 5
24. Companies Interest 5
25. Required By Law Clause 5

MUSEUM FORM A

Only those of the following sections that are completed with respects to limits of liability, rates of premiums shall be deemed to be covered under this policy.

MUSEUM COLLECTION

1. This section covers paintings, etchings, drawings (including their frames, glasses and shadow boxes), rare books, manuscripts, rugs, tapestries, statuary and other bonafide works of art, or rarity, historic value or artistic merit, all constituted as follows:

    (a) Property of the Insured;

    (b) Property of others on extended loan to the Insured for a period of six months or more;

    (c) Property of others offered as gifts to the Insured or for sale to the Insured and while awaiting formal acceptance by the Trustees;

    (d) The Insured's interest in residuary gifts and jointly owned property, but only to the extent of the Insured's interest therein at time of loss or damage;

    all of the above being part of, and known as their Permanent Collection, while on exhibition or otherwise and while in transit within and between the states of the United States, the District of Columbia and the Provinces of Canada.

2. LIMITS OF LIABILITY: This Company shall not be liable under this section of this policy for more than the following sums:

    (a) $ at the Insured's premises

    (b) $ at any other location

    (c) $ in transit on any one conveyance

    (d) $ in any one loss or disaster, either in case of partial or total loss, or salvage charges, or expenses or all combined.

3. PREMIUM: The annual premium under this section of this policy for the policy year _____ to _____ shall be $ _____ and shall be due and payable as of attachment hereof. Subsequent annual premiums under this section for successive policy years shall be subject to recomputation as of each anniversary date of this policy.

4. DEDUCTIBLE: Each claim for loss or damage

separately occurring under this section of this policy shall be adjusted separately and from the amount of such adjusted claim the sum of $ _____ shall be deducted. This clause shall not apply, however, to property described in paragraph 1 (b) or 1 (c).

TEMPORARY LOANS

1. This section covers property of the same nature as described in the above section, and constituting the property of the Insured or the property of others loaned to the Insured and which the Insured has been instructed to insure, covering said property on a "wall to wall" basis from the time said property is removed from its normal repository, incidental to shipment, until returned thereto or other point designated by the owner or their agent prior to return shipment, including while in transit and while on exhibition or otherwise within and between the states of the United States, the District of Columbia and the Provinces of Canada.

2. LIMITS OF LIABILITY: This Company shall not be liable under this section of this policy for more than the following sums:

    (a) $ at premises of the Insured,

    (b) $ at any other location,

    (c) $ in transit on any one conveyance,

    (d) $ in any one loss or disaster, either in case of partial or total loss, or salvage charges, or expenses or all combined.

3. RECORDS AND REPORTS: The Insured agrees to keep an accurate record of the property insured under this section of this policy and on or before the 10th day of each month to report to this Company the total value of all property at risk as of the last day of the preceding month and pay premium thereon at the rate of _____ ¢ per $100.

LEGAL LIABILITY

1. In consideration of premium charged under this policy this section covers the liability of the Insured as bailee of all loan properties on which the Insured has been instructed not to insure (excluding, however, any property for which the Insured has obtained a signed release of liability from the owner) and in the event of any action in-

volving the Insured for loss or damage to such property this Company is to defend (to the monetary extent of its proportionate interest in this insurance) all such actions and to pay its proportionate share of all legal fees, court costs or judgments.

2. The Insured shall not voluntarily assume any liability nor incur any expense nor settle any claim, except at the Insured's own cost. The Insured shall not interfere in any negotiations for settlement nor in any legal proceedings, but whenever requested, and at the Company's expense, the Insured shall aid in securing information and evdence and the attendance of witnesses, and shall cooperate with the Company, except in a pecuniary way, in all matters which the Company may deem necessary in the defense of any suit or in the prosecution of any appeal.

3. LIMIT OF LIABILITY: This Company shall not be liable under this section for more than the sum of $ _____ the aggregate in any one loss.

INTERNATIONAL TRANSPORTATION AND EXHIBITION

1. This section covers the property of the Insured or property of others which the Insured has been instructed to insure while at locations outside the United States and Canada and while in waterborne transit (via passenger liners and Class A-1 vessels) and while in airborne transit (via scheduled air lines or other aircraft as approved by this Company) to and from points and places outside the United States and Canada, attaching from the time such property shall become at the risk of the Insured and covering until the Insured's interest in such property shall cease.

2. This section shall cover in the total amount of $ _____ in any one loss or disaster.

   This insurance, in addition to the foregoing, is also subject to the following American Institute Clauses (February 1949, otherwise as indicated):

   (a) Warehouse to Warehouse

   (b) Marine Extension Clause (4/43)

   (c) Deviation

   (d) Delay

   (e) Both to Blame

All other terms and conditions of the Policy not in conflict with the foregoing remain unchanged, it being particularly understood and agreed that the F.C.&S. clause remains in full force and effect, and that nothing in the foregoing shall be construed as extending this insurance to cover any risks of war or consequences of hostilities.

4. PREMIUMS AND REPORTS: The Insured agrees to keep an accurate record of shipments made under the provisions of this section and on or before the 10th day of each month to report to this Company the total value, points of origin and destination, mode of transit and period of time to be covered at locations, if any, outside the United States and Canada at the risk of the Insured and in waterborne or airborne transit at the risk of the Insured. On values so reported premium shall be payable at the following rates:

VOYAGE	RATES (One Way)	
	Via Vessels	Via Aircraft
(A) U.S. North Atlantic ports to or from		
(1)United Kingdom and European Atlantic Ports		
(2)Scandinavian Countries		
(3)Mediterranean and Adriatic Ports		
(4)Israel		
(5)Central America		
(6)Southern America		
(7)India		
(8)Japan		
(9)Phillipine Islands		
(10)Trans-Mediterranean		
(11)To or from point or places other than listed above		
(B) At locations outside the United States and Canada	c per $100 per month or fraction thereof	

GENERAL CONDITIONS

1. For account of whom it may concern.

2. Loss, if any, payable to the Insured or order.

3. TERM: This policy shall attach at 12:01 A.M., Standard Time at place of issuance,
   and shall cover continuously until cancelled.

4. The Policy insures against all risks of physical loss or damage from any external cause, except as hereinafter excluded.

5. This Policy does not insure:

   (A) Wear and tear, gradual deterioration, moths, vermin, inherent vice or loss or damage sustained due to or resulting from any repairing, restoration or retouching process;

   (B) (1) Hostile or warlike action in time of peace or war, including action in hindering, combating or defending against an actual, impending or expected attack, (a) by any government or sovereign power (de jure or de facto); or by any authority maintaining or using military, naval or air forces; or (b) by military, naval or air forces; or (c) by an agent of any such government power, authority or forces; (2) any weapon of war employing atomic fission or radioactive force whether in time of peace or war; (3) insurrection, rebellion, revolution, civil war, usurped power, or action taken by governmental authority in hindering, combating or defending against such an occurrence, seizure or destruction under quarantine or customs regulations, confiscation by order of any government or public authority, or risks of contraband or illegal transportation or trade;

   (C) Shipments by mail unless by registered first class mail or parcel post provided, however, such shipments by parcel post shall not exceed the sum of $1,000. in value;

   (D) Against loss or damage to property shipped under "on deck" Bills of Lading.

   (E) Against loss by nuclear reaction or nuclear radiation or radioactive contamination, all whether controlled or uncontrolled, and whether such loss be direct or indirect, proximate or remote, or be in whole or in part caused by, contributed to, or aggravated by the perils insured against in this policy; however, subject to the foregoing and all provisions of this policy, direct loss by fire resulting from nuclear reaction or nuclear radiation or radiation or radioactive contamination is insured against by this policy.

6. VALUATION: It is understood and agreed that in event of loss or damage hereunder all property coming under the protection of this insurance shall be valued at and insured hereunder as follows:

   (1) On property of the Insured this Company shall not be liable beyond the current market value of the property at the time any loss or damage occurs. The loss or damage shall be ascertained or estimated according to such current market.

   (2) Property acquired or to be acquired by the Insured as a gift or under wills or similar bequests shall be valued at current market value at time loss or damage occurs. In no event, however, shall this policy cover such property beyond the Insured's interest therein and in event of loss of such property such interest of the Insured at time of loss shall be that as stipulated in the will, bequest, contract or other document executed between the Insured and the donor of said property.

   (3) Property of others loaned to the Insured, and which the Insured has been instructed to insure or for which the Insured may be liable, shall be valued at amounts agreed upon by the Insured and owners, or otherwise this Company shall not be liable beyond the current market value of the property at the time any loss or damage occurs and in no event for an amount in excess of that specified in the policy. Ascertainment or estimate of loss shall be made by the Insured and this Company, or if they differ then the amount of loss will be determined as provided by the Appraisal Clause of this policy.

7. It is a condition of this insurance that the Insured will, to the best of their ability, provide for the insured property being packed and unpacked by competent packers.

8. PAIRS AND SETS: In the event of the total loss of any articles which are part of a set, this Company agrees to pay the Insured, at the option of the Insured, the full amount of the value of such pair or set as determined by the Valuation Clause contained herein, subject otherwise to the applicable Deductible Clause set forth herein, and the Insured agrees, if such option is elected, to surrender the remaining article or articles of the pair or set to this Company.

9. It is understood and agreed that this policy does not cover the insured property on the premises of fair grounds or any national or international exposition unless such premises are specifically described by endorsement hereto.

10. OTHER INSURANCE: If there is any other valid and collectible insurance covering the property insured hereunder, whether prior, subsequent to, or simultaneous with this insurance, which in the absence of this insurance would cover the loss or damage hereby covered, then this Company shall not be liable hereunder for more than the excess over and above such other insurance.

This clause, however, shall not apply to insurance effected by owners of property loaned to the insured and the existence of such insurance or payment of a loss thereunder shall not constitute a defense to any claim otherwise payable under this policy, nor shall such insurance be called on to contribute to any loss payable hereunder.

11. MISREPRESENTATION AND FRAUD: This policy shall be void if the Insured has concealed or misrepresented any material fact or circumstance concerning this insurance or the subject thereof, or in case of any fraud, attempted fraud or false swearing by the Insured touching any matter relating to this insurance, or the subject thereof, whether before or after a loss.

12. NOTICE OF LOSS: The Insured shall as soon as practicable report to this Company or its agent every loss or damage which may become a claim under this policy and shall also file with the Company or its agent within ninety (90) days from date of loss a detailed sworn proof of loss. Failure by the Insured to report the said loss or damage and to file such sworn proof of loss as hereinbefore provided shall invalidate any claim under this policy for such loss.

13. EXAMINATION UNDER OATH: The Insured shall submit, and so far as is within his or their power shall cause all other persons interested in the property and members of the household and employees to submit to examinations under oath by any persons named by the Company, relative to any and all matters in connection with a claim and subscribe the same; and produce for examination all books of account, bills, invoices, and other vouchers or certified copies thereof if originals be lost, at such reasonable time and place as may be designated by the Company or its representatives, and shall permit extracts and copies thereof to be made.

14. SETTLEMENT OF CLAIMS: All adjusted claims shall be paid or made good to the Insured within thirty (30) days after presentation and acceptance of satisfactory proof of interest and loss at the office of this Company.

15. LOSS BUY BACK: The Insured shall have the right to repurchase from the Company property of the Insured that is recovered for the amount paid to the Insured for the loss, plus an amount which represents loss adjustment and recovery expenses.

Damaged property of the Insured, for which a total loss has been paid, may be repurchased by the Insured at the then fair market value of the damaged property.

The Company agrees to notify the Insured of its right to repurchase damaged or recovered property and the Insured shall have sixty days from date of notice to exercise the repurchase right. The Insured, in exercising this right, shall furnish the Company with copies of the proof of loss, police report and claim draft involving such property.

16. NO BENEFIT TO BAILEE: This insurance shall in no way inure directly or indirectly to the benefit of any carrier or other bailee.

17. SUBROGATION: In the event of any payment under this policy the Company shall be subrogated to all the Insured's rights of recovery therefor against any person or organization and the Insured shall execute and deliver instruments and papers and do whatever else is necessary to secure such rights. The Insured shall do nothing after loss to prejudice such rights. This clause shall not apply, however, to museums in which the insured property is being exhibited or on loan.

18. SUE AND LABOR: In case of loss or damage, it shall be lawful and necessary for the Insured, his or their factors, servants and assigns, to sue, labor and travel for, in and about the defense, safeguard and recovery of property insured hereunder, or any part thereof without prejudice to this insurance; nor shall the acts of the Insured or this Company in recovering, saving and preserving the property insured in case of loss or damage, be considered a waiver or an acceptance of abandonment to the charge whereof this Company will contribute according to the rate and quantity of the sum herein insured.

19. SUIT AGAINST COMPANY: No suit, action or proceeding for the recovery of any claim under this

policy shall be sustainable in any court of law or equity unless the same be commenced within twelve (12) months next after discovery by the Insured of the occurrence which gives rise to the claim. Provided, however, that if by the laws of the state within which his policy is issued such limitation is invalid, then any such claims shall be void unless such action suit or proceeding be commenced within the shortest limit of time permitted by the laws of such state to be fixed herein.

20. COLLECTION FROM OTHERS: No loss shall be paid hereunder if the Insured has collected the same from others.

21. APPRAISAL: If the Insured and the Company fail to agree as to the amount of loss, each shall, on the written demand of either made within sixty (60) days after receipt of proof of loss by the Company, select a competent and disinterested appraiser, the appraisal shall be made at a reasonable time and place. The appraisers shall first select a competent and disinterested umpire, and failing for fifteen (15) days to agree upon such umpire, then on the request of the Insured or the Company, such umpire shall be selected by a judge of a court of record in the state in which such appraisal is pending. The appraisers shall then appraise the loss, stating separately the current market value at the time of loss and the amount of loss, and failing to agree shall submit their difference to the umpire. An award in writing of any two shall determine the amount of loss. The Insured and the Company shall each pay his or its chosen appraiser and shall bear equally the other expenses of the appraisal

and umpire. The Company shall not be held to have waived any of its rights by any act relating to appraisal.

22. CANCELLATION: This policy may be cancelled by either the Insured or the Company on giving _____( ) days notice in writing to the other, and upon such cancellation the Insured shall furnish to the Company a complete statement of the Insured property and pay premium to date of cancellation as provided.

23. CHANGES: Notice to any agent or knowledge possessed by any agent or by any other person shall not effect a waiver or a change in any part of this policy or estop the Company from asserting any right under the terms of this policy, nor shall the terms of this policy be waived or changed, except by endorsement issued to form a part of this policy.

24. The interest of each Company hereunder is individual and not joint, and whenever the right or privilege is retained by the Companies, such right or privilege may be exercised by each Company independently.

25. REQUIRED BY LAW: Any provisions required by law to be stated in policies issued by subscribers hereto shall be deemed to have been stated herein.

In event of litigation subscribers hereto upon request agree to issue separate policies covering their subscription.

In witness whereof the Companies hereunder have caused this policy to be signed by a duly qualified officer, attorney or agent, this_____day of_____, 19____.

Company and Policy Number	Percentage Underwritten of each and every loss covered hereunder	Signature for Company
Company _____ Policy No. _____	%	_____
Company _____ Policy No. _____	%	_____
Company _____ Policy No. _____	%	_____
Company _____ Policy No. _____	%	_____
Company _____ Policy No. _____	%	_____

III. MANAGING
MUSEUM SECURITY

5. Museum and Gallery Security Management Techniques

J. L. Paulhus

The practice of security in museums and galleries is affected, as is any component of any organization, by conflicts that are the normal lot of any organization. There are sources of conflict affecting security that appear to be peculiar to museums and galleries. They involve three areas:

1. attitudes involved in problem-solving;
2. multiple authority organization;
3. conflicting interests.

Traditionally, problems were solved by discovering their cause and applying a remedy. This was done by searching for and analyzing the variables and factors which were thought to be relevant, reducing them to a common denominator to understand the problem better and then arriving at an appropriate solution.

In museums and galleries, where, by their nature, there are individuals, linked by a common interest, expert at solving problems and involved with the management of the institution, there will be various solutions advanced for perceived security problems. Because the solutions arise from persons trained in different fields, the perceptions of the problem and the significance of variables and factors, or sets of factors and variables upon which the solutions are predicated, will be different. The solutions may also be influenced by personal biases, status within the orgainzation of the institution, as well as by a focus on different results. When they are divergent or competitive they may be implemented through a "committee" process that accommodates the arguments given in support of the different solutions but begs the security problem; or, by an autocratic application of one of the solutions that will ensure a degree of resistance to the measures required for its application. An example of this sort of failure is the common need to secure and control access to a particular area or building. A "good" solution, let us say, would require a manned post to be established, at certain times, to record and control the coming and going of persons and items. The committee process solution would be to install an impressive lock on the entrance and provide keys to all trusted employees who must have access. This would be considered to meet the different results expected; avoid the cost of paying a guard, which could be applied to a more popular project; not denigrate the trusted employee who would not be subject to identification procedures, searches, and being logged in and out of the area; allow unrestricted access to trusted key holders; and allow all concerned to feel secure now that the problem has been solved.

Unfortunately this would cause the problem to become more serious. There actually would be no control: those responsible for the area would have no assurance that the inventory of the area would remain up to date; should an item not be located, or felt to be lost, searches involving the whole institution would have to be made because there would be no log of the persons who had had access, nor any record of the transactions of items in and out; it would be found that not only trusted key holders had had access but clerks, stenographers, runners, and sundry other persons also had been entrusted with a key because the trusted key holder was too busy; quite as likely it would also be found that extra keys had been cut to ensure that when an original key was forgotten or mislaid there would be another in the custody of a person delegated by the trusted key holder who, in turn, may have repeated the process for the same reason.

In effect, the committee process solution to the problem of securing a particular building or area would have made the problem worse. Not only would it impose the use of keys, which presents its own problems, and waste money on an ineffective endeavor, it would provide no control over the building or area and its contents. Worse yet, the institution would operate with a false sense of security until an unfortunate incident again brought the problem to attention.

Multiple authority within a gallery or museum can be unrecognized. Even when it is, it is rarely seen as a source of conflict in security matters. A museum or gallery can be a complex organization with many departments or areas under the control of a professional, an expert in a field, and responsible for the organization and administration of the department or area. It is, in many ways, an exclusive franchise without competition. If there is no one else doing the same thing within the institution, there is no comparative measurement of how well or how poorly the department or area is operating. As long as appropriate paper is being produced and no apparent mistakes are made, there is little to disturb its existence, nor will there arise any reason to justify its existence. It follows that security, which cuts across or impinges upon all areas of an institution, can be seen, consciously or unconsciously, as a competitor or a source of disturbance. In this context, security may also be seen as a source of manpower to be absorbed to increase the supervisory factor of a position or add to the prestige and authority of a department. It is almost redundant to point out that security operating under such motivations and stresses can be inefficient and possibly misused.

As well as the conflicts that arise from the dynamics of organization, structure, internal relationships, and the attitudes of its members, there is another conflict that operates on a different level. This conflict arises from the interests about the preservation and the presentation of artifacts and art.

It is generally agreed that an object can be indefinitely preserved if it is stored in an airtight container with an inert gas and kept in an appropriate state of heat, light, and humidity. In practice, it is also recognized, that this is not possible if the institution possessing this object is to fulfill its purpose of presenting it to the public. Curatorial and educational staffs agree, in general, that the conservation of artifacts and objects of art has a priority and accept its restrictions, but they have a strong tendency to ignore, or remain unaware of, the fact that human behavior is at least an equally serious hazard. A very common example of this type of conflict of interests involves the fire and theft policies of security and the presentation policies of the institution. Fire-prevention policy requires an open exit and protection against fire; theft prevention requires closed and locked doors and controls. Both of these, in turn, conflict with the aesthetic presentation and preservation policies of curators, educators, and conservators. Fire-detection monitors and the pipes and heads of the sprinkler system are considered to be unsightly and the water dispensed by the sprinklers and other firefighting equipment is considered a threat to the well-being of art and artifacts. The closed or locked doors and the controls to protect against theft, vandalism, bomb threats, and unwelcome visitors are felt to interfere with the comfort of visitors and staff.

This preamble is not intended to be an indictment of the way security is managed in museums and galleries. It is not the opening of a catalogue of security horror stories presented to justify the existence of security measures. The examples are simplified composites. They are meant to draw attention to security as an integral part of an institution subject to strains, internal and external, that can make it ineffectual if not recognized or effective, if taken into account.

SECURITY DIRECTOR

Most professions found in museums and galleries, contrary to popular belief, are neither esoteric nor occult. While they depend, more than the "hard" sciences, on informed opinion and experience, they have developed their own verifiable systems for measuring and quantifying data and applying their knowledge. Security is no different. It is based on solid, hard-nosed, tested experience, hardware, and academic training. It borrows from military and police sciences, psychology and sociology, engineering and electronics, law and management. It conducts research, measures and quantifies data which it authenticates, draws conclusions from formalized analyses, predicts probable events, and recommends appropriate reactions and responses which can be put into practice through a series of formalized decisions.

The first decision for an institution, at the security level, has to be the appointment of a person responsible for the preservation, protection, and safekeeping of the institution's property, staff, and visitors. Generally this is conceded to be the Security Director of the institution who must be provided with the authority and resources necessary to maintain the levels of personnel and equipment to carry out the security task successfully.

While the first decision may have been made by a government department or board of trustees, all subsequent ones, concerning security, should be made by the director. Whether the director deals personally with security or delegates it to another person, the principle of responsibility dictates that the delegate should be knowledgeable in security matters and that there be no intervening authority between the delegate and the director. The application of this simple principle is important. It should ensure that security does not become ineffective because of organizational or administrative problems or become a source of authority operating against the best interests of the institution.

An effective security organization should be designed to provide complete security coverage against loss, damage, and injury to staff and visitors. However well designed, it will not be effective if it is not seen as and integrated as a vital part of the life of the institution. It should not be solely the responsibility of the head of security. It should involve all departments and areas and the security responsibilities should be written into each job description.

A security organization demands a coordination of complex activities with a variety of functions, committed to protecting the institution, by integrating them into a system that detects circumstances that have a potential for loss, damage, and injury and prevents or minimizes their effects.

It is not possible to say which activity takes precedence at any one time, but all the following activities, if integrated, should provide the security functions needed by most museums and galleries:

1. physical controls;
2. guard controls;
3. fire prevention;
4. emergency and disaster controls;
5. identification controls;
6. key and combination lock controls;
7. training of security staff;
8. security training and education of all employees;
9. personnel safety and accident programs;
10. to establish these activities effectively requires:
    a. an awareness of the need for security;
    b. a survey of the security strengths and weaknesses of the institution;
    c. a plan to integrate activities into a system that responds to the resources available weighed against the risks that cannot be eliminated; and
    d. the acceptance of the risks that remain.

These requirements will be better understood if they are considered under the following categories or headings:

1. design and space planning;
2. quantification of risk;
3. surveillance and alarm systems;
4. management and training of security personnel;
5. liaison with local authorities;
6. documentation, records and controls;
7. cost of security personnel, operations, equipment, and insurance;
8. the use of independent consultants.

DESIGN AND SPACE PLANNING

Museums and gallerys have two aspects for security: first, the design of the building with its external interrelationships; and second, the design and arrangements of the areas and displays within the building.

Often designers and remodelers do not consider security as a building function. They may be unaware of security priorities that do not affect more common buildings and, because of the nature of museums and galleries, opt for aesthetic solutions to design problems which may create security problems, particularly where access control, internal traffic flow, and the use of space for security functions are concerned. For example:

Buildings that are part of a community's cultural and social life have operational modes that are different from those used for business and industry. While attention may be given to security in the design of an institution, the interrelationship between security needs and the operational modes of the building can go unrecognized. Unlike banks, for example, that normally have three modes of operation:

1. supervised by security personnel and occupied by staff. Usually on a working day, that is closed to customers, where there is moderate use of security personnel and moderate use of the alarm system;

2. supervised by security personnel and occupied by staff and public. Usually on a working day, that is open to customers, where there is greater use made of security personnel and moderate use made of the alarm system; and

3. supervised by security personnel alone. Usually at night and on holidays, that are closed to staff and customers, where there is least use of security personnel and greatest use of the alarm system.

Museums and galleries have four modes of operation, the three noted above plus:

4. supervised by security personnel and open to customers or public. Usually on weekends, holidays, and evenings, where there is greatest use of security personnel and greatest use of the alarm system.

Planners

Failure by the planners to identify for the designers or remodelers these modes of operation can lead to security problems that will be difficult to solve. It may result in unsatisfactory arrangements such as retrofitting security equipment and space dividers, the use of more guards than otherwise required, and, invariably, unbudgeted expenses. For instance: if the areas of an institution designed as auditoria and special-exhibit areas are not located on the perimeter of the building and capable of being isolated from the rest of the building, during mode three operation, they will escalate the mode of operation to mode four because the building cannot be isolated or made secure without the use of more guards, usually at overtime rates. If the auditoria and special-exhibit areas are designed to be isolated from the rest of the building they can be used by the community, when not required by the institution, without incurring additional costs, which would not be proper for the institution to absorb, or would discourage the community activity concerned.

Failure to identify security requirements and identify them as precisely as possible at the design stage will give security problems it did not create, problems that often have no satisfactory answer, cause operational difficulties, and are invariably expensive.

Security must be involved in the design process until the design also works adequately for its security functions. If the security head, or other person responsible for security, takes the initiative to raise the security consciousness of the planners and designers, it will be found that there is a wide area of adjustment that will allow solutions to the problems raised by the security and other functions of the building because security is, in effect, just another face of good management. Some of the obvious security functions of a building relate to access control, intrusion detection, fire prevention, reaction to natural or man-made emergencies, and traffic flow within and immediately outside the building.

QUANTIFICATION OF RISK

The development of a plan for the introduction of a security system is a process that involves the whole institution. The planner must ensure that security objectives fit into the hierarchy of the institution's objectives. If the security programs, which form part of the security system, are to receive support it is important that the security assumptions about risk and internal and external conditions that define security needs be seen as rational.

The methods of risk analysis are often given as research, screening, monitoring, diagnosis, and prevention or corrective action. The conventional methods of security paraphrase these as security survey for research, screening, and monitoring; analysis for diagnosis; and recommendations for prevention or corrective action. Risk analysis, in security terms for museums and galleries, is a process for quantifying, as much as possible, the risks presented to a museum or gallery by human, societal and natural hazards to which the institution is vulnerable, estimating their effect and the cost of eliminating or mitigating it.

Security Survey

The security survey is a formal process for gathering data about an institution from which recommendations can be made to formulate a new security system, or reformulate an existing one, and prepare a plan for its integration into the overall management system of the institution. Certain steps are essential if it is to produce the data from which an accurate estimate of the institution's needs can be made. These are:

1. determine the objectives of the survey to avoid confusing symptoms with the factors which may be their cause;
2. evaluate previous losses, damage, injuries, reactions to fire or other emergencies, legal suits arising from these, and the types and rates of any insurance coverage involved;
3. check the results of any previous recommendations made to correct security deficiencies;
4. hold preliminary discussions with all managers concerned about the reasons for and the scope of the survey, to ensure that it is seen as a beneficial activity rather than an useless imposition, and arrange timings for subsequent visits and other details;
5. assemble a survey team consisting, if possible, of members familiar with the operation of the institution; make them familiar with the background of the survey and detail their responsibilities;
6. locate the institution on a map or plan large enough in scale to show its relationship to the surrounding buildings and area;
7. interface with local authorities such as are concerned with fire, policing, provision of utilities, and insurance — and also with neighbors;
8. evaluate building plans;
9. review current formal and informal procedures used by the institution and the laws, by-laws, and regulations that affect it; then
10. make a survey checklist; and
11. carry out the survey.

The security survey should then provide the data required for risk analysis and identify the institution's security needs.

The measurement and quantification of risk involves three steps:

1. scaling of each hazard or threat;
2. scaling the institution's vulnerability to each threat or hazard according to its programs, displays, artifacts, works of art, personnel, equipment, and stores; and
3. the correlation of these variables.

The measurement and quantification of risk answer the question; Which of these threats or hazards is the most likely to occur, and if it does, what will be the loss or damage and to what extent will it disrupt programs or close down the institution?

Scaling is the assignment of numbers to objects and events according to logical and acceptable rules. In the case of museums and galleries, where experimentation with fire, theft, or vandalism is not the best way to evaluate threat or hazard, one must rely of the applied science of common sense and experience to assign numbers to the objects and events to be scaled. Any numbering system can be used. Because it is commonly understood, the use of percentages is suggested. For example, opinions about the probability of an event occurring can be translated into measurement with a high degree of significance if it is done as follows:

Almost certain to occur	76 to 100%
Highly likely to occur	51 to 75%
Likely to occur	26 to 50%
Least likely to occur	1 to 25%

The spread of 25 points within each division leaves a wide area for variability of opinion which can help to reconcile differences between individuals expressing opinions, or other subjective statements, about each threat or hazard.

The vulnerability of the institution to loss or damage caused by a threat or hazard event could, in turn, be expressed as:

A.	Would shut down operations permanently or, at least, for a long time	76 to 100%
B.	Would shut down operations for an unacceptable time	51 to 75%
C.	Would curtail operations enough to interfere with the functioning of the institution to an unacceptable degree	26 to 50%
D.	Would interfere with the functioning of the institution but to a tolerable level	1 to 25%

A simple example of the use of these two scales will show how they may be correlated. That is: Threat or Hazard (T) multiplied ($\times$) by Vulnerability (V) will give a correlation value for Risk (R). Abbreviated it reads T $\times$ V = R (see Table 5.1).

Threat or hazard	Probability score (T)	Object of threat or hazard	Vulnerability score (V)	Risk* score (R)
Damage				
Wear and tear	80	Artwork "A"	35	2800
Vandalism	60	Artwork "B"	5	400
Failure of utilities				
Environmental	30	Storage "A"	70	2100
Elevators	60	Visitors	5	300
Visitors				
Illness	90	Area "A"	10	900
Injuries	90	Exhibit "B"	5	450
Assault	60	Main entrance	0	60
Assault	40	Area "A"	2	80
Fire	10	Display "A"	100	1000
	70	Film storage	100	7000
	30	Paint shop	60	1800
Theft	70	In transit	15	1050
	40	Display "D"	5	200
	10	Storage "C"	60	600
	60	Workshop	15	900
	80	Curator's office	5	400

*All items could also be listed in terms of cost of repair, replacement, insurance rate, effect on public relations, and the possibility of litigation. In the case of fire, other emergencies, and utilities there may be costs arising because of laws, regulations or contracts that require reimbursement for services, etc. There may be costs explicit or implied for items on loan. It may be that items cannot be costed because policy will not allow the price of certain items to be made known or because it is not possible to evaluate certain one-of-a-kind or irreplaceable items.

Table 5.1 Risk Correlations

Other items which could have been included were kidnapping and strikes. It is suggested that the problem of kidnapping, which would involve the listing of employees, and sometimes their families, in order of importance is one that raises emotional issues. It would probably be better to treat it as a separate matter. The matter of strikes would involve listing the professions and trades employed in the institution in order of their union's capacity to close down the institution. For example, it could be assumed that the security employees going on strike would close down the institution because of the lack of supervision for the public areas. The effect of sympathetic activity by sister or affiliated unions should not be discounted.

In effect, the procedure of correlation forces the analysis of data in terms of the interrelationships between the components of risk. It casts some light on the assumptions made about threats and hazards and vulnerabilities which may appear incongruous. As shown in Table 5.1, why should an assault on a visitor rate only a risk score of 80 when wear and tear on art-work "A" comes out as 2800? Further analysis may reveal that the frequency of one event is a function of the location of the institution in a disfavored neighborhood, and the value of the item of art to the institution is a function of its being a one-of-a-kind representative item. Whatever the case, correlation allows risk to be listed in order of priority and provides the basis for discussion that should produce agreement about the security needs of the institution and the security measures to be used. The process of singling out threats, hazards, and vulnerabilities as components of risk in relation to individual items, areas, displays, and equipment and correlating them removes the consideration of security measures from subjective feelings, assumptions, and opinions based on erroneous conventions and ex-cathedra solutions. It allows them to be considered in terms of cost and the documentation of risks which cannot be met in a way that forces them to be recognized.

Before recommending any measures to satisfy the institution's security needs they should be questioned to define the scope and character of each measure. The needs should be subjected to the following questions:

1. Is there reasonable evidence to support the existence of each threat or hazard?
2. What are the degrees of vulnerability to each of these threats and hazards?
3. What are the risks?
4. What would be the effect of the various security measures that could be proposed on the efficiency of other areas of the institution?
5. What limitations would be imposed on the proposed security measures by the physical characteristics of the building?
6. What would be the effect of possible budget constraints?
7. To what degree would the maximum security possible with current resources be acceptable?
8. What alternate or short-term measures or techniques are available to provide minimal but acceptable levels of security on a temporary basis?
9. Are the remaining risks acceptable? If not, what activities are available to be cut back to reduce the risk or provide resources for sufficient security measures?

There are conventions, techniques, methods, and procedures for the completion of security surveys but no hard and fast rules. The field is too broad.

Each institution will be similar to another but the differences are too many to allow a cut-and-dried fill-in-the-spaces format to be recommended. If the basic homework is done, the analysis will point out incongruities at some stage of the process which, if not ignored or glossed over, will return the researchers to the survey with more precise or specific objectives.

Risk analysis should be equally effective for large or small institutions; for the whole or part of an institution; for one building or several; for a new building or an old one; and, particularly for the concept of a new building where space, functions, organization, and populations have been estimated or established. Risk analysis can be used as an ongoing process to provide an up-to-date measure of an institution's state of security and the operation of the security measures in use.

SURVEILLANCE AND ALARM SYSTEMS

The ability to respond consistently within a pre-determined time is the most important focus for an institution that uses an alarm system for surveillance and detection. No matter how complex or sophisticated are the lighting and the mechanical and electronic programs installed in an institution, if the response is inadequate to prevent loss or damage, the money and other resources spent on these programs have been lost. All such programs must be considered as supplementing the activities of a person.

Lighting has many functions. When it is used for surveillance, as a security function, care should be taken that it lights and makes clearly visible the critical areas but does not highlight the guard or surveillance instrument.

Locking devices and perimeters, such as doors, walls, fences, moats, and space, should be such that they will gain the response time required by the particular alarm device that is installed outside the perimeter they protect.

The electronic programs should ensure that the monitor is notified immediately and accurately of any alarms without undue false alarms or breakdowns. There are four generally recognized ways to monitor an alarm system which can be used in combination with three categories of alarms and integrated into a system to meet the needs that have been identified for an institution:

1. Ways to monitor:
   a. Central Station — usually operated by a private company which will assume the responsibility for installation of alarms and warning police and fire departments and others.
   b. Proprietary Station — usually installed in the institution where

guards on duty monitor and react to the alarm. It is the property and responsibility of the instittion.

c. Local Station — usually does not report to a central point but sounds a bell, siren, or other device in the immediate vicinity. It is an excellent device for warning persons nearby but of doubtful value against any type of threat if response cannot be certain.

d. Direct Dialing — usually monitored by the local police and fire departments in response to a direct call made automatically when an alarm is given.

2. Categories of alarms:

a. Anti-intrusion — installed for the detection of unauthorized persons in the protective perimeters that should ring the institution and in the areas and spots in between:

   i. Space or motion detectors that operate by A, saturating an area with radio frequency waves that are picked up and balanced at a receiving unit. When something intrudes into the area the reception becomes unbalanced and causes an alarm; and B, by means of a microphone that picks up sounds and transmits them to a monitor or analyzer which initiates an alarm if the sounds are not recognized.

   ii. Photoelectric or laser beam devices, which initiate an alarm when the beam they project is interrupted.

   iii. Capacitance or magnetic field devices, which create a magnetic field and initiate an alarm when the field is altered.

   iv. Vibration detectors, which, when tuned to an appropriate degree of sensivity, initiate an alarm when that degree has been surpassed.

   v. Electromagnetic switches, which create a magnetic field between magnets and initiate an alarm when the magnets are separated.

   vi. Electromechanical switches, which are usually a set of contact switches held in place by springs that initiate an alarm when the contacts are separated.

   vii. Pressure switches, which are balanced to a plus and/or minus degree of pressure and will initiate an alarm when pressure is increased or released beyond the limits to which they have been balanced.

   viii. Taut or trip wires, which are joined to a two-way switch which will initiate an alarm if the wire is loosened or tightened.

      ix. Closed-curcuit television. The proper use of closed-circuit television (CCTV) can often reduce the cost of manpower and in certain cases, with proper interfacing equipment, initiate alarms. It is most useful when installed with two-way voice communication at alarm and perimeter access points where it can provide immediate information and avoid unnecessary dispatching of patrols to investigate.

  b. Fire. Installed according to the appropriate federal, state, provincial and county or municipal standards. They use:

      i. Fire detectors, which may be

        A. Ionization, which initiate an alarm when invisible products of combustion interfere with a current between two electrified plates; or

        B. Thermal, which sense temperature and initiate an alarm when a set temperature is exceeded or when a too rapid rise of temperature, over a certain degree, is sensed.

      ii. Sprinkler systems, which consist of a piping system equipped with sprinkler heads kept closed by a fusible link that separates when a preset temperature has been reached, initiating an alarm and wetting the area below the head if no intervening antiaccident device is integrated into the system.

  c. Environmental. Installed to monitor and report on temperature, humidity, air flow and condition, water pressure, power sources, etc. These may report to other than security monitors.

All three catagories should be integrated to report to a control point that can monitor them twenty-four hours a day. This may not be possible if a central monitoring station is used. The company may not cover environmental or fire alarms. If a proprietary system is used, standards that apply locally may require a separate fire-alarm system. It can report, however, to the same place as the security and environmental alarms. Local alarms should always be installed in the immediate area of a fire monitor as well as at the monitoring station. *Direct dialing should not be used to monitor environmental alarms.*

    If the devices comprising the alarm system have been properly selected, integrated, installed, and adjusted, malfunctions will rarely occur if proper testing and maintenance are regularly carried out. Spare parts must be readily available and regularly inspected or tested, according to the manufacturer's specifications, by a qualified technician. Proper operation of an alarm system requires that

1. Designated personnel should be available to effect minor repairs and maintenance and that service technicians be available, on short notice, to deal with greater problems.
2. Emergency power be available and interfaced with normal sources to ensure changeover without disrupting the alarm system.
3. Plans and diagrams and relevant information about the alarm system should be kept up to date, given necessary protection because it should be classified information, but made readily available to those persons listed as authorized to use them.
4. The control or monitoring area should be suitably located and designed to protect the monitoring personnel and their means of communication. Admittance should be appropriately restricted.

MANAGEMENT AND TRAINING
OF SECURITY PERSONNEL

The management and training of security personnel can easily be done on a person-to-person basis in a small institution where the objectives, organization, and responsibilities of all are known to all. In moderate or larger-sized institutions, the complexities may require an organized procedure to manage and train security personnel. The following procedure can provide guidance if the steps are taken in order:

1. determining the duties;
2. organizing the duties;
3. selecting personnel;
4. training personnel;
5. supervising personnel.

Consideration of design and space planning, quantification of risk, and surveillance and alarm systems steps should determine the duties to be performed by the security staff. They will be easier to recognize if they are placed in one of the following categories:

1. operation and enforcement of a personnel identification and pass systems;
2. control and patrolling of perimeters, areas, and spots in between;
3. operation and enforcement of vehicle access, material and property control programs;
4. monitoring and responding to alarm systems;

5. responding to fire and other emergency procedures;
6. protection of property, material, and exhibits against loss or damage and staff and visitors against injury;
7. statistical or periodic and individual reporting;
8. performance of nonroutine duties; and
9. training.

When the duties have been determined they should be organized according to the location where they will be performed. Such locations are usually called "posts." The number of guards required to carry out the duties at each post are usually called staffers of a post, and the duration of each duty at each post is called shift scheduling. For example, the duties performed at (1) and (3) above, could be performed at one post provided the staff and vehicle entrances are in the same area and adjacent; and those at (4), (5), and (7) could be distributed from the monitoring or control center of the institution.

Once the posts have been identified, staffing requirements can be decided if a thoughtful procedure is followed. The suggested procedure is one that requires making a chart of the posts that includes the assumptions that arise from the duties and the staffing procedure. For example:

It has been decided that the institution will be supervised by security round-the-clock; will be open to the public from 10 AM to 6 PM seven days per week and requires 22 security posts to do this. The requirements could be charted as shown in Table 5.2.

Table 5.2. Chart for staffing requirements

Post no.		Staffed from/to		Days per week							Number of guards	Total Shifts shifts daily weekly	
			S	M	T	W	T	F	S			
1	Staff and vehicle entrance	0001 2400	x	x	x	x	x	x	x	2	3	42
2	Main entrance	1000 1800	x	x	x	x	x	x	x	1	1	7
3–18	16 display areas	1000 1800	x	x	x	x	x	x	x	16	1	112
19	Control room	0001 2400	x	x	x	x	x	x	x	1	3	21
20	Patrol	1800 0200	x	x	x	x	x	x	x	1	1	7
21	Patrol	0200 1000	x	x	x	x	x	x	x	2	1	14
22	Supervisor	0001 2400	x	x	x	x	x	x	x	1	3	21
	Totals		32	32	32	32	32	32	32			224

The assumptions could be:

1. That security employees work 5 eight-hour shifts per week. Therefore to cover 224 shifts would require $224/5 = 44$ persons with 4 shifts left uncovered or 45 persons with one shift to spare ($45 \times 5 = 225 - 224 = +1$). A review of the preceding steps will show whether or not 45 persons should be hired.

2. If the review indicates that 4 shifts can be eliminated the assumption will arise that there may be more economies latent in the security plan. This should require reconsideration of all the factors which may have to be reformulated before being again placed in the chart.

3. If the review shows that the 4 shifts cannot be eliminated and the spare shift, produced by hiring 45 persons, can be absorbed, the assumption arises that further resources may be required to meet the needs of security. This also should require reconsideration and the use of alarms, barriers, and manpower adjusted to suit.

These are not the only assumptions that could be made. There may be assumptions about part-time employees and volunteers; various hours of opening to the public; variations in the daily hours of work; etc. This process of charting should be repeated until there is satisfaction that the functions defined by the charting of duties and posts can be integrated into a coherent security system that meets the needs of the institution.

Once the duties required at each post have been determined and the staffing, or the number of persons required at each post, established, post orders can be written so that each person on each post can understand and carry out its function. These will also define the job specifications and indicate the qualifications required to perform the duties adequately.

At this point it is appropriate, depending on the size of the security force, to survey the employment market to find out if there are enough applicants in the area to be hired and the approximate level of their qualifications. If there is not an adequate source it may be necessary to go further afield or consider a training program and accept the implied costs and lapse of time. To wait longer may result in scuttling timetables, made by other departments of the institution, about publicity for openings, loans, guests, etc. An appreciation of recruiting problems at this time should give enough leeway for the adjustment of the programs of other departments.

Once job specifications are defined and employee qualifications are set, job conditions have to be decided upon before hiring can begin. Such things as hours of work and days off can be arrived at by rearranging the information in Table 5.2 into a shift reconciliation as shown in Table 5.3.

Shift hours	Sun	Mon	Tue	Wed	Thu	Fri	Sat	Weekly Total
0800 – 1600**	4	4	4	4	4	4	4	28
1000 – 1800***	17	17	17	17	17	17	18****	120
1600 – 2400**	4	4	4	4	4	4	4	28
1800 – 0200	1	1	1	1	1	1	1	7
0001 – 0800**	4	4	4	4	4	4	4	28
0200 – 1000	2	2	2	2	2	2	2	14
Daily total	32	32	32	32	32	32	33	225*
Days off	13	13	13	13	13	13	12	90
Total persons	45	45	45	45	45	45	45	

*Each person works five shifts per week; therefore, to cover 225 shifts takes 45 persons (225/5 = 45). Each will have two days off, that is a total of 90 days off (45 × 2 = 90) during the week. Because the institution is open seven days a week these days must be distributed. This is simply done by allocating daily the difference between the total number employed (45) and the number on duty on each day (32). The distribution is shown as days off in the shift reconciliation example above.

**Includes monitor and supervisor.

***Includes main entrance.

****Accounts for the spare shift, previously noted in Table 5.2, which is being used at the main entrance on Saturday when it is very busy.

Table 5.3. Shift reconciliation chart

When union contracts or other regulations require benefits such as annual, sick, statutory, and special leaves, the total value of these, in terms of shifts not worked, should be distributed by means of a shift reconciliation. Where benefits are granted on an annual basis it may be necessary to make a shift reconciliation based on a year instead of a week. A yearly reconciliation could also include the distribution of training time. The basic assumption about the number of days worked and the number of persons required to staff the posts becomes more complex. It should be worked out as follows:

Number of days in a year		365
Number of days off (52 × 2)	104	
Number of days annual leave	15	
Number of days sick leave	15	
Statutory or government holidays	11	
Annual refresher training	7	
Quarterly seminars	3	
Total	155	155
Shifts worked	210	

In the case of yearly computation the number of shifts will also have to be counted by multiplying the weekly total of shifts by the number of weeks in the year. In this example 11,700 (225 × 52 = 11,700), when divided by the number of shifts worked by one person in a year, shows that the staffing of 22 posts now requires 55.71 persons or man years.

The consideration of benefits is important when allocating human resources to meet security needs. The decision on how many posts are required and for how long per day is not as simple as saying "One shift, one man." If a post is to be manned 24 hours per day and the shift is 8 hours long, three shifts will be required. Over a year this adds up to 1,095 shifts. If one person works only 210 shifts per year, as illustrated above, it will require 5.21 persons or man-years to keep the post covered, almost twice the naive assumption of "One shift, one man." It must be a hard-and-fast rule that all the statistics concerning manpower are known, understood, and applied when staffing posts.

The same procedure exemplified for the construction of the weekly charts for staffing requirements and shift reconciliation can be used for distributing shifts, days off, leaves, and training on a yearly or any other length of time basis.

Apart from agreeing to job specifications and possessing the required qualifications, a guard should present a good appearance, speak the languages common to the area, have a pleasant manner, be physically able to carry out the duties, be trainable, and, if possible, have previous experience.

The decision to hire "in-house" guards or contract for them or use a combination of both should be one brought about by circumstances. *"In-house" guards are thought to be more loyal and alert to the needs of the institution* because they can be trained as desired and made to feel that they are an integral part of the institution. They create an administrative burden, however. Contract guards relieve the institution of the greater part of the administrative burden but the institution has no real say in their selection, often suffers a high degree of turnover, and can never be sure of loyalty, which, it is always reasonable to believe, belongs to the contractor company. It may be possible to enjoy some of the advantages and avoid some of the disadvantages of both if a combination of both is used. For example: the basic security of the institution could be carried out by "in-house" guards and the public areas supervised with contract guards.

The subjects to be taught during training should arise directly from the duties to be performed. Bearing in mind that the purpose of museums and galleries is to serve the public, the guard, apart from the performance of security duties, is also the direct contact with the public on behalf of the institution. He is also a symbol of order and good management to the staff. Good public relations can be ensured if the guard is given a good knowledge of the institution and its role, information about other points of interest in the community and their location, other appropriate general information, and how to pass these on to the public in a courteous and professional manner. Because opinion about artifacts and art and their value is prone to provoke arguments, this area of information is properly in the domain of curators. The public-relations training of the guard should indicate quite clearly the limits to which a guard can go in providing this sort of information. The attitudes desired by the institution should be inculcated while training in security subjects is carried out.

Formal and in-job training should be supplemented with staff conferences, employee meetings, discussion sessions, incentive awards, or any process that allows a guard to propose improvements or give opinions in a controlled situation will lead to a feeling of "being part of the team."

The security guard is the most important security tool at the disposal of the institution. He has great influence on the quality of security that prevails. He should be trained to recognize potentially harmful circumstances and motivated to avoid delay in dealing with them so as to minimize risk. *He should never be assigned janitorial or housekeeping roles that detract from his security purpose.* As a rule a guard should be detailed for duty only by a security supervisor and never instructed or taken to task in public.

LIAISON WITH LOCAL AUTHORITIES

Institutions, in the long term, cannot abdicate from the responsibility for protecting themselves, nor can they view their security role in such a way that they exclude others who have a vital concern in their welfare as part of the community. The most important function of security is protection and prevention. When institutional security fails in some degree, it is usually the local authorities such as fire, police, and utilities, who assume responsibility and back up the institution. Liaison with local authorities is an essential part of the security function of a museum or gallery. There should be no reluctance to interface with any local authority at an appropriate level, for

1. it is the immediate back-up for the institution's security system;
2. it should be part of the support required by the institution's emergency programs and plans;
3. it is often the sole source of information about the threat from crime and social disturbances;
4. its specialists are a source of information, advice, and assistance in security matters; and
5. it is the appropriate link with federal, provincial, state, county, and other municipal forces when a security problem exceeds local boundaries.

Liaison by the security head will keep the police aware of the problems peculiar to the institution and often ensure the availability of expert help, advice, and prompt coordination responses to alarms or urgent situations; provide an awareness of the possible links with other authorities with a potential for help; and, not least, is possibly the first and only point where undesirable publicity can be effectively managed.

Liaison with the fire department should also be on a personal level. While the fire chief may be the contact in smaller centers, the inspector for the area and the officer in charge of the station which will respond in the first instance should also be involved in larger centers. They should be kept up to date on the aspects of the institution that are involved with or affecting their response. They should be included in decisions concerning the way firefighters and their equipment will enter the building; the availability and condition of internal support such as pumps, standpipes, firefighting equipment, and operation of elevators; the possible hazards arising from stored combustibles and chemicals; the protection of artifacts and art and persons; the role played by the staff of the institution before and after the arrival of the fire department.

Not as important as the police and fire departments but a good source of advice and information are the insurance companies. They may interfere with the plans of an institution by refusing to give insurance coverage or require very high rates if they feel the security provided to the object or event is inadequate or uncertain. Their information about the security of institutions is often obtained from the local police, and they seem to interact quite freely with one another, making them a reliable source of information concerning the appropriateness of borrowing from or making a loan to another institution, particularly when they are located in other countries. They can also be sources of technical information that should not be ignored, particularly in the areas of hijacking and kidnapping. Liaison with insurance companies should be in person and in writing. Insurance companies may be involved in the recovery of items which may involve crime, as in the cases of art-napping, kidnapping, and theft. No action concerning any crime should be taken in conjunction with an insurance company without prior liaison with the appropriate police force.

Documentation, Records, and Controls

The registration system, and the inventory and stock controls of an institution have a potential for producing losses. They may be manipulated to cover theft and fraud or used to hide or resolve discrepancies that result from inadequate accounting procedures, poor controls, or employee neglect.

Manipulation can be avoided if the registrar and the inventory and stores clerk develop a system by which they mark, for identification, all artifacts, art, equipment, furnishings, and appropriate stores; account for them in registers, inventories, and stock controls; ensure that registers and inventories are checked regularly; and integrate these procedures with the institution's programs for control of access, shipping, and receiving.

The registrar should be aware of

1. the movement of the institution's holdings in and out of and within the institution,
2. the implications of insurance contracts,
3. the requirements of loss reporting and recovery,
4. the essential records required.

If there is no program to notify the registrar of the movement of art and artifacts into and out of and within the institution, there will be no particular concern about their absence until an interested person reports that an item cannot be located. In the case of furnishings and equipment, each display, area, and room should have an up-to-date inventory sheet posted against which the occupant or security guard on patrol can check. This should ensure that discrepancies are immediately reported and actual losses ascertained as soon as possible. Failure to implement this type of control will sooner or later cause unnecessary concern, false alarms, and delays in reporting real losses.

Insurance contracts held by the institution imply the need for appropriate and accurate records. The valuation clauses are usually based on a schedule of insured works or artifacts, actual cost value against a certain amount, and registration or accession records. All these require proof of ownership, proof of condition, proof of value, and satisfactory identification.

The sooner a loss is reported, the greater the probability of recovery. Even when ownership is adequately established, repossession of a recovered artifact or work of art will remain in doubt until it has been satisfactorily identified. Therefore photographs, description in terms of technical data about materials, structure, and physical characteristics as well as evidence of authenticity and continuity of possession are records vital to the final repossession of an artifact or work of art. Essential records should include the following:

1. a record of the introduction of the artifact or piece of art into the institution;
2. a description including, if at all possible, a sharp photograph and a recent condition report;
3. a systematic record of verification of holdings;
4. In and Out registers for storage areas;

5. a record of inspections of items on display by members of the curatorial or registrar's staff;
6. a record of the verification of items out on loan; and,
7. a record of inspections or condition reports on items out on loan.

The stores and inventory clerk should maintain an inventory showing the distribution of equipment, machinery, and furnishings to displays, areas, and rooms with a copy of the local holdings posted in each display, area, or room. This allows the guard on patrol to report variations and assists in the identification of items during searches required to establish a loss or locate a reported bomb. A stock-control program should be maintained to distribute stock and other items to work orders and control the disposal of scrap via the pass system.

COST OF SECURITY PERSONNEL, OPERATIONS, EQUIPMENT, AND INSURANCE

It is paradoxical that institutions which house priceless objects that are often irreplaceable, do not hesitate to acquire new ones and devote resources to the repair, conservation, and protection of these objects against environmental hazards and yet fail sometimes, to devote sufficient resources to protect them from the hazardous effects of human activities. Sound management should not view resources devoted to security as unproductive.

Similar to insurance companies, which insure against intangibles, the production of security cannot be measured directly as cost-effective unless a comparative period of insecurity has been allowed to exist. No security program can present a dollar savings except by comparison. A security system must be judged in terms of its contribution to the well-being of the institution. As long as an institution does not feel secure, it is likely that security will need more resources.

The cost of security arises from the use of equipment, personnel, and insurance.

There is always a tendency to opt for equipment to make up for any inadequacy in the number of guards because it is felt to be a one-time expenditure. This is not necessarily so. When the guarantee period ends, during which the supplier provided the maintenance, parts, and labor, a continuous contract may be required for these services at a cost that may become unacceptable. Equipment, as a general rule, should be purchased, or leased, according to its ability to extend the senses and abilities of a guard; simplicity of installation, operation, and maintenance; and its suitability for future use and adaptability to future generation equipment.

As already indicated, the number of guards is determined by the location and nature of a building and its contents; the layout of its galleries or display areas and presentation of exhibits; the number and nature of its visitors and the freedom they are given; and the capabilities of the alarm system.

Again, there are three ways to provide security personnel for an institution:

1. hire, train, and equip one's own;
2. contract with a security firm; or
3. use various combinations of (1) and (2).

In the long run, if it is to be cost effective, the method used to provide security personnel must be subject to a caution similar to the one made for equipment: it should not be unduly complicated; it should satisfy the need; and should be adaptable to future operations.

Insurance is a partial answer to protection and recovery of losses. It is not a preventive measure. It becomes effective only after a loss has occurred. It is usually an expense without any return other than a feeling of being protected to the extent that can be afforded or allowed. Insurance companies reserve the right not to write insurance when they feel a risk is unacceptable, or they may discourage the purchase of insurance with high premiums. Dollars spent on security measures and loss prevention will usually be reflected in a lower insurance rate, which should be limited to an amount that covers only those risks arising from negligence and incompetence.

USE OF INDEPENDENT SECURITY CONSULTANTS

Most manufacturers or distributors of security equipment and services offer consultant services. While some are very competent, it is useful to keep in mind, others are not. Although they provide technical knowledge, they are sales oriented and often limited to experience with their own products, systems, and services.

It is wise to use the services of an independant consultant when new equipment, services, and systems are being considered. This should ensure that they are properly selected, according to the compromises that have to be made, and properly installed.

In particular, the advice of a consultant should be sought before constructing a new building or reconstructing an old one, to ensure that appropriate security functions are built in. Failure to do this will make the cost of retrofitting security measures and altering the building much greater. This may discourage the use of equipment in favor of more guards than would have been necessary, creating a continuing financial burden.

Many security consultants are generalists and may not have experience with the museum and gallery field. They may not be aware of the intrinsic values that have to be protected and the security weaknesses that are inherent in this type of institution. It is important that the institution considering the use of a security consultant satisfy itself about the following:

1. the credentials of the consultant and the firm he represents;
2. the procedures to be used for the safeguarding and distributing of reports and supporting documentation;
3. that the firm and consultant are free from any affiliation, or financial relationship, with any manufacturer or supplier of security equipment, systems, or services;
4. that the consultant has knowledge of and experience with the aspects of security peculiar to museums, galleries, and similar institutions.

It is a recognized and common practice to use the services of consultants. They are used to audit financial management systems. They provide advice to architects and engineers. They give opinions to financial institutions and investors. Their services are considered as a normal cost to whoever hires them. The same holds true for security. A consultant can provide a different view of a situation that may identify security deficiencies, suggest a more economical use of resources, and prevent potential losses, damage, and injuries from occurring. A consultant's services are valuable for improving an institution's state of security or, at the very least, giving the assurance that it is satisfactory.

Advice concerning the use of security consultants should be sought from museums and galleries who have made use of their services or who have them on staff.

CONCLUSION

Security can be as simple as putting a lock or a guard on a gate or as complex as that required for the protection of a government's property, information, and members. For museums and galleries it lies, depending on size and complexity, somewhere in between. There is no particular mystery about it, although its ramifications can spread throughout an institution. Solutions to its problems are achieved, just as are the solutions to problems in any other field, by the use of common sense, hard work, and tenacity applied through tested procedures by experienced people. It is hoped that some insight has been provided by this brief introduction into some of the techniques that have evolved and are evolving as they are being applied to security problems. At the same time, the reader may also have been exposed to the philosophy that is tacit in a professional approach to museum and gallery security.

6. Common Sense Security for Museum Libraries

Timothy Walch

The theft of valuable cultural materials — manuscripts, books, and art objects — has a long history. The Assyrians and the Greeks knew the problem well and protected their collections of clay tablets by placing curses on those who would dare to steal such treasures. Unfortunately, curses have not proven to be deterrents to art theft, although, even today, much cursing goes on when a theft is discovered.

Although art theft and museum security are popular topics of discussion in the museum world, the security problem in museum libraries also merits attention. These libraries, maintained for the benefit of the scholarly community as well as the curatorial staff, hold valuable collections of prints, books, manuscripts, sketchbooks, photographs, and other research materials. Many of these items are unique and irreplaceable, deserving special protection. Museum library directors should be conscious of the treasures on both library shelves and gallery walls.

Portions of this chapter have appeared in *Archives and Manuscripts: Security*, published by the Society of American Archivists in 1977 and in the *Curator*, a quarterly publication of the American Museum of Natural History. I am grateful for the permission of these organizations to republish parts of my earlier work.

Even though the problem of museum library and special collections theft can be easily identified, the solution is not simple. One of the most frustrating aspects of the problem is that the techniques used by rare-book and manuscript thieves vary widely. The thief may be a clever professional using the same tricks employed by shoplifters, a disgruntled or indebted employee, or a student who cannot afford to do extensive photocopying. A survey of reading room and staff areas does not make predicting who will be a thief or what he or she will steal easy.

RARE BOOK THEFT

Three fairly typical cases from the pages of the Society of American Archivist's *Archival Security Newsletter* illustrate the variety of rare book and manuscript thefts.

"Thou Shalt Not Steal"

The pastor of the First Baptist Church of a small town in Texas was charged recently with the theft of more than $75,000 worth of books and manuscripts from 108 institutions. The good reverend was apprehended after he attempted to sell some of the stolen books to a Dallas book dealer. The dealer had seen a circular identifying the volumes as the property of a local historical society and museum. The minister was arrested and later released on $10,000 bond. His congregation was shocked. The chairman of the board of deacons at the church told reporters that the minister "was doing a good job for the Lord — we thought." The book dealer hypothesized that the minister was able to steal so much because he was trusted by museum staff members. No one suspected that the minister might be a thief. An interesting twist to the case is the fact that the book dealer himself once pleaded guilty to charges of manuscript thievery while he was a student at a major midwestern university.

"Winslow Homer is Missing"

During the first six months of 1976, college and university libraries discovered that prints by Winslow Homer had been systematically cut from magazines in their collections. At least a dozen institutions in the Northeast, Middle Atlantic, and Middle West regions of the country were victimized. In each case, the magazines were shelved in open stack areas where the thieves worked apparently unnoticed by library patrons. Stolen items included the numerous Homer woodcut prints published in *Harper's Weekly* between 1858 and 1875 and in similar journals of the period. There was substantial evidence that the thieves used a special bibliography to locate unsigned lithographs and that their efforts were not limited to Winslow Homer. One library, for example, lost almost 800 lithographs from their issues of *Vanity Fair*. Prints from these and other nineteenth-century journals have a market value of $20 to $100 apiece.

"Extracurricular Activities"

A graduate student in history at a major western university was sentenced to a maximum of ten years in state prison for the theft of rare books. The student admitted stealing over $100,000 worth of valuable literary and historical materials from the Special Collections Department of the university library. The student, who worked in the department, said that he simply snipped the padlocks on the rare-book cages, took what he wanted, and replaced the locks with ones of his own. Beginning in 1974, he stole 198 volumes by stuffing them into his knapsack a few at a time.

Each of these cases illustrates important aspects of museum library security. No patron's honesty can be taken for granted. The good reverend is not the only member of the clergy who has been convicted of manuscript and rare-book thievery. Unique and valuable materials can be overlooked on open library shelves; special collections should have special protection. Thieves can be found among staff members of even the most prestigious institutions.

Planning is the key element of any security system. Museum libraries can implement a number of practical security procedures that cost little or nothing, are minimally disruptive, and offer a definite improvement over the status quo. The museum library director must evaluate the possible impact of new security procedures on employees, patrons, and collections before making final decisions. New procedures can become disruptive and costly if they are not instituted with caution. The director who relies on common sense and ingenuity will have a more secure repository than a colleague who depends primarily on sophisticated security equipment.

STAFF AND PATRONS

The implementation of new security procedures often changes the working relationship among the museum library director, curators, and other museum employees on the one hand and between staff and patrons on the other hand.

If new procedures are not explained to all those involved, the changes will be detrimental to the operation of the museum library. Thus the library director must proceed with caution, remembering to consider the impact of new procedures on staff members and patrons before implementing those regulations. The spirit of a good security system is cooperation!

The professional staff plays the most crucial role in the establishment of any museum library security system. For this reason, the director should give special attention to appointing a staff member to be responsible for quarterly assessments of the security system in operation in the library and for liaison with the museum security officer. It is imperative that this duty be incorporated into the job description and that a certain percentage of the staff member's time be set aside for this responsibility.

The selection and training of security-conscious employees is a critical task in establishing a well-rounded program. The process begins with the employee interview. Prospective staff members should be asked to discuss their interest in working with art books, prints, and manuscripts. Do they collect these items? There is always the possibility that staff members will be overcome with temptation to remove items for their own collection. Employees also might be tempted to remove items from collections and sell them for personal profit. There are numerous opportunities for staff members to steal museum library materials without detection. Directors should take precautions to make sure they are getting staff members of the highest integrity. In addition all employees who handle particularly valuable materials should be bonded under a theft insurance plan.

Staff members also need instruction in how to implement new security procedures. The articles by Philip P. Mason and James B. Rhoads, both listed at the end of the chapter, are useful readings that will explain the procedures to staff members. From there the library director should discuss methods for the observation and detention of suspected thieves. (This matter is discussed in detail at the end of this section.) In all cases, all employees should be encouraged to participate in the discussion and to suggest improvements in procedures. They are likely to know best what will work and what will not. The security orientation should conclude with a presentation by the museum security director, who can give advice on the implementation of other security procedures.

Whenever possible, staff members should be instructed in the techniques of observation. Normally, desk attendants in the reading room will succumb to tendencies that result in biased rather than systematic observation. Untrained observers spend most of their time looking at the bottom half of a scene and ignore the periphery. These are natural tendencies and all employees must guard against them.

There is no standard procedure for observation under all circumstances. The following techniques are useful in many situations. First, desk attendants should quickly scan the room to become familiar with the total picture. They should note areas that deserve more careful attention. Second, they should divide the entire picture into quadrants and in turn analyze the points of interest in each quadrant. Third, they should move to a second location and repeat steps one and two. This will provide a different perspective of the area and may alert the employee to new relationships or suspicious behavior.

The observation of patrons is facilitated by an uncluttered field of vision. Thus the layout of the reading room has a substantive effect on the attendant's ability to observe the actions of patrons. The tables in the reading room should be arranged so that all patrons are clearly visible from the reference desk. In addition, chairs should be arranged so that all patrons face the reference desk. To further improve the field of vision, the reference desk should be raised on a platform about one foot high.

One important maxim in dealing with patrons is that all security procedures should be applied uniformly. Upon arrival at the repository, patrons should read and sign a statement of rules and regulations. In addition, patrons should be asked to complete a researcher registration card, listing their names, addresses, companies or institutions, and research topics. The information on the card should be checked against some suitable form of identification: driver's license, voter registration card, employment identification card, or credit card. In all cases patrons should be asked for identification that includes their picture. After verification of identity, patrons should be allowed to enter the reading room.

Since thieves frequently use false identification, some museum library directors may wish to take further precautions. A number of institutions issue photographic identification cards to all patrons after checking their identification very carefully. An inexpensive alternative is inkless thumb printing, now used to protect shopkeepers against check and credit-card fraud. After checking researchers' conventional identification, a special sticker is removed from a dispenser and placed on the back of the registration card. The patrons' right thumbs are pressed on the colorless ink pad and then on the sticker. The procedure produces a clear image of the prints and leaves no residue on the thumb. The cost of a box of five hundred stickers with an ink pad is minimal.

After completing the registration card, patrons should be asked to store their personal belongings in a locker or secure area provided by the library. Coat racks should also be provided. Brief cases, attaché cases, coats, notebooks, envelopes, padfolders, or purses should not be permitted in the reading room. Patrons should be allowed to bring in pencils, typewriters, cameras, and loose sheets of paper, but these items should be searched before the patron leaves the room. Some institutions may wish to furnish patrons with paper bearing a punched hole. When the patron has finished working, the staff inserts a rod through the hole in the stack of note paper.

The stack is shaken to ensure that no manuscripts have been hidden between the leaves. This procedure is used in the Manuscript Division of the Library of Congress with substantial success.

The amount of material given to patrons at any one time should be limited. The museum library director may wish to assign carts to individual researchers where material can be stacked until needed. Desk attendants should check each box or volume after it has been used by patrons. All folders should be in order and no folder should be empty. Any discrepancies should be reported immediately.

It is very important that patrons have only one unit — box or volume — at any one time. When patrons are through with the box or volume, they can exchange it for another. All folders and volumes should be flat on the table or reading stand; they should not rest against the edge of the table. In addition, patrons should have only one folder open at any one time. Such procedures might seem unduly restrictive, but professional thieves frequently attempt to block the vision of the desk attendant. Nothing should impede staff members from observing the hands of all patrons all of the time. New security procedures may upset patrons, so professional staff should take care to apprise users, especially those visiting the library for the first time, of the reason for these security procedures. This discussion should emphasize the desire for cooperation and assistance to the patron.

When patrons leave the reading room, their notes, typewriter cases, and personal reference books should be checked to make sure that the items from the collections are not being taken by accident or design. Staff members should also instruct patrons to put papers back in their folders and the folders back in their proper boxes each time they leave the reading room. If the patron is leaving for the day, the boxes should be checked to make sure all folders are in order and that there are no empty folders. Patrons should never be allowed to work out of the view of the staff; the temptation might prove overwhelming even for the honest researcher.

LEGAL PROTECTION

The question of what to do if a staff member does discover a theft is a most serious one. Many librarians and archivists have been in such situations and have done nothing for fear of civil prosecution. In most states, museum library directors would do well to stop a theft suspect and call the police. Most state laws offer little protection for the librarian or curator who falsely apprehends a patron. In some states, however, special protection has been provided for cultural intitutions. Museum library directors would do well to discuss appropriate legislation with their superiors and with informed legal counsel. Special protection for archives, libraries, and museums is an important part of any good security program. Without such protection, the prosecution of the museum library thieves will always be in doubt.

In general, laws relating to library security fall into two categories. One type of law makes it a misdemeanor to mutilate or destroy library materials. The second type of law makes it a misdemeanor to fail to return library materials after the expiration of the loan period. These two general laws are on the statute books in most states in one form or another. In some jurisdictions, however, such as Arkansas, Illinois, and Oklahoma, the public library act authorizes the corporation authorities of a municipality to provide by ordinance suitable penalties for the misuse or destruction of archival or library materials. In other jurisdictions, such as Florida and Tennessee, the public library act empowers the library board to fix and impose, by general rules, penalties for loss or injury to archival or library property.

In addition to these two basic types of laws, the actual theft of library materials in most states is covered under the general provisions of the criminal code. In Illinois, for example, the theft of property (including library materials) not exceeding $150 in value is a Class A misdemeanor which carries a penalty of less than one year in a penal institution other than a penitentiary. In the field of public records, there are laws that make it a crime to remove, mutilate, or destroy public records. This prohibition extends to persons who have legal custody of public records and this offense is generally classed as a felony.

Virginia Library Act

One of the most recent and innovative legal enactments in the field of museum and library security is the Virginia Library Act of 1975. The law merits serious attention by all museum library directors because it contains all the components of effective legal protection for museum libraries. The Virginia law contains two unique provisions. The first declares the willful concealment of a book or other library materials to be a separate and distinct crime. Moreover, proof of the willful concealment of a book or other library property constitutes prima-facie evidence of intent to commit larceny. The burden of proof thus shifts to the offender to show that he did not intend to commit larceny.

The second unique provision declares that an employee of an archives, library, or museum shall not be subject to civil prosecution for the detention or false arrest of a patron under special circumstances. The employee, to be protected under this provision, must have "probable cause" at the time of detention to believe that the patron was stealing archival, library, or museum property. "Probable cause" is the vague aspect of this provision and museum library directors should be certain that the actions of the suspected patron warrant such a drastic measure as detention.

This act was drafted by the legal counsel of the University of Virginia at the request of the university library and was supported by the Virginia Library Association. In essence, the Virginia act of 1975 is an adaption of the Virginia shoplifting statute of 1958. On the face of it, the law appears to be a highly desirable measure. The legislative intent is clear. It is designed to combat library, archival, and museum theft by providing a legal mechanism for facilitating the apprehension of an offender and to afford the same legal protection to archivists, librarians, and curators that the Virginia Code provides to merchants in the protection of their merchandise from shoplifters. It appears to be most useful in a situation where the theft is actually observed by a member of the museum library staff. The right to detain an offender for questioning or arrest, without fear of adverse legal consequences, is an important tool that the statute provides.

Shoplifting Laws and Library Legislation. The Virginia law introduces a relatively new concept in library legislation. Shoplifting laws vary from state to state but taken as a whole they contain the following elements:

1. They define the crime of shoplifting as the willful concealment of any merchandise with the intention of converting it to one's own use.
2. They authorize the merchant or his employees to detain the suspect where there is probable cause to believe that the suspect has committed theft.
3. They provide the merchant with a legal defense in civil actions arising out of such detention.

The Virginia act of 1975 has adapted all of these provisions. In the first place it makes a person who willfully conceals a book or other library property guilty of larceny. It also provides that proof of the willful concealment of such book or library property while still on the premises of such library shall be prima-facie evidence of intent to commit larceny. This is highly significant because it prevents a suspected thief from claiming that he forgot to return the manuscript or book, or that he meant to have the material charged out, or from offering some other fabricated excuse.

The Virginia law also incorporates the second element of the shoplifting detention statutes. As mentioned earlier, this is a controversial area of the law and several constitutional prohibitions must be scrupulously observed. On the one hand is the right of property and on the other stands the right of the individual to be free and unmolested. This area of the law is extremely sensitive. Freedom from false arrest, freedom from unlawful search, and the right of privacy are all involved. What is needed is a delicate balance, but balancing property rights with personal rights is not a simple task. How does shoplifting legislation resolve the dilemma? In many states shoplifting deten- tion statutes stipulate that the merchant must have probable cause to believe that the person committed the crime before the merchant could detain him. The term "probable cause" constitutes a dangerous pitfall for the merchant. The courts have denied the existence of probable cause in such cases, for ex- ample, when a suspect merely placed his hands under his shirt and walked off at a rapid pace, and also when a customer merely reported a belief that the suspect had been shoplifting. If, however, the missing items are actual- ly found upon the suspect, or if an employee reports having actually seen the items being concealed by the suspect, then the courts held that there is probable cause.

The third element incorporated in the Virginia law is the provision grant- ing the archivist, librarian, or curator immunity from civil liability for ac- tions arising out of the detention of a suspect. Some statutes merely authorize the detention but do not specifically grant immunity from civil liability. This means that some form of immunity is implied, and the courts must determine whether the statute provides by implication a defense in some types of civil action and not in others, or whether the statute is intended to provide a defense in all actions. There are some statutes that grant immunity from certain civil actions such as false arrest, false imprisonment, and others. The weakness of this approach is the possibility for an ingenious plaintiff to bring an action in a form not covered by the statute. Finally, some statutes grant immunity from all civil and criminal actions. This approach leaves a wronged individual completely without any legal remedy. For this reason most jurisdictions prefer to extend the defense only to certain classes of ac- tions. The actions for which immunity is granted are chiefly false imprison- ment, false arrest, unlawful detention, assault, battery, slander, libel, and malicious prosecution.

It remains to be seen whether Virginia's pioneer effort in adapting the principles of the shoplifting detention statutes to cover library theft should be pursued by other states. Despite the limited applicability of the shoplift- ing detention statutes, and despite the great care taken that must be exercised in not violating the constitutional rights of an individual, the shoplifting statute does provide additional protection not provided by common law or other existing laws both as a punitive force and as a deterrent measure. In a society where law is fundamental, museum library directors have no alter- native but to seek legal remedies to correct inequities. As the thefts from museum libraries increase, it is imperative for museum professionals to take all the necessary steps to protect their collections. Clearly the gravity of the situation calls for new and additional legislation.

Witnessing a Theft

In the event that a staff member does witness a theft in progress, it is important that he or she knows the steps to be taken to stop the thief, protect oneself, and protect the institution. The following points should be incorporated into guidelines for desk attendants and other museum library staff members who come into contact with the public. Only staff members over the age of eighteen should be allowed to detain a patron. Staff members effecting detentions should have probable cause to do so. Ideally, this would include situations when staff members have actually seen suspects conceal items and pass through appropriate checkpoints. Staff members should never rely on the word of a patron as the basis for probable cause that another patron has taken one or more items. It is advisable to conduct a reasonable investigation before any patrons are detained. The purpose of detention is to investigate the possibility of a theft of museum library materials. Any detention, therefore, should be effected and conducted in a reasonable manner. This means avoiding a scene if at all possible. Shouting matches and defamatory language should be avoided at all costs. If staff members follow those simple rules, instances of patron detention can be effected without incident.

Maintaining good relations with staff members and patrons is an important aspect of the museum library director's job. Just as important is protecting the collections themselves against theft. If the director takes the time to explain this situation both to staff and to patrons, long-term problems with both groups can be avoided. The coordinated efforts of staff and patrons will stymie the thief.

THE COLLECTIONS

Providing security for the collections themselves is the most difficult task faced by the museum library director. How is it possible to protect the thousands or perhaps millions of precious items in a museum library? There is no simple solution to this problem, and the security-conscious director must use a variety of techniques to minimize the possibility of theft and maximize the recovery of stolen items. These procedures can be divided into two categories: deterrents to theft and the identification of missing items. Both of these components contribute to providing security for the collections themselves.

The director's first responsibility is the protection of the collections in the library, and this often means preventing theft. This is a special kind of protection, and the director must be highly selective as to how this security is implemented. No one can provide equal protection for every item — book, print, or manuscript — in a museum library, even a small one.

Monetary appraisal of manuscripts and books is not a simple task, and the museum library director may wish to call on dealers for assistance if he or she does not feel able to identify marketable items. Those materials determined to be of significant monetary value — $100 and up — should be scheduled for special protection. This may mean marking every item in collections of eighteenth- and nineteenth-century materials. Archivists should begin by determining the type of protection that is most efficient and economical for each particular collection. There are a number of options and each should be considered before a decision is made.

Separating and Reproducing Marketable Items

The simplest method of protection is the identification of marketable items in a collection. Museum library directors must learn to think like thieves. Which folders are likely to contain autographs of monetary value? Which prints of which artists have recently risen in value? These are items which will need special attention and, if possible, they should be removed from general use. Photocopies or facsimiles can be substituted for originals with no loss of intellectual content. If the number of items is small, the substitution of copies may be the most economical and efficient means of protection. The separated originals should be placed in a vault or other secure area.

Some directors will want to put marketable items in separate folders or boxes that can be easily checked by a staff member both before and after a collection is used by patrons. Although this method does provide a significant measure of protection for valuable manuscripts and prints, it is subject to human error and temptation. Should desk attendants forget to check each folder, or should they overlook one of those folders, the items could be easily stolen. Using this method, desk attendants must check folders both immediately before giving them to a researcher and immediately after they are returned. Should an item be discovered missing after use by a patron, the patron may claim that the item was not in the folder when he used it, putting the staff and the museum in a potentially embarrassing situation. Staff members must be very sure that an item was in the folder before the patron is challenged. If a search of the patron by law enforcement officials proved fruitless, the museum and the staff could be subject to a suit for false arrest — a very expensive proposition. For this reason, separation and substitution are recommended over placing valuable items in individual folders.

Many collections have far too many items to make separation practical. Yet the library director should not overlook a variation on this option. If monetary appraisal by a dealer indicates that there are a substantial number of marketable items in a particular collection, the archivist might consider microfilming the entire collection. The film copy should be used for reference by staff and patrons and the collection should be put into security storage. The prospect of taking whole collections out of circulation and substituting microfilm seems to be a violation of the museum's mission. Yet most museum librarians and curators know of once-valuable collections of manuscripts that have since been decimated by thieves. The library director must weigh the costs and detractions of microfilm against the possibility of losing numerous items from a valuable collection. It is not an easy decision.

Marking the Collection

A final option for protecting individual items is marking. As with separation and substitution, this method must be used selectively. Most museum libraries have far too many items to mark each and every one. Indeed, this is a common problem for archives, special collections, historical societies, and other repositories of unique materials. Almost twenty years ago the Archivist of the United States estimated that it would take five thousand man-years and cost $20 million to mark the holdings of the National Archives. Even though there are no museum libraries with as many items as the National Archives, the cost for any institution would be astronomical. Thus careful planning must precede the implementation of a selective marking program. Institutions must necessarily start with their most valuable collections and stamp selected items in all their collections.

Marking often creates a dilemma for museum staff. On the one hand, marking is a proven deterrent to theft and good legal proof of ownership. On the other hand, marking tends to disfigure and thereby ruin the aesthetics of a manuscript, print, or document. As the number of thefts has increased, however, the decision to mark special items has become increasingly popular.

There are three methods of marking special items: embossing, punching or perforating, and stamping with ink. Paper documents can be embossed by a hand-held device similar to the machine used by a notary public. The device presses paper fibers into the shape of the characters or symbol desired. Embossing can be pressed out and made nearly invisible, but the mark can never be completely obliterated. Because of its vulnerability to partial obliteration and because of the cumbersome nature of the process, embossing has not been a popular means of marking manuscripts, books, or prints.

A second means of marking is perforation. Unlike embossing, perforation cannot be eradicated. At one time perforation was a popular means of marking, but the method has fallen into disuse. In fact, hand-held perforators are no longer manufactured in the United States. A custom-made perforator would be prohibitively expensive, making the method impractical at the present.

The third and most popular form of marking is stamping with ink. The Library of Congress has used this method for many years with great success. Books, prints, and manuscripts may be stamped with either visible or invisible ink. If executed properly, stamping with ink will do minimal damage to the item. The Office of Preservation of the Library of Congress advises museums and other repositories to use an ink that is nonfading, ineradicable with solvents or bleaches, neutral or slightly alkaline in pH, essentially nonbleeding and nonmigrating, stable at heat up to 300 degrees Fahrenheit, to light for at least one hundred years, and slow-drying on the stamp pad but fast-drying on the item. At the time these specifications were promulgated, inks with these requirements were not commercially available.

As a result, the Office of Preservation, in conjunction with the Government Printing Office, formulated and tested such an ink. The ink is available from the Library of Congress free of charge to all who request it. The Library's preservation office estimates that a single two-ounce bottle will last at least ten years if properly used. The formula for this ink will not be divulged since such knowledge might make it possible to develop an effective means of eradication. The Library of Congress advises that ink should be applied by a sharply cut rubber or plastic stamp, which need not be larger than 5/8 of an inch in diameter. The form of the stamp is a matter under discussion by rare-book and library organizations. One noted authority has suggested that repositories use their National Union Catalog symbols, which are easily identifiable. When stamping an item, staff should take care to strike the paper squarely, giving a uniformly inked impression.

There are many opinions as to where the mark should be placed on a document, print, or rare book. On prints, where the reverse side is blank, the mark should be placed there. If there is text on both sides, as with manuscripts, the mark can be placed in any one of a number of locations. Many rare-book and manuscript repositories put their mark in the upper right corner of the front of the document. Other repositories, including the National Archives, have placed their marks in the blank space to the right of the salutation in letters or near the heading in other documents, to the left of the complimentary close or signature, in the indentation of the first line of a paragraph, or after a short line at the end of a paragraph. Guidelines for marking rare books and manuscripts have been prepared by the Rare Books and Manuscripts Section of the Association of College and Research Libraries and are available from ACRL in care of the American Library Association, 50 E. Huron Street, Chicago, Illinois 60611. Summary recommendations are that the ownership mark should be placed out of sight, but where it can be easily located, and away from the text or image, yet where it cannot be excised without injury to the image. Ultimately the location of the mark must be left to the discretion of the museum library director.

Marking offers one of the best means of protecting individual items against theft. Yet staff will find it impossible to mark every item. Thus no matter how contientious the museum is, the collections will always be vulnerable to theft. Determining exactly what is missing can be a difficult if not impossible task since most repositories, museum libraries included, do not have detailed inventories of valuable items in particular collections. Directors should be conscious of the various kinds of item control in their repositories. Card catalogs, manuscript registers, accession records, and call slips all contain valuable information on specific items. Another useful source is the photocopy record. Still a third source is footnotes in scholarly articles citing specific items. One or all of these records can be used in court to prove that a particular item was in the library before it was discovered missing. Such records will also assist museum staff and law enforcement officials in locating missing items and prosecuting thieves.

FIRE PROTECTION FOR MUSEUM LIBRARIES

Securing collections against theft is by no means the only protection that should be provided in the museum library. Areas that are often overlooked are fire suppression and flood control. A recent study of 255 libraries found that 87 percent were without automatic fire suppression systems and 60 percent without fire warning devices. Such statistics are frightening when one considers that 88 percent of library fires occur when these institutions are closed. The museum library without fire alarms and suppression equipment is risking needlessly the loss of a large part of its collections. Equally disturbing are the large numbers of special collections that have suffered severe water damage due to burst pipes or flooding. Few museum libraries have taken precautions against this very serious threat. No one likes to think of such a tragedy, but in the past several years library fires and floods have occured with increasing frequency.

In beginning an evaluation of fire prevention and suppression systems, the museum library director should consult the excellent manuals on museums, archives, libraries, and records centers published by the National Fire Protection Association. These manuals, which are listed in the bibliography, provide the museum library director with a substantial amount of information on the selection of proper equipment. The manuals go a long way toward removing the mystery in fire prevention and suppression.

Museum Location. Several important considerations should be kept in mind when evaluating the quality of fire protection in a museum library. The first is the location of the museum itself. If the facility is near industrial plants, the roof should be fitted with a fire-resistant covering. Burning debris from factories has been the cause of many fires.

Building Interior. A second consideration is the construction and arrangement of the interior of the building. The first principle of fire protection is to isolate a fire in as small an area as possible. Thus, fire-resistant materials should be used on floors and walls, fire doors should close off stairwells, and heating and air-conditioning systems should be isolated to minimize the possibility of a fire moving from one floor to the next. Open, multi-tiered shelves, which allow fires to spread from one stack to the next, should be protected by an automatic fire-suppression system.

Storage. A third consideration is the alignment of files in storage boxes. When record cartons are stored perpendicular to the aisles and the ends of the cartons collapse in a fire, the contents spill into the aisles. This increases the intensity of the fire and helps to spread it to other stacks. Storage of record cartons parallel to the aisle does not contribute to the spread of the fire.

Local Fire Department. A fourth consideration in evaluating a museum library fire-prevention system is the proximity and responsiveness of the local fire department. If the department is distant or overtaxed, more suppression equipment is called for than under other circumstances. Other considerations include the kind and quality of equipment owned by the department and whether the fire-fighters are paid or volunteer. Whatever the circumstances, the museum library director should invite the local fire chief to the museum library to discuss special problems related to fire prevention.

Fire Suppression Equipment. A fifth consideration is the kind of fire-suppression equipment necessary for adequate protection. This is the first line of defense against fires and less than adequate or faulty equipment could prove disastrous. Museum libraries should be equipped with both detection and suppression equipment. Detection devices respond to the heat, smoke, light, change in temperature, or gaseous products of a fire. Every detection system, once triggered, should sound a warning alarm in the library, summon the local fire department, indicate the location of the fire, shut down the building ventilation system, and recall the elevators. A suppression system provides the means to contain the fire and often to extinguish it. In archives, libraries, and in many museums, the most common forms of suppression are the water sprinkler and the gas device.

Of the two, the water-sprinkler system is the most economical. Sprinklers operate by sensing a change in room temperature, with each sprinkler head having its own sensing device. It is important to note that the sprinkler heads operate independently of one another; water is discharged only from those sprinklers activated by flames. Many museum library directors are wary of sprinkler systems because of the potential water damage to collections. Certainly this is an important consideration, but it is no excuse to be without a fire suppression system. A recent test by Factory Mutual Laboratories showed that a library without a suppression system would suffer the loss of 89 percent of the collections in the fire area. The same test was conducted with a sprinkler system and the loss of collections was only 10 percent. This statistic, combined with the improved techniques for restoring water-damaged materials, argues persuasively for sprinkler systems if no other suppression equipment is available or affordable.

A more popular suppression system with museum library directors, as well as with archivists and curators, is the gas device. In the great majority of these devices the gas is carbon dioxide or a chemical compound known as Halon, short for halogenated hydrocarbon, which interferes with the combustion cycle to suppress the fire. These systems are particularly advantageous to museum libraries because they do little damage to books, prints, and manuscripts. The Halon system, which is very popular, is also relatively expensive — 50 cents and up per cubic foot of space. A final caution should be added. Halon will not combat deep-seated fires that may work their way into archival boxes; this increases the risk of a reescalation of the flames. If carefully monitored, Halon is an effective fire suppressant that minimizes damage to collections of paper materials.

Museum library fires should be followed up by the immediate removal of burned materials from the fire locations to the outdoors or other fire-safe locations. Boxes and books should be inspected for deep-seated smoldering. If smoldering is detected, it should be doused with a small amount of water. Fire alarms should be reset and a fire watch maintained for the following twenty-four hours. This will minimize the possibility of a recurrence of the conflagration.

Training. A sixth consideration is training. The museum library staff should be trained to respond to fires and other types of emergencies. All employees should have practical experience in the use of emergency fire equipment, especially fire extinguishers and alarm signals. Procedures should be drawn up for the orderly removal of patrons and staff members from the building should a fire pose a threat. In addition, certain staff members should receive first-aid training. Employees should be trained to work as a team in such emergencies; they should be made aware of the safety and security responsibilities that are part of their jobs.

Water Damage. Even though water is an effective fire deterrent, it also can do serious damage to paper items of all kinds. The museum library director, therefore, must take care to provide security against water damage by flooding, broken or frozen water pipes, and sprinkler systems. Water pipes running through the museum library should be checked regularly to minimize the possibility of disaster. In areas where such damage has occurred in the past and is likely to recur, water gate alarms should be installed to warn of danger. Museum libraries located in basements or on ground-floor levels and those located in flood plains should have emergency plans for the removal of crucial items. When water damage does occur, museum library directors should follow the instructions listed in Peter Waters's excellent manual entitled *Procedures for the Salvage of Water-Damaged Library Materials*, which is available free of charge from the preservation office of the Library of Congress.

The protection of museum library collections lies at the core of any good security system. Museum library directors should periodically reevaluate the deterrents to the theft of their collections, their procedures for the discovery and recovery of missing items, and their protection against loss due to fire and water.

CONCLUSION

The preceding suggestions should help to improve most museum library security systems, and, as noted earlier, they cost little or nothing to implement. They do take time and effort on the part of the museum library director. A caveat should be added at this point. No matter how good their security systems, museum libraries will always be vulnerable to some loss. Missing items should be reported to "Bookline Alert: Missing Books and Manuscripts" (BAMBAM), a not-for-profit service of American Book Prices Current. The charges for listing missing items are minimal and the service will insure that information on the missing item will be available instantaneously, via telephone and computer print-outs, to the thousands of dealers and libraries in this country and in Europe. For more information write BAMBAM c/o American Book Prices Current, 121 E. 78th St., New York, New York 10021.

The protection of valuable and irreplaceable rare books, manuscripts, photographs, prints, and other art materials in museum libraries is the responsibility of everyone working in these institutions. All professionals must ask themselves tough questions about museum library security. What type of identification should be required of patrons? What kind of information should be included on call slips? What should patrons be allowed to bring into the reading room? Should valuable items be marked or stamped? Does the library have adequate legal protection in case of a theft? Does the library have adequate protection from fire and water damage? The answers to these and other museum library security questions are not easily found. Yet as one former Archivist of the United States noted almost twenty years ago, "through our collective efforts, we can make real progress in convincing the document thief that he has made a tragic error in his choice of a career."

7. Fundamentals of Public Relations Communication

Stephen J. Allen

"A man who is too big to study his job is as big as he will ever be." William E. North

Learning the art of communicating is a never-ending process. As in the practice of any profession, to perform satisfactorily demands a great deal of repetition and patience, especially if one is without formal training. A non-professional public relations volunteer or part-time employee can achieve some proficiency in the basics operating in a small institution provided a limited amount of guidance can be made available and the person is willing to practice.

The main ingredients in the application of public-relations communication are consistent with providing the truth — clearly, concisely, briefly, quickly, and correctly — whenever the situation demands, whether the need is mandated within the institution or from an external source.

When the need to communicate is required, whether to inform, instruct, or request, the message must be complete.

As an example of a complete communication, examine a formal invitation to a wedding, a dinner party, or even a ship's launching. Such invitations have all the elements of a complete message, including the suggestion of taking an action by returning your acceptance or regrets. Notice that a complete message will contain five W's: who, what, when, where, and why, and sometimes the 'how,' although not always in that particular order. To become better acquainted with the public relations writing styles for various needs (such as direct-mail announcements and publicity), several textbooks have been recommended in the bibliography for guidance.

AN UNCONVENTIONAL NECESSITY

In the smaller institutions where tight budgets exist that prohibit hiring a professional communicator, it is very possible that the security manager may be assigned to collateral public information duties. The rationale behind this recommendation is that the security person is the logical person who would be the first to know — day or night — of an incident of theft, fire, or vandalism. It would be a security person who would make the first observation and assessment report to the director or curator. It is also the security officer who is first to speak with the police, firemen, or news reporters when they arrive. It is this person who is most likely to be the one staff member self-disciplined enough to avoid panic, stablize others in the area, protect the institution from looters, and maintain the dignity associated with the institution. The security guard's report is very likely to be the base of the museum's later report which establishes the "party line," ensuring that whatever is officially communicated to anyone internally or externally will minimize rumors usually growing from a variety of unofficial explanations.

In the small or medium-sized institution without a public-relations person, this switch in tradition could satisfy the needs of the management, especially in a crisis situation. Just because it may not have been considered before does not mean it is not feasible. Conversely, the security manager, given this confidence and authority, would have to prepare and be willing to assume the responsibilities for an event *which may never occur* or may happen only once in a career.

The art of communicating can be learned and applied at the same professional level as security services even when assigned as a collateral duty.

Then again, there is far more to the art of communicating than merely writing a news release and transmitting information by telephone. Preparing a report and being organized to handle an unusual barrage of complex situations in an emergency are other aspects of the public relations function.

Public relations means dealing effectively and persuasively with people, internally and externally, coworkers and strangers. The traits of good leadership, sound judgment, sensitivity to the problems of others, and honesty are among the major ingredients of the practitioner's personal makeup. The most difficult of all these, for the veteran professional communicator and the novice, is dealing with people, the strongest asset of the security manager.

A Major Reluctance

One drawback to this proposal favoring a security guard having public information responsibilities stems from the exposure to witnessing such responsibilities being assigned to a novice who never before dealt head on with the craftspersons of the mass media.

Professional pride, when fortified with authority, often produces a chemistry likely to erupt or explode when two professionals who have conflicting objectives stand nose-to-nose. A security manager, already suspected of withholding information by the media upon confronting the uniform, will be especially hard pressed by the news reporter. The security manager who may be very personable with people but lack the experience to deal with this special breed of professional is not likely to win the confidence of this "opponent" or be given the opportunity to establish a local reputation for honesty and integrity. This is a difficult handicap to overcome for even the most seasoned public relations veteran.

To expedite the museum's need to communicate, whether it will be achieved by a member of the security force or anyone else, let us explore some fundamentals to obtain an understanding of the mechanics involved in public-relations publicity, lingering on the "why" momentarily before discussing the "how."

ELEMENTS OF PUBLICITY

Why be concerned about publicity anyway? What good can publicity do for the institution? Why tell the news media anything at all?

These were the type of questions usually heard asked by management in the late 1950s. Motion pictures, and later television, helped to remind them of those earlier days of the "huckster" with the gimmicks familiarly associated to the press agent. The media and the public uncovered these "ten percenters" as having little or no integrity in accomplishing their objectives. Over the years, with the development of principles and ethics adopted by the Public Relations Society of America, the media slowly began to gain faith in the honesty of the news releases they received, and the public came to believe more and more of what they read or heard on radio and television. One may still argue the merits of today's news in all the media when the subject of integrity is the focal point; nevertheless, there is a greater mutual respect between the media and public-relations professionals today.

To answer the first question, one reason why publicity has gained momentum is because "the public has a right to know."

The second question is answered with a question: What can publicity do *to* the institution? Adverse publicity will hurt the museum's reputation. Lost public confidence invokes mistrust in its management. Acquisitions of art from donors, or on loan, become more difficult to obtain. The generosity of those public donors and private contributors will decrease tremendously the museum's necessary operating and contingency funds.

There is another dark side to consider about bad publicity. Consider it in a more personal vein. If the bad publicity for a small institution is serious enough to result in the conditions described, the institution may be forced to close its doors, and all persons from the director to the gardener would be required to seek new employment. Understanding this, one can better realize the seriousness and advantages of learning the fundamentals of public relations and adhering to its principles.

UNDERSTANDING PUBLIC RELATIONS

"There is no choice between public relations and no public relations," says Sol H. Marshall, a general practitioner from Hollywood, California. The choice is only between good public relations and poor public relations, he explains. "The choice," he adds, "is making public relations work for the institution, or permitting it to work against the institution."

Marshall's philosophy on the subject is, "Good or bad, public relations is determined largely by the institutional leaders and members themselves. Everyone who speaks or acts for the museum in any capacity, everyone who has a membership interest of some sort, or who represents it in any contact with the public, and even the people who write a check to it, contribute to the PR status of the organization. Once these people are identified to the institution, they affect the PR of that institution, even in their personal and off-duty activities."[1]

One might question what concern others may have for the off-duty activities of a public-relations practitioner, but the Public Relations Society of America makes the concern public in a "Declaration of Principles" in which the first of the four states, ". . . we pledge ourselves: To conduct ourselves both privately and professionally in accord with the public welfare." This and the following statements in PRSA's Declaration which title includes a "Code of Professional Standards for the Practice of Public Relations," helped to bring about the trust, reputation, and integrity the profession enjoys today.[2]

There are numerous definitions of public relations which are acceptable.

Rather than becoming academic, it is sufficient to provide a simple formula as follows: *P*erformance plus *R*ecognition equals PR.

The security officer of any institution probably understands the applicability of this formula more than anyone else in the organization because the security force (whether comprised of a single guard or dozens) represents "the front men for the front man." This is the particular department most exposed to the public on a daily basis, ready to guide, direct, and assist in providing courteous service to the institution's publics. Yes, it is the security people who are the front-line ambassadors of good will, and the first required to put life and limb on the line during a crisis.

PLAYING THE PUBLIC RELATIONS GAME TO WIN

If the security manager is given the secondary role of public information officer, this places him in a strange ballpark where the rules of the game have not been etched in stone. Unfortunately, with institutional public relations it does not take three strikes to be out; one crisis — resulting in a tremendously large vandalism attack or a fire bombing followed by public apathy and possibly general outrage — may be enough to end his ball game with the institution and his primary profession.

When he is required to perform in this secondary role, he may at times be required to perform as a one-man team while the opposing side, also competing to win, has many seasoned players who are skillful, talented, aggressive, tenacious, crafty, demanding, and have the advantage of having written most of the rules which at first glance seem to exist in their favor.

The security officer or other person in public information need not fear this situation. The power to balance or defeat "the other team" lies in the elements of truth, integrity, and sincerity combined with cooperation, compassion, and knowledge of the opponent's strategies, plus a few power-plays not yet recorded in texts or journals but learned from experience in the field, and related in the next chapter.

To understand the gameplay, carefully study that section which deals with coping with the press, which examines the competition's strengths and weaknesses. But first, know something about this competition because even without meeting them personally, without having a crisis, they will also be partners in your news efforts on a regular basis, year in and year out.

Elements of Competition

Before gaining an understanding about writing for and speaking with news reporters, an abstract look at the competition is a necessity. The following description is not to alarm or disarm the communicator, neither is it intended to be defensive of the PR practice, nor an apology for the reporter. Each reporter has a professional mission.

To identify the competition is to label them by their generic title. They are known as "news reporters" to the general public and to their editors. With some respect and some disrespect, they regard themselves as gods. After all, they have in their power ability to create heroes and heroines and motivate people to do great works of charity for real causes; they can persuade others to take sides on important issues, and they work hard to inform the general public of those events to which the public has a right to know. For all the good things they can and do achieve in their lofty positions — for which they are issued a plastic, master pass key to anywhere — they also have the power to destroy a lifetime image built on good will.

A Two-way Sword

In fairness to these "fourth estate" representatives, it should be known they are required to report facts in a fair manner without injecting their personal opinions. They have an important responsibility, and whether or not you cooperate, their job will be done! Take a closer look at this person's top management philosophy, and you can see why they must succeed.

To survive in the business of news reporting, the medium providing this profit-making public service, whether newsprint, radio, or electronic broadcast, must have an audience. The better the news reporting — swiftly and accurately — the larger the following. The larger the audience following, the more leverage is provided that medium for selling advertising. The more advertising sold, the greater the profits, and there is the bottom line — profits.

The reader, listener, or viewer will follow that particular medium providing the nourishment to feed the public's hunger for facts which satisfies their desire to be aware and knowledgeable of what is happening in the world around them, how it affects their life-style now and in the future.

This is the motivation of the news reporter who must report the news in an interesting and factual manner to ensure job retention as well as an eventual promotion. Neither the security manager nor a professional PR practitioner, nor the President of the United States nor the Holy Father in Rome, nor anyone else in the entire world, can escape the thrust of the worldwide army of news reporters assigned to a fast-breaking news story about which the public has a right to know; except, of course, when such intelligence could endanger the lives of millions of people. The competition to report the news out is fierce. You may never be involved with earth-shattering news, or even get a single turn at the bat as a player in the game — if you are lucky — but understanding some of the process may help.

Want not, Cry not!

Years of experience on the street as a news reporter, behind the editor's desk, and on the other side of the fence as an accredited public-relations practitioner do provide some observations and traits to be shared:

1. Ask no quarter, give no quarter, and you won't be disappointed with fair reporting practices.
2. Cooperating with news reporters does not obligate them to favors at any time.
3. When the media want information expect sweet talk, and when you want news space expect back talk.
4. The mass media are in business to make money, not friends; to report the news to the public, not to make a hero out of your boss.
5. Avoid alienating the mass media by being truthful and cooperative even if you haven't anything to gain — except integrity.
6. Ensure the availability of a spokesperson with the freedom to speak with authority.
7. Never speak to news reporters "off the record."

MEDIA FORMATS

Somewhat fortified by the foregoing guidelines, the next step in understanding the mass media is to know the requirements of the editors and news directors in publishing or airing your news. For a more detailed treatment to include the methods of research, the actual writing, editing, proofreading, distribution mechanics, and bulk mailing, refer to the bibliography for this chapter. Knowing the fundamental requirements should be adequate for both normal and crisis public-relations publicity in a small or medium-sized institution with a part-time volunteer serving in public information, or the security manager as suggested.

Each of the three major mediums — newsprint, radio, and television — has different formats, different requirements by which to report the news, and different hours of the day (deadlines) by which the news must be in the hands of the editors and news directors.

Maintaining Media Lists

In time of an emergency the postal service is NOT the method to use to provide the mass media with news copy. The two quickest and most acceptable methods are either to telephone the information or hand deliver your copy. Most media news directors of radio and electronic news feel if you can afford to use the mail and delay relaying information, you either do not have any real news or you simply do not understand what it really is; which makes sense. To service the mass media, you need to know who they are, where they are, what they want, and when they want it, and how.

To reach your medium target, the public information person needs to prepare two media lists, the primary list, containing those media in the immediate metropolitan or megatropolis area, and the second list, comprising those media in the major surrounding cities, towns, and communities beyond the geographical range of the first listing. This second list will include the wire-service bureaus, the Sunday newspapers, and possibly the cablevision companies, too.

Because media people do retire, get promoted, change jobs, are fired, go on vacation, become ill, or take a few days to cover a story, a news release mailed to a specific person may sit for days on a desk without being opened. For this reason, a news release should be addressed to the "editor" of a daily newspaper, the "managing editor" of a weekly publication, and the "news director" of a radio station or television station (or in the latter instant to the "assignment editor" if coverage of an event is desired).

The primary and secondary master media lists on file should also contain the day and night telephone numbers of each medium. Normally, these addresses and telephone numbers can be gleaned from local telephone directories, or by asking the telephone information directory service for a listing.

At the daily newspapers, after normal working hours when the switchboard is secured, the main number automatically switches to the editor's area where a reporter, rewrite person, or even the editor may answer. This is also true of the wire-service bureaus.

In the radio station, after normal working hours, there may be only one or two persons present, one who does the actual broadcasting and, the other being the engineer. In small stations, one person is usually expected to do both. Access to them after normal working hours is gained only by having what is known as the "beeper number." This number is used to obtain live-recorded interviews from the caller, and so-called because of the "beeps" heard while speaking to indicate the message is being recorded. It doesn't automatically happen when the telephone number is called; the broadcaster must set up the system first. When calling this number, some patience is required, obviously.

Should your institution have an incident at night, television — like radio — has diminished crew on duty. The only crews available may be covering a major sports event and a fire, or a testimonial and a late meeting, or one crew may be on the street scene when your call arrives. Unless your request is important, the "assignment editor" will not provide any coverage.

Time and again, this author has argued, when crisis is at your door, depend on the radio. Radio may be your only salvation.

Consider the facts of this statement!

The daily newspapers may have two editions, morning and evening. Television news in depth is four times a day. Radio can bring your message to the public every fifteen minutes. That is why when sending out news releases of future interest to the mass media, some PRs send four copies to radio. When these releases are received they are placed in various segments of the *daybook* for each broadcast period, and from day to day either moved forward or discarded.

Through the radio's telephone "beeper system," your institution's news could be heard within five minutes after both telephones are hung up, and the message carried would in all probability be in your authoritative voice, in your own contrived words.

This would, of course, require you to telephone many radio stations to get your message before the public. Another successful method is to give your story to a rewrite person on the telephone at a wire service bureau. Your message doesn't need to be formally outlined, but all the facts involved would be required to piece the story together. Questions may be asked that you should be prepared to answer or obtain the answers to before the story moves — and how it can move! Unless there is a catastrophe it will not make the "A-Wire" for national use, but the regional "B-Wire" will suffice. All the mass media which subscribe to the services of the wire (mainly the Associated Press and United Press International) will receive the story over a teletypewriter. This copy is scanned for pick-up by subscribers, whether newsprint, radio, or television. The relays are faster than the local newspapers and the television stations in moving the news to where it will be used.

If you are not prepared to telephone your story to every radio station in your area, as well as the newspapers and electronic broadcasters, then you are obligated to use the wire-service bureaus rather than be accused of favoritism.

There is another general rule regarding "exclusives." If one medium telephones about information that medium thus far has the exclusive right to the story. When a second calls, give the caller the story, but explain there was a previous caller. When a third calls, take to the wire services so everyone gets an even break with the news.

PREPARING THE BASIC NEWS RELEASE

As earlier stated, each medium prefers a different format by which the news is prepared. Experience teaches that the better prepared the news release is for use without a staff member having to rewrite your copy, the more probability it will be well received for print or broadcast, rather than be cast aside by a busy news staff without time to rewrite. Remember, the media made the rules, and PR people follow them if they expect to play in the communications game.

It is not necessary that your news release be professionally printed, but it does help to look professional. For this reason a news release letterhead is recommended, printed simply in black ink on any white paper that can be used by a mechanical reproduction machine; i.e., multilith, mimeograph, or copier. To dress up the letterhead, the museum's logo (symbol) may be used.

The first quarter of the page is strictly informational on all releases. In addition to the logo, and the words "News Release," this space must include the name of the institution, its address, zip code, and telephone number. The next line, between borders of a straight line, is information regarding whom to contact for additional information by name with telephone number (and extension).

Below this information on the right side is the date of preparation. On the left the space is used for instructions concerning when the release may be used. First, there must be a determination as to whether the release is "spot" news, which has an immediacy to the reporting process, or whether it is "time" copy and can be released at any time space or air time is available. A third consideration is, is it an "announcement" type of release?

If there is an immediacy to the release, the top left space under the contact's name will have the heading, "FOR IMMEDIATE RELEASE." If the release is purely informational as a "filler," something to take up space which may interest the readership or listening audience, the heading may read, "TIME COPY — RELEASE AT WILL." If the release is to announce a specific event to take place, or to draw foot traffic to a coming attraction, the heading may release the information at a specific time reading, "FOR RELEASE AFTER (date) a.m./p.m."

In an area where there are many weekly community newspapers with one or two dailies, it is a preferred practice to announce board appointments, promotions, and general information with a "HOLD FOR RELEASE ON THURSDAY, (date)," but put the information in the hands of the weekly editors by Monday noon. In this manner, the news breaks equally in weeklies and dailies. This instructional line will also appear on radio and television releases, although announcements for these last two mediums must be in the hands of the news directors about three weeks in advance.

If your institution is a nonprofit corporation with tax-exempt status, it would be to your advantage to state this in the news-release letterhead. If you do, however, ensure a statement to this effect on your institution's letterhead is filed with a list of all the members of the board, their titles within the institution (officers), and their home addresses. Copies are sent to *all* the mass media on your primary and secondary mailing lists. When this is done, your radio and television, and many of your newspaper, releases may begin with the words, "Public Service Announcement," the first line on the top left under the name of the contact person.

Between the date of preparation and the first line of copy, leave a space for the editor or headline writer to enter instructions to the printer. A simple rule to follow is that you allow only one or two paragraphs on the first page. After the last line, if there is a second page to follow, on the next line flush to the right margin, add the word "more . . . ." When you begin the second page, use one or two key words to "slug" or identify the additional page in case the pages become separated by the compositors or are given to more than one person to expedite on a word-processing machine. Follow this method on subsequent pages, numbering each after the slug.

When the last line has been written, use the symbol "-30-" or "###" in the middle of the next line to indicate no more copy follows. For a sample, see Figure 7.1. Note: at the bottom left of the last page, include a block of information similar to the front page of the letterhead concerning the originator.

Radio and Television

The broadcasting industry, linked intimately with the largest audience known to the human race, offers unparalleled opportunities for institutions working in the public interest. To set the record true, broadcasting is under no obligation to grant time to any specific group. There is no law which says a station must devote a fixed amount of time to community or nonprofit groups. Stations do pride themselves on being alert to their needs; however, the major difference is that a nonprofit group does not have to buy the air time (and when having a public service announcement aired free, it had better not come up in a newspaper with a paid ad if additional air time will someday be required).[3]

How do you go about getting your message on radio and television? Like almost everything else, there is a right way and a wrong way. For a most comprehensive learning experience in understanding the operations of both mediums, experts such as Siller (ABC), White (WOR), and Terkel (CBS) in 1960 pooled their backgrounds for Macmillan Publishers in New York to write on *Television and Radio News*. Not only is this book recommended reading, but it is a suggested reference for all communicators.

Competition is very keen for both television and radio time. The basic rules for good publicity apply to news stories and interviews just as they do to newspaper and magazine features. Unfortunately, culture is very low in priority at the news desk, where sensational and controversial news receives most of the attention.

Institutional	Institution's name
logo or symbol	Address
	Telephone number

Name of person to contact: telephone no. and ext.

(release instructions)
FOR IMMEDIATE RELEASE (or)   _____
HOLD FOR RELEASE UNTIL (date)   (date prepared)

> (Begin the first paragraph one-third down this page. Allow this space to be used by the news editor to write a headline and assign the story space.)

Double space all copy, and in this first paragraph, known as the "lead," describe the five W's; who, what, where, when, and why.

The second paragraph is the "bridge" which connects the lead to additional facts or quotations in matters of descending importance. This is known as writing "inverted pyramid style."

Normally, the first paragraph is written to end on the first page. Under the bottom of the last line off to the right margin, type in the word "more" if subsequent page is needed.

more . . . .

. . . .

MUSEUM FEATURES NEWS EXHIBIT–Page 2

The second page begins with an "identifying slug" in case the pages are separated while being typeset by a compositor or word processor given only one page at a time to expedite the typesetting.

or -30-
(The End)

Figure 7.1. Sample news release letterhead

If this game of communications is somewhat restricted to newsprint for the person in the museum's PR role, there is a great deal to be learned in dealing with broadcasting, where there are many opportunities for exposure. The first rule of the game is to study the mediums, hear and see the kinds of news used. To be successful, one should become acquainted with the various ways a station can be of assistance. This can be accomplished by making an appointment with the program director of any station. Basically, public service programming falls into two broad categories: Specials and Segments.

Specials include interviews, panel or group discussions, demonstrations, exhibits in either a series or in a one-time-only presentation.

Segments, similar but short presentations, are inserted as "participating" features of other programs; i.e., a feature on a particular type of art such as sculpturing which may highlight various museums and galleries in the immediate area.

Other on-the-air exposure opportunities include brief spot announcements made at various times during the broadcast day; announcements by on-the-air personalities such as disc jockey, directors of special features or sports figures; short news stories which are included in regular local newscasts and give the brief who, what, when, where, and why of a newsworthy event; and finally, editorials, which are statements prepared by management with its viewpoint on community programs and special projects.

Although television is a "visual" medium, radio and television news release copy may be prepared simultaneously for use by both medums; visuals will be discussed briefly later in this chapter.

Writing for the broadcast media differs substantially from aiming a release for newsprint publication. In the first place, the material is written for the "ear"; it is conversational, and brevity is the key to success. Releases are carefully edited for 10, 15, 30, 45, and 60 seconds, timed by a watch or on the basis of 120 to 140 words a minute. All copy is double spaced, and may be typed in all upper case, or conventionally; however, there is some dispute among communicators today whether stations still prefer numbers spelled out or written in numerals. A few agreed-upon standards remain, such as spelling out within parentheses the phonetic spelling of difficult words and names to pronounce, and avoiding abbreviations such as "Ph.D." or a state's name, for two examples.

Other elements of a radio release include, under the release instructions, the "Time:_____ Seconds" of the release; and under the date of preparation, if a public service announcement, state the specific starting and ending dates the release is to be used, such as "Use between July 1 and July 7" and not the days "Tuesday through next Tuesday"; use an informal style without being too breezy, and send several legible copies at the same time to each station. Also helpful to the broadcaster is that the communicator use paper of good substance which will not rattle while being handled and read over the air. For a sample of radio format, see Figure 7.2.

Writing for television is basically the same as radio; the release is also timed and has many identical requirements. The one outstanding difference is, of course, the visual aspects. The audience will both see and hear the message simultaneously.

There are several ways to accommodate the television medium with visuals. First, with a standard 35mm slide, which could be professionally prepared with an overlay of the museum's name on an exterior picture of the institution or on its logo. At least one of these slides should be sent to the television stations in the museum's geographical area served to be kept on file as an establishing shot for a news announcement at a time of crisis. It can also be used as an establishing shot for a series of other slides to follow in a series describing a new exhibit open to the public. Photographic color prints, in matte finish to avoid a glare, on a format of 9" x 7" horizontally or scaled upwards to a larger size, are acceptable. Sound on 16mm film is acceptable, and a videotape is even better.

Figure 7.2. Sample radio television release

The masthead or letterhead is identical to that used for newsprint, and the variation to be noted is the "timing" and "kill dates" as shown below:

FOR IMMEDIATE RELEASE UNTIL (Date):   _____

                                                                         (Date Prepared)

TIME: :10 Seconds

>   Remember a radio release is written for
>   the ear and should be conversational in
>   style. A brief, concise statement is the
>   key to a good broadcast release.

-30-

If three or more ten-second "spot" news releases are to be used, they

may be prepared on a single sheet. In the space above the "TIME," in-

dicate the release number as "SPOT #1," "SPOT #2," etc.

For the sake of brevity, it is highly recommended that the communicator request copies of radio and television scripts from local stations for study, or from classrooms in audiovisual education at nearby colleges or universities.

THE NEWS CONFERENCE

Press conferences are an excellent method of familiarizing reporters with your institution and providing a livelier understanding of a subject. The conference also encourages press contacts and puts faces behind the names of the PR department and the management. For cultural organizations, the conference provides important visual support.

The press conference should be considered a service to the press, not just a way to create news. The subject must be of definite news value when considered in relation to the many other events competing for the editors' and news directors' attention. The PR person must think like those who pass judgment on the news priorities. As a test, ask the question: If the subject can be adequately covered with a news release, why hold a press conference?

A press conference may be justified to launch a special event that includes a long series of events, to introduce officials or art objects available only for a short duration, or to announce a radical change affecting a large number of people. A press conference is certainly justified during the first hours of a crisis.

When there is a choice, a conference at 10 A.M. on Tuesday will allow metropolitan newspapers to make their Sunday editions, weekly and special newspapers to meet their Thursday edition deadlines, and radio and television crews to be on air for their daily 6 P.M. special newscasts. When in doubt, call several mediums and ask for advice; they can tell you of your competition.

The important aspect of a news conference is to be prepared prior to the arrival of the news reporters; have the area preselected, the proper equipment at their disposal, have your information documented for distribution, and an authoritative spokesperson ready to answer questions — do your homework! The next chapter covers this subject in more detail, and can be adapted to any size institution with a need to communicate to the mass media, especially in time of an emergency situation.

PUBLIC RELATIONS ACTIVITIES

The museum director who understands the ramifications in the performance of public relations services would be a truly unique person because even a PR generalist would experience some difficulties in organizing and managing a museum's day-to-day needs in these changed, and still changing, times. If this statement is acceptable, imagine the problems and responsibilities of a volunteer or a security manager assigned to this role with its complex requirements. The task of managing a museum's public relations cannot and should not be a matter for a person who merely has a background or interest in art, or one whose formal education indicates a flair for the precise and proper word. For an effective and proficient operation, some of the talents to be acquired by the museum's communicator include supervisory skills, managing time and money, cost containment, having an insight into the kinds of information people "have a right to know," and having a good working relationship and knowledge of media operations.

To demonstrate and assist those who may be assigned to such duties on a part-time basis, or as a collateral duty, what is involved, the following list, in no special order, should be considered. While not inclusive, either, the areas with their subordinate needs of attention are fundamental, and, depending on the institution's size and priorities, a planned program of public relations can be prepared with the list used as a guideline.

MAILING LISTS
Board of Directors
Financial Donors
Art Donors
Regional Museums
Legislators
Civic Leaders
Volunteers
Union Leaders
Religious Leaders
Fraternity Leaders
Schools of Art
Historical Groups
Minority Group
   Leaders
Veteran Groups
Accounts Payable
Gift Shop Suppliers
Food Vendors
Law Enforcement
   Groups
Fire Protection
   Groups
Civil Defense Groups
Mass Media

PUBLICATIONS
Newsletter —
   News Gathering
   Writing & Editing
   Graphics & Layout
   Photography
   Cost Containment
   Distribution
Brochures —
   Message Theme
   Selection of Print
   Choice of Stock
   Graphics/Photog-
      raphy
   Cost Containment
   Use of Color
   Distribution
   Evaluation

BULLETIN BOARDS
Effective Locations
Attractiveness/Appeal
Periodically Changed
Position Changes
Materials Relocated

Impact Interest
Message Tested

PHOTOGRAPHY
In-house Availability
Cost Containment
Publicity Prints
Courtesy Prints
Print/Negative Files
Laboratory Skills
Equipment inventory
Legal Release Forms
Historical Files
Archive Preservation
Photographic
   Inventory
Distribution Process

NEWSCLIPS
Historical Files
Publicity Evaluation
Newsclip Service
Employee Pride
Exposure Rating

PUBLICITY
Biographical Files
   Trustees
   Division Directors
   Department
      Directors
   Employees
   Major Donors

MEDIA RELATION-
   SHIPS
General Related Media
   List
Primary Mailing List
Trade Magazine List
Museum Exchange List
"Beeper" Telephone
   List
Wire Service Contacts
Talk Show Contacts
Social Editors
College Media List
Photo Editors List
Network Contacts
Free-Lance Art
   Reporters
Crisis Media Contacts

AUDIOVISUAL
   BASICS
Resources —
   Photo processing
   Equipment Repair
   Equipment Supplies
   Rental Companies
   Photographers
   Sound Technicians
   Video Technicians
   Exhibit Builders
   Floor Stands/Easels
   Electricians
   Security Advisors
Single Lens Reflex
   Camera
Twin Reflex Lens
   Camera
Poloroid 360 Model
   Camera
Electronic Strobe
Floodlights
Copy Camera Stand
Projectors (35mm &
   16mm)
Video Player/
   Recorder

Tape Recorder/
   Synchronizer
Fixed & Portable
   Screens
Dissolve Unit
Storage Area
Utilization Loan
   System
Table Top Podium
   (w/mike)

PRINTING (In-House)
Mimeograph Machine
Multilith Press
Copy Machine
Drafting Table
Graphic Art Supplies
Headlining Equipment
Electric Paper Cutter
Bulk Paper Supplies
Pressman
Graphic Artist
Poloroid MP-4 (Half-
   tones)
Folding Machine
Heavy Duty Stapler
Colating Bench

Areas of the Director-Doer

If the listings in the "activities" section are some of the basic concerns for an effective, organized, and productive public relations department, then consider the following list, which gives evidence that an in-house effort to maintain a constant flow of communication activities, combined with the external needs to communicate, requires an experienced practitioner.

Again, in no special order, are the diversified areas involving the public relations director-doer of a museum:

Publicity
Publications
Bulletin Boards
Photography

Volunteer Recruitment
Donor Cultivation
Employee Social
   Activities

PR Internship Training
Professional Develop-
   ment
Crisis Public Relations

Printing	Anniversary/	Ceremonies and
Guided Tours	Celebrations	Protocol
Speaker's Bureau	Dinner-Tour Rentals	Institution
Personnel Orientation	Budget Preparation	Spokesperson
Civic Meetings	Archives Maintenance	Lobbyist
Newsletter	Open House Planning	Service to Handi-
Travelling Exhibits	City-wide Celebrations	capped
Riot-Disaster Planning	Press Conference	Preventive Safety
Fund-Raising Events	Moderator	Awards Programs
Gift Shop Promotion	Trustees PR Counsel	Office Management

CONCLUSION

The day of the one-person PR shop has been gone since 1965, when consumer advocacy became a prime concern in the operational affairs of not-for-profit institutions and organizations. Too often, the communicator assigned to "mind the store" is greatly handicapped with the added responsibilities of development; publicity is to public relations what fund-raising is to development. This science of obtaining large amounts of funds from private individuals and government agencies requires the experience of a professional who has learned the trade "at the bench." It is not a subject taught in institutions of higher education.

The public relations person so handicapped with this dual role, especially if understaffed, is doomed to fail in either one or both areas, and yet many chief executive officers (CEOs) have added a "third hat" with the role of marketing. That is why it is stated that a CEO with any PR knowledge of the spectrum of responsibilities is a rare person. Budgetary restrictions for this department, often looked upon as a second cousin, non–income-producing department, are a major cause of negative results. It is often said by fund-raising counsel, "When you run a nickel and dime operation, you generally collect nickels and dimes."

What most CEOs fail to realize is that the role of public relations is *their* responsibility, and the public-relations director merely carries the portfolio from which to operate, being careful that it does not get misplaced or misued. The public-relations practice is fundamentally communicating. The need for the PR person in any organization with a department for this purpose is that no one else in the organization or the institution has the time to communicate properly.

NOTES

1. Marshall S. Public relations basics for community organizations manual (Creative Editorial Service, 1972, rev.),p.22.
2. Declaration of principles — code of professional standards of practice of public relations with interpretations. (New York: Public Relations Society of America, 1963), p.1.
3. If you want air time, a handbook for publicity chairmen (Washington, D.C.: National Association of Broadcasters, 1961).

8. Crisis Public Relations Communication

Stephen J. Allen

"The greatest problem of communication is the allusion that it has been accomplished." George Bernard Shaw

Museums, being institutions in which objects of permanent interest in one or more of the arts and sciences are collected, preserved, studied, and exhibited, are also the target for public opinion in time of crisis. The objects, being the works of irreplaceable art, historical artifacts, or scientific specimens that form an important part of the world's cultural heritage, the need to communicate with the public cannot be overestimated or understated. Since these objects are also vulnerable to damage or loss by heat, fire, smoke, water, tornadoes, theft, and vandalism, the need for crisis public relations communication cannot be disputed, nor can the public relations practitioner be denied.

A closer inspection reveals that a fully developed museum serves as a repository for highly valued collections, a center for research, a facility for a broad range of educational and cultural activities. These varied functions result in different occupancies with correspondingly different hazards: exhibit halls, galleries, storerooms for collections, administrative and curatorial offices, conservation and research laboratories, workshops, classrooms, auditoriums, libraries, sales areas and restaurants, in any of which an emergency can arise at any time.

Museums, like hospitals and colleges, exist in a variety of sizes and special interests, each one being established for its own unique needs, to perform a special service according to its resources, opportunities, objectives, and anticipated publics. Because of such differences, every institution must be alert to its own environment when preparing a proficient, viable plan to cope with its communications needs in time of crisis. No two plans will be — or should be — identical among the different types of museums, particularly owing to the variances in staff, location, security support services, or many other reasons. When the completed, workable plan is finalized, the only section similar to other plans may be the methodology of communicating to protect the reputation of the establishment. After all, an institution entrusted to share and safeguard the valuable and irreplaceable art objects preserved for the culture and admiration of future generations must maintain a high standard of credibility and sound integrity with that public, making every honest effort to avoid alienating it by careless loss or damage.

Since it is a traditional assumption, at least among the professional communicators, that *the public has a right to know,* it is as protective to the institution's reputation as it is a service to that segment of the concerned public supporting the institution, that a crisis plan be a basic requirement within the management's operational policy. (The "plan" discussed in this chapter is given the title Crisis Public Relations Communications Plan, or CPRCP, as a descriptive point of reference.)

Preparing this plan requires a task force team effort with the expertise of a professional public relations practitioner in-house or public-relations counsel offering the basic guidelines as the chairperson. That portion of the plan incorporating the methodology of dealing with the mass media and the public should not be left to the whims of the uninitiated novice or an equally uninformed official with rank. The chief executive officer who finally approves the plan must be made to understand that good communication is the key to his or her personal longevity as well as the success of the institution's future.

As mentioned in the previous chapter, an important employee in this planning stage worthy of emphasis is the security manager who has the around-the-clock responsibility for the general safety of the building, its contents, and those people who work and visit within the institution. Deny him not! Break with tradition to isolate security, and elevate these experts to where they may serve to more advantage.

Alan Bart Bernstein, a national authority in crisis planning and founder of PACE, Inc. — a public relations firm dedicated to security — agrees to this concept, writing:

> Security experts often have sophisticated security plans for the emergency itself, but are completely unprepared to speak to the public, employees, or the news media about what has happened. As a result, the damage sustained by poor

media planning and poor public relation responses may prove as costly as the physical losses suffered. There is no reason today why security should fail to work with public relations in developing a coherent program for addressing the public and mass media during an emergency. An emergency public relations plan is not a luxury, but an integral part of contingency planning.[1]

Explaining his recipe for an effective media program, Bernstein, writing in *Security World* magazine (1981), lists the following ingredients: (1) provides emergency information promptly to all audiences speeding relief and recovery efforts; (2) explains the organization's response and ensures the "official" story is told; (3) reduces stress among employees and the anxieties of the public; and (4) minimizes the damage done to the museum's image and credibility, its operating relationships and its contacts.[2]

In this same article, this international expert gives us the basis for what follows when he interprets the nature of the reasoning behind a crisis communications plan, stating, "Two perceptions exist in an emergency. The first is what actually happens — the damage to property and equipment, the death and the injuries. The second is what the public thinks happened, or that which the news media reports and interprets to them."[3]

The course upon which to proceed has been charted. The only choice open is to head for deep waters under full sail, navigating by the precepts of those public relations guidelines which have brought others into safe harbors. Let us together, then, explore those areas where only the fear of the unknown and unexpected are likely to be encountered, and overcome.

INTERNAL COMMUNICATION

When preparing the scene of action after a serious act of vandalism or a theft is discovered during normal working hours, there is usually less chaos than when a situation becomes known at night or in the early morning hours. In this latter instance, dealing with a significant problem is a matter of pre-planning; spelling out, in step-by-step detail, who does what, how it is done, and where the action begins. In the foreground of such instructions, the security personnel, usually the first persons involved in a crisis, know instantly who notifies whom and in what time-saving order. If they don't, they should!

One can reasonably assume the chief executive officer (CEO), the chief security officer, and the public relations director are the first notified. The CEO will then be responsible for determining in what order other key employees are required (which should be listed in the CPRCP with several optional lists depending on the severity of the situation) and in whatever combinations are best suited to the type crisis. Under all crisis categorical listings would be the chief switchboard operator.

The security manager will probably require additional security officers to replace those on duty who will be queried for the preparation of advanced statements to be made to the press. Additional officers will be needed in assisting employees in gaining entrance to the institution after normal hours, in examining press credentials, assisting any injured, and even acting as messengers if necessary until secretarial or other key persons arrive.

When a major crime is committed, in a museum where the security officers are under the employ of a leasing-type agency or company, the reputation of that agency or company is subject to harsh criticism by a fickle public which will invariably want to fix blame on those responsible for security. Does it not, therefore, behoove the security agency or company to have a right to protect its image? When this type of an emergency occurs the public-relations person can be assured that the security guards' employer has issued instructions to remain silent whenever a crime is discovered until an agency or company representative is present, making no statements of an official nature for the institutional victim.

This matter should be given priority attention under such circumstances, or the preparation of an official statement for the press and other concerned parties will be delayed. This could prove awkward for the museum. Anything said to the press to indicate a need for delay would appear to be a ploy to stall for time or to cover up the truth. One question certain to be asked will be, "How good were the security measures in the museum at the time of the crime?"

The question must be answered! Donors have a right to know how their investments or treasured objects are being protected, whether as a gift or on loan.

GETTING IT ALL TOGETHER

The public relations director will require all the details up to the hour, the names of persons on duty, and information relative to preparing an initial statement for study and approval by the CEO before the latter approves any release of information to an external source. Too, the DPR will prepare a variety of notes, especially to internal security, to reinforce such policy matters relative to talking with the press or civil law enforcement personnel — uniformed brothers for whom some preferential treatment might be shown — as well as to the recalled personnel. Everyone must understand the policy that no information on any subject concerning this crisis is to be volunteered to anyone except the CEO and DPR, either one or both normally being the only designated official spokespersons for the institution. If no such policy exists for all personnel, now — today — is the time to originate and distribute an instruction to this effect to all employees, volunteers, and trustees.

Additional personnel to be recalled, or at least notified, would probably be the institution's legal counsel and the insurance representative. The museum's attorney should have an understanding or at least some knowledge of the DPR's role, for experience has shown that legal counsel, rightfully concerned with protecting the client from making statements to the media, may inadvertently ill-advise the CEO when the DPR is in fact the professional communicator who knows the dangers of withholding from the media information which "the public has the right to know."

One mutually agreed-upon reason for legal counsel to intercede is the caution for preparing news releases with words that are considered danger signals. For example, in preparing the initial news statement for a release after the fact, care must be exercised to avoid a single expression to be printed deliberately or accidentally that can be the basis of a libel suit if it slips by the copyreader at the newspaper or a broadcaster called on a direct line.

Some of these danger signals are found in such words as blackmailer, charlatan, conspirator, criminal, crook, degenerate, embezzler, forger, fraud, imposter, maniac, racketeer, rascal, scoundrel, shyster, swindler, and thief. A good rule to remember is, "When in doubt, leave it out."

Another important point to remember is that the only ironclad defense against a libel action is proof that the truth was told without malice, without distortion and false emphasis, and in the public interest. Haste, gullibility, and good intentions count very little with either judge or jury; it is what is said, not the thought behind it, that counts in the courtroom.

DELAYING THE ACTION

For the obvious reason, the recommendation to notify the civil law enforcement authorities immediately upon discovering an act of major vandalism or a theft has been held in abeyance pending further discussion.

A major advantage for this delay in notifying the police is to provide the museum officials and staff the opportunity to "get their act together." Everyone involved must be on the same wavelength, without any static, with no possibility that anyone will contradict another's comments. The moment the police officials are notified by a telephone call, a "beat reporter," one who is assigned to cover police news, need only hear the words "museum theft" and the action begins. These words, like a starting gate bell, send the seasoned reporter off at a gallop for the institution, with the intent of being the first media representative to cross the main threshold. The race is on to get the story and file it!

In a city which has more than one daily newspaper — competition — or in a major city having a news wire bureau office, the activity becomes tremendously vicious in the race to compete. Every minute the CEO can afford to delay the initial telephone call to the civil police is a plus for the museum to establish its posture, gather the facts, reinforce the present security staff, select areas for directing the press and others with an interest, prepare statements (handouts) for the media, and notify its own personnel of the situation.

Too many institutions, cold and impersonal, look upon the employees as numbers belonging to a time clock instead of considering them as part of the "family." As such, employees should not have to read a newspaper or obtain their news from the electronic broadcast media, as if they were second cousins. To allow this to happen endangers internal morale and gives vent to rumors, speculation, and criticism of the management. Notices should be posted over the time clocks and in employee lounges and on bulletin boards as soon as possible when a crisis situation arises.

THE OBJECTIVE PLAN

What is done is done. What must be told will be told.

The museum being the recipient of public donations, federal grants, state and city support, and private gifts, the objective plan is to maintain the museum's credibility and integrity as the protector of its contents, and to ensure the continued public and private support. If public sympathy is earned, a bad situation can be reversed in favor of the museum, into a lucrative opportunity even if the art or artifacts stolen or destroyed can never be replaced or duplicated. The damage done, why not take advantage of this opportunity for fund-raising?

NEED FOR PHOTOGRAPHY

With all the preliminary problems to think about, the need for photography is often overlooked even at this stage of readiness. In the case of vandalism or theft, public interest will be more aroused by a visual account of the object(s) damaged or stolen than by a mere verbal announcement of the loss. The availability of an in-house or commercial reproduction photographic facility, therefore, would be an advantage. Needed would be a facility with the capabilities to produce a color slide from a photograph on file, or a color print with the imaged subject 7" X 9" horizontally as preferred by television, or a black and white glossy print in such numbers as may be required for press kits, and in the shortest possible time. This service would be beneficial to the museum to gain public support and gain cooperation from the media for the management's attitude.

In the case of vandalism, the PR person, if not equipped or qualified to photograph the situation, should have a number of resources to call upon instantly, day or night, to make the required photographs. As an alternative, although temporary, the PR office should have available the use of a Polaroid #360 Land Camera. This camera accepts a #197 film pack with a film speed of 3,000 index (nearly six times faster than traditional black and white film, requiring very little light source). While this method would not generally be accepted for media use, such prints do have an important role if used properly.

If time permits, such photographic evidence could be mounted on a large cardboard, placed on an easel, and used to describe the situation and the physical plant of a particular area to the media. Used in a conference room, highlighting an area distant from the news broadcaster may help to describe the area which, because of security reasons, cannot be exposed. When the media have departed, this display could then be mounted in the employee cafeteria or lounge to share information with the "family" as a warning against complacency. The same display, dismounted by individual prints, will later be filed in the museum's own historical archives to be used in a future anniversary booklet. These photographs could be the only visual record of the crisis ever made; don't count on the press photographer for prints.

DECISION-MAKING ASSESSMENT

The events resulting in emergency press are generally of such a nature that when reported by the media the public will quickly draw definite conclusions and will be the first to pass judgment on the institution's incident. Unfortunately, in the more serious instances, while those people with a special interest in the arts will probably assess this single event honestly and fairly, the fickle public will focus on the entire spectrum of the museum industry, and all institutions will be judged by "association," as being good or bad institutions depending on the public's available information. Losses from whatever the cause rarely result in "good" publicity, and intelligent management does not expect any PR person to turn a disaster into a success. A bad situation, however, can be made worse if ignored, or if the news media are hampered in their efforts to obtain the news. Accurate information from a primary source — your museum — is better than inaccurate information from a secondary one. As Bernstein points out, the accepted philosophy of PR practitioners is, bad news which leaves a bad taste is easier to digest in one swallow than in sips as reporters uncover fresh information leading to new accusations.[4] This fact will be discussed later in more detail.

For the museum involved, the bad news is embarrassing. Still, the adverse news must not be repressed. One reason the story must be told is purely a practical one. Attempts to hide bad news will cause the museum to appear dishonest. Refusal to cooperate with the news media for whatever reason during the first few hours results in speculation, rumor, and conjecture among employees as well as the public. This is especially true while becoming organized during an emergency.

Usually, in the hustle to get organized, the public relations person, acting for the CEO, is the "fact-finding body" with whom all personnel queried should provide their complete cooperation. Personnel employed must not take it upon themselves to censor the facts, withhold information, or attempt to cover up the truth, even though it is human instinct to remain blameless. Eventually, all the true facts will be revealed. Precious time is saved through cooperation.

The public relations person's task is to gather the facts in order to relate them clearly and concisely to the CEO, provide counsel as to what information should be accurately released and with what dispatch, including a recommendation on how the information is to be transmitted. The CEO, of course, makes all the final decisions after an assessment of all the information presented.

The time for decision-making is at hand. Appraisal of the situation was made without exaggeration or panic. Eliminated were any thoughts of what the board members, or other museum PR persons, might think when they learn of the crisis. Concentration is on what will be told to the general public, remembering that those persons momentarily feared may be critical, but that they are also part of the institution's publics.

Another consideration entering into the decision-making process was that of holding a press conference. Before jumping into a full-scale press conference, however, consider the alternative of a brief "press advisory," a statement of fact given to the wire services, acknowledging the basic facts, and assuring editors and news directors of the mass media that further information will be forwarded when becoming available. This delaying tactic provides the pause allowing the staff to gain their composure, establish a plan of alternate action if it becomes necessary, and time to put that alternative into play. Before releasing any plan of activities, however, officials should make a last review, in-depth, of the actual situation.

ASSESSING THE EMERGENCY

For a mother, the newborn held in her arms may be the most important event in her life at that moment, but for the world's millions of mothers who have enjoyed a similar experience — many more than once — such news is of minor interest. Conversely, what appears to be an emergency close to the hearts of the museum's management may be blown out of proportion as to its true importance to the general public, and as far as media personnel are concerned.

What the public has the right to know is, what was lost, how much money is involved, and who is at fault. They may also need to know who the culprit(s) was and if he is in police custody. These are the usual prime concerns. The public's reaction to any statements on the matter depends heavily on the degree of the crisis. In reading of the national reports on economy, spending, and waste, seven- to ten-figure currency denominations are so commonplace it would be difficult to raise any body temperatures among the general public in reportng a mere million-dollar loss. Their first reaction would probably be, "So what? The insurance company will make good the loss." The level of public apathy is staggering, especially in the absence of any proximity.

The matters of what is lost or destroyed, and how much money is involved, are really secondary in the public's concern. The public does enjoy being able to sit in judgment, and the big question would be, "Where do you fix the blame?" They not only want to know how it happened, but they want reassurance the incident is not likely to recur. In the event of a robbery or wanton destruction, the foolish public accept this as a way of life today; this is the bottom line in satisfying the public's knowledge as well as their curiosity, because "these things do happen." In the case of death or injury, the public is much more vocal and opinionated. They could have little to say, of course, if the destruction was caused by a flood or a tornado.

An emergency suggests urgency. What, then, does a disaster suggest? One sophisticated definition is, "A disaster is a disruption in the normal flow of energy that is uncontrolled." Another is, "The impinging upon a structured community of an external force capable of destroying human life or its resources, on a scale wide enough to disrupt normal patterns of behavior."[5]

In examining these two definitions, it would appear that disasters, regardless of how or by whom defined, have certain common attributes. They include injury, suffering, damage or destruction to property, and death. There is no commonly accepted system for categorizing disaster beyond the two main divisions — man-made or naturally caused. Among those events suggested as disasters recognized by the American Red Cross are hurricanes, tornadoes, other windstorms, floods, flash floods, explosions, fires, and wrecks (ship, train, airplane, etc.). Another would be a war.

ANY EMERGENCY IS NEWSWORTHY

In our quest to protect and preserve the art objects of the world which have survived for generations, one cannot be parochial on the subject of museum emergencies. For those persons with an appreciation and love of art and a dedication for such preservation and display of culture within the museum industry throughout the world, even a minor loss under whatever circumstances would be of interest to such people whether in Sydney, Australia, or Jacksonville, Florida.

An early assessment of the event to be classified as an emergency, therefore, cannot be considered to be a mere matter of local news just because of the museum's location or proximity to any particular media, but should be looked upon with the broadest scope possible. In whichever city the news is first released, if important enough, the wire services will pick up on the local source and transmit the news around the world in the amount of time normally needed to empty a coffee cup.

At a time when new acquisitions have become a must for drawing foot traffic for gate receipts and selling souvenirs to survive, and when the art business is booming for reasons of feeding the culturally hungry, or for the purpose of investment, no institution should push itself into a corner of mistrust. The greater the loss, the more public interest will be shown, and the more attention will be given the matter by the press.

At the scene of the incident, news representatives are just that — representatives of the public who have a right to know. Through the reporters' eyes and ears, the public learns all the available details. The public's first impression of the museum will be formed from what they read in their newspapers, hear on the radio, see on television, or scan in their monthly magazines. They will naturally assume all museums are similar except for content. It is important to the entire industry, then, that these impressions be unbiased and undistorted from the beginning. It is the earliest stories that receive the biggest headlines, and the first impressions are likely to be the most enduring.

The important considerations, then are; How serious is the emergency situation, and is the museum prepared to cope with the media for favorable results?

TOWARD A BETTER UNDERSTANDING

One of the many problems confronting the CEO of any institution in time of stress is how to tell the corporate story without getting into difficulty with experienced reporters. The CEO realizes he is at a disadvantage in being interviewed by a skilled newsprint reporter for whom he holds the same respect as those from the mediums of radio and television. He knows only too well that they ask provocative questions in order to get provocative, interesting, and controversial answers. But the advantage need not be so one-sided if museum administrators will accept the fact that when you know the rules of the reporters' game, you can communicate your corporate story effectively.

This particular section is for CEOs and their designated representative who need to understand the basic rules:

The more intelligently you speak, the more details you provide, the fewer the questions left to be asked. The more plausible you appear to sound, the easier it will be for the news reporter to relate the story "you" want the public to know. Remember, the news reporter must turn in a story. That story must be interesting and informative, leaving no questions in the mind of its readers or listeners. The reporter may even attempt to obtain a statement which is controversial and, if possible, detrimental to the interviewee representing the institution. For a newspaper, this kind of information is what helps to write the headlines that sell newspapers, which carry the advertising, which makes the publication its money. This is the bottom line for all the media.

Knowing this, executives tremble in fear of being asked questions for which the answers are open to the "interpretation" of the interviewer. Another fear is that of being misquoted, or having a comment taken out of context. It happens! The first time you are caught in a contradiction or make reference to the major reason for the interview, all media representatives present will pick up on this one point, which may or may not be a deliberate attack on the integrity and credibility of the institution or its management.

One of the reporters' means of drawing the executive into such a conversation is to ask, "How could such an event been prevented?" That puts the interviewee on the defensive, and if there is a satisfactory answer readily available, the next question may be, "Knowing this, why didn't the museum's authorities take corrective action *before* the incident?" The CEO now gets wedged into a corner with this line of questioning, but he must remain calm and confident.

Today it is normal to fear the young reporters assigned to a crisis who will accidentally or deliberately pull words out of context, or purposely write their personal observations into a story. Every reporter knows, too, that such repeated behavior will endanger his or her longevity since editors and news directors dislike having errors constantly cropping up on their desks.

Some precautions the CEO may want to consider are general rules that are applicable to similar situations in any type of institution.

Put your best foot forward by approaching the interview with a positive attitude. Don't underestimate the news reporter who appears in bluejeans, sport shirt, and looking like a "flower child." You have in your midst an intelligent professional member of the working press, according to the credentials inspected by the security officer. You, as the CEO, on the other hand, have the advantage of knowing more about the subject to be discussed than any other individual present. Project competence. Avoid any attitude displaying arrogance or portraying false humility. Above all, to beg for mercy — so to speak — is as foolhardy as asking for crucifixion. If you act in such a manner you will not be disappointed by this warning.

Before meeting the press representatives, prepare a factual, detailed summary of events to answer the who, what, where, when, why and how of the crisis situation. Conduct your own investigation, interviewing security personnel, telephone operators, volunteers, and others if during normal working hours. Record all comments "for the record." Read and reread your own notes over and over. Commit the ideas, not the words, to memory. Do not use a prepared statement if appearing before the press in a news conference.

An executive should never report "off the cuff" since reporters have no obligation to keep any confidence. If any statement cannot be made for the record, do not say anything. The public relations practitioner, playing the role of the devil's advocate, can prepare a series of questions likely to be asked by the press to better prepare the executive for the barrage of in-depth questions to follow at the conclusion of the CEO's opening statement.

During a live press conference, at this point the questioning should be done in an orderly manner with preconference instructions stressing to those present that each will have a turn-around-the-table, and then anyone can jump in with a question until all questions have been answered. After the press conference, the CEO may be required to be interviewed on video tape or by a radio reporter with a recorder. Do not add anything to what has already been said or you will be accused of giving some reporter an "exclusive."

The key to success with the mass media simply remains, as always, to be cooperative.

COPING WITH THE MEDIA

Earlier it was hinted that when the civil police are telephoned to report an event, there usually is a news reporter, known as the "beat reporter" at the station. The news reporter, serving a daily, is not a photographer. Unionization prevents this, and conversely, photographers do not write stories.

You can safely assume the tip received by the beat reporter when the initial call is received triggers a message back to the city desk requesting a photographer. This request is relayed by telephone, by mobile telecommunication while the reporter is enroute to the museum, or by high-powered "walkie talkie" receiver-transmitter equipment. Teams of reporters-photographers will follow. They will not be arriving together, but at staggered intervals. Photographers may be delayed owing to the completion of other assignments.

The PR person and the security chief must have an harmonious working relationship as well as an agreed-upon plan to account for these anticipated media representatives, showing a professional respect for each other. Each must have an understanding of the others' role during a crisis.

SCREENING THE PRESS

The first policy rule to be agreed upon is that only those with "acceptable" press credentials will be honored at the main entrance. This will help exclude many nonaccredited free-lancers seeking the sensational news from crashing and upsetting the museum's staff with their zealous efforts to scoop the professionals. This breed often lacks the professional ethics of their competition.

Screening is difficult because of legitimate card-bearing photojournalists, known as *stringers* (paid for their works monthly according to the string of inches accumulated to their credit). This causes much confusion for the newer security guard.

So how does the security guard differentiate between correspondents? Many college newspapers even issue press cards, as do their university radio and television stations. Good judgment must be exercised by the security officer, who acts in a diplomatic and tactful manner to avoid offending an important media representative. In major cities such as Chicago, New York, Los Angeles, and others, it is not unlikely to have a correspondent representing an art magazine, a wire service, or a general publication of distinction. The guidelines here are (1) when in doubt, play it out. Telephone the media stated to be represented and verify the representatives' credentials, or (2) call out the public-relations person to make the final decision if doubt persists.

Expecting the media to converge on the museum during a crisis, the DPR will have prepared in advance to use for such occasions a stack of log sheets. These log notes request the usual basic information; name of medium represented, address of the medium, telephone number, time in, and time out. These accumulated listings also serve to provide names to whom updated information may be released later, as well as "thank you" letters and a survey questionnaire (these will be discussed under "evaluation" later in this chapter).

If the newsperson is not the person he or she professes to be, the visitor could be backed off with the hint of prosecution as a trespasser. Having the visitor present when the security guard checks credentials may also discourage the free-lancer. These defensive tactics will prevent a three-ring circus from emerging from what otherwise should be an orderly, dignified scene.

The security officer posted at the main entrance to screen the press and others will reflect the first impression visitors will receive of the institution's management. The officer, therefore, must be a mature, pleasant, and a patient diplomat. If the reporter anxious to gain entrance to get to his work assignment is met with hostility, this attitude will reappear in the reporter's attitude during the interview process. Hostility, like courtesy, is also contagious. The guard should not be a person who is likely to transform a neutral friend into an aggressive enemy. Regardless of the reporter's pushiness, attire, personal appearance, or manners, all museum employees must remain friendly, cooperative, and understanding of the mission of the press. The reporter has a job to do. One way or another, it will be done, even if the news must come from a somewhat unreliable source.

DEADLINE PRESSURES

To help cope with news-gathering people, it is essential to understand what makes them aggressive, tenacious, and successful.

Reporters are under the pressure of meeting a deadline. In this respect, you need to imagine yourself in their position.

First, newsprint reporters must gather all the details possible, interview people for quotation or attribution to their own commentaries, arrange for a photograph if considered needed, absorb all the technical background information in the press-kit handouts, and then either return to their desks to write the story or telephone the information to a "rewrite person" back at the newspaper who prepares the final draft while accepting the facts as transmitted. All this is to be achieved in the shortest possible time. Although it sounds very routine, it is not as simple as tying shoelaces or combing hair. The process of news gathering is nervewracking under the pressures of deadlines. Quite possibly, the reporter may have another assignment or an emergency to cover when leaving the museum.

Second, the radio broadcast journalist or radio reporter has the same problem, but with a slight edge over newsprint competitors. That edge is that every fifteen minutes this reporter has the opportunity to file the story gathered and at will can feed it back to the radio station in bits of information to be put together by another broadcast news reporter who meanwhile has set these short takes up for immediate broadcast, promising the station's listeners an update at the next station break. This can be achieved by using the telephone relay or a taped cassette from a recorder using special devices, thus having the added plausibility of the museum's spokesperson's voice on the air.

Parenthetically, consider the situation. If a crisis occurred after 3 A.M., a daily newspaper with only a morning edition must wait one whole day to report the item to its subscribers. The radio station can be reporting to the working "night people," tell the story again during breakfast hours, and again during "drive time" for those heading out to work, and again to all the housewives long before the newspaper reaches its publics even with an evening edition.

The television crew can also produce instant live direct-beam broadcasts — if the timing is right for the regularly scheduled news telecast, and during station breaks as well; however, most networks are off the air by 1 A.M. Only when there is a serious crisis of national significance would a TV station break into a program in progress. When a video tape film is produced, it must be returned to the station's studio and edited for the next telecast, probably no longer than three hours apart. Even in this medium, the news reporters and studio partners are pressured by deadlines. Too, the TV crew requires a reporter, a cameraman, and a soundman, and after normal working hours at many stations only a single crew on duty may be at another emergency at the time of a museum's crisis period. And if not, they, too could have an assignment to cover when leaving the institution, and again with a deadline to meet. Life-and-death matters take precedence over robberies and destruction with any medium reporting news.

WHEN THE DUST SETTLES

Suppose the newspaper can make the last deadline. Suppose, too, the third shift has taken over and an important piece of art is discovered stolen. What can be expected? The story will either make the front page with the space given the item depending on other national, international, or local news or end up on the inside front page, the inside back page, or the last page. These are the last four pages (called a "signature") held until the last edition is put to bed with space saved for fast-breaking news. With good fortune, the story may get very little play, in which case no one will pay much attention to the item.

If the story is considered important, a reporter on the next shift will be assigned to write a follow-up piece and will be on the telephone shortly after the museum's employees report to work.

The lines of communication between the media and the PR person must be constantly open until the matter subsides. Each media call should be logged until the PR person reports to work to ensure none will be overlooked when their telephone calls are returned.

Setting the Scene for a Crisis

Careful preassessment of institutional needs in time of emergency, developed with the input of all department managers likely to be involved, is finally converted into a written plan for approval by the CEO. The CPRCP, to be widely distributed throughout the institution, defines the roles and responsibilities of the PR person as an official spokesperson in all relationships with the media and the general public. This is also the person who is most likely to respond to the inquires from the police, fire, government agencies, and the institution's immediate "family" of employees, volunteers, officers, and trustees.

With the CEO's guidance, the spokesperson will put into writing all policy statements and information to be related to the media making telephone requests for interviews. Both persons should address themselves to the needs of internal personnel, the press, and all other interested parties, around the clock if necesssary. In large institutions, the PR person will need to rely on the building superintendent or the security manager for commentaries, guidance, and related facts. In the smaller institutions, the security manager may need to be the official spokesperson.

PERSONNEL INVOLVEMENT

The CPRCP must emphasize that personnel are prohibited from divulging any information voluntarily to media representatives, law enforcement agencies, or other officials without express permission from the CEO or PIO (an interchangeable term for public relations director is the "public information officer" or the person who does not have the *primary* function of public relations). This regulation is necessary because (1) such personnel may not have all the facts or be privy to all the correct information; (2) volunteered information may be contradictory to the detailed statement approved for dissemination by the CEO; (3) a statement off the record may invade the privacy of, or shift a nonexisting suspicion to, another employee; and (4) the action indicates to the media the institution is disorganized and destroys the credibility of the management.

The switchboard operator supervisor in a large institution needs to have available the name, home address, and telephone number of *every* employee, trustee, conservation member, and volunteer. During a crisis, it may be necessary to recall various persons, or to ask specific questions helpful to the situation. Too, in case of injury or death, the next of kin must be notified *before* any information regarding this person(s) can be released to the press. In the absence of this listing, access to personnel files becomes essential. Knowledge of access to these files' keys could be posted with the security manager or the officer on duty.

The institution's legal, insurance, and fire representatives should also be notified of a crisis situation to alert them of the possible need for consultation services. The legal officer should also assist in planning the CPRCP. Employees when hired are seldom required to execute a waiver form giving permission to be photographed. If it happens during a crisis, it is news, true, but the museum would be on firmer ground to have employees or security guards sign a "Photographic Waiver Form" authorizing the institution to use their photograph for publication if necessary on a need-to-have basis in connection with the normal or unusual operation of the museum. This action would be taken even if the picture were to be used in a widely distributed brochure. Not to do so can result in another type crisis in a courtroom if there was an objection later by a subject claiming an "invasion of privacy."

The extent of personnel involvement does depend on the size, location, and varied policies from institution to institution, as well as geography. As previously pointed out, where one museum may be subject to flooding, another may be in an area subject to the types of blizzards experienced in New England during the late 1970s. Then, too, there are international areas where people are engaged in internal strife and full-scale war.

An acquisition on loan which is partially or completely destroyed in any location becomes the subject of crisis for both the loanee and the exhibitor. In such cases, the CPRCP should include safeguards and policies relative to international implications where appropriate.

CRISIS INFORMATION CENTER (CIC)

Centralizing the two-way flow of communication is a task coordinated from the Crisis Information Center, an area set aside such as a board room, conference room, or office, where the public can be avoided and the information team can be isolated until ready to conduct a news conference or meet the press. The preselected space is usually outfitted with a special telephone jack which has two internal lines and one private-external line to be used exclusively for crisis communication, with the number included in the overall plan. The external line should also be known to the media as an "emergency-crisis telephone number" and secondary to the PR person's home telephone number for night calls. This avoids delay for the media and also enables them to call direct without overloading the switchboard, or being delayed. Too, in this manner of direct dialing, the press is denied the opportunity of questioning switchboard operators who may unknowingly, despite their usual efficiency, leak a helpful hint to the media which the PIO is not ready or willing to divulge.

CONVERSION FOR PRESS CONFERENCE

In preparing a statement for the press for the CEO, the PIO should anticipate the questions to be asked during a press conference if such is to be necessary. The prepared questions and answers in writing will serve as a guide for interviews whether live, recorded for radio on tape cassette, or on video tape. The CIC, now converted to a press conference room, should include a portable desk-top podium with battery-operated microphone and speaker attachments for overcrowded situations. One advantage to having this equipment is its overpowering volume level if needed when a questioning period becomes too noisy or unruly. The spokesperson or moderator should repeat each question asked before replying. This pause technique provides for thoughtful reply and ensures the question was heard by everyone present, and restated correctly as asked.

An employee-manned table by the conference room entrance is an excellent means for logging in attendees, providing each with an identification badge, and distributing handouts, press kits, and note-taking supplies.

Electrical extension cords may be required by broadcast media with tape recorders (and weak batteries), and for television crews with special lighting equipment. To protect the furniture and flooring from those who must smoke, ashtrays of glass or porcelain are better than aluminized paper types.

ONE-UPMANSHIP

If the activities occur around midnight, consider the possibility of conducting the conference in the employee cafeteria or a lounge where soft drinks and hot refreshments may be served or set out on a table. Planning for crisis public relations communication is often a matter of awareness and creativity.

One must anticipate the needs of the media and be prepared to offset their gameplan with superior courtesies. For example, if damage or loss involves a special piece of art on loan, perhaps the registrar's office may have a photograph of the art which can be displayed on an easel or mounted on a wall behind the podium, off-center of the speaker's position. You can easily anticipate the pleasure of the television medium and news photographers for such thoughtfulness. Each institution has different needs and varied opportunities to relate its particular story, and these needs should be included in drafting the CPRCP.

Giving specific attention to such details as to who does what, when, and under what circumstances may even require a rehearsal or drill once or twice a year. Although this may be costly in overtime, perfecting the plan will prove the worth of this expenditure in time of a real crisis. It may be the only manner by which to test for flaws in the plan, and it should be as welcome to employees as an "abandon ship drill" is to sailors. Only by drills can such plans be executed orderly and proficiently. For the most effective drills, have each department conduct its own for closer inspection, and once a year have a full-scale drill utilizing department managers as observers to critique the event. Special considerations will be required for evacuations, riots, and bombing when persons are likely to be injured. Civil defense, American Red Cross personnel, and hospital volunteers can be of immeasurable aid in drafting plans for these instances.

CRISIS PUBLIC RELATIONS COMMUNICATIONS PLAN

The time to prepare a crisis plan is before a disaster occurs. To think any institution is immune to an emergency or a disaster is to believe that life on earth is forever. Whatever the cause of either an emergency or a disaster, it can be happening right now, next week, or a year hence. A crisis can occur anytime. The conservative, complacent executive can heed the writings of philosopher Alexander Pope, who teaches, "To know yourself diseased is half the cure." Because a museum is highly susceptible to the illnesses of a constantly changing society, prescribing the means for any prevention is not enough to deal with the side effects of a crisis when it involves people. Even though some regional weather reporters can predict oncoming high-velocity winds and the dangers of flooding with some degree of accuracy, thieves, arsonists, protestors, drug addicts, and vandals are all totally unpredictable as well as devastating in creating their own individual types of destruction.

Whatever the cause of a crisis, it has an immediate negative effect, physically and emotionally, in-house and among the public who have the right to know the true facts surrounding the event. To deal responsibly with a crisis situation, and minimize the potential for error during such stressful conditions, every institution, regardless of its size, should have available for immediate utilization a pre-prepared written plan outlining in detail the public relations guidelines to be followed. This is a fact which needs repeating.

The CPRCP should be as comprehensive and practical as is consistent with the size, scope, economics, and content of the museum and as is necessary and affordable by finances and manpower.

COMPREHENSIVE PLANNING

The New England region is not likely to experience the type of flooding familiar to southwestern residents, nor will the people of the southeastern states likely be victims of snowstorms that are normal for those ranchers in the Northwest. All types of emergencies must be considered in planning consistent with the geographical area as well as the contents of the individual museum.

The cause of crisis may be flood, bombing or bomb threat, or fire, all of which require evacuation, while theft and vandalism would require much different treatment in the initial planning. It becomes quite evident, therefore, the CPRCP must be *comprehensive,* providing for the right action, at the right time, for the right reason, by the right people, for the ultimate right result.

While an emergency plan may be considered a noncatastrophic situation (usually a minor event on a local scale), a disaster-crisis would be more difficult for which to plan on a local, regional, or national scale because of the extremely unusual circumstances involved, and the urgency of tremendous pressures from the news media, especially when one or more deaths are involved. When a disaster of such proportions does occur, many duties must be performed almost simultaneously.[6]

For example, while one person is responding to the telephone inquiries, another may be notifying the next of kin of the injured or dead, the legal department, and others required to serve in a designated, preestablished Crisis Information Center.

In all probability, before this litany of telephone calls has been completed, news media reporters, family and friends of employees, visitors, and the institution's officials are enroute or have arrived at the main entrance. Police and other civic officials also become instantly activated. Without adequate assistance, the institution can erupt into chaos, especially if those employees who could assist have not been preassigned or prerehearsed in a special function or specific duty during normal working hours *before* the crisis. A disaster with chaos and frustration invites additional danger. During the confusion of organizing there is the added danger of theft, since opportunity is present during normal visiting hours. The security force, therefore, must be an integral part of the planning process to provide input into the overall finalized plan. Their problems at such times are compounded. They are responsible for the protection of the institution's contents, the safety of the employees and the public, and they must control foot traffic and avoid panic, screen the oncoming rush of news reporters and officials with a desire to gain access, and yet may be in the process of evacuating people from within and ensuring that all the visitors leave without carrying off the museum's valuables. Through it all, they are also required to remain efficient, calm, dignified, courteous, alert, and protective. That's a tall order for any security officer, whether a professional or a part-time (second-job) moonlighter, especially if he is asked to put his own life on the limb.

The CPRCP must be specific in the responsibilities assigned to each security person, of which there are never enough to serve the needs of the security manager during a disaster-crisis; at least not immediately. For this and other obvious reasons, the CPRCP as prepared in advance needs to ensure that each person, or that for each assignment made, someone knows exactly what he or she must do instantly. Some plans currently in force around the nation have taken as long as two years to finalize, an additional few months to orient the entire staff, and longer still to conduct drills to perfect the plan so it will work precisely and effectively.

How to Begin

Begin with investigation. Make a list of every conceivable type of crisis possible in your own institution. Consider the various groups of people who may be affected. Know the difference between an emergency and a disaster situation and determine how many persons can be relied upon for manpower assistance in each instance during and after normal working hours.

Establish an ad-hoc committee of only a few key persons to brainstorm the immediate needs during a crisis for temporary fire-fighting or fire containment until the professionals arrive (screen employees for former military personnel, usually trained for this). Select reliable, mature persons for manning the telephones in key offices, and for handling office equipment to reproduce instructions, releases, important messages, and establish a secretarial pool.

When the initial research is exhausted, develop each crisis possibility by generic title, one at a time, to completion. Be realistic, yet imaginative, about the methods of operations required to handle each situation. List the main objectives which must be accomplished on a priority basis in each instance. Do not become overwhelmed with the "how to" at this stage of providing general information to be developed or used as a springboard for finalizing the details.

How Large a Plan?

How many bricks are required to build a house depends on how big a structure is needed. Each of the various types of crisis events which could occur can be appended to the "overall plan," preceded by instructional guidelines; i.e., one letter with multiple enclosures. These guidelines may be contained in a single page, or may be manual-size if specifics are listed to include every possible crisis event as a whole. Each institution must decide which system would best meet its own needs.

One of the first specifics to be considered is who notifies whom and in what order. This is essential, especially after normal visiting hours, such as between midnight and 8 A.M. For an efficient system when manpower is required, each person called can call two others preassigned. Remember, leave some flexibility in this plan. In some instances, it may be required that the security supervisor on duty initially recall or hire additional security personnel even before the chief executive officer is notified. Every plan, no matter how official, must allow for this flexibility, initiative, and keen judgment to be used by responsible persons. In other instances it may be far more appropriate to have working secretaries and switchboard operators immediately available for duty than have untrained executives to cope with the needs. The plan must be precise, with the recall section listing each person by name, title or position, home telephone number and working telephone number, and recommended is a telephone number of a next of kin.

Expect the plan to grow before finally submitting it for approval. Once approved, there should be very little to add to the plan if careful and serious thought is given to the basic needs. Changes will come after rehearsals or the real thing; the important matter is to get it down on paper, get it right, and get it out.

The Right Person for the Right Task

At this particular time of explanations, the opportunity is compelling to comment about those officials and employees who have never participated in a disaster-crisis situation — and many never will in their entire employment career — who for the first time will perceive the public relations function in a different light. Disaster-crisis in all its ramifications is the supreme test of the PR practitioner, for job security, peer review, family respect, self-esteem, professional satisfaction, media relationships, and belief in the power of prayer. It is at such times that many PR persons on the sidelines have mumbled those oft-repeated words, "There but for the grace of God. . . ."

This commentary serves more as a warning than a justification; a warning to those who flex their muscles at the board-room level and advocate that public relations is one of those jobs anyone can be left to do who "relates well to people," or who has majored in the English language, and then with the reasoning of a close-minded executive leaves that person to work out of a vacuum.

An early factor, then, is having a professional practitioner or PR consultant from an agency in charge of the initial planning to ensure a great measure of success for crisis communication. This would be the person who most likely will execute the CPRCP after the fuse has been lit.

Keeping it Basically Simple

Because a crisis is instantaneous, every ounce of energy expended in pre-planning will result in excellent dividends. Like preventive maintenance, such planning may not eliminate the probability of an emergency any more than carrying an inflated spare tire in an automobile trunk will prevent a blowout, but it will sharply reduce the impact and the consquences of being unprepared. As previously stated, an important element is knowing how to apply the plan at the right time, in the right place, for the right reason, by the right person, to which is now added, with the right equipment. Without all the required equipment, negative factors take over energy and clear thinking. Frustration takes hold, and then panic. Panic will overcome all logic and good judgment. Avoid this. Stay close to basics during the initial planning stage.

BASIC PLANNING

Press room. A preselected area in which to confine and converse with all news-media persons. An area which will provide for easy access to and by public relations personnel, easily converted into a conference room and equipped with extra telephone jacks and instruments for media use. Also needed will be typewriters, paper supplies, correction tape or erasers, paper clips, pencils, pads, handout materials, stock photographs, large manila envelopes, and if a long period is to ensue, obviously some light refreshments.

Telephone switchboard. The "nerve center" of any institution from which a caller receives a first and possibly a lasting impression begins with the telephone operators. The chief operator is the person who can best determine, from experience and from the telephone company's guidance, how much of a load of incoming and outgoing calls can be handled without delays; be responsible for the recall of other off-duty operators if they are needed, and keep tabs on the crisis team members' whereabouts at all times, especially the PR person and the security manager. The operators also provide services to the media on the premises with need to reach their external contacts to relay their information which is rewritten on the other end as a matter of expediting their job and in meeting their deadlines. The switchboard is really the only link internally and externally for instant communication unless other equipment is available.

Radio communication. Should the normal telephone operation be disrupted, short-circuited, or overloaded, a Citizens-Band (CB) radio or short-wave radio emergency system will bring cooperative outside agencies or private citizens to aid the situation by providing a relay system to those with whom officials need to make contact. A 40-channel CB hook-up with the PR department could also maintain contact with security by using the lower-numbered channels available on the CB-portable transmitter unit, similar to the "walkie-talkie."

Portable equipment. Should the electrical system fail, a portable public-address system, also needed for special events, should always be available to security personnel. Similarly, an electronic "bull horn" can project a voice up to 1,500 feet distant; ideal for crowd control and making announcements from wing to wing along corridors, up and down stairwells, or as an aid if escorting a group of media to an on-site area.

Report system. Arrange for one or two persons to circulate, run errands, handle special assignments, and report back at regular intervals in person or by walkie-talkie to ensure knowledge of activities in various areas which are not accessible in any other way. These "floaters" should also provide liaison with the security manager, the personnel and maintenance managers, and replenish as required the press facility, visitors lounge, and crisis information center.

Second holding area. There is a need for a second conference room or lounge to be established for relatives, friends, civic officials, donors, or any other persons not connected with the media who have a "reason" to be present owing to special interests. The chief executive officer, the curator, or other designated person should be available to this group to answer questions briefly, postively, and with discretion. Telephones and refreshments for this area should not be overlooked, as a courtesy if not for good will.

Being organized. The "take charge" PR person should fight off the temptation and desire to be where the action is taking place. There are enough details needing attention at the established CIC. Normally there is an horrendous amount of details to be supervised, the PR person being responsible for all matters of public information, coordination, media decisions, and other matters of lesser importance to be handled personally. Leaving this station unattended could result in wasted time for others trying to make one-on-one contact. Even if to visit a rest room, the PR person should notify someone left in charge, and at any other time when moving from one location to another.

Keep people separated. One ploy recommended is to ensure that the media, victims, and visitors are never brought together in the same room, but kept apart, and all questions asked are to be answered by one person in charge of each room assigned. It has been said, "A rumor is as hard to unspread as butter." The security manager, therefore, must be instructed that each guard on duty at the only entrance open to the institution knows where to direct, or dispatch under escort of another guard, each person arriving at the building in time of crisis. Each person will be required to log in and, if required, establish some identity or provide some evidence of relationship with a person injured, or with some other person in the institution.[7]

Delegate authority. If the institutional PR has only a secretary, or if there isn't any PR person employed, the crisis becomes even more difficult to handle. Reliable persons must be assigned immediately to handle inquiries even if not so trained (provided for in the overall plan), to speak with the press reporters, and do all the chores required, ensuring that all statements are the "party's line" without any contradiction by any other official or crisis team member. *The CEO establishes the statement to be disseminated.* Unfortunately, a working CPRCP must be custom-tailored to a particular institution. No one plan will meet the needs of all museums no matter how similar the crisis. Each will, of course, vary in scope, and so will the results.

News of the injured. As a word of caution, coordinate communication plans with your local health care institution. If there is more than one hospital nearby, it may prove beneficial to designate one for treatment of employees and visitors, especially if one has a burn center. Obtain the name of the PR spokesperson with whom to coordinate patient information. Hospitals do observe local press codes established by the American Hospital Association (often revised by the state's hospital association), which provides guidelines for releasing basic information; i.e., that which is required for public record in addition to diagnosis, but not prognosis. Usually *after* the next of kin have been notified, this information is available to reporters and police. Since the innovation of the "Patient Bill of Rights," however, some hospitals may balk until the patient gives permission to release such information. A museum official with rank should be designated as a hospital contact to share information with the museum's legal representative for obvious reasons.

PLANNING SUMMARY

Start with a written plan. No one could possibly commit to memory all the dos and don'ts of so complex an operation, which may be in effect for months and even years before it becomes activated. Turnover of personnel, too, requires that orientation programs be repeated. Initially distribute copies to all key persons required to participate, and arrange for all future assignees to sign a custody card to indicate having received a copy from the person they succeed. This will ensure some continuity. Changes must be distributed to all holders of the plan whose names appear on the master list as having received a personal copy.

Don't leave anything to chance or error. When a crisis strikes without warning, as it will, there is no time to look for the Plan in the files, in a drawer, or on a bookcase and then go through a detailed review to recall one's responsibilities. Only by regularly scheduled rehearsals will employees and others learn their assigned duties by rote and execute their duties without hesitation.

Personnel turnover, new construction, and other changing conditions make revisions imperative. Updating the Plan should occur at regularly scheduled intervals with suggested changes that have been received between the promulgation of other official changes. Keep these suggestions with the master copy for quick reference.

Even the best of plans may appear error-proof when confined only to paper. The true test is both in the rehearsal and the actual circumstance. Like a parachute, one never knows how effective or successful it will be until put into actual use. If the chute doesn't open . . . well, the CPRCP may not work as well as hoped, but at least a second chance is available, with the opportunity to correct the defects. Ideally, then, the plan — like the parachute — may never be needed to bail out of a serious situation which can injure the reputation of the museum, or the integrity of those responsible for its operation, but proper attention to details in the first place will help ensure success to a satisfactory degree.

RESPONDING TO INQUIRIES

In replying to the media about the aspects of a crisis, making a decision to be candid but careful is commendable providing you know when to be either. Once you have decided it is mandatory to reply to media inquiries, all facts must be honestly chronicled. The time to be careful is after you receive the first wave of publicity. The aftermath of public information, once reexamined by media personnel, often leads to new slants by which to write the follow-up stories.

The seasoned public relations practitioner, often posttreated for the media's preheat, will respond only to responsible critics. The PR person will avoid those with large national circulations having a reputation for highlighting only the sensational news. Such reluctance avoids giving legitimacy to such publications. Another safeguard relative to responding to media inquiries is to determine whether they are being controversially critical — which is all right, too — and whether they respect the institution's officials as moral people. If not, do not respond.

When under media attack, make every effort to keep the internal organization and the constituency informed by providing them with answers to questions arising from the crisis or emergency. People in general become uncomfortable being associated with any institution subject to criticism, especially board members who hold similar posts elsewhere.

Out-of-town visitors to the museum during the next day's public session are certain to ask questions of the staff on contact. It may be from curiosity. It could be an ego trip to show off their own knowledge on the subject. It could be a free-lance correspondent known as a "stringer." Questions asked will be aimed at obtaining more intimate details not read, heard, or seen previously. The PR person must ensure that everyone exposed to the institution's publics (including one's own family, friends, and neighbors) is telling the same story, free of contradiction, without any exaggeration, and certainly without criticism of "those who put the bread on the table" or the security system.

When the media exaggerates, or disseminates information contrary to the actual facts, don't counterattack the writer or the medium, but do counterattack the misinformation, and use the occurrence as a means to gain positive coverage.[8] If it is decided that a response must be made, do so only in the medium which carried the criticism or misinformation. Address all the points to be corrected without adding new information to rekindle the cooled embers.

The important matter is to get into print refuting such information, however done, even if the museum's own newsletter is the only means, but get on record with your institution's side of the story.

Even the best-prepared museum cannot anticipate everything during a crisis planning period. When museum officials, by tradition, muzzle the PR person with such statements as, "First, let's not give out any information until all the facts have been gathered and studied," they are in essence establishing a low profile, and when this is on paper in the overall plan, a decision to say nothing has already been made. Unfortunately, corporate executives who have survived their careers without ever living through a weekend of a public relations crisis situation are the first to rely on the PR person's talent and skills as a substitute for good business practice, believing that by sheer words, with a friendly and warm smile supported by a few refreshments, they can maintain credibility with the media whether warranted or not. At this particular time it would be far better to trust in God than in the PR person if such is the case. This may be especially true when the crisis becomes one of such significance as to involve the lives of people.

If the manpower in the PR department is limited to handle a serious emergency crisis, it should be allowed for in the Plan to provide for this contingency by listing those public relations firms which specialize in PR crisis management and can be called upon to take charge of the PR needs in a matter of hours.

EVALUATING YOUR EFFORTS

Rehearsals held at least semiannually should be conducted during and after normal working hours, each with a different theme applicable to the particular institution. Immediately following the rehearsal, supervisory management should attend a critique to discuss any flaws in the operation and execution of the Plan. Did everyone perform in accordance with the job assigned? Was a temporary first-aid station established for any injured? Were all the supplies needed available? Did persons assigned to fire-fighting containment stations bring with them the proper apparatus? Were fire doors and windows secured immediately? Did the switchboard notify the proper civil officials? Did the guard force set up a screening system at the main entrance? Was the nearby hospital notified in order to determine the number of beds available? Did anyone think about having stretchers available to move injured persons? Were enough blankets available? Was someone assigned to direct the fire-fighters when they arrived? These are some of the questions which could be asked. Reporters who are familiar with these scenes may ask the same questions when injury or death is involved.

AFTER A CRISIS

When the crisis subsides, evaluate your Plan as quickly as possible. Include in the Plan a sample questionnaire appended for later guidance; some people may not know what it is they are expected to report about. Send questionnaires to all management personnel (including those persons on duty during the crisis period who participated in order to learn and correct any difficulties they encountered in locating equipment, supplies, gaining access to storerooms or other areas), consultants, and the news media attending the news conference, requesting them to evaluate your effectiveness.[9]

These questionnaires, studied for comments when returned, can provide information necessary to revise and update the CPRCP. In a cooperative effort to ensure an overall public appreciation for museums, the director who has experienced a crisis could be of tremendous service to similar type institutions by making the results of this survey available with a copy of the revised Plan at the cost of printing and postage. After all, if the preservation and presentation of all art throughout the world should be shared, why not include the management of other institutions in which such treasures are housed?

A final step in the Plan after documentation is writing a letter of commendation to those staff persons assisting throughout the various areas during the crisis. File copies of commendations with the personnel department for insertion into the individual's file jacket. If that person's department head is eventually succeeded in this post, or if the director of persons responsible for the employee's evaluation leaves the institution, these commendations will serve as reminders to their successors of the justification for an employee's wage increase, merit raise, or promotion or to support requests of a special nature.

Dispatch "thank you" letters — also known as the "bread and butter letters" — to those reporters who did an exceptionally outstanding job in reporting the news, with copies of these letters mailed to the managing editors of newspapers and to news directors of radio and television stations.

COUNTING YOUR MEDIA BLESSINGS[10]

Another aspect in the evaluation process worthy of mention is the value of newsclips. They not only verify what the public has learned of the institution's crisis, but provide a record for the museum's own archives. They also provide a broad base of what is known and understood by the public of the institution in terms of its services, history, and availability.

A newsclip received from a clipping service bureau has affixed to the top of the clipping the name of the newspaper in which the item or feature appeared and the circulation of that medium. The circulation figure, multiplied by 2.5, gives the total average readership of that newspaper, which, when translated in numbers, indicates the "exposure rating." Equally important, using a ruler or a line count on the clipping (fourteen lines to an inch without a ruler) provides the total column inches of space given to each item or feature. This includes the space given to photographs.

By telephoning several daily and weekly newspaper advertising departments of those who used the story, and obtaining the column-inch advertising rates, an "average" monetary factor can be determined. The average costs have often worked out to be about $18.50. Once the total column inches have been tallied, multiply that number by the predetermined average cost figure. This final figure is the total sum worth of your newsprint exposure. This dollar amount of publicity should be included in the evaluation report submitted to the CEO after a crisis, and in the public-relations department annual report to the CEO and board of directors. For a sample, see Figure 8.1.

If the institution is not a subscriber to a state, regional, or national newsclip service bureau (and the larger institutions should be to keep abreast of the competition and trends), the PR person may be able to call upon a colleague who does subscribe to a service and request a temporary "piggy back" for the duration of the crisis. Make an offer to provide reimbursement for the newsclips received. This helps to defer paying a flat monthly fee for only a week of newspaper attention. Usually a subscriber only pays a small

The exposure rating itself explains in circulation numbers the newspaper readership on the subject of the museum's crisis. The total figure may be compared with the population of any preselected area; i.e., a 1 million exposure rating can be translated as one-fifth of the population of the Commonwealth of Massachusetts.

As a sample, the exposure rating report may be prepared as follows:

July 1981	Number of newsclips	Number of circulation	Column inches	Dollar value*
Week of 7/1 – 6	156	15,334,211	1092	$15,834
Week of 7/7 –13	84	11,401,003	611	8,859
Week of 7/14–21	42	614,316	290	4,205
Week of 7/22–29	5	131,114	18	261
Totals:	287	27,480,644	2011	$29,159

Exposure rating: 68,701,610**

*   This value is based on the local *average* advertising rate of $14.50 a column inch.
** This figure represents the average readership, excluding exposure provided by the broadcast/electronic media, and is equal to the population of....

Under normal circumstances, subscribers to a newsclip service can provide these statistics for their own information on a monthly, quarterly, semiannual basis in preparation for their annual department report. The total sum in dollar value usually far exceeds the entire budget of the PR department, thereby giving evidence of the intangible benefits of a communications person or a public-relations consultant with excellent media relationships serving the institution.

Figure 8.1 Computing exposure rating in newsprint after a crisis

additional fee for all newsclips over a maximum of 100 clips, about 25 cents each. A colleague may not receive the maximum in a given month; therefore, the cost factor is reduced to even less than anticipated.

If the colleague is willing, a telephone call to the service bureau will immediately activate the search for newsclippings. Within two weeks, all newsclips on the subject of the museum's crisis should be in the hands of the institution's spokesperson.

Monitoring radio and television coverage works on the same principle;

however, it is far more costly to obtain copies of the broadcast radio cassettes or videotapes. This decision depends on the need to have the service or the tapes in the files.

NOTES

1. Berstein AB. Supporting the security expert: a new job for public relations and social science. In: Fennelly L., Tyska L. Cargo theft. Boston: Butterworth, 1982.
2. Bernstein AB. Crisis reporting. Security World Jan. 1981: 35.
3. Ibid.
4. Berstein AB. Cargo theft.
5. U.S. Navy rate training manual, non-resident career course. Washington, D.C.: U.S. Government Printing Office, 1978, NavEdTra 10295B (stock no. 0502-LP) ch 6 p. 161.
6. Barbour RL. Guidelines for drawing up public relations emergency & disaster plans, part one. PR Reporter supplement Tips & Tactics 1977; 15:21:1.
7. Barbour RL. Who does what in emergency public relations, part two. PR Reporter supplement Tips & Tactics 1977; 15:22:2.
8. PR Reporter 1979; 22:33:1.
9. Smith S. How to plan for crisis communication. PR Journal Mar. 1979; 18.
10. Allen SJ. Blueprint for image engineering. Publication pending.

IV. Fire Prevention and Emergency Planning

9. Building Security and Fire Safety

Byron M. Johnson

Those concerned with fire safety want as many exits as are economically possible; those concerned with security want as few as possible. Both groups have compromised, especially security personnel, despite increasing life and property losses resulting from crime in recent years. At present, fire and crime result in property losses and personal injuries of equal magnitude. Specialists in security, building design, building management, and sociology have discussed the importance of building design in relation to this problem at the Division of Building Research, National Research Council of Canada. They concluded that relatively simple modifications to building design and the specification of better hardware and construction would greatly reduce crime, without jeopardizing fire safety.

To provide measures that are sufficient to deter the opportunist without being too elaborate or too expensive involves an assessment of the risk to the building, its contents, and the occupants. Among the factors that determine the risk of criminal attack are location of the building, value of contents, and type of building.[1] Consideration must be given not only to the costs of building repairs or replacing valuables but also to those resulting from personal injury, legal proceedings, and the wider social costs of

This chapter originally appeared in *Specifying Engineer,* May 1980. Permission obtained to reproduce.

support for convicted criminals and their families. Compared with these, the additional cost of providing adequate protection to most buildings is negligible.[2]

HOUSING

Housing is by far the most burglarized building type. Usually burglary is opportunistic and localized, with the greatest increase in burglary rates in middle-income housing. Generally this housing has been equipped with poor-quality doors, windows, and locks. According to the United States report, 53 percent of illegal entries were through doors and almost all were gained by defeating the lock! Many types of locks are available but few are effective. The mortise dead-bolt shown in Figure 9.1 with a 25 mm (1 in.) throw will withstand most assaults if mounted in a strong door and frame. Such locks are readily available integrated with a knob-or lever-controlled latch. Other locks tend to be either more expensive or less effective. If a lock is being added to a door that has already been installed, one with a vertical bolt may be the most cost-effective. A key should not be required to open the door from the inside, because this is too dangerous in case of fire.

The 25 mm (1 in.) dead-bolt lock requires that the door frame and supporting studs be at least 100 mm thick. This frame would also be more difficult to pry apart and less susceptible to warping. If the door frame is not thick enough, more expensive locks are available that clamp the strike plate to the lock. The screws supplied with the lock will often need to be replaced with screws 75 mm long. The door should be of solid construction and in high-risk areas may need special treatment with metal or similar sheathing. It is necessary to ensure that the door adequately supports the lock. Standards have recently been developed in the United States for specifying door construction.[3]

Figure 9.1. Mortise dead bolt.

Fire exit doors open outwards but can be secured even after the exposed pins are removed by providing "jimmy" pins which connect the leaves of the hinges. Alternatively, the pins can be held in place by bolts or screws. Rim-mounted emergency (panic) latches are preferable, but mortise-type hardware can be made secure by installing an escutcheon plate to stop the hardware from being released by wires worked through the frame separation. In double-leaf exit doors a removable mullion should be used along with rim-mounted latches. If such doors are not to be used for entry they should not have hardware on the outside.

Standards have been developed in the United States to deter the use of windows as a point of entry in all types of buildings. Windows are frequently broken by vandals and can be lifted out of their mountings either by prying or unscrewing. They can be secured by stronger frames, nonretractable screws on the outside, or by pins through the frame and mullion. These pins should be designed to be easily removed for windows that might be used as emergency exits.Casement windows are the most difficult to force open; sash and pivot-hung windows are easier to force open; sliding windows generally provide little security. Sliding patio doors can be secured by placing screws in the top track to prevent the window or door from being raised. Laying a rectangular wood board in the lower track will stop forcible sliding; round sections can be rolled out of place.

The use of plastic glazing can serve to stop vandalism to inaccessible windows, but in high-risk buildings such as schools, such material is easily marred. Windows should be protected by meshing in such location. Expanded metal of similar size to ornamental leaden windows can be used to make illegal entry difficult. In general, bars or meshings should be positioned on the inside of windows.

NONRESIDENTIAL BUILDINGS

In nonresidential occupancies, the resolution of the conflicts between building security and fire safety requires an understanding of the needs of the occupants and method of operation of the building.

Over the past five years DBR/NRC has investigated the movement of spectators in theaters, arenas, and grandstands. These studies were concerned with evacuation time and safety and security procedures that affected evacuation were identified. Such procedures were most apparent at the Olympic Games in Montreal, when all exits were constantly surveyed and complex arrangements made for the protection of dignitaries.

Places of assembly are usually not concerned with preventing unpaid entry, either by guarding the exits or locking them during performances. Guards, however, are expensive because of the number required. Even where exits are close together at least one guard may be required at each door. In one Canadian arena two guards are needed for hockey games or rock concerts to prevent groups of spectators inside from assaulting solitary guards and letting friends in.

Where regulations permit, exit doors can be locked either by manual latches or solenoid holders. The solenoids have the obvious advantage of allowing rapid release from a central control, overcoming many of the problems associated with manual latches; but they need to meet strict (in some cases impossible) regulations to prevent electric shock or failure to function. In addition, a manual lock must be installed to ensure that doors remain locked during power failures.

Several factors have contributed to the rising rate of the theft from office buildings. Increased area and open working arrangements make it possible for strangers to walk unchallenged through work areas, steal an article, and escape by way of exit stairs. Calculators, electric typewriters, and specialty equipment are prime targets. Very often security systems have been designed to prevent illegal entry for the purpose of industrial espionage or similar crime, but petty theft is a greater problem, possibly of the order of $75,000 for every ten stories of office space (10,000 m²) every year. In Canada, as elsewhere, government agencies require provisions for security in the design of all new buildings.[4]

The main problem with offices results from the ease of movement between floors via stairs or elevators, particularly after hours (i.e., silent hours). The importance of control at elevator lobbies has long been recognized and specific recommendations have been made. Entry to the offices can be controlled by a simple installation of a contact switch that sounds a buzzer when a person opens the door from the lobby.

It is suggested that passage via elevators should be made more difficult by enclosing and locking each elevator lobby when no one is working on the floor. An exit stair off the elevator lobby would be required, and it could be designed for smoke-pressurization to provide temporary refuge in the event of fire for anyone having difficulty using the stairs.

Most building regulations require at least one exit stair directly to the outside, and this makes it difficult to prevent "grab-and-run" techniques. This direct exit is required for its assumed usefulness in evacuations, but research has revealed that during evacuations 40 percent more people, on average, use the stair that terminates in the main lobby than the stair that does not.[5] There are several possible explanations for this, but the main one is familiarity, a conclusion that is reinforced by other studies.[6] Pauls recommends that the lobby stair be designed to encourage normal use as well as efficiency during evacuations.[5] In buildings with central service cores, exit stairs often pass through the basement if they do not terminate at the lobby. As fires frequently start in the service area beneath the lobby level, it is worth re-examining requirements that result in exits through basements.

One solution for such stairs would be to construct an emergency door in the stairwell at lobby level that, if opened, would activate an alarm to give security personnel sufficient time to apprehend the thief; such a door and wall could also reduce smoke movement (Figure 9.2). Alternatively, if all stairs and elevators from upper stories terminate in the main lobby, then everyone would pass security personnel either to exit directly outside or indirectly through parking or service areas.

Nonemergency use of exitways results in the common problem of exit-doors being held open, allowing smoke movement in the event of fire. Although this problem is not related to security, it emphasizes the importance of understanding and planning for the desired traffic patterns in buildings. This means that integration of fire emergency systems and security systems is essential, as advocated by Fitzpatrick and Ruchelman: "Rather than oper-

Figure 9.2. Cross stairwell barrier.

ating as separate activities, the two functions must be seen as comprising a total security package for high-rise buildings."[7]

Schools are an example of a building type where the complexity of the activity patterns creates problems. Night-time use presents significant problems of vandalism even where schools are used only by adults in the evening. This raises the issue of master keying and a mechanism for key control.[9] As with office buildings, there is value in analyzing activities and zoning the building so that everyone does not have free access after hours when few supervisory staff are present. Zeisel[8] has made recommendations on design and hardware selection that allow designers to produce good buildings with proper consideration given to the occupancy patterns of the schools. In correctional institutions the conflict between security and evacuation needs is paramount; recent disasters have made it imperative to reconcile them.

SECURITY HARDWARE

There are two basic types of security hardware: passive and active. The first attempts to delay or discourage an intruder by presenting obstacles. Active hardware announces an intrusion or retaliates. This type is often advocated, however, without adequate recognition of the inherent difficulties. Many types of active hardware, such as electric fences, can be dangerous and may make a building owner liable to an extent greater than his potential loss would justify. As well, alarm systems depend on having someone to react quickly. They are frequently installed on exit doors to deter thieves from grab-and-run techniques. Although no definitive studies have yet been done, it seems probable that in most cases these installations are ineffective. Security personnel can seldom react fast enough to reach an exit in time to apprehend the culprit. The same seems true of preventing illegal entry. By the time security personnel can reach the door there will probably be no sign of the intruder, and it is uncertain whether the alarm was activated as a result of malfunction or hard knocking. Video cameras can be useful for observing an entrance when an alarm sounds, but are very expensive and would only be warranted where the risk is very great.

Passive hardware may also present difficulties. The homeowner particularly is faced with the difficult problem of deciding just what quality (cost) of hardware he needs. In this regard several books on home security are valuable.[10] Institutional hardware is only slightly less difficult to choose. For exit doors the required panic bar is most unsuitable for security. Tests have shown that it is easily cheated unless special door frames are installed and, if used frequently, it breaks down because people often exert force on the door before the bolt can retract.

OCCUPANCY/MANAGEMENT RELATIONS

Hostile occupants. Despite the emotive strength of this term, there are many occupancies where the occupants would not try to prevent a crime. The inmates of correctional institutions are, in general, hostile to management or administration. Less obviously hostile are those who use public assembly buildings, yet seldom will a visitor or spectator try to prevent a criminal action. Other occupancies such as schools and universities are subject to circumstance. As a general rule, the determining factor is whether occupants would be expected to prevent or aid a crime. In most instances hostile occupancies require some security staff to protect either the building or its occupants from other occupants. If either illegal entry or exit is the main security problem, then large numbers of security staff may be needed.

Responsible occupants. Occupants of this type would in the majority of cases be held responsible if they did not sound the alarm or question doubtful behavior. Most office buildings fall marginally into this category. Generally, the number of security personnel is few and the occupants are implicitly expected to perform this function, although they have not been given clear directives or training. Residential buildings also belong to this category, where the peer pressure or guilt would be great if a person allowed someone else to commit a crime without taking some action. A consequence of this criterion is that residential complexes where people cannot or will not challenge intruders should be considered to belong to the hostile category. Occupants' reasons for not accepting responsibility might include risk to themselves in challenging intruders or lack of opportunity to alert authorities.

Security-conscious occupants. Few buildings have occupants trained to take definite action toward someone committing a crime. Military establishments and similar occupancies are of this type, but they face little risk of the type of crime that can be prevented by environmental design. Other occupancies where people perceive intervention to be in their interest might include airports, owing to the common fear of terrorist action, or banks where fear of financial loss might prevail.

TOPOLOGY OF EXITS

The categories first described help to define how occupants use entrances and exits of buildings and their attitude toward them. Frequent use of an exit door and failure to ensure that it is properly closed can allow an intruder to enter illegally. This often happens in office or apartment buildings where considerable caution is, at the same time, being taken to ensure that garage or main entrance doors are kept locked. The problem of exit doors requires a classification scheme for the topology of exit doors.

Open Exits These are generally the main or front entrances of buildings. They are locked or unlocked according to the amount of supervision available and the general level of security. They can often be observed from a desk or from the road (i.e., from patrol cars). Ironically, these doors have received the greatest attention for security, yet they are probably the least vulnerable. (A problem beyond the scope of this chapter concerns the requirement for determining who should be allowed to enter, one of the unresolved problems in crime prevention.)

In many instances front entrances may need to be only class I or class II, according to the classification system of the National Institute of Law Enforcement and Criminal Justice (NILECJ)[3].

Enclosed Exits. Most buildings contain several exit stairs that are completely enclosed and exit directly to the outside. They can only be surveyed by cameras, prohibited for normal use, or given special security treatment. The problem with such exits is manyfold: easy escape for thieves, occupants using the stair to travel to prohibited floors or to avoid being questioned by receptionists, occupants using the exit on a day-to-day basis (thereby wearing out hardware that later allows entrance to unauthorized persons), and persons who cheat the exit door from the outside. This last problem of unauthorized entry concerns both door manufacturers (i.e., to produce hardware that cannot be defeated easily) and designers of security systems in trying to design a system that reacts quickly to illegal intrusion. These exits should be at least class III of the NILECJ classification system, but if there is no external hardware they can easily be built to class IV.[3]

Special Exits. Special exits are those at which users can expect to be challenged, for example, exits from workrooms, basements, or perhaps such facilities as freight doors. Use of such exits would require good knowledge of the building. Generally they share the problems of enclosed exits, but have the advantage of being isolated when the building is unoccupied and perhaps even when it is occupied. Exits in this category can easily be determined by considering the level of risk and the occupant/management relation.

REQUIREMENTS OF EXIT DOORS

If an analysis is undertaken of occupancy/management relations and the topology of exit doors, the requirements given in Table 9.1 can be used to de-

Occupancy/management relations

TOPOLOGY OF EXITS	Hostile	Responsible	Security Conscious
Open exits	– Easily opened in confirmed emergency but otherwise controlled – Hardware should give good security when building unoccupied	– Door needs surveillance but entry/exit is uncontrolled – May be required for evacuation of crowds – Hardware should give good "silent-hour" security	– Usually needs to be controlled – Method of detecting "unwanted" visitors may be required – May require 24-hour "guarding" or alarm
Enclosed exits	– Surveillance required when building occupied – Easily inspected from outside, should be very secure	– Surveyed or set with alarms that allow adequate response – No exterior hardware – In some locations may be locked unless confirmed emergency	– Alarm on an exit is needed – Possible surveillance by cameras
Special exits	– Isolated from main building unless controlled – Secure hardware, possible alarms	– Should be controlled when building occupied and locked or isolated when unoccupied	– To be avoided unless doors are locked by remote control

Table 9.1. Requirements for exit-door design

BUILDING: High School

CONTEXT OF PATTERN: Emergency Exit-Door from Stairs

REQUIREMENTS	RECOMMENDATIONS	PATTERNS
Surveillance required when building occupied	• Glass doors to stairwell to allow doors to be seen	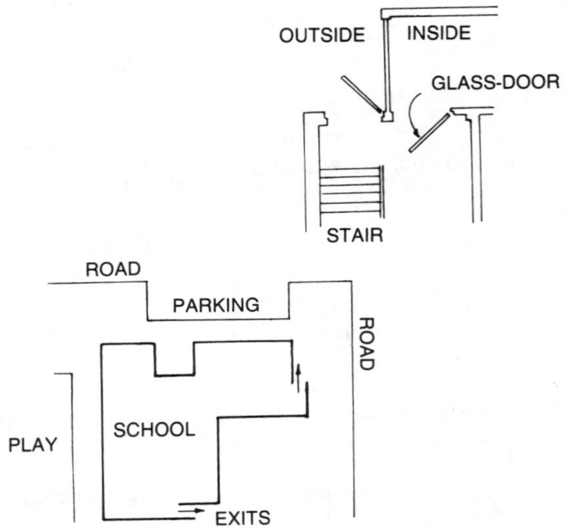
	• Alarm on opening	
Easily viewed from outside	• Position facing road	
Very secure, class III NILECJ	• Firm frames	
	• No exterior hardware	

Figure 9-3. Requirements of service doors.

velop specific design recommendations for individual buildings. A series of patterns can be drawn and taken by the designer to produce hard-line drawings. This technique of pattern drawing was strongly advocated by Alexander[11] as a method of expressing requirements.

The use of patterns of requirements is shown in Figure 9.3 for a hypothetical high school. Several topologies and functions of exits are analyzed. The occupancy/management relation is considered hostile, primarily because of the number of students with this attitude. The main concern, however, is illegal entry plus theft or vandalism rather than illegal entry alone (e.g., at dances) or uncontrolled escape during school hours. It is further assumed that the school is used in the evening despite the management problems this creates.

In the development of these patterns of NILECJ classification system[3] was used for describing the level of resistance of the doors. It has the advantage of ready use in producing a specific statement of what should become established tests on doors. To some extent, however, it must be admitted that the classification system did not relate well to the problems of the types of door in the example chosen, primarily because of its apparent orientation to domestic situations.

CONCLUDING REMARKS

This discussion has suggested an approach to the design problems of exit control. In many ways its success is dependent upon the usual procedures of the designer and his awareness of the requirements of the occupants and management. It is hoped that those using these or similar methods to design secure buildings will communicate to the author their experiences in resolving the requirements of security and emergency evacuation.

This chapter is a contribution from the Division of Building Research, National Research Council of Canada, and is published with the approval of the Director of the Division.

REFERENCES

1. Scarr HA. Patterns of burglary. 2nd ed. Washington, D.C.: United States Government Printing Office, 1973.
2. Johnson BM. Crime prevention through building design. Specification Associate, 1978; 20:8-9.
3. NILECJ, Standard for the physical security of door assemblies and components. National Institute of Law Enforcement and Criminal Justice, Law Enforcement Assistance Administration, U.S. Department of Justice, May 1976.
4. Building Security. Public Works Canada. August 1975 (Briefing Document D-9).

5. Pauls JL. Building evacuation: research findings and recommendations. To be published.

6. Johnson, BM, Pauls JL. Pilot study on personnel movement in office buildings. In: Health impacts of the use, evaluation and design of stairways in office buildings. Health and Welfare Canada. 1977; 1 April 1977: 75-92.

7. Fitzpatrick DR, Ruchelman L. Integrating fire and crime control systems in highrise office buildings. Skyscraper Management July 1974.

8. Zeisel J. Stopping school property damage. American Association of School Administrators 1976.

9. Lesniak J. Master keying. Problems, solutions, alternatives. Doors and Hardware October 1978.

10. Rhodes RC, ed. Home owner's security handbook, Philadelphia American Society for Testing and Materials, 1976.

11. Alexander C. Notes on the synthesis of form, Cambridge, Mass.: Harvard University Press, 1967.

10. Fire Protection Systems and Fire Prevention Techniques

Stephen W. Weldon

Before commencing this chapter, I would like to clarify a term I will use frequently. Throughout I will use the term "arts facilities" which will incorporate museums, art galleries, libraries, and historical sites. In other words, any facility containing works of art, historical or religious treasures, and other irreplaceable artifacts including important architectural elements will be included in the term arts facilities.

The basic procedures and systems discussed, however, can be readily related to corporate offices where critical records are maintained, and even within private residences. Although the records or objects may not be of historical or monetary value to arts facilities, their value to corporate offices and homeowners is equally important.

WHY A SPECIALIZED FIRE ACTIVITY FOR AN ARTS FACILITY?

Within this section, I will speak to four basic points that make any arts facility fire prevention-suppressant program a highly specialized activity.

Artifacts — Specialized Hazards

First, one must consider the contents housed within an arts facility — especially in a museum. Museums, by their very nature, contain a heavy concentration of fire loading material. I am, of course, referring to artifacts. These items are collection pieces because they have acquired age, and the very process of gaining age has created a drying of the object, whether it be furniture, tapestry, rugs, paintings, books, flooring, paper, paneling, etc.

An arts facility has the obligation to show the treasures to the public. In many cases, especially with the historical type of institutions, these artifacts will be shown in such a manner to offer realism to the pieces (See Figure 10.1). Usually this is accomplished with older flooring and paneling (in some cases the flooring, paneling, ceiling, etc., will be the same age as the objects). So we not only have a potential hazard with the object(s), we have now compounded that hazard by installing the object within an envelope of hazardous materials.

The illumination of art treasures is another potential area of hazard. Lighting requirements (which I cover in more detail under the heading Electrical Hazards) run the gamut from very low light levels in historical facilities — which is usually accomplished through electric candles — to intense lighting loads within a gallery displaying modernistic treasures. The key factor here is the word specialized. Any time one deals with specialized activities or services, one must consider the fact that they are specialized because they differ from the norm. Thus, special care and attention must be paid to the items used to provide the "specialization." In this particular case, it would include everything from wax bases for electrified candles to heavy-duty fusing and wiring for spotlights and floodlight arrangements.

In addition to having the responsibility to display these art objects to the public, arts facilities have the equally challenging responsibility to preserve the treasures for the future.

I feel that the conservation and preservation aspects of the art facility offers, in many cases, a more serious fire hazard potential than does the displaying of the objects.

To assist in preserving and caring for collection pieces, we use everything from the basic wax to more sophisticated fabric and material preservers. Modern science and technology have been a tremendous help in developing compounds and liquids utilized to repair and extend the life of art objects. But this is critical: many of these compounds possess highly flammable and explosive ingredients; even the most simple wax formula contains compounds that can burn.

I will not attempt to list all of the items used within the many and varied art conservation and preservation activities that are potentially

Figure 10.1. Artifacts—specialized hazards

dangerous; to do so would require a list that would take up the largest portion of this chapter. I do have a few suggestions, however. The first one is: read the labels carefully. The government requires manufacturers to list clearly the hazards contained within specific formulas. That requirement should be taken advantage of. Also, although not so important from a fire or explosion standpoint, is the potential hazard the product offers in the way of breathing in fumes and/or skin or eye burns. On the other hand these products, in many cases, are the only thing that will accomplish certain tasks or functions. Under your responsibility to protect and preserve the collection, you must use many of these items. Learning to use hazardous chemicals is like learning to swim. Don't fear and shun the water; learn by studying and listening to instructions, followed by proper movements. Then acquire a respect for water and its hazards.

In some of the smaller institutions, many staff members must wear many hats. Consequently, handling and usage of potentially dangerous chemicals may not be as familiar to them as with staff members in larger operations where they have the staff and time to specialize.

One of a Kind — Priceless — Uninsurable

The items in the arts facility have to be protected carefully, which is an awesome responsibility. In most cases, they are one of a kind, and that brings up several factors that again point out the need of "specialization." In industry or commercial environments, the treasures could be computer tapes — billing or other operational files. In the home it could be a family heirloom. If any of these items are lost through fire, no amount of insurance can replace or restore them. At this point, however, the difference between valuable items in an art facility and valuable items in a business or home environment can be noted.

Many times, arts facilities cannot afford to carry insurance on their collections. These irreplaceable artifacts carry cost factors so astronomical that institutions would go broke in attempting to pay the insurance premium. This fact makes a tremendous difference in the entire scope of fire protection considerations required within the facility. These points will be discussed throughout this chapter and will be important agenda in the topics of Fire Prevention, Fire Detection, and Fire Suppressant.

Unquestionably, based on this line of reasoning, you *cannot afford a fire*. I will say more about this in the section Hazards of Fire Extinguishing Services and also in the section Standard Fire Service Salvage Activities.

I was once associated with S.K.F. Industries in their Jet Aircraft Precision Bearing Division. The motto of their operation was "Zero Defects." This premise was based on their very logical reasoning that it was too late to correct a defect in a critical engine bearing at 50,000 ft. So you checked and rechecked during the manufacturing stage. You inspected and reinspected, you instituted and maintained a system of counterbalances all aimed at eliminating a defect before it became a defect. In the long run, it was easier and less costly to stop a defect from occurring than to not only correct a defective component, but prevent a catastrophe and to survive with the irreversible damage done.

We must adopt the same type of philosophy, only our goal must be zero fire hazards. We may never entirely accomplish that goal, but with the right attitude, guided by checks, inspections, habits, and plain old common sense, we can greatly reduce the percentage in our favor.

An ironic fact is that these safeguards are completely inexpensive. Yet, they are more critical to the protection of your treasures than the best, most expensive fire detection and suppressant system.

I am not downgrading a good, reliable, fire detection and suppressant system within your facility. I will write in some detail about such protection systems later under the headings Fire Detection and Fire Suppressants.

When these systems come into play, however, you have a problem! Your treasures may well depend on how good a detection and suppressant system you have and how it will react. My goal is to stop that defect, that situation, before it progresses to the point that it requires action by your fire detection and suppressant system. These systems are good backup but, if at all possible, let's keep them as backup. Don't get your facility in the situation where all the eggs are in one basket, so to speak. Your collection should not depend solely on the capabilities of a mechanical or electronic device. Utilize the best, most reliable device known for fire protection — the human element.

If at the beginning of this chapter, now, and at the end I were asked to sum up in a few words the reasoning and goals behind this article, I would quickly reply with just two words — "fire prevention." Fire detection and fire suppressant are important, but if your prime, total emphasis is on fire prevention, hopefully you will eliminate the need for fire fighting within your facility.

With this thought on your mind, I want to jump quickly to the next point, hazards of fire extinguishing services.

Hazards of Fire Extinguishing Services

I hope to accomplish two goals during the course of this section: (1) add to the urgency of the need for specialized fire protection systems within your facility and (2) point out that you could be next door to the best paid fire department in your city and still experience considerable damage to your collection, even if the fire situation were minor in nature.

I'd like to begin by making a statement with which some people will take issue. I feel that no fire organization, whether it be a volunteer or paid department, can appreciate the special needs dictated by any arts facility — *period!*

These fire-fighting organizations and their personnel are trained and gain experience in combating fires in industrial, commercial, and residential facilities. All fire-fighting forces are schooled and trained religiously in the fact that their primary reason for existence is to extinguish a fire in the quickest possible time with whatever resources and actions are available and required.

This usually results in an abundance of water, the ventilation and opening of areas by fire axes or jam bars, and the dragging in of heavy equipment without undue concern about objects. The concentration is on extinguishing the blaze.

What I am saying is not to be construed in any way as a belittlement or down-grading of any fire department or its personnel.

Every fire company performs an invaluable service. They deserve all the credit they get; it is a tough, dirty, dangerous, and thankless job. I know from experience: I have spent many years in various types of fire service activities. I am, however, being realistic and stating proven facts, not hearsay.

Today firemen are underpaid and their departments are undermanned in just about every location where a paid fire department exists. To fill this void, the firemen must use water to a greater extent than if additional manpower were available that could be engaged in more exploratory work in and around the area involved prior to the discharge of water.

A line officer knows fully well he has a limited roster of personnel available and, if he waits too long, the chance of losing control of the fire increases with each minute, so he does what he must do. The hoses are turned on and the fingers of water enter through broken-out windows and battered-down doors; ventilation holes are cut in roofs, hopefully keeping the fire within the smoke-filled interior of the building. The same procedure holds true for the volunteers whose roster of trained personnel is limited during critical time periods. This situation will worsen as governing bodies attempt to cut manpower and equipment costs to balance already overloaded operating budgets.

At the same time I would be the first to state that the procedures and methods employed by the firefighters are correct. Remember, the largest percentage of their response in combating fire is in industrial, commercial, and residential establishments. These same procedures will play havoc with an arts facility.

What can be done? We can't expect professional firemen to restructure their training to encompass the handling of art treasures under fire conditions. The same firemen who handle an oil refinery fire would handle an arts facility fire. There is no way a parallel can be drawn between fire combating procedures in industrial, commercial, and residential facilities. The cost to establish a comprehensive training program for firemen outlining the requirements that should be employed in an arts facility would be too costly (remember the overtaxed cities and towns) and would actually get in the way of standard fire-fighting techniques employed to combat the majority of fires they will encounter.

Just for conversation purposes, however, let's say we could get the funds to acquire more manpower and institute arts facility training programs; a very important ingredient would still be missing. The handling of an antique or other art treasure with "tender, loving care" comes only from someone who is trained and associated with art objects.

Another point that needs to be made to highlight the difference between a fire situation within an arts facility and that of the other categories of environments is that even a minor fire in an arts facility could cause thousands of dollars of damage or even destroy artifacts completely. By this I am referring to the elements associated with a fire activity — water, especially under pressure; smoke; the passing of fire combat materials and equipment through an area not threatened by the actual fire situation.

Fire hoses, fully charged, must be dragged through areas not endangered by the actual fire; these hoses are stiff, sometimes soiled, and in many cases have couplings notorious for leaking.

The hoses are heavy and rather clumsy to handle. They are unwieldy and can cause serious damage to objects with which they come into contact. Smoke, filtering back from a fire, is another threat to collection items not exposed to the actual fire situation. Finally, the firemen in their protective clothing present a serious hazard to items as they make their way through unaffected areas to reach the fire scene. Normally, a human's mind will automatically allow for the safe passage of one's body through rather narrow, restricted areas. But when you add to the body bulky items such as helmets, large coats, tool belts holding spanner wrenches, a door-forcing bar, and axe — these items are often not taken into consideration in the passage through restricted areas.

Even in minor fire situations where smoke exists, a fireman wears life-support equipment. This includes a restrictive face mask and a large tank on his back connected to the mask by two stiff hoses. Couple these bulky items with the restricted vision of the eye pieces on the mask, the dragging in of heavy equipment, smoke, the urgency of an unknown fire situation, and the unfamiliarity of the area and you have a very real potential of damage to art treasures even though they may not be actually endangered by the fire. Later we will illustrate some steps you can take to reduce the hazards discussed in this section. Note that I said *reduce* the possibilities, not eliminate them. There is only one sure way to accomplish that goal and that is to eliminate the need to call a fire department into your facility. The fire department will be as happy as you are — "fire prevention" is the secret.

Standard Salvage Activities

The standard salvage activities used by fire departments, although workable and even acceptable in the majority of fire situations they encounter, would most likely create damage rather than protect objects in an arts facility. I base this assumption on numerous facts.

One of the most important hazards is the material used to protect items removed from an involved facility. I am speaking primarily of salvage covers. These large canvas covers are carried on fire vehicles and are used to provide a protection cover for objects removed from the actual fire scene. The standard canvas covers are large, heavy, and stiff. Even though the firemen attempt to keep them clean, they do become soiled. More importantly, these covers become impregnated with industrial chemicals. Many times this saturation of chemicals becomes firmly entrenched in the canvas blanket fibers and is not readily noticeable to the eye. When the cover becomes wet from water, especially the chemical used by the fire-fighting service to create "wet water," the chemicals will reappear.

Consequently, collection items that may have survived the hazards of fire, smoke, and handling could be damaged or destroyed through the salvage operation.

Still another point that needs to be made regarding potential hazards is transporting collection items from the fire scene to the salvage staging area. If you have had the opportunity to come in contact with a fireman's fire-fighting attire you know that it is well constructed, heavy, and designed to protect the fireman, as it should be. It provides a definite hazard, however, to any type of art treasure. The coats are usually made from heavy canvas with bulky stitching and raised, reinforced seams. The coat is held together by metal snaps which protrude from the coat. Every fireman wears a tool belt, also made from heavy, webbed canvas on which the fireman hooks tools he will need to combat the fire effectively. In addition, he wears life-support equipment, as mentioned earlier. Firemen wear heavy, steel-toed boots, which many times are folded down from the top of a position just above the knee. This fold exposes coarse tape lining that protrudes from the firemen's legs.

Most of the time the firemen will wear rather stiff gloves usually coated with a rubber solution to make them waterproof. The glove, even at its cleanest, presents a very definite hazard to fragile art objects.

A salvage staging area is usually established outside of the facility experiencing a fire. The objects are usually stacked and sometimes roughly piled in groups on which the canvas salvage covers are spread over for added protection against the elements. The elements could range from a hot and humid environment to a bone-chilling winter day which will not be shut out by the canvas covers.

Another important fact that certainly must be considered is the curiosity seeker, or worse yet, the thief. In the hundreds of fires I have been involved with, I would say we experienced a 70 percent ratio of curiousity seekers and vandals. Earlier I stated that art facilities in many cases do not have insurance on their art objects because of premium costs, or, even if they had insurance, how do you replace a one-of-its-kind object?

On the other hand, the larger percentage of alarms that the firemen respond to are covered by insurance, and this makes a difference. I am not implying that firemen deliberately man-handle objects within a fire situation. I am saying that the handling objects by the firemen will cause damage to art treasures because of all the ramifications created by the emergency.

The issue of insured versus uninsured does also make a difference. The difference may be psychological but it is a real difference. It is like the bull in the china shop theory.

Now that we are firmly convinced fire departments using standard procedures and equipment can cause havoc within the facility, what can be done? As I have stated numerous times before and will continue to do so throughout this chapter, you must concentrate on *preventing* a situation from developing that requires calling a fire department.

This can be done by launching a comprehensive program of "fire protection," which serves as the lead into the next section — Fire Prevention (Top Priority). One might say that all this information is well and good, but what if the art facility is hit by an act of God — lightning or another catastrophe — and our facility becomes involved in a fire? Under the section entitled Emergency Management, I will discuss in detail the things that can be done to lessen all of the hazards you may encounter with a fire department responding to your facility.

FIRE PREVENTION (TOP PRIORITY)

The real problem should be fully known and understood by all in the very first stages of developing a comprehensive fire prevention program. Your attitude (and the attitude of those who will be working with you) must be positive and you must believe in what you are doing. If I were asked to lay an importance on the benefits of a good fire prevention program, I would say a good attitude is 90 percent of a good fire prevention program.

How real is the problem of fire prevention? To establish the reality of the problem firmly I would like to quote from the N.F.P.A. Master File Protection Handbook, Fourteenth Edition.

First, let's review the number of fires by occupancy between the years 1970 and 1974. I will use only those types of facilities that parallel an arts facility in one way or another (see Tables 10.1, 10.2, 10.3).

As you can see, the trend is accelerating at a breath-taking pace. Although statistics are not fully developed at this writing, the present rate has greatly surpassed the past frequency rate.

I could continue to illustrate this material with charts and graphs indicating just about any fire statistic conceived, e.g., frequency rate, most dangerous operations and activities within an arts facility regarding fire hazards, etc., but I am a firm believer in not using statistics unless they prove a point. The three tables shown illustrate one important fact: fires are on an ever-increasing frequency rate and we must acknowledge them the greatest threat to art facilities and their collections.

Security is important. In no way do I downgrade security services. My responsibility at Winterthur Museum also included security operations. If a

	1970	1971	1972	1973	1974
Public assembly	31,000	31,700	37,900	34,100	47,000
Educational assembly	17,000	20,500	22,400	24,100	35,500
Institutions (general)	14,000	18,200	21,200	21,600	31,500

Reprinted by permission of the publisher, from National Fire Protection Association Master File Protection Handbook, Fourteenth Edition.

Table 10.1 Number of fires by occupancy

	1970	1971	1972	1973	1974
Public assembly	$119,400	138,900	153,200	155,000	181,400
Educational assembly	77,800	87,000	90,900	99,000	124,800
Institutions (general)	17,200	22,400	24,800	23,900	39,400

Reprinted by permission of the publisher, from National Fire Protection Association Master File Protection Handbook, Fourteenth Edition.

Table 10.2. Fire losses by occupancy

	No. fires $250,000-over	No. fires $750,000-over	No. fires $3,000,000-over	No. fires $10,000,000-over
1974	615	177	31	8
1973	501	157	22	4
1972	574	158	12	0
1971	499	132	10	1
1970	504	149	21	4

Reprinted by permission of the publisher, from National Fire Protection Association Master File Protection Handbook, Fourteenth Edition.

Table 10.3. Large-loss fires by size of loss

theft takes place within our facility, it is very distressing and everyone is very concerned. It usually involves a small number of objects, however, and there is always the hope that they can be recovered intact. Through a lot of hard work, cooperation, and planning among art security services throughout the world, the recovery rate today is impressive.

Mechanical and physical plant operations are another threat to art treasures. Constant and correct temperatures and humidity controlled environments are critical. Again, I know this from experience since this also falls within my area of responsibility. If a physical plant failure occurs, it is usually for short periods of time. In addition, most art facilities have a conservation staff that is able to repair artifacts damaged by a temporary change in environment.

On the other hand, even a minor fire can and will destroy many artifacts. The damage need not only be the actual flames. As stated previously, there are eight hazards associated with a fire: (1) fire or flames; (2) smoke; (3) water; (4) rough handling; (5) salvage; (6) equipment and materials used to combat the fire; (7) element exposure; (8) theft/vandalism.

If the loss of an art treasure occurs by fire, the loss is complete. There is no hope of recovery. No amount of conservation work can restore what has been consumed by flames. As emphasized earlier, art treasures not threatened by the actual flames can be destroyed or damaged by the very forces, equipment, or material used to protect them in eliminating the fire condition.

Many times an art treasure can be a total loss, simply because it is rendered useless because the damaged appearance defaces or distorts the historical significance of the piece. Also, unlike security-related problems, *the fire hazard is always within your facility.* Neither elaborate security systems nor highly sophisticated physical plant systems can protect your collection from this unseen, always-present danger.

Push back from your desk for a minute. Think of the points I have made so far about fire and its hazards in conjunction with your collection. If this scares the hell out of you, it is meant to. This means two things: you are being realistic and you care about your collection. Now let's get down to the nitty-gritty of what we can do.

Electrical Hazards

My intention is to begin each subsection under the Fire Prevention category with a general outline of the problems associated with that heading, and then finish with a guide on how to establish programs that will minimize the hazards for that particular element.

Without reservation, I can state that the greatest hazard to your collection is electrical. Electricity is a boon to our modern civilization. It is a bargain (even at today's high rate), and, if handled and supervised properly, it is perfectly safe.

There is an old adage that states, "We are our own worst enemy," and, although I don't know what the original author had in mind when he or she coined the phrase, I can assure you it very aptly applies to electrical usage and arts facilities. We have very beautiful, very important, and very historical art treasures to show. Our pride is reflected in the way we display these treasures. Nothing gives a director or curator more satisfaction than to stand back and listen to the words of admiration from visitors who view their collections.

To display these articles and treasures most effectively, we use many varied and special lighting arrangements, and this is as it should be. This does bring some hazards into play, however. If these hazards are known, they are relatively safe.

Electricity can become a fire hazard through arcing or overheating of electrical components. Both of these hazards can be triggered by lighting systems. So, let's start with the basics. To minimize these hazards, only tested and approved material recognized by testing U.L. laboratories should be used. Equipment should be sized according to the safe electrical circuits that will feed the components, and vice versa.

Wiring, Fixtures, and Fuses. Equipment should be installed in conformity with accepted standards. Such installations should be included in a preventative maintenance schedule (N.F.P.A. WO 70) that deals with maintenance and operation of electrical systems. Loose connections will create an arc which will result in heating due to the high resistance of the loose connection. The intensity of the arc and temperature of the heat produced will depend on the current and voltage flowing through it. You would be surprised at the quick heat buildup within a faulty electrical circuit. Unfortunately many times the arc or heat buildup occurs within a wall or other normally out-of-the-way locations. The temperature generated can easily be of such magnitude that it will ignite any combustible material around it such as the very insulation covering the wire. If hot enough, it could also cause the metal of the conduction to fuse or to be joined together by melted metal. This hot metal could be scattered about and set fire to other combustible material.

Wire is designed to allow the passage of electricity through it in direct proportion to the resistance of the conductor. This simply means that the wire is designed to do a specific job; the wire comes in many sizes so that it will operate the components or heavier, brighter lighting beyond which the circuit was originally designed to handle. Like your body, which gives you signs when you are overworking — shortness of breath and tired muscles — the overworked electrical system will let you know: fuses will start failing when you add, start, or plug in added components. A solution is to install heavier fuses. This can be a good move provided you are careful about installing them. Know the size of your wiring (look at an electrical print). Know the electrical load (wattage) of the components you are adding. Insert only a fuse slightly higher to handle the stated load; don't jump up two or three sizes above the original size because it works well and never blows. Remember, the blown fuse, normally, is the power circuit saying, "Hey — I'm overworked." If you don't adhere to your body warnings you could have a stroke or a heart attack; failure to adhere to the circuit's warning could result in a serious fire.

Circuits or wiring fires are a hazard for other reasons. Wiring is buried in walls, floors, or ceilings. Problems occurring within these wires will usually start with smoldering. This smoldering effect may start at 2 P.M. when you were at the peak of your lighting load due to a special display. Everything went fine; the special display was well received. At 2 A.M. you get a call from the fire department that a fire is now in progress within your facility. This may be a dramatic way to present this example, but believe me, an overloaded circuit has that capability. When reviewing electrical load requirements to be added to existing circuits, unless you have an engineer on staff, have a survey conducted by a qualified, licensed electrical engineer. The cost for such a survey could very well be the most economical investment you ever make.

Temporary Displays. A very important facet in the life of any arts facility is the arranging, setting up, and dismantling of temporary displays. Although these types of displays are important, even vital to the function of the arts facilities, they do introduce additional hazards to the facility. In fact, I would venture to say that the arts facility is probably passing through one of its most hazardous times when involved with temporary displays.

By the very nature of "temporary," there is a very real and valid implication that a certain amount of danger will exist no matter how careful we are. Temporary lighting must be established. Many times, because of the concentration of this lighting, circuits are temporarily overloaded and extension cords are used rather freely.

Extension cords. If I could write these two words in glaring red that would jump out at you every time you read them, I would do so. They are the arms of an octopus that can very easily reach out and strangle all of the safeguards built into an electrical system. They should be outlawed, disposed of, and destroyed. If you get the feeling that I am strongly against the usage of extension cords, you are right. Having now stated and established my strong feelings against extension cords, I will do a complete about face and state why we use them, and I am sure you will, too.

Unless your facility differs from Winterthur Museum (which I doubt) tight budgets are a way of life, especially in setting up a temporary display. To get electricity from Point A to Point B (where lights must be installed) you must run an extension cord. The proper way to accomplish this feat would be through the usage of conduits, fused circuits, panel boxes, and wall outlets. This is the proper way to do it if you have the budget, which none of us has.

There are things, however, that can be done to reduce (not eliminate) the hazards associated with extension cords: (1) make certain cords are heavy enough to carry anticipated loads; (2) if using one extension cord to feed a gang box, make certain, again, that the cord is heavy enough to carry the combined loads of the outlets available. Purchase or rent a gang box that is fused. That way, if a problem develops in one of the cord circuits, the fuse will blow and stop the electrical feed to that particular circuit.

Tripping hazards are always a threat with extension cords. The tripping potential can physically hurt someone, but also, importantly, it can snatch a cord from an outlet and turn over a lighting fixture, etc., all of which can result in an electrical short circuit.

Other hazards are bracing for backdrops and lighting fixtures which are not as firmly mounted as permanently installed fixtures. Usually they are not firmly mounted, especially if they were installed under the hectic frenzy that usually accompanies the time period as you approach the opening. Carefully check all bracing and light brackets regularly during the life of your temporary display. Papier-maché or other flammable fabrics or material sometimes hang dangerously close to lighting sources of heat. Make certain they do not touch hot lights; allow for limpness that will set in on some items used in temporary displays. When this occurs the original clearance between light fixtures and the material will shrink. Check daily and readjust, especially in the latter days of the display. There is usually a tendency to become lax about a display that has been up for a considerable period of time.

There are several good fire-resistant solutions that can be applied to cardboard panels and other combustible display material to greatly reduce their flammable qualities. The solutions can be sprayed on or applied with a brush and they won't affect color or stability of the sets. Paint, turpentine, and other flammable liquids usually are used extensively around temporary displays. Care and attention must always be given to the storage and usage of combustible ingredients around temporary display projects.

Fire extinguishers should always be available. Please don't take a fire extinguisher from another spot to use with a temporary display. Purchase extinguishers to be used exclusively with temporary displays. If need be, pro-rate their cost against several displays, but purchase them. If your display (as most do) contains important artifacts, purchase Halon 1211 fire extinguishers. These are the best all-around extinguishers for the classes of fire situations you may experience with a temporary display without *damaging art objects* (more on this later under the heading Fire Suppressants).

Transformers – disconnects. According to the N.F.P.A. the phrase "Tired" or "Worn-out" defines equipment that is actually worn out. This is a natural reaction, similar to growing older. We humans (although we don't want to admit it) wear down with age. We can't carry the loads we did in our younger years. We don't have the endurance. To do much of a particular physical activity can actually break us down.

The same principle holds true for wires, fixtures, appliances, cords, heating components, and, the leading item within this category, the electric motor. Aging of electric equipment results in the deterioration of insulation, corrosion, and plain fatigue of the wires and cables. Unfortunately, many see the electrical motor only as a simple gadget that starts when you flip the switch and runs until you shut it off. They don't realize the danger of not instituting a preventative maintenance program, which does much more than postpone the payment for a new motor. One of the greatest benefits of a good preventative maintenance program is that it will greatly reduce the hazard of an electrical fire. Remember, the electric motor was responsible for almost 6 percent of 415 actual documented fires. Even more impressive, however, is the fact that the electric motor caused nearly 30 percent of documented fires that occurred within a building.

A preventative maintenance program will also reduce the possibility of a motor failure at a most critical period of time! In the middle of a well-attended display or on the hottest, most humidity-laden day of the year, your air-conditioner will fail. Finally, the preventative maintenance program will definitely extend the life of the motor, thus reducing your operational costs. Not to mention a savings of energy cost, which is the thorn in the side of just about all art facilities today.

Once more, I want to point out that an electrical preventative maintenance program is very reasonable since you already have most ingredients on hand, including good *common sense.*

One of the highest failure factors of the electric motor is dust. An accumulation of dust on an electric motor restricts the air cooling capabilities of vents on the motor housing and can cause the motor to overheat. If left to accumulate for an extended period of time, dust will attract grease, which, combined with dust, will create an added fire hazard. A simple dusting will greatly reduce or eliminate this hazard from the motors within your facility.

Transformers come in all sizes and shapes. Their usage is equally as diversified. Many times, especially in period room settings, we use fixtures of lower than standard 115 volts A.C., such as electrified candles. In order to lower the standard 115 volts to 12 or 16 volts normally used in special displays, a step-down transformer is used. A step-down transformer, in oversimplified terms, is like a dam holding back a river and only letting a specific amount of water pass through.

The step-down transformer will hold back the voltage it is receiving and, based on its winding, allow a smaller voltage to pass through. There are two characteristics of a step-down transformer that, if realized, respected, and allowed for, will not create any additional hazards: (1) transformers are ugly; there is no other way to state it. When you take the natural ugliness of a transformer and attempt to locate it within an arts facility, the ugliness goes from repulsive to downright unbearable. The first thought is to hide it, bury it, put it anywhere it cannot be seen, not only by visitors but also employees.

Unfortunately this line of reasoning makes for a very tough maintenance activity; so, usually it will not get the attention it should receive. The out-of-the-way location of units are confining and restrictive, and that leads to the second characteristic: (2) heat buildup. This is a natural reaction of trans-formers. By holding back or restricting the passage of electrical current, a certain amount of friction will occur which results in the heat buildup. To compensate for this characteristic, there are two types of coolants used to keep the heat within acceptable ranges. One type of transformer is air cooled and, consequently, requires fairly open spaces in which air can freely flow around the transformer. Restrict this by hiding or burying your transformer and you have created a hazard that did not exist.

The second type of transformer is oil cooled and does not need the air circulation that the air-cooled transformer requires. It will build up a certain amount of heat, however, and can add to the drying out of electrical compo-nents within a confined space. The greatest danger is, as noted earlier, that a confining space will restrict proper electrical preventative maintenance. The oil within the transformer will need changing on a fairly frequent schedule based on its usage factor and restriction of electrical current.

A qualified electrical engineer or electrical contractor will take samples of your oil and analyze them for a moderate fee; the cost is very reasonable when compared to the alternatives.

Every art facility from the smallest to the largest utilizes some type of transformers. Treat them right and a transformer will give years of problem-free operation.

Computer-Data Processing Centers. Modern art facilities, on an ever-increasing basis, are becoming part of the trend of utilizing computer-data or word processing centers. This is the way it should be. Computers and data processing centers are an important asset to modern arts facilities, en-abling them to cope with accelerating manpower and operational costs. These installations do bring into play certain hazards that, up until recently, were only associated with the industrial and commercial sector. Within these two sectors the installation of these systems was considered another facet of the necessary machinery to widen the profit margin or to accelerate operations. Consequently, it received top priority. This same format is being considered by the arts facilities with several modifications. Within the industrial or com-mercial sector, the installation was given a priority on its value to operations and profits with no undue concern about *location or appearance*. If a room or building was needed to be constructed or altered to house the facility, it was done.

Within the arts facility sector, several other points come into play. No arts facilities that I know of have any extra available space without major problems associated with the shifting of support services such as conserva-tion shops and studies and/or vital storage for material and equipment used in continuing and changing exhibits.

For some reason, which I don't understand, an arts facility will expand into every nook and cranny within its building(s) with vital, absolute, necessary operations (or at least every curator, registrar, conservator, librarian, etc., utilizing that particular space will so attest). This makes the selection of an area for computer or data processing centers within an arts facility rather sticky and, unfortunately, the selection many times will be made not on critical installation and operational reasoning but rather on appeasement.

Everyone wants a center until it intrudes into their particular hallowed space. This is wrong. Once the collective decision is made that a computer or word processing system is required, one of the most important considerations has to be the safest, most economical location for the installation. ECDP (Electronic Computer Data Processing) centers are particularly susceptible to severe damage from fire and the accompanying heat and smoke. Temperatures in excess of 140 degrees Fahrenheit can and will upset components within the electronic circuit.

ECDP installations bring additional hazards to an art facility in the areas of heat buildup within components, and also additional and substantial electrical feed circuits, along with their own special HVAC (heating, ventilation, air conditioning) requirements. Physical plants with humidity and temperature limitations that parallel those required for the protection of a collection are, in some instances, even more stringent.

All of these additional hazards will be taken care of by the computer systems design engineer. Unfortunately, some arts facilities will employ such an engineer or company and then qualify the assignment with a list of restrictions, or worse yet, appoint a space allocation committee from the staff whose reasoning will be biased for reasons stated above. The unfortunate company or engineer, if he wants to sell a system (and that is what he is in business to do), will reluctantly design a system to operate within a space that is not ideal. If this happens, you may have increased your hazards.

Finally, budget restraints are very tight within an arts facility. Unlike the industrial or commercial sector, where increased cost can be passed on to the consumer, the arts facility must look to government and/or the private sector for grants and gifts.

This is becoming increasingly difficult because of the recent slash in sums set aside for the arts by the government and unfortunate tax allowance changes that don't make gifts as attractive in the public sector.

Don't let your installation experience important component cuts due to restrictive budgets. A penny saved here can prove to be very, very costly even to the point of the loss of critical tapes, or even more scary, the loss of irreplaceable art treasures. Think about it.

Inspections — Preventative Maintenance. In summation, I would like to restate some facts that should be apparent from this section on electrical hazards: *the danger is very real.* It exists everywhere in your facility — it's as real at 3 A.M. when no one is in the building as it is at 3 P.M. when you are open to the public. Every wall, ceiling, and floor contains the single most dangerous hazard of electrical systems — wiring.

My goal at Winterthur is to have all wiring circuits tied into centralized disconnects. When the museum closes both to guests and visitors, we will disengage the switches feeding the numerous circuits running through the walls, floors, and ceilings. Our reasoning is that when the building is operating with greatly reduced manpower, the various feeder circuits will be free from electrical feed. Thus, if a faulty wire or component fails during these closed hours, the danger of sparking, shorting, and combustion will be eliminated totally. This arrangement is not as hard as it sounds to accomplish.

A check through panel boxes will clearly show the feeder circuits that are not required in after-hours operations. For each circuit removed from service, you eliminate one more potential electrical hazard. Many times a single main switch can be thrown that will remove electrical feed to several panel boxes which feed many circuits. If your facility possesses an up-to-date set of electrical prints, I would suggest having an electrical consultant review your system and make suggestions. You must not shut down circuits feeding HVAC components. I would most certainly make this program part of any alterations involving lighting and appliance circuits. This safety precaution could be done during construction at no additional cost. For details in establishing a comprehensive electrical preventative maintenance program, I recommend the following:

- N.F.P.A. Fire Protection Handbook, Section #7, Chapter 2, Electrical Systems and Appliances.
- N.F.P.A. Inspection Manual, Chapter 12, Electrical Wiring and Apparatus.
- N.F.P.A. Manual 911, "Protection of Museums and Museum Collections," Chapter 4-2.

All of these publications can be purchased at reasonable prices by writing to National Fire Protection Association, Inc.

Electrical Preventative Maintenance. The following suggestions can be used in all areas of electrical wiring, fixtures, cords, etc., whether they be located in either a permanent or temporary environment.

Actual experience is worth a thousand words printed in an instruction book. The N.F.P.A. is a firm believer in using actual experience in determining where a problem may arise within your facility. I most strongly recommend that you use this experience within your facility as the foundation on which to build your electrical preventative maintenance program.

The following information was taken from the N.F.P.A. Fire Protection

Handbook, 14th Edition, which incidentally is the fire services' Bible. The purchase of this book would greatly enhance your ability to establish a fire prevention function.

I will list the most probable cause of electrical fires within your facility based on the N.F.P.A. text.

1. Cords — all types — out of 494 fires studied almost 7 percent were attributed to cords.
2. Christmas decorations — which could include specialty types of temporary lighting for displays. Out of 30 fires reported, percentage was 0.399.
3. Heating appliances — incandescent lamps were 10.5 percent responsible for a reported 787 fires.
4. Motor windings were some 5.5 percent of 415 reported fires.
5. Transformers represented 1.6 percent of 124 reported fires.
6. Audio visual equipment a reported 0.745 percent of 56 fires.
7. Television receivers were reported at almost 6 percent of 443 reported fires.
8. Miscellaneous wires, devices and appliances (which abound in every facility) was a staggering 52.1 percent of 3,924 fires.

All right, now that we know the primary culprits, let's try to determine where they may occur.

Outside buildings are rated at 4 percent, with 2 percent being attributed to lighting and feeder cables each.

Inside buildings — an alarming 93 percent — let's try to narrow that down to specific areas:

- Meters — approximately .½ percent.
- Panelboards — 1 percent.
- Wires — 15 percent.
- Transformers — 3 percent.
- Fixtures, outlets, switches, receptacles, sockets — 12 percent.
- Cords — 9 percent.
- Appliances — 52 percent — 30 percent of which is attributed to motors.
- Miscellaneous equipment — 3 percent.

With the aforementioned information, you should be able to single out the areas where the probability of a fire occurrence is the greatest. Concentrate your electrical preventative maintenance program on the most critical. A good program will encompass all areas within its operation.

Electrical fixtures, plugs, cords, and wiring should be inspected at least every six months.

Many times, art facilities will use electrified candles and special hidden spotlights or wall washers. During the course of usage, these items have a tendency to develop dried-out wiring and sockets, which is attributed to the heat of the fixture lighting.

Cords become frayed, especially if used in activities where they are frequently moved.

Although it is taboo and a definite no-no, how many times have you seen someone pull a plug from the wall by holding and pulling on the cord, rather than the body of the plug? This is a very bad practice. Plugs will become loose within the housing from being mishandled frequently.

Remember, we are talking about an overall frequency rate of 7 percent that cords could cause a fire. When you narrow this down to a probable location within your facility, the percentage jumps to over 9 percent. You can very easily, with very little out-of-pocket-cost, reduce the percentage to less than ¼ of 1 percent.

How? Institute a regular inspection of these items. Check cords for fraying. Check cords that may have cracks showing through the cord insulation. Normally, you will need to flex the cord gently, looking for tell-tale cracks. Look closely at the plug; move the prongs gently and check the screws holding the wires to the plug. Do they show signs of becoming frayed? Remember, it only takes a few strands from the hot wire to touch the ground wire, and you have a short.

Check outlet boxes on cords and check the wall outlets. Do they show weakening by moving within the outlet cavity? If so, tighten them up.

Although you should refrain from splicing cables as much as possible, there will be times, especially when setting up temporary displays, when you need to splice.

Make certain splices are firm, with wires pulled back against the cord shank after the first primary wrap, then wrap the entire splice with good, waterproof electrical tape. Remember, the splice, no matter how well done, could prove to be the weakest link in the cord and will become faulty from abusive use. Check them frequently

Lightning (N.F.P.A. Code No. 78). Earlier I mentioned that an unforeseen act of God could hit your facility. I am, however, a firm believer that even the so-called "Acts of God" — floods, storms, earthquakes, etc. — can be planned for and, although you may not be able to eliminate damage, you can minimize it.

My purpose in this chapter is to speak to fire prevention, and one of the "Acts of God" would include lightning. No arts facility, large or small, rich or poor, should be without some means of lightning protection, unless, of course, you live in an area that does not experience lightning in all its shattering brilliance. Lightning is a frequent cause of fires and indeed, in some areas, is one of the leading causes. Due to the fact that lightning is instantaneous and unpredictable it is feared as a cause of loss of life. We cannot stop lightning from occurring. We can and should plan to harness its destructive capabilities, especially in the arts facility sector.

"The theory of lightning is simple: provide means by which a lightning discharge may enter or leave the earth without damaging the property protected" (quoted from the 14th Edition of The N.F.P.A. Fire Protection Handbook).

Your lightning protection system has only one function: to intercept a lightning charge before it strikes your facility and then to discharge the current harmlessly to earth. Although the theory is simple the actual design and installation of a good functional lightning system is somewhat complex. Much variance will be experienced, not only by the type of facility that houses your collection, but also by the environment that surrounds it. A word to the wise would be advise you to contact a contractor who specializes in lightning arrestor systems.

Mechanical Hazards

I am a firm believer in preventative maintenance programs for every activity: electrical, security, fire, housekeeping, even administrative functions. I don't believe that anything should be let go until it fails or simply wears out. One of the most complex preventative maintenance programs for any facility — arts, industrial, or commercial — is a mechanical preventative maintenance program. What I am going to attempt to do in this section is to pull those items from an overall mechanical preventative maintenance program that relate only to potential fire hazards rather than general mechanical operations.

This will not be easily accomplished since a good mechanical preventative maintenance program is so closely related to all facets that to separate any one function is a challenge.

Duplicating machines — friction. For instance, photo-duplicating equipment. Copy units range from the small desk-type versions to the large computer-operated units. Two primary hazards can be directly related to copiers or duplicators. There is a significant heat buildup within the unit that must be taken into consideration, especially in the larger units. They must be installed within an area with adequate ventilation. Unfortunately, sometimes within an arts facility, a medium to large photo-duplicating unit is placed in an area formerly used as an office or storeroom.

The exhausting requirements for a standard office and certainly a storeroom are not adequate for medium to large photo-duplicating units. Inadequate ventilation will increase heat buildup within the room, resulting in premature aging and drying out of the electrical components and wiring, hence increasing the potential fire hazard of the unit and the circuits within the room. Sometimes, where duplicating is done by various staff members rather than one person, a unit will inadvertently be left on after closing. Again, we are faced with heat buildup, only this time it is totally unnecessary and could present a problem before it is noticed the next morning. Many use a sign that clearly states, "Please Shut the Unit Off After Using." But who reads signs?

The best solution is to install a timer which shuts off the power at a preset time. If preferred, you can install a keyed timer so that someone needing duplication services after hours can sign for the key and assume the responsibility to see that the unit is shut down. Also, there is always the potential of a friction-caused fire within a copier. A case in point: a large amount of paper is placed on an automatic feeder tray and the operator leaves for a cup of coffee or to talk to a person in an office down the hall while the load runs through. A sheet of paper becomes jammed in a roller; the friction of the rollers against the paper will cause a buildup of heat to the point that it will ignite the paper. The small print in the machine operations manual may or may not state that the automatic failsafe will shut down the machine should this occur. That may or may not occur.

Let me state Murphy's Law about failsafes: "A failsafe component will usually fail by failing to be failsafe."

In an arts facility, you can't afford the unnecessary risk, no matter how slim. Remember, our entire theme is fire prevention — by eliminating hazards wherever possible. Two things can be done. First, operators should never leave a duplicating unit (or for that matter any other piece of equipment in which friction heat could result) while it is in operation. Second, in most rooms converted from offices or storerooms, there is a standard fixed temperature detector. (More on detectors later in the section on Fire Detectors.)

Remove the heat detector and replace it with a product of combustion ionization detector head. This unit will sense a problem before it even becomes apparent to the operator — and certainly the operator who walked down the hallway.

Ideally it would be tied to a smoke detector which would back up the alarm coming from the first detector. If both units agree a problem is developing, they would automatically discharge a suppressant: sprinklers or Halon 1301 (more on these later under Fire Suppressants). If this proves too costly for your budget, how about simply having the detector(s) wired to the electrical feed and an alarm bell? If a problem develops, the detector shuts off the power and rings an alarm bell which will probably cause the missing operator to spill coffee on his/her lap.

Dust is another problem associated with a duplicator. Heat attracts dust and dust creates a fire hazard in itself (ignition by heat) or by collecting to the point where it constructs a bridge between hot and ground circuits and you have a short. Here is where a good standard preventative maintenance program would come into play. An important part of the program would include checking the unit on a regular schedule for dried-out wiring and to remove dust. I know many have service contracts. But look at your contract closely. Does it state that a service technician will respond *if you have a problem?* At this point, it's too late — you needed him before the problem existed. *Remember: Zero Fire Hazards.*

Pumps, Circulators, Fans. At the beginning of this section, I stated that it was very tough to separate a standard mechanical preventative maintenance program from that of a preventative maintenance program dealing with fire protection. The reasons are obvious; a comprehensive preventative maintenance program will maintain moving equipment at peak operational condition and, consequently, greatly reduce the possibility of failure and the fire-producing hazards associated with the failure. All moving equipment has potential fire-producing hazards because of friction. I am speaking about pumps, circulators, and fans. Friction occurs if a bearing fails and a shaft drops down and jams; if a fan blade moves and jams within its housing; or if an object becomes jammed within the moving parts. When this happens, several things will occur. Heat will immediately build up and, if continued in a jammed mode, the hear will be capable of igniting combustible-support material-like insulation.

Sometimes a jammed unit will cause a serious overload on an electric motor. If the unit does not kick out on overload (remember my comment on failsafes) you will shortly thereafter experience an electrical fire. Vibrations can also add to the hazards. Because they revolve, some at high speeds, there is always the possibility of the unit's being thrown off balance, resulting in excessive vibrations. This will create a dangerous situation as pipe and electrical connections can be shaken loose.

The oil level in bearings can become low, to the point where heat buildup will occur within the bearing housing and eventually the unit will seize and fail. Oil is another hazard associated with pumps, circulators, and fans. Usually there will be oil lying in and around the "oil fill" openings and, if not cleaned on a regular schedule, it will saturate material and fabric around the unit. Needless to say, oil is a real hazard around any type of igniter.

These and other hazards are associated with normal operations of the units. You can greatly reduce the hazard frequency percentage, however, with a good preventative maintenance program.

I am listing some guidelines that can easily be adapted to your particular facility. Once more let me point out the cost is nil — especially when you compare it to eliminating hazards.

One more stumbling block occurs before a preventative maintenance program can be instituted which, unfortunately, is more likely to occur within arts facilities than other sectors. Space limitations will always plague arts facilities. I said it before and will undoubtedly mention this fact several times in this chapter when attempting to make a point. It is a real problem, as a hazard-producing potential, and, unhappily, something that we in the arts facility field must learn to live with. This creates two problems: it compounds the hazard of combustible material in an area of potential ignition. The presence of stored material greatly complicates any preventative maintenance program by blocking or impairing free access of personnel and equipment. In addition, in many areas, you are operating against code by using mechanical spaces as storage areas.

Finally, there is a very good chance you are violating your insurance policy. If you are unfortunate enough to experience a fire situation traced to one of your illegal mechanical storage rooms, the insurance company may very well refuse to pay on the loss. Pumps, circulators, and fans carry a higher noise level than many other types of operating equipment. This is distracting within an arts facility, especially if it is in close proximity to the interpretational areas. In an attempt to hold the noise level to an acceptable level, various types of sound-deadening materials are used within the enclosure. Care must be exercised to see that the sound-deadening components are fire resistant and that their installation does not impede or eliminate air flow.

A positive schedule of maintenance should be carried forward on all pumps, circulators, and fans. The following suggestions should be considered minimum; you will have to adapt a schedule for your particular facility based on the usage factor.

Daily
1. Check oil levels and grease fittings — add as necessary.

Weekly
2. Check filters (if applicable).
3. Dust.
4. Clean up oil spills or leakage.
5. Check shaft and bearing for alignment. This can be done by slowly rotating (by hand) shaft and checking play in shaft to bearings.
6. If bearings are water cooled, check feed piping and connections; open adjustment valve and allow full flow of water for a few minutes to clear lines, then reset.

Annual
1. Bearings — remove, inspect, and clean. Replace if wear is evident.
2. Clean housing and bearing body with cleansing solution. Do so by disassembling unit.
3. Replace old packing.

4. Check alignment.
5. Check (and blow out if necessary) all lines including cooling water lines. Oil lubrication lines, vents, etc.
6. Check, recalibrate, and replace all gauges.

Boilers, Heaters, Air-Conditioning Plants. I feel that this section should begin with a very strong statement: "If you, or other members of your staff, don't fully know and understand boilers and air-conditioning plants, leave them alone." Have these highly technical facilities under full service. There are no alternatives. The price of a service contract, although fairly expensive, is one of the best investments you can make to protect your art treasures from fire and environmental hazard.

I can offer some suggestions that will assist you in determining the action that must be taken. Remember that service contracts are important, even vital, to an art facility. But the serviceman only comes (other than routine maintenance) when you call him. Consequently, although your background and experience may be in the arts and education fields, you have to possess at least enough mechanical ability to make the first evaluation. Let's review some general hints to assist in reducing hazards associated with boiler or heating plant operations. *Don't* use a boiler or heating room for the storage of combustible items like fabric, paper, liquids, or wood.

Another danger, especially in the arts facility sector, is to use one corner of the boiler or heating room for a mechanical workshop which includes the storage and usage of solvents and cleaners and painting material. Be careful not to store or in some other way place materials or supplies in front of fresh-air intake louvers. This problem can also occur on the exterior of your facility by allowing foliage to grow in front of air intake openings. Air in proper amounts is ultracritical to the proper combustion of your boiler no matter what fuel is used.

Have an Emergency Instruction card prepared and installed in a location from which a person can safely make an evaluation but at the same time be in no danger from the boiler. If your boiler or heating plant goes off the line due to a failsafe device (low water, inadequate air, loss of fuel, high load demand, etc.), don't attempt to reset and reignite the boiler unless you clearly understand what the problem is and what to do about it. If this is not the case, call your service company.

Miscellaneous

Indoor Housekeeping. If I have not yet provoked the wrath of my peers by referring to the habit at arts facilities of filling every nook and cranny — or territorial prejudice — I will probably do so with my thoughts on housekeeping.

Arts facilities in general (usually behind the scenes) are not the best of housekeepers.

Our collection and display areas are the epitome of beauty and sparkling neatness, but behind those doors marked "Staff Only" it is a completely different world.

Our Museum Service Section, which has the responsibility of taking care of the collection and cleaning and maintaining offices, studios, and work rooms, is headed by a very good, conscientious supervisor — his staff of thirty-nine men and women are equally good employees — yet, we have a continuing "housekeeping problem."

I don't actually know why. I can speculate that we have too much for too little space and feel that I am pretty safe in my assumption.

If you are going to turn up your nose with a smug "Not us," you have already closed your eyes to the problem — and, with your eyes closed, you will never be able to see the "housekeeping hazards."

Do yourself a favor however; before you close your eyes, check your facility: walk out into the public area and then come back through the "Staff Only" doors slowly; compare. I feel confident many of you will think exactly what I thought: "I really never noticed; there is a difference."

The poor housekeeping habits to which I am referring are not the dirty, unkempt kind, but rather the piling of materials, boxes, papers, and books upon other piles of materials, boxes, papers, and books which are already piled upon other piles of materials, boxes, papers, and books, and so on. Push back from your desk and slowly pivot around, looking closely at the desk, tables, furniture, and even the floor. See any piles?

I know a curator who has not seen his desktop for a long period of time. There is a librarian who only has one chair in his office to sit on that is not loaded with books — *his*. Or an educator with sheaves of papers that keep slipping off his desk. And finally, a building superintendent who fights the battle of the paper bulge each day. They all have one thing in common: these stacks and piles are "fire hazards." A misplaced ash from a cigarette, an overheated desk lamp, a shorted wire; any of these ignitors left smoldering among or touching the piles of class A fire concentrations could easily be the beginning of a serious situation.

Overflowing trashcans are another very real hazard. A match (thought to be out) carelessly dropped into a trashcan could easily smolder until the occupant of the office leaves for the day. Or, the tidy person who dumps a loaded ashtray into a trashcan without feeling for heat among the cinders.

Closets are another prime culprit. I remember telling my son, who wanted to go out to play in a softball game, "Not until you straighten your room." To my surprise, the room was straightened ten minutes later. Twenty to fifty various-sized articles were gone. So, true to my word, I let him go out. My wife went to my son's room about half an hour later to get his jumper (from the closet) to wash. I heard the door open, followed by a substantial crash and a shriek.

Fibber McGee and Molly (for us old-timers) always had problems with a jammed closet. I do not know if it is the child within us or Fibber McGee's reasoning, "Out of sight, out of mind," but we do have a tendency to stuff our closets, producing another Fire Hazard that did not previously exist.

The following are general comments to assist you in establishing a "Housekeeping Fire Prevention Program."

Materials stored in heavy concentrations or density loading, whether it be stacks of paper on your desk or loaded closets and boxes, present a hazard in two ways: first, the hazard of their burnable content, and second, if a fire should develop, their density will greatly restrict the fire-extinguishing capabilities of the suppressant — Halon 1301, CO_2, or water.

Keep areas in a neat, orderly fashion. Leave passageways in and around piles of materials.

Make certain that desks, filing cabinets, and other objects do not block breathing louvers for air-moving systems. Do not block doors that could be used for emergency exits.

Establish a procedure in which inspections are made on a frequent basis with concentration on staff and janitorial closets. Many times hazardous cleaning cloths impregnated with oils and cleaning solutions are carelessly stored in closets in nonapproved "storage cans." This is a very real problem and will require continual monitoring.

Smoking. A continuing war is being waged between the smokers and the nonsmokers with cries of injustice and foulness. As a result, various areas are classified and declassified as smoking areas. One point is certain: *smoking is a fire hazard.* As I have stated throughout this chapter, we live with and adjust to many potential fire hazards within our facilities, and smoking is one of those hazards with which you must live and adjust. A Blanket rule that states, "No Smoking, anywhere at anytime" cannot be established without risking several problems. (1) The majority of "true smokers" will not obey the rule. Somehow, someway, they will find a place to "sneak a smoke." There is a good chance that the place they select will be a more hazardous area than if you permitted smoking in a controlled environment. (2) More important, the smokers will not only be smoking illegally but forced to do it in an illegal area. Consequently, from a fire-protection standpoint, there will be a tendency for the smoker to be nervous and careless with the culprit — the cigarette and its hot ashes — increasing the chance of a fire.

Select an area for smoking. Furnish ample ashtrays and have a frequent cleaning schedule established within the area.

Do not use wooden trashcans. Although they make a more striking appearance in certain areas, they present an additional potential hazard due to discarded matches and hot contents from ashtrays. There are nice-looking office trashcans on the market that are specially treated to prevent fires caused by smoldering igniters.

Do not let trashcans fill to overflowing.

Do not permit sweeping to be dumped into a trashcan that contains paper.

Outdoor Housekeeping. A program for rubbish and other discarded combustible material removal should be firmly established. The frequency rate will depend on your needs. Monitor the accumulation of material for a certain period, and then set a schedule based on that observation. Allow extra load removals for special programs and activities at your facility.

All grass and weeds around your facility should be cut on a regular basis. Piles of cuttings should be raked and removed from buildings and shrubs.

Select a point where rubbish can be stored temporarily away from buildings and trees. Contact a local trash-removal company and think about renting large metal bins for housing trash until it is removed.

If you elect to burn rubbish at your facility, certain guidelines should be established. (1) Get approval from state, county, or city for a permit. Many areas have firm laws against such practice and you could be heavily fined. (2) Select a location that is away from all other combustible material. Prune trees if in the area. Skim back the grass around the fire location.

If possible, burn in a slight pit area within a heavy, closely knitted metal mesh enclosure to prevent flying sparks from passing beyond the clearance.

Have a charged hydrant connection and fire hose at the burning location.

Last, but certainly not least, have the operation supervised.

Packaging Activities. Within an arts facility include packing materials such as excelsior and strawlike material. These each offer added fire hazards and should be handled as noted:

1. Maintain only small amounts of such materials in the building.
2. Keep stored in properly constructed bins which should be built of substantial noncombustible material or wood lined with metal. They should have a cover that will close automatically in case of fire.
3. No smoking rules should be enforced in the packing area.

Storage of combustible material should never be located in congested, out-of-the-way areas. In arts facilities there is a tendency to store old and unused furniture and equipment, paper, magazines, files, fabric, and crates in the basement or other remote unoccupied areas.

Construction — Alterations

When involved in construction and alteration projects, the arts facility will experience some of the greatest fire hazard potentials of its daily operations. (See N.F.P.A. 241: Safeguarding Building Construction and Demolition Operations.)

Someone must be assigned the responsibility to check on a continual basis the construction and alteration side for potential hazards. It must be pointed out that the construction industry on the whole will not consider items with the same initial emphasis that an arts facility will.

Remember: the same type of comparison that we used in reviewing fire department operations must be employed when reviewing general contractors. Do not expect them to appreciate your special needs — then you will not be disappointed.

Check on a daily basis to see that construction debris is not stacked against your building. Contractors would rather accumulate debris until a sizable load is gathered before assigning a truck to haul the load away. This practice saves the contractor money, but increases your fire hazard.

If for some reason the trash cannot be removed daily, at least have the accumulation located away from your building. The cleared area between the pile of debris and your facility will be governed by the amount of debris. If this debris should ignite, the cleared area will stop the fire from spreading to your facility.

Construction workers will not be as careful when discarding cigarettes as your arts-oriented staff. Welding and/or sparks, melting pots for lead, hot tar heating pots — any of these igniters could set the rubbish pile on fire.

Make sure that cords tied into your outlets to power construction operations do not overload your circuits.

FIRE DETECTION

You have at your beck and call the best-trained and equipped fire-fighting group possible, but if you don't get early detection of a fire in an arts facility, your losses and damages to artifacts will be staggering, and, in many cases, a complete disaster, for reasons already stated.

At Winterthur, we have what I feel is one of the most highly trained and best-equipped fire departments in the art facilities sector: three fire trucks, thirty-two men, training every two weeks for four hours in specific collection areas, a full-time fire marshal with over twenty years' experience, and our own fire school. I am not bragging about our organization because no matter how good they are, no matter how much equipment they have, no matter how well they train, if we don't get early detection of fire situations there is a very good chance we will lose hundreds or thousands of collection pieces and indeed the entire collection. A good, well-trained fire-fighting activity can and will save the building or adjacent structures, and indeed that is the purpose of a fire department. But in the case of an arts facility, the reasons for your very existence, "your collections," if lost, would terminate those reasons. What would Winterthur Museum be without its collection?

Later, under the heading of fire fighting, I will review how we train our fire department, what our goals are, and how you can use this knowledge to train your employees whether they be four or forty. But the critical, down-to-earth, tell-it-as-it-is, bottom line is *early fire detection* — period! As you may have gathered, my comments up to this point have concentrated on the top priority of *fire prevention*; second, fire detection; and third, fire extinguishment. Yet I would be quick to admit that it's like the chicken and the egg: which came first? A total fire protection package would not be reliable if it did not provide provisions for all facets of fire activity.

The Human Element

One of the best sources of fire detection is the human factor. Certainly there are a host of electronic sensing detectors available to an arts facility today. Many of these are good and I will discuss and illustrate them in this portion of my presentation.

The human factor, however, goes one step beyond. People cannot only sense and detect through three important detectors, sight, smell, and sound, they have the added important factors of being able to make a determination with their minds, use their voices to call for assistance and their hands to close doors or move other objects to retard the spreading of a fire and its damage. But even more important, if the fire is in the incipient stage (more on this later), they can extinguish the fire without damage to any other artifacts. This can be accomplished by a small Halon 1211 extinguisher, which can be carried in a belt holster by a Detex clock roundsperson. More on this extinguishing agent under Fire Suppressants.

But, like any good product, it has its drawbacks. These you must acknowledge and do something about. Reduce the risks. Remember, always strive for zero fire defects in all areas as much as humanly possible. The very reason that makes this human detector such a good factor could also make him or her a poor detector. Let me explain.

If you notice, I will continually refer to this function as a clock roundsperson, and for a very good reason. You cannot rely on a person to (1) walk through a building, especially at 2 or 3 A.M. or into a room at the top or bottom of a long stairway, or into a hot boiler room, to name a few unpopular locations; (2) this same roundsperson would not necessarily choose to walk through areas prone to hazard potentials: laboratories or lunch areas where hot plates or coffee pots could have been left on. Finally, and equally important, this same person would not make the inspections on a regular schedule if left to his own choosing. You must take the initiative. Walk through your facility. Pick out critical areas. Time your walk. Allow time between locations, but not too much. Finally, install your clock keys. Review the clock tapes daily. Make certain the roundsperson is indeed making his rounds, checking all areas you prescribed on a regular schedule — possible problem areas. Inspect the key locations on a regular basis. Rounds-persons have been known to remove keys from locations at the beginning of their shift and then punch or turn the keys into the clock without leaving their desk for the remainder of the shift.

Closely check links of the chain holding the key to the wall holder. Sometimes they will loosen one link very slightly so links will come apart. Sometimes they will remove the chain holder pin which holds the key to the key cabinet or wall. On occasion, they will use a mixture of flour and water to hide the pin removal scratches around the hole in a plastered wall. Evidence of key removal will show up on close inspection.

Don't make the mistake of installing a security system (ultrasonic, infrared, motion detectors) that is so space-consuming that it prevents a clock roundsman from passing through critical areas during "closed hours."

Fire protection of an arts facility must be a combined effort of all divisions and offices within the facility, but — most critical — between security and fire protection priorities.

Personally, I am a firm believer in a good perimeter security system that surrounds the arts facility with a security envelope, but, at the same time, permits passage through all areas during closed hours by "human detectors." Also, a perimeter system is in service when the facility is open as well as closed. This benefit is not applicable to many ultrasonic, infrared, and motion detector systems.

Smoke Detectors — Ionization — Photoelectric

As I stated earlier there are many good electronic detectors (see Figure 10.2). The best detector available for an arts facility is the products of combustion ionization detector head. I will attempt to explain how these detectors function. Each detector contains a minute quantity of Americicum 214, a radioactive isotope. This material ionizes or charges the air within the detector and makes possible the early detection of fires. Each chamber contains minute sources of alpha-emitting material which ionizes the air in their respective chambers, making the air electrically conductive. When no combustion gases

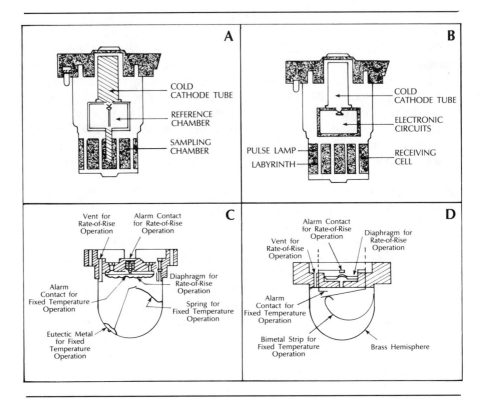

Figure 10.2. Types of standard detector heads. A. Ionization. B. Photoelectric. C. Rate-of-rise fixed temperature eutectic metal. D. Fixed temperature, bimetal element.

are present, the chambers are electrically balanced and the tube is non-conductive.

When combustion gases enter the open chamber, however, the electrical conductivity of the chamber is decreased, increasing the voltage drop across the chamber and increasing the voltage on the starter electrode of the tube. When the voltage reaches the ignition potential of the tube, the tube fires and becomes a low-resistance path for current flow. The minimum potential (voltage) increase necessary for ignition is the sensitivity of the detector.

The sensititivy is changed by changing the amount of ions picked up by the starter electrode and hence the effective resistance of the outer chamber. This is important, and the bottom line, the detectors can be adjusted to provide coverage in, say, a rare-book area where you want the utmost sensitive setting to a work area or conference room, in which you have people and equipment and the sensitivity need not be so critical. One system provides diversified coverage. These types of detectors are recommended for use in areas where the air movement is relatively high (over 25 feet per minute). They will protect a 1,000-square-foot area with a normal ceiling height of 8 to 16 feet — no barriers.

The second-best detector for an arts facility is the smoke detector, photoelectric type. In fact, I feel a good detection system is one comprised of products of combustion and ionization detector heads intermixed with the photoelectric smoke detectors — cross zoned. This assures the best overall coverage no matter how the fire situation develops.

These units are usually employed in areas where a lot of smoke may be generated prior to temperature increases sufficient to sound a heat detection system. Very simply, this type of detector operates on a light principle where smoke enters a light beam and either obscures the beam's path or reflects light into a photocell.

These types of detectors are available in the spot type, the refraction type, and the beam type. A fire system designer engineer would recommend the best type for your particular facility after reviewing your site and its collection.

There are two other types of detectors available. First, the fire detectors rate of rise principle consists of an air chamber, a flexible metal diaphragm and a moisture-proof vent which is carefully calibrated. When fire occurs, the air temperatures rise very rapidly and the air in the chamber expands faster than it can be vented. This creates a pressure which distends the diaphragm and closes electrical contacts.

The rate of rise action is not related to any fixed temperature level, but responds with the utmost promptness when the rate of temperature rise exceeds fifteen degrees per minute. If the heat is removed, the air within the chamber contracts, relieving the pressure and restoring the electrical contacts to a normally open circuit position. Although I feel the ionization products of combustion detectors are the most suitable for the protection of arts and artifacts, the rate of rise detectors can provide a suitable coverage factor for some areas. I must point out, however, that, with the rate of rise detector, it could be too late in alarming and dropping suppressants if the fire is of the slow developing type. It is possible that the temperature may not increase rapidly enough (fifteen degrees per minute) to operate the rate of rise element. This brings us back to ground zero. I feel the products of combustion–ionization is the very best detector.

The last type of detector is the fixed temperature unit, which melts when the temperature reaches a preset heat. This will in turn sound an alarm. If at all possible, I recommend that the fixed temperature dectector not be used in an art facility. By the time one of these units sounds an alarm, you are in very serious trouble.

Finally, before closing out the fire detection segment, I would like to discuss the four stages of a fire (see Figure 10.3) as a further illustration

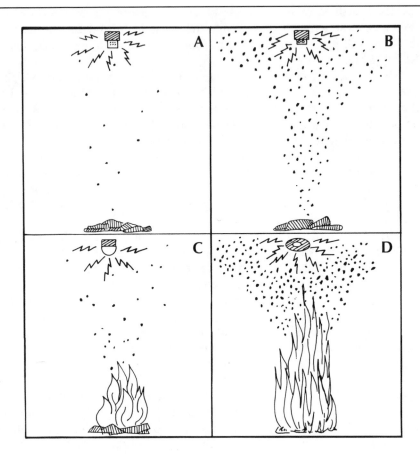

Figure 10.3. Smoke detectors and four stages of fire. (a) Incipient stage. Products of combustion are present in the room but contain few or no large particles; also there is little heat and no visible flame. The products of combustion ionization detector is the only detection device capable of detection at this point. (b) Smoldering stage. Some large and small products of combustion are present again, with little heat and no visible flame. The photoelectric or smoke detector would alarm at this point. (c) Flame stage. Follows smoldering stage, large and small products of combustion but in lesser amounts. Visible flame is present, heat begins to build up at ceiling, rate of rise detector would alarm. (d) Heat stage. Large and small products of combustion are highly visible, flame has broadened, heat and gas builds up quickly. Fixed temperature or thermal detectors would alarm at this point.

of why I feel certain detectors just described are the best suited for the arts facility.

The incipient stage: no visible smoke, flame, or any significant heat is yet developed. But a condition already exists which generates a significant amount of combustion particles. These particles have mass, but are too minute in size to be visible to the human eye. This stage usually develops over an extended period of time lasting minutes or hours. Chances are, you would not even know the condition existed if you were in the area, but an ionization product of combustion detector head would sense, alarm, and drop Halon 1301, CO_2, or sprinkler suppressants.

The smoldering state or smoke stage occurs as a fire condition develops and the quantity of the combustion particles increases to the point where the collective mass now becomes visible. During this stage, there is still no flame or significant heat. A smoke detector would likely alarm at this point.

The flame stage means that the fire condition has developed to the point where ignition actually occurs. Infrared energy is now given off from the flames. The level of smoke will usually decrease in the flame stage and the amount of heat developed will increase. At this point, the rate of rise detector heads should alarm.

The heat stage. Tremendous amounts of heat, flame, smoke, and toxic gases are produced. This stage develops very quickly and usually follows the flame stage in only seconds, and your facility is in serious trouble.

FIRE SUPPRESSANTS

The subject of this section is the desirability of having the best described fire suppressant system available with fully automatic detection capability. Then, hopefully, you will never need to have the local fire-fighting companies come to your facility under actual fire conditions.

Halon 1301, Halon 1211, CO_2

Without hesitation, I feel the best suppressant system to protect an arts facility *collection* is Halon. Many questions are asked about Halon, such as: Will it hurt people? Can you breathe it? What is its effect on people? What effect does it have on artifacts? How does it work? How does it differ from other fire suppressants? I hope to answer these questions and many more during this segment. Before jumping into the Halon 1301 fire suppressant capabilities, I think I should highlight a few standard fire-fighting statistics.

To burn, a fire must have all three sides of the "need-to-burn" triangle as seen in Figure 10.4.

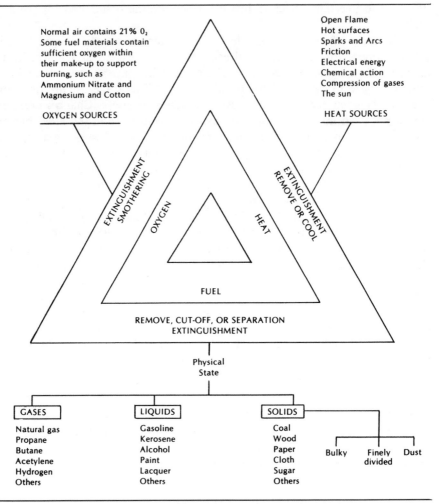

Normal air contains 21% O_2
Some fuel materials contain
sufficient oxygen within
their make-up to support
burning, such as
Ammonium Nitrate and
Magnesium and Cotton

OXYGEN SOURCES

Open Flame
Hot surfaces
Sparks and Arcs
Friction
Electrical energy
Chemical action
Compression of gases
The sun

HEAT SOURCES

EXTINGUISHMENT
SMOTHERING

OXYGEN

HEAT

EXTINGUISHMENT
REMOVE OR COOL

FUEL

REMOVE, CUT-OFF, OR SEPARATION
EXTINGUISHMENT

Physical
State

GASES	LIQUIDS	SOLIDS			
Natural gas	Gasoline	Coal			
Propane	Kerosene	Wood			
Butane	Alcohol	Paper	Bulky	Finely	Dust
Acetylene	Paint	Cloth		divided	
Hydrogen	Lacquer	Sugar			
Others	Others	Others			

Figure 10.4. Fire triangle. (From Berger D.L., *Security for Small Businesses*, Butterworth Publishers, Boston, 1981.)

1. Fuel in whatever form must always be present because there must
   be some type of combustible material for the fire to consume.
2. Oxygen in sufficient quantities for the fire to feed upon is necessary,
   and the supply of oxygen must be present in varying degrees of volume if the fire is to be sustained. The larger the fire, the greater
   the quantity of oxygen to sustain it.
3. Heat or friction is the third element required to start a fire. Ignition
   sources can range from unseen spontaneous combustion to the sim-

ple ignited match. Most extinguishable agents work physically. In other words, they attack the fire by smothering or cooling or separating fire from oxygen.

This is the theory: a fire is extinguished by one of the following actions: cooling, oxygen exclusion or smothering, or mechanical separation of fuel oxidizer. Remember the triangle: remove one of the sides and the fire cannot burn. Now that I have explained all this, I must tell you that none of these actions explains the reaction of Halon. Some cooling can be expected due to the low burning point of Halon 1301 (minus 72 degrees Fahrenheit) but it is low in comparison to the heat generated by the fire. That blows the cooling theory. Halon 1301 is heavier than air, so you would think it would smother the fire by laying down a blanket over the burning material. Wrong! This theory could be true if the fire occurred in a leak-proof container where it would hold its concentration and not be diluted by air movement.

Have you ever seen one of those exciting airplane movies when, an engine ablaze, the hero manages under great strain to reach out at the most critical moment and pull a lever? Suddenly the blazing fire goes out in the engine and all are saved. Guess what put out the fire? Right — Halon. The Air Force and now all commercial aircraft use Halon for this purpose. Where would you have any more tremendous air movement and turbulence than in an aircraft engine? That blows the blanket-smothering theory.

Halon 1301 is actually a low-boiling, colorless, liquefied compressed gas having high density and low viscosity. The halogen compound reacts with transient combustible products which are responsible for rapid and violent flame activity. This chemical reaction terminates the combustion chain reaction and thereby stops the flame activity. There are two theories offered that explain the actual extinguishment process. One is referred to as the free radical process; the other is based on ionic activation of oxygen during combustion. In spite of the theory and confusion, it works. If you want further details, I suggest you write the Halon 1301 Division of the Du Pont Company, Wilmington, Delaware.

CO_2 will also extinguish a fire by removing the oxygen from the area in which the fire occurs. This is critical, however, and the reason it is not more widely used in fire suppressant service is that it is very dangerous and can prove fatal to humans if they do not immediately clear the area.

On the other hand, only a 5 percent concentration by volume of Halon 1301 is needed to stop most fires. The range of concentration could be 3 percent to 7 percent based on the fire loading material it would protect. These concentrations leave ample oxygen in the environment for people to breathe while they exit the fire scene in an orderly fashion. Halon 1301 does not damage artifacts because it leaves no foam, powder, or other residue behind.

Is Halon 1301 harmful to persons after exposure to a discharge? Halon 1301 has been used in fire fighting for over fifteen years without a single reported injury resulting from exposure to its vapor. Incidentally, detailed reports are available on the safety of Halon 1301. In addition, Halon 1301 has been the subject of some twenty-five years of comprehensive medical research. Based on the results of these tests, the National Fire Protection Association set up guidelines which state: "In concentrations by volume of Halon 1301 at 7 percent or lower, humans could be exposed to the gas vapor for at least five minutes." Since most fires are extinguished with a 5 percent concentration within a few minutes, no ill effects can be expected. Does Halon 1301 provide any hazard if it is released during a very hot fire? The question could be answered if your facility is protected by Halon 1301 and a total flooding system triggered by ionization products of combustion detector heads, in that you should never experience "a very hot fire." (see Figure 10.5).

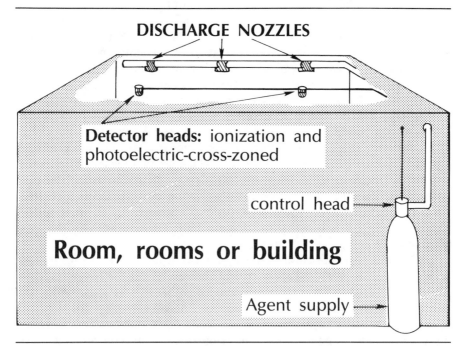

DISCHARGE NOZZLES

Detector heads: ionization and photoelectric-cross-zoned

control head

Room, rooms or building

Agent supply

Figure 10.5. A total flooding system. A problem develops within the facility; the products of combustion ionization head detects the problem, the second head, a photoelectric, verifies the problem, the units alarm, the control head fires and the extinguishing agent is injected into the facility at a preset concentration which puts out the fire.

But, for conversational purposes, let's say Halon 1301 is released in a hot fire — what happens?

As Halon 1301 extinguishes a fire, it produces primarily hydrogen bromide and hydrogen fluroide. In some fire situations where Halon 1301 systems have been used, the concentrations of HF and HBr have been recorded at below twenty parts per million. This is barely detectable to the nose.

To highlight the further versatility of Halon in protecting your collection, I need to spend a few minutes on some basic fire principles. Let me review the four categories in which fires are classified. This classification is important in knowing what particular type of extinguishment to use to put out a fire (see Figure 10.6). If the extinguisher is to be effective, it must remove at least one of the elements that is necessary to sustain the fire (remember the triangle). Each fire class has been assigned a color-coded symbol to identify the type of extinguisher to be used in an attack upon that particular fire.

Class A fire occurs in ordinary combustible material, such as paper, wood, pulp, and grass. These fires are normally extinguished by quenching them with water. The water lowers the temperature of the burning mass below the kindling point necessary for continued fire action to be sustained, thus removing one of the sides of the triangle.

Class B fire occurs in flammable liquids, such as gasoline, oils, paints, and cooking fats. Burning liquids require a smothering action to extinguish a fire. Extinguishers generating foam and dry chemical extinguishments are normally used in subduing the class B fire. Water may be used if nozzles and water pressure will create a "fog" by breaking the stream of water into minute droplets.

Class C fire occurs in electrical equipment, such as motors, switches, and appliances. A nonconducting extinguishing agent is required in class C fires. Carbon dioxide or a general or special purpose dry chemical extinguisher is normally used.

Class D fire occurs in flammable metals, such as magnesium and certain other special metals which will burn when chemical changes are in correct proportion. Special-purpose dry chemicals, powdered graphite, and other specially prepared powder are used to extinguish these fires, which normally are related to industrial operations.

It is very important that you use the right portable hand extinguisher for the right class of fire. The result of using the wrong extinguisher would create a worse situation than a fire. Problem: most areas could have either an A, B, or C class fire, a combination, or two or more. Consequently, you should have several types of extinguishers available at several locations. One must still be careful not to grab the wrong extinguisher. A Halon 1211 extinguisher which is rated for A, B, or C classes could be used. More importantly, it would not damage collection objects as would the other ex-

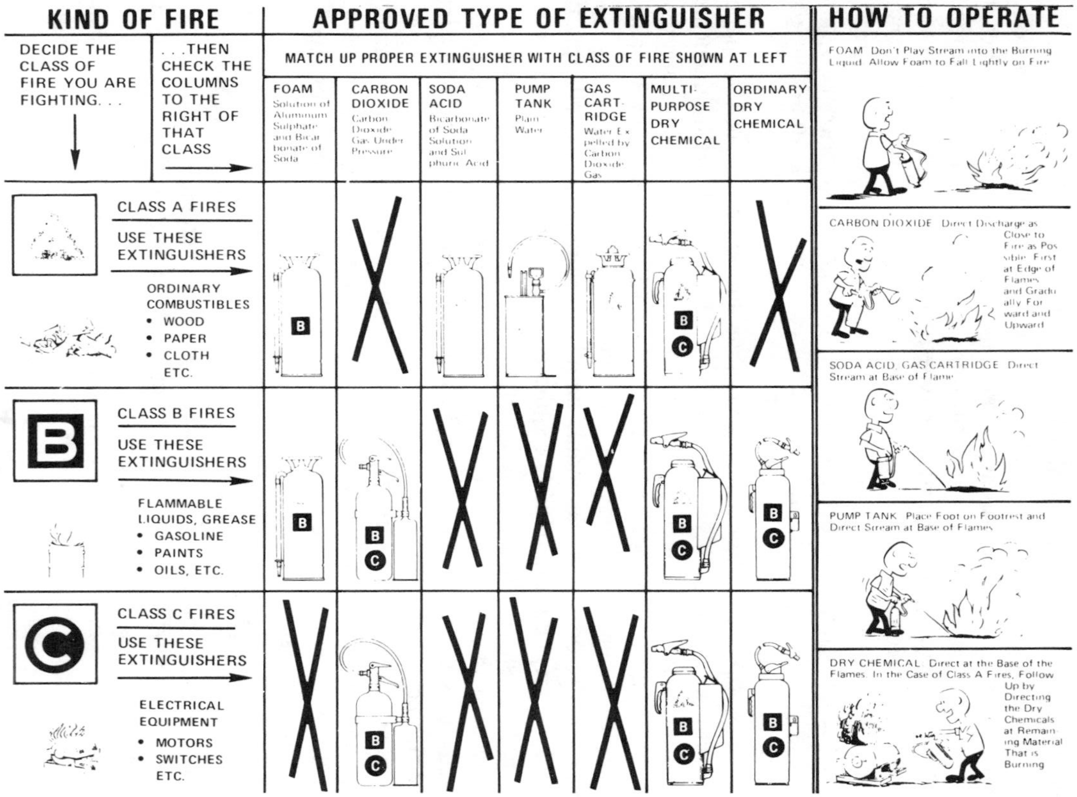

Figure 10.6.   Classes of fires and extinguishing methods. (Courtesy of National Institute for Occupational Safety and Health)

tinguishers. A seven-and-a-half-pound Halon 1211 portable extinguisher is available and is listed by the Underwriters Laboratories.

As I have already stated, one of the particularly attractive benefits of a total flooding system is the very high degree of extinguishing effectiveness and low toxicity. These two features combine in providing an inert atmosphere, while at the same time presenting a low risk of personal exposure.

Incidentally, a total flooding system is a system designed to release a predetermined amount of agent into an enclosure that will develop a uniform extinguishing concentration throughout. There is a potential problem, if you can call it that, within the "A" fire classification. The "A" classification, if you remember, contains wood, paper, fiber, and has two burning characteristics: (1) flames; (2) deep-seated char.

Normally Halon 130l can extinguish fires within this classification in seconds with a concentration as low as 3 percent. But the second characteristic, "deep-seated char," requires a Halon 1301 "soaking time."

A deep-seated fire represents a large amount of heat contained in the fuel; for instance, an overstuffed chair or mattress. Surface water or Halon 1301 will not touch the deep seated char on the first discharge. The first discharge, however, will halt the oxidation reaction, but the heat remains. The fuel will continue to produce heat and the "deep-seated char" will expand. This must be dissipated by radiation and conduction, since Halon 1301 has only minor cooling power. Thus, to dissipate the heat and cool the temperature below its ignition point, the Halon 1301 must remain in its discharge concentration for x number of minutes. All of this is taken into consideration by the design engineer when the proposed system is developed for the facility it will cover. To prevent a "deep-seated char" and to lessen the danger to artifacts, the Halon 1301 should be applied at an early stage of combustion. At this point, the fire is smaller and has not become fully involved. If you will recall, the idea is to sense, alarm, and discharge the Halon 1301 under stage one — the incipient stage. This is before the appearance of smoke, flame, or appreciable heat.

In areas used for the storage of art and artifacts, an automatic carbon dioxide system could be employed with the use of the same types of products of combustion detectors. The system is capable of providing protection with little danger to certain types of collection objects. The discharge of a CO_2 system would result in a very rapid temperature drop, which would create snow or fog. Even more critical is the fact that CO_2 could prove fatal to humans who did not exit the problem area immediately on the discharge of the system. Taking these points into consideration, a CO_2 system could be utilized in nonvisitation areas with ample safety alarms and override switches at a cost somewhat below the Halon 1301 system.

Finally, I will speak about water sprinkler systems that could be used in an art facility with the least amount of danger to the collection. There are faults and benefits associated with a modern-day sprinkler system. Without reservation, as previously stated, I firmly believe the Halons are the best fire suppressant mediums in existence today for, and this is important, the protection of an arts facility *collection*.

Notice I said arts facility *collection*. Halon in a total flooding condition will put out a fire in a specific area in which it is installed provided (key point) the envelope or the building remains intact. Break out a window or smash open a door and you have defeated the designed concentration of the Halons by introducing excessive air within the facility. The Halon people will quickly point out that if the problem is internal, the Halon will suppress the fire before it gets to the window or door-smashing stage — right. The sprinkler people would reply that the penetration of the building structure could come from the outside by a serious accident or explosion and then the Halon system would be ineffective — right.

Sprinkler System

Most curators, directors, and conservationists will react strongly against water being employed, indeed even considered, as a possible fire suppressant system.

Their reasoning is both right and wrong. I know that sounds confusing, so let me expand. I will use some statements made by museum professionals illustrating their fears of water. The reasoning is based on the fact that water could indeed cause more harm to artifacts than the actual fire. This could be correct. Even if the fire threatened only one small area, water could damage art treasures in other areas not even endangered by fire; this could also be true. A small fire could cause a whole string of sprinkler heads to open, spraying water in all areas, even where a fire doesn't exist. This is wrong; it is an old wive's tale. Some people would say that once those sprinklers go on, they stay on until they are manually shut off by the fire department. By that time, your entire collection is washed out in the street. Again this is wrong reasoning and it is an old wives' tale. This is not true with a modern sprinkler system.

I would make a good politician by agreeing with both sides; however, both are right. A Halon system is basically designed to protect the *contents* of an arts facility; the sprinkler system is designed to protect the *building* that houses the collection.

Hopefully, a properly installed and operating Halon system will eliminate the need for ever bringing the sprinkler system into operation. If needed, however, nothing will put out a major fire more positively than a properly installed and operating modern sprinkler system. I would like to mention another point that has been made by curators and conservators: "We will never use water in our arts facility." Contrary to this statement, water will be used in any arts facility by firemen responding to an alarm. They will use hoses under pressure to spray into your facility with a swinging back-and-forth motion.

Visualize this versus a sprinkler head spraying down a gentle umbrella of water in a pattern over the fire area. The choice is yours, but rest assured, water will be used in your facility if the fire is of major proportions and your building exterior is penetrated. Don't despair; the situation is far from bleak. Let me review modern sprinkler systems. I'm confident it will prove enlightening if your conception of sprinklers parallels the feelings encompassed thus far.

The first automatic sprinkler system was devised and installed in England in the 1800s. This system was simple and effective. A series of holes were drilled in pipes that ran overhead through areas to be protected. The water was kept from entering the pipes by a rope which held the valve closed. When the rope was burned through by the fire, the valve opened. Water surged through the pipe, out the holes, and put the fire out. Today, although much more sophisticated in detection and operation, the basic principle is the same.

There are four basic types of sprinkler systems available today. I will briefly explain the systems and point out some questions that may be answered by a specific system.

1. Wet pipe system. Standard system designed to operate by having water available throughout the entire system of pipes which flows immediately when a sprinkler head is ruptured (see Figure 10.7A).
2. Dry pipe system. Uses compressed air and has valves at the riser location to prevent water from entering the piping installed in the protected area until the sprinkler has been ruptured. When the compressed air escapes out the ruptured sprinkler head and its pressure drops below the water pressure, the valve opens and the water enters the system (see Figure 10.7B). This eliminates the fear of many of leaking pipes in collection rooms, as is possible in the wet pipe system.
3. I feel the best system for arts facilities is the preaction system. This system is designed primarily to protect facilities where the danger of serious water damage could be caused by damaged sprinklers or broken piping.

The principal difference between a preaction system and a standard dry pipe system is: the preaction system contains a water supply valve that is activated independently of the opening of the sprinklers. In other words, the water supply valve is opened by the operation of an automatic fire detection sys-

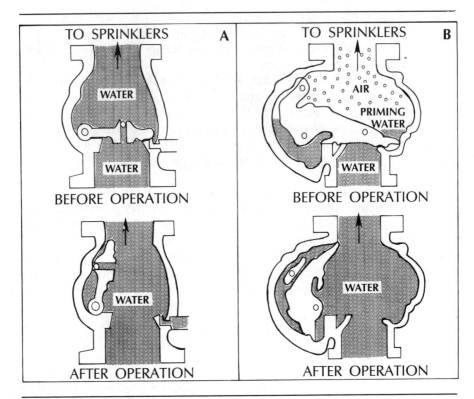

Figure 10.7. Two types of standard sprinkler systems. A. Wet pipe-lines filled with water. When sprinkler head opens, water flows, lifting valve. B. Dry pipe-lines filled with air when sprinkler head opens; air flows, relieving pressure against valve, which opens and allows water to enter.

tem, (same detection used for the Halons system can be employed) and not by the fusing of a sprinkler head.

The preaction system has several advantages over a dry pipe system. The valve is opened sooner because the fire detectors have less thermal lag than sprinklers. The detection system also automatically rings an alarm. Fire and water damage is decreased because water is on the fire more quickly and the alarm is given when the valve is opened.

Because the sprinkler piping is normally dry, preaction systems are non-freezing and therefore applicable to dry pipe service. The detection feature of a preaction system can also be added to a conventional dry pipe system.

Finally, there is the deluge type of sprinkler system, which is better suited for industrial and commercial use. I feel this system is totally unacceptable in an arts facility.

Sprinkler heads. First let me state without reservations that the accidental rupture of sprinkler heads occurs *very, very infrequently* and, in my estimation, carries very little danger to a collection.

The sprinkler head is the heart of the sprinkler system and it is the head which ruptures and discharges an amount of water in a predetermined pattern on the fire.

There are several different types and shapes of sprinkler heads. The type of head and rating are very technical and vary with the requirements in the areas they cover. This information would be gathered and evaluated by a fire design engineer when he studied your particular need.

Most sprinkler heads are set at approximately 135°. This means the fusible link (a soft metal seal which melts when the temperature reaches this setting) will allow the water pressure to bear upon the struts, forcing them out of position, and a free stream of water will flow under pressure.

Only the sprinkler heads experiencing the heat buildup will open and discharge water. Contrary to popular belief, all of the sprinkler heads will not open at one time and flood your facility.

For the same reason I recommend the preaction sprinkler system for all arts facilities, I would recommend on and off sprinkler heads. These units will open per design to spray water on the fire. *Important!* When the temperature recedes (hopefully when fire is put out), the head will reseat and shut off the flow of water.

In conclusion, none of us likes to think about water being sprayed in our collections. If the reasoning is being concerned about our collections (and it is), that same reasoning should require us to approach the question of sprinkler systems with an open mind.

FIRE FIGHTING

The following will list in detail what we are attempting to establish at Winterthur in a fire-fighting activity devised and established especially for an arts facility housing irreplaceable artifacts. Although our operational personnel may be larger or smaller in number than yours, I feel the basic concepts are the same. For instance, under each category, you may have only one person assigned to that particular responsibility. The key is that you do have a person specifically assigned to accept the responsibility to carry out a specific act during an emergency. Each separate function is designed to dovetail into an overall 'fire-fighting activity."

Too many times, in an emergency situation, people panic and become excited. Important items are overlooked in the confusion. You cannot stop people from becoming excited and feeling panicky. You can, through a regular training program, have each person respond with only his area of responsibility to worry about. This in itself will greatly help in reducing the natural confusion of thinking — what should I do? As previously stated in my section on Why a Specialized Fire Activity for an Arts Facility, I noted that the responding fire department or fire company will want to extinguish the fire in the quickest possible time.

We, too, want to extinguish a fire in the quickest possible time and this is what we have attempted to formulate in our training program, but we are going to take other steps to protect the collection at the same time we are combating the fire.

Our fire fighting is subdivided into four primary categories: (1) fire fighting; (2) collection protection and salvage; (3) security of the collection; (4) mechanical. All of these categories will be activated and busily engaged in their particular assignment at the same time (see Figure 10.8). Each group is to be trained to handle their assigned tasks independently and yet, at the same time, be coordinated into a fire protection system. The overall coordination of these activities will be handled by the person in charge.

Each section will have an officer assigned to head the group who is

Figure 10.8. Fire fighting activity plan

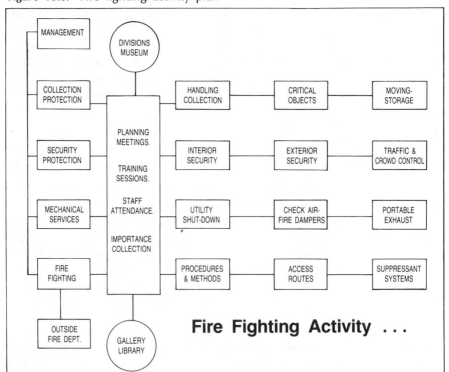

well versed and trained in the particular service his group will be responsible to provide. For instance, fire-fighting efforts will be directed by the fire marshal and his staff; the collection protection and salvage, by the museum services supervisor and his staff; and the security during the emergency will be furnished by the security supervisor and his staff. Mechanical shut-offs, smoke injectors, and disengaging electrical pullboxes will be handled by the mechanical supervisor and his staff. Overall coordination of these activities will be the responsibility of the buildings superintendent.

Through splendid cooperation with the curator and her staff, who are furnishing advisors at all drills involving the collection, we are able to train our people in the proper methods to employ in handling and storing objects during an emergency.

Before outlining how we are training the individual sections of the fire brigade and what we will expect from them, I would like to recap our earlier efforts. I had thought when I first learned that the fire brigade responsibility came within the structure of Museum Buildings Division it would be treated like any other private fire-fighting organization. As plant engineer at several industrial plants, I also had the responsibility for fire-fighting protection. Consequently, I assumed that it would simply mean transferring ideas, schedules, and procedures from past experience and that activity could be re-adjusted to incorporate our needs at Winterthur.

With this thought in mind, I observed the fire brigade in training and discussed in detail its activity with the brigade officers. Training programs were being held in the use of water and chemicals, pit fires, smoke masks, ventilation, fire truck handling, ladders, field fires, which were all standard procedures. I thought the time schedule was a little loose, but nevertheless a good basic structure for an efficient fire group did exist. This was in my earlier stages of association with Winterthur. As I became more and more aware of what the Winterthur Collection actually consisted of and the historical significance of these pieces, some shadows of doubt crept into my mind as to my earlier evaluation of our training efforts.

I must admit that the more knowledgeable I became about the magnitude of the irreplaceable pieces in the Winterthur Collection, the more doubt entered my mind. My first optimistic evaluation was replaced with anxiety that we were indeed not preparing properly to assume the awesome responsibility for the fire protection of the collection.

From past fire-fighting experience, education, and an accumulation of fire activity manuals (primarily designed for industrial and commercial establishments), I came to the conclusion that if we were to create a fire protection service relevant to Winterthur Museum, we had to initiate our own program. This fact is the foundation on which our entire fire training activity is based. In 1972, our first full year under our newly formed format, we made many gains and made many mistakes.

In the 1980–81 program we made tremendous increases in our entire fire protection activity including a full-time fire marshal with over twenty-five years of professional fire service experience. We added our third fire truck and changed the title of the group from Winterthur Fire Brigade to the Winterthur Fire Department, an important morale booster for the men operating the department. Another very important addition to the fire department's capability was to establish our own F.M. two-way radio system, with each member of the fire department wearing beeper units tied into this system.

But, all in all, we are still training every other Monday for four hours; we are still learning and still making mistakes, but the mistakes made during training, hopefully, will reduce the mistakes made when responding to an actual emergency.

Our collection areas are under the constant surveillance of an ADT system that not only senses within each collection room but, equally important, senses within the air movement risers feeding the collection from six fan rooms. This system is part of an ADT network that is being monitored in an ADT central station and at our security desk location. When receiving, an ADT will automatically dispatch three local volunteer fire companies to Winterthur. Security sounds a large siren on the roof of the nine-story building and sets off thirty beeper units. The location of the alarm is given over the radio to the beeper units. These units are worn by key personnel. At the same time, air handling units and fire dampers in the affected area will be shut down automatically. Evacuation bells, which are automatic, sound throughout the building and guests and employees commence a preplanned evacuation schedule. Men are assigned the responsibility of bringing the three fire trucks to the location at the museum. A mechanical maintenance employee will report to the fire pump house in response to the first call. Here, three fire pumps will be placed on the line to supply nine critical fire hydrants located around the museum with a constant stream of pressurized water.

Fire Fighters

We do not have the manpower and equipment to combat a major fire within the present structure of our fire department, but we do have a trained group of fire department members who intimately know and appreciate the Winterthur Collection and the structures that house it. Our people will work closely with the three companies responding.

We have found that outside fire-fighting groups welcome the assistance of persons who know the structure and utilities within a smoke-filled building that they must penetrate. In a small, minor situation, it is our intention to handle the problem with our forces. Our training within this group specializes in the following areas: the importance of the collection, access routes to and from the collection areas, routes to move bulky and heavy fire-fighting equipment to the scene, proper ways to carry fire-fighting tools in collection areas, extinguishing the fire with the least amount of water possible, carrying small involved objects outside for extinguishment, exit areas, light switches, location of portable fire extinguishers, standpipes, hose stations, preventing damage by smoke, smoke injector usage, preventing damage by water.

In addition, of course, our people are trained in all the standard fire procedures and equipment, such as operation of fire-fighting equipment, masks and respirators, ladders, structural and pit fires, fire hydrant system, hose lays, brush and woods fires, and, finally, an in-depth study of the fire suppressant system used at Winterthur.

We have converted one of the smaller concrete barns to serve as a fire school. We set smokey fires within the building and let the men enter wearing respirators. They attempt to put out the fire with booster hoses, working together as a team.

Collection Protection and Salvage

As I stated earlier, the curatorial division furnishes us with advisors who attend all collection fire training sessions. Through their excellent suggestions and recommendations, we are training the museum services supervisor and his personnel in the proper methods to employ in moving and storing objects during emergencies. Fortunately, many of the members of the museum services group are fairly well versed in the proper methods to employ in the normal everyday handling of objects. This makes the training sessions a little easier to administer.

We have purchased and made various-sized covers and bags from the light weight, fire-resistant material called Nomex (made by the Du Pont Company). These bags and covers will be employed to shield and protect collection items from the danger of the actual fire and damage caused by the elements employed to combat the fire.

The collection of Nomex bags and the covers are maintained at our central base of operations. In time, our plans call for the installation of Nomex bags and covers on each floor of the museum.

On notification of an alarm, the museum services staff (preassigned) will report to the central location, pick up their equipment, and proceed to the scene of the fire. Under the direction of the museum services supervisor, they will start to cover, protect, and move the collection, if required, to a safe location. Nomex cloths, precut to door size, with a header strip already attached to the top of the cloth with nails driven halfway through, will also be taken to the area so the rooms can be sealed off as further protection.

Other supplies picked up by these men responding to an alarm at the central base are mops, buckets, brooms, and cleaning cloths. Their training includes the importance of the collection, the critical pieces within the collection, covering and carrying collection objects under emergency conditions, temporary and permanent storage areas, access routes for larger pieces, protection against water, and protection against smoke.

Security

Upon the receipt of an alarm, the security supervisor will report to the fire scene. He will assign and supervise all security activities within the fire area.

This will include stationing personnel at all windows and doors broken open for ventilation and emergency access to the fire; the observance of all strangers in and around the fire area; posting security personnel around any items or objects removed from museum protection systems due to a fire or elements used to extinguish the blaze.

The security supervisor will also oversee the operation of the fire-police activity. Training will consist of the importance of the collection, access routes through the collection areas, exit facilities, and all standard security procedures which they employ in their normal observations to carry out the protection of the collection.

Another group, under the security captain, will specialize in traffic and crowd control, working on the exterior of the museum.

Mechanical Maintenance

Members of mechanical maintenance will report to the central station on the sounding of an alarm. Under the direction of the mechanical maintenance supervisor, they will take smoke injectors and heavy-duty extension cords to the fire scene.

Upon arrival on the fire scene, the supervisor will report to the fire marshal. He will then direct the shutting down of all utilities (gas, electric) within the fire area.

Smoke injectors will be installed at key locations on request of the fire marshal.

Training consists of the importance of the collection, utility shut-off locations within the areas under training, access routes, ventilation procedures, and protection of the collection.

In summation, an actual procedure in an emergency would function as follows (it will take longer to relate than it actually takes to respond):

A guide within the collection notes smoke on the seventh floor. She immediately proceeds to one of the emergency phones located in three critical locations on all nine floors. When this phone is picked up, it automatically rings at the central control desk.

The person on duty takes down the information, noting all pertinent facts, while at the same time pushing buttons that bring thirty radio beepers into play. "I have a reported fire situation on the seventh floor" (gives exact location), repeating the message twice.

At the same time, the exterior heavy-duty siren located on the roof of the ninth floor is started. In addition, the evacuation bells are sounded. While this is taking place, a call is dispatched to the fire board, who automatically dispatch three volunteer fire companies to the scene.

(Up until this point, the same procedure would have been employed if the alarm came from a pull-box or automatic detectors. The only difference is that the pull-box or automatic detector alarms would have been transmitted directly to ADT rather than our having to alert the fire board.)

The fire fighting group reports to the central control station and receives their instructions from the fire marshal.

Preassigned men respond to the fire house and bring over the three fire trucks, two pumpers, and an 85' high-riser platform truck. Another man responds to the fire pump house to start and maintain the emergency hydrant system.

As soon as the evacuation bells are sounded, the museum service group goes into operation. Museum service personnel normally assigned cleaning assignments on specific floors start through their floors making certain that all guides and guests are clearing the floor. If they meet a group with a wheelchair or elderly guest, they call a number where an emergency evacuation group is standing by.

Within the four floors of offices in the Washington Wing, volunteer monitors walk through their respective sections making certain employees have vacated the premises, closing all doors as they leave.

The Museum services supervisor takes up a position at the main exit doors. On a preprinted form, he checks the monitors as they exit the building, noting that their area is reported clear. If a monitor does not report, a search group (2 men) is dispatched by radio to the area in question.

When the building is cleared, the museum services supervisor reports to the building superintendent, who has taken a position at the base station and emergency telephone desk.

The fire-police group swing into action by taking up strategic locations in front of the building to keep positions open for the fire trucks now under way.

Since Winterthur grounds consist of 960 acres and some 26 miles of roads, our motor patrol vehicle is radio dispatched to the exterior gate to lead fire trucks to the location requested by the fire marshal.

Transportation section personnel (three buses, two vans, and a carryall) report to a preplanned staging area for the purpose of moving guests and employees to the pavilion about three-quarters of a mile from the museum.

Once the museum service supervisor has seen to the evacuation of the building, he proceeds to the fire scene with members of his group, stopping to pick up equipment enroute. He then reports to the fire marshal at the fire scene to commence whatever collection protection services that are required.

A man will be assigned to either side, atop and below, the fire area, paying particular attention for possible smoke and water seepage.

On hearing the alarm and getting the location over his beeper unit, the mechanical supervisor and members of his group swing into action. All control boards are checked to see that all smoke dampers and air handling units are shutdown. Another man pulls all elevators to the main floor, unloads them, then locks them into a shutdown mode.

The supervisor, along with other personnel, picks up smoke injectors and heavy-duty extension cords and reports to the fire scene. Enroute, he shuts down all utilities feeding the affected area.

Depending on the severity of the fire, we will broaden or reduce operations with all instructions and communications being funneled through the control desk via our radio and telephone systems.

Within this framework, we train every other Monday for four hours. These training programs take place within a different collection area each time.

All supervisors view the area carefully, looking for and making notes, on procedures they can employ if they are called to this area under actual fire conditions.

Hoses are layed, standpipes tested, emergency exits checked.

After a training session, a debriefing is held where actions and procedures employed during the drill are discussed. On drills within the fire training barn, only members of the fire-fighting group attend.

We have some 191 buildings on 960 acres, which include many acres of woods and fields. There is a good chance that we will experience fires within these categories more than an alarm at the museum building, and, fortunately, experience has proven this theory.

Since we maintain three large parking lots, our fire department also trains in oil pit–type fires, using foam, which we feel the best training for a possible automotive fire.

We see no need to train the museum services and mechanical maintenance group in these types of fires.

EMERGENCY MANAGEMENT

Nothing — *I repeat,* nothing — can be done toward establishing a realistic fire protection activity without the full backing and support of the management of any Arts facility.

At Winterthur we are very fortunate in having not only a great spirit of cooperation between the members of the fire department, but also the full backing of critical divisions such as curatorial, conservation, registrar, etc. In addition, we have full backing from our management and, equally important, our board of trustees.

I would like to close this report with this segment. I will summarize and discuss activities designed for an arts facility relying on you to establish your own fire protection plan. You must preplan. Review and discuss it with all personnel involved, including all divisions and offices. Request suggestions and recommendations and be prepared to get many unproductive comments.

There will be definite territorial comments made from staff. This is, unfortunately, the makeup of many arts facilities. If you are a dreamer or, like the ostrich, stick your head in the sand and don't acknowledge this problem exists, you will not succeed.

Know it for what it is. Each division or operation has a tendency to believe its particular service or activity is the most crucial to the overall operation of the arts facility. Your job is to acknowledge these territorial claims without letting biased thoughts enter your emergency planning.

You must continually ask yourself, "What is the best procedure to employ in protecting the collection during a fire emergency?" This point must be continually brought out at every meeting. Slowly but surely, the territorial disputes will fade away, to be replaced with a unified effort. Have patience until that change takes place. Each step of your emergency procedures must be well thought out, placed in writing.

Don't expect personnel to know and understand every facet of the emergency action procedure. Instead of helping, this approach could easily impair the success of your program.

By now I think you will agree that the overall fire protection is extensive and very complex. One person attempting to learn and fully understand each facet could easily confuse procedures when an actual emergency occurs and urgency and confusion reign supreme.

You will never be able to eliminate fully the urgency and confusion that will occur when a fire situation hits your facility. Consequently, you plan around it. You minimize the confusion by (1) establishing procedures in clear, simple segments and assigning that responsibility to one person. If a larger group exists, assign one person to transmit information to those assisting (him or her). (2) During training sessions and meetings you review how each facet is designed to dovetail into an overall fire protection activity, at the same time stressing that each assigned person have only one primary function for which responsible.

For each person assigned a particular responsibility, you must have at least one backup person. At Winterthur each supervisor is backed up by his foreman. They are instructed to choose separate vacation periods.

Ask for volunteer monitors from each floor. Their assignment, when receiving or hearing an emergency call, is to check their location to make certain that persons have cleared the area and that all doors are closed.

Although I have not spoken of life safety during this article, it is not because we don't train on life safety programs. It is simply because in this article I have attempted to speak of fire hazards, activities, and equipment relating to a fire emergency in an arts facility. Life safety is our first goal. In no way do we differ with any fire department or code regarding an all out emphasis on life safety.

The monitors are our best means of accomplishing that goal in our buildings. In addition, closing doors after clearing an area will help to prevent the spread of a fire.

Once you develop your procedures and personnel, train on a regular basis. Again, be realistic. Training can be very boring. The assignment is not without hard work and frustrations. Stay with your program. Do something extra for the people participating in your fire protection operation: a free lunch once in a while, consideration in pay raises, time off for services rendered, etc.

The four critical areas of responsibility within your fire protection program should include (1) fire fighting; (2) care of collection; (3) security of collection; (4) mechanical systems. In smaller institutions this could mean only one person within each heading.

Remember that the primary goal is to have a person thinking clearly and to be knowledgeable in specific areas of activities during an emergency.

One person working with an outside fire department can go a long way in informing the fire department of the physical layout of your facility. This will remove much uncertainty as to where the fire is actually located and how to get there.

Someone who knows, understands, and, very important, appreciates your collection can be an invaluable asset when firemen are working within your facility, especially in the area of salvage. The same logic holds true for security and for any person who knows where to shut down critical utility feeders.

Establish a program where at least responding fire department officers and their wives are brought to your facility for a free luncheon and tour. Have an impressive member of your curatorial or public-relations department explain the importance of your collection, not in dollars but in historical and educational content. Do this on a regular six-month basis. Remember, these same officers will be the men in charge when they respond to an actual fire situation. If your tour and narration on the importance of your collection cause them to think twice before ordering the opening of a hose into a smoke-filled room, without a preliminary investigation, your effort has been worthwhile.

EMPLOYEE FIRE AWARENESS PROGRAM

Provide opportunities for employees to practice using fire extinguishers and fire hoses. If at all possible, set a small fire in a protected area. Allow the employees actually to put out the fire using the extinguishers and hoses.

Actual use of an item is worth a thousand words. The use of a fire extinguisher to put out a fire does four things: (1) It allows the employees to gain confidence in the extinguishing agent and their ability to use the extinguisher. (2) It removes doubt about the ability of the unit to do the job. (3) It allows the employees to become familiar with the noises and the characteristics of the unit, such as the hissing or pressure of the expelling fluid or powder. (4) Finally, the information and confidence gained by the employees in actually operating the unit are much more impressive then merely reading instructions on the unit's use.

Provide all employees with instructions on how to work daily on a fire-loss-prevention approach to their respective jobs. I am reminded of the old Indian who told the missionary, "Indian not need one day a week as worship day, every day is his worship day." The same principle holds true for a fire prevention program. Don't wait for Fire Prevention Week to do something impressive; do something less impressive but meaningful every day of the week. This should include shutting down continuously running equipment and safeguarding records, papers, and files.

Educate persons as to the importance of maintaining clear aisles and corridors. Prevent overcrowding of all items. Don't block passageways or doors. Review emergency evacuation procedures with all employees. Always allow room for easy access of emergency fire-fighting equipment and personnel to your facility.

Continually review and update emergency procedures.

Make certain that emergency procedures are posted in easily accessible locations.

Hold practice sessions and drills on a regular basis.

CONCLUSION

Sometimes we, who are fortunate enough to be affiliated with arts facilities, need every once in a while to step back and admire that which we many times take for granted in a work-a-day approach to our jobs.

Every afternoon, when possible, I push away from the desk and take a stroll through our nine floors of collections. The public has left for the day. Many of the period rooms are lighted only with the last rays of the afternoon sun. The silence is so complete I can hear the floors creaking back into their resting position. Somewhere down the hall a grandfather clock chimes 5 P.M.

With the thought of how fortunate I am to be associated with these beautiful, irreplaceable artifacts, I also have a sobering thought. How unfortunate I am to have the responsibility of protecting these one-of-a-kind items from fire.

No matter how many times I experience these two lines of thought, I always arrive at one conclusion, "fire fighting" is not the answer. The most experienced, the best trained, the most sincere fire-fighting group in existence cannot entirely stop these treasures from being damaged or destroyed.

We must do everything that is humanly, electronically, and mechanically possible to eliminate the need to employ a fire-fighting activity with our collections: *Zero Fire Hazards*.

Appendix 10.1

Fire Training Program

The following is the reproduction of an actual training program dated August 10, 1981. By reviewing the format, you can see how we preplan a drill. In addition it may suggest some points you could utilize in establishing your own activity.

WINTERTHUR FIRE DEPT. FIRE TRAINING

Simulated Fire Situation, Museum, 4th Floor, Fraktur Room.

TIME: 1:30 P.M.

OBJECT: Confine fire to the Fraktur Room, prevent horizontal and vertical extension.

CONFINING HORIZONTAL EXTENSION: After stretching hose lines for service, using ceiling hooks, open up ceilings in Dunlap Room and adjacent hall. This would expose fire traveling horizontally.

CONFINING VERTICAL EXTENSION: Stretch hose lines to 5th floor floor Marlboro Room (above the fire), feel walls for extreme heat. Open necessary walls (partitions), extinguish any fire extending upward in partitions. Be prepared to open up roof to draw fire up and out, confining it to this wing.

WATER SUPPLY: Interior   #1.   Standpipe, Pine Hall, 4th floor.
                                       #2.   Standpipe, Latemeria Room, 4th floor.
                                       #3.   Standpipe, Montmorenci Hallway, 5th floor.
                Exterior   #1.   Hydrant, Hillside, West of Fraktur Rm.
                                       #2.   Hydrant, Walkway, N.E. of Conservatory.
                                       #3.   Hydrant, So. side of Port Royal Circle.
                                       #4.   Hydrant, Stairs West of Reflecting Pool.

HOSE LINE ACCESS FROM EXTERIOR:
1.   Exterior door to Fraktur Rm. S.W. corner of Wing.
2.   Exterior stairway down into flower room, then to Pine Hall.
3.   Phyfe Entrance, down steps to Pine Hall.
4.   Port Royal Entrance.
5.   Vauxhall Entrance.

Transmissions

1. Simulated Fire Situation, Museum, 4th Floor Fraktur Room. Active Pagers, Museum Fire personnel, activate Standpipe, Pine Hall, lead to fire in Fraktur Rm. Sound Siren, review and simulate fire alarm procedure by Reception desk.
2. Mini Pumper . . . Come in, road to Conservatory, lead off from hydrant on hill. (Place 2½" siamese to opposite opening of hydrant, stretch two 1½" lines for service to exterior door to Fraktur Room.)
3. Engineer Cahall, man the Pump House.
4. Pumper . . . To Garden Lane, down hill to area of Conservatory, stretch 1½" line down steps into Flower Room, then to Pine Hall, etc. Stretch a backup line to hydrant #2 by walkway. Place 2½" Siamese to opposite opening of hydrant.
5. Aerial . . . Respond to area of Conservatory using Pumpers route. Raise bucket, for ventilation, be prepared to open up the roof. Place portable ladders for service.
6. Object Removal: Bring two lengths of 1½" hose line from Brigade Locker with spanner, Stretch hose from Standpipe, Latemeria Rm., 4th floor to fire area. Commence sealing off room openings.
7. Place Air Paks into service. Bring ceiling hooks to fire area, open ceilings, prevent horizontal spread of fire.
8. FIRE-POLICE: Assist with evacuation of the Building. Unlock and stand by access points for outside fire units. Port Royal Entrance, Conservatory Entrance, Phyfe Entrance, Vauxhall Entrance. Station a man to direct outside fire units, Museum Road, East and West of the Museum.
9. MECHANICAL MAINTENANCE: Bring Air Paks and Exhaust fans to fire floor from Brigade locker. Simulate Power shutdown in fire wing. Respond with chair stretcher to Kershner Hall, remove injured Object Removal member to Port Royal Circle. (Ambulance)
10. Stretch 2½" water lines to Aerial truck, place master stream into service.
11. OUTSIDE FIRE UNITS RESPONDING:
    First Engine and Ladder Co. . . . Water from Hydrant #1 (Mini Pumpers hydrant). Stretch 1½" hose line into Conservatory, then to 5th floor Marlboro Rm. (Above Fire. Check partitions for vertical extension. Ladder Co. main ladder to the roof.)
    Second Engine Co. . . . Water from Hydrant #2 (Winterthur Pumpers hydrant). Stretch 1½" hose line into Phyfe Entrance, down stairs into Pine Hall to fire.
    Third Engine Co. . . . Water from Hydrant #3 (South side of Port Royal Circle). Stretch 2½" water line into Port Royal Entrance, lead North (left) to fire.
    Fourth Engine Co. . . . Water from Hydrant #4 (Steps above Reflecting Pool). Stretch 2½" water line into Vauxhall Entrance. Ambulance to Port Royal Circle.
12. Fire under Control. . . . Begin overhauling and removal of debris to the outside.
13. Secure the Fire Pump House.

11. Museum Disaster Planning

John E. Hunter

AUTHOR'S PREFACE

The purpose of this chapter is (1) to acquaint persons working in museums with the fundamental principles of emergency planning and disaster preparedness and (2) to provide references to publications and organizations that can be of help in preparing emergency and disaster plans for a museum. It must be noted here that the guidance presented in this chapter can be equally useful to persons who are responsible for emergency planning in archives and libraries.

While there are a number of excellent books and journal articles in print on the subject of disaster preparedness and planning, very few of them were written specifically for museum use. I hope that this chapter will fill this gap. I also hope that its readers will let me know how well it has served their needs and will suggest any corrections or improvements that it may need.

TERMS AND DEFINITIONS

In order for us to deal intelligently with the subjects of planning for emergencies and preparing for disasters, we need to become familiar with some basic terms and principles.

The following chapter is considered a U.S. Government work, and no copyright for this information is asserted by the author or this publication. Published with permission of the National Park Service, United States Department of the Interior.

The first term needing definition is *emergency*. According to Webster's Third New International Dictionary, an emergency is "an unforeseen combination of circumstances or the resulting state that calls for immediate action." In this definition, the important words are *unforeseen* and *immediate*.

The dictionary definition of *planning* is "to devise or project the realization or achievement" of something. Planning is also a process of imagining and evaluating possible futures. The steps involved in this process are the identification of problems, the definition of goals, the gathering of relevent information, the design of strategies for solving problems and achieving goals, and the assessment of those strategies. These steps are all directed toward one end: to provide a rational basis for determining the best future or the best solution to a given problem.

The dictionary defines *disaster* as "a sudden or great misfortune" and goes on to say that it carries an implication of "unforeseen mischance bringing with it destruction of life or property or utter defeat." Other definitions have been used by various authors; among them are:

- A disaster is any unnatural event that is likely to cause significant disruption of one's operation for a given period of time.
- A disaster is an event that occurs unexpectedly and results in serious destruction.
- A disaster situation exists anytime your normal resources of personnel and equipment are unable or insufficient to cope with the emergency at hand.

From these definitions, a workable definition of *disaster* can be created: A disaster is an emergency event that occurs with little or no warning and that causes more destruction or disruption of operations than the museum can correct by application of its own resources.

According to this definition, disasters are a class of emergencies: not all emergencies become disasters but all disasters are emergencies that have gotten out of hand.

It must be understood that whether or not a given emergency event is considered to be a disaster depends to some extent upon the circumstances of its occurrence. The difference between a disaster and a serious emergency can be determined by such factors as the number of casualties, the extent of property damage, the length of time the destructive forces are at work, the capacity of available resources to cope with the event, and the psychological effect of the event on its victims. A flood in a museum storeroom could be a disaster, but a flood in a museum classroom or restaurant might not be. The loss by fire of an exhibit such as "The Treasures of Tutankhamun" would be more disastrous than the loss of a Smithsonian SITES exhibit containing nothing but replaceable photographs. The total loss by tornado of a small town's only history museum might well be considered more disastrous by that community than the total loss of a large art museum in a city 3,000 miles away.

The last term that needs to be defined is *preparedness*. The dictionary defines it as "the quality or state of being prepared." It then defines *prepared* as "made ready, fit, or suitable beforehand."

These definitions can be combined and adapted to our purposes to create working definitions for *emergency planning* and *disaster preparedness:*

- Emergency planning is the process of identifying those events that might occur unexpectedly and cause injury or property damage in the museum and of designing and assessing strategies for immediately coping with such events as they occur.
- Disaster preparedness is being prepared for and able to cope with unexpected and seriously destructive emergencies that can occur in the museum and that cannot be contained solely with the museum's own resources.

Having adopted these definitions,[1] we will be concerned primarily with those events that occur with little or no warning and that require immediate concerted response by the museum staff in order to avert or minimize potential damage. Excluded, therefore, will be such recurring or chronic problems as insufficient staffs or budgets, inadequate storage space, and poor environmental control. Also excluded will be such problems as burglary, robbery, employee theft, most kinds of vandalism, and pilferage from exhibits. While such events may require some kind of immediate response, the response would not necessarily be by the museum staff and normally would not require the entire resources of the museum to be effective. Such events seldom assume the proportions of true disasters, serious though they may be.

TYPES OF MUSEUM DISASTERS

The most common and often the most devastating disasters are those caused by Nature. Tornadoes, hurricanes, and floods are chief among the natural causes of severe and extensive damage. Tornadoes destroy through the action of high winds; their damage often is compounded by accompanying torrential rains. Hurricanes also destroy through wind action and are almost always accompanied by tidal waves and widespread coastal flooding; they also can cause river flooding far inland.

Floods can occur because of heavy rains, such as those associated with hurricanes, or because of broken dams or rapidly melting snow. Slow rising floods may cause more of their damage to building contents; however, rapidly rising or rampaging floods can completely destroy buildings as well.

Damage from the water itself can be compounded when the flood deposits mud, wastes, chemicals, and liquid fuels in the museum.

Less common natural causes of severe damage to museums include heavy snows, ice storms, earthquakes, and volcanic eruptions. Generally, ice storms and heavy snows affect museums indirectly by bringing down power lines and blocking access by the staff. However, given enough buildup, snow can collapse roofs. In addition, the snow or ice on the collapsed roof can melt and cause water damage inside the building.

The damage to museums from downed utilities and blocked roads usually is minimal and of brief duration. But, a prolonged loss of power or fuel for humidity and temperature control can result in damage to some kinds of artifacts and can even cause irreparable structural damage. Problems of this nature were experienced in several northeastern and New England states in the winter of 1976-1977.

An earthquake probably will cause minimal damage to a museum if the building is well constructed to withstand seismic shock. Tremors, however, may knock objects and books off shelves and cause objects in exhibits to fall over; glass may break, plaster may crack, and pictures may fall off walls. On the other hand, if the building is not designed or remodeled to be earthquake resistant, a severe earthquake could cause its total collapse and destruction of its contents. In many instances on record, much of the damage from earthquakes has been of secondary origin. Such damage can include fires set off by broken gas mains, damage from broken water and sewer mains, and flooding due to collapsed dams.

Volcanoes have the potential for causing total destruction. I have found no record of a museum having been destroyed by a volcano, although it is likely that some have been damaged by the earthquakes that often accompany violent eruptions. Unless the museum is on the flanks of the volcano, the danger to it from lava should be minimal because lava flows slowly enough to permit evacuation of the collections. Of course, clouds of pumice and ash could turn a museum into a instant Pompeii and cause nightmarish problems for curators and conservators attempting to keep the ash off of objects. The experiences of museums in the Northwest following the eruptions of Mount St. Helens in May 1980 are adequate testimony to these kinds of problems.

These then are the major types of natural events that can cause disasters. I doubt that any museum is vulnerable to all of them. But every museum is vulnerable, to one extent or another, to some of these events. You know best which ones you need to be prepared for. You also recognize others that I have not mentioned, events peculiar to your particular location.

The remaining emergency events that can turn into disasters for museums are ultimately man-made in origin. The most common of these nonnatural or technological causes of disasters are fires, bombings and other explosions, structural collapse, accidents involving hazardous chemicals or radioactive materials, utility failure, warfare, and civil disorder.

Fire probably is the single most devastating disaster that can strike a museum; and fire probably is the one disaster most likely to strike any museum. There are no hurricanes in Utah, no ice storms in Hawaii, no volcanoes in Georgia; but fire can strike anywhere, anytime. No museum is immune. The effects of a major structural fire are doubly devastating: what the fire does not burn, water may damage or destroy. If your museum happens to be in a wooded area, you may also have to be concerned with forest fires in addition to fire originating within the building.

Explosions caused by faulty heating equipment, accidents to fuel lines, carelessly handled gas bottles, and bombs may actually cause little direct damage. The damage may be confined to just one room. All too often, however, the explosion leads to fire, resulting in two destructive forces to contend with, the fire being the more serious. Explosions caused by accidents and faulty equipment usually occur without warning. Bombings, on the other hand, may be preceded by a warning, giving you a chance to act to minimize potential damage and injury.

Structural collapse may be due to faulty construction or an accident, such as a runaway truck or a plane crash, or may be a result of a natural event, such as an earthquake. As with collapse due to natural events, the extent of damage can vary widely and secondary problems, such as fires and broken water lines, can occur.

Among the hazards of modern technology are those associated with transporting, processing, storing, and using hazardous and radioactive materials. Spills, fires, or explosions occurring from overturned tank trucks or derailed tank cars constantly threaten facilities near major highways and railroads. Entire communities have had to be evacuated because of accidents to shipments of hazardous materials such as ammonia, chlorine, gasoline, nitric acid, and radioisotopes. Many of the substances that are hazardous to life are also highly corrosive and potentially damaging to museum collections. Nuclear power plants and nuclear weapons on military bases constitute potential threats to nearby museums: a serious accident could either obliterate a museum or render the community uninhabitable for generations. The same problem also exists in respect to agents of chemical and biological warfare stockpiled at some military bases.

Earlier I referred to damage to utilities from bad weather. A museum's gas and electricity can be cut off by accidents and human error just as easily. Burst water mains or back-up sewer lines can flood a museum just as thoroughly and just as devastatingly as can a nearby river. Even a sprinkler system, installed to protect against fire, can malfunction and cause water damage. Such malfunctions are rare, however, in systems that are properly installed and maintained.

Warfare can be conventional, involving chemical explosives and localized actions of air and ground troops, or nonconventional, involving thermonuclear bombs with resulting large-scale destruction and fallout. The potential for wartime damage to museums ranges from zero to total, depending upon location. The Geneva (1949) and Hague (1954) Conventions afford some degree of protection for museums and other cultural institutions against bombing, shelling, looting, and vandalism by enemy troops. Under the terms of these conventions, however, cultural properties located near strategic targets will not necessarily be spared. Should a conventional war be fought in the United States, museums are most likely to be severely affected by losses of personnel, utilities, and essential services than by direct physical damage to the museum facility. On the other hand, it is almost impossible to predict the effects of a nuclear war on this country's museums. Certainly, some museums would be vaporized and many would cease to operate for an extended time because of heavy damage. Very few would come through completely unscathed. And most, if not all, would be in the path of radioactive fallout.

As is the case with natural disasters, your museum may not be vulnerable to all of the various man-made disasters. In all probability, you have recognized that some of these disasters, such as fire, explosion, and accident, are more likely to happen than some of the natural events we examined earlier. The extent to which your museum might suffer from a disaster of technological origin depends upon many factors; among them are: the quality of your maintenance program; the quality of your fire prevention program and of the local fire department; the construction of your building and the nature of the utilities and equipment supporting it; and the proximity of the museum to other buildings and activities and to such facilities as rail yards, ship yards, and highways. Again, you will know best which types of emergencies threaten your museum.

RATIONALE FOR PLANNING AND PREPAREDNESS

As we have seen, some types of emergencies, such as floods and hurricanes, are somewhat predictable. The destructive forces of such disasters cannot be avoided. But it is possible to take advantage of the warning time to minimize damage from the initial impact. We also have seen that some types of emergencies, such as explosions and earthquakes, are not predictable. When these events occur, it may be impossible to avoid or minimize the initial impact. By placing an emergency plan immediately into operation, however, it may be possible to avoid additional costly or fatal damage and to prevent a disaster from turning into a tragedy.[2]

In her very useful booklet *Disaster Prevention and Disaster Preparedness,* Hilda Bohem of the University of California Library System quotes someone as having said, "A disaster is what happens only if you are not prepared for it." At first glance, this sounds rather like a folk remedy: washing your car to make sure it rains, or, conversely, carrying an umbrella to make sure it does not. But, on closer consideration, this description of a disaster says a great deal more. Because, if a disaster strikes and you are prepared for it, its impact will be a great deal less disastrous.[3] Good planning can prevent an emergency from turning into a disaster and a disaster from turning into a tragedy.

Keeping an emergency from developing into a disaster often depends upon three factors. First, how well you have planned for meeting all possible emergencies. Second, how well you and your staff react when an emergency occurs. And third, how much you and your staff learn from your experiences during actual emergencies and how well you apply that learning to preparing for the future.

According to the security and disaster planning expert Richard J. Healy, the primary goal of emergency preparedness is avoiding the loss of one's resources. Advanced planning is the key to achieving this goal. Calm deliberation during the planning process will result in speeding decisions and actions during an emergency so that effective response will be ensured even in the face of disaster. How effective you are in keeping a disaster from developing will depend upon how well you have planned in advance.[4]

When disaster strikes, confusion can be expected, communication links will be disrupted, and chaos will reign. With a disaster control plan, those responsible for the museum during the emergency can focus on solving major problems rather than having to bring order out of chaos due to a lack of prior planning. If all predictable and routine concerns are covered by the plan, those in charge of the museum will be able to deal with the unpredictable or unusual situations that always develop.[5]

Developing an emergency plan may appear to be a very difficult task. Since one has to consider the many peacetime disasters that may occur as well as the possibility and consequences of enemy attack, developing a good plan may seem almost impossible. As Healy puts it, "The futility of attempting to make a plan to cope with enemy attack with modern weapons may tend to obscure the objective to such an extent that the entire effort may seem hopeless." Nevertheless, it must be kept in mind that the museum can be destroyed or badly damaged by a variety of disasters not involving enemy action. Any of these peacetime disasters could happen at any time and all of them are far more likely to happen than is an enemy attack. Or at least, let us hope so. Consequently, as Healy suggests, one method that can be used to make the task of preparing a plan less daunting is "to initially disregard enemy attack completely and concentrate only on planning to cope with the more immediate problems — peacetime disasters."[6]

THE EMERGENCY PLANNING PROCESS

Following Healy's suggestion, museum emergency planning should be done in two phases. In Phase I you would plan for all of the natural and industrial disasters that we examined earlier. When this work has been completed, Phase II would be concerned with the more complex problems arising out of enemy attack. Unless the Cold War escalates and the threat of nuclear attack becomes more imminent than it is at present, you might even consider beginning the implementation of Phase I plans before proceeding with Phase II planning.

A comprehensive emergency plan for a major museum may take a year or more to implement entirely. It should be noted that a plan can be designed and written in a relatively short time. It is the effective implementation of the plan that will take time. Therefore, Healy suggests that you establish realistic dates for completion of each part of the plan and use milestone charts to control the progess of its implementation.[7]

There are ten steps in developing and implementing an emergency and disaster control plan for a museum. These steps are outlined in the following paragraphs.

Step 1. Designation of a Disaster Organization

The first step in the planning process should be the appointment of a senior member of the musuem staff to be responsible for preparing the plan and to serve as Emergency Services Officer in the event of an emergency. The individual should be selected by the museum's director and should be capable of dealing effectively with management and employees at all levels. Normally, the Emergency Services Officer (or ESO) should not be the museum director; the director will have enough to do during an emergency without having to assume the task of coordinating reaction and recovery plans. In a large institution, the security director or perhaps the building manager would be a logical choice for ESO. Of course, in a museum with a small staff, there may be no one other than the director to assume the responsibilities of ESO. The appointment of the ESO should be made in writing and his responsibilities and authority should be defined clearly and fully. The director and the board of trustees must be willing to give full support to the ESO and to his development of an emergency and disaster control plan.

The ESO should be delegated full responsibility and authority for developing the museum's plan and for implementing a disaster control program. He or she will coordinate all actions carried out under the plan during an emergency and will draft any policies and administrative directives that may be issued by the director to properly establish the program.

In all but the smallest museums, a committee should be appointed to advise and assist the ESO in developing and implementing the plan. In large institutions, the committee might logically consist of department heads or their assistants, someone from the director's administrative staff, and perhaps someone from the board of trustees, if someone on the board has had experience with planning in his own business or industry. This committee eventually will become the museum's disaster organization and its members will be the persons in charge of disaster mitigation and recovery efforts. In small museums, it is quite possible that the entire staff will constitute the committee and, subsequently, the disaster organization.

The museum should not develop a new organizational structure just to handle emergency and disaster situations. The existing administrative and supervisory structure and the personnel responsible for day-to-day operations should also handle emergency problems. The existing chain of command will be well known to the entire staff and will be less subject to breakdown during an emergency than will an *ad hoc* structure.

Step 2. Liaison with Local Protection Agencies

The second step in the planning process requires that the ESO contact local public protection agencies and the local civil defense organization. These agencies and organizations can provide valuable assistance and technical advice in the development of an emergency plan. Through such contacts, the ESO can also determine what plans have already been developed by local officials for dealing with emergencies and disasters. It is crucial that such plans be known to the museum so that it does not count on using outside resources that may be committed to higher priority disaster operations elsewhere. Likewise, it is important that the police and fire departments, the civil defense organization, and other public protection organizations know of the plans the museum is making so they can coordinate efforts to support the museum appropriately in time of disaster. It would be a good idea to also establish contact with other local museums with the idea of setting up mutual aid agreements.

Step 3. Vulnerability Assessment

The third planning step is to identify the emergency and disaster situations that can occur in the museum. Earlier we looked at a variety of natural and man-made events that can impact on communities and their museums. This third step involves determining which of these events are possible and therefore have to be planned for. But it is not sufficient simply to identify each potential threat. Most museums have only limited resources that can be applied to the protection or recovery of their assets. It is essential that these resources be applied wisely. Therefore, it is necessary to determine the probability or likelihood of each disaster event actually occurring as well as its criticality, that is, the impact or effect upon the museum's assets if the event does occur. These determinations become the act of vulnerability assessment and result in an indication of which disaster events need to be planned for first.

There are sophisticated formulas for determining the probability of an event occurring. For our purposes, these formulas are of little value. Instead, we shall employ a more basic, but equally useful concept: The more ways a particular event *can* occur in given circumstances, the greater the probability that it *will* occur.

In determining loss event probability, it will immediately be apparent that some potential events cannot occur or cannot impact upon the museum. For example, if the museum is in the desert Southwest, there is little point in being concerned about the possibility of a hurricane. On the other hand, this same museum might be at considerable risk from flash floods or water supply failure. Once the impossible loss events have been eliminated, all remaining threats are at least possible to some extent and their probabilities must be determined.

Richard J. Healy and Timothy J. Walsh, in their book *Industrial Security Management,*[8] suggest determining an institution's vulnerability by applying a grading system that places each possible loss event on a scale according to how probable it is to occur and how critical it would be if it did occur. Each possible loss event is given a probability rating of A to E. Assignment of a rating is made without consideration of any precautions or countermeasures that later may be taken to reduce or eliminate the threat. The loss event probability rating scale is shown here:

A.	Virtually certain	Given no changes, the event will eventually occur
B.	Highly probable	The likelihood of occurrence is much greater than that of nonoccurrence.
C.	Moderately probable	The event is more likely to occur than not to occur (between probabilities of 0.333 and 0.749)
D.	Improbable	The event is more likely not to occur than to occur but is still possible.
E.	Probability unknown	Insufficient data are available for an evaluation to be made.

In assigning these probability ratings, the past loss history of the museum will have to be acknowledged. But other factors will also influence the ratings. For example, recent flood control work may have lessened the chance of flooding in a community with a history of floods. Or the local civil defense organization may have instituted better tornado warning procedures. On the other hand, there may be additional industry or heavier truck traffic in the vicinity of the museum or there may be heavier air traffic overhead. Thus, looking only at the past loss history will not be enough.

Assignment of ratings will be, to some extent, subjective. It is not essential to achieve exact precision. But it is vitally important to be able to distinguish all threats of virtually certain probability from all others. To compensate for inexactness and subjectivity, the higher of two possible ratings should be assigned when in doubt. Moreover, a rating of Probability Unknown must be changed to one of the other four ratings before assigning priorities for protective measures.

Once loss event probability ratings have been assigned, you next assign ratings for loss event criticality. Highly probable threats may not require much in the way of preventive or counteractive measures if the net loss or damage they would produce is small. Likewise, moderately probable or improbable threats might command greater attention if the impact of the loss would be great. Thus, while it should be considered highly probable that a museum in a northern climate will be in an ice storm some day, the potential effects from the storm might be so slight as to be ignored. On the other hand, it may be that a structural fire in the same museum is only moderately probable or improbable; but the impact of the building's loss would be so great — so critical — that it deserves the application of full protective measures. Therefore, the criticality rating of each possible event must be determined.

The loss event criticality rating scale below is based on that suggested by Healy and Walsh.

1.	Fatal to business	A loss would result in the abandonment or long-term discontinuance of the museum
2.	Very serious	A loss would be a subject for deliberation by management as to whether or not to continue the museum's operation
3.	Moderately serious	A loss would have noticeable impact upon the museum and would require attention from senior management and the governing authority.
4.	Relatively unimportant	A loss would be covered by normal contingency planning within the museum's own resources

5.   No real effect   The impact of the loss would be so
                               minimal that it would have no adverse
                               effect; the loss would be absorbed

When all acknowledged threats have been given a probability rating and a
criticality rating, they must be arranged in priority according to these ratings.
In assigning priorities, criticality is weighted heavier than probability. The
fatally critical threats are ranked higher in priority than all others regardless
of their respective probabilities. When several threats have the same probability of occurrence, rank them according to their respective criticality ratings.
It is permissible, when desired, to rank two or more threats alike. When you
have completed the listing of all threats in priority, you will know which
disaster events to plan for first. You also will know where first to apply the
museum's resources of manpower and funds. Without conducting an analysis
of this type, you might eventually discover that a disproportionate amount
of time has been spent preparing for dangers that probably will not occur
or that would have little overall impact on the museum if they did occur.[9]

(A detailed explanation of the above-mentioned ranking system can be
found in another work by Walsh and Healy. It is their *Protection of Assets
Manual,* which is published by the Merritt Company, Santa Monica, California. The system is explained in Chapter 10 of that publication. See the
notes to this chapter for a fuller citation.)

Step 4.   Identification of Assets and Assignment of Priorities

The fourth step in the emergency preparedness process is a survey of the
museum to identify what assets will require protection in case of a disaster.
The survey should be made by the persons on the staff most familiar with
the assets to be evaluated: the curatorial staff will evaluate the collections;
the registrar will evaluate collection records; the conservator and the exhibits
preparator will evaluate their laboratory and shop equipment; the building
manager will evaluate the building, its equipment, and its fixtures; and so
forth. These evaluations will result in a listing of all the museum's assets
in priority according to how important they are to the museum and its
operation. Do not forget people: people will always be considered the most
important asset. The protection of the museum's staff and visitors always
must come first in any of your planning.

If yours is a large museum it probably will not be practical to give critical evaluation to each individual object in the collection, except perhaps
for paintings, sculpture, furniture, and certain groups of archival materials.
Instead, each subcollection or group of objects should be evaluated as a
unit. Most archival collections and objects historically associated with indi-

viduals are best evaulated this way. In a small collection, it may be possible to evaluate each object individually.

Evaluation of the museum's collection will result in each object being assigned to one of three priority groups according to its value and irreplaceability. The priority groups could be as follows:

Priority 1   Objects of such importance that they must be protected at all costs

Priority 2   Objects of great importance, the loss of which would be serious but not catastrophic; such objects ususally are those that are replaceable, though perhaps at great cost

Priority 3   Objects of relatively little importance, the loss of which would not create a major problem; such objects usually are easily or inexpensively replaced if they have to be

As I just noted, objects will be assigned to one of these three (or perhaps more) groups on the dual bases of irreplaceability and value. The specific criteria used in the evaluations will depend upon the nature of the collection being evaluated. Original works of art, historic buildings, manuscripts, scientific specimens, and ethnographic and archeological artifacts are usually, by their nature, unique and therefore irreplaceable. Books and periodicals and manufactured objects, especially those of the last hundred years, can more often than not be replaced, though at a cost.

In determining irreplaceability, the cost and practical difficulty of the museum's replacing a given object should be considered, as well as the theoretical possibility of its replacement based on the existence of other known copies. Such works of art as posters, prints, lithographs, and bronzes of which there may be several extant copies ordinarily will not have the same degree of irreplaceability as original paintings and other unique objects. Taxidermic specimens and other items created expressly for exhibits likewise can be replaced and should be given relatively low priorities.

The practical difficulties of replacing books will, of course, depend upon the existence of other copies, their cost, and perhaps the existence of the information they contain in some other form, such as microfilm. The irreplaceability of manuscripts and archival materials will depend upon the existence of microfilm, photocopies, or completely edited printed copies elsewhere. An historic building may be considered replaceable to some extent if detailed drawings and photographs of it exist to permit its accurate repair or reconstruction. Naturally, microfilm, photocopies, drawings, and photographs must exist somewhere besides in the museum in order for them to be considered safe and, therefore, available for copying or acquisition following the loss of the museum's originals.

The possibility of having to replace an entire collection also must be considered, for the value of a collection often depends upon its completeness. This is particularly true for systematic natural history collections. Moreover, the value of an object within a collection often is enhanced by its association with related objects.

The criteria for determining the value of museum objects are even less precise than those for determining irreplaceability. Among the considerations that will affect the relative values assigned to different objects or collections are the following:[10]

1. Intrinsic or sentimental value attributed to the object itself. Examples of objects with high intrinsic value include the Declaration of Independence and the Constitution; they are considered priceless, even though the materials of which they are made have almost no value and the texts of both documents can be found in innumerable copies.

2. Aesthetic value. Examples of objects with high aesthetic value include such works as the *Mona Lisa,* the *Pietà,* and many other works of art as well as historic buildings preserved because of their appearance.

3. Legal and administrative value. Few museum objects will have any legal or administrative value, except perhaps for certain type specimens in natural history collections. But, the museum's catalog and accession records, conservation reports, photograph files, and administrative files will have such values and must be protected on an equal basis with the collections themselves.

4. Research value. This will be a basic consideration in evaluating library materials, manuscript collections and archives, and museum specimens collected specifically to support research. Not to be overlooked are the potential research values of current museum administrative records. Also consider the importance of general and specialized library card catalogs and bibliographical files.

5. Monetary value. Considerations of monetary value may be less important to historical collections but undoubtedly will be of major concern to art museums. To some extent, monetary value is considered when making all of the other types of evaluation. It has a particularly important bearing, however, on the practicality of replacing objects that may be damaged or destroyed and, therefore, must be considered in the relative evaluation of the various assets of the museum.

In general, Priority Group 1 will contain relatively few objects. It is these objects that will receive the maximum possible protection. Priority Group 2 will be somewhat larger. The objects in this group will receive special protection within the limits of available personnel, facilities, reasonable expense, and time. Priority Group 3 will contain the bulk of the collection. Objects in this group will receive only the protection afforded by the museum building, at least initially. Only after objects in the first two groups have been protected appropriately will any further resources be devoted to protection of objects in the third group.

In setting your priorities for protection of the museum building, fixtures, and operating equipment, a similar ranking process can be used. Normally, monetary value and ease of replacement will be the primary determining factors, although the length of time the museum can be without a given asset until it is replaced or repaired also should be considered.

Step 5. Formulation of Protection Methods

After you have selected those objects or collections that are to be given special protection in event of a disaster and have determined their relative priorities for receiving protection, the fifth step in the preparedness process is to decide upon the particular methods to be used in their protection. This decision will have to be based on six factors.[11]

1. The degree of danger to which the objects would be exposed in a disaster.
2. The extent of protection currently afforded the objects by the museum building and by their exhibit and storage cases.
3. The physical characteristics of the objects; that is, what they are made of and how fragile or sturdy they may be.
4. How the objects are being used; that is, whether they are on exhibit, in storage, being conserved, being used for demonstrations, etc.
5. The values assigned to the objects in Step 4.
6. The funds and personnel available for providing protection.

There are many different ways to protect museums and their contents in the face of disaster. It is not possible to examine all of them in the scope of this chapter. Therefore, only the five principal protective methods will be considered here. You may refer to the works listed in the notes for further details and explanations of other protective methods. The book cited as note 10 will be the most useful.

The first protective method is protection and reinforcement of the museum building in advance of the disaster. This is the most basic protective method and one that should always be considered in all museums except perhaps those occupying historic buildings which cannot be modified. Reinforcement can be permanent or temporary. Protecting the building not only minimizes the chances of damage to the museum collection but also will reduce the damage to the building itself. This method of protection is the most appropriate one when earthquakes are being planned for.

The second method is protection in place of museum collections and other assets. This method is applicable to objects too heavy or too fragile to be moved, objects that can be replaced if protection in place fails, objects not easily damaged, and equipment and records that must remain in use during the emergency. Protection in place entails some degree of risk; it cannot ensure complete safety of the museum's assets in the face of some types of disasters, such as earthquakes, hurricanes, tornadoes, and floods. However, this method does have the advantage of relatively low cost and is the method that can be executed most quickly.

The techniques used to protect property in place will vary considerably according to the nature of the threat and the nature of the property. Some examples are:

1. Covering glass exhibit cases with quilts to minimize the potential for broken glass or taping the glass of cases and framed works to hold the glass in place if it is cracked.
2. Rearranging objects on storage shelves so that large, heavy objects are on the lowest shelves where they cannot fall and damage objects below.
3. Packing books tightly together on shelves to prevent them from falling off due to shock.
4. Elevating objects off the floor, especially in basements, if floods are expected or if water is being used to fight a fire.

The third protective method is relocation of collections, records, and other assets to safer storage within the museum building. This method is applicable to fragile objects that cannot be protected in place with confidence or evacuated. It is also applicable when the museum has a vault or other secure area that can accommodate (at least temporarily) those parts of the collection requiring protection.

The fourth protective method provides for evacuation of collections, records, and other assets from the museum into a building in some location that is not exposed to danger. This often is the best method of protection and, if the museum has been badly damaged, may be the only method that can be used. Evacuation, however, does require more preplanning and labor and may require construction of crates, locating of vehicles for transportation, and hiring of drivers for the vehicles. Movement of collections outside the museum exposes them to additional dangers from environmental changes, theft, and damage in transit. And it is essential that the temporary repository be secure, free from agents of deterioration, and climate-controlled. Evacuation becomes more practical when the distance between museum and the repository is short and the move can be accomplished quickly, easily, and inexpensively.

If you contemplate using evacuation as a method of protection, it is essential that evacuation plans be worked out as thoroughly as possible in advance. An inadequately or hurriedly planned evacuation could be as dangerous to the collections being moved as the disaster that called for the evacuation. Evacuation plans should include the following six elements:

1. Legal clearances and authorizations, such as contracts with moving van companies and storage warehouses, authorizations from persons owning objects on loan to the museum, and agreements with your insurance carriers that collections will remain protected when off the museum premises.
2. All objects to be evacuated must be identified in advance and lists of those objects must be kept up to date to permit quick preparation of packing lists and to ensure that all objects are evacuated that should be.
3. The repository to house the collections must be selected in advance and made ready for use. If you plan to use a commercial warehouse, you must have assurances that it will have all the space you may require and be capable of suitable climate control and security. If the museum will be using a building under its control, it must be staffed adequately once it is placed in use.
4. Packing methods must be determined in advance and packing supplies and materials stockpiled for use. If the probability for ever having to evacuate your collection is high, you might want to consider building shipping containers for your Priority 1 objects and keep them on hand in the museum. Containers for Priority 2 objects can be constructed but stored off-site and brought in if they are ever needed. Containers for other objects can be designed and the materials stockpiled for their construction; however, the containers would not be constructed until they are needed. In the meantime, containers for objects in Priority Groups 1 and 2 could be used whenever the objects go out on loan.
5. Advance arrangements must be made for transportation. The mode of transportation to be used will depend upon the value and condition of the objects to be moved, the distance to be covered, and costs. The manner of packing will be determined to some extent by the mode of transportation selected. Therefore, the choice of transportation must be made at an early date.
6. Provisions must be made for inspecting and guarding the collections in their temporary location. If the museum is operating its own repository, it might be practical to station some of its own staff there, particularly if the museum has been severely damaged and the staff would otherwise have no place to work.

The fifth protective method calls for restoration or replacement of damaged assets. It should be immediately apparent that this method is not truly a protective method because it assumes the loss of certain assets. As a practical matter, however, some museum property cannot be protected by any of the other four methods. In addition, certain classes of property may cost more to protect than to replace, such as library books, custodial and office supplies, and office furniture. Therefore, it can be appropriate to make a conscious decision to sacrifice some property, to assume its loss, and to plan for restoring, repairing, or replacing it later.

While replacement of lost or damaged property is a method most suited to operating equipment and supplies, it also may be possible to replace objects from the museum's collections. Such items as lithographs, prints, posters, and bronzes produced in multiple copies still may be available. Original and unique objects, of course, cannot be replaced, although similar ones perhaps can be substituted for them in some instances, such as with period furnishings in historic house museums.

Museums having collections of original and unique objects may want to consider large-scale programs of photographing their objects and keeping the photographs with copies of accession and catalog records in an off-site repository. If the objects are ever lost, there will at least be an accurate visual and written record of them. Naturally, photographs made for such purposes must be of the highest quality and stored under conditions that will minimize color shift and other deterioration.

Step 6. Formulation of Recovery Plans

We are now ready to consider the sixth step in preparing a museum to deal with emergencies. This step involves formulation of plans for recovering from the unavoidable effects of disaster, just as Step 5 involved formulation of plans for trying to avoid those effects.

In point of fact, few of the disaster events potentially affecting museums can actually be prevented or totally avoided. The most we can hope to accomplish by emergency planning is to minimize the loss of assets and otherwise lessen the impact of losses as they occur. Consequently, all emergency planners must recognize that some disasters will occur and that recovery from them also will have to be planned for.

If the organization of restoration and recovery efforts has been well planned in advance, recovery will be less difficult, less costly, more efficient, and probably more productive. The most critical part of a recovery plan is providing for the protection of supplies and equipment that will be needed to begin the recovery effort. Such materials are much more valuable and much harder to obtain after a disaster than they might be under normal circumstances. The supplies and equipment you may want to obtain for stockpiling in advance will be used for two primary purposes: (1) repairs to the museum building, its operating equipment, fixtures, and protection systems and (2) emergency stabilization and conservation of the collections and collection records. Stockpiled supplies and equipment must be given the same degree of protection from disaster as the collections themselves. Emergency supplies and equipment can be classified into the following groups:

- Materials for mucking out and cleaning up
- Tools and equipment for demolition, repairs, and rescue
- Construction materials
- Emergency equipment
- Materials for protection and safety of personnel
- Conservation supplies and equipment
- Miscellaneous supplies and equipment

A suggested list of supplies and equipment is included at the end of this chapter. As you look at that list, you will discover that your museum probably keeps most of the items on hand routinely. If so, it remains only for you to ensure their protection during a disaster so they will be on hand afterwards for use.

Perhaps the most important tool to secure against damage or loss is at least one copy of the museum's emergency plan, particularly the recovery portion, so that those engaged in recovery operations will know what to do. Because the plan will contain instructions for emergency stabilization of the collection and how to call for assistance, the importance of its protection cannot be overemphasized.

The recovery plan needs to contain the following four sets of instructions at a minimum:

- How to assess damage.
- How to assign priorities for recovery efforts.
- How to select recovery methods according to damage sustained.
- How to request outside assistance.

Damage assessment consists mainly of determining the answers to these three questions:

1. What has been damaged?
2. What is the extent of the damage?
3. Where is the damage located? (That is, what portions of the building and which portions of the collection?)

Those persons making the assessments must be trained to recognize the types of damage that can occur to museum collections and other property, including the physical plant itself. The recovery plan should assign responsibilities for making assessments according to the abilities of the staff and other persons who will be involved. For example, do not assign curators to look for gas leaks; that task is best left to the utility company or to the museum's maintenance personnel. Conversely, do not assign the janitors to look at wet paintings; that task is more properly assigned to curators or conservators. Among the signs of damage to look for in your collections are:

- Mold growth on organic materials.
- Rust or corrosion on metals.
- Warping and splitting wooden objects and furniture.
- Blanched varnish on furniture and paintings.
- Stains on upholstery and other textiles.
- Broken and cracked porcelain, glass, and other fragile objects.

The person responsible for developing damage assessment procedures and for carrying them out should work with conservators and building managers to come up with a checklist of potential damage that should be looked for; this checklist would become part of the recovery plan.

Generally speaking, the priorities for recovery will be the same as your priorities for protection of assets in advance of a disaster. If an object is important enough to be evacuated or relocated first, then it is important enough to receive emergency stabilization treatment first. Although your previously established priority lists will be your primary guide to setting recovery priorities, you will need to exercise some judgment when deciding what damage must be tackled first.

Your highest priority objects may receive only minor damage that does not require prompt corrective action, but lower priority objects may receive major damage. In such an instance, it would make sense to apply emergency stabilization and conservation efforts first to those objects requiring the earliest attention to forestall further deterioration. The slightly damaged objects can then await the later attentions of professional conservators.

On the other hand, you may find that high priority objects have sustained so much damage that any effort to salvage them would be futile. With this possibility in mind, you need to develop guidelines for deciding what can be saved and what cannot. The recovery staff must have an officially approved, preconceived basis for making their decisions. Charles W. Bahme, in his book *Fire Officer's Guide to Disaster Control*, likens this decision-making process to the principle of *triage*, a term applied to military and medical decision-making when casualties (usually from warfare) occur and choices must be made quickly on which persons to save and which to let die.[12]

Selection of which recovery methods to employ, based on damage sustained, is largely a function of the materials the objects are made of. During the initial assessment of priorities for protection of collections from disaster, you should note what kinds of objects are in the collections and from what materials they are made. This evaluation will enable you to determine the range of emergency stabilization and conservation methods that may have to be employed some day. If your collection contains furniture, oil paintings, watercolors, glassware, porcelain, textiles, furs, leather, books, and firearms, you will very likely have to employ a wide variety of conservation procedures to prevent or minimize deterioration after a disaster. On the other hand, if your collection consists only of paintings and prints, the range of conservation methods that might have to be employed will be somewhat limited.

There is a considerable body of literature on emergency conservation techniques, particularly in regard to water-damaged books, records, and works of art. You should review this literature and select the most appropriate recovery methods for your collection. It is imperative that you consult a conservator before deciding on which methods to prepare for. There may be some value to preparing for several different recovery methods, varying in levels of sophistication, so that those executing emergency conservation efforts can select the one deemed most appropriate under the prevailing circumstances.

After the potentially useful conservation methods have been selected, if the chances of ever needing to use them are considered to be even or higher, you should stockpile the supplies and equipment that will be needed to put those methods into effect. You cannot wait until after a flood to order Thymol from a conservation supply house or to order a dozen dehumidifiers from the manufacturer. You must keep on hand at least enough of the necessary supplies and equipment to begin the recovery effort; additional quantities can be brought in later if they are needed. Be sure to secure and protect these materials from prior use and against damage from disaster. The towels and rust-preventive lubricants you will need for drying and preserving wet firearms will be useless if they are floating around in a flooded basement or have been consumed by the museum's maintenance staff in cleaning shop tools.

How to request assistance with recovery operations is the last element of the recovery plan. Highest on your list of outside sources of assistance probably will be nearby museums. Bear in mind, however, that the effects of many disasters will be widespread and other museums in the area very likely will also have sustained damage. Therefore, if you plan to depend upon local museums, you would do well to develop alternative plans in case they are unable to help. Next on your list of possible sources of outside help might be local or regional conservation centers and conservators in private practice as well as such persons as local art and antique dealers, art-school faculty and students, and practicing artists and craftsmen.

Do not forget the museum's supporting volunteer organization; most such organizations can provide a very valuable pool of labor: persons with previous experience working in your museum. You might even be fortunate enough to have as a volunteer someone who has had experience with emergency planning or recovery, such as a retired fire chief or a military officer. If you do anticipate using volunteers, be sure they receive the same disaster recovery training that your staff receives. You should not wait until after a disaster strikes to train volunteers in what they are to do.

Step 7. Writing the Plan

After you have completed Steps 1 through 6, you are ready to commit your emergency plan to paper. There are a number of good reasons why the plan must be written. The chief reason for writing the plan is to avoid the weaknesses inherent in the "one-man show." You as museum director or Emergency Services Officer may have a good plan; but if the plan in only in your head and not on paper, it isn't going to do anyone else any good. If you drop dead of heart failure at the news that your museum was flooded during the night and you are the only person who knows what to do about it, your staff is going to be in big trouble.

Drawing from the works of other authors, we can discover more reasons for writing out the emergency plan. Several reasons for a written plan can be based on suggestions of Charles W. Bahme in his book *Fire Officer's Guide to Disaster Control.*[13] They are:

- A written plan will point out gaps in your planning.
- A written plan will define the chain of organizational command and the scope of each person's authority; it will also fix responsibility.
- A written plan may be required if the museum is part of a larger organization, such as a city, county, or university. The museum's plan would then become part of the plan for the overall organization.
- Writing the plan in full ensures that its objectives are reasonable and accurately conceived and defined.
- Writing the plan will point out needed improvements in the museum's day-to-day operations, such as the need for improved fire prevention, better organizational structure, or better means of communications within the building.
- The written plan brings together in one document all information about the museum's disaster control organization so that it can be reviewed comprehensively to determine if the organization itself will be sufficient to control disaster or to recover from it.

- Having a written plan will reduce the time required to act when disaster strikes. Without a written plan, everyone with some responsibility for action would have to sit down at a table and decide in conference who is to do what.

Looking to the work of Timothy J. Walsh and Richard J. Healy in their *Protection of Assets Manual,*[14] we can find other reasons for written plans:

- Only a written plan can serve as an assessment and inventory of the resources that will be needed to support the museum during and after the disaster. Rapid accessibility to personnel and supplies can be the key to success of your disaster plan and essential to your recovery efforts. You must record where these resources will come from.
- Writing the plan can suggest preventive measures that can either reduce the probability of a disastrous occurrence or minimize its effects.
- A written plan can be — and should be — used in training all employees, including volunteers, so that they will be prepared no matter what happens.

The written plan should be characterized by flexibility, simplicity, detail, and adaptability. The plan should be flexible to allow for changes in your staff, in the availability of outside help and recovery supplies, and in the threats to which the museum may be vulnerable. The plan should be simple enough to be easily understood and quickly executed. Yet it must be detailed enough to minimize the number of decisions that must be made during an emergency. The plan should be adaptable to any situation that it may not be specifically designed to cover. It should be designed around the effects of disasters, not their causes. For example, instead of having one plan for floods, another for broken pipes, and a third for water damage due to fire-fighting, you should consider having a single plan, that being for water damage in general.

There is no standard format for a museum disaster plan. I have seen suggested plans with as many as thirty different sections. Some of the standard works on the subject recommend seven to ten sections. I believe, however, that most museums will find that a plan consisting of four major sections and a series of appendices will best suit their needs. The four major sections are Introduction and Statement of Purpose, Authority, Scope of the Plan, and Emergency Procedures. This last section could easily be divided into two if desired; one would be Disaster Mitigation and Prevention Procedures and the other would be Disaster Recovery Procedures.

The first section, Introduction and Statement of Purpose, states why the plan has been developed and written and what it is intended to achieve.

This is a good place to say something about how the plan was developed and how it is to be kept current.

The Authority section documents the authority for preparation and implementation of the plan. Normally, the plan will be prepared under the authority of the museum's board of trustees and implemented by the Emergency Services Officer under delegation from the director. This second section also designates the Disaster Control Organization and indicates by name those persons responsible for deciding when and under what circumstances to execute the plan and for coordinating all emergency actions during its execution. At this point, you should note that implementation of the plan is different from execution of the plan. The plan is implemented when the Disaster Control Organization does everything called for by the plan in advance of disaster, such as acquisition of supplies and equipment, training of staff, and assignment of priorities for recovery. The plan is executed when an emergency occurs and the staffs respond with mitigating, preventive, or recovery actions in accordance with the plan.

Section Three, or Scope of the Plan, identifies each of the emergencies or disasters the plan is intended to cover. Here you list and describe each of the events that could occur in the museum; you will have identified these events during vulnerability assessment in Step 3 of the planning process. For each of these events, indicate how probable it is to occur and what the expected impact of the event would be on the museum's operation. The most serious events probably should be listed first. Be sure to consider the "trigger effect," wherein one event triggers others leading to a total disaster situation of greater seriousness than would exist with just one event. For example, when describing the potential impact of a tornado, you should note that the damage may not be limited to wind damage but may include death and injury, water damage, fire, contamination by chemicals and fuels, and looting. Responses to each of these events, including those "triggered" by others, will be detailed subsequently in Section Four (or Sections Four and Five).

If the museum consists of several buildings, particularly if they are widely scattered, you have the choice of developing a complete, independent plan for each building or developing a single plan for the entire institution. If you elect to create only one plan, Section Three should describe the extent to which the plan applies in each building. Section Three also should describe how the disaster plan relates to any other operating plans that might exist, such as a medical emergency plan, a fire reaction plan, or a plan for dealing with criminal activity. It will be a good idea to describe how all plans relate to and supplement each other and to indicate the circumstances under which they may be executed individually or simultaneously. This section also is a good place to describe how the museum's plan relates to or integrates with disaster plans for the local community or for the state, particularly if other agencies have some responsibility for supporting the museum in times of emergency.

Section Four — or Sections Four and Five if you choose to divide them- — is the heart of the disaster plan because it describes what is to be done to prevent, minimize, or cope with each of the emergencies or disasters that may occur in the museum. This section will be derived from the decisions made in Steps 5 and 6 during the planning process; these steps determined which protection and recovery methods will be used. In this Section, you indicate who will participate in executing each part of the overall plan, under what circumstances the plan is to be partially or fully executed, and how all necessary procedures are to be carried out. In short, this section tells who, when, what, where, and how.

Usually it will be best to devote individual subsections to each of the emergency or disaster events already itemized in Section Three. For each of these events, describe what is to be done in advance of the event, if there is sufficient warning. Describe what, if anything, is to be done during the event. And describe what is to be done after the event by way of recovery.

Plans for those emergencies commonly preceded by a warning will emphasize preventing loss or minimizing the impact of the event as it happens. For example, plans for dealing with a hurricane will place emphasis on weather-proofing buildings, relocating artifacts and records to inner rooms of the museum or evacuating them to safer quarters, and covering large objects that cannot be moved. Of course, this same plan must include procedures for recovering from the effects of the hurricane. But these procedures might not have to be fully executed if the prehurricane portion of the plan were successfully carried out.

Plans for dealing with those disasters that strike without warning will place primary emphasis on recovery. For example, plans for recovering from a major structural fire probably will include: evacuation of objects threatened by building collapse or looting; freeze-drying of water-soaked papers, books, and textiles; immediate drying of metals subject to rusting; and attention to locating all pieces of broken objects during removal of debris. The emphasis of this type of plan is not on prevention of damage from the fire but on prevention of further damage afterward.

The "guts" of your emergency plan will consist essentially of the four or five major sections I have just outlined. But these sections, by themselves, will not be enough. They will have to be supported and supplemented by appropriate appendices containing information that must be at your fingertips but that may change too often to be included in the major sections of the plan. You will have to determine what kinds of information to include in the appendices, but here are ten suggestions.

Appendix 1 should include a staffing chart of the museum, showing all divisions and at least the key positions. If the museum is part of a larger organization, such as a city or county government or a university, this appendix should include a chart to show the museum's position within the overall organization and its relation to sister agencies, such as the zoo or the library. Being able to refer to these charts in time of emergency will facilitate communications and maintain the chain of command. These charts should be as simple as possible and easy to understand. Usually it will be sufficient to show only division and office names and perhaps functions, as well as names and titles of key personnel. Members of the disaster control organization should be indicated on the charts or perhaps on a separate chart showing only that organization. Colored markers can be used to highlight the key personnel or activities.

Appendix 2 can consist of call-up lists of key personnel who will be needed for execution on the plan. The list should include each person's name and his or her title, home address, and home telephone number. This list also may include a brief résumé of each person's duties and responsibilities under the plan. This same appendix would be a good place to have a roster of the museum's entire staff. Such a roster can be handy in case there is an incident requiring a head count to determine if everyone is safe.

Appendix 3 can consist of a listing of emergency contacts outside the museum. Such contacts would include: the police and fire departments; the FBI; the local Civil Defence organization; local utility companies, hospitals, and ambulance companies; plumbers, electricians, and glass companies; local and regional conservators and curators; key staff persons of nearby museums; your museum's insurance agents; and any other organizations or persons whom the museum might have to contact in case of emergency. Both daytime and after-hours telephone numbers should be listed. Where known, also give the names of your contacts in the listed agencies. It is critical that this and all other call-up lists be kept current; revision at least every thirty days is suggested.

Appendix 4 can be a description of the circumstances that would require a call to each outside agency or person and what kinds of services or assistance you should expect to receive as a result of your call. It might be desirable to combine appendices 3 and 4 if doing so would not make them too cumbersome to use.

Appendix 5 could include floor plans of the museum and maps of its surroundings. Floor plans can show those parts of the museum that are most vulnerable or that contain the most valuable assets. They should show emergency exits and evacuation routes, the locations of gas and electric cutoffs and telephone closets, the locations of fire-fighting equipment, the locations of burglar and fire alarm devices and controls, the locations of emergency supplies and equipment stockpiles, and other such information. Maps can show sidewalks, streets, driveways, gates, fences, buried and overhead utility lines, fire hydrants, manholes, and other information that might be needed quickly. Floor plans and maps will prove particularly useful if you have to depend upon volunteers or other nonstaff personnel for help. Certain floor plans also can be posted in chart form at key locations around the non-public parts of the museum to facilitate movement during an emergency and to assist outside maintenance and service crews. It should go without saying that the inclusion in this appendix of sensitive information, such as information about intrusion detection systems, may require the control of who sees copies of the museum's plan or may dictate that certain portions of the plan be kept in sealed envelopes.

Appendix 6 might be an inventory of all collections, records, and other vital or valuable property that must be saved and the priority for their protection. With this record could be a floor plan that shows the location of each object or group of objects on the inventory. A similar plan can be posted in chart form in the museum's storerooms and conservation labs to facilitate quick access to these objects by emergency evacuation personnel who may be unfamiliar with your holdings. I would suggest, though, that you exercise caution in just how much detail you include on a posted plan. You wouldn't want to make it a shopping list for any burglar who might break in. Some sort of coding, such as with colors, might eliminate this problem.

Appendix 7 could be a summary of what arrangements have been made for evacuation and relocation of the collection. This appendix would include packing and crating instructions and information about what supplies and materials are available and where they can be found. This appendix also would include names of persons to contact when temporary space is needed as well as contacts to make for alternative spaces in case the primary site you have chosen is affected by the same disaster that has struck your museum.

Appendix 8 could be instructions for emergency management of the building's utilities and for service and operation of vital building operating systems. Such systems might include: burglar and fire alarm systems, fire suppression systems, fire fighting equipment, elevators and escalators, emergency lighting, emergency generator, heating and air conditioning equipment, humidifiers, and dehumidifiers. This appendix could include information copied from manufacturers' instruction manuals or could simply refer to the manuals kept elsewhere. If the vital information is only referenced, however, it will be necessary to protect the manuals to the same extent that the emergency plan itself is protected.

Appendix 9 is one of the most important appendices; it contains a list of local resources that you might need in case of emergency. You will have stockpiled certain emergency supplies and equipment. Record what they are (description, quantity, etc.) and where they can be found. Also record who is to be responsible for the issue and use. You will have arranged to borrow personnel from nearby museums or sister organizations for assistance in evacuation or recovery operations. Record what these arrangements are and who the appropriate contacts are. You will have arranged to borrow certain equipment such as a portable generator, power tools, fans, and dehumidifiers. Record what you have arranged for and who is to provide it and transport it. You will have arranged to purchase certain supplies, such as plywood, nails, plastic sheeting, tissue paper, cardboard boxes, tape, and disinfectants. List what you may need, where you can get it, and how it is to be paid for.

You will have arranged to call upon outside curators and conservators for advice and assistance. Record who they are, what their specialties are, and how they are to be contacted. If they are supposed to actually come to your museum, record how they are to be transported and whether or not you will be responsible for their lodging, meals, and other expenses. List any volunteers you may need to call upon, along with their special skills. If anybody on the staff, including volunteers, has promised to bring certain equipment and supplies with him for personal or museum use, indicate what they are. Keep all of this information current.

Appendix 10 might be a glossary of terms used in the emergency plan. Such a glossary will ensure that everyone using the plan will be speaking the same language.

An index to the entire plan would make a highly useful addition or a final appendix. However, because the plan will change through time and may change fairly frequently, it may not be practical to keep updating an index. Nevertheless, an index should be considered and included if practical.

The written plan can be kept most conveniently in a three-ring binder. I suggest that you make several copies of the plan and put the original in a safe or other secure, fire-resistive container. The Emergency Services Officer will be responsible for keeping the plan updated; he should have a copy handy for constant revision. As he makes changes to his copy, the typed original can be changed by a typist. Other copies should be kept by the key personnel in the Disaster Control Organization. If the museum occupies more than one building, at least one copy of the plan should be placed at critical spots around the museum, such as with fire-fighting equipment and stockpiles of emergency supplies. Each copy of the plan should contain a record of where all other copies may be found. It is vital that the original and all copies be updated as often as necessary; changes should be posted as they occur and changed pages should be retyped on a regular schedule. Remove and destroy obsolete pages and date all changes.

At least one copy of the plan kept in the museum should be accompanied by selected publications that will be needed for reference during emergency stabilization and conservation efforts following a disaster. The bibliography cites several useful publications, particularly those dealing with water damage. If your museum has a conservator on the staff, you may prefer to have that person prepare instructions specifically for your collections, rather than use existing published instructions. If so, then these instructions would be kept with the plan or perhaps even made part of it.

I suggest that your plan also be accompanied by a carefully selected assortment of blank forms, typing supplies, and other such materials that may be needed for preparing purchase orders and reports during and after an emergency. In case the museum office is damaged by a disaster, you will have these materials with the emergency plan and can carry on with vital administrative duties.

Step 8. Training the Museum Staff

The emergency preparedness process does not stop with preparation of a written disaster plan. The effectiveness of your plans during an actual disaster will depend upon prior training of all personnel who will execute the plan and upon regular testing of the plan under simulated conditions. The continued usefulness of the plan also will depend upon how well it performs during actual emergencies, as determined by postevent evaluations.

The eighth step in the emergency preparedness process is training of the museum staff. The three purposes of training are

1. To guarantee that every employee will react automatically in an emergency.
2. To ensure that each person on whom execution of the plan depends will know his or her responsibility.
3. To ensure that each responsible person has acquired the skills to do his or her job efficiently.

Training should be conducted regularly by the Disaster Control Organization and can be in conjunction with other regular museum employee training and skills development programs. The personnel appointed to the Disaster Control Organization probably should take appropriate courses offered by local and state Civil Defense organizations; these programs usually are free and are considered to be excellent training opportunities. Major businesses and industries often have disaster preparedness training courses for their own employees and may be willing to allow museum staff people to sit in. Reading the literature in print on the subjects of emergency planning and disaster preparedness also will be educational. Do not forget to rely upon your local public protection agencies, particularly the fire department, for training in such skills as fighting fires with hand-held extinguishers and controlling crowds during emergencies.

Step 9. Testing the Plan

The ninth step in emergency preparedness takes place after the plan has been written and training of the museum's staff has begun. This step is testing the plan.

To ensure that your plan will be effective and work as intended under actual disaster conditions, you should thoroughly test it under simulated disaster conditions. As Timothy J. Healy warns, the effectiveness of your plan should not be determined for the first time during an actual disaster. By testing the plan, you will discover its deficiencies and unrealistic features. The tests may show that procedures require revision or that additional procedures are needed. Also, those responsible for execution of the plan will receive very valuable training in how to react under emergency conditions.[15]

Testing consists of holding periodic exercises involving the full range of emergency situations that can be expected. Actual test problems can be written for each potential emergency situation and then presented for solution. Senior administrative and curatorial personnel should test the plan first. After they have participated in a series of exercises and after the plan has been improved as a result of those exercises, the entire museum staff and the staffs of agencies that will support the museum in time of disaster can be tested. All exercises should be as realistic as possible and held with as little advance notice and preparation as feasible. Test exercises should be as realistic as possible and be concerned with the full range of possible emergencies, from minor incidents all the way up to total disasters.

Step 10. Evaluating the Plan

Constant evaluation of your plan is essential to ensure that it is always up to date. Evaluation is the tenth and last step in the emergency preparedness process. The most effective way to evaluate a plan is to see how well it functions during actual emergencies. For this reason, it is vital that you keep records of what happens anytime you have to execute any part or all of your plan. When time permits, after the crisis has passed, all those involved in executing the plan should meet to discuss any problems that might have developed. They should determine how the plan should be improved so that similar problems do not arise during future emergencies.

As part of the evaluation, it is very important to observe and record exactly what damage resulted from the disaster and why it occurred. Photographs are particularly useful for this purpose. Such records may even be damanded by your insurance carriers. Such records also will enable you to refine your emergency plan so that it pays more attention to the kinds of damage that actually occur than to the kinds that you originally believed might occur. Furthermore, determining the causes of damage might permit the rebuilding or remodeling of the museum so that it becomes more physically resistant to the same kinds of damage in the future. It is important that an appropriate camera and accessories and a quantity of film be included as part of your stockpile of protected emergency supplies.

SUGGESTED EMERGENCY SUPPLIES AND EQUIPMENT

The supplies and equipment listed here include a variety of items that may be needed to cope with emergencies or disasters; some items can be used to prevent or minimize damage and others can be used afterwards to clean up or recover from damage. Few museums will need to use all of these items. Each museum should acquire only those items that will be needed to cope with the range of emergencies and disasters that it can expect. On the other hand, this list is not all inclusive; it is intended only as a guide. Any museum may find that it will require items not listed here.

Items listed here do not necessarily have to be obtained or stockpiled exclusively for use in an emergency. Some of the listed items will be found in all museums as a matter of routine. They can be diverted for use in cleanup and repair operations when they are needed. Keep in mind, however, that the items you may count on using in an emergency may be damaged or destroyed by the disaster. Therefore, those items that will be critical to the survival or recovery of the museum and that cannot be procured promptly from elsewhere after the disaster should be set aside (stockpiled) in a safe place so they will be available if ever they are needed.

Remember, too, that some items — such as dry-cell batteries and certain first-aid supplies — have a limited shelf life. Plan on replacing such items periodically so that fresh stock is always on hand in your stockpile.

Finally, remember always to include operating manuals or instructions with items of mechanical and electrical equipment in case persons not experienced with their operation are required to use them.

Supplies and Equipment for Mucking Out and Cleanup

> Low-sudsing detergents
> Bleaches
> Sanitizers (such as chloride of lime or high-test hypochlorite)
> Fungicides
> Disinfectants
> Ammonia
> Scouring powders or other household cleaners
> Rubber gloves

Brooms
Dust pans
Mops, mop buckets, and wringers
Scoops and shovels
Scrub brushes
Sponges and rags or cloths
Buckets and tubs
Water hoses and nozzles
Throw-away containers or bags for trash
Vacuum cleaner with accessories

Tools and Equipment for Demolition, Repairs, and Rescue

Hammers (both claw and machinists)
Wrenches (pipe, channel lock, and Vise Grips in various sizes)
Pliers (adjustable, lineman's, and needle nose in various sizes)
Screwdrivers (straight blade and Phillips in various sizes)
Wood saws
Hand drill with bits (power saws and drills may be selected if a source of electricity can be assured)
Metal saw with blades
Utility knife with extra blades
Wire cutters with insulated handles
Tin snips
Pipe cutters and possibly pipe threaders
Bolt cutter
Pry bar or crowbar
Axes, including fireman's axe
Rope
Dollies or handcarts
Folding rule or retractable tape measures
3-ton hydraulic jack
Sledgehammer
Block and tackle
Pit cover hook (if applicable)
Hydrant and post indicator valve wrenches (if the museum has a sprinkler or hose and standpipe system)
Staple gun and staples
Ladder(s) and step-stool(s)

Construction Materials

Plywood for covering or replacing windows
Dimensional lumber
Nails, screws, and assorted fasteners

Tapes of various kinds (masking, duct, electrician's, etc.)
Glue
Twine and cord
Plastic sheeting for protection against leaks and splashes
Binding wire

Emergency Equipment

Emergency gasoline powered electrical generator
Portable lights (to be powered from the generator if electricity un-
    available)
Emergency lights with extra batteries
Flashlights or lanterns with extra batteries
Fire extinguishers (ABC type recommended)
Battery-operated radio(s) with extra batteries
Walkie-talkie radios with extra batteries
Portable public address system or bullhorn, electrical or battery-
    powered
Geiger counter and dosimeters
Gas masks with extra canisters
Air breathers with extra oxygen tanks
Resuscitation equipment
Gasoline-powered water pump (or pump that can be powered from
    the electrical generator) with hoses
Extension cords, preferably equipped with ground fault interruptors

Personal Equipment and Supplies (some of these items may be provided by
the individual employees and volunteers who are to use them)

Necessary protective clothing
Rubber boots or waders
Hard hats
Rubber lab aprons
Protective masks
First-aid kits and medical supplies
Food and food-preparation equipment
Potable water
Sanitation facilities
Changes of clothing
Sleeping bags and blankets

Conservation Supplies and Equipment

Polyester (Mylar) and polyethylene film (in rolls)
Newsprint (unprinted)

Polyethylene bags, various sizes (such as Zip-Lock and produce bags)
Plastic garbage bags
Thymol
Ethanol
Acetone
Industrial denatured alcohol
White blotter paper
Weights (such as shot bags)
Various sizes of thick glass or smooth masonite
Japanese tissue
Towels or clean rags
Clothes pins
Scissors
Sharp knives
Water displacement compound (such as WD-40)
Waxes and dressings (determined by nature of collection)
Other preservatives

Miscellaneous Supplies

Boxes for packing and moving artifacts, records, and equipment (record transfer boxes are the easiest to use, carry, and store. They come flat for storage and are set up as needed; they may be reflattened for future use)
Box sealing and strapping tapes
Tissue paper, clean newsprint, plastic "bubble pack," foam "noodles," and other such materials for packing and padding artifacts for movement
Marking pens, preferably ones that are not water soluble
Insecticides and rodenticides

Miscellaneous Equipment

Fans
Space heaters, either electric or gas operated
Portable dehumidifiers
Hygrometers
Photographic equipment (camera, lenses, flash, light meter, etc.)
Essential office equipment (manual typewriter, pocket calculator, pencil sharpener, stapler, rulers, scissors, etc.)
Essential stationery and blank forms and other such supplies to ensure continuity of minimal administrative operations

CONCLUSION

In conclusion, let me remind you that emergencies are a part of the life of a museum. You may never have been involved personally in a serious emergency, let alone a disaster. If so, you may count yourself lucky or you may already be prepared. In either case, constant awareness that disaster can strike anytime should keep you vigilant and generate an incentive to become prepared if you aren't already. Whether or not an emergency turns into a disaster and whether or not you are able to cope with that disaster depend upon planning.

To repeat: *The primary goal of emergency planning is avoidance, and advanced planning is the key to achieving that goal.* Some emergencies cannot be prevented. The impact of some disasters cannot be avoided. But, you can plan in advance. You can commit that plan to paper. You can keep your plan up to date. And you can train yourself and your staff to use that plan. By taking these steps, you will achieve the capability to immediately cope with any emergency that cannot be prevented or avoided.

When you have that advance capability — and are confident that you have it — you will be prepared. That's what disaster preparedness is all about: being prepared.

NOTES

1. In the numerous and varied activities associated with disaster prevention and preparedness, a number of terms and expressions are entering into common usage. In the interests of uniformity and in order to avoid confusion, it is desirable that each of these terms and expressions should have a meaning that is widely accepted. The office of the United Nations Disaster Relief Co-ordinator (UNDRO) is considering this subject and, as an interim measure, has provided the following list of terms together with their meanings.

   Disaster prevention may be described as measures designed to prevent natural phenomena from causing or resulting in disaster or other related emergency situations. *Prevention* concerns the formulation and implementation of long-range policies and programmes to prevent or eliminate the occurence of disasters. On the basis of vulnerability analyses of all risks, prevention includes legislation and regulatory measures, principally in the fields of physical and urban planning, public works, and building.

   Disaster preparedness may be described as action designed to minimize loss of life and damage, and to organize and facilitate timely and effective rescue, relief, and rehabilitation in cases of disaster. *Preparedness* is suppported by the necessary legislation and means a readiness to cope with disaster situations or similar emergencies which cannot be avoided. Preparedness is concerned with forecasting and warning, the education and training of the population, organization for and management of disaster situations, including preparation of operational plans, training of relief groups, the stockpiling of supplies, and the earmarking of the necessary funds.

The above information was quoted from *Guidelines for Disaster Prevention and Prepared-ness in Tropical Cyclone Areas* prepared jointly by the Economic and Social Commission for Asia and the Pacific, the World Meteorological Organization, and the League of Red Cross Societies, published in Geneva and Bangkok in 1977.

2. Richard J. Healy, *Emergency and Disaster Planning* (New York: John Wiley and Sons, 1963), p. 1.
3. Hilda Bohem, *Disaster Prevention and Disaster Preparedness* (Berkeley, Calif.: The Univer-sity of California, Office of the Vice President for Library Plans and Policies, 1978), p. 1.
4. Healy, op. cit. p. 3.
5. Timothy J. Walsh and Richard J. Healy, *Protection of Assets Manual,* (Santa Monica, Calif.: The Merrit Co., 1976), Chapter 10, p. 2.
6. Healy, op. cit. p. 5.
7. Ibid., p. 6.
8. Richard J. Healy and Timothy J. Walsh, *Industrial Security Management* (New York: American Management Association, 1971), pp. 4-21.
9. David L. Daughters, "The Basic Goal of Emergency Planning — Avoidance." *Security Man-agement*, May 1978, p. 15
10. Committee on Conservation of Cultural Resources, *The Protection of Cultural Resources Against The Hazards of War.* Washington, D.C.: National Resources Planning Board, February 1942, pp. 8-9.
11. Ibid., p. 9.
12. Charles W. Bahme, *Fire Officer's Guide to Disaster Control* (Boston: National Fire Pro-tection Association, 1978), p. 10.
13. Ibid., pp. 12-13.
14. Walsh and Healy, 1976, Chapter 10, p. 20.
15. Healy, op. cit., p. 24.

Appendix 11-1

EMERGENCY PROCEDURES FOR LIBRARIES

Lawrence J. Fennelly

INTRODUCTION

For library security purposes, an EMERGENCY EXISTS WHEN THERE IS THREAT OF PERSONAL DANGER OR SIGNIFICANT POTENTIAL DAMAGE TO OR LOSS OF PROPERTY.

To be prepared for an emergency in a library, you must be familiar with the following:

1. The layout of the library and its emergency systems, including:
   a. Fire alarm boxes
   b. Fire extinguishers
   c. Fire hoses
   d. Smoke detectors
   e. Intrusion alarmed doors
   f. All annunciator panels
   g. Offices, study rooms, toilets, storage areas, shipping room
   h. Keys that provide access to the above
2. The meaning and operation of alarm systems
3. How to respond to emergencies
4. Follow-up procedures after an emergency ends

If you have any questions, please ask a senior staff member immediately and remember that in a community the size of Harvard there is almost always someone or some "agency" immediately available for help.

These procedures have been reviewed and approved for use by the director of the library, the fire and police departments, and the Environmental Health and Safety Office.

This appendix has been written in the form of a sample guideline which would be distributed to every library employee. It is based on information provided by Alan E. Erickson, Librarian, Cabot Science Library, Harvard University.

SUMMARY OF EMERGENCY PROCEDURES

Emergency	*Action*	*Name or Title of contact*
Fire (alarms not ringing)	Call 555-111 or pull fire alarm in library.	(This line is direct to the fire department and is monitored by police, security, and building engineers.)
Fire or smoke alarms sound	Evacuate library, *all* rooms, and *all* floors, with help of staff. Users take personal belongings, but leave library materials.	
Intrusion alarm rings	Check annunciator panel and exit violated for source of problem.	
Malfunction of intrusion alarm.	Call responding alarm company — 555-1101.	
Medical asistance	Call ambulance service company for transportation — 555-1102	Or local police department
Disturbance or "suspicious person"	Call responding police agency.	Police and Security Director
Fire or water damage to books	Call 715-5990.	LIBRARY DIRECTOR
Emergency utility or building problems	Call 715-2627 during weekday hours. Call 715-5560 evenings and weekends.	Director's Office Security Director's Office Operating engineers

EXPLANATION OF ALARMS IN LIBRARY

There are three alarm systems in the library. The fire and smoke alarms have a gong signal. The door or intrusion alarm and display case alarm have both buzzer and bell alarms.

Gong Alarms

Fire Alarm: A double series of four gongs
FIRE/FIRE . . . FIRE/FIRE . . . FIRE/FIRE . . .
The fire alarm is activated only by an intentional pull of one of the fire alarms in the library (or by a "power dip," a temporary drop in current in power lines, which may also cause a momentary dimming of lights immedieately before the alarm sounds).

Smoke Detector Alarm: A double series of five gongs:
SMOKE/SMOKE . . . SMOKE/SMOKE . . . SMOKE/ SMOKE . . . This alarm is activated by an increase in particulate matter in the air detected by smoke detectors located on the ceiling throughout the public area of the library and in each room (i.e., office, study, toilet, closet, etc.). A small pilot light goes on at the side near the top of the smoke detector that has been activated, the annunciator goes on in back of the circulation desk, and the alarm sounds. All detectors on the first floor are linked to a single red annunciator button on the panel in back of the circulation desk. Second floor smoke detectors are all linked to another single button and all basement detectors to a third red annunciator button on the panel.

Note: *Gongs stop ringing after eight series have sounded. This does NOT mean that the emergency is over. They stop so emergency crews can communicate in the affected area.*

Bell Alarms:

Door Intrusion Alarm: When any of the "armed" doors to the library are violated (i.e., opened), a bell alarm sounds at the door and a buzzer sounds at the annunciator panel at the circulation desk. A light on the panel, corresponding to the door in the violated zone, turns on. During working hours, the front door alarm (and on occasion the shipping door alarm) are deactivated.

Display Case Alarm: The alarm for protection of the display cases was added in 1980. Violation of the exhibit cases causes the alarm marked "Projection and Exhibit" to ring. In this case, however, there is no bell at the exhibit case but only over the projection door immediately adjacent to the alarm annunciator panel at the circulation desk.

To be sure that the intrusion alarm system functions properly, the bells are tested daily and the doors are opened on a regular basis. The alarm system is wired to the police station. An alarm rings at the station only when the board is set on "Secure" or when there is a power failure. By setting the panel on "Secure" at closing time, responsibility for monitoring the system is transferred to the police.

If the door intrusion alarm system fails to operate properly, call the police. The police will determine if it is necessary to call for outside service. The contractor for service is − − − (state the name of service to be contacted to respond to an alarm for service.)

HOW TO RESPOND TO EMERGENCIES

Fire

Discovery of fire or smoke. If the fire or source of smoke is trivial, e.g., contents of a wastebasket, pull the alarm and extinguish the fire, but only if you can do so without danger of being trapped. If it is not trivial, pull the alarm and evacuate the library as quickly as you can.

With assistance from other staff members, go through the entire library, checking ALL areas, rooms, offices, toilets, and stairways. When evacuating the library provide as much information as possible so that people will understand the need for quick movement. A satisfactory message would be:

"Please clear the building immediately. Take your personal belongings with you, leave library materials. Use the main exit, please. The fire alarm has been pulled (or a smoke detector has been activated)."

During normal weekday hours, staff responsibilities are as follows:

Second floor: cleared by reference staff.
First floor: cleared by staff assistant with help from technical services.
Basement: cleared by technical services.

Circulation staff will move to the door to assist checkers in monitoring exit and materials being removed by users.

On evenings and weekends, circulation will clear the library with the checker doing his best to monitor exiting material. Remain near library entrance if practicable. If not, go to the main annunciator panel in the east corridor opposite the administrative office to direct firemen.

Fire or smoke alarm sounds. Check annunciator panel to find out on which floor the smoke detector was activated. If the panel is lighted up, proceed to the source of the problem. Clear that floor of the library first. If the fire is trivial, e.g., contents of a wastebasket, extinguish it. If the annunciator panel is not lighted up, clear the entire library. Remain near the library entrance if practicable. If not, go to main annunciator panel in the east corridor opposite the administrative office to direct the firemen.

Intrusion

Intrusion alarm sounds. If an alarm rings, a member of the circulation staff (or a guard if designated by the person in charge) should push the acknowledge button on the annunciator panel, pick up the alarm key, proceed immediately to the violated door, and try to determine why the door was opened by looking for someone who either has continued out the door or is returning from the door, or by inquiring of people in the vicinity. (In the past, alarms have usually been activated by visitors too preoccupied to notice the warning signs on the doors.) Close the door. Insert the alarm key into the keyhole beside the door, and turn the key. The bell should stop ringing. THEN TURN THE KEY BACK TO THE ORIGINAL POSITION TO RESET THE ALARM BELL. Now withdraw the key.

Return to the annunciator panel in back of the circulation desk and push the "reset" button. Record information about the incident (including time) in the guard's notebook.

Display case alarm sounds. Both the exhibit case and projection door should be checked. (State name of person who should be contacted for help in deactivating the alarm.) Sometimes flickering lights in the exhibit case can set off the alarm. A temporary solution under such circumstances is to turn off the lights in the exhibit case by flicking the switch between the cases.

Disturbances

Contact the librarian in charge. Call police if the problem does not appear to be amenable to normal procedures. If you *suspect* that something is amiss or that a person is likely to cause trouble call the police. It is better to have erred on the side of safety than to lose valuable response time. ALWAYS avoid physical contact. Try to enlist the aid of witnesses.

Medical Emergencies

Call the police who will respond with assistance and transportation if needed. In addition you may wish to call the hospital emergency room. State that it is an emergency. A physician or nurse will then ask what the problem is and will direct you to do whatever is medically appropriate.

In A DIRE EMERGENCY IN WHICH THE PATIENT'S HEALTH WOULD BE JEOPARDIZED BY DELAY, go to the emergency room of the nearest hospital.

Bomb threats

If you receive a telephone call in which a bomb threat is made, obtain as much information as possible, particulary about the expected time of detonation and location (building, floor, room, nature of container, etc.). Make a note of everything and anything you can (voice, accent, background noise) during and after the converstaion. Relay all information to the police immediately, then to the director of the library, and then to the librarian. Do not evacuate the library unless instructed to do so. ASK for instructions. If the library is evacuated, the library staff should remain in the vicinity to receive instructions about reporting back to work so that the library can be reopened as promptly as possible.

Utility or Other Building Problems

During normal 9-to-5 weekday working hours, please notify the library secretary, who in turn will notify the director's office of any problems, and who, perhaps with your assistance, will make sure that appropriate attention is given to the problem. After 5 P.M. and on weekends, call the building engineers to report any problems. Call again if you believe adequate time has elapsed and the problem still has not been resolved. It is not unusual for the computer to shut down the air-handling equipment at 5 P.M. after the library goes off the 9 A.M. to 5 P.M. intersession or vacation schedule. The library "dies" under such circumstances, i.e., all air movement ceases. Call the engineers and ask them to reactivate the air-handling systems.

FOLLOW-UP PROCEDURES AFTER AN EMERGENCY ENDS

As soon as the procedures outlined in this chapter have been complied with, the person in charge of the library during the emergency should contact the following persons as seems appropriate:

1. Notify the library director at work or at home. If he cannot be reached, contact any other department head.
2. If none of the above can be reached, notify one of the senior librarians if you believe someone in the library should be appraised of the problem.

CONCLUSION

As much information as possible should be included in the emergency procedures. Assume that a new part-time employee is on duty and a crisis arises, the procedures should specify everything that this employee should do. As a working guide, these procedures should include:

1. Floor plans of smoke detectors, fire alarms, and fire extinguishers.
2. Instructions about how to operate Halon if it is present in the library.
3. A floor plan of the intrusion alarm system, showing the locations of each component.
4. A list of the staff members, with their home addresses and phone numbers.
5. A list of all people to be called in the event of specific emergencies.

Appendix 11-2

SALVAGE OF WATER-DAMAGED LIBRARY MATERIAL.[1]

SUMMARY OF EMERGENCY PROCEDURES

1. Seek the advice and help of book and paper conservators with experience in salvaging water-damaged materials as soon as possible.

2. Turn off heat and create free circulation of air.

3. Keep fans and air-conditioning on at night, except when a fungicidal fogging operation is in process, because a constant flow of air is necessary to reduce the threat of mold.

4. Brief each worker carefully before salvage operations begin, giving full information on the dangers of proceeding except as directed. Emphasize the seriousness of timing and the priorities and aims of the whole operation. Instruct workers on means of recognizing manuscripts, materials with water-soluble components, leather and vellum bindings, materials printed on coated paper stock, and photographic materials.

5. Do *not* allow workers to attempt restoration of any items on site. (This was a common error in the first 10 days after the Florence flood, when rare and valuable leather- and vellum-bound volumes were subject to scrubbing and processing to remove mud. This resulted in driving mud into the interstices of leather, vellum, cloth, and paper, caused entensive damage to the volumes, and made the later work of restoration more difficult, time consuming, and extremely costly.)

6. Carry out all cleaning operations, whether outside the building or in controlled-environment rooms, by washing gently with fresh, cold running water and soft cellulose sponges to aid in the release of mud and filth. Use sponges with a dabbing motion, *do not rub*. These instructions do not apply to materials with water-soluble components. Such materials should be frozen as quickly as possible.

7. Do not attempt to open a wet book. (Wet paper is very weak and will tear at a touch. *One tear costs at least one dollar to mend!*) Hold a book firmly closed when cleaning, especially when washing or sponging. A closed book is highly resistant to impregnation and damage.

8. Do not attempt to separate single-sheet materials unless they are supported on polyester film or fabric.

9. Do not attempt to remove all mud by sponging. Mud is best removed from clothes when dry; this is also true of library materials.

10. Do not remove covers from books, as they will help to support the books during drying. When partially dry, books may be hung over nylon lines to finish drying. Do not hang books from lines while they are very wet because the weight will cause damage to the inside folds of the sections.

11. Do not press books and documents mechanically when they are water soaked. This can force mud into the paper and subject the materials to stresses which will damage their structures.

12. Use soft pencils for making notes on slips of paper but do not attempt to write on wet paper or other artifacts.

13. Clean, white blotter paper, white paper towels, *strong* toilet paper, and unprinted newsprint paper may be used for interleaving in the drying process. When nothing better is available, all but the color sections of printed newspapers may be used. Great care must be taken to avoid rubbing the inked surface of the newspapers over the material being dried; otherwise some offsetting of the ink may occur.

14. *Under no circumstances should newly dried materials be packed in boxes and left without attention for more than a few days.*

15. Do not use bleaches, detergents, water-soluble fungicides, wire staples, paper or bulldog clips, adhesive tape, or adhesives of any kind. Never use felt-tipped fiber or ballpoint pens or any marking device on wet paper. Never use colored blotting paper or colored paper of any kind to dry books and other documents.

EVALUATION OF LOSS

When a flood- or fire-damaged collection is covered by insurance, full settlement of a claim cannot be realized until the lost and damaged materials have been listed and their values have been established. The extent and success of possible restoration must also be determined. In the event that a claim is anticipated as a result of such damage, every item should be salvaged, frozen, and dried. After drying, the affected materials should be shelved in a specially equipped environment storage area, isolated from the main stacks, and there inspected and monitored over a period of time. Such a policy is the best guarantee of sound judgments by custodians, consultants, and adjusters when they must calculate the degree of loss as a basis for compensation.

SOURCES OF ASSISTANCE

The following organizations are known to have had actual experience in the salvage and preservation of flood-damaged materials:

Conservator
The Newberry Library
60 West Walton Street
Chicago, Ill. 60610
(312) 943-9090

Book Conservator
68 Divisadero Street
San Francisco, Calif. 94117
(415) 626-8626

Director/Conservator
New England Document
  Conservation Center
800 Massachusetts Avenue
North Andover, Mass. 01845
(617) 686-9669

Conservator
Carolyn Horton Associates, Inc.
430 West 22nd Street
New York, N.Y. 10011
(212) YU 9-1472

Physical Scientist
Research & Testing Office
Library of Congress
110 Second Street, SE.
Washington, D.C. 20540
(202) 426-5607

Chief, Conservation-Analytical
  Laboratory
Museum of History and Technology
Smithsonian Institution
Washington, D.C. 20560
(202) 381-5592

Conservator
American Philosophical Society
  Library
105 South Fifth Street
Philadelphia, Pa. 19106
(215) WA 5-9545 or 567-4566

Restoration Officer
Library of Congress
110 Second Street, SE.
Washington, D.C. 20540
(202) 426-5634

Graphic Arts Conservator
612 Spruce Street
Philadelphia, Pa. 19106
(212) MA 7-2303

The Library of Congress will gladly act as an information source for technical advice where needed.

NOTES

1. *Procedures for Salvage of Water-Damaged Library Material* by Peter Waters, Library of Congress Publication, U.S. Government Printing Office, Washington, DC, 1975, pp. 26-27.

V. SECURITY METHODS
FOR MUSEUMS,
ART FACILITIES,
AND LIBRARIES

12. Security Theory For A Large Museum

Alain Goffier

In museum security, the scientific approach must be looked at from the viewpoint of how it can be achieved. This means finding the right components for the system that is to be devised, and today art security can be effective only by following this approach. In discussing museum security the primary concern is how the artwork itself can be conserved, since conservation per se is the scientific task of the specialists, namely, museum curators.

The work of curators, therefore, is to detect risk, to transmit information, to quantify the methods of intervention, and then to act, which implies intervention by stopping the intruder. Although many levels of security have to be taken into account, three simple concepts can be defined: *Complete Security,* which means that all means of detection are in effect, and all areas are "frozen"; *Partial security,* which means that, when functions must be filled, a concept of services is used that leads to a form of *gradual security*; and *Basic Security, which corresponds to a fundamental, rock-bottom level of security.*

Within this framework of three concepts, two notions need to be highlighted: The notion of *Open Time* — the period of time during which the misdeed can take place, which must be minimal. The notion of *Required Time* — the time needed for security to intervene, which must be maximal.

CONCEPT OF DETECTION

Misdeed Detection

Since the public is present, this is the *Daytime* mode of detection. It can also be used at night, and thus become a permanent characteristic of the security plan.

Detection of Burglary Attempts

Since the public is absent, this is the *Night-Time* mode of detection. It can also be used on holidays or during strikes, for instance.

Detection When Services Are Operating

In this mode of detection the public is not present but personnel and services are in operation. This is the *Services* mode, in which the form of detection can be quantified and localized but should be managed in a flexible manner. This method reduces open time and has a dissuasive effect because of its secrecy, the way in which it is carried out having been left up to the discretion of the museum authorities.

CONCEPT OF TRANSMISSION

Transmitting information is one of the most important factors in being successful when taking action. If news of a misdeed is transmitted *Rapidly*, intervention *Open Time* is reduced and owing to mobile detection, a dissuasive surprise effect can be achieved. This method allows for the installation of alarm clusters that become dangerous for chance events.

The antenna detection units are autonomous, reliable, well performing, and portable anywhere. Because the antenna must submit its information in a code that cannot be counterfeited, the code number must vary according to the detection unit. It should be easy to establish programs either for variable periods or for very short amounts of time. This information should be transmitted to portable receivers by roundsmen or supervision inspectors. At the same time, however, it should reach the central zone stations and the central supervision station.

CONCEPT OF CENTRALIZATION

We next consider the necessity of *Three-level centralization*, which is defined as: (1) Mobile centralization (portable); (2) Local centralization (central zone station); and (3) Centralized centralization (central supervision station).

CONCEPT OF PROCESSING

Information is processed by applying the following kinds of regulations: (1) General Regulations; (2) Regulations specific to the museum; and (3) Specific guidelines (general, punctual, per station). These three points make up the framework of security organization and are to be entered into a file. Today the computer index provides the best way of applying the components of these regulation systems. They should be applied according to priority and as quickly as possible. A map of the premises may also be incorporated into the plan and an intervention plan devised.

Data process directly the conditions of *Open Time*. It must be rapid, and thus organized and premeditated, for everything takes place in real time.

CONCEPT OF INTERVENTION

Intervention means that a decision has been made. Decisions must be studied beforehand, and action must be preestablished. One can try to think up all possible cases, but here again, the system must be flexible enough to incorporate immediately any new contingency that arises from an occasional occurrence, or in extraordinary circumstances.

CONCEPT OF BACKUP SECURITY

At the individual level, backup security is ensured by supervisory inspectors, as well as central zone stations and the central supervision station. As far as the grounds are concerned, they are covered by outside intervention, such as fire stations or police forces.

CONCEPT OF SECURITY MANAGEMENT

Because security is, obviously, not a science, preliminary analysis of security management and prevention must be subject to constant revision by experience, events, and human beings. The study of security represents only the past, the sum of what is known; however, the past is the basis for the present, namely, action. Although action is taken a posteriori, it determines the future, for statistics are collected on all phenomena. They are sorted out according to their affinities, specific characteristics, and functions. Analysis of these statistics can improve the system and lead to greater efficiency. For this reason data must be revised continuously. Data must distinguish among: Route information; general instructions in a regulation framework; particular instructions within known patterns; and multiple warning instructions for ambivalent action (in the case of a series of attacks launched simultaneously against the museum). Until recently, the only type of effective service adapted to the inherent complexity of a large museum was by live caretakers. This system is very flexible. The field covered by the guard is well mastered, and risk and required action are correctly estimated. Nevertheless, this task is so monolithic that weariness or bad habits may arise and cause mistakes. In addition, in the case of an accident the guard is always held responsibile, for he is the number-one witness and is subject to investigation as to responsibility or information. Reliable automatic appliances now exist that are of help to the guard by the very fact of their being automatic.

However, automatic caretaking does not mean the replacement of human caretaking. Rather, it is a way of reducing tension among supervisory personnel by freeing them from certain chores of observation and prevention, thus allowing them to concentrate on evaluating risks and perceiving the limits of their action and responsibility. Any study of automatic caretaking requires perfect knowledge of the premises, and the quality of an installation is based just as much on engineering problems as on the study of the premises. Machines are expected to be trustworthy and to operate constantly in order to guarantee permanent supervision, but they are limited and lack the ability to quantify action according to risk.

This is why a joint *human + machine service* must be developed. People must be freed from sensory tasks so that they can have greater availability and be more broadly active. Experience proves that if the means at our disposal must evolve in order to obtain an operational and efficient security service, people must evolve along with the equipment.

The fundamental difficulty lies in the ambivalent mission of a museum which creates two contradictory aspects for museum security: (1) conservation of the artistic, historical, and scientific patrimony of our civilization for the coming generations; (2) offering the current generation wide-ranging possibilities for exhibits.

The risk of theft includes outside as well as inside theft. *Theft from the outside* — in other words, a holdup — is organized and implies previous visits to the museum, plus the possibility of an inventory of security installations having been made. How to prevent holdups is well known today, but great care must be taken that the automatic detection instruments be as invisible as possible as well as being immune to tampering. They should also be mobile. For then they will create doubt, cause surprise, and ultimately lead to failure.

Theft from the inside is the disappearance of a work of art organized from within the museum. Preventive measures are more difficult to take because a museum also contains study and research offices, shops, archives, libraries, and educational institutions. In addition, a museum is closed to the public for longer periods than it is open, at which time the number of security personnel is reduced.

Finally, there is the risk of often irreparable mutilation of a work of art. This possibility causes the greatest worry, for while it is possible to organize fire and theft prevention to a certain extent, museums are totally unprepared against vandalism under the current caretaking system. In my opinion, this is the number one risk, since fire and theft prevention are a routine part of the security job.

This triple pattern of risk (theft from the outside, theft from the inside, and vandalism) covers all high-risk periods and places. These include temporary exhibits, transportation, temporary installations, work on the buildings, restoration of artworks, workshops, storerooms, exceptional visits, motion-picture filming, authorized photography, and so on.

We are henceforth faced with the problem of detecting the misdeed, with this problem being subject to the nature of the exhibit, the architecture, the artwork environment, and to changes in presentation. Accordingly, the choice of the means of detection is of major importance.

In fire detection, instead of choosing one type of detector, it is necessary to consider the largest possible number of different kinds of detectors with a wide range of functions, based on the particular grounds and risks. For example, the following kinds of detectors could be used:

- Ionic ambient smoke detector (should be about 0.04 microcurie of americium)
- Optical smoke detector (Tyndall effect)
- Ultraviolet flame detector
- Ionic sampling smoke detector (analysis chamber depressed by suction device)
- Ionic sampling smoke detector for airduct mounting (analysis chamber depressed by venturi)
- Rate of temperature rise detector
- Thermostatic detector
- Optical smoke detector by infrared radiation (opacimetric method)
- Rate of temperature detector by burst of microcapsules of rare gas (microphonic alarm reception of increase in temperature of electric cables, for example, or of motors, transformers, electric cabinets, connecting boxes, or very high storage)

In theft detection, again, instead of choosing one detector, it is necessary to consider a group of different kinds of detectors that offers the best technical protection of the premises. The following kinds of detectors could be used:

- Punctual detection of a shock, contact, or opening
- Detection by capacitive fields
- Detection by infrared, ultrasonic devices, or radar
- Detection by the use of photographic circuits or television

In general, what qualities are required in a detector? The qualities can be listed in the following order: reliability, sensitivity, untamperability, and purchase and maintenance cost. What are the installation requirements? These can be listed as follows:

- In new galleries, or in galleries undergoing rearrangement, *integrated security*, which is the best kind of security, can be practiced.
- In galleries that are already set up only *added security* can be practiced.
- For galleries that are listed as "historical monuments," where the installation of wires and detectors is a problem, (hence the usefulness of mobile instruments), all security equipment must respect the work of art, its environment, and the museum infrastructure.

In particular, the use of wiring must be avoided as this may involve expensive modifications in the architecture.

Detection instruments that are designed for a specific use must be easily and rapidly transported, since the works exposed are moved frequently and the exhibit galleries changed. Such instruments must not disfigure or harm the premises. A good choice is the use of portable detection units in which the alarm is transmitted by portable radio (STARP: Système de Télétransmission d'Alerte à Récepteurs Portatifs).

PERSONNEL REQUIREMENTS

It is advisable for all personnel to be employed by the museum directly. The museum guard should be divested of any mythical quality — he is not a town watchman, for what is at stake has a completely different value. The guard must become, because of the increasing use of technical equipment, a true technician in the surveillance field. This ability must be accompanied by a notion of the value of the art being protected.

Personnel must be informed and consulted in order to be motivated, and also must undergo training in order to be efficient, responsible, and conscientious about their duties. The following responsibilities can be specified:

- Responsibility for analysis and coordination — museum director
- Responsibility for decisionmaking — head of security
- Responsibility for action — guard

In determining security requirements the following studies are undertaken:

1. site and operation analysis
2. studies of intervention diagrams or risk analysis
3. intervening caretaker
4. central zone stations and central supervision station
5. security director and the need for evidence
6. personnel training requirements
7. maintenance

SITE AND OPERATION ANALYSIS

The first step is to study the goals to be attained, and then to look for the material means of reaching them within the framework of the budget.

An absolute requirement is to cover the premises without abolishing the principle of permanent detection (thus volumetric detection is not turned off during rounds, for instance, enabling supervision centers to follow the guard on his round through the alarm system).

Areas covered by supervision (necessary passage points, high-risk areas, etc.) are designed with an overall security plan in mind and the guards are armed with detection units (theft, fire, sabotage, etc.) with a coded HF portable transmitter.

STUDY OF INTERVENTION DIAGRAMS

These secret diagrams are drawn up according to the possible risks. The means of carrying out the various interventions are estimated in terms of personnel and instruments, which determine in advance how much intervention time is required. For a large museum, having only one supervision office would be insufficient and therefore central zone stations must be set up. Intervention is guided by information; which must be simple, for clarity in visualizing instructions leads to a reduction in intervention time (see the section, Long-Range Security Plan).

INTERVENING GUARD

Many levels of intervention are set up:

- Assigned station level (guards)
- zone level (supervision inspectors)
- museum level (security director)

Responsibilities

Responsibilities should not be diluted by assigning overly vast territories to each guard or by setting up rounds that are too long and that tire the guard and impair his sense of observation.

Constant reception of information is necessary. When on rounds, the supervision inspector should always carry a portable microcentralizer (HF receiver).

Each guard must be attached to his equipment by a sense of ownership, the ability to use it, and an awareness of its cost and usefulness. The guard must gain confidence in the equipment through training, for often his first reaction is to reject any new system. Often criticism is expressed, but this can also be constructive.

CENTRAL ZONE STATIONS AND CENTRAL SUPERVISION STATION

This connection is the "on-the-spot" joining of the guard and the inspector, the set point in local centralization. Guards collect security data by geographical sector and transmit it to the other central zone stations for correlation and then to the central supervision station, which is in charge of filing the data and also providing backup security, if it is needed.

Accordingly, the central supervision station and roving agents must be equipped with HF receivers that decode data and give alert information.

The system must be designed so that in every zone supervision rounds can be carried out by security personnel without impeding permanent detection. Indeed, suspending electronic supervision, in order to avoid meaningless alerts during the rounds of security agents, is out of the question. This would lead to the suppression of the positive aspect of this security measure and isolate the security agent from the equipment designed to assist him.

The solution is to set up renewable rounds that enable the central supervision station to locate and follow the roving security agent each time he passes a detector.

While maintaining a permanent detection infrastructure, this major principle in solving protection problems makes it possible to:

- Supervise rounds
- Control personnel movement
- Insure the safety of the supervision agent by detecting unexpected intrusions for him at the central supervision station level as well as

becoming aware of any abnormalities along a round that has been preprogrammed as to time and route

- Determine whether the detection and transmission units are operating correctly during each round

This last characteristic requires the central supervision station to have alert receiving and signaling equipment (along with the receiver carried by agents on patrol) with outstanding receiving and recording capabilities; for example, a printing time recorder.

Finally, we have seen that a security installation of this type (with transportable detection points and portable receiving units) is much less vulnerable to attack, especially by professional burglars who may already have detailed knowledge of the premises and who may have made an inventory of the protective installations.

The central supervision station will be expected, first of all, to administer and compile information in order to formulate instructions for action that is commensurate with the risks; print and keep records of all events and operations; and finally, record all messages, calls, and instructions given by telephone in order to keep track of the progressive events.

SECURITY DIRECTOR

The security director needs the evidence provided by the printed logs and the systematic recording of all messages and calls made to the outside (e.g., police, fire department, public services). By studying this information, he can reconstruct the course of events and explain what has occurred to the administration, the authorities, and to the operating personnel. These pieces of evidence are the basis for a study that he must make after a "security event." This study enables him to diagnose the system, and instructions for action that were established before the event took place can be modified and improved in order to ensure a better operating system.

PERSONNEL TRAINING REQUIREMENTS

In order for personnel to become more proficient in handling the increasingly complicated security equipment, it is vital to provide training in operating these new devices. Practical courses and drills, both by night and day should be given. Although it is often difficult to find time for this training, it is worthwhile, for personnel is thus furnished with a real career and their increased qualifications become "profitable" for everyone. It is in the museum's best interest as well as necessary for job promotion.

MAINTENANCE

Maintenance is necessary to keep the equipment in a permanent state of working order. Two phases are included:

- A *preventive* phase, which is normal, recurrent, and planned, consisting of routine upkeep, control, and testing;
- A *curative* phase, which is exceptional and unforeseen (e.g., repair service), requiring rapid intervention because until the work is finished, the equipment is not functioning completely.

For maintenance cost is often responsible for its being irregular or nonexistent. It should be realized, however, that the cost of maintenance is always low when compared to the cost of a breakdown or other consequences that could have been avoided.

In the security field, technical supervision equipment can be compared to the oil pressure gauge in an automobile. The consequences of a "burned-out" gauge caused by an oil circuit leak are easy to imagine, which can be summed up cost-wise as follows: the gauge or the motor!

For the detection of a fire or a malevolent action, however, it is more difficult to draw a parallel, for it is not easy to oversee the maintenance of machinery that is in steady use. It is necessary to the uncommon event that, hopefully, will never take place. And yet the same kind of maintenance plan should be applied, since a fire detector that is out of order can mean the cost of refurbishing a gallery or an isolated alarm opening can mean the loss of a work of art. For a security installation to remain in working order, maintenance is needed just as it is for any machine or equipment; but for security installations, maintenance must be of exceptional quality, especially during the "repair" phase.

In security, it is never possible to catch up on breakdown time. If the installation is not in working condition and nothing occurs, so much the better, but if the uncommon event does take place, then it can mean a serious loss.

Upkeep must be ensured by periodic inspections, a minimum of four times per year. Some equipment is routinely checked if the technology warrants it. The running order of the entire system is tested. Instruments are cleaned, readjusted, and regauged by rotation, by lots or groups. In this way, each year all of the machinery in the entire system can be treated.

Emergency repairs belong to the curative phase of maintenance. For emergency service to be rapid, efficient, and of high quality, it is necessary to have good installation engineering. Therefore detectors are grouped by geography, function, and according to the technology required to fulfill the security need. It is necessary to have a basic technician who is well trained and who knows the equipment and the security requirements. The equipment must be easily reparable and allow for the installation to be put back into normal operating order in a minimum of time. In this last aspect, STARP is totally satisfactory, since it allows for an immediate standard exchange of either the entire detection unit or the CD 1211 transmitter, the RC 1311 receiver, the printing module PR 1410, or the receiver RC 1302 within the CT 1400 centralizer. All this kind of work is done on the spot, which means "first-level" repair service. For "second-level" repairs, which are carried out in the workshop, the various components of the detection units should allow for rapid equipment rotation and a minimum of downtime.

The strong points of an efficient repair service include portability of equipment, having equipment in modular units, and the standard exchangeability of parts!

LONG-RANGE SECURITY PLAN

For a large area, such as the premises of a vast museum, security problems should be approached with a long-range security plan from an overall perspective. Otherwise, it is not materially possible to secure the entire area. The reasons are obvious: the size of the budget, works of art on a large scale, too many rooms closed to the public, too many workmen present at any given time, and so on.

All these factors indicate that a security plan can be accomplished only by spreading it out over many years, perhaps even a decade. This raises the question whether the partial system installed today will be compatible with the complementary equipment added one, two, or three years later? In addition, any installations that are satisfactory should be retained. But will these systems become outdated because their central components differ from the others?

Today, we use many autonomous and portable detection and transmission units. The very nature of the medium of information transmission, the UHF radio channel, eliminates the interconnection problem between instruments, which is no small advantage. Since the message format is defined, equipment is immediately compatible notwithstanding the development of technology over several generations. Only the number of units and the size of the departments covered can cause problems in the development of the centralization station. The latter must be able to evolve in order to allow for future expansion.

The problem is to choose a coherent system that can be adapted to every new need, foreseen or unforeseen (and often unforeseeable). Choice is no longer based exclusively on finding equipment with the capacity to hypothetically centralize an estimated number of detection points. Rather, equipment is chosen according to basic principles and philosophical directives set by the security plan. In other words, the equipment is chosen according to the security needs of the museum. The availability of equipment with modular programmable microprocessors has enlarged the horizons of those who plan and use security system installations. This type of equipment is similar in concept to a computer; with input, output, and a "heart" or central unit (CPU). This equipment, following the software, orders action in output according to data in input, which is entered on a control and display unit. The installation can thus conduct an entire process. It must be offline, however, in order to ensure the execution of this process up to an advanced operating level. This system is called an Autonomous Processor for Security Data (APSD).

The originality of APSD lies in its equipment makeup. For instance; it has C/MOS integrated circuit technology, and thus uses little energy. It provides optimal autonomy for a given capacity of batteries, autoprotection against dismantling and opening, and locking up of the control keyboard, output module, input module, signaling module, and control module, all of which respond to security operational requirements. This equipment becomes a key element in the security installation, both as hardware and as software, thereby guaranteeing that instructions (schedules for supervision, predetermined action) will be transmitted accurately. The level of equipment is defined by the curator of the museum.

A museum is not a strongbox that can be opened or closed. It is a world with its own rhythm. If it is paramount to ensure tight security over well-defined premises, we must also avoid imposing useless constraints that would imperil the very life of the museum.

With APSD the temptation is to manage hundreds of detection points with only one machine while also watching for an uncommon breakdown, which can always occur, and also being beware of the possibility of sabotage of the central element, which would paralyze the entire installation.

Beyond a certain number of detectors, which vary according to type, we must have a "group of systems" to develop the fundamental level of security operations, to decentralize an overly centralized system, to spread out the system's autonomy, and to create an organization that allows for a minimal level of security to remain operative when any one element in the system becomes defective.

For example, one department or a group of departments may be linked to a zone control and command post equipped with APSD. All APSDs are linked to a central minicomputer whose sole purpose is to manage the whole security network. The minicomputer is not — in this case — a security element. It is a management tool that reduces the number of permanent staff at the central station. If the central managing unit breaks down, each APSD "takes the situation in hand," the continuity of security at the fundamental level is ensured, and it is carried out locally.

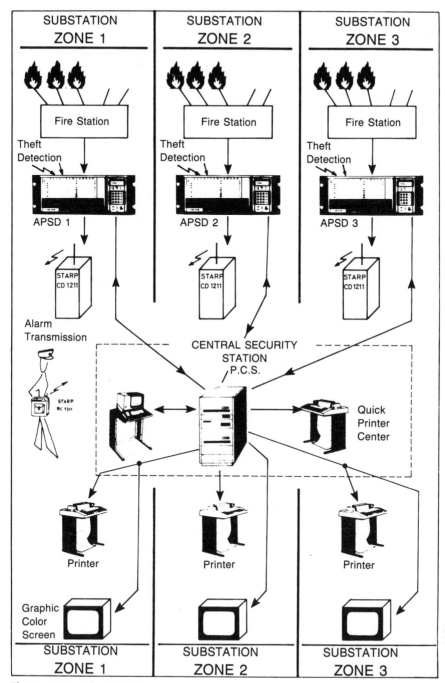

Figure 12.1. The STARP system

Thus, in a nearly permanent manner (more than 95 percent of the time), the computerized security command post allows for supervision of all security systems and, if necessary can send orders from a distance by planning supervision periods and automatic instructions. Later, the log is processed in order to assemble statistics that point out abnormalities, as well as provide diagnostic information for improving the installation.

When the minicomputer is under maintenance or has broken down (less than 5 percent of the time), an APSD that has not received information by echo from the command post reacts according to its "autonomy" programming, and its vital security functions are still carried out. The log of the zone is consigned to memory. An APSD could also receive wired installations as well as data emanating from units such as the CD 1211 (UHF detector/transmitter) of the STARP and transmit, or retransmit, data to the RC 1311 receivers carried by the security agents, whatever the type of data. This kind of reception extends to existing older systems and makes their data conform to others. This is the ultimate result of the standardization of different installations when employed as an entire unit. One three-zone application of this system is given in Figure 12.1. This type of installation does not offer the advantages of a security command post equipped with double computers fed by a standby electric network, but it has the advantage of being realistic budget-wise and it respects the principles of levels of security. It remains open to other forms of use, including the use of computer equipment for security.

Whether this reasoning is conducted on the hardware, software, or operational levels, the goal of "security and safety" can be approached only with a conception based on modules and autonomous units that guarantee minimal damage in case of a breakdown. These units must be organized as a whole with their interconnections and intercommunications integrated so that they can respond to one-directional action.

13. Intrusion Detection Systems for Residences, Libraries, Small Museums, and Art Galleries

Albert S. Janjigian

PHYSICAL SECURITY

A physical security system is comprised of products that physically deter a potential burglar from attempting to enter a premise. These devices range from locks on doors to bars or grates on windows, many of which make a burglar's job almost impossible. However, experts in the security field are emphatically against the use of many of the physical security products on the market today. A product such as a grate or a thick wire screen that, once installed, cannot be removed without a lot of work becomes a "double-edged sword" in terms of security and protection. Although the product renders the door or window on which it is installed virtually burglarproof, it also eliminates the door or window as a means of egress in the event of a fire, with potentially catastrophic consequences. No physical security product should be installed that cannot be removed by a resident or employee with a minimum of force, unless there is absolutely no chance that the opening (door or window) the product secures could be used as an escape route in a fire.

Nevertheless, there are many effective and safe ways to construct a physical security system. Steel doors with strong locks (morticed brass deadbolts are strongly recommended) provide an effective deterrent to burglars; however, they are not always aesthetically pleasing. Doors that contain glass should be avoided. Chain-link fences have been proven to deter burglars, although they, too, are not always aesthetically acceptable, and other types of fencing can be equally effective.

The benefits of extensive outside lighting should not be underestimated. No burglar wants to work where he can be seen. In addition, good lighting allows neighbors and police to observe the premises better, a desirable benefit when buildings are unoccupied.

Physical security products frequently do not provide a coordinated approach to protection. The products perform individually. For overall protection you must turn to an electronic security system.

ELECTRONIC SECURITY SYSTEM DEALERS

When purchasing an electronic security system it is imperative that a reputable dealer is chosen. It is a good idea to consult a state burglar and fire alarm association or the National Burglar and Fire Alarm Association (NBFAA) in Washington, D.C., which has over 400 alarm dealers in its membership who offer reliable equipment, installation, and service. You should also ask for customer references and not be afraid to check them out.

A great deal can be learned about a company through its sales representative. A sales representative should be knowledgeable about all areas of the alarm industry. It is his job to "tailor" a system that will provide the level of protection needed with as little disruption as possible to the facility. This can generally be accomplished through an effective system design.

To design an alarm system, a sales representative chooses from among the many alarm products available to him those products that best suit the individual application. You should be cautious if a representative is not flexible with regard to the products he chooses. This may mean that the representative has a limited knowledge of the alarm industry.

A good electronic security system should be presented as a group of services, not as a group of products like a physical security system. The electronic security system dealer should become an *active* participant in the protection of a facility by designing, installing, servicing, and perhaps even monitoring the security system. Any electronic security system that is not presented as a group of services should be scrutinized closely.

The services offered by alarm companies vary, with some companies providing more than others, but all alarm companies should be able to provide the basic services. The following list of alarm company services is explained later.

ALARM COMPANY SERVICES

BASIC

SECURITY SURVEY–DESIGN SYSTEMS
SYSTEM PROPOSALS (at least two)
INSTALLATION / TESTING / DEMONSTRATING
SERVICE DEPARTMENT
LOCAL ALARM SYSTEM

OPTIONAL

CENTRAL STATION SERVICE

Direct Wire System
    Uses leased telephone line
- 24-hour monitoring/tamperproof
- Police notification
- Homeowner notification
- Other notification (optional)
- Alarm company guard service (optional)
- Alarm company guard service with keys (optional)

Communicator (digital or tape) System
    Uses existing telephone line
- Homeowner notification
- Police notification
- Other notification (optional)
- Alarm company guard service (optional)
- Alarm company guard service with keys (optional)

The security survey and system proposal are self-explanatory. You should be particularly careful that the alarm company uses capable installers. Wiring should be concealed wherever possible, and if it is not, it should be run neatly and be protected. Sloppy installations can cause false alarms. The service department should also do neat work and be available on short notice.

All alarm companies install "local alarms." This means that when it is violated, the system will actuate devices (bells, sirens, etc.) on the property.

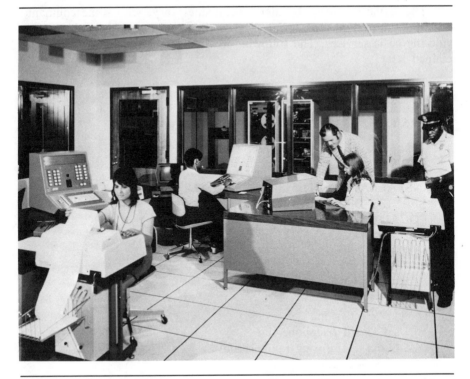

Figure 13.1. A fully computerized alarm company central station. It is capable of receiving an alarm signal from thousands of customers. This is often the most expensive and most reliable service.

Some companies utilize some type of "central station" to receive and respond to an alarm signal. These central stations vary in sophistication from a simple electronic box in a dealer's facility to a fully computerized, guarded, almost military-like plant (see Figure 13.1). The direct wire service and the communicator service are explained later.

Generally, a system purchased from a smaller company is less expensive. Small companies do not have the overhead that a large company has; however, they often are not capable of providing all the services that a large company can (i.e., central station). Larger companies are often better equipped to protect objects of substantial value, such as art treasures.

THE ELECTRONIC SECURITY SYSTEM

Every electronic security system consists of three basic elements: the alarm sensors, the control panel, and the reporting devices (see Figure 13.2). Alarm

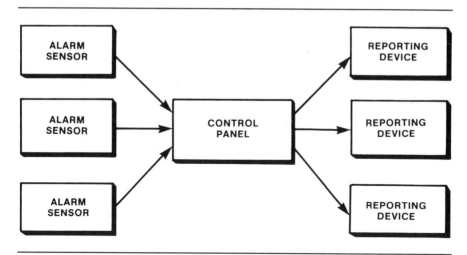

Figure 13.2. The electronic security system

sensors are the protective devices installed to monitor different parts of the building. A sensor reports, usually by way of wires, any change in the status of whatever it is monitoring to the control panel, which interprets this report and decides whether or not to activate the reporting devices. The sensors are like the nerve endings in a human body; the control panel is like the brain; and the reporting devices can be compared to the mouth.

Alarm Sensors

Alarm sensors can be divided into two categories: space protection devices and perimeter protection devices. A perimeter protection device does exactly what its name suggests: it notifies the control panel if any perimeter door or window is violated. Different products do this in different ways, however.

Magnetic Contacts. The most widely used device for protecting a door is the magnetic contact. A magnet is attached to the door and a contact (electrical switch) is attached to the door frame. When the door is closed the magnet and the contact line up close together and the control panel, to which the contact is connected by way of a wire, "sees" a "good" circuit. Upon opening the door, the magnet moves away from the contact. When this occurs, the control panel sees a "break." The control panel must then decide whether or not to activate the reporting device.

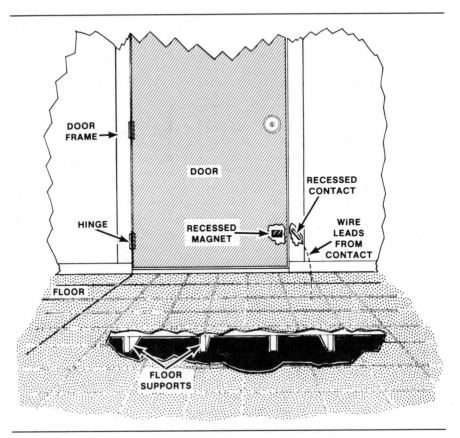

Figure 13.3. Installation of a recessed magnetic contact

There are many kinds of magnetic contacts. The most popular model is a recessed type, which means that, once it is installed, it is not visible (see Figure 13.3). To install a recessed contact in a door, the installer drills a small hole through the door frame and then drills either down into the cellar or up into the attic. A tube-shaped contact is sunk into the hole. This contact has wires attached to it that connect to the alarm circuit. Another hole is drilled in the door for a tube-shaped magnet so that when the door is closed the ends of the two "tubes" line up. When these holes are filled and painted, that alarm connection virtually disappears. Other types of magnetic contacts can be mounted on surfaces where aesthetics are not a prime concern.

Magnetic contacts are often used to protect windows; however, they do not protect against glass breakage because they do not operate unless the window is physically opened. A window contact can be avoided by a burglar who breaks the glass and climbs through the opening.

Figure 13.4. Window bug. (Courtesy of United Security Prod., Inc.)

Window Bug. A more effective way of window protection is to combine the use of a magnetic contact with a window "bug," which is a small electronic device that, when adhered to a window, alerts the control panel when it "hears" the sound of breaking glass (see Figure 13.4). The bug contains a small microphone that is calibrated to recognize the sound frequency emitted by breaking glass. The disadvantage of a window "bug" is that the device itself and most of its wiring must be visible. The "bug," however, is small enough to be hidden by curtains in many instances.

Shock Sensor. Shock sensors are perimeter protection devices that are used to protect both doors and windows. They are about the size of a matchbook (Figure 13.5) and are mounted on the door or window frame. Any intrusion attempt such as pounding on a door or window transmits high-frequency shock waves that the shock sensor detects and reports to the control panel. Shock sensors also must be visible, but they can be mounted close to the floor and frequently be painted to match the wall color.

Window Foil. Window "foil" is the most effective way to protect glass. No electronic or mechanical device has been developed that provides as much reliability with as much resistance to false alarms; however, window foil is

Figure 13.5. Shock sensor. (Courtesy of Litton)

quite unattractive, being designed primarily for commercial use. Foil is recommended strongly in areas where aesthetics are not a concern, such as cellar windows. Foil is also highly visible from the outside thus alerting a potential intruder to the fact that the building has an alarm system, which may in itself be a deterrent to crime.

Security Screens.   Other effective and, at the same time, attractive devices used to protect windows are security screens. These screens look and function the same as ordinary aluminum insect screens; however, tiny wires woven in them detect when a screen is removed or cut. Window screens may be the most expensive way to protect windows because each screen must be custom made, but they can be virtually foolproof and they do allow for ventilation without sacrificing security.

   Other perimeter protection devices are:
   • Reed switches
   • Wire lacing
   • Ball traps
   • Breakaway cords
   • Leaf switches
   • Push button switches
   • Roller switches

Space Protection

The major function of space protection devices is to establish burglar "traps." The number and extent of these traps depend on what you want to protect and how much you want to spend. Basically, a trap is established either in an area that contains an item or items of great value or in an area through which a potential burglar is likely to travel.

Switch Mats. Switch mats are one of the simplest and least expensive space protection devices available. They are installed on the floor, under a rug or on the bare floor, and alert the control panel when they are stepped on. Switch mats are particularly effective when installed on a stairway with a minimum of three steps. This type of "trap" in effect cuts one floor of a house off from another. If wall-to-wall carpeting has to be moved in order to install switch mats, you should make sure that it is replaced properly so that a burglar will not notice that a security device has been installed. It often makes sense to have a professional carpet installer participate in the work.

Stress Sensors. Like switch mats, stress sensors detect where an intruder walks. However, they do so by monitoring the structural stress caused by an intruder's movement. The installer epoxies the stress sensor to floor beams under areas where a "trap" is to be established. One stress sensor can protect an area as large as 300 square feet (27 square meters) depending on structural characteristics. Stress sensors automatically adjust to changes in the weight on the floor, which might be caused by rearranging the furniture in a room. In addition, they work extremely well for protecting the roof of a building.

Photoelectric Beam. A photoelectric beam, commonly known as an electric eye, detects an intruder passing through an invisible beam of light that is transmitted from one strategic location to another. The control panel "sees" this interruption in the beam and decides whether or not to activate the reporting devices. Photoelectric beams often are quite unobtrusive, looking like standard electrical outlets when they are recess-mounted (see Figure 13.6). Photoelectric beams are particularly effective for "trapping" long hallways or when aimed through doorways to cut off a whole section of a house. Small rooms limit the effectiveness of a photoelectric beam. The longer a beam travels, the more cost-effective protection it provides.

Ultrasonic. The space protection device most widely used by alarm companies is the ultrasonic motion detector. While a photoelectric device transmits an invisible beam of light, an ultrasonic motion detector transmits high-frequency (ultrasonic) sound energy. This forms an invisible three-dimensional

Figure 13.6. A photoelectric beam recessed into a wall as part of a home alarm system. As stated, the device looks much like an ordinary electrical outlet. (Courtesy of Korday)

pattern within a protected area that echoes back to the motion detector. Movement in the protected area disrupts this pattern, causing the frequency of the sound energy to change. The detector interprets this frequency change as the motion of an intruder and notifies the control panel.

Figure 13.7 shows the invisible protective pattern of high-frequency sound energy produced by an ultrasonic motion detector. An intruder is detected when he walks into the balloon-like pattern. As the illustration shows, there are corner-mount and wall-mount units. There are also ceiling-mount units. Some units produce two patterns for protecting larger areas.

The first ultrasonic detectors, appearing on the market in the early 1970s, revolutionized the alarm industry. The prospect of having one detector protect a whole room instead of having to wire every door and window appealed to alarm dealers. Installation time was cut drastically. Like most new products, however, the first ultrasonic detectors were accompanied by several "bugs." In certain instances they would mistake normal movement or noise, such as vibrations, air turbulance, telephone bells, or hissing from a heater, for an intruder and cause a false alarm to go off. These problems have been virtually eliminated with the evolution of ultrasonics into its present state.

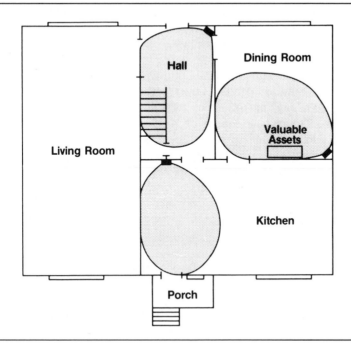

Figure 13.7. Protective pattern of an ultrasonic motion detector. (Courtesy of Aritech Corp.)

There are many good detectors on the market. One recent development, "balanced signal processing," makes a detector virtually immune to false alarms while increasing its sensitivity to the movement of an intruder. Ultrasonic detectors featuring balanced signal processing are ideal for high-security areas containing valuable objects.

Passive Infrared. Unlike ultrasonic detectors, passive infrared (PIR) intrusion detectors do not transmit any energy. Rather, PIRs contain a sensing element that "looks" out over parts of a "trap" area measuring the invisible (infrared) energy emitted by the objects in the area. The viewing pattern of the sensing element (or what part of a trap area is seen by the sensing element) is determined by a group of mirrors in the detector. The viewing pattern can be thought of as a group of protective "fingers" spread through the trap area. The length and width of these fingers are determined by the design of the mirrors. When an intruder crosses a protective finger the sensing element "sees" an increase in the infrared energy caused by the heat of the intruder's body. This causes the PIR to report an intrusion to the control panel.

The drawings in Figures 13.8A and B illustrate the protective fingers of a passive infrared intrusion detector. When an intruder crosses a finger, which is actually a viewing area through which the detector's sensing element measures infrared energy, he is detected. The size and length of the fingers are determined by the mirror construction within the detector. Different trap areas in a home require different finger patterns. The long-range unit is designed to protect long, narrow areas such as hallways, while the wide-angle unit is designed to protect square or rectangular areas such as rooms.

Because PIRs respond to a change in infrared energy resulting from a change in temperature, care should be taken by the installer not to locate a detector where it could mistakenly see any object that changes temperature rapidly. These objects include heaters and walls or windows that are exposed to solar heat. In addition, the homeowner should be certain that any PIR installed comes equipped with the following features, both of which resist false alarms:

STEP–FOCUS–OPTICS   Design of mirror provides for optimum detection of man-sized targets while ignoring small nuisance targets.

BALANCED DETECTION: Each protective "finger" is actually split in two, and an alarm is initiated only when both sections of a finger are crossed.

Figure 13.8.　Passive infrared. Wide angle coverage. (Courtesy Aritech Corp.)

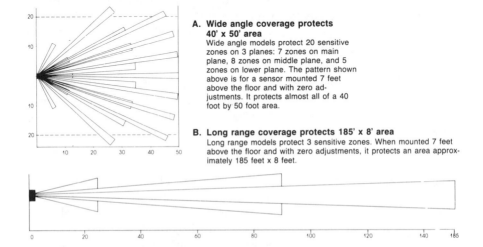

A. Wide angle coverage protects 40' x 50' area
Wide angle models protect 20 sensitive zones on 3 planes: 7 zones on main plane, 8 zones on middle plane, and 5 zones on lower plane. The pattern shown above is for a sensor mounted 7 feet above the floor and with zero adjustments. It protects almost all of a 40 foot by 50 foot area.

B. Long range coverage protects 185' x 8' area
Long range models protect 3 sensitive zones. When mounted 7 feet above the floor and with zero adjustments, it protects an area approximately 185 feet x 8 feet.

Microwave. A microwave intrusion detector transmits microwave energy toward a potential target. This energy is reflected back to the receiver portion of the device. The information is processed similar to that of a radar set to indicate movement. Shape of the coverage area is controlled by the placement and shape of the unit's internal antenna. Range of the unit is adjustable with models available in 20-feet to as much as 100-feet pattern configurations. The patterns are three-dimensional and shaped like tear drops similar to the ultrasonic pattern.

Most microwave motion detectors are self-contained transceivers usually incorporating a standby power supply.

It may seem that ultrasonic, passive infrared, and microwave detectors all do exactly the same thing — provide space protection in alarm systems — and they do. The different principles of operation employed by these sensors however, cause them to respond differently to different ambient conditions in a so-called trap area. Some conditions affect the operation of one type of sensor while not affecting the others. This gives alarm dealers the ability to choose the right sensor to provide the best protection with the least problems. Figure 13.9 shows what kinds of conditions may affect the detectors. If, however, any of the three types can be used, ultrasonic sensors tend to be the least expensive.

Control Panel

The control panel is the "brain" of an electronic security system. Through its circuitry, the alarm is turned on and off. It determines if and when to actuate the reporting devices. Most home alarm control panels are powered by 6 to 24 volts of alternating current (A.C.) supplied by a transformer that plugs into an ordinary electrical outlet (similar to the plug-in transformer connection for a calculator). Some control panels must be wired directly to the building's electrical system. In the event of a power blackout or in case a potential intruder interrupts the building's current (e.g., by smashing the outside electrical meter), it is imperative that a control panel have a standby battery as an auxiliary source of power. Some control panels are equipped with an automatic charging circuit to keep the battery at full strength at all times. The capacity and quality of the control panel determine the capacity and quality of the entire system. Some panels are more complex than others, but complex control equiment is not a necessary criterion for a home alarm. There are, however, certain features that every home alarm control panel should have.

Zoning. The panel should have the capacity for at least three separate zones of protection. One should be a 24-hour zone that is active all the time,

ENVIRONMENTAL AND OTHER VARIABLES	ULTRASONIC	PASSIVE INFRARED	MICROWAVE
Vibration	No problem with balanced processing, some problem with unbalanced	Very few problems	Can be a major problem
Effect of temperature change on range	A little	A lot	None
Effect of humidity change on range	Some	None	None
Reflection of area of coverage by large metal objects	Very little	None, unless metal is highly polished	Can be a major problem
Reduction of range by drapes, carpets	Some	None	None
Sensitivity to movement of overhead doors	Needs careful placement	Very few problems	Can be a major problem
Sensitivity to small animals	Problem if animals close	Problem if animals close but can be aimed so beams are well above floor	Problem if animals close
Water movement in plastic storm drain pipes	No problem	No problem	Can be problem if very close
Water noise from faulty valves	Can be a problem Very rare	No problem	No problem
Movement through thin walls or glass	No problem	No problem	Needs careful placement
Drafts, air movement	Needs careful placement	No problem	No problem
Sun, moving headlights, through windows	No problem	Needs careful placement	No problem
Ultrasonic noise	Bells, hissing, some inaudible noises can cause problems	No problem	No problem
Heaters	Problem only in extreme cases	Needs careful placement	No problem
Moving machinery, fan blades	Needs careful placement	Very little problem	Needs careful placement
Radio interference, AC line transients	Can be problem in severe cases	Can be problem in severe cases	Can be problem in severe cases
"Piping" of detection field to unexpected areas by A/C ducting	No problem	No problem	Occasional problem where beam is directed at duct outlet
Radar interference	Very few problems	Very few problems	Can be problem when radar is close and sensor pointed at it
Cost per square ft. large open areas	In between	Most expensive	Least expensive
Cost per square ft. divided areas/multiple rooms	Least expensive	Most expensive	In between
Range adjustment required	Yes	No	Yes
Current consumption (size of battery required for extended standby power)	In between	Smallest	Largest
Interference between two or more sensors	Must be crystal controlled and/or synchronized	No problem	Must be different frequencies

Figure 13.9. Space protection guide-what detector to select. This is intended as a guide only and does not represent absolutes but suggests areas for consideration. (Courtesy of Aritech Corp.)

whether the alarm is turned on or off. It can be used to protect valuable objects 24 hours a day.

This zone should also include a "tamper" circuit to protect any alarm devices that are mounted outside the building (bell, sirens, etc.) from being tampered with. The second zone should be comprised of all the perimeter protection devices, and the third zone should include all the interior space protection devices.

Zoning an electronic security system in this fashion provides three stages of protection. One zone is active all the time; this is stage one. The perimeter zone is stage two. When it is on by itself, all the perimeter openings are protected. Stage three, the space protection zone, can be added to the other stages to provide maximum protection.

This kind of zoning provides a great deal of flexibility in using the system. For example, when the building is unoccupied, all three stages of the alarm system can be armed. However, when the building is occupied, you may opt to arm only stage two. In this application, the perimeter openings and all 24-hour devices are protected, but the space protection devices are off, allowing for normal movement throughout the interior.

Remote Arming and Disarming. Another feature that an alarm control panel should have is the capacity for remote *arming and disarming*. This means that the alarm can be turned on and off from convenient locations around the premises, as opposed to having to operate the system only from the control panel. These on/off remote stations should allow you to select which zones will be on in different situations, as well as to arm and disarm the system.

In addition, on/off remote stations should be equipped with lighted indicators that display the status of the system. These "status" indicators should provide the operator with the ability to easily and quickly recognize (1) whether the alarm is on or off; (2) if any and/or all of the protective zones are secure; and (3) if the alarm has been violated. See Figure 13.10 for different types of on/off stations.

Exit/Entry Delay. Every alarm control should be equipped with an *exit/entry delay* feature. This allows you to arm the system from an on/off station inside and then leave within a set amount of time. Conversely, you may enter the building and disarm the system within a set amount of time. Some dealers do not utilize the exit/entry delay feature, but instead install on/off station(s) on the exterior of the building to provide for arming and disarming the system when the building is unoccupied. You should be aware that the operation of an exterior on/off station can sometimes be affected by the weather.

An exterior on/off remote station should also be made electronically tamperproof to prevent a potential intruder from disarming the system from outside.

Reporting Devices

The function of the reporting devices in an electronic security system is two-fold: to alert the residents that the alarm has been violated, and to alert another party or parties so that a predetermined response can be initiated (see

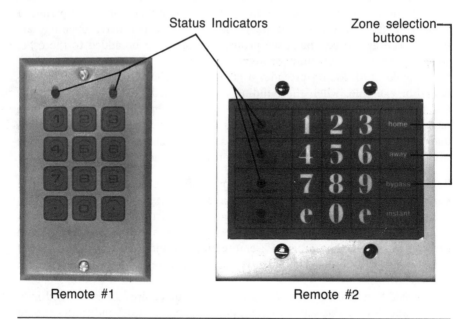

Figure 13.10. Two types of remote on/off station. On both a secret number code is pushed to arm or disarm the alarm system. Both have "status indicators." Remote #2 is also equipped with buttons that allow the homeowner to select which protective zones will be armed. Pushing the "home" button activates zones one and two. Pushing the "away" button activates all three zones providing maximum security

Figure 13.11). Every home security system should have at least one audible reporting device (bell, siren, etc.) located inside the house to alert residents (strobe lights are recommended for alerting deaf residents). More audible devices are strongly recommended for outside the house to alert neighbors and aid police in finding the residence, as well as to scare an intruder away. There is no such thing as too much noise when a home alarm is violated. The homeowner should be sure to abide by any local laws or ordinances governing the length of time that a device can sound. Any audible device mounted on the outside of a house should be secured with bolts that go through the walls to the inside of the house (toggle bolts). An exterior audible device should also be made electronically tamperproof.

As stated earlier, a local alarm system, when violated, actuates an audible and/or visible reporting device on the property. In many cases, a local alarm provides adequate protection; however, when a residence contains valuable objects such as an art collection, it is recommended that the homeowner supplement the local alarm system with central station service.

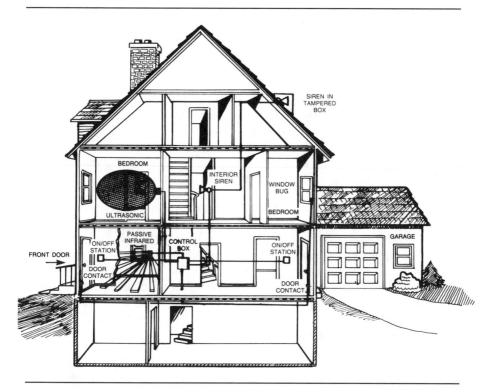

Figure 13.11.   Home alarm system. The drawing illustrates a home alarm
system. The front door contact, rear door contact and the window bug are on the perimeter zone. The ultrasonic detector
and the passive infrared detector provide "traps" for the interior zone. There are two on/off stations by the front and
back doors. There is both an interior and an exterior audible
reporting device. Wires connect all of these to the control
panel which is the "brain" of the alarm system

Central Station.   A central station is a control center located at an alarm
company's facility where alarm systems are monitored. If an alarm is violated, the central station receives a signal and notifies the local police. Sometimes the central station will initiate an independent response. As stated
earlier, these central stations vary in sophistication. Thus the services offered
can vary greatly. Some alarm companies employ guards who can be dispatched when an alarm signal is received. Often these guards are supplied
with the keys to a residence to initiate a rapid investigation of an alarm and
to provide access for the police.

There are two ways to transmit an alarm message to a central station:

over existing telephone lines or over separate leased telephone lines that directly connect the home alarm system to the central station (direct wire system). Not all alarm companies can provide direct wire service, which obviously provides the highest degree of protection. The following devices are the different kinds of reporting devices that connect an alarm to a central station.

Tape Dialer.   The simplest and least expensive notification device is the tape dialer, which uses an eight-track tape to telephone the central station and/or the police or any other party and deliver an alarm message. The amount of times a tape dialer will attempt to dial out is limited to the length of the tape. This can be a problem when the number dialed is busy.

Digital Communicator.   A digital comminucator is a solid-state reporting device that sends an electronically coded message to a special receiver in an alarm company central station. It connects to the existing telephone lines in a residence. Upon receiving this code, the central station notifies the police department and any other party you designate of an alarm. Digital communicators provide greater assurance of the transmission of an alarm signal than a tape dialer because the alarm company controls each phase of the transmission from the installation of the communicator to the monitoring of the receiver in the central station.

Direct Wire System.   The highest degree of home security provided by a notification device is through a direct connection to an alarm company central station. This system is also the most expensive. A wire, run by the telephone company (and for which there is a monthly fee), connects the building directly to the central station. The alarm signal is monitored around the clock by the alarm company. The connecting wire itself is monitored to preclude tampering. A direct connection provides immediate response to an alarm signal and is recommended for use in facilities that contain valuable art objects. There are some direct wire systems that connect an alarm to the local police station; however, the police are not always able to monitor these systems as closely as an alarm company might.

CONCLUSION

The priciples for security stated in this chapter are designed to educate you about what a basic security system should entail. It cannot be stressed too strongly that each application of a security system is different (i.e., no two alarms are alike). Before contacting alarm companies, you should have an idea of what you want to protect.

Appendix 13.1

Specifications for a Fully-Zoned Ultrasonic Intrusion Alarm System*

I.   General

1.0 *Introduction*

The following specifications outline the requirements for a fully-zoned intrusion detection system which provides individual alarm indications from each sensor in every area protected. Included in the specifications are detailed elements which are essential for maximum system stability and integrity. Also for the same reason, certain features and concepts have been specifically prohibited.

The sensors must be able to accommodate changing levels of environmental interference such as air turbulence, without false alarming or losing substantial protection capability. However, to prevent system compromise, no manually adjustable turbulence compensation or other device affecting the system response may be employed.

1.1 *Sensors*

Each remote sensor must be capable of identifying itself visibly as the source of an alarm signal, retaining that information and, if required, activating remote visual registers to provide a fully-zoned system. All remote sensors shall have their coverage patterns/ranges individually adjustable. However, the system shall not include a common adjustment whereby the remote sensors are collectively adjustable.

1.2 *Mode Control*

System zone indications shall be remotely controllable in three modes: "reset," "latch," and "freeze," as hereinafter described.

1.3 *Zone Indication*

Optional remote zone display shall be by collective register or duplicate graphic display or both if required and shall display alarm status.

1.3.1 The zone display must be capable of being coupled with any required peripheral device such as a local alarm, access control or multiplex transmission system.

_____

*Prepared by Aritech Corp., Framingham, Mass., 01701.

1.3.2   For greater visibility, zone alarm indications at the remote sensor, remote register or graphic display will be by means of a flashing light emitting diode (L.E.D.) with a duty cycle of 10%.

1.4   *Operating Frequency*

Operating ultrasonic frequency shall be nominally 26 kHz. In any case, the frequency shall be above 24 kHz to prevent sound induced physiologically disturbing stresses and fatigue, and below 30 kHz to avoid undue attenuation of the signal.

1.5   *Operating Power*

Maximum peak power output of the transmitter shall not exceed 105 dB SPL at any angle, 1 meter or greater range per safe levels as stated in U.S. Environmental Protection Agency Report 550/9-73-002.

1.6   *Interconnection*

DC Power, Transmit Reference, and Signal Conductors are to be carried throughout the system in a common cable from the control unit to the remote sensors.

1.6.1   If remote zone register or graphic display is required, additional wiring shall be limited to one conductor per remote sensor.

1.6.2   The system must be capable of utilizing multiple branch circuits. Each branch shall not exceed 1,000 feet of cable, nor shall the total cable exceed the maximum specified for the system used.

1.7   *UL Listing*

The intrusion alarm system must be listed by Underwriters' Laboratories for local and central office alarm service.

1.8   *Control Unit Relays*

There shall be separate alarm and tamper/supervisory relays. Each relay shall be energized in the normal non-alarm condition. The alarm relay shall provide both normally-open and normally-closed contacts; the supervisory relay contacts shall be closed in the non-alarm state. The system alarm relay shall operate on system detections or remain in the protection mode, as appropriate, regardless of the presence, absence, or status of sensor or remote zone indicators. Alarm relay contacts shall be rated at 1 ampere at 115 VAC.

1.9   *Other Alarm Indicators*

In addition to alarm relay operation, the sensors shall be capable of providing a visual alarm indicator at each sensor, independent of other sensors.

II.   Detailed Specifications — Master Control

2.0   *Master Control, General*

The master control unit shall consist of a power supply, crystal oscillator reference circuit, alarm relay, optional add-on tamper circuitry, supervisory relay and remote sensor-interface electronics. All circuitry must be solid state. (The control unit shall not contain a sensitivity control of any type capable of adjusting overall system sensitivity.)

2.1 *Master Control Unit Power Supply*
The power supply shall be capable of operating with an input voltage of
18-24 volts ± 15% AC, 50/60 Hz, single phase. During power failure, a
standby battery shall power the system for at least 8 hours under normal
room temperatures with a minimum of 6 hours at 32°F (0°C). A step down
transformer shall be supplied for low AC voltage operation at 18 VAC, if
required. The transformer shall be a U.L. listed, Class II transformer with a
rating of at least 0.84A at 18 VAC.

2.2 *Transceiver Unit Signal-Processing Circuitry*
The system shall employ signal processing for high immunity to interference.
2.2.1 Detection capability: within the area covered by each ultrasonic
sensor, the signal processing circuitry shall be capable of detecting
intruder movement down to 0.4 feet per second.
2.2.2 Sensitivity Control Restriction: A sensitivity control capable of
adjusting overall system sensitivity shall not be employed. Within the
area covered by each passive infrared sensor, the signal processing
circuitry shall be capable of detecting a change in radiation contrast
down to less than 3° centigrade.

2.3 *Master Control Unit Sensor-Driver Circuit*
The driver circuitry shall be capable of supplying sufficient power to ener-
gize up to 15 sensor units.

2.4 *Master Control Tamper and Cable-Supervisory Circuit*
Electronically controlled tamper/supervisory circuits added to the master
control unit and employing end of line supervisory resistors in the last sensor
of each branch circuit shall be provided. A tamper/supervisory alarm shall
result from shorting or opening transmit or power conductors in the
common cable interconnecting the control unit and each sensor.

2.4.1 In addition, the control unit and each sensor enclosure shall contain
provisions for a tamper switch to detect unauthorized entry.

2.4.2 This entire circuit shall be isolated from external alarm loops by a
tamper/supervisory relay.

III. Detailed Specifications: Sensor Unit

3.0 *Sensor Unit: Ultrasonic*
Each remote ultrasonic sensor unit shall consist of a transmitting and receiving transducer, associated electronics, alarm indicating system, control and
related electronics; all contained in a single case.

3.1 *Sensor Unit: Passive Infrared (wide angle)*
Each wide angle remote passive infrared sensor unit shall consist of an
infrared sensing element, multifaceted optical system, with a detection angle
of not less than 110° and a range of not less than 30 feet. Associated electronics, alarm indicating system, control and related electronics are all contained within a single case. Detection capability shall be less than 3° Celsius
radiation contrast. Internal tamper protection shall be provided.

3.2   *Sensor Unit: Passive Infrared (long range)*

Each long range remote passive infrared sensor unit shall consist of an infrared sensing element, narrow beam width optical system, with a detection angle of not more than 10° and a range of not less than 100 feet. Associated electronics, alarm indicating system, control and related electronics are all contained within a single case. Detection capability shall be less than 3° Celsius radiation contrast. Internal tamper protection shall be provided.

3.3   *Sensor Unit: Universal Interface Unit*

Each universal interface sensor unit shall consist of circuitry converting the output of equipment using normally open or normally closed contacts to that which is compatible with the alarm initiating circuitry of the master control unit. The interface shall accept normally open or normally closed contacts, provide for negative and positive closed circuit loops, and accept fast acting contacts such as vibration sensors and photoelectric devices. Onboard alarm indicating circuitry as well as remote capability shall be provided. Internal tamper protection shall be provided.

3.4   *Sensor Indication*

Each sensor shall provide suitable electronics to provide for preamplification and control of the received signal and to recognize and display an individual alarm condition for that sensor only. Display shall be by means of a "blinking" light emitting diode (L.E.D.) located in the individual sensor; additionally, each sensor indicator shall be capable of remote display, should it be required.

3.5   *Mode Control*

The display logic circuitry and indicator must respond to three modes of operation.

3.5.1   *Reset,* which clears an alarm indication.

3.5.2   *Latch,* which acts as a memory of an alarm event by causing the display indication to be initiated on alarm and retained until reset.

3.5.3   *Freeze,* which inhibits additional responses to the latch mode and prevents a change in display status by personnel responding to the alarm.

3.6   *Deletion of Indicator*

Additionally, the individual sensor LED indicator shall be capable of being deleted or removed without interfering with remote displays, if required. The function of the system alarm relay shall not be affected by the presence, absence, or status of any zone indication.

3.7   *Operating Power*

Maximum peak power output of the transmitter shall not exceed the specifications as set forth in paragraph 1.5 of this specification, nor shall the operating frequency be less than 24 kHz nor more than 30 kHz for ultrasonic sensors.

3.8   *Range Control*

An adjustable range control shall be located within each sensor enclosure.

Adjustment shall be for ultrasonic sensors only and shall not affect or interact with the adjustment of another sensor.

3.9 *Walk-test*

Each sensor shall provide for a "day or partial occupancy walk test" for that sensor only, utilizing the visual alarm indicator on each sensor.

3.10 *Tamper*

Each sensor unit shall be capable of employing an isolated tamper-circuit switch and shall be capable of adapting to the tamper/supervisory system outlined in paragraphs 2.4 and 2.5.

IV. Component Physical Specifications

4.1 *Control Unit*

For ease of shipment and installation, the control unit shall not exceed the following dimensions: 4" (10.6 cm) x 10" (25.40 cm) x 15" (38.10 cm). Control unit weight should not exceed twelve (12) pounds, (5.4 kg).

4.2 *Sensor Units*

For reasons noted in paragraph 4.1, sensor enclosure dimensions shall not exceed 3½" (9 cm) x 2½" (5 cm) x 11" (28 cm). Weight is not to exceed 1.2 pounds (0.6 kg.).

4.3 *Operating Temperature*

The system control unit shall be capable of normal operation in ambient temperatures ranging from 32°F to 120°F (0°C to 50°C): remote sensors from 15°F to 120°F (–10°C to 50°C).

V. Installation Information

5.0 *Manual*

A complete installation and instruction manual of commercial quality must accompany each control unit.

5.1 *Substitution*

Substitution on an "or equal" basis will be permitted only on demonstration of equivalency of all specified features and characteristics. Final decision of qualifications lies solely with the specifying authority.

Notice to Specifying Authority:

Proper installation and service of any ultrasonic system requires an experience factor beyond the normal skills of wiring and hook-up. This experience is available only through regular burlgar alarm companies and electrical contractors regularly engaged in the alarm business. It is, therefore, strongly recommended that the following paragraphs concerning contractor qualifications be included in the specification.

Suggested Contractor Requirement Under General Conditions or Contractor Requirements

Each bidder must be a burglar alarm and service company contractor who has been regularly engaged in the installation and maintenance of similar intrusion alarm systems for a period of three years. The contractor must show proper evidence, if required, that he is accustomed to performing work of the specified technical scope and project size.

In the event the contractor cannot qualify under the three year experience clause above, evidence of being a known operator of an established burglar alarm central station or listing as as Underwriters' Laboratories-qualified burglar alarm installation company, or full membership in the National Burglar and Fire Alarm Association, or Central Station Electrical Protection Association will be accepted as an alternative.

Appendix 13.2

Application Guidelines For
Exterior Intrusion Detectors*

Many false alarms can be prevented by selecting the proper sensor for the application and by using good installation practices. Guides listed below should be considered in the intrusion detection system design along with the guides recommended in the manufacturer's installation manual for the specific equipment being installed.

Before listing guides for specific exterior detectors, some generation guidelines are listed that are applicable for all detectors. The guides are not listed in any order of priority.

General.
a.   Check all equipment for shipping damage prior to installation.
b.   Check the equipment after installation for damage.
c.   Check that all electrical connections are secure.
d.   Mount detector transducers, especially active motion detector transducers, rigidly on vibration-free surfaces.
e.   Adjust detector sensitivity level for adequate detection in the worst case operating environment.
f.   Areas containing sources of electromagnetic energy (radio transmitters, radar, electrical switches, large motors, generators, etc.) could cause severe operational problems.
g.   Avoid adjusting any detector sensitivity so high that it will be susceptible to false alarms.
h.   Detector enclosures should be tamper-protected and the tamper alarms monitored continuously.
i.   Detector processor units installed out-of-doors should be in weatherproof enclosures and the circuit boards should be conformal coated.

---

*From *Intrusion Detection Systems* by Robert Barnard, Butterworth Publishers, 1981.

j.   All interconnecting cables should be installed in sealed conduit and, where applicable, buried in the ground.

k.   Exterior detection zone lengths should be limited to about 300 linear feet.

Fence Disturbance Sensors.

a.   The fence fabric should be reasonably tight and the fence posts well anchored.

b.   All fence signs should be removed or secured so they will not rattle.

c.   Gates should be well secured so that they will not rattle.

d.   Bottom of fence fabric should be in close proximity to the ground or, better yet, anchored down.

e.   All brush and tree branches should be cut or removed so they will not rub against the fence.

Microwave Detectors.

a.   Ground should be level with no dips or obstructions between the transmitter and receiver.

b.   Zones of detection should be overlapped (approximately twice the distance from the transmitter to where the beam touches the ground).

c.   Grass should be removed or maintained at a length of no greater than 4 inches between the transmitter and receiver.

d.   Snow should not accumulate more than about 4 inches.

e.   Dectectors should be located far enough from the fence that the fence will not interfere with the microwave beam.

Infrared Detectors.

a.   Ground should be level with no dips or obstructions between the detector columns.

b.   Bottom beam should be no greater than 6 inches above the ground.

c.   Top infrared beam should be at least 4 feet above the ground.

d.   Zones of detection should be overlapped or top of detector columns protected with pressure switch.

Electric-Field Detectors.

a.   When detector is installed on chain-link fences, the fence fabric should be reasonably tight.

b.   All vegetation must be removed from under the electric-field fence.

Geophone Sensors.
    a.   Locate sensor to avoid objects anchored in ground that could move in the wind.
    b.   Backfill dirt for geophone trench should be well tamped.

Strain/magnetic Line Sensors.
    a.   Locate sensor cable to avoid objects anchored in the ground.
    b.   When crossing over or under power lines with the sensor line can not be avoided, then cross perpendicular to them.
    c.   Avoid routing signal and power cables in the same trench with the transducer cable.
    d.   Backfill dirt should be well compacted.

Appendix 13.3

Application Guidelines For Interior Intrusion Detectors*

The intent of this summary is to present a list of basic guidelines that should be considered in the selection, design, installation, and operation of interior intrusion detectors.

Ultrasonic Motion Detectors

a.　Avoid using ultrasonic detectors in areas with large volumes of moving air caused by open windows, doors, vents, etc.

b.　Avoid directing the transceivers at large glass windows, nonrigid partitions, warehouse doors, etc., that might vibrate and cause false alarms.

c.　Avoid directing transceivers directly at each other unless they are separated by an adequate distance to prevent interference (usually about 60 feet).

d.　Avoid locating individual receivers or transceivers close to air conditioning and heating registers.

e.　Position the transceivers and separate receivers at least 10 feet from telephone bells or any type of bell (unless otherwise indicated by the manufacturer).

Microwave Motion Detectors

a.　Avoid locating detectors closer than 10 feet to bare fluorescent lamps, especially if the detector will be pointed toward the lamp, without first determining that the fluorescent lamps will not affect the detectors.

b.　Avoid directing the transmitted energy toward nonrigid metal partitions, thin metal walls, or large metal doors that might be vibrated by wind, passing trucks, airplanes, etc.

---

*From *Intrusion Detection Systems* by Robert Barnard, Butterworth Publishers, 1981.

c. Avoid directing the transmitted energy toward windows, wooden walls, or any wall that the energy can penetrate and perhaps detect outside movement.

d. Avoid directing the transceivers toward rotating or moving machinery.

e. After an installation is complete, check movement outside the protected area that might cause alarms. (Remember, cars and trucks are larger targets and can cause alarms when at greater distances than human movement.)

Sonic Motion Detectors

a. Consider the fact that sonic detectors generate an audible high frequency tone that might be heard several hundred feet from the area being protected, depending on the building construction.

Infrared Motion Detectors

a. Avoid directing the detectors toward heat sources that cycle on and off.

b. Avoid directing the detectors toward burning incandescent lamps.

c. Avoid mounting the detectors over heat sources such as radiators or hot pipe lines.

d. Avoid directing the detectors toward windows where sunlight enters.

Audible Detectors

a. Avoid locating the receivers close to inside noise sources or near outside walls or doors where exterior noises could be a problem.

Vibration Detectors

a. Both structural and glass breakage detectors should be well secured to the surface where they are detecting penetrations.

b. Structural vibration detectors should be connected to a pulse-accumulating supervisory circuit that can be adjusted for the specific application and not alarm on a single impact.

Operable Opening Switches

a. Doors and windows should be well secured to prevent excessive motion that might cause false alarms.

Photoelectric Detectors

a.   Mount transmitters and receivers along with any mirrors securely on vibration-free surfaces.
b.   Avoid using mirrors with detectors covering long ranges or ranges over 100 feet.
c.   Conceal transmitters and receivers to reduce compromise.

Capacitance Proximity Detectors

a.   Avoid using wooden blocks to isolate the protected metal object from the ground plane.
b.   Reference ground plane should be well grounded to provide adequate electrical potential differential between the metal object and ground.

Pressure Mats

a.   Conceal pressure mats to reduce compromise.

Appendix 13.4

Terms and Definitions for Intrusion Alarm Systems*

Access Control — The control of pedestrian and vehicular traffic through entrances and exits of a **Protected Area** or premises.

Access Mode — The operation of an **Alarm System** such that no **Alarm Signal** is given when the **Protected Area** is entered; however, a signal may be given if the **Sensor, Annunciator,** or **Control Unit** is tampered with or opened.

Access/Secure Control Unit — See **Control Unit.**

Access Switch — See **Authorized Access Switch.**

Accumulator — A circuit which accumulates a sum. For example, in an audio alarm control unit, the accumulator sums the amplitudes of a series of pulses, which are larger than some threshold level, subtracts from the sum at a predetermined rate to account for random background pulses, and initiates an alarm signal when the sum exceed some predetermined level. This circuit is also called an integrator; in digital circuits it may be called a counter.

Active Intrusion Sensor — An active sensor which detects the presence of an intruder within the range of the sensor. Examples are an **Ultrasonic Motion Detector,** a **Radio Frequency Motion Detector,** and a **Photoelectric Alarm System.** See also **Passive Intrusion Sensor.**

Active Sensor — A sensor which detects the disturbance of a radiation field which is generated by the sensor. See also **Passive Sensor.**

Actuating Device — See **Actuator.**

Actuator — A manual or automatic switch or sensor such as **Holdup Button, Magnetic Switch,** or thermostat which causes a system to transmit an **Alarm Signal** when manually activated or when the device automatically senses an intruder or other unwanted condition.

Air Gap — The distance between two magnetic elements in a magnetic or electromagnetic circuit, such as between the core and the armature of a relay.

Alarm Circuit — An electrical circuit of an alarm system which produces or transmits an **Alarm Signal.**

Alarm Condition — A threatening condition, such as an intrusion, fire, or holdup, sensed by a **Detector.**

Alarm Device — A device which signals a warning in response to a **Alarm Condition,** such as a bell, siren, or **Annunciator.**

Alarm Discrimination — The ability of an alarm system to distinguish between those stimuli caused by an **Intrusion** and those which are a part of the environment.

Alarm Line — A wired electrical circuit used for the transmission of **Alarm Signals** from the protected premises to a **Monitoring Station.**

Alarm Receiver — See **Annunciator.**

Alarm Sensor — See **Sensor.**

Alarm Signal — A signal produced by a **Control Unit** indicating the existence of an **Alarm Condition.**

Alarm State -- The condition of a **Detector** which causes a **Control Unit** in the

---

*Courtesy U.S. Department of Justice, Law Enforcement Assistance Administration, National Institute of Law Enforcement and Criminal Justice.

Secure Mode to transmit an **Alarm Signal.**

Alarm Station—(1) A manually actuated device installed at a fixed location to transmit an **Alarm Signal** in response to an **Alarm Condition,** such as a concealed **Holdup Button** in a bank teller's cage. (2) A well-marked emergency control unit, installed in fixed locations usually accessible to the public, used to summon help in response to an **Alarm Condition.** The **Control Unit** contains either a manually actuated switch or telephone connected to fire or police headquarters, or a telephone answering service. See also **Remote Station Alarm System.**

Alarm System—An assembly of equipment and devices designated and arranged to signal the presence of an **Alarm Condition** requiring urgent attention such as unauthorized entry, fire, temperature rise, etc. The system may be **Local, Police Connection, Central Station** or **Proprietary.** (For individual alarm systems see alphabetical listing by type, e.g., **Intrusion Alarm System.**)

Annunciator—An alarm monitoring device which consists of a number of visible signals such as "flags" or lamps indicating the status of the **Detectors** in an alarm system or systems. Each circuit in the device is usually labelled to identify the location and condition being monitored. In addition to the visible signal, an audible signal is usually associated with the device. When an alarm condition is reported, a signal is indicated visibly, audibly, or both. The visible signal is generally maintained until reset either manually or automatically.

Answering Service—A business which contracts with subscribers to answer incoming telephone calls after a specified delay or when scheduled to do so. It may also provide other services such as relaying fire or intrusion alarm signals to proper authorities.

Area Protection—Protection of the inner space or volume of a secured area by means of a **Volumetric Sensor.**

Area Sensor—A sensor with a detection zone which approximates an area, such as a wall surface or the exterior of a safe.

Audible Alarm Device—(1) A noise-making device such as a siren, bell, or horn used as part of a local alarm system to indicate an **Alarm Condition.** (2) A bell, buzzer, horn or other noisemaking device

used as a part of an **Annunciator** to indicate a change in the status or operating mode of an alarm system.

Audio Detection System—See **Sound Sensing Detection System.**

Audio Frequency (Sonic)—Sound frequencies within the range of human hearing, approximately 15 to 20,000 Hz.

Audio Monitor—An arrangement of amplifiers and speakers designed to monitor the sounds transmitted by microphones located in the **Protected Area.** Similar to an **Annunciator,** except that supervisory personnel can monitor the protected area to interpret the sounds.

Authorized Access Switch—A device used to make an alarm system or some portion or zone of a system inoperative in order to permit authorized access through a **Protected Port.** A **Shunt** is an example of such a device.

B.A.—Burglar alarm.

Beam Divergence—In a **Photo-Electric Alarm System,** the angular spread of the light beam.

Break Alarm—(1) An **Alarm Condition** signaled by the opening or breaking of an electrical circuit. (2) The signal produced by a break alarm condition (sometimes referred to as an open circuit alarm or trouble signal, designed to indicate possible system failure).

Bug—(1) To plant a microphone or other **Sound Sensor** or to tap a communication line for the purpose of **Surreptitious** listening or **Audio Monitoring;** loosely, to install a sensor in a specified location. (2) The microphone or other sensor used for the purpose of surreptitious listening.

Building Security Alarm System—The system of **Protective Signaling** devices installed at a premise.

Burglar Alarm (B.A.) Pad—A supporting frame laced with fine wire or a fragile panel located with **Foil** or fine wire and installed so as to cover an exterior opening in a building, such as a door, or skylight. Entrance through the opening breaks the wire or foil and initiates an **Alarm Signal.** See also **Grid.**

Burglar Alarm System—See **Intrusion Alarm System.**

Burglary—The unlawful entering of a structure with the intent to commit a felony or theft therein.

Cabinet-For-Safe—A wooden enclosure having closely spaced electrical **Grids** on all inner surfaces and **Contacts** on the doors. It surrounds a safe and initiates an alarm signal if an attempt is made to open or penetrate the cabinet.

Capacitance--The property of two or more objects which enables them to store electrical energy in an electric field between them. The basic measurement unit is the farad. Capacitance varies inversely with the distance between the objects, hence the change of capacitance with relative motion is greater the nearer one object is to the other.

Capacitance Alarm System—An alarm system in which a protected object is electrically connected as a **Capacitance Sensor**. The approach of an intruder causes sufficient change in **Capacitance** to upset the balance of the system and initiate an **Alarm Signal**. Also called proximity alarm system.

Capacitance Detector—See **Capacitance Sensor**.

Capacitance Sensor—A sensor which responds to a change in **Capacitance** in a field containing a protected object or in a field within a protected area.

Carrier Current Transmitter—A device which transmits **Alarm Signals** from a sensor to a **Control Unit** via the standard ac power lines.

Central Station—A control center to which alarm systems in a subscriber's premises are connected, where circuits are supervised, and where personnel are maintained continuously to record and investigate alarm or trouble signals. Facilities are provided for the reporting of alarms to police and fire departments or to other outside agencies.

Central Station Alarm System—An alarm system, or group of systems, the activities of which are transmitted to, recorded in, maintained by, and supervised from a **Central Station**. This differs from **Proprietary Alarm Systems** in that the central station is owned and operated independently of the subscriber.

Circumvention—The defeat of an alarm system by the avoidance of its detection devices, such as by jumping over a pressure sensitive mat, by entering through a hole cut in an unprotected wall rather than through a protected door, or by keeping outside the range of an **Ultrasonic Motion Detector**. Circumvention contrasts with **Spoofing**.

Closed Circuit Alarm—See **Cross Alarm**.

Closed Circuit System—A system in which the sensors of each zone are connected in series so that the same current exists in each sensor. When an activated sensor breaks the circuit or the connecting wire is cut, an alarm is transmitted for that zone.

Clutch Head Screw—A mounting screw with a uniquely designed head for which the installation and removal tool is not commonly available. They are used to install alarm system components so that removal is inhibited.

Coded-Alarm System—An alarm system in which the source of each signal is identifiable. This is usually accomplished by means of a series of current pulses which operate audible or visible **Annunciators** or recorders or both, to yield a recognizable signal. This is usually used to allow the transmission of multiple signals on a common circuit.

Coded Cable—A multiconductor cable in which the insulation on each conductor is distinguishable from all others by color or design. This assists in identification of the point of origin or final destination of a wire.

Coded Transmitter—A device for transmitting a coded signal when manually or automatically operated by an **Actuator**. The actuator may be housed with the transmitter or a number of actuators may operate a common transmitter.

Coding Siren—A siren which has an auxiliary mechanism to interrupt the flow of air through its principal mechanism, enabling it to produce a controllable series of sharp blasts.

Combination Sensor Alarm System—An alarm system which requires the simultaneous activation of two or more sensors to initiate an **Alarm Signal**.

Compromise—See **Defeat**.

Constant Ringing Drop (CRD)—A relay which when activated even momentarily will remain in an **Alarm Condition** until **Reset**. A key is often required to reset the relay and turn off the alarm.

Constant Ringing Relay (CRR)—See **Constant Ringing Drop**.

Contact—(2) Each of the pair of metallic parts of a switch or relay which by touching or separating make or break the electrical current path. (2) A switch-type sensor.

Contact Device — A device which when actuated opens or closes a set of electrical contacts; a switch or relay.

Contact Microphone — A microphone designed for attachment directly to a surface of a **Protected Area** or object; usually used to detect surface vibrations.

Contact Vibration Sensor — See **Vibration Sensor.**

Contactless Vibrating Bell — A Vibrating Bell whose continuous operation depends upon application of an alternating current, without circuit-interrupting contacts such as those used in vibrating bells operated by direct current.

Control Cabinet — See **Control Unit.**

Control Unit — A device, usually **Electronic,** which provides the interface between the alarm system and the human operator and produces an **Alarm Signal** when its programmed response indicates an **Alarm Condition.** Some or all of the following may be provided for: power for sensors, sensitivity adjustments, means to select and indicate **Access Mode** or **Secure Mode,** monitoring for **Line Supervision** and **Tamper Devices,** timing circuits, for **Entrance** and **Exit Delays,** transmission of an alarm signal, etc.

Covert — Hidden and protected.

CRD — See **Constant Ringing Drop.**

Cross Alarm — (1) An **Alarm Condition** signaled by crossing or shorting an electrical circuit. (2) The signal produced due to a cross alarm condition.

Crossover — An insulated electrical path used to connect foil across window dividers, such as those found on multiple pane windows, to prevent grounding and to make a more durable connection.

CRR — Constant ringing relay. See **Constant Ringing Drop.**

Dark Current — The current output of a **Photoelectric Sensor** when no light is entering the sensor.

Day Setting — See **Access Mode.**

Defeat — The frustration, counteraction, or thwarting of an **Alarm Device** so that it fails to signal an alarm when a protected area is entered. Defeat includes both **Circumvention** and **Spoofing.**

Detection Range — The greatest distance at which a sensor will consistently detect an intruder under a standard set of conditions.

Detector — (1) A sensor such as those used to detect **Intrusion,** equipment malfunctions or failure, rate of temperature rise, smoke or fire. (2) A demodulator, a device for recovering the modulating function or signal from a modulated wave, such as that used in a modulated photoelectric alarm system. See also **Photoelectric Alarm System, Modulated.**

Dialer — See **Telephone Dialer, Automatic.**

Differential Pressure Sensor — A sensor used for **Perimeter Protection** which responds to the difference between the hydraulic pressures in two liquid-filled tubes buried just below the surface of the earth around the exterior perimeter of the **Protected Area.** The pressure difference can indicate an intruder walking or driving over the buried tubes.

Digital Telephone Dialer — See **Telephone Dialer, Digital.**

Direct Connect — See **Police Connection.**

Direct Wire Burglar Alarm Circuit (DWBA) — See **Alarm Line.**

Direct Wire Circuit — See **Alarm Line.**

Door Cord — A short, insulated cable with an attaching block and terminals at each end used to conduct current to a device, such as **Foil,** mounted on the movable portion of a door or window.

Door Trip Switch — A **Mechanical Switch** mounted so that movement of the door will operate the switch.

Doppler Effect (Shift) — The apparent change in frequency of sound or radio waves when reflected from or originating from a moving object. Utilized in some types of **Motion Sensors.**

Double-Circuit System — An **Alarm Circuit** in which two wires enter and two wires leave each sensor.

Double Drop — An alarm signaling method often used in **Central Station Alarm Systems** in which the line is first opened to produce a **Break Alarm** and then shorted to produce a **Cross Alarm.**

Drop — (1) See **Annunciator.** (2) A light indicator on an annunciator.

Duress Alarm Device—A device which produces either a **Silent Alarm** or **Local Alarm** under a condition of personnel stress such as holdup, fire, illness, or other panic or emergency. The device is normally manually operated and may be fixed or portable.

Duress Alarm System—An alarm system which employes a **Duress Alarm Device.**

DWBA—Direct wire burglar alarm. See **Alarm Line.**

E-Field Sensor—A **Passive Sensor** which detects changes in the earth's ambient electric field caused by the movement of an intruder. See also **H-Field Sensor.**

Electromagnetic—Pertaining to the relationship between current flow and magnetic field.

Electromagnetic Interference (EMI)—Impairment of the reception of a wanted electromagnetic signal by an electromagnetic disturbance. This can be caused by lightning, radio transmitters, power line noise and other electrical devices.

Electromechanical Bell—A bell with a prewound spring-driven striking mechanism, the operation of which is initiated by the activation of an electric tripping mechanism.

Electronic—Related to, or pertaining to, devices which utilize electrons moving through a vacuum, gas, or semiconductor, and to circuits or systems containing such devices.

EMI—See **Electromagnetic Interference.**

End Of Line Resistor—See **Terminal Resistor.**

Entrance Delay—The time between actuating a sensor on an entrance door or gate and the sounding of a **Local Alarm** or transmissionof an **Alarm Signal** by the **Control Unit.** This delay is used if the

Authorized Access Switch is located within the **Protected Area** and permits a person with the control key to enter without causing an alarm. The delay is provided by a timer within the **Control Unit.**

E.O.L.—End of line.

Exit Delay—The time between turning on a control unit and the sounding of a **Local Alarm** or transmission of an **Alarm Signal** upon actuation of a sensor on an exit door.

This delay is used if the **Authorized Access Switch** is located within the **Protected Area** and permits a person with the control key to turn on the alarm system and to leave through a protected door or gate without causing an alarm. The delay is provided by a timer within the **Control Unit.**

Fail Safe—A feature of a system or device which initiates an alarm or trouble signal when the system or device either malfunctions or loses power.

False Alarm—An alarm signal transmitted in the absence of an **Alarm Condition.** These may be classified according to causes: environmental, e.g., rain, fog, wind, hail, lightning, temperature, etc.; animals, e.g., rats, dogs, cats, insects, etc.; man-made disturbances, e.g., sonic booms, EMI, vehicles, etc.; equipment malfunction, e.g., transmission errors, component failure, etc.; operator error; and unknown.

False Alarm Rate, Monthly—The number of false alarms per installation per month.

False Alarm Ratio—The ratio of **False Alarms** to total alarms; may be expressed as a percentage or as a simple ratio.

Fence Alarm—Any of several types of sensors used to detect the presence of an intruder near a fence or any attempt by him to climb over, go under, or cut through the fence.

Field—The space or area in which there exists a force such as that produced by an electrically charged object, a current, or a magnet.

Fire Detector (Sensor)—See **Heat Sensor** and **Smoke Detector.**

Floor Mat—See **Mat Switch.**

Floor Trap—A **Trap** installed so as to detect the movement of a person across a floor space, such as a **Trip Wire Switch** or **Mat Switch.**

Foil—Thin metallic strips which are cemented to a protected surface (usually glass in a window or door), and connected to a closed electrical circuit. If the protected material is broken so as to break the foil, the circuit opens, initiating an alarm signal. Also called tape. A window door, or other surface to which foil has been applied is said to be taped or foiled.

Foil Connector—An electrical terminal block used on the edge of a window to join interconnecting wire to window **Foil.**

Foot Rail—A **Holdup Alarm Device**, often used at cashiers' windows, in which a foot is placed under the rail, lifting it, to initiate an **Alarm Signal**.

Frequency Division Multiplexing (FDM)—See **Multiplexing, Frequency Division**.

Glassbreak Vibration Detector—A **Vibration Detection System** which employs a **Contact Microphone** attached to a glass window to detect cutting or breakage of the glass.

Grid—(1) An arrangement of electrically conducting wire, screen, or tubing placed in front of doors or windows or both which is used a part of a **Capacitance Sensor**. (2) A latice of wooden dowels or slats concealing fine wires in a closed circuit which initiates an **Alarm Signal** when forcing or cutting the lattice breaks the wires. Used over accessible openings. Sometimes called a protective screen. See also **Burglar Alarm Pad**. (3) A screen or metal plate, connected to earth ground, sometimes used to provide a stable ground reference for objects protected by a **Capacitance Sensor**. If placed against the walls near the protected object, it prevents the sensor sensitivity from extending through the walls into areas of activity.

Heat Detector—See **Heat Sensor**.

Heat Sensor—(1) A sensor which responds to either a local temperature above a selected value, a local temperature increase which is at a rate of increase greater than a preselected rate (rate of rise), or both. (2) A sensor which responds to infrared radiation from a remote source such as a person.

Hi-Field Sensor—A **Passive Sensor** which detects changes in the earth's ambient magnetic field caused by the movement of an intruder. See also **E-Field Sensor**.

Holdup—A **Robberty** involving the threat to use a weapon.

Holdup Alarm Device—A device which signals a holdup. The device is usually **Surreptitious** and may be manually or automatically actuated, fixed or portable. See **Duress Alarm Device**.

Holdup Alarm System, Automatic—An alarm system which employs a holdup alarm device, in which the signal transmission is initiated solely by the action of the intruder, such as a money clip in a cash drawer.

Holdup Alarm System, Manual—A holdup alarm system in which the signal transmission is initiated by the direct action of the person attacked or of an observer of the attack.

Holdup Button—A manually actuated **Mechanical Switch** used to initiate a duress alarm signal; usually constructed to minimize accidental activation.

Hood Contact—A switch which is used for the supervision of a closed safe or vault door. Usually installed on the outside surface of the protected door.

Impedance—The opposition to the flow of alternating current in a circuit. May be determined by the ratio of an input voltage to the resultant current.

Impedance Matching—Making the **Impedance** of a **Terminating Device** equal to the impedance of the circuit to which it is connected in order to achieve optimum signal transfer.

Infrared (IR) Motion Detector—A sensor which detects changes in the infrared light radiation from parts of the **Protected Area**. Presence of an intruder in the area changes the infrared light intensity from his direction.

Infrared (IR) Motion Sensor—See **Infrared Motion Detector**.

Infrared Sensor—See **Heat Sensor, Infrared Motion Detector**, and **Photoelectric Sensor**.

Inking Register—See **Register, Inking**.

Interior Perimeter Protection—A line of protection along the interior boundary of a **Protected Area** including all points through which entry can be effected.

Intrusion—Unauthorized entry into the property of another.

Intrusion Alarm System—An alarm system for signaling the entry or attempted entry of a person or an object into the area or volume protected by the system.

Ionization Smoke Detector—A **Smoke Detector** in which a small amount of radioactive material ionizes the air in the sensing chamber, thus rendering it conductive and permitting a current to flow through the air between two charged electrodes. This effectively gives the sensing chamber an electrical conductance. When smoke particles enter the ionization area, they decrease the conductance of the air by attaching themselves to the ions causing a reduction in mobility. When the conductance is less than a predetermined level, the detector circuit responds.

IR — Infrared.

Jack — An electrical connector which is used for frequent connect and disconnect operations; for example, to connect an alarm circuit at an overhang door.

Lacing — A network of fine wire surrounding or covering an area to be protected, such as a safe, vault, or glass panel, and connected into a **Closed Circuit System**. The network of wire is concealed by a shield such as concrete or paneling in such a manner that an attempt to break through the shield breaks the wire and initiates an alarm.

Light Intensity Cutoff — In a **Photoelectric Alarm System**, the percent reduction of light which initiates an **Alarm Signal** at the photoelectric receiver unit.

Line Amplifier — An audio amplifier which is used to provide preamplification of an audio **Alarm Signal** before transmission of the signal over an **Alarm Line**. Use of an amplifier extends the range of signal transmission.

Line Sensor (Detector) — A sensor with a detection zone which approximates a line or series of lines, such as a **Photoelectric Sensor** which senses a direct or reflected light beam.

Line Supervision — Electronic protection of an **Alarm Line** accomplished by sending a continuous or coded signal through the circuit. A change in the circuit characteristics, such as a change in **Impedance** due to the circuit's having been tampered with, will be detected by a monitor. The monitor initiates an alarm if the change exceeds a predetermined amount.

Local Alarm — An alarm which when activated makes a loud noise (see **Audible Alarm Device**) at or near the **Protected Area** or floods the site with light or both.

Local Alarm System — An alarm system which when activated produces an audible or visible signal in the immediate vicinity of the protected premises or object. This term usually applies to systems designed to provide only a local warning of **Intrusion** and not to transmit to a remote **Monitoring Station**. However, local alarm systems are sometimes used in conjunction with a **Remote Alarm**.

Loop — An electric circuit consisting of several elements, usually switches, connected in series.

Magnetic Alarm System — An alarm system which will initiate an alarm when it detects changes in the local magnetic field. The changes could be caused by motion of ferrous objects such as guns or tools near the **Magnetic Sensor**.

Magnetic Contact — See **Magnetic Switch**.

Magnetic Sensor — A sensor which responds to changes in magnetic field. See also **Magnetic Alarm System**.

Magnetic Switch — A switch which consists of two separate units: a magnetically-actuated switch, and a magnet. The switch is usually mounted in a fixed position (door jamb or window frame) opposing the magnet, which is fastened to a hinged or sliding door, window, etc. When the movable section is opened, the magnet moves with it, actuating the switch.

Magnetic Switch, Balanced — A **Magnetic Switch** which operates using a balanced magnetic field in such a manner as to resist **Defeat** with an external magnet. It signals an alarm when it detects either an increase or decrease in magnetic field strength.

Matching Network — A circuit used to achieve **Impedance Matching**. It may also allow audio signals to be transmitted to an **Alarm Line** while blocking direct current used locally for **Line Supervision**.

Mat Switch — A flat area switch used on open floors or under carpeting. It may be sensitive over an area of a few square feet or several square yards.

McCulloh Circuit (Loop) — A supervised single wire **Loop** Connecting a number of **Coded Transmitters** located in different **Protected Areas** to a **Central Station** receiver.

Mechanical Switch — A switch in which the **Contacts** are opened and closed by means of a depressible plunger or button.

Mercury Fence Alarm — A type of **Mercury Switch** which is sensitive to the vibration caused by an intruder climbing on a fence.

Mercury Switch — A switch operated by tilting or vibrating which causes an enclosed pool of mercury to move, making or breaking physical and electrical contact with conductors. These are used on tilting doors and windows, and on fences.

Microwave Alarm System—An alarm system which employs **Radio Frequency Motion Detectors** operating in the **Microwave Frequency** region of the electromagnetic spectrum.

Microwave Frequency—Radio frequencies in the range of approximately 1.0 to 300 GHz.

Microwave Motion Detector—See **Radio Frequency Motion Detector.**

Modulated Photoelectric Alarm System—See **Photoelectric Alarm System, Modulated.**

Monitor Cabinet—An enclosure which houses the **Annunciator** and associated equipment.

Monitor Panel—See **Annunciator.**

Monitoring Station—The **Central Station** or other area at which guards, police, or commercial service personnel observe **Annunciators** and **Registers** reporting on the condition of alarm systems.

Motion Detection System—See **Motion Sensor.**

Motion Detector—See **Motion Sensor.**

Motion Sensor—A sensor which responds to the motion of an intruder. See also **Radio Frequency Motion Detector, Sonic Motion Detector, Ultrasonic Motion Detector,** and **Infrared Motion Detector.**

Multiplexing—A technique for the concurrent transmission of two or more signals in either or both directions, over the same wire, carrier, or other communication channel. The two basic multiplexing techniques are time division multiplexing and frequency division multiplexing.

Multiplexing, Frequency Division (FDM)—The multiplexing technique which assigns to each signal a specific set of frequencies (called a channel) within the larger block of frequencies available on the main transmission path in much the same way that many radio stations broadcast at the same time but can be separately received.

Multiplexing, Time Division (TDM)—The multiplexing technique which provides for the independent transmission of several pieces of information on a time-sharing basis by sampling, at frequent intervals, the data to be transmitted.

Neutralization—See **Defeat.**

NICAD—(Contraction of "nickel cadmium".) A high performance, long-lasting rechargeable battery, with electrodes made of nickel and cadmium, which may be used as an emergency power supply for an alarm system.

Night Setting—See **Secure Mode.**

Nonretractable (One-Way) Screw—A screw with a head designed to permit installation with an ordinary flat bit screwdriver but which resists removal. They are used to install alarm system components so that removal is inhibited.

Normally Closed (NC) Switch—A switch in which the **Contacts** are closed when no external forces act upon the switch.

Normally Open (NO) Switch—A switch in which the **Contacts** are open (separated) when no external forces act upon the switch.

Nuisance Alarm—See **False Alarm.**

Object Protection—See **Spot Protection.**

Open-Circuit Alarm—See **Break Alarm.**

Open-Circuit System—A system in which the sensors are connected in parallel. When a sensor is activated, the circuit is closed, permitting a current which activates an **Alarm Signal.**

Panic Alarm—See **Duress Alarm Device.**

Panic Button—See **Duress Alarm Device.**

Passive Intrusion Sensor—A passive sensor in an **Intrusion Alarm System** which detects an intruder within the range of the sensor. Examples are a **Sound Sensing Detection System,** a **Vibration Detection System,** an **Infrared Motion Detector,** and an **E-Field Sensor.**

Passive Sensor—A sensor which detects natural radiation or radiation disturbances, but does not itself emit the radiation on which its operation depends.

Passive Ultrasonic Alarm System—An alarm system which detects the sounds in the **Ultrasonic Frequency** range caused by an attempted forcible entry into a protected structure. The system consists of microphones, a **Control Unit** containing an amplifier, filters, an **Accumulator,** and a power supply. The unit's sensitivity is adjustable so that ambient noises or normal sounds will not initiate an **Alarm Signal**; however, noise above the preset level or a sufficient accumulation of impulses will initiate an alarm.

Percentage Supervision — A method of **Line Supervision** in which the current in or resistance of a supervised line is monitored for changes. When the change exceeds a selected percentage of the normal operating current or resistance in the line, an **Alarm Signal** is produced.

Perimeter Alarm System — An alarm system which provides perimeter protection.

Perimeter Protection — Protection of access to the outer limits of a **Protected Area**, by means of physical barriers, sensors on physical barriers, or exterior sensors not associated with a physical barrier.

Permanent Circuit — An **Alarm Circuit** which is capable of transmitting an **Alarm Signal** whether the alarm control is in **Access Mode** or **Secure Mode**. Used, for example, on foiled fixed windows, **Tamper Switches**, and supervisory lines. See also **Supervisory Alarm System**, **Supervisory Circuit**, and **Permanent Protection**.

Permanent Protection — A system of alarm devices such as **Foil**, **Burglar Alarm Pads**, or **Lacings** connected in a permanent circuit to provide protection whether the **Control Unit** is in the **Access Mode** or **Secure Mode**.

Photoelectric Alarm System — An alarm system which employs a light beam and **Photoelectric Sensor** to provide a line of protection. Any interruption of the beam by an intruder is sensed by the sensor. Mirrors may be used to change the direction of the beam. The maximum beam length is limited by many factors, some of which are the light source intensity, number of mirror reflections, detector sensitivity, **Beam Divergence**, fog, and haze.

Photoelectric Alarm System, Modulated — A photoelectric alarm system in which the transmitted light beam is modulated in a predetermined manner and in which the receiving equipment will signal an alarm unless it receives the properly modulated light.

Photoelectric Beam Type Smoke Detector — A **Smoke Detector** which has a light source which projects a light beam across the area to be protected onto a photoelectric cell. Smoke between the light source and the receiving cell reduces the light reaching the cell, causing actuation.

Photoelectric Detector — See **Photoelectric Sensor**.

Photoelectric Sensor — A device which detects a visible or invisible beam of light and responds to its complete or nearly complete interruption. See also **Photoelectric Alarm System** and **Photoelectric Alarm System, Modulated**.

Photoelectric Spot Type Smoke Detector — A **Smoke Detector** which contains a chamber with covers which prevent the entrance of light but allow the entrance of smoke. The chamber contains a light source and a photosensitive cell so placed that light is blocked from it. When smoke enters, the smoke particles scatter and reflect the light into the photosensitive cell, causing an alarm.

Point Protection — See **Spot Protection**.

Police Connection — The direct link by which an alarm system is connected to an **Annunciator** installed in a police station. Examples of a police connection are an **Alarm Line**, or a radio communications channel.

Police Panel — See **Police Station Unit**.

Police Station Unit — An **Annunciator** which can be placed in operation in a police station.

Portable Duress Sensor — A device carried on a person which may be activated in an emergency to send an **Alarm Signal** to a **Monitoring Station**.

Portable Intrusion Sensor — A sensor which can be installed quickly and which does not require the installation of dedicated wiring for the transmission its **Alarm Signal**.

Positive Noninterfering (PNI) And Successive Alarm System — An alarm system which employs multiple alarm transmitters on each **Alarm Line** (like McCulloh Loop) such that in the event of simultaneous operation of several transmitters, one of them takes control of the alarm line, transmits its full signal, then release the alarm line for successive transmission by other transmitters which are held inoperative until they gain control.

Pressure Alarm System — An alarm system which protects a vault or other enclosed space by maintaining and monitoring a predetermined air pressure differential between the inside and outside of the space. Equalization of pressure resulting from opening the vault or cutting through the enclosure will be sensed and will initiate an **Alarm Signal**.

Proprietary Alarm System — An alarm system which is similar to a **Central Station Alarm System** except that the **Annunciator** is located in a constantly manned guard room maintained by the owner for his own internal security operations. The guards monitor the system and respond to all **Alarm Signals** or alert local law enforcement agencies or both.

Printing Recorder — An electromechanical device used at a **Monitoring Station** which accepts coded signals from alarm lines and converts them to an alphanumeric printed record of the signal received.

Protected Area — An area monitored by an alarm system or guards, or enclosed by a suitable barrier.

Protected Port — A point of entry such as a door, window, or corridor which is monitored by sensors connected to an alarm system.

Protection Device — (1) A sensor such as a **Grid**, **Foil**, **Contact**, or **Photoelectric Sensor** connected into an **Intrusion Alarm System**. (2) A barrier which inhibits **Intrusion**, such as a grille, lock, fence or wall.

Protection, Exterior Perimeter — A line of protection surrounding but somewhat removed from a facility. Examples are fences, barrier walls, or patrolled points of a perimeter.

Protection Off — See **Access Mode**.

Protection On — See **Secure Mode**.

Protective Screen — See **Grid**.

Protective Signaling — The initiation, transmission, and reception of signals involved in the detection and prevention of property loss due to fire, burglary, or other destructive conditions. Also, the electronic supervision of persons and equipment concerned with this detection and prevention. See also **Line Supervision** and **Supervisory Alarm System**.

Proximity Alarm System — See **Capacitance Alarm System**.

Punching Register — See **Register, Punch**.

Radar Alarm System — An alarm system which employs **Radio Frequency Motion Detectors**.

Radar (Radio Detecting And Ranging) — See **Radio Frequency Motion Detector**.

Radio Frequency Interference (RFI) — **Electromagnetic Interference** in the radio frequency range.

Radio Frequency Motion Detector — A sensor which detects the motion of an intruder through the use of a radiated radio frequency electromagnetic field. The device operates by sensing a disturbance in the generated RF field caused by intruder motion, typically a modulation of the field referred to as a **Doppler Effect**, which is used to initiate an **Alarm Signal**. Most radio frequency motion detectors are certified by the FCC for operation as "field disturbance sensors" at one of the following frequencies: 0.915 GHz (L-Band), 2.45 GHz (S-Band), 5.8 GHz (X-Band), 10.525 GHz (X-Band), and 22.125 GHz (K-Band). Units operating in the **Microwave Frequency** range are usually called **Microwave Motion Detectors**.

Reed Switch — A type of **Magnetic Switch** consisting of contacts formed by two thin moveable magnetically actuated metal vanes or reeds, held in a normally open position within a sealed glass envelope.

Register — An electromechanical device which makes a paper tape in response to signal impulses received from transmitting circuits. A register may be driven by a prewound spring mechanism, an electric motor, or a combination of these.

Register, Inking — A register which marks the tape with ink.

Register, Punch — A register which marks the tape by cutting holes in it.

Register, Slashing — A register which marks the tape by cutting V-shaped slashes in it.

Remote Alarm — An **Alarm Signal** which is transmitted to a remote **Monitoring Station**. See also **Local Alarm**.

Remote Station Alarm System — An alarm system which employes remote **Alarm Stations** usually located in building hallways or on city streets.

Reporting Line — See **Alarm Line**.

Resistance Bridge Smoke Detector—A **Smoke Detector** which responds to the particles and moisture present in smoke. These substances reduce the resistance of an electrical bridge grid and cause the detector to respond.

Retard Transmitter—A **Coded Transmitter** in which a delay period is introduced between the time of actuation and the time of signal transmission.

RFI—See **Radio Frequency Interference**.

Rf Motion Detector—See **Radio Frequency Motion Detector**.

Robbery—The felonious or forcible taking of property by violence, threat, or other overt felonious act in the presence of the victim.

Secure Mode—The condition of an alarm system in which all sensors and **Control Units** are ready to respond to an intrusion.

Security Monitor—See **Annunciator**.

Seismic Sensor—A sensor, generally buried under the surface of the ground for **Perimeter Protection**, which responds to minute vibrations of the earth generated as an intruder walks or drives within its **Detection Range**.

Sensor—A device which is designed to produce a signal or offer indication in response to an event or stimulus within its detection zone.

Sensor, Combustion—See **Ionization Smoke Detector, Photoelectric Beam Type Smoke Detector, Photoelectric Spot Type Smoke Detector** and **Resistance Bridge Smoke Detector**.

Sensor, Smoke—See **Ionization Smoke Detector, Photoelectric Beam Type Smoke Detector, Photoelectric Spot Type Smoke Detector** and **Resistance Bridge Smoke Detector**.

Shunt—(1) A deliberate shorting-out of a portion of an electric circuit. (2) A key-operated switch which removes some portion of an alarm system for operation, allowing entry into a **Protected Area** without initiating an **Alarm Signal**. A type of **Authorized Access Switch**.

Shunt Switch—See **Shunt**.

Signal Recorder—See **Register**.

Silent Alarm—A **Remote Alarm** without an obvious local indication that an alarm has been transmitted.

Silent Alarm System—An alarm system which signals a remote station by means of a silent alarm.

Single Circuit System—An **Alarm Circuit** which routes only one side of the circuit through each sensor. The return may be through either ground or a separate wire.

Single-Stroke Bell—A bell which is struck once each time its mechanism is activated.

Slashing Register—See **Register, Slashing**.

Smoke Detector—A device which detects visible or invisible products of combustion. See also **Ionization Smoke Detector, Photoelectric Beam Type Smoke Detector, Photoelectric Spot Type Smoke Detector**, and **Resistance Bridge Smoke Detector**.

Solid State—(1) An adjective used to describe a device such as a semiconductor transistor or diode. (2) A circuit or system which does not rely on vacuum or gas-filled tubes to control or modify voltages and currents.

Sonic Motion Detector—A sensor which detects the motion of an intruder by his disturbance of an audible sound pattern generated within the protected area.

Sound Sensing Detection System—An alarm system which detects the audible sound caused by an attempted forcible entry into a protected structure. The system consists of microphones and a **Control Unit** containing an amplifier, **Accumulator** and a power supply. The unit's sensitivity is adjustable so that ambient noises or normal sounds will not initiate an **Alarm Signal**. However, noises above this preset level or a sufficient accumulation of impulses will initiate an alarm.

Sound Sensor—A sensor which responds to sound; a microphone.

Space Protection—See **Area Protection**.

Spoofing—The defeat or compromise of an alarm system by "tricking" or "fooling" its detection devices such as by short circuiting part or all of a series circuit, cutting wires in a parallel circuit, reducing the sensitivity of a sensor, or entering false signals into the system. Spoofing contrasts with **Circumvention**.

Spot Protection—Protection of objects such as safes, art objects, or anything of value which could be damaged or removed from the premises.

Spring Contact — A device employing a current-carrying cantilever spring which monitors the position of a door or window.

Standby Power Supply — Equipment which supplies power to a system in the event the primary power is lost. It may consist of batteries, charging circuits, auxiliary motor generators or a combination of these devices.

Strain Gauge Alarm System — An alarm system which detects the stress caused by the weight of an intruder as he moves about a building. Typical uses include placement of the strain gauge sensor under a floor joist or under a stairway tread.

Strain Gauge Sensor — A sensor which, when attached to an object, will provide an electrical response to an applied stress upon the object, such as a bending, stretching or compressive force.

Strain Sensitive Cable — An electrical cable which is designed to produce a signal whenever the cable is strained by a change in applied force. Typical uses including mounting it in a wall to detect an attempted forced entry through the wall, or fastening it to a fense to detect climbing on the fence, or burying it around a perimeter to detect walking or driving across the perimeter.

Subscriber's Equipment — That portion of a **Central Station Alarm System** installed in the protected premises.

Subscriber's Unit — A **Control Unit** of a **Central Station Alarm System.**

Supervised Lines — Interconnecting lines in an alarm system which are electrically supervised against tampering. See also **Line Supervision.**

Supervisory Alarm System — An alarm system which monitors conditions or persons or both and signals any deviation from an established norm or schedule. Examples are the monitoring of signals from guard patrol stations for irregularities in the progression along a prescribed patrol route, and the monitoring of production or safety conditions such as sprinkler water pressure, temperature, or liquid level.

Supervisory Circuit — An electrical circuit or radio path which sends information on the status of a sensor or guard patrol to an **Annunciator.** For **Intrusion Alarm Systems,** this circuit provides **Line Supervision** and monitors **Tamper Devices.** See also **Supervisory Alarm System.**

Surreptitious — **Covert,** hidden, concealed or disguised.

Surveillance — (1) Control of premises for security purposes through alarm systems, closed circuit television (CCTV), or other monitoring methods. (2) Supervision or inspection of industrial processes by monitoring those conditions which could cause damage if not corrected. See also **Supervisory Alarm System.**

Tamper Device — (1) Any device, usually a switch, which is used to detect an attempt to gain access to intrusion alarm circuitry, such as by removing a switch cover. (2) A monitor circuit to detect any attempt to modify the alarm circuitry, such as by cutting a wire.

Tamper Switch — A switch which is installed in such a way as to detect attempts to remove the enclosure of some alarm system components such as control box doors, switch covers, junction box covers, or bell housings. The alarm component is then often described as being "tampered".

Tape — See **Foil.**

Tapper Bell — A **Single-Stroke Bell** designed to produce a sound of low intensity and relatively high pitch.

Telephone Dialer, Automatic — A device which, when activated, automatically dials one more pre-programmed telephone numbers (e.g., police, fire department) and relays a recorded voice or coded message giving the location and nature of the alarm.

Telephone Dialer, Digital — An automatic telephone dialer which sends its message as a digital code.

Terminal Resistor — A resistor used as a **Terminating Device.**

Terminating Capacitor — A capacitor sometimes used as a terminating device for a **Capacitance Sensor** antenna. The capacitor allows the supervision of the sensor antenna, especially if a long wire is used as the sensor.

Terminating Device — A device which is used to terminate an electrically supervised circuit. It makes the electrical circuit continuous and provides a fixed **Impedance** reference (end of line resistor) against which changes are measured to detect an **Alarm Condition.** The impedance changes may be caused by a sensor, tampering, or circuit trouble.

Time Delay—See **Entrance Delay** and **Exit Delay.**

Time Division Multiplexing (TDM)—See **Multiplexing, Time Division.**

Timing Table—That portion of **Central Station** equipment which provides a means for checking incoming signals from **McCulloh Circuits.**

Touch Sensitivity—The sensitivity of a **Capacitance Sensor** at which the **Alarm Device** will be activated only if an intruder touches or comes in very close proximity (about 1 cm or ½ in.) to the protected object.

Trap—(1) A device, usually a switch, installed within a protected area, which serves as secondary protection in the event a **Perimeter Alarm System** is successfully penetrated. Examples are a **Trip Wise Switch** placed across a likely path for an intruder, a **Mat Switch** hidden under a rug, or a **Magnetic Switch** mounted on an inner door. (2) A **Volumetric Sensor** installed so as to detect an intruder in a likely traveled corridor or pathway within a security area.

Trickle Charge—A continuous direct current, usually very low, which is applied to a battery to maintain it at peak charge or to recharge it after it has been partially or completely discharged. Usually applied to nickel cadmium (NICAD) or wet cell batteries.

Trip Wire Switch—A switch which is actuated by breaking or moving a wire or cord installed across a floor space.

Trouble Signal—See **Break Alarm.**

UL—See **Underwriters Laboratories, Inc.**

UL Certificated—For certain types of products which have met UL requirements, for which it is impractical to apply the UL Listing Mark or Classification Marking to the individual product, a certificate is provided which the manufacturer may use to identify quantities of material for specific job sites or to identify field installed systems.

UL Listed—Signifies that production samples of the product have been found to comply with established Underwriters Laboratories requirements and that the manufacturer is authorized to use the Laboratories' Listing Marks on the listed products which comply with the requirements, contingent upon the follow-up services as a check of compliance.

Ultrasonic—Pertaining to a sound wave having a frequency above that of audible sound (approximately 20,000 Hz). Ultrasonic sound is used in ultrasonic detection systems.

Ultrasonic Detection System—See **Ultrasonic Motion Detector** and **Passive Ultrasonic Alarm System.**

Ultrasonic Frequency—Sound frequencies which are above the range of human hearing; approximately 20,000 Hz and higher.

Ultrasonic Motion Detector—A sensor which detects the motion of an intruder through the use of **Ultrasonic** generating and receiving equipment. The device operates by filling a space with a pattern of ultrasonic waves; the modulation of these waves by a moving object is detected and initiates an **Alarm Signal.**

Underdome Bell—A bell most of whose mechanism is concealed by its gong.

Underwriters Laboratories, Inc. (UL)—A private independent research and testing laboratory which tests and lists various items meeting good practice and safety standards.

Vibrating Bell—A bell whose mechanism is designed to strike repeatedly and for as long as it is activated.

Vibrating Contact—See **Vibration Sensor.**

Vibration Detection System—An alarm system which employs one or more **Contact Microphones** or **Vibration Sensors** which are fastened to the surfaces of the area or object being protected to detect excessive levels of vibration. The contact microphone system consists of microphones, a **Control Unit** containing an amplifier and an **Accumulator**, and a power supply. The unit's sensitivity is adjustable so that ambient noises or normal vibrations will not initiate an **Alarm Signal.** In the vibration sensor system, the sensor responds to excessive vibration by opening a switch in a **Closed Circuit System.**

Vibration Detector—See **Vibration Sensor.**

Vibration Sensor—A sensor which responds to vibrations of the surface on which it is mounted. It has a **Normally Closed Switch** which will momentarily open when it is subjected to a vibration with sufficiently large amplitude. Its sensitivity is adjustable to allow for the different levels of normal vibration, to which the sensor should not respond, at different locations. See also **Vibration Detection System.**

Visual Signal Device—A pilot light, **Annunciator** or other device which provides a visual indication of the condition of the circuit or system being supervised.

Volumetric Detector—See **Volumetric Sensor.**

Volumetric Sensor—A sensor with a detection zone which extends over a volume such as an entire room, part of a room, or a passageway. **Ultrasonic Motion Detectors** and **Sonic Motion Detectors** are examples of volumetric sensors.

Walk Test Light—A light on motion detectors which comes on when the detector senses motion in the area. It is used while setting the sensitivity of the detector

and during routine checking and maintenance.

Watchman's Reporting System—A **Supervisory Alarm System** arranged for the transmission of a patrolling watchman's regularly recurrent report signals from stations along his patrol route to a central supervisory agency.

Zoned Circuit—A circuit which provides continual protection for parts or zones of the **Protected Area** while normally used doors and windows or zones may be released for access.

Zones—Smaller subdivisions into which large areas are divided to permit selective access to some zones while maintaining other zones secure and to permit pinpointing the specific location from which an **Alarm Signal** is transmitted.

14. Designing Security Alarm Systems for Libraries, Museums, and Art Facilities

Charles Schnabolk

INTRODUCTION

All too often, the alarm systems installed in museums, art galleries, and historic sites are identical to the systems used to protect private homes, supermarkets, and warehouses. Rarely does the alarm installer (who typically regards every building the same) consider the unique factors relative to buildings housing works of art. As a result of this inflexible attitude, most museums are installing expensive and sophisticated systems that are totally unrelated to their particular needs. The result of this misapplication of alarms is the fact that, although the art community spends more money each year to protect their collections, the rate of recorded art theft is at an all-time high. While there is no perfect alarm system, there are devices and techniques available that could significantly improve this situation.

This increase in art theft is not a result of poorly designed alarm systems alone. No matter what system is installed, it cannot prevent a curator from "borrowing" objects from his/her vault storage area, nor can it discourage the poorly paid guard from stealing a small painting, or the museum director from walking out the front door with a painting. Yet with a forceful and intelligent approach to security, the museum can establish an atmosphere that will discourage the normally honest individual from temptations, and make it difficult for the professional thief as well.

Security is a twenty-four-hour obligation which cannot be limited to night-time use of contact switches on exit doors. All too often, this type of system is not activated until the thief leaves the building with the painting under his coat. The fact that a guard is on duty inside the building all night does not serve as an adequate deterrent to art theft. Most guards are ill-equipped, untrained, underpaid, and, often, too old to offer effective resistance to a determined thief.

Alarms, *when properly applied,* can be cost effective, since they usually reduce guard personnel needs. While it may be true that all alarms can be circumvented, they cannot be corrupted, nor do they fall asleep — situations that are occurring all too frequently with reference to guard forces employed by museums.

The primary aim of this chapter is not to make economic and technical comparisons between a guard force and an alarm system but to show that security alarm systems must be customized to the needs and vulnerabilities of buildings exhibiting works of art to the general public. The final decision on security system design cannot be left to the architect or the local alarm installation company, who often do not have an adequate understanding of the special characteristics and problems unique to a museum or museum-type facility. (The term "museum" when used in this chapter will include fine art museums, historic sites, science museums, natural history museums, children's museums, planetariums, library exhibits, and art galleries.)

This chapter will present enough basic information to encourage the museum administrator to participate in the design and selection of an alarm system. The final decision on the alarm configuration should never be left to the subjective discretion of alarm installation companies because they tend to concentrate on night-time protection, without any thought to the museum's vulnerability during daytime visiting hours. Most museum administrators avoid decisions in areas relating to security because (1) they feel that the technology involved is too complicated and is outside their area of responsibility, and (2) they consider the alarm salesperson as an experienced and knowledgeable expert in the field. Both these assumptions have proven disastrous to many museums, including those that have delegated the responsibility to a full-time security director. Many museum directors are retired law enforcement officials who have as little knowledge on the technical aspects of security protection as the registrar or curator.

This chapter will attempt to clarify and simplify the technology so that administrators can be called upon to assist in the design of the security system. The material presented will not make an expert out of the reader, but it will remove some of the mystery that is associated with the subject of security. Administrators (registrars, curators, and security directors) must be encouraged to participate in the security design process — a procedure that is rarely followed in most museums.

While the cost of providing a total protection system can be expensive, it can be justified by the reduced cost of insurance. There are several factors that influence the premium a museum pays for its fire, safety, and theft insurance. They are:

- Guard service
- Alarm systems
- Sprinkler systems
- Fire detection
- Crowd-control procedures
- Museum staff
- Quality of packing and shipping department
- Fine arts loan procedures
- Registration procedures

Insurance for museums and historic associations is classified as "uncontrolled." In the field of fine arts, an insurance company has wide flexibility regarding rates and, in many cases, may provide an organization with what the insurance company — by its own standards — decides it deserves. Many insurance policies include fidelity exclusion. This concerns the possible dishonesty of personnel working in the museum. This factor alone justifies a better daytime security system, since statistics indicate that most thefts are inside jobs. An art object is insured for X number of dollars; if it is lost, the museum is paid X number of dollars. From the writing of the policy to the time of loss, the object may have doubled or tripled in value, but since museums do not continuously upgrade their policies, a significant differential exists between insured and market value. Therefore, a system that was installed in the mid-1970s is not only obsolete from the technological standpoint, it is inadequate when balanced against the new evaluation of the collection in today's market.

Today, museums regularly lend objects of art to other museums as part of a traveling exhibit, and, of course, borrow pieces as well. Very often, the loan agreements are verbal, and loose agreements exist between lender and the borrower. This increases the need to furnish adequate protection while an exhibit is on tour. The cost of a premium on loan exhibits is relatively low, but alarm systems protecting borrowed objects will make the underwriting of this type of insurance more attractive to the agent.

ALARM SYSTEM CONFIGURATION

Museums require reliable protection in five major areas:

1. *Collection (Object Protection).* Works of fine art must be protected against damage from the innocent art lover inspecting the piece too intimately, or the malicious malefactor intent on creating severe damage for one reason or another.
2. *Physical Plant (Building Security).* The physical plant can be protected against the threat of a devasting fire by the prudent use of early warning smoke detection. The thought of the potential loss created by fine arts going up in flame sickens any museum director or curator. Priceless works of art can be completely lost (never to be replaced) in such a conflagration.
3. *Visitors (Surveillance).* Visitors, while on the premises, are entitled to enjoy themselves in a safe and congenial atmosphere. Closed-circuit TV can be employed to provide surveillance over the galleries, so that a centrally stationed guard can observe any disturbing situations. Periodic, centrally supervised patrol tours will force the visit of a guard to all areas of the museum at which hazardous situations could occur. These patrol tours provide the existing "in place" guard posts with periodic support and visitation.
4. *Staff (Access Control).* The staff, utilizing an access control system, will be regimented so that only authorized personnel are allowed in areas in which they belong at authorized times. This can help protect the staff against a member who has a grievance against the museum management and seeks revenge.
5. *Reputation.* Every museum holds its reputation most high. If a museum acquires a bad reputation, other organizations are apathetic toward lending it works of art, insurance rates rise, and staff morale plummets. Fire and security alarms can minimize damage and losses and directly maintain the museum's reputation at a high level. In the museum community, reputation is an important asset. Not only does a good reputation attract contributors, it also makes it easier to get good loan exhibits which, in turn, bring revenue. Art thefts often go unreported for the purpose of preserving a museum's high reputation.

A properly designed, and periodically upgraded, alarm system can help protect all five areas.

Other security problems encountered by museums include

1. Vandalism
2. Souvenir collectors
3. Terrorism (particularly in Europe)
4. Armed robbery — hit and run (rare, but it does happen)
5. Internal theft
6. External theft

At any given time, only a third of the museum's total collection may be on view. The balance is in various curatorial storerooms. Each of the curators has his/her own storage areas, including high security vaults. Access to these areas has to be available to the staff. Curatorial staff members consider themselves scholars and are not overly concerned with security details. This problem can be solved with a sound access control system.

Art that moves across national borders is difficult to trace. The country of origin of any master work does not like to have it leave the country because of this, but will allow it to be loaned, however, if proper security is observed.

Object Protection

Frequently, alarm systems concentrate on protecting the building from unauthorized entry after visiting hours and very little emphasis is placed on protecting works of art during visiting hours. This represents a total misapplication of alarm equipment. Increasing security by hiring more guards sometimes compounds the problem because of the questionable integrity of a guard who is often paid the minimum wage allowed by law. The most effective technique in protecting art objects during daytime hours is to alarm the object (painting, pedestal, display case) rather than to alarm the entire room. Visitors can now move about the room without being made to feel that "big brother" is watching. Guards and TV cameras can make visitors feel so uncomfortable that they tend to avoid visiting the museum. By protecting the object, constant surveillance is achieved without discouraging visitors from moving close to the object. This approach will stop thefts and discourage a growing phenomenon in museums called vandalism. The incidents of vandalism have reached disastrous levels, and these acts cannot always be blamed on children. The attacks on the *Pieta* and Rembrandt's *The Night Watch* were carried out by mature persons with mental problems. In the decade of the 1970s, art thefts rose to an estimated $100 million a year, about half of it (13,000 objects) in the United States. The only way to stop this trend, short of closing the building to the public, is to alarm the object.

Painting, Pedestal, and Display Cases. There are a few devices available today that will protect paintings and free-standing pedestals. The most popular are

1. Light beams focused along and parallel to the wall.
2. Magnetic contact switches, attached to the painting frame.
3. Mercury switches that are activated if tilted.
4. Capacitance protection that "senses" human movement near the surface of the painting.
5. Shock sensors on display-case glass.
6. Panic buttons mounted beneath the pedestal.

All of the above are workable systems that require hard wire between the object and the alarm control panel. This is an expensive and often awkward method of alarming a painting. There are two new techniques available that are wireless and more effective than the normal hard-wire systems:

1. Wireless transmitter attached to a shock sensor.
2. Ultrasonic transmitter mounted on the ceiling with ultrasonic receivers mounted inside the display case.

The actual selection of the protection device will depend on the knowledge of the alarm system, funds available, and the environment in the room.

Light beams are a rather crude method since they are easy to spot and, with a little practice, may be easily defeated. The beam is usually mounted in the corner of the room and focused along the surface of the wall at two or more heights. If someone tried to grab a painting, the hand motion would disturb the beam and an alarm would be sounded. By careful observation, the actual path of the beam can be determined and the painting removed without disturbing the beam. This type of system is generally used on less valuable paintings, and it keeps the curious visitor from touching the canvas. Noted on a scale of 1 to 10 (10 being the most effective), the beam would be rated as a 4.

Magnetic contact switches and mercury switches are attached to the rear of the frame and wired directly to a control panel. Any movement of the frame away from or off the wall will cause this sensor to send an alarm signal. While a strategically mounted light beam can protect groups of paintings along the wall, the magnetic switch can only protect a single frame. This means that each painting has to be wired to the control panel, an expensive and time-consuming technique. This system would be rated as a 2.

Capacitance detection can provide effective protection if certain precautious and installation practices are followed. A metallic antenna must be installed on the back of the painting, beneath the pedestal, or under a tablecloth (when used in historic sites). Since most paintings are hung on walls, the makeup of the wall behind the painting can affect operation of the system. If the wall behind the painting is not well grounded (reinforced concrete is usually a good ground), then a metal ground screen has to be added to the wall area behind the painting (see Figure 14.1). When used with pedestal-mounted sculptures that are nonmetallic, a special metallic antenna must be added in the form of a copper fly screen. While the process sounds complicated, it does provide the same sensitivity as the capacitance sensor used on safes. Due to the expensive maintenance involved, this technique would be rated as a 6.

Figure 14.1. Capacitance detection system

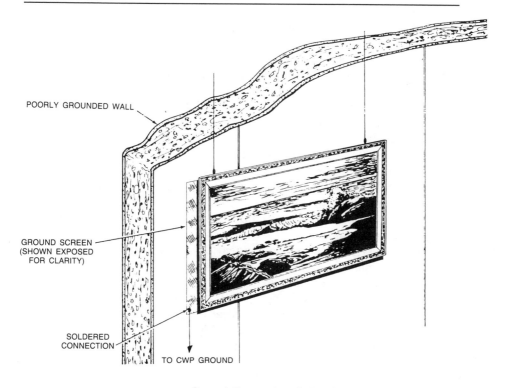

Ground Screen Installation for
Paintings.

Shock sensors and vibrators are effective when mounted on the glass partitions used on wall enclosed and free standing display cases. These small devices are capable of reading the "sound" of cracking or shattering glass panels. Each sensor must be wired directly to the control panel. Their value is rated as a 6 if properly installed.

WIRELESS SYSTEMS

Probably the most effective technique for painting protection is the *combination* of an FM wireless transmitter and a shock sensor. The wireless transmitter is hidden behind each painting and attached through short cable to a sensor that is mounted directly onto the frame or even onto the canvas back (See Figure 14.2). Any sudden movement of the painting will activate the sensor, causing the transmitter to send a signal to a receiver located within 150 feet of the transmitter. A single receiver can monitor an unlimited number of transmitters scattered throughout the museum. Furthermore, by carefully selecting (tuning) the individual transmitter, actual locations of the disturbance can be monitored. One such system can distinguish up to fifteen frequencies through the use of a single receiver and the main annunciator panel. The only wiring that is required is between the centrally located receiver and the annunciator.

The same transmitter can also be used to protect pedestal-mounted sculptures or a display case. The pedestal sensor would be in the form of "plunger" switch while the glass sensor would be the same type used on the painting frame. The wireless transmitters are not the popular wireless unit used for protecting doors and windows. These ordinary transmitters are similar to garage-door openers; they do not supervise the wire between the sensor and the transmitter (protects against cutting), nor can they react to microsecond shock (cutting of the canvas) or be tuned to separate fifteen frequencies over a single cable.

The wireless RF transmission system described here is specifically designed for museum use and has no relationship to the "garage-door opener" type normally associated with wireless security systems. The fact that it can "read" the touch of a vandal's razor blade separates this system from other wireless systems and makes the device ideal for all types of paintings, pedestals, and display cases. When used with lithium batteries it can function for over seven years without requiring battery replacement. This system rates a 9½ on a scale of 10.

Ultrasonic transmission with remote receivers can be used on free-standing display cases. The ultrasonic transmitter is mounted within the room that houses the display case. It is powered from the nearest outlet so that the

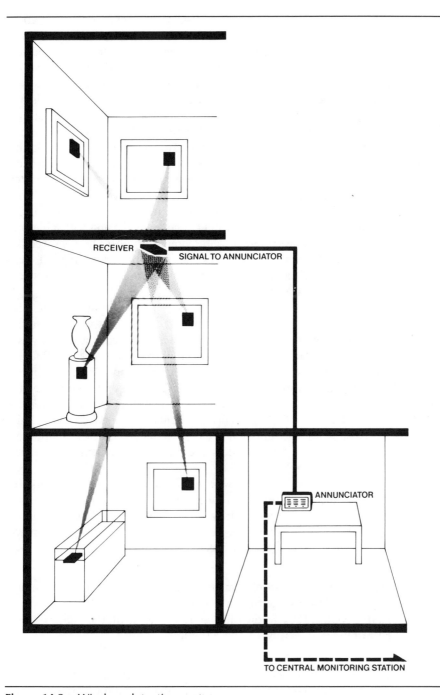

Figure 14.2. Wireless detection system

unit is continuously transmitting a high-pitched sound-wave signal (well above the hearing range). The receiver is designed to react when it "hears" the particular transmitted ultrasonic frequency. The receiver is battery operated and mounted under a display case. Under normal conditions, the receiver cannot hear the transmitter, but if the glass is broken or the case opened, the sound waves would enter the case and activate the receiver. Since the receiver is battery operated, it cannot power a loud siren, so all it is doing is activating a relatively low-level siren for a brief period. Someone has to be near the unit to hear the siren before the battery goes dead. To overcome this shortcoming, some museums have added a simple garage-door-opener-type transmitter that is connected to the receiver. When the receiver hears the ultrasonic transmitter, it sends an RF signal to a wall-mounted RF receiver. This rather complicated system rates a 6 on a scale of 10. (It should be noted that if the ultrasonic transmitter is silenced by pulling out the plug or covering the unit with a blanket, the entire system fails. To overcome this shortcoming, another ultrasonic receiver must be mounted on the wall, this one designed to remain dormant if it hears the ultrasonic transmitter, and go into alarm when it does a sort of reverse of the unit mounted inside the display case.)

Any type of ultrasonic alarm can adequately protect a museum building during the night-time hours. The most popular system appears to be ultrasonic units, even though some curators feel that the constant ultrasonic waves can eventually cause some deterioration to the oil base on works of fine art. This theory is not widely accepted. The second most popular device is the passive infrared unit, followed by the use of microwave and audio detection units. A brief outline of their operational theory is being presented to remove some of the mystery surrounding security systems and to encourage administrators to assist in the design of a security system. The fact is apparent that administrators have a better understanding of the problems and vulnerable areas than the alarm salesmen.

Electronic protection systems, whether used in a museum, bank, or school building, consist of four basic elements. Each of these elements is equally important to the overall security of the building. Unless all four are carefully analyzed, balanced, and integrated, the resultant security system will be practically useless. The elements are:

1. DETECTION (ultrasonic, microwave, magnetic switches, beams)
2. TRANSMISSION (getting the signal out)
3. ANNUNCIATION (indicating and recording of the signal)
4. RESPONSE (reacting to the situation)

Each category requires a realistic approach with a practical knowledge of the needs of the particular situation, as well as the limitation of the responding authority. All too often, expensive and sophisticated intrusion detectors are installed in a museum, while annunciation is limited to a bell located on the roof of the building. The building may be two miles from the closest person, and the ringing bell alerts no one, while wasting electricity.

Just as often, there are facilities which have a direct wire connection to a central answering service (the most secure method of transmitting an alarm signal), but the alarm inside the museum is limited to a light beam along the four interior walls. The professional thief has only to step around, or over, these easily spotted beams to enter and leave the premises.

Stressing one element at the expense of the others accomplishes very little protection and creates a false sense of security. The installation of a sophisticated alarm system requires an intelligent balance of sensors and transmission in order to be effective. A sensor (or detector) may function correctly, but if the transmission medium is defective the signal goes unrecorded. This situation, which is quite common, has contributed toward the rising rate of art theft within these four basic elements.

Another highly successful use of electronics is the locking of secondary exits that are usually hidden behind large works of art. All these so-called "fire exits" have panic hardware to allow exiting of the premises in case of fire or other emergencies. Most of these doors are equipped with some type of local bell contraption, so that whenever the door is opened the bell will annunciate the fact that the panic hardware was pushed and the door opened. Most of these local alarms are powered by batteries which are rarely replaced, and often dead. They generally are considered useless security hardware.

The most practical approach to controlling these doors is to lock them so that the panic-bar hardware cannot be used to open the door. A regular lock cannot be installed due to the fire regulations covering these exits. But, if the lock is magnetically controlled, and the power to support the holding force is funneled through the fire-alarm system, the chance for fire department approval is excellent (see Figure 14.3). Whenever a fire signal is detected (pull boxes or switch detectors), the power to the lock is cut off and the regular panic hardware can release the door latch. It is a brand-new concept and very few alarm companies are aware of its flexibility in situations where exit doors are remote and tempting to a would-be thief.

All the preceding ideas were designed by building managers and are typical of the common-sense approach that can be used to develop special devices and techniques for museums. While there are many more ideas that are just as applicable, these examples are cited to encourage more curators to participate in the design of alarm systems.

The remainder of this chapter is dedicated to a description of the basic alarm devices so that some of the mystery associated with them may be removed. It is not intended to make an expert out of the reader because, all

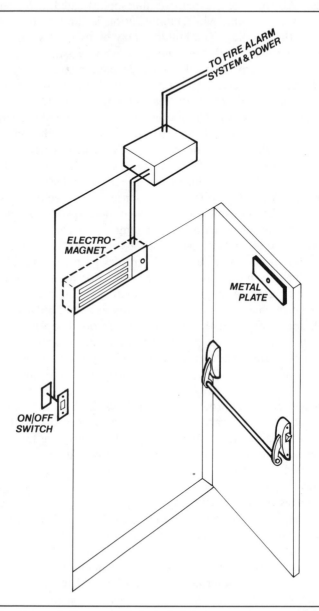

Figure 14.3. Magnetically controlled panic bar

too often, the alarm salesperson is not an expert either. Since this individual usually does not understand the flexibility and wide range of devices available, he or she often designs a system around a very limited scope of knowledge. The aim of this chapter is to assist museum administrators in finding alternative methods for selecting and designing alarm systems.

INTRUSION DETECTORS

As was previously mentioned, most museums, historic sites, and galleries rely on standard magnetic door switches and light-beam devices to protect their premises during night-time or nonoperating hours. When this traditional approach failed to provide adequate protection, a whole new set of devices was developed to cover not only the perimeter of museum, but also the critical interior areas. These new devices were found much more difficult to compromise than door switches and beams. These devices are called *volumetric alarm systems.*

The word "volumetric" indicates a flooding of an area with unseen "waves" detecting movement in three dimensions — area, as opposed to the conventional two-dimensional narrow beam. Volumetric devices have been available for over twenty-five years, but very little technical information is available to describe the operational differences among each of the major techniques used to protect space against intrusion. A brief description of the four most accepted techniques are as follows:

1. *ULTRASONIC/ULTRASOUND:* sends high-frequency (above the normal human hearing range) sound waves into an area the size of an average classroom. Detection is in response to changes in the sound waves caused by movement within the protected area.
2. *MICROWAVE:* operates on the same general theory of ultrasonic detection with an important difference in the frequency of the transmitter and receiver. It operates in extremely high radio frequency ranges, and is capable of penetrating some kinds of wall material and can be directed to protect areas as long as 400 feet.
3. *AUDIO:* highly sophisticated amplifier that is critically tuned to "listen to" sounds in specific bandwidths. This discriminating feature eliminates reaction to outside noise and detects sounds made by human movement. This is the primary distinction between a *detector* and a simple *amplifier.*
4. *PASSIVE INFRARED:* usually confused with the light-beam detector that uses an infrared colored filter.

A more detailed explanation of these devices follows.

Ultrasonic/Ultrasound Detectors

The oldest and most widely used volumetric device on the market today is the ultrasonic detector. This device sends out high-frequency sound waves and responds to changes in those waves caused by movement within the protected area.

Sound may be defined as the range of frequencies between 30 Hz and approximately 18,000 Hz that can be heard by most people. Any sound below or above this range of frequencies cannot be heard by the average human ear. Sound above this "normal" range of human hearing is called *ultrasound* or *ultrasonic*. Hearing does not stop abruptly at 18,000 Hz, particularly if the sound is strong enough and the listener has good hearing. Frequencies up to 22,000 Hz can be heard by some people (for some reason, women are more likely than men to possess sensitive hearing abilities). Animals are very sensitive to extremely high frequencies, particularly dogs, who respond to dog whistles which are undetected by most humans.

The manufacturers of ultrasonic alarms usually select frequencies slightly above human hearing for their ultrasonic alarms. The most popular frequencies fall in the range of 19,200 Hz, 21,000 Hz, and 40,000 Hz. The exact selection of frequency is based on various technical factors and practical considerations.

There is no single "perfect" frequency, since each frequency offers some advantages as well as disadvantages. The final choice is a balance of the many technical considerations that define sound waves. The industry generally tries to stay as close to the audible range as possible, but high enough so that the ultrasound does not penetrate the room barriers or become confused by common noises such as hissing radiators or ringing telephone bells.

The frequency chosen should be above 20,000 Hz so that a burglar would be unaware of its presence and location; however, it should be lower than 50,000 Hz since frequencies at higher ranges are easily absorbed by the air (any absorbtion significantly reduces the distance a detector can cover). Higher frequencies do offer certain advantages since barriers (walls, ceilings, floors, and windows) cannot vibrate at higher frequencies. This means that more ultrasonic energy is forced back into the protected area. Very low frequencies (falling within the audible range) are not absorbed by the air, but can lose some of their overall effectiveness by vibrating the walls and windows. This lowers the important "bounce" or reflex characteristic. There are products on the market that are called *sonic* detectors because they operate in the audible range in a deliberate attempt to scare away, rather than capture, intruders.

An alarm condition would occur if someone walked into the area covered by the detector, thus altering the sound-wave pattern. The better ultrasonic detectors are designed to ignore very small changes. This capability is needed to keep the system from reacting to air in motion (drafts) and the movement of draperies or curtains. If the intruder moved very, very slowly, he could possibly defeat the system, but would require a long time to move across a thirty-foot room. The major drawback of ultrasonic alarms is the belief by many museum curators that the vibrating sound waves bouncing off the oil paint will eventually cause some deterioration to the surface (flaking, etc.). Theoretically, there is some justification for this belief, but since the power of the ultrasonic detector is so small, the actual sound wave would be too weak really to have any significant effect on the painting, but the concern of the curator is understandable and since there are adequate substitutes for ultrasonic, the use of another device would at least bring about some peace of mind.

Microwave Detection

The microwave-detection field grew out of the need for a sophisticated device that would effectively detect motion without being distracted by external environmental stimuli (e.g., air currents, insects). The first microwave devices were installed around 1968 at a time when the industry was just beginning to accept ultrasonic technology. As a result, sales representatives for the one company which manufactured microwave alarm units spent more time educating the alarm installer on microwave theory than "selling" the device. Because of the unfamiliarity of the industry with microwave theory, the device was frequently misapplied and misinstalled, and many component failures and false alarms occurred.

Theory of microwave detection. Microwave detection, over the years, has been identified by several different (and sometimes confusing) names: RF (radio frequency), radar detection, radiation resistance detection, and, finally, microwave.

The earliest versions of microwave detectors did not use the frequency shift effect to detect motion. They operated in the lower radio frequency range and, while sometimes referred to as microwave frequencies, they really were not high enough to be considered microwave. Those first units utilized a simple pole-shaped antenna that radiated RF energy in every direction surrounding the antenna. Any movement within its range reflected energy back into the antenna, changing the pattern of the antenna radiation. It was not until the late 1960s, when the government permitted operation at extremely high frequencies, that microwave came into its own.

ULTRASONIC VS. MICROWAVE

Ultrasonic units operate in the 20,000 Hz to 40,000 Hz range. AM broadcast frequencies are around 1,000,000 Hz and microwave systems generally operate at the 10,000,000,000 Hz range, which is also called the 10.5 Giga Hertz range. It is included in what is called the "X" band.

In accordance with FCC regulations, microwave detectors are only permitted to operate within a limited microwave power range, and at only five specific frequencies.

Method of operation. High frequency microwave signals are generated by a solid-state device called a *gunn diode.* These diodes consume relatively small amounts of power in order to remain within the limits mandated by the FCC. The power generated is less than 10 millivolts or 1/100 of a watt. This low power is sufficient to drive a signal up to 400 feet, but cannot (as some microwave critics claim) affect the operation of a pacemaker or cause other physical damage to humans.

In order for the gunn diode to radiate the required microwave energy, the transmitter and receiver must be installed in a metal box with one side open. This enclosure is called a *microwave cavity.* The same cavity can cover different areas simply by changing the antenna shape. The overall volume of coverage remains constant, but the coverage pattern can be altered from a narrow path of 300' by 2' by 1' (600 cubic feet) to cover a room that is 10' by 10' by 6' (also 600 cubic feet).

The shape changing ability is a favorable feature since one basic shortcoming of other devices is that they are difficult to modify for different situations. Each microwave unit transmits the wave into a protected area, striking stationary objects in the room. These waves are reflected back to the receiver. The receivers are adjusted to ignore the signals from stationary objects because they do not create a doppler shift. They are sensitive, however, to anyone moving within this field of coverage. This is similar to the operational theory of ultrasonic devices, but there are two characteristics that make microwave unique, and, in many situations, superior to ultrasonic systems: (1) the signals can be controlled to project in fairly precise directional patterns (this enables coverage of areas that vary widely in size and configuration); and (2) microwave signals are not affected by either air turbulence or low-frequency noise (both conditions can cause havoc with ultrasonic devices).

Besides its long-range capability, the most unique characteristic of the microwave detector is its ability to penetrate most building material and actually "see" into another room or series of rooms. The energy to penetrate ceilings, floors and walls around the microwave transceiver can be very useful, particularly in a cargo storage area. One unit, placed in an attic and pointed down, can protect two entire floors within being seen. This capability could cause trouble if the unit were pointed toward an outside wall where the energy would continue to the exterior of the building, and could detect a car moving on a road 200 feet away, or a truck even farther away. Microwaves are reflected and contained by metal (which is grounded), concrete, and dense building material. Microwaves penetrate glass, light, dry wood, plaster and plaster board, most fabrics, and fiberboard.

One microwave unit can cover a 400-foot corridor, yet 10 ultrasonic transceivers are often selected to cover the same area. This fact has encouraged microwave manufacturers to produce mini-units that protect a maximum of 30 to 40 feet and can compete with ultrasonics for small area requirements. Even at these limited distances, microwaves offer the unique advantage of being immune to the external stimuli (e.g., air currents) which plague ultrasonics, causing false alarms.

Audio Detection

One of the most familiar concepts in the field of electronics is the function of the microphone and its sensitivity to even the slightest sound levels. The microphone (or speakers which are used like microphones) operates by converting sound into an electrical impulse that can be amplified. In a similar manner, the cycle of sound–electrical impulse–sound is the basis for the audio detection system.

Audio detection systems are designed to "read" the signatures of sounds picked up by strategically located microphones. If the detected sound is loud or continuous enough, or at a specific frequency, it will cause the system to go into alarm.

The principle of audio detection is based upon the theory that intruders will create noise of known frequency and volume as they move around a room. Almost every movement creates a detectable noise even before the creator of the noise enters the protected premises. The audio detector can often "sense" intrusion before it occurs (e.g., a key being placed in an outside door lock, physical attack against a building). Ultrasonic and microwave units do not have this capacity.

Audio and vibration detection are the acceptable techniques approved by insurance companies to be used inside bank vaults. In the quiet atmosphere of the small vault area, the audio detection microphone can sense the burning, drilling into concrete and steel, hammering, or shoveling around the outside vault area. It "sees" what is not there!

Even a low-level noise can be detected by an inexpensive microphone mounted high on a wall or ceiling, amplified, and analyzed for frequency patterns. When used in a bank vault, no frequency discrimination is necessary, since all detectable sounds in this normally quiet environment are suspicious. A great deal of ambient noise is present, however, when used in a cargo building. In this environment, special electronic circuitry is required to distinguish intrusion sounds from recurring common sounds.

Theory of audio detection. The primary difference between ultrasonic and audio detection units is the fact that ultrasonic units are active; they transmit their own sound patterns and actually control their operating frequency. Audio units, on the other hand, are passive since they do not transmit signals. They are only receivers and must be accurately programmed to detect the frequencies of sound created by human movement.

Most nonaudio protection systems on the market today are the silent type, with the alarm signal transmitted through a phone line to a remote central station. The signal is annunciated on a control panel. The operator, alerted to the alarm condition, must take responsible and corrective action to record this alarm condition. The only way to determine the reason for the alarm is to send someone to survey the building where the alarm condition occurred. This often proves to be a time-consuming and frustrating process, since alarms transmitted are frequently false.

The audio detector is superior, in some situations, to ultrasonic and microwave devices, and may prove appropriate for many museums. This is due to the fact that it possesses the special advantage of allowing the central station operator actually to "listen in" on the source of the alarm condition. With a little practice, any operator can identify the familiar sounds of banging pipes, airplanes, traffic noise, or can even monitor and record actual conversation of burglars. The audio detector is the one method currently available to analyze false alarms, thus avoiding false responses without resorting to desensitizing the alarm system.

Use of audio detectors in special situations. There are numerous self-contained audio detection units designed for home use only. These portable units are made to look like hi-fi speaker cabinets and contain sirens as well as detector circuits. This type of detector frequently reacts to lightning, thunder, traffic, animals, and other external stimuli. Hopefully, it would also go into alarm if a would-be intruder tried to force a window. Although the unit's siren might frighten the intruder away, it probably would not bring the police (or even the neighbors) since its known proneness to false alarm has caused others to disregard it. When this self-contained unit is used in commercial establishments, it has produced less than satisfactory results and is sometimes stolen along with the merchandise.

There are many situations in which audio detection can be superior to other alarm devices. One example is in buildings that possess a public address (P.A.) system with speakers installed through the entire structure. This existing network of speakers can be easily converted into an audio detection system when the speakers are utilized as microphones.

The primary advantage of audio detection systems is their ability to detect sounds and to transmit these sounds over a phone line for determination of the source or type of sound being detected. This capability is becoming more and more important in an industry which produces equipment that is frequently activated by false signals. This ability has given audio detection a potential to recapture a significant portion of the credibility it has lost in the last decade to other alarm detectors.

AUDIO DETECTORS: PRIMARY CHARACTERISTICS

1. Discriminate all sounds that fall outside the 1500 Hz to 6000 Hz range (except bank vaults).
2. Count pulses of sounds while disregarding single disturbances.
3. Have an effective sensitivity control.
4. May be matched electronically to public address speakers or microphones.
5. Possess a cancellation circuit to eliminate persistent outside noises.
6. Provide for supervised protection of the cable between the main panel and the microphones.
7. Incorporate high-fidelity amplification to permit listening from a central station.

Passive Infrared Detectors

During the Vietnam War, the federal government perfected, as a surveillance device, a technique to detect the motion from low-flying reconnaissance aircraft. This system was different from all existing methods of motion detection and possessed the following unique characteristics:

1. It did not require visible light, as camera surveillance techniques did.
2. It did not (like radar, microwave, and ultrasonic) require a transmitted (active) signal to measure movement.
3. Its detection (unlike audio systems) was totally unrelated to noise or sound.

With the development of small elements (transducers), which changed in electrical characteristic when bombarded with infrared energy, came the revolutionary passive IR motion detection system.

Passive infrared detection was not really an offspring of the Vietnam War. The theory had its origins in a technique developed many years earlier for use in the detection of breast cancer. Medical laboratories were the first to apply the passive IR principle when they discovered that carcinogenic tissues projected more IR energy (because of a higher oxidation rate) than healthy ones. Although major modifications had to be made to adapt equipment developed for the detection of malignant tumors to use in aircraft surveillance and the protection of commercial property, the basic passive IR concept remained the same.

Theory of passive infrared detection. The passive IR detector is basically an optical device that utilizes a lens system to focus IR radiation into a component called a *thermocouple* or *thermistor*. This element receives radiation (heat) from the human body and converts it into an electrical signal. The focusing of IR energy on to the transducer is similar to the action of a camera focusing light onto the film surface behind the lens. Passive IR detectors are so sensitive to heat that they are able to distinguish between temperatures that are within a fraction of one another, and can accomplish this feat from a distance of 2,000 feet.

PRIMARY CHARACTERISTICS OF IR RADIATION

1. Infrared is a form of transmittable energy normally emitted by every object because of its temperature.
2. Infrared energy is transmitted without physical contact between the emitting and receiving surfaces.
3. Infrared energy warms the receiving surface and can be detected by any device capable of sensing a change in temperature.
4. Infrared energy is invisible and completely silent.

Once the optical IR detector adjusts to the amount of IR radiation being emitted from the surrounding environment, it is sensitive to any sudden changes in emitted IR radiation. Small movements in the environment are usually ignored, but whenever a body that has more than a 0.5° F temperature differential moves between the detector and the background upon which it is focused, it will be detected. Since every solid object in a room emits different amounts of IR energy, it is almost impossible to build a shield at one ambient temperature that could hide a moving intruder.

IR motion detectors do not measure actual temperature, but, rather, react to the difference in the radiated heat of the objects captured by the special lens systems. Although heat is not an actual measurement of temperature, radiated infrared energy bears a close relation to temperature. The higher the temperature, the greater the infrared radiation. IR energy does not travel slowly, like heat waves, but moves rapidly through space at the speed of light. Consequently, infrared detectors are infinitely more sensitive to changes in temperature than thermometers.

> The mercury tilt switch in a wall-mounted thermostat automatically controls the heat given off by the furnace and radiators when a bimetallic strip tilts the switch. The mercury moves back and forth, making and breaking the contact, depending on the fluctuating temperature. Infrared-sensitive elements (transducers) also react to temperature change — only at a much faster rate — and can be focused on a small spot in a room rather than having to sense the ambient temperature surrounding the device.

Use of passive IR detectors in the security protection field. The passive IR device used in the protection field surveys the area directly in front of the lens, up to a distance of 30 feet. Unless the intruder is at room temperature, or the room at 98.6 degrees, the IR radiation difference will be detected by the sensor.

Once again, it must be pointed out that there is a great deal of confusion in the security protection field regarding the use of the photoelectric light beam (which often uses an infrared color filter) and the passive infrared motion detector. *The two are alike in nomenclature only.*

The photoelectric light beam device requires a transmitter and is therefore, like ultrasonic and microwave units, considered an ACTIVE alarm device. The passive IR unit does not require both a sender and receiver. The infrared energy of the human body acts as a sender, and the device is therefore considered a PASSIVE system.

Although not the panacea to all protection woes, passive IR sensors are immune to many environmental conditions, such as humidity, air currents, sound-wave disturbances, etc. They provide another alternative to the space protection problem and are as effective as any sensor on the market for their particular application.

SELECTION OF INTRUSION DETECTORS

Due to the peculiar configuration of most museums, care must be exercised in the selection of one device over another. The detectors selected must be able to "flood" areas. This may require that, instead of a single detector being mounted on the east wall, a second detector may have to be mounted on the west wall, as well. The most effective system is to align the detectors in a checkerboard pattern, so that there is a criss-cross effect through the room area. The exact location may only be determined after the pattern coverage is known.

During the early 1970s, almost all detectors were ultrasonic because most companies promoted this technique. When it was demonstrated that microwave detectors were able to protect larger areas than the conventional 30' by 30' configuration of most ultrasonic units, they began to capture a good share of the market. In the late 1970s and early 1980s, the passive infrared device began to make inroads into the market when better optics were perfected that allowed the unit to directly change the old-fashioned light beams in distance of coverage. There are passive IR devices available today that can protect an area 150' by 7'. Simply by changing the optics, this same unit can cover an area 40' by 40'. This flexibility can be very useful in a building such as a museum.

TRANSMISSION OF THE ALARM SIGNAL

Much emphasis is placed upon the selection of an appropriate sensor for an alarm device; however, many false alarms are actually due to the improper selection of transmission media. All too often, the sensor may be the only component functioning in an alarm system. Bells ring in museums; sirens wail all night in deserted galleries; and central station services can fail to detect the fact that a system was never turned on or that a connecting phone line has been out of order for months. Often the only person aware of these deficiencies is the burglar.

Installing a sophisticated type of sensor is a waste of money unless it is accompanied by a transmission system that is just as reliable. Although a sensor may function correctly, its reaction is futile if it goes unrecorded and uninvestigated. Although transmission is as important as the other elements which comprise a complete alarm system, it is too often selected with a minimal amount of forethought or investigation.

From a security standpoint, the transmission of an alarm signal to a location remote from the protected museum is infinitely more desirable than any local alarm system. Alarm devices, such as sirens and strobe lights and the local systems which use them, are rapidly being replaced by central station systems. This is largely due to the fact that local alarms are too often ignored, and even criticized, by the very community that the devices rely upon to summon help.

The local alarm has some value as a deterrent, but even in this area its value is questionable. Intruders have learned that a siren indicates that the security system is not connected to a central station, and that once the local alarm is disabled, there is nothing remaining on the premises to detect their movements. In fact, the constant activation of local alarm systems due to false alarms has become so annoying that a growing number of municipalities have begun to establish "noise-abatement ordinances" controlling the use of local alarms (maximum duration of alarm must be fifteen minutes; volume level of the sounding device must be severely limited, etc.).

A silent alarm transmitted to a location that is sometimes miles away is generally superior to most local alarms for a multitude of reasons. The use of the phone line not only enables the alarm signal to be transmitted over long distances, but it can, in some situations, also be designed to permit the remote operator actually to "listen in" to the sounds originating at the protected premises to determine the cause of the alarm — intrusion or non-intrusion disturbances. This listen-in technique is the only effective method for minimizing false alarms since it may provide the intelligence needed to identify or verify the actual event which activated the alarm signal.

There are numerous methods for transmitting the alarm signal to a remote monitoring system. Some of these techniques even require elaborate computerized panels at central control stations; others only require a standard phone line in police headquarters. Most popular systems in use today require the services and cooperation of the phone company.

The use of leased telephone lines to carry the alarm signal has become such a convenience that almost all systems rely upon this transmission medium. If the alarm industry loses this easy and relatively inexpensive communication link, they may have to replace most existing equipment. This possibility is now threatening many central station companies whose future, to a significant extent, is controlled by the FCC and company policies and tariffs. Until some radical changes are made, however, the alarm industry will continue to rely on the telephone line as the principal connecting link between the monitoring service and the protected premises.

There are five primary communications/transmission systems in use today. Four require telephone links. They are:

1. Tape dialers
2. Digital communicators (dialers)
3. Dedicated/leased direct wire phone lines
4. McCulloh loop and multiplexing networks
5. Radio transmission (FM)

The Tape Dialer

Though tape dialers are inexpensive, easy to install, and somewhat reliable, many police departments have refused to respond to them, and, in some municipalities, their use has been banned.

The first dialer was introduced in the early 1940s. It had a wind-up motor coupled to a metal finger which was used to dial a standard telephone. When triggered, the device would dial a preset number and play a recorded message (e.g., "This is 15 Park Avenue, Hoboken, N.J. Suspected burglary in progress. Send help.").

The tape dialer filled a need during a period when there was no other choice in self-contained and portable communications equipment. The machine, once activated, sent a message over the existing phone to any phone number preprogrammed on the tape. Once the proper series of numbers is dialed, a delay (blank tape) is built in to allow for time duration of about three rings, after which the programmed message is given. Then a simulated signal would, in effect, hang up the receiver. The tape dialer is capable of transmitting two or three additional numbers and repeating the same message on one run of the tape. At the end of the tape, the machine would be ready to send the same series of messages if activated again.

Tape dialers can be made to dial anywhere in the United States, and messages can specify situations other than intrusion. If, for example, the dialer were connected to the fire alarm, the preset number would be that of the fire department, and the message would explain that a fire emergency existed. The tape dialer could also be connected to a thermostat and could be programmed to start when the temperature on the premises went below freezing (or to go off when the refrigerator went above freezing).

The major advantages of this "blind" obedience to a preprogrammed tape are also the reasons for most of its shortcomings. The tape machine has no control over the sensor or communication link to the answering phone. If the intrusion alarm sensors are false-alarm prone, the dialer will continually go off.

There are other factors that have limited the acceptance of the tape dialer. Since there is no way to test the system from a remote location, its use as a high security device is questionable. For example, the sensor could be broken, or the phone line cut (or out of order). If the sensor were broken, the dialer would not operate. Similarly, if the phone line were cut, the dialer would operate but would deliver its message to a dead phone line. Perhaps the most critical limitation is the fact that even when the sensor and phone are in perfect working order, the dialer has no way of determining if anyone is actually listening to its message. It can, and often does, deliver an emergency message to a busy signal.

Even though the popular attitude is to blame tape dialers for false-alarm messages, it is usually the activating sensor that is at fault. Nevertheless, the trend has been to prohibit, or control by municipal ordinances, the use of tape dialers. A growing number of municipalities have restricted their use to individual installations approved by the police. In these situations, only approved dialers are given a "secret" police number. If there are too many false alarms by any user, that person is either fined or the use of the special number is rescinded. In this way, the police can establish some control over the tape dialer problem.

Only the better-made dialers are constructed in such a manner that, even if not used for years, they will operate when called upon to do so. Most dialers, like any electromechanical device, will tend to "stick" or break down after lying dormant for two or three years. The most common complaint received about telephone dialers from the industry itself is the fact that the programmed tape must be made at the factory or by the installer. This necessitates a dangerous delay when the tape message and/or phone number must be changed. While all manufacturers sell a programmer capable of making tapes, there are so many different and noninterchangeable models that the cost of purchasing programmers becomes exorbitant. There are now products on the market that come with built-in programmers including microphone, tape, and dialing device. This solves the problem of inconvenience, but not the problem of potentially faulty equipment.

The Digital Dialer (Communicator)

The widespread acceptance of the automatic tape dialer has encouraged the development of a more sophisticated device — *the digital dialer.* In order to differentiate this device from the tape unit, the industry has been attempting to change the nomenclature to "digital communicator."

Aside from the fact that tape and digital devices both rely upon existing phone lines, there are virtually no similarities between the two. Unlike the tape dialer, the digital communicator does not send an audible voice message but transmits tone-coded signals which are decoded by a special digital receiver. While the tape dialer is comprised of a single sending unit, digital communicator systems require two components: the transmitter (at the sensor location) and the receiver (at the monitoring station). The tape dialer, as previously explained, has no interconnection with the number being called. The digital communicator, on the other hand, relies upon communication with a programmed receiver at one particular location.

Digital communicators cannot send messages to just any phone location as tape dialers can. A digital communicator can only transmit to a special digital receiver which possesses the capability of decoding the message(s) sent. Although the digital transmitter unit can be programmed to dial any number, that number must be at a location where the phone line is connected to the special receiver. One receiver can monitor hundreds (usually up to 1,000) of communicators.

The programming of each communicator is stored in a small electronic component called a "memory chip." Since all chips look alike, it is not possible, by mere appearance, to decipher anything about the coded message. In lieu of chips, some units use plug-in cards and others have switches mounted directly on the digital transmitter. These units are more vulnerable to deciphering than those which utilize memory chips.

The memory chip, along with the other circuitry in the digital communicator (or transmitter), electronically simulates the dialing of the phone. This number can be addressed to any phone, anywhere in the country, equipped with the special receiver.

> One of the largest communication monitoring systems in the United States is located in a city on the East Coast from which it controls alarm systems located in forty-eight states. If a call comes in that the temperature in a refrigerated area in a warehouse in Kansas has dropped below a certain point, the receiving unit immediately records the situation. An operator then dials the police station nearest the building to alert them to the situation.

The transmitting communicator will continue to dial until it gets a special signal back from the receiver (similar to hearing the phone picked up at the other end). This "handshake" signal initiates the electronic conversation and verifies that a connection to a "live" receiver has been made. At this point, the only useful knowledge communicated is that the receiver has been placed into the system and is awaiting further communication to identify the sender.

Next, a series of coded numbers appear in the receiver to identify the caller. The Kansas farmer might be designated "067," while a factory in New York City would be "939." If more than 999 locations are required, a second receiver would be connected to a second incoming phone line, etc. The information given must be repeated twice, one behind the other, to satisfy the receiver and to overcome jamming by a third party.

After the receiver properly identifies the sender's location, the transmitter is alerted to send still another type of coded signal. This last signal indicates the type of problem by listing an "04" to indicate a burglary, and "02" for a fire, etc. When all this information is displayed on the receiver panel, a signal is sent back to the transmitter to reset (hang up) and get ready for future intrusion, etc. Some types will send a full message up to twenty-four times. Typical receiver codes are established by the central station. Generally, the lower the number, the more threatening the situation is to human life. For example:

01......	Medical emergency	05......	Reset
02......	Fire	06......	Test
03......	Hold-up	07......	Extra
04......	Burglary	08......	Battery low
	09...... Extra		

There are many features which cannot be accomplished with tape dialers that can expand the system. For instance, the digital dialer can be programmed to dial a second receiver if there is line trouble at the first location. Since the communication link can create a situation where two phones are electronically connected, a microphone can be connected to the transmitter, permitting the receiver actually to listen in to the protected premises. This feature is usually free since the price schedule used generally covers a full three minutes of time, and the coded signals establishing location and trouble rarely take longer than fifteen seconds. This leaves two minutes and forty-five seconds for listening in without additional phone charges.

Digital communicators are the fastest-growing devices in use for transmitting the alarm signal to the central station. They are infinitely more reliable than the tape dialer and provide almost as much information as a human conversation. Their primary drawback as high-security devices is the fact that they rely on existing switched phone circuits to transmit their messages. While it may be inexpensive to use this type of telephonic transmission, phone lines are vulnerable to cutting. Since the connection between the transmitter and the receiver utilizes normal switched telephone circuits, there is no way to "supervise" the line between the protected premises and the central station. Some of these weaknesses may be overcome by using two separate incoming phone lines at the protected premises. Using this method, the digital transmitter would be connected in such a way that if one line were cut, it would send notification of this event via the second phone line (of course, this method would be ineffective if both lines were cut simultaneously). There is another device available which reads the phone line voltage on the outgoing line. If the voltage goes to zero (cut wire), a local bell or siren is activated in the protected building to alert someone to the defective phone line. This device, of course, relies on someone's being in the area to notice the alarm.

Because it offers a reasonable alternative to equipment requiring the rental of special phone lines, the digital communicator is a technological advancement exercising a profound effect on the entire security industry.

The Leased/Dedicated Phone Line

Tape dialers and digital communicators function more or less as telephone extensions which connect into existing phone lines, but require special or extra interface equipment (other than an interface jack) from the phone company. *Leased (or dedicated) phone lines,* on the other hand, require special connections between the protected premises and communication centers (e.g., central service stations, police departments). Alarm companies are no longer permitted the convenience of running wires over rooftops to their customers' properties. As they did sixty years ago, they are again forced to lease lines from phone companies.

Leased lines can be run into any building that can have telephone wire running into it. They represent the most practical transmission method since they make use of an existing pair of cable wires running between the protected premises and the central station by "dedicating" them to alarm service. This method involves no switching at phone company terminals and no change in phone instruments. A single pair of wires is selected out of a cable and run from the protected premises to the phone exchange. There it is connected to another pair of wires that run from the phone exchange to the central station. The major problem with leased lines is their increasingly higher rental cost. There have been runs made of over 100 miles, but generally the phone company would rather use the leased line for regular phone service than lease it to an alarm company. For just one customer's use, the phone company can place hundreds of phone conversations on that pair of wires and collect much more than they would with a fixed-rate leased line. In addition, alarm lines (which must be in perfect working order at all times) require close attention from the phone company.

The McCulloh Loop and Multiplexing Networks

The McCulloh loop is another system of transmission universally used by central stations to overcome the cost factor of leased lines. This system of connecting several locations into one incoming line connected to the central station has been in use for almost 100 years. The McCulloh circuit is, essentially, a form of "party line" through which several protected premises share a single loop or circuit and are wired in series from the phone company terminal. A single pair of wires is then run from the terminal to the central station. Identification is accomplished by programming each sensor on the circuit to transmit a unique signal so that the receiver can determine which sensor is alarming. The code is usually presented in the form of a gearlike apparatus that, when activated, hits a series of contacts which transmit the code set by the spacing of the gear teeth. The system is wired in such a way that if there is a break in the phone line, there is a way for the phone company immediately to determine the exact location of the problem.

Radio Transmission. The obvious need for an alternative method to phone line transmission has encouraged a rapid advancement in low-powered radio transmission technology. The result of these efforts is a system of transponders capable of communication between the protected premises and the central control station. Multiplexed FM-coded signals can reliably send messages up to thirty miles in flat, unobstructed terrain, and ten to fifteen miles in the commercial centers of large cities. This distance directly competes with phone line communication links because almost all subscribers to central station services lie within a fifteen-mile radius. Distances greater than that become economically inefficient since phone line rental costs become greater at longer distances.

The initial application of electronics to identify automatically a specific transmitter occurred after World War II, when the need for such a device became critical. Radar systems, although able to detect flying objects, could not distinguish one object from another (or one "blip" from another on the radar screen). The use of transponders was successfully demonstrated during World War II under the system known as "Identification: Friend or Foe" (IFF). Since many aircraft were operating within radar range, it was essential to identify a friendly "blip" from an enemy one. The IFF system consisted of a transceiver at the ground radar station and a transponder on all friendly aircraft. The radar station would continually transmit a radio signal to the aircraft within the radar surveillance area each time the radar antenna pointed to the specific aircraft during a 360-degree cycle. The aircraft would translate the radar station "impulse" or interrogation and automatically transmit back the proper code of the day (or mission). As the radar antenna continued to sweep the sky, it would continue to receive the coded signals from all friendly aircraft. If no signal were received, or if the code were incorrect, the aircraft would be considered unfriendly.

This system is now in use in all military and commercial aircraft and in most private aircraft. A modified version is in use as a security device. The transponder identifies the protected premises after being interrogated by a central monitoring station.

The system used by the military was very powerful. It utilized large ground antennae and required a roomful of computerized electronics. The security systems which function on the same concept use low-powered (about 1–1½ watts), small, integrated circuits and omnidirectional antennae. The identifying code is present before the transponders are installed in the subscriber's building. The power and frequency assignment of the equipment is dictated by FCC regulations which allocate frequency and power according to need, and in order to avoid interference with other radio communication equipment in the area (the same frequency can be assigned to several central stations as long as they are separated by hundreds of miles). The use of very high frequency (VHF) or ultra high frequencies (UHF) may limit the useful distance to thirty miles, but it also eliminates the "skip" problems often associated with low-frequency AM radio (CB band, etc.).

Technical operation. Each set of protected premises requires a transponder that, when triggered by the activation of a sensor, notifies the central service of the event. If, instead of a transponder (which is basically a combination of a receiver and transmitter), the protected premises have only a transmitter, the system would function in one direction only. This would mean that when an alarm device was activated, the transmitter would send an encoded signal to the controlling central service receiver. If two or more alarms come in simultaneously, the encoding allows for separating the multiple signals. The problem with this system is that there is no way of telling if the transmitter is in working order. It functions as an unsupervised system and is unacceptable for high-security situations.

The more sophisticated transponder system receives signals from the central station every few seconds and reports back that there is no intrusion. This reaction also indicates that the transmitter is in working order. Time-sharing techniques permit the typical radio transmission central service to monitor 500 subscribers over a single transmitter/receiver network. The central service sends 500 identical signals over the omnidirectional antennae, one at a time, to all subscribers. The returning signal from the protected premises is different for each subscriber, enabling the central station to know whose premises it is interrogating at any particular instant. When the protected premises receive the proper code, they immediately retransmit a condition code back to the central station. Up to eight conditions may be transmitted from each location with most commercially available systems. After this condition code is recorded, the central station goes on to interrogate other premises. The 500 subscribers can transmit special codes, but since the transponder is programmed to do this only when interrogated on a sequential time-sharing basis, the central station knows its exact status because of its position on the sequence cycle. It will only take a few seconds to interrogate all 500 subscribers.

The primary reason for the slow acceptance of FM radio transmission is the high cost of reliable equipment, the stability of frequency assignments by the FCC, and the fact that the typical alarm installer is unfamiliar with radio transmission. Radio transmission should grow significantly in the 1980s as the equipment becomes less costly and the assignments of frequency become fixed and permanent. It should prove to be the logical replacement for the difficult-to-obtain dedicated phone line.

Transmission of the alarm signal is, and will continue to be, one of the most important phases in the alarm system. Faulty transmission is a major contributing factor to the high false-alarm rate which has caused many police departments to ignore, and even ban, certain alarm devices. The customary use of wire to interconnect sensors, control panels, and annunciators provides the most effective transmission technique; however, the world's supply of copper is diminishing, and easy accessibility to phone-company connections is slowly disappearing. The constant threat of the phone company to curtail use of dedicated copper wires for alarm use has led to a great many techniques that allow "shared" lines. Time Division Multiplexing and Frequency

Division Multiplexing are growing slowly in popularity, and this shift in technique is being encouraged by the phone company. The growth of radio transmission as an alternative to all types of phone line connections indicates that ingenuity and innovative approaches to security controls are still a major part of the industry. New techniques will be developed as the need arises, and it is predicted that, with the growing use of cable television, both phone line connections and radio transmission will be replaced in a few years with this new communication method.

15. Standards for the Design, Installation, Testing, and Maintenance of Interior Intrusion Detection/Alarm Systems

John E. Hunter

INTRODUCTION

These Standards are to be applied to the design, construction, performance, installation, operation, maintenance, and testing of medium- and high-security interior intrusion detection/alarm equipment and systems that are

The following article is considered a U.S. Government work, and no copyright for this information is asserted by the author or this publication. Published with the permission of the National Park Service, U.S. Department of the Interior. First Draft: November 1976; Second Draft: July 1977; Third Draft: July 1981; Rewritten: December 1981.

to be used for the protection of buildings in units of the National Park System. Included in the scope of these Standards are local, proprietary, police-connected, and central station alarm systems. Not included are electronic building automation and energy management systems, outdoor perimeter intrusion detection systems, and fire detection or suppression systems. These other systems will be covered in companion standards yet to be developed. However, many of the principles contained in these Standards can be applied successfully when writing specifications for the other types of systems.

These Standards were based largely on two previously published documents: Federal Specification W-A-00450B "Components for Interior Security Alarm Systems," published by the General Services Administration,[1] and "Model Burglar and Holdup Alarm Business and User Statute," published by the International Association of Chiefs of Police in 1977. These Standards also are based on alarm specifications developed by the Department of Defense and on performance specifications developed and provided by several alarm companies for use in preparing this document. Heavy use was made of the various standards published by Underwriters Laboratories, Inc. (UL) and the standards developed by the National Institute of Justice or NIJ (formerly the National Institute for Law Enforcement and Criminal Justice or NILECJ) under the Law Enforcement Standards Program at the National Bureau of Standards.

This document makes frequent reference to both the UL and the NILECJ/NIJ standards. In all cases both the standard name and its number are cited. In citing NILECJ and NIJ standards, the standard numbers have been modified to delete reference to a particular edition. For example, the standard covering magnetic switches is NILECJ-STD-0301.00. The "00" signifies that this is the first edition of the standard. Subsequent editions will be numbered "01," "02," etc. In citing such numbers in this document, the last two digits have been replaced by "XX." This will signify that the *latest* edition is intended for reference. Older issues of these Standards are prefixed "NILECJ" while newer editions are prefixed "NIJ"; both are products of the Law Enforcement Standards Laboratory. Copies of all are available at nominal costs from the Government Printing Office.

These Standards are not intended to supplant or be used instead of existing standards from GSA, NIJ, UL, or any other agency. They are intended to supplement the other standards by treating types of equipment they do not cover and by treating the subject of alarm systems rather than just components, an approach not fully taken by the other standards. Terminology

---

1. Fed. Spec. W-A-00450B is dated February 16, 1973. A revised edition is scheduled for publication in mid-1982. The reader is advised that references to paragraphs in the 1973 edition may not be accurate when using the 1982 edition. Editions of this document prepared after 1982 will reference the 1982 edition of the Federal specification.

in this document is in accordance with LESL–RPT–0305.00 "Terms and Definitions for Intrusion Alarm Systems" published by NILECJ in October 1974.

The first four drafts of this document were entitled "Design Criteria for High-Security Interior Intrusion Alarm Systems." The title has been changed on this version to more accurately reflect the true purpose of the document. It is not a set of design criteria which would be used to select equipment and to determine the nature and extent of an alarm system. Rather, it is a set of standards by which the quality of selected equipment and the quality of the installation work should be judged.

The first draft of this document was reviewed by the following agencies which furnished comments and suggestions for changes and improvements: Underwriters Laboratories, Inc., National Bureau of Standards, American Society for Industrial Security, National Burglar and Fire Alarm Association, and the National Crime Prevention Institute. The assistance of these agencies in preparing the second draft is greatly appreciated. Subsequent revisions have been necessitated by changes in the state-of-the-art of alarm systems and are based on field experiences with actual installations.

Technical comments and suggestions concerning any aspect of this present document are invited from all interested parties. Comments should be addressed to: Physical Security Coordinator, National Park Service (MWR), Room 474, Federal Building, Lincoln, Nebraska 68508; telephone (402) 471-5392.

CONTENTS

Section
Paragraph   *Title*

Purpose of the Standards

1.0   General Provisions
     1.1   Standards
     1.2   Federal Specifications
     1.3   Departure from Standards and Specifications
     1.4   Standard Products
     1.5   Product Quality
     1.6   Capabilities of the Alarm Contractor

2.0   System Philosophy
     2.1   Design Concept
     2.2   Resistance to Defeat of System
     2.3   Immunity from Electromagnetic Interference
     2.4   Power for the System
     2.5   Operating Modes
     2.6   Tamper Protection
     2.7   Tamper Switches
     2.8   General Technical Requirements

Section
Paragraph　*Title*
3.0　　　　　Planning and Layout
　　3.1　　　　System Plan
　　3.2　　　　Wiring
　　3.3　　　　Power Source

4.0　　　　　System Wiring
　　4.1　　　　Wiring Requirements
　　4.2　　　　Wiring Supervision
　　4.3　　　　Wiring Installation

5.0　　　　　Controls and Control Cabinet
　　5.1　　　　Cabinet Construction
　　5.2　　　　Controls
　　5.3　　　　Power Supply
　　5.4　　　　Cabinet Labeling

6.0　　　　　Authorized Access and Shunt Switches and
　　　　　　　Access Controls
　　6.1　　　　Switch Type
　　6.2　　　　Switch Operation
　　6.3　　　　Switch Housings
　　6.4　　　　Switch Housing Mounting
　　6.5　　　　Access Controls
　　6.6　　　　Shunt Switches

7.0　　　　　Detectors and Sensors
　　7.1　　　　General
　　7.2　　　　Detector Specifications
　　7.3　　　　Magnetic Switches
　　7.4　　　　Balanced Magnetic Switches
　　7.5　　　　Mechanical Switches
　　7.6　　　　Mercury Switches
　　7.7　　　　Conductive Foil
　　7.8　　　　Breakwire, Screens, and Grids
　　7.9　　　　Mat Switches
　　7.10　　　Capacitance (Proximity) Sensors
　　7.11　　　Infra-Red Photoelectric Beam Detectors
　　7.12　　　Infra-Red Motion Detectors (Passive)
　　7.13　　　Light Threshold Motion Detectors
　　7.14　　　Sound Sensing Detectors (Passive Audio)
　　7.15　　　Audio Frequency (Sonic) Motion Detectors
　　7.16　　　Ultrasonic Motion Detectors
　　7.17　　　Microwave Motion Detectors

Section
Paragraph   *Title*

7.18   Vibration Sensors
7.19   Audio Detection for Vaults
7.20   CCTV Motion Detectors
7.21   Fixed Duress Alarm Initiating Devices
7.22   Portable Duress Alarm Initiating Devices
7.23   Products of Combustion Detectors

8.0   Local Alarm Signaling Devices
8.1   Bells
8.2   Sirens
8.3   Visually Indicating Alarm Devices

9.0   Telephone Dialing and Reporting Devices
9.1   Performance
9.2   Construction
9.3   Power Supply
9.4   Telephone Line Connections

10.0   Monitoring Units for Proprietary Alarm Systems
10.1   Operation
10.2   Secure/Access and Reset
10.3   Annunciator Readout
10.4   Annunciator Construction
10.5   Annunciator Connections

11.0   Police Connected and Central Station Units
11.1   General
11.2   Line Supervision
11.3   Digital Communicators
11.4   Compliance with Standards

12.0   Auxiliary Devices and Equipment
12.1   Compatibility
12.2   Compliance With Standards
12.3   Power Requirements

13.0   False Alarms
13.1   Introduction
13.2   Definitions
13.3   Expected Performance

14.0   System Test
14.1   Initial Acceptance Test
14.2   Periodic Testing

Section
Paragraph   *Title*
15.0   Documentation and Training
   15.1   Operation and Maintenance Manual
   15.2   Record Drawings
   15.3   Training of Operating Personnel

16.0   Warranty
   16.1   General
   16.2   Reinstatement of Time

17.0   Reference Publications
   17.1   Standards and Codes
   17.2   Other References

PURPOSE OF THESE STANDARDS

These Standards were developed to guide Park Services engineers and others who plan or supervise the installation of intrusion detection systems. Such systems are installed both in new buildings as they are constructed and in existing buildings. These Standards do not tell how to design an alarm system nor can they be used to decide what components to include in an alarm system. These Standards are to be used after such decisions have been made. They will be found most useful when preparing plans and specifications for systems to be procured by the competitive bidding process. Also, they can be given to alarm companies who have been invited to submit proposals for alarm systems as a means of informing them of the Service's standards. These Standards can be used by contracting officers to establish quality control measures and to judge a contractor's performance as he installs a system. Finally, these Standards can be given to contractors who should be encouraged to use them for establishing their own quality control measures.

Cursory readers of this document may conclude that these Standards are intended to apply only to high-security alarm systems of the type used on military bases and at nuclear power stations. While these standards could be used successfully at such facilities if fully adhered to, it is unlikely that most Park Service alarm systems will have to adhere to all the provisions of this document. Park Service systems generally are relatively small and simple in comparison to the complex systems used to protect military information and hardware or nuclear materials.

The major difference between simple and complex systems in Park Service buildings is in respect to: the types of detectors and sensors used; the number of zones of detection required; the nature of required signaling devices; and the degree of supervision needed for alarm signal transmission lines. Thus, one park structure might require a single zone control panel, one alarm bell, magnetic switches on all doors, and a photoelectric beam device in front of non-opening windows. Such a system would be considered simple. Another park might have to protect a dozen or so buildings scattered throughout an historic district; it might want to use a proprietary alarm system. Such a system could consist of: multiple zones of detection in each building, some of which would use motion detectors; holdup alarms; audible and visible alarm devices on each building; individually operable premises control units; card access readers; a multi-zone annunciator console with event recorder in a guard office; and high-level line supervision on circuits connecting each protected building to the office. Such a system would be considered complex.

Yet both systems would have a number of important features in common. These common features would not include the *kinds* of equipment used; the systems would differ considerably in this respect. Rather, the common features relate to the *quality* of the installed equipment, that is, how well it is made, and to the quality of the installation work, that is, how well the alarm company does its job. These Standards are intended to establish what level of quality the Service should ask for and expect in its alarm systems.

It is Service policy that the simplest alarm system should be planned as thoroughly and installed as carefully as the most sophisticated system. There is no reason why wiring, for example, should be sloppily installed in a simple system but properly installed in a complex one. There is just as much reason to pick reliable detectors for a simple system as for a complex one; we want both to work properly and all the time. In short, all of our systems should be quality systems, no matter how small or large, no matter how simple or complex.

As previously stated, not all of the provisions of these Standards will apply to all systems. The following paragraphs indicate when and to what extent each section is to be used in developing plans and specifications and in monitoring an alarm company's work.

Section 1, General Provisions, should apply to all systems regardless of their type, size, or complexity.

Parts of Section 2, Design Concept, will not apply to all systems. The paragraphs dealing with resistance to defeat and immunity from electromagnetic interference (EMI) should be applied differently for different systems. For example, where the level of criminal attack sophistication is very low, the defeat resistance standards can be relaxed somewhat, in the interest of obtaining simpler, less expensive equipment that could not be used where sophisticated attacks against alarm systems are common. Likewise, where EMI levels are low, as in some rural areas, the standards can be relaxed somewhat, permitting the use of unshielded cable and simpler circuits and resulting in less expensive systems; such systems might not function properly where EMI levels are high. However, the provisions of Section 2 relating to tamper protection should be applied in common to all types of systems because all systems should have a high degree of tamper resistance.

Section 3, Planning and Layout, will apply equally to all systems.

Section 4, Wiring, will apply equally to all systems. However, simpler systems with lower requirements for defeat resistance may not require as much system wiring to be in conduit.

Section 5, Controls and Control Cabinet, will apply to all systems. However, the power supply requirements, particularly the standby battery capacity, will vary according to the sophistication and size of the system and will depend upon the reliability of local AC power. In areas with a history of intermittent power failures, a longer standby capacity may be needed.

Section 6, Authorized Access and Shunt Switches and Access Controls, will apply to all systems using the kinds of equipment covered by this section. It is recognized that many systems will not require such devices as access controls and card readers.

Section 7, Detectors and Sensors, will apply equally to all systems as far as the quality standards are concerned. Certainly, few if any systems will utilize all the different sensors and detectors covered by this section. However, to the extent that a given detector is selected for a given system, the standards for that detector will apply.

Section 8, Local Alarm Signaling Devices, will apply to all systems using such devices.

Section 9, Telephone Dialing and Reporting Devices, will apply to all systems using such devices, although the requirements for standby battery capacity usually will vary according to the requirements of the overall system.

Section 10, Monitoring Units for Proprietary Alarm Systems, will apply only to proprietary systems. Some of the standards in this section can be applied, if desired, to the configuration of multi-zone control panels used in local and police-connected systems.

Section 11, Police Connected and Central Station Units, will apply only to systems that transmit alarm signals to police or other law enforcement agencies or to commercial central stations. This section has only minimal standards for the equipment located at the police station or central station because the Service normally has little control over the quality of such equipment. It is suggested that alarm systems in park facilities not be connected to central stations without thorough investigation into the reliability of the alarm companies being considered for providing that service.

Section 12, Auxiliary Devices and Equipment, will apply to all systems using such equipment.

Section 13, False Alarms, generally will apply to all systems. The extent to which this section should or should not apply to a given system is summarized in Table 1 in this section.

Section 14, System Test, will apply to all systems. However, the nature of the required test and the time allotted for it will vary widely according to the nature and size of the system.

Section 15, Documentation and Training, will apply to all systems. Formal training of the type described in this section may not be absolutely necessary when extremely simple, unsophisticated local systems are involved. However, such training is always advisable regardless of the size or nature of the particular system.

Section 16, Warranty, will apply to all systems.

1.0 GENERAL PROVISIONS

1.1 Standards

Alarm systems shall comply with all applicable Federal, state, and local building, electrical, and safety codes, including the latest edition of the National Electrical Code (NFPA 70). All materials and equipment installed shall conform to the standards of Underwriters Laboratories, Inc. or other similar nationally recognized testing organization. Equipment shall bear the approval or listing mark of the testing organization unless the specifying engineer approves the use of non-labeled equipment.

1.2 Federal Specifications

All equipment and material used in the alarm system shall be of sufficiently high quality to comply with Federal Specification W-A-00450B "Components for Interior Security Alarms." While it may not be necessary for a particular alarm installation that all components and materials used therein actually be accepted and qualified in accordance with Section 4 of W-A-00450B, it is intended that they be designed and manufactured in accordance with its philosophy and intent. Materials that are qualified in accordance with Section 4 shall be so labeled.

1.3 Departure from Standards and Specifications

No departure from the contract drawings or specifications will be permitted without written approval from the Contracting Officer. If the alarm Contractor considers any changes to the contract drawings or specifications to be necessary, he shall so advise the Contracting Officer within 30 days of award of contract.

1.4 Standard Products

Unless otherwise specified or approved, all materials and equipment to be furnished as part of an alarm system shall be new and shall be the standard products of manufacturers of established reputation regularly engaged in the production of such equipment. All materials and equipment shall be of the latest design current at time of delivery. All devices incorporated into the alarm system shall meet the intent of the system philosophy and design.

1.5 Product Quality

As full use as practical shall be made of high reliability solid state electronic devices. Materials and workmanship shall be consistent with the best commercial practices. Furnished components of the system shall be clean, well made, and free of defects that might affect appearance or serviceability. Defective equipment and materials, or equipment and materials damaged in the course of installation or testing, shall be replaced or repaired in an approved manner to the satisfaction of the Contracting Officer.

1.6 Capabilities of the Alarm Contractor

The installing Contractor shall have an established reputation and shall be regularly engaged in the design, installation, and maintenance of electronic security systems. He shall be able to refer to similar installations made by him that are rendering satisfactory service. The Contractor shall be skilled in the maintenance of the installed system and shall be capable of providing timely and efficient maintenance to the system as required. [Allowable response time for a service call will be specified separately for each installation.] The Contractor shall maintain in his inventory sufficient stocks of spare components, modules, and parts to be able to perform maintenance of the installed system when called upon to do so.

2.0 SYSTEM PHILOSOPHY

2.1 Design Concept

Design of an intrusion detection system and selection of its components should be basically conservative to ensure that the system is inherently stable, defeat-resistant, fail-safe, durable, reliable, and suitable in every respect for satisfactory, long lasting, and continuous operation. The design should be such that the system will require a minimum of maintenance and adjustments.

2.2 Resistance to Defeat of System

The intrusion detection system shall be designed to maximize the detection and reporting of intruders and to minimize false alarms due to equipment malfunction and operator error. The system shall be designed to alarm if system devices or wiring are tampered with whether the system or any zone is in the ACCESS or the SECURE mode. The system shall be designed and installed to resist countermeasure attempts. The system shall register an alarm if countermeasure attempts are made using resistance or impedance substitution methods, potential or current substitution methods, equipment substitution, signal substitution, signal synthesization, or any other such compromise methods. The system shall alarm also if any detection component or detection loop wiring is cut or shorted to other wires. Overall defeat resistance should be equivalent to UL Grade A or AA depending on circumstances.

2.3 Immunity from Electromagnetic Interference

The system and all components thereof shall be designed and installed to minimize or eliminate interference to and from other audio and radio frequency devices. The system shall be highly immune to transients or spikes on the power lines and to alarm transmission line noise, such as crosstalk, hum, transients, and the like.

2.4 Power for the System

The system shall be designed to operate from standard 120-volt[2] commercial power and to automatically switch over to operation from standby batteries upon the loss of commercial power. It is the intent of the system philosophy that active devices be powered from the master control cabinet and be compatible in voltage, current, logic levels, impedance, etc., with the control cabinet and with other elements of the system. Where system peripheral devices must be powered from sources other than the control cabinet, these sources shall meet the standby power, tamper resistance, and supervisory spe-

---

2. Other voltages (110,115, etc.) may be specified when appropriate.

cifications of the overall system. When independently powered devices are used in a system, power failure to or at such devices will create an alarm condition.

2.5 Operating Modes

The system shall have at least three major modes: ACCESS, SECURE, and MAINTENANCE or TEST. These three modes shall be controlled by a high-security key switch or digital key (touch pad) located on the control cabinet face. In the SECURE mode an alarm condition shall be caused by the tripping of any detection device, by the opening and/or shorting of any door or window switch, by the cutting of any cable or foil in the system, or by the tampering of any of the system devices containing tamper switches. The system shall alarm in the ACCESS or the SECURE mode when any of the system devices are tampered with or when any system cable is cut. The system, once in an alarm status, shall have the option of remaining in that status until manually reset at the control cabinet with the correct high-security key or digital code *or* shall automatically reset itself after a specified time period; the time period should be field-adjustable over a range of five minutes to sixty minutes. The system shall provide the capability of testing the status of the detection and alarm circuits from the control cabinet without initiating an actual alarm. Provisions (such as a momentary contact switch) shall be made in the system design for rendering it difficult or unlikely for the system to be left in the MAINTENANCE or TEST mode. Systems that can be tested completely in the ACCESS mode are not required to have a MAINTE-NANCE or TEST mode.

2.6 Tamper Protection

Detectors and sensors, the control cabinet, detection circuits, signal transmission equipment and lines, and auxiliary devices shall be so designed, constructed, and installed as to resist attack and tampering and to minimize vulnerability to countermeasures. The system shall be so designed that it will be difficult to "jumper out" or by-pass sections, loops, or components of the system. All system detection devices shall have covers protecting their electrical terminals. After the system is installed, no terminals shall be accessible without first removing the protective covers. In the case of outside bells or siren housings, it shall be impossible to gain access to the electrical terminals without first opening or removing outside and inside covers. Any single wire in the system that can be cut without an alarm occurring shall not cause loss of the system's ability to detect intrusions and tampering.

2.7 Tamper Switches

Enclosures and cabinets used in an alarm system (as for control panels, bell and siren housings, motion detectors, power supplies, and telephone dialers) shall be provided with tamper switches. All such enclosures will have cover-operated switches, arranged to intitiate an alarm signal when the cover or door is moved as much as ¼ inch from its normally closed position. Such enclosures will have tamper switches to detect removal of the enclosure from its mounted position when removal can compromise the operation of the system. Movement of the enclosure as much as ¼ inch will initiate an alarm signal. Tamper switches shall remain inaccessible until they have been activated. Tamper switch mounting hardware shall be concealed so that the location of the switch cannot be visually detected from the exterior of the enclosure. Tamper switches shall remain supervised at all times, whether the alarm system (or zone) in which they are installed is in the ACCESS or the SECURE mode. Tamper switches on doors that must be opened to make normal maintenance adjustments to the system shall be of the push-pull set, automatic reset type.

2.8 General Technical Requirements

Intrusion detection system components and parts shall meet the following miscellaneous technical specifications.

A. *Maintainability.* Devices and equipment shall be designed and constructed to facilitate modular, unitized component replacement to the maximum extent feasible. Components shall be so arranged and assembled that they are readily accessible to maintenance personnel without compromising the defeat-resistance of the system. Controls and adjustments inside enclosures, requiring manipulation by maintenance personnel, shall be readily visible and accessible with minimum disassembly of the equipment being needed.

B. *Interchangeability.* Like units, assemblies, sub-assemblies, and replaceable parts shall be physically and functionally interchangeable as complete items, without modification thereof and without modification of other parts with which the items are used. Individual items shall not be hand-picked for fit or performance unless so specified. The extent to which it will be necessary to provide readily replaceable, modular subassemblies and parts will be stated in the system specifications.

C. *Environmental Requirements.* Unless specifically stated otherwise in the system specifications, all components of the system shall be capable of full, continuous operation under the following conditions:

1. Relative humidity of 0 to 85%.

2. Ambient indoor temperature in the range of 32 to 120 degrees Fahrenheit.

D. *Environmental Precautions.* Appropriate precautions, by enclosure or otherwise, shall be taken to ensure that as far as practicable no part of the alarm system is adversely affected by the environmental conditions to which it is likely to be exposed. Special precautions shall be taken where parts are likely to be exposed to the weather, dampness, corrosion, oil, heat, adverse industrial atmospheres, or mechanical damage.

3.0 PLANNING AND LAYOUT

3.1 System Plan

Installation work shall be carefully laid out in advance. Where cutting, drilling, channeling, chasing, etc., is to be accomplished for proper installation or for anchorage or support of conduit or devices, the work shall be carefully done after approval by the Contracting Officer. Damage to walls, ceilings, floors, piping, or other elements or fixtures of the building caused by the Contractor shall be repaired to the satisfaction of the Contracting Officer at no additional cost to the contract prior to the acceptance of the system.

3.2 Wiring

All wiring shall be run in enclosed spaces such as attics, walls, etc., to the maximum extent possible so that wiring will not be visible or readily accessible to unauthorized persons. Wherever possible, all detector heads shall be recessed so as not to be visually obtrusive. Installation of recessed devices shall cause no permanent damage to the fabric of the building or to any fixtures. When recessing a device would cause structural weakening of the building, the device will be surface mounted. It will not be necessary to recess any device when the wiring to or from that device has to be mounted on the same surface because of structural considerations.

3.3 Power Source

The intrusion alarm system will be connected to existing 120-volt,[3] 60-cycle unswitched AC power source(s) by the Contractor. If the contractor has reason

3. Other voltages (110, 115, etc.) may be specified when appropriate.

to believe or suspect that connection of the system or any portion thereof will overload existing AC circuits, he must so advise the Contracting Officer well enough in advance to permit the separate installation of additional circuits by an electrical contractor. The Contractor may be requested to advise on the location and capacity of any new circuits that might be needed.

4.0 SYSTEM WIRING

4.1 Wiring Requirements

A. The intrusion detection system shall employ wiring utilizing a minimum of two separately insulated UL listed copper conductor wires as recommended by the manufacturer(s) of the components being interconnected. Either solid or stranded conductors may be used, depending on the requirements of the installation. Single conductor perimeter loops (i.e., a single conductor run to a device and back to the control cabinet) shall not be permitted. Water pipes, steam pipes, gas pipes, drain pipes, or conduit within the building used for carrying building electrical service shall not be permitted to be used as elements of intrusion detector loop wiring. A cold water pipe may be used as a system grounding point if permitted by the manufacturer of the equipment being grounded and if permitted by the National Electrical Code. This provision is not to be construed as excluding supervised ground connections that may be required by UL standards.

B. Where voltages are less than 30 volts dc, system wiring shall be no smaller than #22 AWG solid conductor UL listed wire. Where voltages are greater then 30 volts, wiring shall be accomplished in accordance with Article 725 of the National Electrical Code. In most alarm systems, the detection loop and signal circuit wiring will be somewhat heavier than #22 AWG, though it will seldom be necessary to use wire heavier than #18 AWG except for ac power connections. Where elements of the system are installed in hazardous locations, the equipment therein installed shall meet the requirements of Article 500 of the National Electrical Code.

4.2 Wiring Supervision

Wiring shall be accomplished in such manner that it will be continuously supervised whether the system is in the ACCESS or the SECURE mode. An alarm shall occur if any system wiring is cut or shorted to other wires in the system or if the system devices are tampered with. The form of alarm (i.e., INTRUSION or TAMPER) will depend upon the design of the system and the type of alarm notification desired. The system shall be so designed and installed that it will alarm when any of the countermeasures or defeat efforts described in Paragraphs 2.1, 2.5, and 2.6 are attempted. Signal transmission lines shall be protected in accordance with Paragraph 3.5 of Federal Specification W-A-00450B; the class of supervision selected (A, AB, or B) will depend upon the level of security required.

4.3 Wiring Installation

A.   The system shall be installed and wired by the Contractor in accordance with the instructions provided by the manufacturers of the components being used in the system and in accordance with the codes, specifications, and standards referenced by the contract specifications.

B.   Splices shall not be permitted in system wiring between components of the system, such as control panels, detectors, audible devices, etc. Single runs of wiring must terminate at each end at a system component or at a junction box where wiring is interconnected using terminal strips or blocks. Wire ends shall be prepared (tinned, lugs soldered on, etc.) for attachment to component terminals in accordance with the recommendations of the equipment manufacturer(s).

C.   *Open Wiring.* When wiring has to be run in the open (i.e., not in conduit or raceway), it shall be installed in the following manner.

1.   Wiring shall follow the general contours of the building and shall be run as high as practicable. Wires shall not be strung from beam to beam beneath a ceiling unless protected against physical damage. In joisted construction, unless run parallel with the joists, wires shall be placed in conduit, metal-clad cable, or raceways OR shall have a solid backing strip (such as wood) not less than 2 inches wide to protect the wires from damage. Wires shall be protected from abrasion due to sharp corners or projections by at least four layers of vinyl (or at least two layers of cloth) electrical insulating tape or the equivalent.

2.   Connecting wires may be attached to plaster, plaster board, or wood surfaces by means of approved types of staples, insulated-head brads or nails, porcelain or other non-absorptive insulating knobs or cleats, bridle rings, or tie wires. Adhesive clips made of plastic may be used for short runs of lightweight wire where other forms of attachment are not practical or possible (e.g., on a window frame). For attachment to masonry surfaces, expansion bolts, fiber or plastic plugs and screws, toggle bolts, or the equivalent shall be used. Non-absorptive, non-combustible supports shall be used to set wires out entirely clear from walls subjected to dampness.

3. Uninsulated saddle (U-shaped) staples may be used only on telephone cable or similar cable that is round in cross section and must be used in such a way that the cable is not pinched and its outer jacket is not cut.

4. Staples or brads shall be spaced not more than 2 feet apart on wood, plaster, or plaster board surfaces, except that where wires are run along the top of molding, cabinets, etc., and thereby receive additional mechanical support, brads and staples may be spaced not more than 4 feet apart. Bridle rings, porcelain knobs, or cleats shall be spaced not more than 4 feet apart; tie wires and adhesive clips shall be spaced not more than 2 feet apart.

5. Open wires shall be kept at least ½ inch from other signal wires, pipes, conduit, fixtures, and other grounded objects or, where is it necessary to run them closer than this, two or more layers or electrical insulating tape, or the equivalent, shall be provided where the wires cross.

6. Wires shall be run over rather than under steam, water, drain, and sprinkler pipes wherever possible.

7. Wires shall be spaced at least 2 inches from electrical light and power lines unless one of the circuits is in conduit or the circuits are separated by a continuous and firmly fixed insulator. Porcelain or non-metallic-flexible tubing extending for 2 inches beyond the wires and taped at the ends will provide the necessary continuous separation. Tape alone is not acceptable protection. Shielded cable may be used for alarm system wiring to provide the necessary electrical isolation in some cases.

8. Wires bunched together in a vertical run from one floor to another shall have a fire-resistive covering to prevent the travel of fire. For protection against mechanical damage, wires passing through floors or walls shall be in conduit, tubing, or some form of bushing. In some cases, a heavy wrapping of electrical insulating tape may provide the required protection. When it is necessary to penetrate concrete fire walls or floors with system wiring, approved fire barrier gaskets or other approved material shall be used to prevent the travel of fire from one side of the barrier to the other.

9. Connectors intended to carry circuits onto movable openings shall be of a type listed by Underwriters Laboratories for burglar alarm system wiring.

D. *Concealed Wiring.* When wiring is to be run concealed (i.e., in conduit or raceway), it shall be installed in the following manner.

1. Wiring shall be run in a rigid, thinwall, or flexible metal conduit or in Wiremold or other approved raceway at any point where the wiring must be surface mounted within 10 feet of the floor. Where wiring has to be run outside the protected area, it shall be in rigid or thinwall metal conduit and shall be routed and secured to the structure in such a manner as to render it difficult of access. Surface mounted conduit and raceway normally should be painted to match the surface on which it is run.

2. All conduit shall be run concealed within ceilings, walls, etc., to the maximum extent possible, except that in mechanical rooms and similar non-public areas, conduit may be run exposed. Exposed runs of conduit shall have supports at all bends except when bends are within 2 feet of an equipment cabinet, supported outlet or junction box, or other fixture that is itself supported. In addition, supports shall be placed not more than 8 feet apart on straight runs. Changes in direction of conduit shall be made with symmetrical bends or with metal fittings designed for the purpose. Bends and offsets shall be made with an approved hickey or conduit bending machine. Conduit that has been crushed or deformed in any way shall not be installed. Not more than four bends shall be permitted in any one run. When more than four bends are required, pull or junction boxes must be used to reduce the number of bends.

3. Conduit shall be supported on approved factory manufactured type steel wall brackets, ceiling trapeze, strap hangers, or pipe straps. Such supports shall be fastened to the structure as follows: on masonry surfaces, use toggle bolts, expansion bolts, or fiber or plastic plugs and screws; on metal surfaces, use "butterfly" or toggle bolts or machine screws; and on wood, plaster, or plaster board surfaces, use "butterfly" or toggle bolts or wood screws. The use of wood plugs and screws in masonry or plaster and the use of nails shall not be permitted.

4. Care shall be exercised to prevent clogging of conduit with dirt or other debris. All cut ends of conduit shall be reamed or smoothed before assembly and shall be securely fastened to all junction and pull boxes and equipment cabinets with two steel locknuts and bushings drawn up tight. Approved connectors may be used to splice lengths of conduit for long runs.

5. Conduit and bushings that penetrate through air ducts or through exterior walls or roofs shall be caulked or otherwise rendered airtight and watertight. Penetration of hot air ducts (supply side) shall be made only when allowed by the National Electrical Code and then in a Code-approved manner.

6. Where junction boxes, pull boxes, conduits, or pulling els are used, they shall be mounted as specified above in 4.3.D.3. Such fixtures shall be furnished with steel covers which shall be secured with one-way or other type of temper-resistant screws. When it is necessary to install such fixtures outside of the protected area, they shall be protected by tamper-switches under the covers. Alternatively, covers may be welded to the boxes with not less than 8 spot welds or a continuous weld around the edge of the cover.

7. Conduit for enclosure of telephone circuits, where required, shall comply with the above specifications provided that no single run shall exceed 90 feet and shall have no more than 3 bends between outlet or junction boxes or equipment cabinets.

8. Conduit normally will be installed in accordance with Articles 345, 346, and 348-352 of the National electrical code.

E. *Grounding*. Neutral conductors, conduit, raceways, junction boxes, cabinets, cable messengers, and all non-current carrying metallic parts of equipment shall be grounded in accordance with The National Electrical Code, especially Article 250.

5.0 CONTROLS AND CONTROL CABINET

5.1 Cabinet Construction

The control cabinet shall be fabricated of at least 16 gauge (0.063 inch) steel, flanged and constructed to prevent forceable entry. Cabinet exterior and interior surfaces shall have a rust inhibiting prime coat and at least two coats of baked-on enamel or equivalent finish. Finish coats shall be even and free from runs, sags, or blemishes. There shall be no unused knockouts, holes, or other openings to the cabinet. The cabinet shall be free of any burrs, shavings, or sharp edges. Wiring entering the cabinet shall enter through tightly grommeted holes or in conduit. Excess air space around the wiring inside grommets shall not be permitted. Where wiring enters or leaves the cabinet in conduit, the conduit shall be secured with two locknuts and need not meet the grommet and air space requirements of this paragraph. Any ventilation openings shall be protected by internal baffling. The cabinet shall be lockable with its own high-security, pick-resistant lock. This lock shall be keyed alike with locks on other cabinets housing components of the alarm system. A cabinet formed from high-impact plastic may be used in lieu of a steel cabinet provided it: (a) affords security and physical protection equivalent to a steel cabinet meeting these specifications and (b) offers a means of securely terminating runs of steel conduit when conduit is being used.

5.2 Controls

The control cabinet shall contain the system electronics logic, switching devices, and power supply. It shall be equipped with tamper switches front and rear which shall alarm the system if tampered with, whether the system is in the ACCESS or the SECURE mode. Any fuses required by the system shall be contained within the control cabinet and no external fuse holders, terminals, or adjustments shall be permitted. (Exception: Separate components, such as telephone dialers, may have their own internal fuses.) Devices within the control cabinet shall be essentially maintenance free. Electronic circuitry shall be readily replaceable and ideally should be modules or PC boards of the slide-in, readily connected type. The control cabinet shall contain on its face at least the following components: high-security locking cylinder, high-security key-operated Operate/Reset switch or digital key (touch pad) unless located elsewhere in the system, zone indicators (when required), necessary zone reset switches (when required), and a means of indicating whether the system is operating on commercial or standby power. Other components and visual indicators may be on the face of the cabinet as required or permitted.

5.3 Power Supply

A. Power supplies shall operate normally on AC power supplied in the protected area and shall be capable of stable operation if the supply voltage varies up to 10% and/or the frequency varies by two cycles. Batteries should be sealed nickel-cadmium or lead acid "gel-cell" types.

B. The control cabinet should be large enough to contain the system power supply. When normal commercial power is interrupted, power to the alarm system shall be provided from continuously charged standby batteries within the control cabinet. When commercial power is restored, the standby batteries shall recharge and maintain their full charge continuously. No intrusion alarm shall be signaled when the standby batteries are switched in or out of the power circuit; however, there shall be a visible indicator on the control cabinet (and an audible indicator when required) to show when the system is operating on standby power. System standby batteries should be sealed, requiring no water to be added, essentially maintenance free, and capable of operating in any position or labeled to show the correct operating position. Lead-acid type batteries (i.e., auto batteries) may be required for some installations; such batteries shall be housed in a ventilated cabinet or in a room where they can be maintained easily. Suitable precautions must be taken to protect against personal injury from battery acid.

C. In the event of commercial failure, the standby power supply shall be capable of powering the system with no local alarm for at least 24 hours, during which time the system shall be capable of detecting an intrusion and of reporting it to the proper authorities with commercial power still off. When system function is impaired or after 24 hours[4] of commercial power failure, an intrusion alarm shall be initiated so that prompt response by appropriate personnel will leave the protected area vulnerable for the least amount of time. The declining standby power notification shall be independent of an intrusion alarm notification and shall not compromise or affect detection of an intrusion.

D.   During the first 12 hours of commercial power failure, the standby power supply shall be capable of powering all system sirens or bells to full output specifications for a minimum of 30 minutes. When commercial power is restored to the system with completely discharged batteries, the batteries shall recharge to 85% of rated capacity within 24 hours and to full rated capacity within approximately 36 hours. The system shall be fully operational during the recharge cycle. The standby power supply and charger system shall be capable of operating with ac input voltage of 120 volts $\pm 15\%$.

E.   The Contractor may elect to house the power supply in a separate cabinet in lieu of having it in the control cabinet. If a separate power supply cabinet is used, it must be constructed to the same specifications as the control cabinet and must be located immediately adjacent to the control cabinet. Wiring runs between the two cabinets shall be in rigid conduit or else the two cabinets shall be touching in which case locking bushings shall be used to connect knockouts on the two cabinets. The power supply cabinet shall be equipped with a high-security locking cylinder keyed alike to the lock on the control cabinet.

5.4   Cabinet Labeling

Functions controlled from the surface of a cabinet, such as OPERATE/RESET, shall be labeled. Function switch positions shall not be labeled as to functions "in-the-clear" but shall be numbered or lettered in a code so that the meaning of each position will not be apparent to a casual observer. (This requirement can be waived if the control cabinet is located where there can be no casual observers, such as in a mechanical room; in such circumstances, control cabinet functions may be labeled with words denoting the functions.) Cabinet labeling shall be accomplished permanently and legibly in a professional manner. Embossed plastic tape will not be an acceptable form of labeling. The foregoing requirements also apply to function controls inside a cabinet except that labeling normally will not have to be coded.

---

4. Longer intervals may be specified when desired. Normally 72 hours will be the maximum practical limit to operation on standby power.

6.0 AUTHORIZED ACCESS AND SHUNT SWITCHES AND ACCESS CONTROLS

6.1 Switch Type

System key switches shall be UL listed for use in burglar alarm systems (Standard for Connectors and Switches for Use With Burglar Alarm Systems, UL 634, ANSI SE2.6-1973 or latest edition). Switches shall be multiple pin tumbler, pick-resistant, and drill-resistant, housed in a hardened barrel. Key switches shall be continuously supervised; if the wiring to the switch is opened or shorted, the system shall initiate an alarm

6.2 Switch Operation

The remote key switch cover plate shall contain one or more visual indicators (as required) that shall be highly reliable (LEDs are suggested) and have an indefinitely long life. Should any of the intrusion sensors be in an alarm condition, a protected opening be unsecured, the control cabinet key switch be left in the RESET or TEST position, or a tamper condition exist anywhere in the system, the remote key switch visual indicator shall so indicate in order that corrective action can be taken before the remote key switch is turned to the SECURE position. Once the remote key switch is turned to the SECURE mode, an intrusion or faulty circuit anywhere in the system shall cause the system to alarm. The remote key switch cover plate shall be secured with one-way or other type of tamper-resistant screws.

6.3 Switch Housing

Remote key switches shall be contained in a housing of at least 16 gauge (0.063 inch) steel with stainless steel cover plate of the same thickness. The remote key switch housing shall be designed for flush mounting in concrete, brick, or block walls and, when used outdoors, shall be completely weatherproof. The housing shall contain a tamper switch that will alarm the system if the cover is removed whether the system is in the ACCESS or the SECURE mode. If it is necessary for structural reasons to surface mount the switch housing, it shall be equipped with a rear tamper switch as well.

6.4 Switch Housing Mounting

Wiring from the control cabinet to a remote key switch shall run in rigid conduit at any point where it is surface mounted or run outside the protected area. Cracks, chips, or gaps in a wall surface created by the installation of a remote key switch housing shall be filled, patched, smoothed, and painted (if appropriate) to match the surrounding wall surface to the edges of the switch housing. The material used for filling and patching shall be of at least the same strength, durability, and hardness as the material of the wall on which it is used.

6.5 Access Controls

Electronic locking devices or access controls (card reader, remote digital touch pad, etc.) may be used separately or in combination with a remote key switch if it can be demonstrated that security would be materially enhanced or at least not be diminished by their use. Where electronic locking devices or access control systems are utilized, they shall be of the solid-state, high-reliability type and shall not be solely dependent for their power on commercial power sources but shall have the capability of being powered by standby batteries that meet the requirements for standby power for the overall alarm system. These access control systems shall be fail-safe: should the commercial and standby power fail, they shall permit entry to the protected area only after causing an alarm. Access control systems not directly connected to the intrusion detection alarm system may not be required to meet the standby power requirements of these standards although they must have some form of standby power. This paragraph shall not be construed as requiring the use of electronic access controls in conjunction with intrusion alarm systems.

6.6 Shunt Switches

Shunt switches designed to temporarily shunt out sensors at a protected entrance shall meet the requirements of paragraphs 6.1, 6.2, 6.3, and 6.4 above. Any visible indicator present on the cover plate shall indicate only whether or not the protected entrance is shunted in or out of the protective circuit, not whether the alarm system itself is in the SECURE or the ACCESS mode.

7.0 DETECTORS AND SENSORS

7.1 General

All detectors and sensors shall initiate an alarm signal under any of the following conditions: (1) when sensing a stimulus or condition to which it was designed to react; (2) if primary power fails and secondary power does not take over properly (for powered devices only); (3) if the detector's circuitry is opened, shorted, or grounded and if such condition is capable of compromising the device's normal operation; and (4) if a tamper switch or other tamper-detection mechanism is activated. To the extent feasible, the device shall be designed to initiate an alarm if any part or component fails or ages to such an extent that the detector will be rendered ineffective. Terminals shall be located within the detector enclosure and be readily accessible to permit wiring the detector into the protective circuit. All controls and terminals that are not required for operation of the detector shall not be readily accessible. All controls that affect the sensitivity of the unit shall be located inside the tamper-resistant enclosure.

7.2 Detector Specifications

All detectors and sensors incorporated into an alarm system shall meet the performance, construction, and installation specifications given in the remaining paragraphs of this Section 7. Unless specific construction or installation specifications to the contrary are given, it may be understood that the installation instructions provided by the manufacturers of equipment meeting the performance specifications will be deemed adequate. In any event, the Contractor is expected to follow the highest professional standards in installing all components of an alarm system.

7.3 Magnetic Switches

A. The switch shall be designed so an alarm is initiated whenever the magnet housing is moved as much as 1 inch (2 inches for heavy-duty switches on overhead rollup doors) from the switch housing. The switch shall be rated for a minimum of 10,000,000 activations without malfunctioning. Switches shall be intended for use in normally closed two-wire protective circuits. In installations requiring high security, but where the ultimate protection of a balanced magnetic switch is not needed, NC/NO switches (opens and crosses or opens and grounds on activation) may be used.

B. The switch and the magnet shall be enclosed in separate housings of molded plastic, stainless steel, aluminum, or some other non-magnetic material; housings shall be sealed against moisture and dirt. Switches intended for use out of doors shall be capable of operation under all weather conditions and in 100% relative humidity. Switch terminals shall not be accessible after housing covers are installed. Contact surfaces shall be made of metals that will give long life and high reliability. Contacts shall have a self-wiping action or equivalent protection against "freezing."

C. The switch and magnet housings shall be secured to the two sides of a movable opening (door and frame or window and frame, for example) with appropriate screws (self-tapping metal screws or machine screws tapped in advance on metal surfaces or wood screws on wood surfaces) or a RTV compound approved by the switch manufacturer.

The use of one-way or other type of tamper-resistant screws is suggested. When offset angle brackets must be used to ensure correct alignment or separation of the switch and the magnet, the housings shall be secured to the brackets with machine screws, lock washers, and nuts. Brackets shall be of stainless steel or other non-magnetic metal or high-strength plastic of substantial thickness to ensure dimensional stability and permanency of mounting.

D. The use of recessed housings is encouraged to eliminate the accessibility of the switch and for aesthetic purposes. When recessed switches are used, the manufacturer's mounting instructions should be followed rather than the instructions in paragraph C above.

E. Switches shall meet the requirements of Standard for Connectors and Switches for Use With Burglar Alarm Systems, UL 634, and Standard for Magnetic Switches for Burglar Alarm Systems, NILECJ-STD-0301.XX.

7.4 Balanced Magnetic Switches

A. The switch mechanism shall be of the balanced magnetic type and shall initiate an alarm upon increase, decrease, or attempted substitution of an external magnetic field when the switch is in the secure state. The switch shall be electrically protected so that a sudden surge of voltage will create an alarm. The switch shall be designed so an alarm is initiated whenever the magnet housing is moved as much as 1 inch (2 inches for heavy-duty switches on overhead rollup doors) from the switch housing. The switch shall be of the type that opens and crosses or opens and grounds the circuit when activated. The switch should be rated for a minimum of 10,000,000 activations without malfunctioning.

B. All provisions of paragraphs 7.3B, 7.3C, and 7.3D above also shall apply.

7.5 Mechanical Switches

Specific standards for mechanical switches and their installation have not been drafted. Switches shall meet the requirements of Standard for Connectors and Switches for Use with Burglar Alarm Systems, UL 634, and Standard for Mechanically Actuated Switches for Burglar Alarm Systems, NILECJ-STD-0302.XX.

7.6 Mercury Switches

Specific standards for mercury switches and their installation have not been drafted. Switches shall meet the requirements of Standard for Connectors and Switches for Use With Burglar Alarm Systems, UL 634, and Standard for Mercury Switches for Burglar Alarm Systems, NILECJ-STD-0303.XX.

7.7 Conductive Foil

A. This material is intended for application to glass and other surfaces to detect surreptitious and forcible penetrations.

When properly installed and connected into an electrically supervised "double circuit" detector circuit, breaking, grounding, or crossing the foil circuit shall cause an alarm to be initiated.

B. Foil used on glass surfaces shall be not more than ½ inch wide and not more than 0.0015 inch thick for plain glass and not more than 0.003 inch thick for wired glass. Foil used on walls and doors shall be not less than ⅜ inch nor more than 1 inch wide and not more than 0.003 inch thick. Foil shall not exceed 1.2 pounds in tensile strength and shall be capable of carrying a maximum electrical current of 60 milliamperes (60 ma) at 60 volts with a temperature rise of not more than 1 degree Celsius.

C. Adhesive and protective coating materials shall be of the type resistant to aging, moisture, and temperature changes.

D. Foil shall be applied evenly and secured to the surface so that it will not blister or loosen in service. Cracks shall not be bridged with foil except that small cracks in plate glass may be reinforced and foiled across if a section of the glass cannot be removed without breaking the foil at other points.

E. At the junction of glass and frame, foil shall be reinforced to protect it against breakage in normal service. Foil shall be completely protected against mechanical damage where necessary.

F. Walls of plaster, concrete, or similar absorptive materials shall be covered with moisture-retardant paper or the equivalent before application of the foil. Hardboard or similar material may be foiled directly, provided reinforcement for the foil is afforded where it crosses joints in the panel.

G. Conductive foil shall be manufactured and installed to meet all requirements of Standard for Installation and Classification of Mercantile and Bank Burglar Alarm Systems, UL 681, and Standard for Metallic Window Foil for Intrusion Alarm Systems, NIJ-STD-0319.XX.

7.8 Breakwire, Screens, and Grids

A. Breakwire is intended to be used in fabricating screens and grids, grooved stripping, and open wiring in various arrays and configurations neces-

of acoustic energy above a frequency of 18 kHz. Movement of a human (minimum size 5 feet tall and weighing 80 pounds) within the protected area for a distance of 5 feet or more at any velocity between 20 and 600 feet per minute in any direction shall cause the control unit to initiate an alarm signal.

B. Controls shall be provided in the master control unit to adjust the system sensitivity. Each monostatic type unit shall contain its own sensitivity control for precise individual sensitivity adjustment to accommodate varying room geometries and acoustics. Each motion detection system shall have a fail-safe circuit coupled with the system oscillator circuit that will activate an alarm in the event of intermittent or complete oscillator failure. The application and installation of systems with two or more master control units shall not generate random alarms caused by a hetrodyne frequency between oscillators. When master controls operate near each other, the oscillator output of each master control shall be wired in parallel or a separate master oscillator shall be provided and wired in parallel with each master control oscillator output. It shall be possible to zone and synchronize using two or more master control units. Each detector shall be equipped with a visual indicator to indicate when that detector has been activated as an aid to walk testing the unit and as an indication of when a unit has caused a false alarm; the visual indicator can be at the control or at the detector. Each unit shall have a background disturbance indicator as an installation aid. Remote readout of alarm indication shall be an available option.

C. The control cabinet may provide for removal of ultrasonic energy from the dector heads when the system is in the access mode in order to prevent annoyance to persons with sensitive hearing. However, other circuitry, such as battery charging and processing circuitry, within the control cabinet or the individual detectors must continue to be powered in order to ensure stability of the system. Transmitter and receiver transducers shall be available in uni-directional and omni-directional configurations.

D. Detectors shall meet all requirements of Standard for Intrusion-Detection Units, UL 639, particularly Section 37, and Standard for Ultrasonic Motion Detectors for Burglar Alarm Systems, NILECJ-STD-0309.XX.

7.17 Microwave Motion Detectors

A. This detector shall consist of transmitter/receiver elements and necessary control circuitry to saturate the protected space with electromagnetic energy. Movement of a human (minimum size: 5 feet tall and weighing 80 pounds) within the protected space for a distance of 5 feet or more at any velocity between 20 and 600 feet per minute in any direction shall cause the detector to initiate an alarm signal.

B. The detector shall be designed so that nuisance alarms due to electromagnetic emissions from other equipment such as fluorescent lights and motors are prevented; the system also shall be immune to nuisance alarms caused by changes in environmental relative humidity, temperature, air pressure, noise, or air motion. Microwave detectors shall operate within a frequency range and power output allocated by the Federal Communications Commission. Units shall be provided with a tunable oscillator to allow field selection of operating frequency within the allowed bandwidth. Additionally, the units should provide a doppler cycle counter or other circuitry to enable small background movements to be ignored. Controls shall be provided to adjust the range of the microwave detection circuit and the alarm signal threshold. The controls shall not interact with each other and not affect the specified sensitivity of the detection circuit. The controls shall allow the coverage of the detector to be confined to a small area, to saturate a large area, or if required, to penetrate soft walls, glass, or other similar material to achieve detection beyond such material. Confinement or penetration of microwave radiation also can be achieved by proper selection of the most appropriate operating frequency band.

   C.   Detectors shall meet all requirements of Standard for Intrusion-Detection Units, UL 639, particularly Section 37, and Standard for Microwave Motion Detectors for Intrusion Alarm Systems, NILECJ-STD-0310.XX.

7.18   Vibration Sensors

   A.   This sensor shall consist of piezoelectric pickup devices designed to be mounted on masonry or reinforced concrete surfaces connected through an amplifier/accumulator designed to initiate an alarm signal in response to structurally borne vibration caused by an explosion or a single heavy blow, a series of lighter blows, or similar phenomena characteristic of attempted forcible entry. The amplifier/accumulator shall integrate the amplitude of input stimuli with respect to time up to a preset alarm level. In addition, the amplifier/accumulator shall be so designed that stimuli of insufficient magnitude to initiate an alarm are bled off to the normal quiescent level at a rate of decay from the level immediately below alarm to 10% to 15% of alarm level in not less than 10 nor more than 30 minutes. Amplifier/accumulator adjustments shall include, at a minimum, gain control and repetition rate.

   B.   The performance of the detector system shall be adjustable so that at mid-range sensitivity, with pickup devices mounted on 6-inch thick monolithic reinforced concrete (or hollow masonry concrete block walls 8 inches thick), it shall be capable of initiating an alarm whenever the protected surface is struck on the exterior side, within a minimum radius of 15 feet from a pickup device, by 10 or fewer blows at 5-second intervals, from a 1½-pound steel ball free-falling through a 90-degree arc at a radius of 12 inches. With the controls set at minimum sensitivity, the detector shall not respond to the above impact test beyond a radius of 10 feet from a pickup device. When tested in the SECURE mode, an alarm can be initiated even if a single inoperable sensor exists, regardless of the gain setting and the accumulator level.

C.   Vibration sensors shall meet all requirements of Standard for Installation and Classification of Mercantile and Bank Burglar Alarm Systems, UL 681, particularly Sections 14.22 through 14.31, all applicable requirements of Standard for Intrusion-Detection Units, UL 639, and Standard for Microphone Vibration Sensors for Intrusion Alarm Systems, NILECJ-STD-0311.XX.

7.19   Audio Detection for Vaults

A.   This type of detection system is intended *only* for use in vaults or other confined spaces in which the ambient noise level during secure periods is 55 decibels or less. The space to be protected shall be tested for ambient sound level. The level shall not be determined in the presence of sounds that are to be canceled or otherwise prevented from causing false alarms by the system.

B.   The detection system shall consist of one or more sensitive microphones mounted within the volume to be protected and connected to an amplifier/accumulator control unit designed to initiate an alarm signal in response to stimuli characteristic of unauthorized or forced entry. The system will initiate an alarm when there is a single sound of 4 decibels or more or when there is a series of five sounds of 2 decibels or more.

C.   The control unit shall contain an amplifier of the low band pass type, a resistance-capacitance time constant accumulator circuit, and a means of integrating the amplitude of input signals with respect to amplitude and time. The integration circuit shall be so designed that an alarm signal shall be initiated in response to a single loud sound or a series of normal sounds. In addition, the accumulator shall be so designed that stimuli of insufficient magnitude to initiate an alarm are bled off to normal zero level at a rate of decay from the level immediately below alarm level to zero in not less than 10 or more than 30 minutes. The amplifier/accumulator shall have adjustable gain and accumulator controls. Controls in the unit shall be accessible only to maintenance personnel. The control enclosure and power supply shall comply with requirements of Sections 2 and 5 of these Standards.

D.   Audio sensors shall be of the piezoelectric or reluctance type designed to give peak response to sound which would be associated with unauthorized activity in the protected area. Each sensor shall contain a preamplifier with an adjustable gain control.

E.   Audio detection systems shall meet all applicable requirements of Standard for Intrusion Detection Units, UL 639, and Standard for Sound Sensing Units for Intrusion Alarm Systems, NILECJ-STD-0308.XX.

7.20 CCTV Motion Detectors

A.   This detector shall detect the presence of an intruder by electronically comparing successive scenes for differences in images. An alarm shall be initiated when the compared images differ by more than 6%. The detector shall be capable of desensitizing portions of the viewed space where naturally moving objects occur. Comparison of the video information within the protected space shall occur at not less than one sample per second. Failure of the camera shall produce an alarm independent of that caused by the detection of an intruder in the protected space. The CCTV motion detector shall be designed to operate with cameras that automatically compensate for scene illumination.

B.   The CCTV detection system shall be compatible with any CCTV surveillance system that already may be installed and shall use the existing surveillance cameras wherever possible. If surveillance cameras are equipped with pan, tilt, and zoom features, the CCTV detection system shall provide for automatic disconnect of these features during such times as the cameras are in the intrusion detection mode; the disconnect shall provide for manual override. Authorized operation of manual override shall not cause an intrusion alarm to be sounded.

C.   The CCTV detection system shall be equipped with a video recorder as a means of identifying the nature of the intrusion that initiated the alarm. The recorder shall be activated automatically by the alarm and shall record as long as the detection system indicates activity in the protected area or until manually turned off by responding personnel. A recorder existing as part of an installed CCTV surveillance system may be used.

D.   The system shall meet any applicable UL or NIJ Standards which may be published in the future to cover such equipment.

7.21 Fixed Duress Alarm Initiating Devices

A.   Every duress alarm device (commonly referred to as "holdup alarms") shall be a closed-circuit device, wired in a supervised closed-circuit protective loop.

B.   The mechanism activated to create an alarm condition shall not produce perceptible noise, nor shall obvious body movement be necessary to activate it. A means of indicating which particular device has operated shall be provided, but it shall be so designed and situated as to be unlikely to be noticeable to an intruder.

C.   The operating portion of every hand-operated device shall be flush or recessed with respect to the surrounding surface and protected from accidental activation. Foot-operated devices must be reliable, easy to operate, securely mounted, and protected from accidental activation. Care must be taken to protect operating mechanisms from the effects of mechanical damage, dust, and moisture.

D.   Once activated, alarm-initiating devices shall lock in the signal until manually reset with a key or similar device.

E.   Such devices shall meet all requirements of Standard for Hold-Up Alarm Units and Systems, UL 636, and any applicable NILECJ Standards which may be published in the future to cover such devices. Devices employing mechanical switches also shall meet all applicable requirements of Standard for Mechanically Actuated Switches for Burglar Alarm Systems, NILECJ-STD-0302.XX.

7.22   Portable Duress Alarm Initiating Devices

Specific standards for portable duress alarm-initiating devices have not been drafted. Such devices shall meet applicable regulations of the Federal Communications Commission governing radio-transmitted alarm signals (47 CFR Part 15) and, where applicable, meet all requirements of Standard for Hold-Up Alarm Units and Systems, UL 636. Such devices also shall meet requirements of any NIJ Standards which may be published in the future to cover such devices.

7.23   Products of Combustion Detectors

To detect safe and vault attacks from a cutting torch or an oxygen lance (burning bar), the employment of products of combustion detectors will be permitted and encouraged. Products of combustion detectors shall be compatible with the intrusion detection system and shall initiate an intrusion alarm if triggered. Such detectors should be on a separate detector circuit from other devices used to protect the same safe or vault so that, if the conventional detectors are compromised, the products of combustion detector still may initiate an alarm. Active products of combustion detectors shall meet the standby power requirements of the alarm system.

Products of combustion detectors used for vault protection also may be used as part of a building fire detection system provided that the control circuitry can discriminate between a vault attack and a fire and sound the proper alarm. Products of combustion detectors shall meet all requirements of Standard for Combustion Products Type Smoke Detectors for Fire Protective Signaling Systems, UL 167, and relevant portions of Standard for Intrusion-Detection Units, UL 639. In addition, such detectors shall meet applicable requirements of any NIJ Standard which may be published in the future to cover such devices.

8.0 LOCAL ALARM SIGNALING DEVICES

8.1 Bells

Specific standards for bells have not been developed. However, bells shall meet all applicable requirements of Standard for Audible Signal Appliances, UL 464, and the audibility requirements of Section 33.5 of Standard for Local Burglar-Alarm Units and Systems, UL 609. In addition, bells should meet applicable requirements of any NIJ Standard which may be published in the future to cover alarm signaling devices.

8.2 Sirens

A. Electronic sirens shall be capable of providing ____ decibel[5] output at 5 feet. The electronic tones shall be selectable or adjustable for pitch and period without compromising the output decibel level. Electronic sirens shall be compatible with the specified control panel and shall be capable of being driven directly from the control panel, although higher output sirens may require a separate driver in its own cabinet. The siren electronics shall be located within the control panel or in a cabinet of equivalent construction located immediately adjacent to it and connected to it by rigid conduit. It should be possible to connect more than one siren speaker to the siren output.

B. Electronic sirens to be used inside of buildings only and for remote indoor annunciation at another premises shall meet all specifications of Paragraph 8.2A but normally will operate at a lower decibel level than outdoor sirens, usually in the 85-105 decibel range. However, higher output can be specified when needed. It shall be possible to silence the remote siren audible sound at the remote location but any visual remote indicator shall remain lighted or engaged until the alarm system has been reset at the protected premises.

C. In order that fire alarm systems may be compatible with intrusion alarm systems, two inputs to an electronic siren driver may be provided. One input shall provide an alternating high-low tone (Europen siren) or a steady wailing tone suitable for warning of an intrusion; a different input shall provide a slow whoop (ascending low to high-repeated) tone suitable for warning of fire. Tones shall be non-interfering and the fire alarm tone shall preempt the intrusion alarm tone. The same siren speaker shall be capable of emitting either warning sound, which one depending upon the nature of the emergency.

---

5. The required output will be specified for each installation. Normally at least 95 decibels will be required; however in some cases, up to 130 decibels may be required.

When an intrusion alarm system utilizes bells as the audible alarm signal and a fire alarm system in the same premises utilizes sirens as its audible signal, it will not be necessary for the sirens to have the dual tone capability. Likewise, systems employing sirens for intrusion alarms and bells for fire alarms will not require dual tone sirens.

    D.   Sirens mounted outside of the protected perimeter of a premises shall be contained within tamperproof housings. Housings shall be made of steel or cast aluminum and shall be double, the outer shell having a minimum thickness of 0.085 inch and the inner shell having a minimum thickness of 0.63 inch. Anti-tamper switches shall be mounted front and rear and shall initiate an alarm if the cover is removed, if the housing is pried from the mounting surface, if the housing is taken apart, or if the housing is drilled. An alarm shall occur from any of these actions whether the system is in the ACCESS or the SECURE mode.

    E.   Wiring to outside sirens shall enter the siren through the wall into the back of the housing or, if exposed wiring is necessary, in steel conduit secured with two locknuts and bushings at the housing. Wiring to outside sirens shall not be run exposed to the weather.

    F.   Sirens shall comply with all applicable requirements of Standard for Audible Signal Appliances, UL 464, and Standard for Police Station Connected Burglar Alarm Units and Systems, UL 365. In addition, sirens shall meet applicable requirements of any NIJ Standards which may be published in the future to cover audible alarm devices.

8.3 Visually Indicating Alarm Devices

Specific standards for visual alarm devices have not been developed. Such devices are intended to be used in conjunction with audible devices and include strobe lights, rotating beacons, and similar devices. Generally, such devices will have two purposes: (a) to help call attention to an alarm situation or to help better locate the source of an alarm or (b) to remain active after an audible device has been shut down by automatic system reset in order to call attention to the fact there has been an alarm.

9.0 TELEPHONE DIALING AND REPORTING DEVICES

9.1 Performance

Telephone dialing and reporting devices shall provide at least two channels and be designed to accept two or more separate input signals from the alarm system control unit. Telephone dialing and reporting devices shall provide output for dial pulse or dial tone and for the messages applicable to the emergency situation. Units shall provide for automatic start in the event of an alarm and for automatic stop after completing the message cycle. Telephone dialing devices using magnetic tape drives shall provide 5 minutes of tape for each complete cycle and shall provide a second means of automatic cut-off in the event the tape drive mechanism fails to stop from the impulses on the tape. Magnetic tape operated dialers shall provide enough time on each channel for three to five complete numbers to be dialed with complete messages to each number dialed. The unit shall contain provision for one of the channels to be the priority channel. Thus the priority channel, when activated, shall always override the non-priority channel. The unit shall have the capability of line seizure. Telephone dialing and reporting devices shall be listed in the UL Classified Products Directory under Telephone Dialers.

9.2 Construction

Dialer covers and housings shall be a minimum of 16 gauge (0.063 inch) steel and shall be capable of preventing erasure of the audio tape when a hand-held magnet of fixed strength is held to the cover. The dialing equipment shall contain provision for electrically trapping the wiring to it so that, should the telephone line plugs or jacks be removed by an unauthorized person, the system will alarm, whether it is in the ACCESS or the SECURE mode. Internal electronics should be readily replaceable plug-in circuit boards. The housing shall be equipped with a high-security, pick-resistant locking cylinder which should be keyed alike to other cabinet locks in the alarm system.

9.3 Power Supply

Power may be obtained through the control panel or from some other source of unswitched 120-volt[6] ac power. The unit may obtain standby power from the alarm system standby batteries within the control cabinet or may contain its own rechargeable standby batteries that are maintained on float charge. In either case, a precisely regulated power supply shall be provided, with provision for prevention of overcharge and for automatic switchover to standby batteries in the event of commercial power failure. Standby batteries shall be sealed, essentially maintenance free, and capable of operation in any position or labeled to show the correct operating position. (See also Paragraph 5.3 of these design criteria.) The standby batteries shall be capable of powering the device through at least three complete cycles with commercial power off. The

---

6. Other voltages (110, 115, etc.) may be specified when appropriate.

standby batteries shall meet the minimum system standby power requirements specified in Paragraph 2.4 of these Standards. If the dialer utilizes its own self-contained standby batteries, provision shall be made for monitoring the status of the batteries at the system control cabinet if the dialing device is located out of sight of the control cabinet. Otherwise, the power supply monitor may be located on the face of the dialer housing.

9.4 Telephone Line Connections

The dialing device shall be provided with a means for direct connection to the telephone line or for connection to a telephone line coupler of a type acceptable to the operating telephone company. Line seizure capability shall be provided. Connection points or terminals shall not be exposed after the cover is installed.

10.0 MONITORING UNITS FOR PROPRIETARY ALARM SYSTEMS

10.1 Operation

Annunciator units shall be so designed that, when connected with their ancillaries into a detection and alarm system, they provide the means to monitor the condition and control the operation of the alarm system at a location removed from the protected premises. Annunciator units shall be electrically compatible with the detectors and circuit supervisory equipment and shall be of modular design capable of being installed with other annunciators in a rack, console, or cabinet. When specified, individual annunciator units shall be furnished in appropriate enclosures. To the extent practicable, equipment related to the annunciator, such as standby power supply, audible alarms, and circuit supervisory circuits, shall be contained in the same enclosure. Generally, when annunciator panels accept modular annunciator units, the individual units will share a common alarm module or display.

10.2 Secure/Access and Reset

The annunciator panel shall have a SECURE/ACCESS switch and an alarm reset switch. An alarm shall create a lock-on condition which shall require manual restoration and controls shall be provided to reset the system. The annunciator shall have a means of silencing the audible signal from a particular zone during prolonged alarms. However, a visible signal shall remain illuminated on the annunciator panel until the system is restored to normal operation at the protected premises. The silencing control shall be so connected that the audible alarm signal will be re-activated upon receipt of an alarm from another zone. When a detection circuit is conditioned for authorized entry into the protected area (in ACCESS mode), the annunciator shall continue to indicate alarms (or trouble, depending upon equipment design) if circuit supervisor limits are exceeded, if any tamper switches are disturbed, or if any detection circuit is cut or shorted.

10.3 Annunciator Readout

A. The annunciator shall be equipped with a readout of the type specified in B or C below.

B. *Electronic or solid-state type readout.* This type of readout uses either a cathode-ray tube (CRT), a nixie tube. or a light-emitting diode (LED) type of display and a printer (inking register) for recording alarm conditions. The electronic or solid-state type of display shall have an average life expectancy of not less than 100,000 hours and, at a minimum, shall display any location that has a change of status and show the present status of that location. The printer shall print out any location that has a change of status, the present status of that location, and the time of day the change occurred.

C. *Colored signal lights type readout.* This type of readout shall indicate by colored lights of not less than 50,000 hours of life expectancy the following conditions:

1. Green lights: detectors and circuits are in the SECURE mode.
2. Red lights: that a detector in the protected premises is in an alarm condition, or that power failure or malfunction of a component has caused the alarm system to be inoperative, or that circuit supervisor limits have been exceeded, or that a tamper switch has been activated.
3. White lights: that the system is operating in an ACCESS mode.
4. Amber or yellow lights: that the system is operating on standby power or that trouble has developed.

(In some systems, amber lamps may signify the ACCESS mode and there is a common trouble lamp which may be red, amber, or white.)

In addition to the visible signal lights, an audible signal shall sound whenever the system changes status or condition. However, the audible signaling device need not be part of each individual annunciator module.

10.4 Annunciator Construction

Individual annunciator modules of a given manufacturer shall be interchangeable to facilitate maintenance. Plugs and sockets shall be used to the maximum extent possible. All parts of the annunciator shall be easily identified and readily accessible for authorized access and maintenance. All controls required for normal operation shall be permanently and conspicuously marked. All controls not required for operation of the system shall not be readily accessible to the operator when the equipment is installed in a rack or console.

10.5   Annunciator Connections

The annunciator shall be provided with terminals for the purpose of connecting the power supply (normal and standby) and for interconnecting with other annunciators, detection circuits, alarm transmission lines, and other peripherals.

11.0   POLICE CONNECTED AND CENTRAL STATION UNITS

11.1   General

Premises and police or central station connected units shall be compatible with each other and with the rest of the intrusion alarm system. They shall be designed in such manner that the police or central station unit will initiate an audible alarm in the event of an intrusion or trouble on the line. The remote unit shall have a reset capability for the audible alarm. The police or central station unit also shall display a visual indication for line trouble or intrusion, resettable at the police or central station only if the line trouble or intrusion condition has been corrected. The police or central station unit shall indicate an alarm condition if an intrusion occurs, if the protected system is tampered with, if potential, impedance, resistance, or similar substitutions are made on the alarm line, or if the alarm line is opened or shorted. If the premises unit is not housed within the system control cabinet, it shall meet the control cabinet construction and locking specifications in Paragraph 5 of these Standards, including the standby power requirements.

11.2   Line Supervision

Line supervision for direct-connect (leased line) systems shall be accomplished in accordance with Paragraph 3.5 of Federal Specification W-A-00450B. Systems requiring exceptionally high line security should employ random-digital interrogate/reply systems in either the double or single scan mode, depending on the degree of telephone line noise.

11.3 Digital Communicators

Specific standards for digital communicators have not been developed. Digital communicators shall be used in lieu of tape-type telephone dialers whenever possible.

11.4 Compliance with Standards

Police connected alarm systems shall comply with Standard for Police-station Connected Burglar Alarm Units and Systems, UL 365. Central station connected alarm systems shall comply with Standard for Central Station Alarm Units and Systems, UL 611. Such systems also shall meet applicable requirements of any NIJ standard which may be published in the future to cover them.

12.0 AUXILIARY DEVICES AND EQUIPMENT

12.1 Compatibility

Auxiliary devices and equipment include all alarm system major components not described in other parts of these Standards. Auxiliary devices shall be compatible with each other and with the overall system and shall meet the intent, philosophy, and design requirements of the system. Such devices, where applicable, shall meet the minimum housing or enclosure requirements of Paragraph 5.1 and the anti-tamper requirements of Paragraph 2.6. Auxiliary devices,when used as part of an overall security system, shall meet the minimum standby power requirements of Paragraph 5.3. Auxiliary devices shall not be susceptible to false alarms due to audio or radio interference and shall not cause interference to other audio or radio frequency devices.

12.2 Compliance with Standards

Where auxiliary devices perform a signaling or communications function, they shall conform to the electrical and safety requirements of the relevant UL Standard. Such devices should be UL listed whenever possible.

12.3 Power Requirements

Auxiliary devices may be powered from the control cabinet or may contain their own standby batteries. Self-contained power supplies shall meet the power requirements specified in Paragraph 5.3.

13.0 FALSE ALARMS

13.1 Introduction

This section is intended as a guide to the level of reliability that might be expected from an alarm system designed, installed, operated, and maintained in accordance with these Standards. It is impossible to objectify or quantify the matter of false alarms *vs.* true alarms or to establish strict criteria for system reliability because each protected premises possesses its own unique characteristics and each alarm system will consist of different kinds and qualities of equipment. Therefore, this section should be taken only as a general guideline.

13.2 Definitions

A. *Burglar Alarm:* a single initiated by an alarm system responding to an actual or an attempted intrusion.

B. *Valid Alarm:* a signal initiated by an alarm system when it detects a break in security not related to an actual or an attempted burglary. For example, a window broken out by a vandal who makes no effort to enter the building will be detected and an alarm will be initiated. Likewise, a pedestrian on a sidewalk might be detected by a microwave motion detector if its area of coverage were spilling outside the walls of the building in which it is located. The pedestrian is not an intruder but the system will perceive him as one. In both examples the detection system is doing what it is supposed to do but it has delivered a "false" alarm.

C. *Infraction Alarm:* a signal caused by the system due to the action or inaction of someone authorized to be at the protected premises or perhaps at an alarm monitoring post. Causes of such alarms could include: improper operation of system equipment; failure to close a protected door or window; entering a protected area without turning off the system; testing the system without notifying the police or other responding agency; failure to notify a central station of work schedule changes; or someone unwittingly left behind in the protected premises after hours.

D. *Environmental Alarm:* a signal caused by detection equipment responding to stimuli caused by environmental conditions in the protected premises. For example, an audio sensing system might respond to vibrations caused by rattling light fixtures or air ducts or to structurally transmitted motor noises. An ultrasonic motion detector might respond to air turbulence from a hot radiator, an air conditioning system, or a strong draft. A passive infrared motion detector might sense a fly crawling in front of its sensing element. In all these cases, the detection equipment is responding to stimuli it is designed to detect but the stimuli are not caused by human intruders.

E. *Equipment Alarm:* a signal occurring because of a failure in the hardware of the alarm system in the protected premises or in the monitoring station or along the alarm transmission line (when there is remote transmission, as in a police-connect, central station, or large proprietary system). Program or software failure in a computer-based system also would be equipment failure. Such failures could include: battery failure, loose wiring connections; cut or frayed wiring insulation; loose door and window switches; motion detectors knocked out of alignment; and natural age deterioration of electronic components. Such failures should be rare if the system is well designed, installed, and maintained and if good equipment has been installed.

F. *Single System:* an interconnected assemblage of detectors, sensors, signaling devices, and related circuitry all controlled and operated by one control panel. Examples of single systems would include: a local system protecting one building or a part thereof; a system protecting a single building but with alarms transmitted to a central station or to a police station; and a proprietary system protecting several buildings from a single central control/annunciator panel.

Single systems may have one or more zones of detection/annunciation and may incorporate sub-control panels as needed for operation of such devices as sound sensors, capacitance detectors, and ultrasonic motion detectors. A central station that monitors a number of premises control units is not a single system; neither is a proprietary system if the protected buildings have their own premises control units and the central panel only monitors their status.

G. *Proper Detection Sensitivity:* the ability of the alarm system to detect an intruder in the secured area(s) 95 times out of 100 under the conditions stated in the performance criteria for each type of detection device or for the complete alarm system.

13.3 Expected Performance

Under normal environmental conditions, a single alarm system installed in accordance with these Standards and with the codes and standards herein referenced should perform as stated in Table 1 while maintaining proper detection sensitivity. The figures given in the table are averages based on a 10-15 year life expectancy for an alarm system. These figures may vary from year to year, depending upon the quality of operating and maintenance personnel and upon such factors as changes in the environment. New systems will experience a "burn-in" period during which equipment failure alarms may be high; old systems will experience a gradually increasing rate of equipment failure alarms as components wear out. The rate of infraction alarms will depend upon the

Type of Alarm	Type of Alarm System		
	Single Premises with Local Alarm	Single Premises with Remote Alarm	Large Proprietary system
Burglar	As required	As required	As required
Valid	Depends on system	Depends on system	Up to 12 OK
Infraction	None acceptable	1-2 acceptable	1-4 acceptable
Environmental	1-4 acceptable	1-6 acceptable	1-12 acceptable
Equipment	1 acceptable	1-2 acceptable	1-24 acceptable

Table 15.1. Acceptable Frequency of Alarms per Year for Single Systems

quality of employee training and supervision. Environmental alarms and some valid alarms can be eliminated by "fine-tuning" the system so that it responds only to actual and attempted intrusions while maintaining proper sensitivity.

14.0 SYSTEM TEST

14.1 Initial Acceptance Test

A.   Upon completion of installation of the system, tests shall be conducted to determine whether it meets all specifications and will perform as intended. The tests shall be conducted by the Contractor during a continuous period of 48 hours. Tests shall be conducted in the presence of the Contracting Officer or his authorized representative who may suspend or discontinue the tests at any time performance is considered unsatisfactory. The tests will resume upon correction by the Contractor of any elements of the system found to be performing unsatisfactorily. The resumed testing will cover any previously untested elements, and any previously tested elements at the discretion of the Contracting Officer. The Contracting Officer will develop a checklist of elements to be tested in advance of the tests and will use the checklist to record performance of the system as it is tested. The time, cause, and other conditions prevailing will be recorded for each alarm and trouble signal received. The Contractor shall furnish all test personnel except for those required to maintain alarm records for the Contracting Officer. Test instruments and equipment of the accuracy necessary to perform the tests shall be furnished by the Contractor. If test equipment is furnished to the Government as part of the contract, then this equipment should be used for conducting the acceptance tests.

B.   The tests shall include — but not necessarily be limited to — the operation of all sensors and detectors, the operation of all signaling and annunciation devices, the activation and operation of all remote, shunt, and SE-CURE/ACCESS switches, the activation of all card readers and other access controls, and the operation of all controls (both externally and internally mounted) on the control panel(s) and on any annunciator panels. In addition, the satisfactory operation of the standby power supply and its batteries shall be demonstrated; this demonstration shall include operation of the entire system on standby power for at least 12 hours or for one-half the time the system can be operated on standby power, whichever is greater. Tamper switches shall be tested if they are accessible; when tamper switches are not accessible, at least their wiring should be tested. Line supervision equipment shall be tested to the extent that testing is non-destructive to the line, its terminals, and attached components and to telephone company equipment.

14.2 Periodic Testing

A.   In consultation with the Contractor, the person responsible for security at the protected facility (herein referred to as the Security Officer) shall establish a schedule for periodic inspections and tests of the system. Some elements of the system may have to be tested weekly or even daily, although many routine tests can be conducted monthly or even quarterly. Equipment that is operated or "exercised" daily may never require special testing. The schedule shall provide for complete testing of each element of the system at least annually; this provision can be met by testing different elements of the system at regular intervals so that all of them are tested each year. Daily, weekly, and monthly inspections and tests usually will be conducted by operating security personnel. Quarterly and any needed annual tests usually will be conducted by the installing contractor or by the person or agency responsible for system maintenance and repair.

B.   The nature and frequency of tests necessary to ensure continued satisfactory operation of a system will depend to a large extent upon the types of equipment comprising the system and upon the system's overall level of sophistication. In general, large proprietary alarm systems will require more frequent testing than local systems. Table 2 provides general guidelines for the frequency of inspection and testing normally considered necessary for medium- to high-security alarm systems. This table includes both operator-conducted inspections and tests and contractor-conducted tests.

C.   Routinely scheduled inspections and tests should include the following at a minimum:

1. Check the installation and location of system elements against installation plans and specifications to verify that all required elements are in place.

2. Wherever practicable, inspect the equipment and wiring with particular reference to the security of doors, windows, and their frames. Where wiring is protected against mechanical damage in conduit or is concealed, the inspection may be an electrical test of wiring and a visual examination of its terminations for mechanical damage, corrosion, frayed insulation, or other faults that could affect the electrical circuit.

3. Wherever practicable, check that there is no apparent corrosion of metallic parts and no visible defect, such as cracking or retraction, in insulation, nor mechanical damage to the base laminate of printed circuits, of such nature as to impair the effectiveness of the system. Check that there is no evidence of abrasion, particularly on connections, and that all contacts are in good condition. Check that all mechanical connections (electrical wiring terminals, box mounts, cover screws, etc.) are firmly fixed.

4. Check window and cabinet foil for blistering or loosening. Inspect take-off blocks and connections for damage and deterioration and for evidence of tampering. Restore the moisture-resistant coating wherever necessary.

5. Wherever possible, check the operation of all detection devices. Check that door and window switches are in good repair, properly positioned, and securely fastened. Wherever possible, open all doors, windows, and other movable openings fitted with switches to ensure correct operation of the contacts.

6. Check duress and holdup alarm devices for correct operation and, in particular, check to make sure alarm indicators do not operate without an alarm being sent and that an alarm is not sent without indication.

7. Check the normal and standby power supplies.

8. Check the control equipment and maintain it in accordance with the manufacturer's instructions.

9. Check the operation and reliability of all telephone dialers using taped messages and ensure that the messages is intelligible.

10. Check the operation of digital dialers and direct-connect equipment in cooperation with the police or central station concerned.

11. Check the operation and proper audibility of all audible alarm devices. Check the operation and proper visibility of all visible alarm devices. Ensure that alarm devices are not blocked or attenuated by growth of trees and shrubs or by new construction.

12. Obtain a signature and written certification from the person or company performing the test that it has been conducted and that the submitted written report is true and complete.

D. The Security Officer shall be notified immediately should any test reveal: a weakness in the degree of security provided by the system; evidence of tampering with equipment, detection and tamper circuits, signaling circuits, or remote alarm transmission circuits; unauthorized adjustments made to equipment; or that any equipment or sensitive element has been moved or removed.

E. If regularly scheduled tests reveal that adjustments need to be made to equipment, the adjustments shall be made. If such adjustments affect the sensitivity or reliability of the alarm system, the Security Officer shall be so informed. Parts that have failed or that are likely to fail before the next scheduled test also shall be replaced during the inspection/test.

F. A written report shall be made of each test conducted by the Contractor and of each other test for which the Security Officer requires a written report. At a minimum, the report will include such information as: records

Table 15.2. Suggested Frequency for Testing Medium- to High-Security Systems

System Element	Visual Inspection	Performance Test
Audible and visible alarm devices	Weekly	Monthly
Telephone dialers (tape and digital)	Weekly	Monthly
Proprietary remote monitoring equipment	Daily	Weekly
Police-connected remote monitoring equipment	Daily (by police)	Monthly
Premises control unit and alarm transmitters	Daily	Monthly
Remote, shunt, and SECURE/ACCESS switches	Daily	As operated
Standby power supply batteries and charger	Monthly	Quarterly
Tamper switches that are accessible	Monthly	Quarterly
Tamper switches that are not accessible	Quarterly	Annually
Detectors on movable openings	Weekly	Quarterly
Mat switches and trapping devices	Weekly	Quarterly
Window foil	Monthly	Annually
Breakwire (open, grids, screens, etc.)	Monthly	Annually
Capacitance detectors	Monthly	Quarterly
Photoelectric beam devices	Weekly	Quarterly
Passive IR motion detectors	Weekly	Monthly
Light threshold motion detectors	Weekly	Monthly
Sound sensing detectors (passive sonic)	Weekly	Monthly
Sonic (audible frequency) motion detectors	Weekly	Monthly
Ultrasonic motion detectors	Weekly	Monthly
Microwave motion detectors	Weekly	Monthly
Vibration sensors	Weekly	Quarterly
Audio detectors in vaults	Weekly	Quarterly
CCTV motion detectors	Daily	Monthly
Duress/hold-up alarm devices	Daily	Monthly
Products of combustion and heat detectors	Weekly	Quarterly

of battery voltages found; the nature of and reasons for any adjustments that were made; a list of parts that were replaced and an explanation of why they were replaced; and descriptions of any evidence of tampering that may have been found.

G. Tests and inspections made by operating personnel can be scheduled for any hours by the Security Officer. Tests to be conducted by the Contractor should be performed between the hours of 8:00 A.M. and 5:00 P.M. exclusive of weekends and holidays, except when special security requirements make other hours necessary. Alternative hours shall be designated by the Security Officer and will be mutually agreeable to the Contractor.

15.0 DOCUMENTATION AND TRAINING

15.1 Operation and Maintenance Manual

A. Upon completion of acceptance testing but prior to certification by the Contractor that the system is ready to be placed into operation, the Contractor shall furnish three copies (or more if so specified) of a manual containing complete operating and maintenance instructions for the system. This manual shall be prepared in a manner and form best suited for providing technical data required by operating personnel to operate, test, and maintain the system. (The manual is not required to contain information needed only by the Contractor if he is to provide continued maintenance on the system. Should another contractor assume maintenance responsibilities, this proprietary information should be turned over to the new contractor.) The manual shall include text, drawings, schematics, tables, charts, and photographs as appropriate. It can include literature (or copies thereof) provided by the manufacturers of installed equipment. A draft of the manual shall be submitted for the Contracting Officer's approval as to adequacy prior to its preparation in final form. The draft should be submitted far enough in advance that the final manual will be ready upon certification of the system for service.

B. The form and content of the manual will be determined by the Security Officer and the Contracting Officer based on the needs of operating and maintenance personnel. The following outline is suggested for consideration:

1. *Covers.* Front and back covers should be of durable stock or a three-ring binder can be used. The design of the cover should permit easy replacement of obsolete pages and insertion of new ones but should also provide for positive retention of the pages. The cover should bear substantially the same information as required for the title page (see below).

2. *Title Page.* The title page should contain the following information in an attractive, easily readable format and letter style and size:

- Title, such as "Operating and Maintenance Manual for Intrusion Detection System in (name of building or site)."
- Name and location of the protected facility or site.
- Date of publication. (When changes are made to the manual, subsequent dates will follow the original date.)
- Security classification, if any, will be prominently marked.
- Proprietary notice to read "Prepared under Contract No. by (Name of Contractor) for (name of Department of Agency)."

3. *Table of Contents.* The table of contents shall list all important divisions and sub-divisions of the manual and shall be in a format to facilitate easy reference.

4. *General.* The general section shall contain an overall narrative description of the system, including the nature, extent, and sophistication of detection, the types of equipment installed and their basic purposes, how the system is arranged and laid out (using diagrams as necessary), and a summary of the points made in Section 2 of these Standards.

5. *Technical Section.* This section should contain detailed information on the equipment comprising the system. It should include the following at a minimum: general theory of operation; installation, maintenance, and adjustment; and troubleshooting. It is particularly important that this section be easy to use and to understand. This section usually will rely heavily on literature published by manufacturers of installed equipment.

6. *Operation Section.* This section shall contain recommended procedures for routine operation of the system and its constituent components. The instructions shall be clear and easy to follow and understand. They should be written expressly for the system rather than simply copied from manufacturers' literature, although the language may be substantially the same. If the system is to be connected to a police station, this section shall contain instructions which may be reproduced and given to police personnel answering alarms. If the system is to be connected to a central station, this section should contain at least a summary of what actions central station personnel will take upon receipt of an alarm.

7. *Emergency Service Section.* This section shall contain full details about how operating personnel can request emergency repair services from the Contractor or from the person or agency that will be maintaining the system if it is not maintained in-house. This section should outline the circumstances under which emergency service may be requested, the proper way to request service (phone numbers, times of day, names of service people, etc.), and what kinds of emergency service can be expected. If this information is brief enough or can be condensed without loss of vital information, it should also appear on the inside of the front cover of the manual.

8. *References.* This section should contain information about the nature

and location of contract documents (plans, specifications, etc.) that may be needed for reference at some time. This section also may include a marked-up (i.e., "as-installed") drawing of the system unless the drawing would be more conveniently kept elsewhere, in which case its location shall be noted.

15.2 Record Drawings

Upon completion of the installation and final certification that the system is ready to be placed into operation, the Contractor shall furnish to the Contracting Officer three copies of system plans. Such plans can be either (a) shop drawings neatly and legibly modified to show as-installed conditions or (b) prints made from original drawings made by the Contractor to show as-installed conditions. (The Contractor may be required to turn over the original drawings in some cases where high-security systems are involved or if the Contractor will not be providing any further services, such as systems maintenance.) These drawings shall indicate locations and descriptions of all installed equipment, routing of all wiring, and such installation details (such as how equipment was mounted) as may be necessary or asked for by the Contracting Officer. Block diagrams and schematic diagrams may be requested but can be incorporated in the operating manual or the drawings as mutually agreed upon. Drawings shall be clearly labeled as to the name of the system, its location, the name of the agency, the name and address of the contractor, the date of the drawings and all revisions, contract number, and number of related specifications in book form.

15.3 Training of Operating Personnel

The Contractor shall conduct a training program for operating personnel who will be designated by the Security Officer. The training program will be conducted as soon as possible after completion of acceptance testing of the system and can occur prior to its final certification by the Contractor. The program shall include, at a minimum, the following: procedures for gaining authorized access to protected premises; procedures for actuating, securing, and resetting the system and its operating equipment; operating of monitoring equipment; and procedures to be followed in requesting emergency service. Training shall be presented by one or more qualified instructors who can be employees of the Contractor or representatives of manufacturers of installed equipment. The instructor(s) shall use drawings, charts, diagrams, training aids, demonstration equipment, films, slides, and any other media needed to make the system and its operation fully understandable. It is suggested that the training also include familiarization with the operating manual. If the agency operating the system is to do some or all of its own maintenance, the training shall cover all aspects of maintenance as well.

16.0 WARRANTY

16.1 General

The Contractor shall fully guarantee the system against defects in materials, design, workmanship, and installer labor for at least one full year from the date of acceptance thereof, either for beneficial use or final acceptance, whichever is earlier. The Contractor shall provide for periodic inspections and maintenance at quarterly intervals or more frequently during the warranty period. During the warranty period, the Contractor shall replace or repair without charge to the Government any elements of the system that have failed in normal operation (excluding damage caused by operator failure or user error, acts of God, civil disorder, vandalism, and natural disaster).

16.2 Reinstatement of Time

When equipment and labor covered by the Contractor's warranty or by a manufacturer's warranty has been replaced or restored because of its failure during the period of that warranty, the warranty period for the replaced equipment or restored work shall be reinstated for a period of time equal to the original warranty period and commencing with the date of completion of the replacement or restoration work. (For example, if a magnetic switch has been warranted for one year beginning on July 1, 1981, and it fails on April 19, 1982, and is replaced on April 21, 1982, the warranty for the new switch will extend from April 21, 1982, to April 20, 1983.)

17.0 REFERENCE PUBLICATIONS

17.1 Standards and Codes

The standards and codes referenced in this document can be obtained from the following sources:

A. *Federal Specifications*
Standardization Division
Federal Supply Service
General Services Administration
Washington, D.C. 20406

B. *NIJ and NILECJ Standards and Reports*
Single copies of most publications and a current publications list can be obtained at no cost from:
    Law Enforcement Standards Laboratory
    National Bureau of Standards
    U.S. Department of Commerce
    Washington, D.C. 20234
Multiple copies and publications that must be purchased can be obtained from:
    Superintendent of Documents
    U.S. Government Printing Office
    Washington, D.C. 20402
C. *UL Standards*
    Underwriters Laboratories, Inc.
    Publications Stock Department
    333 Pfingsten Road
    Northbrook, IL 60062

17.2 Other References

Anyone not experienced in the design and installation of alarm systems will find the following publications very useful. The first book should be required reading by facilities managers considering the installation of an alarm system. The remaining publications will be most useful to engineers and designers but may be of interest to the layman who is interested in learning as much as possible about alarm systems in order to better communicate with alarm system specialists. The publications are listed in order of their overall estimated usefulness to the layman, sources also are noted.

BIBLIOGRAPHY

Sher, A.H., and Gerard N. Stenbakken. SELECTION AND APPLICATION GUIDE TO COMMERCIAL INTRUSION ALARM SYSTEMS. (Washington, DC: Law Enforcement Standards Laboratory, National Bureau of Standards, August 1979). NBS Special Publication 480-14. 40 pp., illus.

Barnard, Robert L. INTRUSION DETECTION SYSTEMS: PRINCIPLES OF OPERATION AND APPLICATIONS. (Woburn, Mass.: Butterworth Publishers. 1981. 339 pp., illus., biblio. (Butterworth, 10 Tower Office Park, Woburn, MA 01801)

Prell, J.A. INTERIOR INTRUSION ALARM SYSTEMS. (Washington, DC: U.S. Nuclear Regulatory Commission, February 1978). 41 pp., illus., biblio. (U.S. Government Printing Office, Washington, DC 20402)

Greer, William A. (editor). ALARM INDUSTRY QUALITY CONTROL MANUAL. (Washington, DC: National Burglar and Fire Alarm Association, 1980). Ten sections, paginated separately; updated by subscription. (NBFAA, 1101 Connecticut Avenue, NW, Washington, DC 20036)

Kmet, Mary Alice. "The Proof Is in the Planning." SECURITY MANAGEMENT, Vol. 24, No. 7 (July 1980): 69-71. (American Society for Industrial Security, Suite 651, 2000 K Street, NW, Washington, DC 20006)

Post, Deborah Cromer. "Specifying A Security System." SECURITY WORLD, Vol. 18, No. 2 (February 1981): 29-31. (Security World Division, Cahners Publishing Co., 5 South Wabash Avenue, Chicago, IL 60603)

Sandia National Laboratories, Nuclear Security Systems Division. INTRUSION DETECTION SYSTEMS HANDBOOK, 2 Volumes. SAND 76-0554. (Washington, DC: U.S. Department of Energy, November 1976, updated through July 1980). (Assistant Director for Research and Development, Safeguards and Security, Department of Energy, Washington, DC 20545)

Trimmer, William. UNDERSTANDING AND SERVICING ALARM SYSTEMS. (Woburn, Mass.: Butterworth Publishers, 1981). 277 pp., illus. (Butterworth, 10 Tower Office Park, Woburn, MA 01801)

16. Museum Television Security

Closed circuit television (CCTV) provides an important contribution to safeguarding works of arts in museums. The CCTV system extends the eyes of the museum staff to a given area in order to prevent vandalism or theft of precious works of art. The success of CCTV in the prevention of these crimes is a result of: (1) the deterrent effect of a visibly displayed CCTV camera; (2) the current use of CCTV cameras to provide surveillance of potential vandals or thieves; (3) the availability of low-cost, high-quality television systems; (4) the ability of a guard force to respond immediately when a criminal act is observed; and (5) the ability of the CCTV video recorder to provide a permanent record for later viewing by police or in courtroom use for conviction.

The use of small hidden cameras and lenses has proven very effective for identifying criminals. Camouflaged cameras in simulated decorations, paintings, lamps, fixtures, etc., prove very effective in observing museum visitors without their knowledge.

More advanced CCTV museum installations utilize television image motion detectors to alert the guard force to movement by an object or person in a pre-designated area. Most of these systems operate by detecting the change in light received by the CCTV camera from the ambient lighting. Another system utilizes a "wall of light" to separate the public from the work of art. Whenever the light wall is penetrated, an intrusion is detected and the guard is alerted via the CCTV monitor picture.

By covering the fundamentals of CCTV systems, this chapter presents the functions of lenses, cameras, monitors, recorders, transmission means, and special equipment particularly suited for museum security. It analyzes some specific applications and gives practical solutions. A checklist for designing a museum CCTV system is accompanied by a glossary that defines commonly used terms in the industry.

ONE CAMERA/MONITOR CCTV SYSTEMS

A large number of museum CCTV applications require only one television camera. Figure 16.1 shows a simple, but frequently encountered, problem: the monitoring of people entering and leaving the front lobby of the museum building with a one camera CCTV system. The monitor is located at a remote guard station, and the camera is located in the lobby, close to the ceiling. The camera looks at a scene with a lens with a field of view (FOV) large enough to see most of the lobby, the front door, and the internal access door.

The parts of this CCTV system have the following functions:

- Lens — Collects light from the scene and forms an image of the scene on the camera tube.
- Camera — Converts the visible scene into an electrical signal suitable for transmission over a coaxial cable.
- Coaxial Cable — Transmits the camera scene signal from the camera to the remote monitor.
- Monitor — Displays pictures that the camera takes by converting the electrical signal back to a visible picture.

Although this is a simple system, there are a number of questions to be answered and decisions to be made before a system can be specified and installed. Some of these questions, which can serve as a convenient checklist during a survey and quotation, are:

1. Camera/Lens
   - Where should the camera be located so that all people in the lobby as well as the doors can be viewed?
   - In what direction should the camera be pointed so that the sun, or doors opening to the outside, have minimum effect?
   - Should the camera have a ⅔-inch or 1 inch diameter image tube?
   - What field of view should the camera lens cover?
   - Should a fixed focus or zoom lens be used and what focal length is best?
   - How much lighting is available? Is daytime and/or night-time operation required?

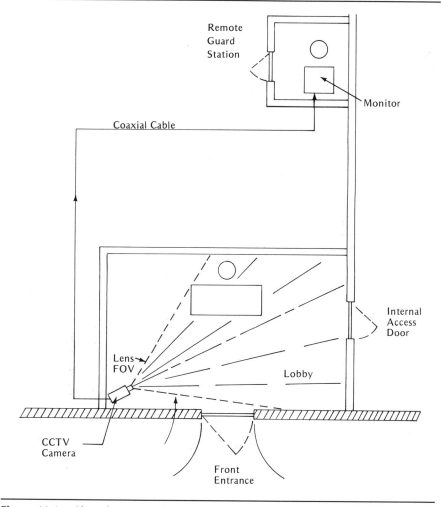

Figure 16.1. Closed circuit television system

- Should the camera be mounted with brackets, recessed in the walls or ceiling, or be installed in a housing?
- Should the camera voltage be 117 VAC or 24 VAC?

2. Cabling
   - What is the distance between the camera in the lobby and the monitor at the remote guard location?
   - What coaxial cable type should be used: RG 59, RG 11?

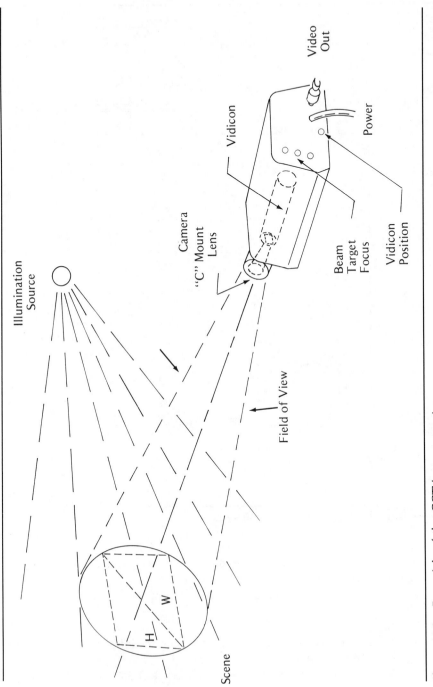

Figure 16.2. Essentials of the CCTV camera system

3. Monitor/Switcher
- What size monitor screen should be used?
- How is the monitor connected to the switchers?
- What type of switcher is required?

4. Lobby Camera Location

Aside from choosing the equipment, camera location is most important. The camera lens should never be pointed in the direction of the sun or toward an outside door. Large light-level changes degrade the picture quality. The camera in Figure 16.1 is pointed toward the inside of the building, thereby receiving relatively constant illumination. If the camera uses a standard vidicon tube, direct sunlight or a bright target (common tungsten bulbs) will burn a spot on the image tube, leaving a white image on the monitor screen. With the camera location shown, it views people coming in and out of the museum, almost all of the lobby, and the internal access door.

CAMERA SYSTEM

Figure 16.2 shows the essentials of a CCTV camera, including the lens and the field of view (FOV), or scene, that the camera "sees."

The camera sees the scene in the following manner. A light source (sunlight, lamps) illuminates the scene. A part of the light reaching the scene from the source is reflected toward the camera, and is intercepted and collected by the camera lens. The camera lens collects the reflected radiation much like the lens of the human eye or a film camera lens. The lens focuses the scene onto the television image tube, which acts like a detector similar to the retina of the human eye or the film in a camera. The image tube and camera electronics convert the visible image into an equivalent electrical signal suitable for transmission to a remote monitor. Although the scene image is focused onto the image tube continuously, the camera electronics transforms the visible image to an electrical signal point by point. The camera video signal (containing all picture information) contains frequencies from 30 Hz (cycles/second) to 4 MHz, which are transmitted via the coaxial cable. Most cameras external controls include: (1) mechanical focus (vidicon, position), (2) focus (electronic), (3) beam current, and (4) target voltage.

VIDICON CAMERA SIZE

All standard CCTV cameras use either a ⅔-inch diameter or 1-inch diameter vidicon image tube as shown in Figure 16.3. Which tube to use is determined

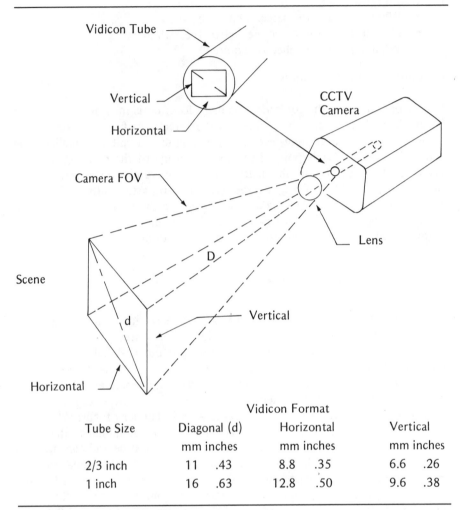

Vidicon Format					
Tube Size	Diagonal (d)		Horizontal		Vertical
	mm	inches	mm	inches	mm	inches
2/3 inch	11	.43	8.8	.35	6.6	.26
1 inch	16	.63	12.8	.50	9.6	.38

Figure 16.3. Camera tube geometry and formats

primarily by cost factors. A ⅔-inch tube has a .25 inch x .35 inch (6.75 mm x 9 mm) image format, that is, the visible scene falling in the central 6.75 mm x 9 mm (11 mm diagonal) region of the vidicon is later displayed on the monitor. Likewise, a 1-inch diameter vidicon has a .38 inch x .50 inch (9.6 mm x 12.8 mm) active area (16 mm diagonal).

If cost is a primary factor, the ⅔-inch system should be chosen. If the best image quality and reliability are required, the 1-inch system is superior. It is somewhat like comparing a super 8 mm to a 16 mm film movie system. Because the ⅔-inch system costs less, it is the size most commonly used in museum security systems.

Camera Field of View (FOV)

The task of choosing the right lens to do the job is perhaps the most difficult part of designing a CCTV system.

Just as a person's eyes have a FOV, that is, the scene that one can see, so also does the television camera. The camera FOV is determined by the simple geometry shown in Figure 2. The scene has a width (W) and height (H) and is a distance (D) away from the camera lens. Once a decision has been made about the scene the camera should view, there are three factors that determine what is the correct focal length lens to use: (1) size of the scene to be televised (height, width); (2) distance between the scene and camera lens, (distance); (3) image tube size, ⅔-inch or 1-inch diameter. Table 16.1 lists the scene sizes viewed by 1-inch cameras for common lens focal lengths and for a range of subject distances. A simple multiplication factor converts the numbers to a ⅔-inch tube format. Understanding Figure 16.3 and Table 16.1 makes it easy to choose the right lens for most applications. For example, choose a lens for viewing all of a 10-feet high by 15-feet long wall from a distance of 30 feet, with a 1-inch diameter CCTV camera. Table 16.1 indicates that a 25 mm F.L. (focal length) lens will do the job.

If in the example just given a ⅔-inch vidicon would have been required, then multiply the required scene size by 1.43 to get 1.43 × (10 ft. × 15 ft.) = 14.3 ft. × 21.45 ft. Then proceed as before. A 16 mm (.63 inch) F.L. lens will do the job. Table 16.2 summarizes the camera angular view versus lens focal length.

Several comments and observations can be made about CCTV lenses:

- Lenses invert the picture image (the camera electronics reinverts the picture so that it is displayed right side up on the monitor).
- A short F.L. lens has a wide FOV (Table 16.1: 6.5 mm, 1-inch tube, sees 59.1 ft. × 44.4 ft. at 30 ft.).
- A long F.L. lens has a narrow FOV (Table 16.1: 150 mm, 1-inch tube, sees 2.5 ft. × 1.9 ft. at 30 ft.).
- The 25 mm F.L. lens is considered the "standard" or reference lens and has a focal length in between the two lengths just mentioned. It is defined to have a magnification (M) of 1. Using the 25 mm lens as a reference with M = 1, the 75 mm lens has a magnification of 3, and the 8.5 mm, a magnification of ⅓. In general, the magnification of a lens is as follows:

$$\text{Magnification} = \frac{\text{Lens focal length (mm)}}{25 \text{ mm}}$$

or

$$M = \frac{\text{F.L. (mm)}}{25 \text{ mm}}$$

Table 16.1. Camera scene FOV vs lens focal length

Lens		Distance (D) In Feet (Note 1)		
mm	inch	W×H	W×H	W×H
		5	15	25
4.0*	.16	16x12	48x36	80x60
4.8*	.19	13.3x10	40x30	66.7x50
6.5	.26	9.8x7.4	29.4x22.2	49x37
8.5	.33	8.2x5.9	24.6x17.7	41x29.5
12.5	.5	5x3.8	15x11.3	25x18.8
16	.63	4x3	12x9	20x15
25	1	2.5x1.9	7.5x5.6	12.5x9.4
50	2	1.3x.9	3.8x2.8	6.3x4.7
75	3	.8x.6	2.5x1.9	4.1x3.2
100	4	.6x.5	1.9x1.4	3.1x2.3
150	6	.4x.3	1.3x.9	2.1x1.6

Lens	F.L.	Camera to Scene Distance (D) in Feet (See Note 1)									
mm	inch	10	20	30	40	50	60	70	80	90	100
		W+ x H+	W x H	W x H	W x H	W x H	W x H	W x H	W x H	W x H	W x H
4.0*	.16	32x24	64x48	96x72							
4.8*	.19	26.7x20	53.3x40	80x60							
6.5	.26	19.7x14.8	39.4x29.6	59.1x44.4	78.8x59.2	98.5x74	118x88.8				
8.5	.33	16.3x11.7	32.6x23.4	48.9x35.1	65.2x46.8	81.5x58.5	97.8x70.2	114x81.9			
12.5	.5	10x7.5	20x15	30x22.5	40x30	50x37.5	60x45	70x52.5	80x60	90x67.5	100x75
16	.63	8.1x6	16.2x12	24.3x18	32.4x24	41x30	48.6x36	56.7x42	64.8x48	72.9x54	81x60
25	1	5x3.75	10x7.5	15x11.25	20x15	25x18.75	30x22.5	35x26.25	40x30	45x33.75	50x37.5
50	2	2.5x1.9	5x3.8	7.5x5.6	10x7.5	12.5x9.4	15x11.3	17.5x13.1	20x15	22.5x16.9	25x18.7
75	3	1.7x1.3	3.3x2.5	5x3.8	6.7x5	8.3x6.3	10x7.5	11.7x8.8	13.3x10	15x11.3	16.7x12.5
100	4	1.3x0.9	2.5x1.9	3.8x2.8	5x3.8	6.3x4.7	7.5x5.6	8.8x6.6	10x7.5	11.3x8.4	12.5x9.4
150	6	0.8x0.6	1.7x1.3	2.5x1.9	3.3x2.5	4.2x3.1	5x3.8	5.8x4.4	6.7x5	7.5x5.6	8.3x6.3

*4.0 and 4.8mm lenses are available *only* for ⅔" format. Multiply W x H by 0.7
+ W and H is width and height in feet.

Notes: 1) Scene sizes (W x H) are for 1 inch vidicon. 2) To get scene size for ⅔ inch vidicon, multiply W by .7 and H by .7. Example: For a F.L. = 25mm and a ⅔ inch vidicon at 20 ft., W = 10 ft. x .7 = 7 ft. H = 7.5 ft. x .7 = 5.25 ft.

Lens F.L.		Max. Lens Aperture*	Camera Angular FOV (Degrees)+			
			⅔" Vidicon		1" Vidicon	
mm	inches		Horizontal view angle	Vertical view angle	Horizontal view angle	Vertical view angle
4.0	.16	f/1.4	96	79	N/A	N/A
4.8	.19	f/1.8	86.3	70.2	N/A	N/A
6.5	.26	f/1.8	69.4	54.8	89.1	72.9
8.5	.33	f/1.5	54.8	42.5	78.3	60.8
12.5	.5	f/1.4	38.7	29.5	54.5	42.1
16	.63	f/1.6	31	23.4	44	33.3
25	1	f/1.4	20	15	28.5	21.5
50	2	f/1.4	10	7.5	14.5	11
75	3	f/1.4	6.7	5	9.6	7.2
100	4	f/2.8	5	3.7	7.1	5.3
150	6	f/2.8	3.4	2.5	4.8	3.6

*These values are for common CCTV lenses.
+ For any distance (D).

Table 16.2.   Camera angular view versus focal length

ZOOM LENSES

A zoom lens is a variable focal length lens. Several elements in these lenses are physically moved to vary the F.L. and thereby vary the angular FOV and magnification. The F.L. is varied manually by a simple control knob, or electrically from a remote location. These lenses have the advantage that a range of focal lengths can be dialed in, thereby accommodating a variety of fields of view with one lens. Zoom lenses generally cost two to ten times as much as fixed F.L. lenses.

SCENE LIGHTING

The CCTV camera image tube responds to the reflected light from the scene. If the scene is illuminated, via sunlight or artificial lighting (fluorescent or tungsten), a standard vidicon (using an antimony trisulfide target) will probably be satisfactory. This vidicon has advantages and disadvantages. Its primary advantages are (1) good image resolution and (2) the ability to be controlled over wide variations in lighting levels, from a bright sunlight scene (8,000 ft. cd.) to a relatively dim indoor scene (1 ft. cd.). This represents a variation of 8,000 to 1 in light level. A third advantage is its low cost and availability. A disadvantage of this type vidicon is that (1) a fixed scene being viewed will slowly "burn" into the vidicon and (2) if the camera inadvertently receives light directly from the sun (or bright reflection) or from a common tungsten light, the tube will be damaged, and a burn spot (white spot on the monitor) will be seen.

When an application requires viewing bright lights or, occasionally, the sun or its reflections, a vidicon that has a silicon target or Newvteon* (instead of antimony trisulfide) are better choices. These tubes are also between 10 to 100 times more sensitive (able to see at dusk or in very low lighting) depending on the type of illumination, and they will not burn. These lower light level tubes are not a panacea, however. They cannot operate over more than about 100 to 1 change in light level. An application that has a larger light level change requires an additional automatic optical attenuator (automatic iris) for proper operation.

The illumination that is present in the scene, as well as the amount of light ultimately reaching the television camera, is an important factor in successful CCTV operation. The illumination either can be from natural sources such as the sun, moon, or starlight, or from artificial sources such as tungsten,

---

* Trademark of Radio Corporation of America

Table 16.3. Source light level variations and applicable cameras

Illumination condition*	Illumination (ft cd)	Camera tube sensitivity range +			
		Standard Vidicon	Silicon/ Newvicon	SIT	ISIT
Direct Sunlight	10,000				
Full Daylight	1,000				
Overcast Day	100				
Very Dark Day	10				
Twilight	1				
Deep Twilight	.1				
Full Moon	.01				
Quarter Moon	.001				
Starlight	.0001				
Overcast Night	.00001				

*Natural light illumination (sun, star, or moonlight) using an f/1.4 lens and viewing a scene with 50% reflectance.

+Shaded region indicates useful operating range of TV camera.

fluorescent, sodium, or Xenon lamps. It almost goes without saying that the more light available on the scene the better the ultimate television picture. Some factors that must be considered in the source illuminating the scene include: (1) the source spectral characteristics, (2) the beam angle over which the source radiates, (3) the intensity of the source, and (4) the variations in the source intensity. Factors to be considered in the scene include: (1) the reflectance of objects in the scene and (2) the complexity of the scene. The CCTV camera image tube responds to the reflected light from the scene. Figure 16.2 shows the illumination source, the scene to be televised, and the camera with the lens. As shown in Figure 2 the radiation from the illuminating source reaches the television camera by first reflecting off the objects in the scene.

If the scene in Figure 2 is illuminated by sunlight or moonlight, the illumination will be relatively uniform. On the other hand, if it is illuminated by several sources, that is lamps, the illumination may vary considerably over the field of view of the camera. Table 16.3 summarizes the overall light level variations produced, ranging from direct sunlight to overcast night. For outdoor conditions the camera system must operate over the full range of direct sunlight to night-time conditions. It must have an automatic light control means to compensate for this light level change.

Artificial light or illuminating sources consist of several types of lamps. These lamps may be used either in outdoor conditions, such as parking lots, outdoor storage facilities, or fence lines, or in indoor environments, such as general room lighting, hallways, work areas, or elevator locations. The lamps are of two general types: (1) tungsten or tungsten iodine lamps with solid filaments, and (2) gaseous lamps with either low- or high-pressure gas in an envelope. Examples of gaseous lamps include mercury, low- and high-pressure sodium, fluorescent, multi-alkali, and xenon. For special applications, some of these lamps are covered with a dark filter so that only invisible or infrared radiation illuminates the scene. Since the different camera types respond to different colors, it is important to know what type of illumination exists in a typical surveillance area, as well as what type might have to be added in order to get a suitable television picture. Figure 16.4 shows the light output characteristics of the various artificial sources available, as well as the radiation characteristics of natural sunlight and moonlight. Superimposed on Figure 16.4 are the spectral sensitivities of the different types of cameras that are available. As can be seen readily, each of the different sources produces light in different wavelengths or colors. In order to obtain the maximum utility from any television camera, it is important that the camera be sensitive to the light produced by the artificial or natural source. It is evident that sunlight, moonlight, and tungsten lamps produce energy in a range in which most TV cameras are sensitive. For this reason low light level cameras are sensitive in both daylight and night-time environments. Vidicon and Newvicon tubes are more sensitive to

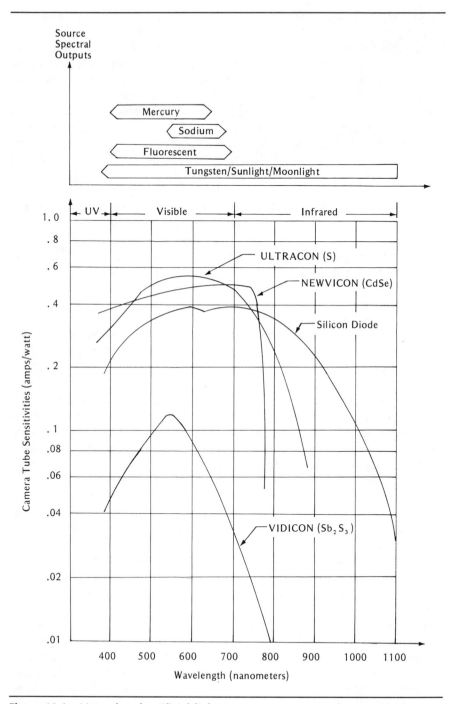

Figure 16.4. Natural and artificial light sources vs camera tube sensitivities

the visible wavelength (tungsten, mercury, or sodium) than the silicon television tube. For covert applications the silicon, SIT, or ISIT tubes are best although the Newvicon tube has some sensitivity in the near infrared region.

Another characteristic important in determining the amount of light needed for a scene is the beam angle over which the source radiates. It is obvious that the sun and moon radiate over the entire scene. Man-made light sources and lamps can be adjusted to produce narrow or wide angle beams. If a large area is to be viewed, it is necessary to have either a single wide beam source or multiple sources located within the scene to illuminate the scene fully. On the other hand, if a small scene at a long range is to be viewed, it is necessary only to illuminate that part of the scene to be viewed with the beam, thereby reducing the total power needed from the source.

SCENE CHARACTERISTICS

The quality of the television picture is dependent on various scene characteristics. These characteristics include the contrast of the object(s) to be observed relative in the scene background, and whether the object(s) to be viewed are in a simple uncluttered background or in a complicated scene. Actually how well a television system operates depends on what the information required to do the job consists of: (1) detecting an object or movement in the scene; (2) recognizing the type of object in the scene (i.e., whether it is a man or child, or dog or cat; and (3) identifying the object (if it is a person, who is the person, and if it is a dog, exactly what kind of dog it is). Whether or not these distinctions can be made, and if so, how well, depends on the resolution of the system and the contrast obtained at that resolution.

CCTV EQUIPMENT

Lenses — Fixed Focal Length

The majority of lenses used in CCTV applications are referred to as fixed focal length lenses. All of these lenses have "C" type (1-inch × 32 threads/inch) mounting. They are used on a ⅔-inch or 1-inch vidicon cameras and have a fixed field of view (FOV). Commonly used focal lengths vary from 4.0 mm (wide angle) to 150 mm (telephoto). Most of the available focal lengths between these values and their corresponding areas of coverage are shown in Tables 1 and 2. Most of these lenses are available with a manually adjustable iris, and the lenses with focal lengths down to approximately 8.5 mm are available with an adjustable focus ring. The 4.0 mm to 4.8 mm focal length lenses are available for ⅔-inch vidicon cameras only and show some image distortion in the picture. The 4.0 mm lens has a 96-degree horizontal by 79-degree verti-

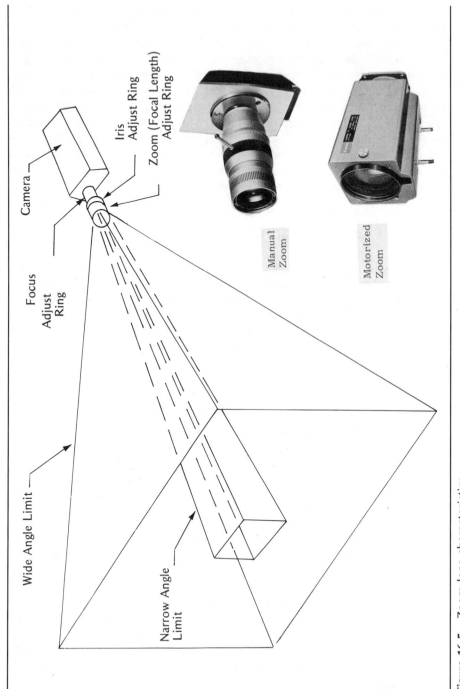

Figure 16.5. Zoom lens characteristics

cal FOV and considerable distortion, but it can view an extremely wide area in close quarters. Table 2 shows the angular FOV obtainable with lenses from 4 mm focal length up to 600 mm focal length. Above approximately 150 mm focal length, lenses become large and expensive. Although long focal length lenses can be designed with small lens or mirror elements, the amount of light passed through these lenses to the television camera is too small to be of practical use. Therefore, as the focal length becomes longer and the diameter of the lens increases, costs increase substantially. Most fixed focal length lenses are available in a motorized or auto iris form for use in remote control applications. When they are used with low light level television cameras, such as the Newvicon, Silicon, SIT, and ISIT types, the iris or light level control must be varied depending on the scene illumination. This is usually accomplished via automatic iris, and neutral density filters.

Zoom Lens

The zoom lens is a second class of lenses used especially in remote control applications (pan/tilt) where the FOV seen by the lens and camera must be varied from wide angle to narrow angle and vice versa (Figure 16.5). The zoom lens has a variable focal length (variable magnification) and the ability to change its FOV. This lens permits viewing narrow, medium, and wide angle scenes depending on its setting (which may be motorized), thereby permitting initial wide field viewing of an area and then close-in telephoto viewing of one portion of the area. Focal length ranges for various classes of zoom lenses vary from 20 to 200 mm and anywhere from 3 to 1 focal length change to 20 to 1 focal length change. These lenses are available for either manual or motorized operation.

CCTV Cameras

Most cameras used for security have a ⅔-inch vidicon format, and use a standard antimony trisulfide (Sb2S) tube. One-inch vidicon cameras are used when the highest level of reliability and the best resolution are required. All vidicon cameras utilize automatic light control (ALC), which changes the camera amplification to adapt to large variations in light level conditions. ALC compensation over a 10,000 : 1 range is standard, although cameras with a 100,000 : 1 ALC capability are available. When the ALC capability of the camera, in addition to the auto iris mechanism in a lens, is utilized, light level compensation of 660,000 : 1 or more is achieved for low light level cameras. Other features available as options in many cameras include: (1) camera identification number, (2) electronic screen splitter, (3) RF modulator, and (4) external synchronization. The RF modulator option permits taking the composite video output from the camera and connecting it directly into the antenna input of a home-type television receiver.

When standard vidicon cameras do not produce an adequate picture, lower light level cameras using the Newvicon, Silicon, or Ultracon tube are used. These cameras have a sensitivity between 10 to 100 times better than that of the standard vidicon. In general all three of them are relatively immune to image burn, which can occur in standard vidicon cameras when they are pointed at bright lights or the sun, or continually at the same scene. When the available scene illumination is in the visible spectrum, the Newvicon is the better choice since it has slightly better resolution than the silicon types. When these lower light level cameras cannot produce an adequate picture, very low light level cameras such as the SIT (silicon intensified target) and ISIT (intensified SIT) cameras are required. These cameras are extremely sensitive and must use lenses with special automatic iris characteristics. Likewise these cameras are expensive and are justified only when the light level cannot be raised by providing additional lighting.

A very small new type of camera is available but not yet widely used in security applications. It is the charge transfer device (CTD) camera. There are currently two types available, the CCD (charge couple device) and the CID (charge injection device). These solid-state silicon cameras utilize no vidicon tubes but instead use a single chip of silicon.

Figure 16.6 shows one of these CCD cameras in which the imaging sensor (CCD chip) is remotely located from the camera electronics via a ribbon-type cable. This results in an extremely small camera "head," approximately

Figure 16.6. Photo of CTD solid state camera with remote sensor

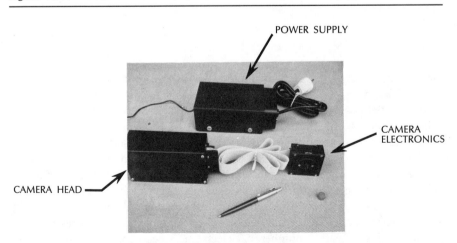

1.5 inches by 2 inches by 1 inch thick. Adding an automatic iris to this camera results in a size of 2 inches by 4 inches by 1.25 inches deep.

CCTV Monitors

Standard television monitors are available with screen sizes from 5-inch to 23-inch diameter diagonal with the 9-inch diagonal monitor in most common use. These monitors are available for 117-volt operation. Several are available for 12-volt operation. Connections are made via UHF or BNC connectors on the rear, and terminated in either 75 Ohm or high impedance inputs. If only one monitor is used, the switch on the rear of the monitor is set to the 75 Ohm or low impedance position for best results. If multiple monitors are used, all but the last monitor in the series is set to the high impedance position and the last monitor to the low impedance position. All cameras and monitors have a 4 by 3 format, that is, horizontal size is in a 4 to 3 ratio to the vertical size.

Small viewfinders and portable-type monitors are available in 1½-inch to 4½-inch diameter tube sizes and are powered by 9 or 12 volts or 117 VAC. These monitors are used in portable applications and for servicing equipment in the field.

Once the single camera lens system is understood, most of the design toward achieving multiple camera systems has been accomplished. The question remains whether an individual monitor is sufficient to display each camera or whether the picture from each camera should be switched into a single display monitor via an electronic switcher. Depending on the preference of individual viewers, the number of people entering and leaving each of the camera areas, and the activity in the scene(s), one or the other system will be chosen. If the scene activity, that is the number of people passing into or out of an area is relatively high, all cameras should be displayed on separate monitors. For installations with infrequent activity, or casual surveillance, an electronic switcher should be used. There are switchers available that have manual and automatic switching sequences.

VIDEO SWITCHERS

There are many different types of video switchers available for connecting multiple cameras to a single monitor or multiple monitors. The simplest type of switcher is a manual switcher (Figure 16.7), which provides the function of choosing one camera from among a number of cameras and presenting that camera on a single video monitor. The switcher contains a number of switches that are activated manually by the operator to connect the individual cameras

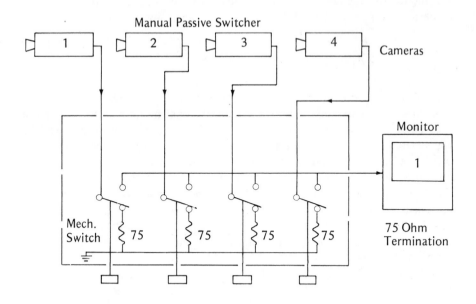

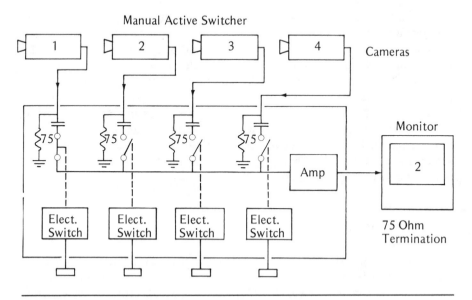

Figure 16.7. Manual CCTV switching system

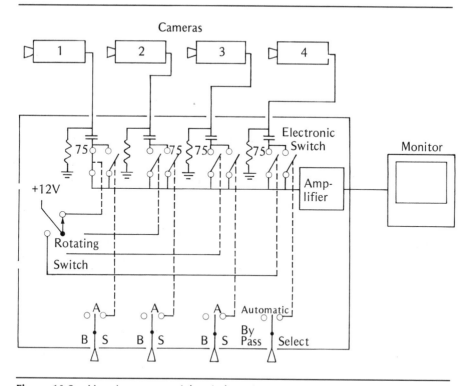

Figure 16.8. Housing sequential switcher system

to the monitor. The two basic types available are shown in Figure 7: (1) manual passive switcher and (2) manual active switcher. The basic difference between them is that the passive switcher uses a simple contact switch whereas the active switcher uses an electronic switch. Switchers are generally built to accommodate from 4 to 16 different cameras.

Figure 16.8 shows a second type of switcher called a homing sequential switcher. This switcher can operate in an automatic sequencing mode whereby each of the individual cameras is presented on the television monitor, one after the other, automatically. The length of time each camera picture is presented on the monitor can be varied by the operator. The three-position front panel switches provide three separate functions for operation: (1) automatic sequencing, (2) bypass, and (3) select (homing). When a switch is set on "bypass," that particular camera is not displayed. When the switch is set on "select," that camera picture is presented continuously on the monitor and in essence

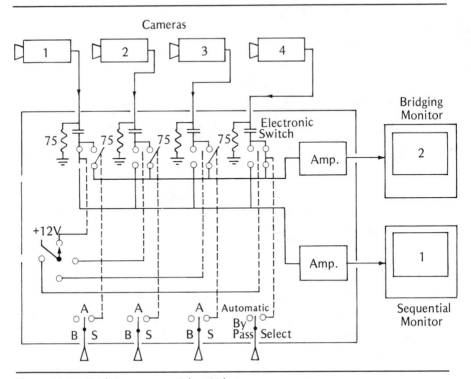

Figure 16.9. Bridging sequential switcher

overrides the automatic sequencing function. This permits continuous observation of any particular camera at the operator's command.

Figure 16.9 shows the block diagram for a bridging sequential switcher. This switcher system operates in a similar way to the homing sequential switcher but has the additional feature that two monitors can view the television cameras. The first monitor, the sequential monitor, has all the functions of the homing sequential switcher. The bridging monitor sees whatever camera is selected on the switcher when it is in the select mode of operation. When the particular camera is selected for the bridging monitor, the automatic sequence continues for the sequential monitor.

Figure 16.10 shows the block diagrams for looping homing and looping bridging sequential systems. The looping homing system is similar to the homing sequential switchers with the additional capability that all camera inputs can be brought out to a second switcher, which in turn operates as a homing sequential switcher. The looping bridging sequential switchers operate in the same manner as the bridging sequential switchers except that the looping input capability is added.

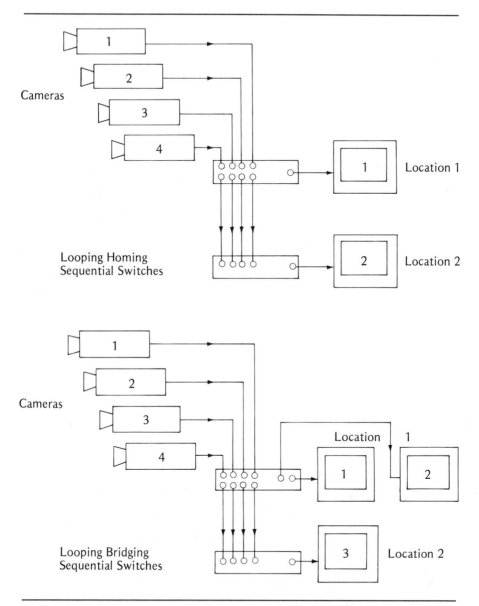

Figure 16.10. Looping housing and looping bridging sequential switcher systems

Another type of switcher is the alarming switcher. This switcher displays a picture on a monitor or starts a video tape recorder each time a camera is activated by a motion detector system or another type of alarm. When it is used with a video cassette or tape recorder, a switch closure on the back of the switcher turns on the recorder, which can be set up for either a real time or time lapse mode of operation.

Video Tape and Cassette Recorders

For many years the reel to reel video tape recorders (VTR) have dominated the security field. This type of recorder provided real time recording of the television picture, as well as time lapse recording for long periods of time. The ease of use of video cassettes and video cassette rcorders (VCR) has resulted in their widespread use. Present real time recording systems record 2, 4, or 6 hours continuous black and white or color recording with more than 300 line resolution. Time lapse recorders have total recording time up to three hundred hours and an alarming mode in which the recorder reverts to real time recording when an alarm condition exists. Every television scene that can be displayed on a monitor is capable of being recorded on a VCR for a permanent record for later use. The tapes can be erased and reused many times so that tape cost remains relatively low.

Figure 16.11 shows a 300-hour time lapse video cassette recorder. It can be activated by an external switch closure. This recorder would normally operate in the time lapse single frame mode and automatically switch into a real time recording upon activation by the external alarm.

Figure 16.11. Time lapse video cassette recorder

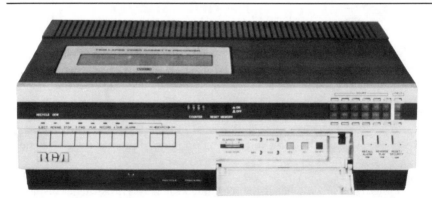

Pan and Tilt Systems

There are many accessories available for CCTV cameras and systems. Included are pan/tilt mechanisms to rotate and tilt the camera to the direction of interest. These mechanisms are available for lightweight duty, indoor, small camera applications as well as large, heavy-weight outdoor systems for larger lens and camera installations. These mechanisms can operate in an automatic mode or via control from a remote control joystick mounted on a control console. Figure 16.12 shows typical indoor and outdoor pan/tilt systems.

There are several techniques for transmitting the video signal from the CCTV camera to the monitor. The most common, reliable, and lowest cost way is via coaxial cable. There are basically four types of cables for use in video transmission systems: (1) 75-ohm unbalanced coaxial cable for installations in buildings, (2) 75-ohm coaxial cable for outdoor use, (3) 124-ohm balanced indoor coaxial cable, and (4) 124-ohm balanced outdoor cable. The type of cable used for a particular installation depends on the environment in which the cable will be used and the electrical characteristics required for the system. By far the most common forms of coaxial cable used are the RG-59/U and the RG-11/U, 75-ohm impedance type. Common forms of this coax cable are RG 59/U and RG 11/U. For short camera to monitor distances (a few hundred feet), preassembled sections of RG 59/U coaxial cable with connectors at each end are used. These cables come in lengths of 25, 50 and 100 feet, with either "UHF" or "BNC" type of connectors attached. Long cable runs (several hundred feet and up) should be run with a single length of coaxial cable with a connector at each end. For most interior CCTV installations, 75-ohm unbalanced coaxial cables should be used. When very long cable runs (several 1,000 feet or more) are used, particularly between several buildings, the balanced 124-ohm cable system should be considered. The equipment at the ends of the cable run, for example, if it is in two different buildings, may be at a slightly different ground potential, hum may be impressed on the video signal and show up as an interference (wide bars on the video screen) and make the picture unacceptable. A two-wire balanced cable can eliminate this problem.

Television camera manufacturers generally specify the maximum distance between the camera and monitor over which their equipment will operate. Table 16.4 is a guide for choosing the right type of cable for the application.

Where cable runs of several thousand feet are required, video amplifiers are also required. These amplifiers are located at the camera output and/or somewhere along the coaxial cable run. These amplifiers permit camera to monitor distances up to 3,400 feet for RG 59 cable, to 6,500 feet for RG 11 cable.

Most cameras operate from 117 VAC or 24 VAC. If a 117-VAC outlet is available at the camera location, it should be used. If power is to be run from a remote location to the camera, a 117-VAC to 24-VAC step-down trans-

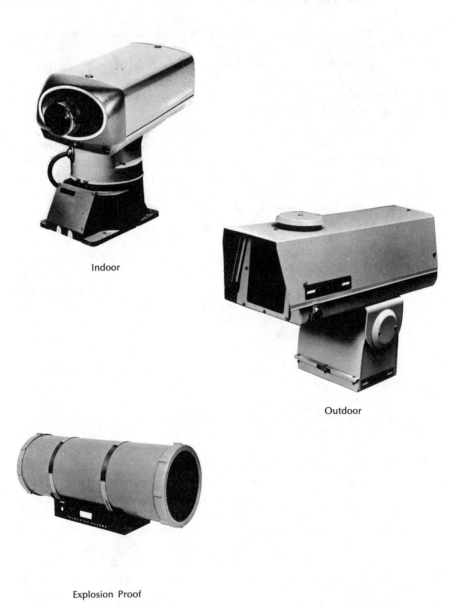

Indoor

Outdoor

Explosion Proof

Figure 16.12. CCTV pan-tilt mounts and housings

Cable type	Maximum Recommended Camera to Monitor Range For Each Type Cable*		
	Cable only[1]	With video amp [2]	Powered[2] Coax
Rg 59/U	500 ft.	3400 ft.	2000 ft.
Rg 6/U	750	4800	
Rg 11/U	1000	6500	3000 ft.
Rg 15/U	1500	8600	

[1] All cables have a 75 ohm impedance necessary for CCTV.

[2] The video amplifier is connected at the camera output to extend the coaxial cable effective range.

*If a coaxial cable can't be installed, the video signal can be transmitted over a twisted pair of telephone wires. A special transmitter and receiver permit transmission over a range of 4000 ft. using #22 or #24 wire.

[3] Single coax cable powers the camera and transmits the video signal.

Table 16.4. CCTV coaxial cable characteristics

former powering a 24-VAC camera has an advantage; any technician can install it and an electrician is not required. A 50-volt-amp (VA) power rating on the transformer is readily available and adequate to power the camera.

There are cameras available that require only a coaxial cable for operation. Figure 16.13 shows two examples of this type of camera. The coaxial cable (RG 59 or RG 11) transmits both the camera power and the video signal, which is referred to as vidiplexing. This single cable camera model reduces installation costs, eliminates costly utility wiring and conduit, and is ideal for installing in places that are hard to reach.

If a coaxial cable is not available or difficult to install (perhaps because two buildings are separated by a street or for some other reason), a technique exists for transmitting the television picture over a dedicated pair of wires. These wires can be run parallel or as a twisted pair but they cannot run through a telephone switching station. The system uses a small transmitter and receiver at each end of the pair of wires and can transmit the picture over a maximum distance of about 3,000 feet. Surprisingly good quality television transmission is obtained. In addition, a variation of this system includes transmitting CCTV pictures simultaneously in both directions, with half of the resolution of a normal picture. This is real time duplex television. Two-way voice communication and control signals for switching cameras, adjusting the camera lenses, and other functions can be added. This system is shown in Figure 16.14.

POWER:
120 VAC

SINGLE COAX CABLE
BETWEEN CAMERA AND
POWER CONTROL UNIT

POWER:
12 VDC

SINGLE COAX CABLE
BETWEEN CAMERA AND
POWER CONTROL UNIT

Figure 16.13. Vidiplex CCTV camera systems

Other means for transmitting television pictures without cables (wireless) include the use of microwave transmission and gallium arsenide (GaAs) infrared laser transmission. The microwave system has a range of approximately 3,500 feet with excellent picture quality, but it may require an FCC license for operation. On the other hand, the infrared laser transmission does not require FCC approval, but it has a shorter range, generally 2,000 feet or less in good visibility conditions and down to a few hundred feet in poor visibility conditions. A microwave system exists that has a built-in intrusion detection

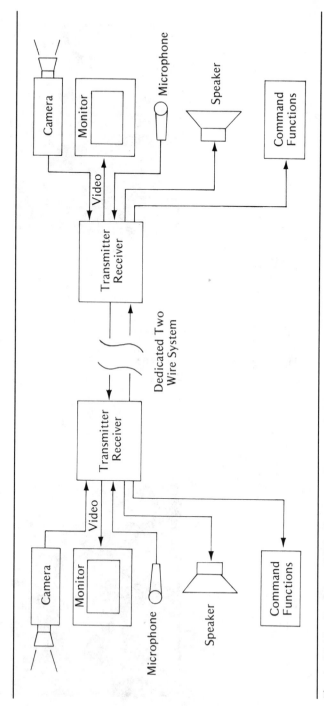

Figure 16.14. Realtime CCTV Transmission via telephone lines

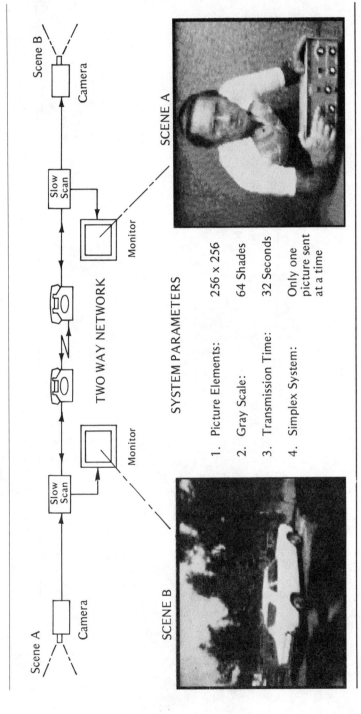

Figure 16.15. Slow scan television transmission and resulting snapshot pictures

function, so that if the beam is disturbed by a person walking between the transmitter and receiver an alarm output is registered. Both of these systems permit independent placement of the CCTV camera in locations that might be inaccessible for a coaxial cable transmission.

The above wireless transmission systems all result in real time television transmission. A scheme for transmitting the television picture over large distances, that is, anywhere in the world, makes use of what is called slow scan television transmission. This non-real time technique involves storing one television picture (snapshot) and sending it slowly over the telephone network anywhere within a country or from one country to another. The received picture is reconstructed to produce a continuously displayed television snapshot. Each snapshot is transmitted in 32 seconds, with the resulting picture having a resolution of approximately half that of a conventional closed circuit TV system. Every subsequent scene is transmitted in 32 seconds so that a time lapse effect is achieved. Shorter transmission times are possible at corresponding decreases in picture resolution. Figure 16.15 shows the system and examples of the picture.

Split Image Lenses

A special lens for imaging two independent scenes onto a single television camera is called an image-splitting optical or bifocal system. The lens system views the two scenes with two separate lenses with the same or different magnifications, and combines them on the camera tube (Figure 16.16). Depending on the orientation of the lens system on the camera, either a vertical or horizontal split is obtained. The C mount lenses can have the same or different focal lengths, and any lens that mechanically fits can be used. The adjustable mirror on the side lens permits looking in many directions. The adjustable mirror can be oriented so that it is pointing at the same scene as the front lens. In this case if the front lens is a wide angle lens (e.g., 6.5 mm focal length) and the side lens is a narrow angle lens (e.g., 75 mm focal length), a bifocal length system results; that is, *simultaneous* wide field and narrow field coverage *with one camera* results. The split FOV covered by each of the lenses is half of the total lens FOV. For example, with the 6.5 mm and 75 mm focal length lenses, on a ⅔-inch camera and a vertical split, the 6.5 mm lens will display a 49.3 ft. by 74 ft. scene, and the 75 mm lens a 4.1 ft. by 6.3 ft. scene at a distance of 50 ft. The horizontal FOV of each lens has been reduced by one-half. The bifocal lens inverts the picture on the monitor, a condition that is rectified by either inverting the camera or its vertical deflection coil.

Another image-splitting lens that can produce a three-way optical image is shown in Figure 16.17. The lens is designed primarily for viewing three hallways at one time. This lens provides the ability to view three (3) different

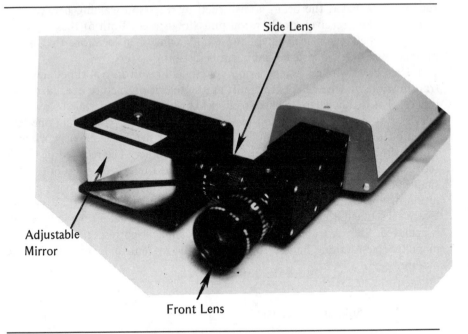

Figure 16.16. Image splitting optics

scenes with the same or different magnifications on one monitor with one camera with no electronic splitters required, thereby replacing two cameras and two monitors. Each scene occupies one-third of the monitor face. Adjustable optics in the lens permits changing the pointing elevation angle of the three front lenses so that they can look close in for short hallway applications, and all the way out for long hallways. This lens inverts the monitor image as does the bi-split lens.

Right Angle Lens

Another very useful lens for mounting cameras parallel to a wall or ceiling is shown in Figure 16.18. This right angle optical system permits use of wide angle lenses (4.0-mm, 100-degree) looking at right angles to the camera axis. This cannot be accomplished by using a mirror and a wide angle lens directly on the camera, since the entire scene will not be reflected by the mirror to the lens on the camera. The edges of the scene will not appear on the monitor because of picture vignetting. The right angle adapter permits the use of any focal length lens that will mechanically fit into its C mount. It is designed for ⅔-inch or 1-inch camera formats.

Front section moves up and down
to point lenses far out or close in

Side
Looking
Lens

Front
Looking
Lens

Side
Looking
Lens

Figure 16.17. Tri split lens

CAMERA INSTALLATIONS

There are many ways to install the television camera, including a simple camera bracket, camera recessed in the wall or ceiling, and an attractive wall- or ceiling-mounted housing. Indoor and outdoor camera installations generally require protection from vandalism. Figure 16.19 shows three attractive camera housing systems.

The indoor corner housing will accommodate most ⅔-inch cameras, fixed focus lenses, and low light level cameras (Newvicon or Silicon) with auto iris lenses. The camera is mounted in the housing pointed up at a moveable mirror (azimuth and elevation adjust) to obtain the proper pointing angle.

The spherical dome housing is available with either a clear or tinted (one-way mirror) dome configuration. The tinted form usually requires that the camera be of the low light level type, but it provides the advantage of no one being able to see where the camera is pointing.

The outdoor environmental housing houses ⅔-inch or 1-inch cameras with fixed focus, zoom lenses, or image-splitting optics. The housing is lightweight

Iris

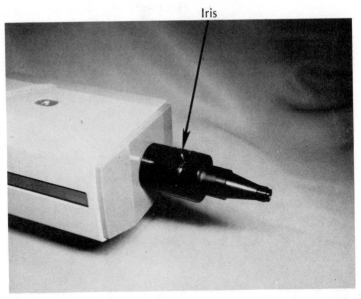

Straight

Iris

Right Angle

Figure 16.18. Right angle and auto iris right angle lenses

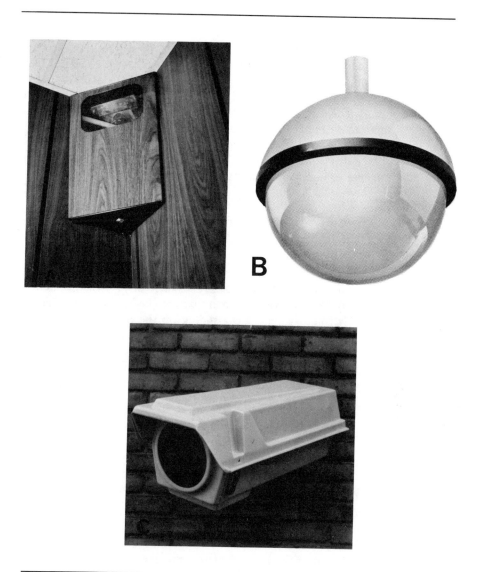

Figure 16.19. Examples of attractive unobtrusive housings

(4 lbs.) and is constructed of tough, durable, weather-resistant plastic. The housing can withstand direct sunlight and precipitation for many years. The housing is vandal-proof, has a locked cover, and is attractive.

CAMERA POWER

Most cameras operate from 117 VAC or 24 VAC. If a 117-VAC outlet is available at the camera location, it should be used. If power is to be run from a remote location, especially for the camera, a step-down transformer has an advantage; anyone can install it and an electrician is not required. The transformer chosen depends on the power requirements of the camera. The wattage or volt-amp (VA) rating on the transformer should be equal to or higher than the camera power rating. Today some cameras that require only a coaxial cable for operation are available. The coaxial cable (RG 59 or RG 11) transmits both the camera power *and* video signal.

MULTIPLE CAMERA CCTV SYSTEMS

Once the single camera lens system has been mastered, most of the design creating a multiple camera system has been accomplished. A question remains, however — will an individual monitor be sufficient to display each camera or will the picture from each individual camera be switched into a single display monitor via an electronic switcher? Depending on the preference of the individual customer, the budget for the project, and the number of people entering and leaving each of the camera areas, one or the other system will be chosen. If the scene activity, that is, the number of people passing into or out of an area, is relatively high, all cameras should be displayed on separate monitors. For installations with infrequent activity, or casual surveillance, an electronic switcher should be used.

Wide FOV CCTV

There are generally four techniques for solving the wide FOV CCTV application: (1) a camera on a pan/tilt platform with a fixed focus or zoom lens, (2) multiple cameras to split the wide FOV into narrower FOVs, (3) a camera with a fixed, wide FOV lens, and (4) a camera on a pan/tilt with two lenses with a wide FOV and a narrow FOV lens. The last technique (4) provides maximum surveillance of the area.

The pan/tilt system permits the television camera to rotate in a horizontal and vertical plane, thereby permitting the camera to look at scenes substantially outside the FOV of the lens used. The fixed lens and camera systems (single or multiple cameras), on the other hand, look at the FOV only as determined by the lens F.L. and the camera tube diameter (see Tables 1 and 2).

Each of the four techniques has distinct advantages and disadvantages. The pan/tilt system has a primary advantage in that it can look at any part

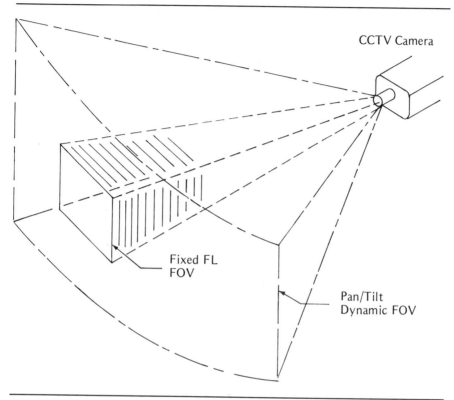

Figure 16.20. Static lens FOV vs pan/tilt dynamic FOV

of the scene by changing the pointing direction of the lens and camera. If a zoom lens (variable focal length and therefore a variable FOV) is used, it can provide excellent resolution when it is in the high magnification mode and good area coverage when it is in the low magnification mode. The main disadvantages of the pan/tilt installations are: (1) high initial and maintenance costs; (2) inherent optical dead zone, and (3) the need for operator time and dexterity to manipulate pan/tilt and zoom functions. Maintenance costs come from periodically replacing electric motors, gearing, limit switches, and so on. An additional maintenance item is the coaxial cable that bends and flexes each time the camera is moved, which therefore must be replaced periodically.

The inherent optical dead zone of the pan/tilt system originates because the system cannot be looking everywhere at the same time. When it is pointing in a particular direction, all areas outside the FOV of the lens *are not under surveillance,* and hence there is effectively no surveillance in those areas part of the time. Figure 16.20 illustrates this condition. The cross-hatched area is the instantaneous FOV of the camera (fixed focus lens FOV shown). The outer

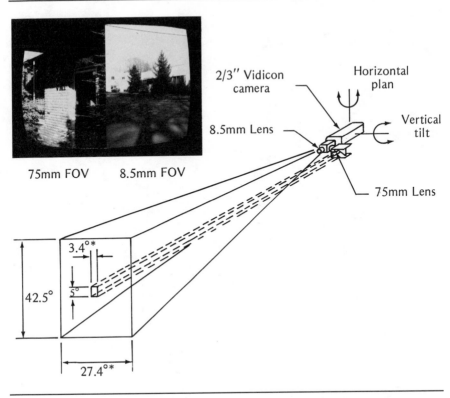

2/3" Vidicon camera

Horizontal plan

8.5mm Lens

Vertical tilt

75mm Lens

75mm FOV   8.5mm FOV

3.4°*

42.5°

5°

27.4°*

Figure 16.21. Bifocal split image lens FOV

lines show the total pan/tilt dynamic FOV and lens FOV, and represents the total angular coverage that the pan/tilt camera system can view. At any given time, most of the area for which surveillance is desired is not being displayed on the television monitor. To overcome this shortcoming, if someone hiding from the camera is out of the instantaneous FOV of the CCTV, the camera and pan/tilt mechanism is sometimes hidden, so that this person does not know where the camera is pointing at any particular instant.

The primary advantages of the fixed CCTV camera installation over the pan/tilt type are: (1) low initial installation costs, (2) low maintenance costs, and (3) lack of an optical dead zone. The primary disadvantage is that only a small FOV can be viewed with good resolution, that is, the wider the FOV the smaller the amount of detail that can be seen.

The bifocal optical image-splitting lens (Figure 16.21) offers a unique solution to the problem of displaying a wide FOV and narrow FOV (telephoto) scene *simultaneously* on one monitor. It is particularly advantageous when expensive low light level cameras (Newvicon, Silicon, SIT, ISIT) are used since only *one* camera is used (Figure 16.21).

For instance if an 8.5 mm lens and 75 mm lens are used with the optical image splitter shown, FOVs of 27.4 x 42.5 degrees and 3.4 x 5 degrees, respectively, would be viewed (see Figure 24). At a distance of 50 ft., this represents views of 40.8 ft. x 58.5 ft. and 4.2 ft. x 6.3 ft., respectively. If the FOV of the telephoto lens is centered on that of the wide FOV lens, a very effective CCTV surveillance system results. When the system operates with pan and tilt, wide area coverage is always displayed *simultaneously* with a closeup view of the area of interest. A pan and tilt system with or without a zoom lens cannot accomplish this. To obtain maximum flexibility and wide angle area coverage, a bifocal lens, with a zoom lens and a narrow angle (75 mm to 200 mm F.L.) lens, is an excellent solution. The zoom lens permits a variable FOV coverage from wide angle (40 degrees) to medium coverage (4 degrees).

This combination is particularly good for outdoor parking lot and fence line (perimeter) and indoor Hallway surveillance applications. In the fence line application, if the pan/tilt is left in normal pointing combination, so that the telephoto FOV is looking at a perimeter gate or along the fence line, a video motion sensor programmed to respond only to the narrow FOV scene can be used to activate an alarm, guard cue, or VCR. Simultaneously, the wide FOV zoom lens scene assures no dead zone in the scene. Similar requirements can be met for a hallway application.

Another technique for hallway surveillance utilizes the tri-split lens. The CCTV requirement is to view down as many hallways as possible to show who is in the hallway, where they are going, and what they are doing. Figure 16.22 illustrates the problem of monitoring the activity at an elevator lobby on one level of a museum.

An important feature of fixed camera systems is that the guard viewing the monitor sees a stationary picture (no pan/tilt movement) in the hallway or elevator. This would not be acceptable since the guard would have to view too many monitors if each hallway were to be monitored by a separate camera. Even if they were switched the guard still would be overburdened and ineffective. An improvement would be to connect the three cameras to two electronic splitters and display the three cameras on one monitor.

The most cost-effective solution is to use one camera and tri-split lens (Figure 17) and display the three scenes on one monitor. The lower cost of the tri-focal lens solution is emphasized when the cost of one low light level camera is compared to the cost of three cameras required in the other solution. The complete tri-split system can be housed in either a dome-shaped or rectangular-type enclosure with a clear or tinted one-way mirrored surface.

110 DEGREES FOV CCTV

A system specifically designed to provide 100-percent surveillance of a room, elevator, loading dock, lobby, small room, and so on, is shown in Fig-

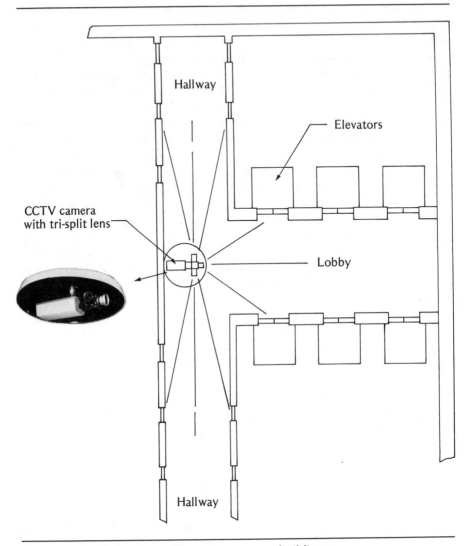

Hallway

Elevators

CCTV camera
with tri-split lens

Lobby

Hallway

Figure 16.22. Hallway surveillance in museum buildings

ure 16.23. By using a very wide angle lens, a horizontal FOV of approximately 95 degrees is obtained. The lens has an iris diaphragm for light level
control and uses a ⅔-inch vidicon (see Tables 1 and 2 for FOV coverage).
The key feature of this system is an attractive customized unobtrusive housing
— only 10½ inches high — which makes it suitable for mounting in the ceiling
corner of any front lobby — because the monitor sees a stationary picture (no
pan/tilt movement). He can thereby detect moving objects with high probabil-

Figure 16.23.   Wide angle vandalproof elevator CCTV system and monitor picture

ity and accuracy. The system is ideal for elevators since it is compact and it views the entire elevator; thus no one can hide in the elevator. A monitor in the lobby or security room permits the elevator patron and/or security guard to view who is in the elevator. In an elevator installation, the coaxial cable is laced in with the existing elevator cab power and signal cable.

COVERT CCTV SYSTEMS

The use of small hidden cameras and lenses has proven very effective for identifying criminals. Camouflaged cameras in simulated decorations, lamp domes, and so forth, have also been effective in deterring crime.

Although there are many applications for overt television systems with the lens and camera in full view, museum applications often require a covert or hidden system. This section discusses unique pinhole cameras and lenses required for successful covert CCTV installations. The use of lenses in which the front lens elements are small in diameter, making it possible for the lens and camera to view the scene through a small hole, are analyzed. Most of these lenses have moderate fields of view (FOV) — from 40 to 60 degrees (9 to 11 mm focal length) — in order to cover a large scene area but still provide identification of persons and recognize activities and actions. Special pinhole lens variations, including right angle, auto-iris versions, and others with unique features, are discussed.

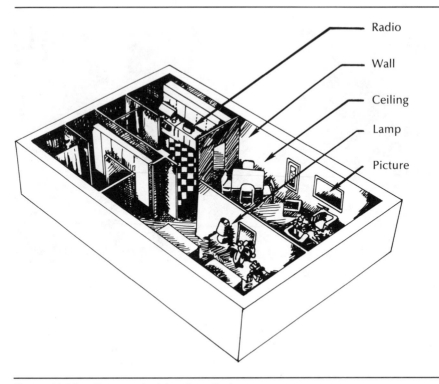

Radio

Wall

Ceiling

Lamp

Picture

Figure 16.24. Covert television installations

DEFINING THE PROBLEM

Figure 16.24 shows a room for which television surveillance is to be provided. A number of possible lens/camera locations are shown: (a) ceiling, (b) wall, (c) fixture, (d) furniture, or (e) other articles normally used in a room. Depending on the location of the activity in the room, the television system can be installed in one or more locations. Lens concealment is accomplished by viewing through a small hole.

OPTICAL CONSIDERATIONS

Covert CCTV systems offer unique optical problems. Since the diameter of the front lens viewing the scene must by necessity be small, only a small amount of reflected light from the scene reaches the television vidicon. As a consequence, lenses generally referred to as pinhole lenses are designed to

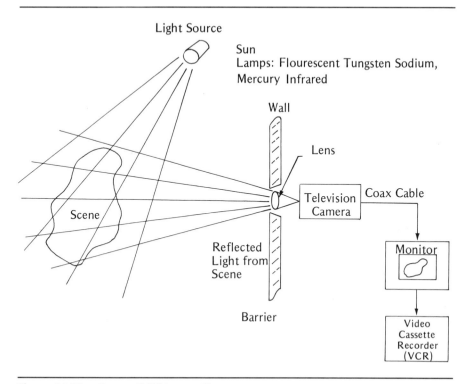

Figure 16.25. Covert CCTV surveillance system

be optically fast and collect and transmit as much light as possible from the scene to the television vidicon tube.

There are many misconceptions regarding the factors determining a good pinhole camera or lens system for covert applications. Since the lens and camera for these systems and the installation are a significant capital investment, an understanding of what constitutes a good system is important.

Figure 16.25 shows the general covert, visual surveillance problem. The requirement is to receive reflected light from an illuminated scene and transmit the light to the camera vidicon tube and then transmit the video signal to a video monitor and/or VCR. Most covert lenses are designed for ⅔-inch vidicon TV cameras. Indoor light sources are usually either fluorescent or tungsten lamps. Outdoor light sources are sunlight during the daytime, and mercury, tungsten, sodium, or Xenon lights at night.

There is a basic difference between the covert pinhole camera installation and the normal overt camera installation. In the covert system, the lens and camera are located behind a small hole in an opaque barrier (wall, ceiling, etc.). In the overt system they are located in front of the barrier in full view.

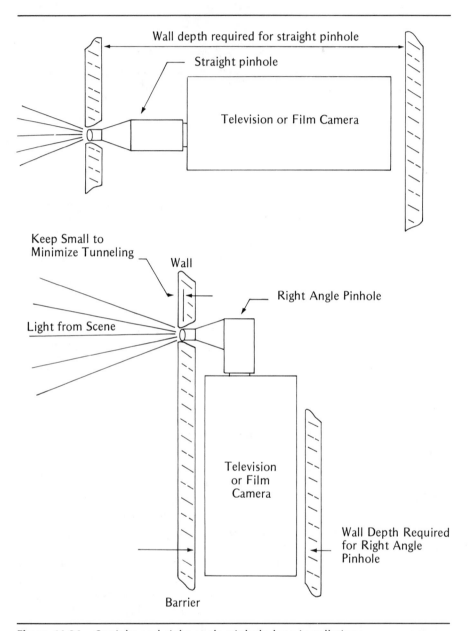

Wall depth required for straight pinhole

Straight pinhole

Television or Film Camera

Keep Small to
Minimize Tunneling

Wall

Right Angle Pinhole

Light from Scene

Television
or Film
Camera

Wall Depth Required
for Right Angle
Pinhole

Barrier

Figure 16.26. Straight and right angle pinhole lens installations

Figure 16.26 shows two basic configurations of the pinhole lens and camera located behind a barrier. When space permits, the straight type of installation is used. In confined or restricted installations in which there is a limited depth

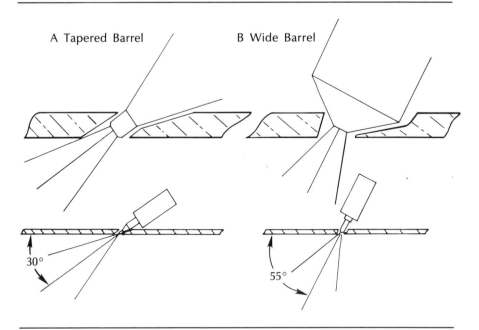

Figure 16.27. Pinhole lens pointing angle. Tapered vs wide barrel

available behind the barrier, a right angle pinhole camera installation is used. In both installations, however, it is imperative to locate the front lens element of the pinhole lens as close to the front surface of the barrier as possible in order to avoid "tunneling" of the light to the lens. When the front element of the lens is close to the front barrier, the full lens field of view (FOV), as defined later, is obtained. When the front lens element of the pinhole lens is back from the front of the barrier, the lens is in effect viewing through a "tunnel"; therefore, the view as imaged on the camera has a narrower FOV. This is seen as a porthole-like (vignetted) picture on the screen. An important installation problem often initially overlooked is the lens pointing angle required to see the desired FOV (see Figure 16.27a). Many applications require the lens axis to point at a small angle as shown in Figure 16.27a. Not all lenses can be mounted at a small angle to the ceiling because of the particular lens barrel shape as shown in Figure 16.27b. Lenses with a large barrel diameter at the front cannot be mounted at the shallow angles required. Their large barrel would require a large hole that would expose the lens.

Figure 16.28 shows the pinhole lens geometry. The pinhole lens parameters of interest are: (1) optical speed (f/number), (2) field of view (FOV), (3) focal length (F.L.), (4) entrance diameter (d), and (5) image size. The best theoretical f/number (f/#) a lens can have is equal to the focal length divided by the entrance diameter (d) of the lens:

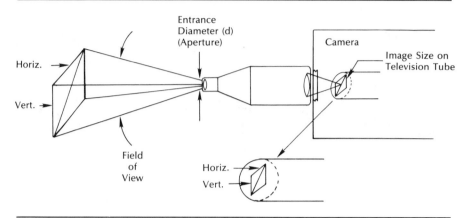

Figure 16.28. Pinhole lens design

$$f/\# \; = \; \frac{\text{Focal Length}}{\text{Diameter}} \; = \; \frac{\text{F.L.}}{d}$$

In practice the f/# obtained is worse than this because of various lens losses caused by nonperfect lens transmission (reflection and absorption) and lens-imaging properties. For a pinhole lens, the light getting through the lens to the television is limited primarily by the diameter of the front lens or mechanical opening. Therefore the larger the entrance diameter, the more light gets through to the television vidicon. More light means better picture quality, assuming all other conditions remain the same. The amount of light passing through a lens system is a strong function of the lens f/#. This means that if the lens diameter is increased a small amount, the light passing through the lens increases a large amount. Actually it increases as the square of the lens diameter increases. If the lens diameter is doubled (factor of two), the light getting through is quadrupled (factor of four). This relationship is crudely analogous to water flowing in a pipe, that is, if the diameter of the pipe is doubled, four times as much water flows through it.

HIGH LIGHT POWER PINHOLE CAMERA

A unique pinhole camera (Figure 16.29) is now in use; it combines a very fast pinhole lens — f/1.8 — with a new television camera design. Unlike all other covert pinhole lens and camera combinations, this system integrates the fastest pinhole lens into the camera. The lens has a 11.5 mm F.L. and a front barrel diameter of ⅜ inch (9.5 mm) and a taper that makes it easy to mount behind a barrier (see Figures 16.26 and 16.27). A means of focusing the lens while it

Figure 16.29. Pinhole camera systems. Top. Complete camera power: 120 VAC (non vidiplex). Bottom. Camera with remote power unit (vidiplex).

is installed is located at the rear of the camera. Table 16.5 summarizes the characteristics of the pinhole camera and commercially available pinhole lenses. In order to compare different lenses with respect to their ability to transmit light to the camera tube, a light power factor is defined with an f/4.0 lens as a base or reference. Note the difference in light passing through the pinhole camera as compared to the pinhole lenses. The f/1.8 pinhole camera transmits five (5) times as much light as an f/4 pinhole lens.

MANUAL IRIS PINHOLE LENSES

There are several covert lenses commercially available for CCTV applications (Table 5). Most of these lenses are designed for a ⅔-inch vidicon format since

System type	Lens focal length	Lens diameter	Lens f/#	Light* power	Camera FOV horiz X vert	Configuration
Pinhole Camera	11.5mm	.25 inch (6mm)	1.8	5	47 x 38	Straight
	11.5mm	.25 inch (6mm)	1.8	5	47 x 38	Right angle
Manual Iris	9mm	.10 inch (2.3)	4.0	1	58 x 48	Straight
	9mm	.125 inch (3.2)	4.0	1	67 x 53	Straight
Pinhole Lenses	9mm	.100 inch (2.5)	4.0+	0.9	67 x 53	Right angle
	11.5mm	.25 inch (6mm)	2.5	2.6	47 x 38	Straight
	11.5mm	.25 inch (6mm)	2.8	2.1	47 x 38	Right angle
Auto Iris Pinhole Lenses	11.5mm	.25 inch (6mm)	2.5	2.6	47 x 38	Straight
	11.5mm	.25 inch (6mm)	4.0	1	47 x 38	Right angle

*Light Power is a figure of merit for the lens system based on the f/4 pinhole lens having a lens efficiency of 1 (one). The *higher* the number the better the system. Example:

$$\text{Light Power for Pinhole Camera} = \frac{(4.0)^2}{(1.8)^2} = 5$$

Table 16.5.   Pinhole camera lens characteristics

this size camera is small and in widespread use, and the best image detail is not usually required. Some lenses have a very small entrance aperture, i.e., .10 inch (2.5 mm), and are therefore optically slow by design. A lens with a focal length of 9 mm (50-degree vertical by 60-degree horizontal FOV) on a ⅔-inch vidicon with a 2.5 mm aperture has at best a theoretical f/# of:

$$f/\# = \frac{9 \text{ mm}}{2.5 \text{ mm}} = 3.6$$

Other lens losses result in an f/# of approximately f/4.0. Another covert lens available has a focal length of 11.5 mm with an aperture of 6 mm resulting in a theoretical f/number of:

$$f/\# = \frac{11.5 \text{ mm}}{6 \text{ mm}} = 1.9$$

Other lens losses result in an f/# of approximately f/2.5. The advantage of the 6 mm aperture lens is that it can be used in applications where a larger hole, i.e., 6 mm diameter, adequately conceals the lens and there is insufficient light available for the .10 hole. To emphasize, the most important characteristics of the pinhole lens are (1) fast optical speed, meaning how low is the f/# (the lower the better), and (2) ease of installation and use. Table 5 summarizes the characteristics of these manual iris lenses.

Figure 16.25 illustrates the usual covert lens/camera installation problems. A small hole on the scene side of the barrier and some area cut out of the barrier behind it to permit the front lens element to be located close to the front of the barrier surface are shown. A lens having a small front diameter mechanical configuration (shown) is simple to install. Figure 16.27 illustrates the problem of installing the two types of pinhole lenses available. The tapered barrel Type A can be mounted at a smaller angle to the barrier than the wide barrel Type B. This feature allows pointing the Type A lens over a larger part of a room than the Type B lens. Depending on the space available behind the barrier, the camera must be mounted approximately parallel or perpendicular to the barrier. In general, a straight pinhole lens performs better than a right angle version (because it has better light throughput) and should be used whenever possible.

Figure 16.30 shows examples of straight and right angle pinhole lenses with 9 and 11.5 mm focal lengths and optical speeds from f/2.5 to f/4.0. The lenses are designed for C mount, ⅔-inch vidicon cameras and have manual iris diaphragms for initial level adjustments to the camera. The lenses invert the picture; therefore the camera or the vertical deflection coils must be inverted to get a normal picture. Although most pinhole lenses available are fixed focus, the 11.5 mm F.L. lenses are available with an adjustable focus.

Figure 16.30. Typical straight and right angle pinhole lenses. Left, tapered barrel. Right, wide barrel

AUTO-IRIS PINHOLE LENSES

When the covert surveillance application is in a low light level area (which often is the case) or when some lights in a well-lighted area are turned off, a more sensitive camera than the standard vidicon camera is required. This

Figure 16.31. Auto iris pinhole lenses. Top, straight. Bottom, right angle.

can take the form of a Newvicon* or silicon target camera. These camera types require an automatic iris diaphragm to control the light reaching the camera tube. Figure 16.31 shows straight and right angle auto-iris pinhole lenses with optical speeds of f/2.5 and f/4, respectively. The video signal from the camera controls the auto-iris mechanism in a way similar to other auto-iris lenses, and adjusts the light level to the camera over a 300,000 : 1 dynamic range. Table 5 summarizes the characteristics of these lenses.

RIGID FIBER OPTIC PINHOLE LENSES

All of the previous lenses find wide application when the barrier is thin, for then the lens and camera can be mounted directly behind the opening in the

* Trademark of Matsushita Electric Co., Inc.

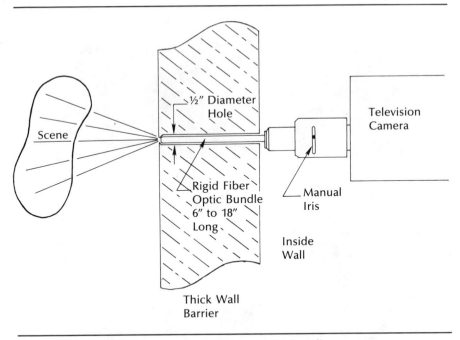

Figure 16.32. Rigid fiber optic installations in thick walls

barrier. What if the barrier is a thick concrete wall: 6, 8, or 12 inches thick? By combining lenses with coherent fiber optic bundles, a long, small diameter optical system is produced that requires only a ½-inch diameter hole to be drilled to position the front lens near the front side of the barrier. A smaller aperture hole (dependent on light) is drilled completely through the wall and the camera on the opposite side is protected. Figure 16.32 shows this problem and its solution. This type of lens–camera system solves many automatic teller machine (ATM) security problems encountered by banks.

Figure 16.33 shows a photograph of a rigid fiber optic lens. The 7/16-inch diameter fiber optic lens extension can be up to 18 inches in length. The optical speed of this lens is approximately f/4, slower than "all lens" type lenses but adequate for many applications. A minor disadvantage of all fiber optic systems is that the picture obtained is not as "clean" as that obtained with an "all lens" pinhole lens. There are some cosmetic imperfections that look like dust spots, as well as a slight geometrical pattern caused by fiber stacking. For most surveillance applications these imperfections do not result in any loss of intelligence in the picture.

As with the standard pinhole lenses, the rigid fiber optic pinhole lenses are available with adjustable focus, manual or automatic iris diaphragms, and have a ⅔-inch image format.

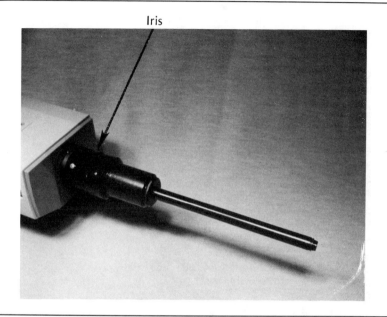

Iris

Figure 16.33. Rigid fiber optic pinhole lens

FLEXIBLE FIBER OPTIC PINHOLE LENSES

When utmost flexibility is required between the front objective lens (pinhole or otherwise) and the camera, a flexible fiber optic bundle is used. Figure 16.34 shows a flexible C mount fiber optic bundle 36 inches long. The front can be a pinhole lens or any other kind of lens. At the rear of the bundle, a relay lens re-images the scene onto the ⅔-inch format television or film camera. The 36-inch length can be twisted through more than 360 degrees (Figure 16.34) with no image degradation. This lens will show some cosmetic imperfections as described previously. Table 16.6 summarizes the specifications for several rigid and flexible fiber optic systems.

MOTION AND INTRUSION DETECTORS

The output of a television camera when provided with appropriate processing electronics can make the camera operate as an alarm sensor. The processing electronics (motion detector) memorizes the instantaneous television picture, and then if the light level in the television picture changes by a prescribed amount somewhere in the scene, an alarm signal is generated to alert a guard

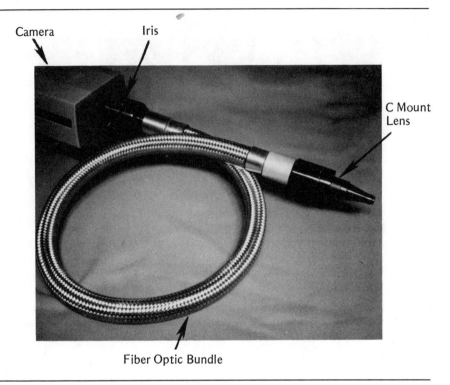

Camera　　**Iris**

C Mount Lens

Fiber Optic Bundle

Figure 16.34. Flexible fiber optic pinhole lens system

System Type	Lens focal length	Lens diameter	Lens F/#	Light* power	Camera FOV horizontal x vertical	Configuration
Manual	11.5 mm	.25 inch	4	1	47 x 38	Fiber Length 6″
Iris	11.5 mm	.25 inch	4	1	47 x 38	Fiber Length 8″
Rigid Fiber	11.5 mm	.25 inch	4	1	47 x 38	Fiber Length 12″
Auto	11.5 mm	.25 inch	4	1	47 x 38	Fiber Length 6″
Iris	11.5 mm	.25 inch	4	1	47 x 38	Fiber Length 8″
Rigid	11.5 mm	.25 inch	4	1	47 x 38	Fiber Length 12″

*Light Power is a figure of merit for the system based on the f/4 pinhole lens having an efficiency of 1 (one). The higher the number, the better the lens.

Table 16.6. Fiber Optic Pinhole Lens Specifications

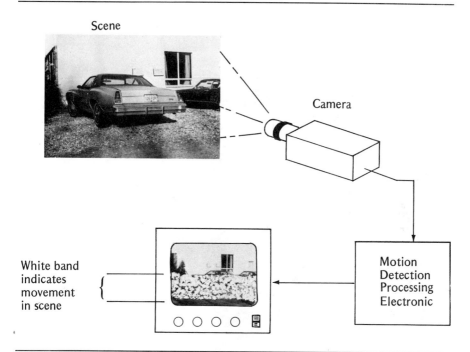

Figure 16.35. CCTV motion detection system

or record the video scene on a VCR. Although two general types of processing electronics have been used, analog processing and digital processing, the digital form provides more capability and reliability. The digital processor analyses the picture and presents information such as: 1) location in the picture where a motion or intrusion has occured, 2) a record of the intrusion through the use of the VCR, 3) various audible and visible alarm signals to the operator. Figure 16.35 shows the block diagram for the motion detection system and illustrates in principle the type of information which can be obtained.

A second type of intrusion motion detection system is described below. Combining a low-power laser with a CCTV system provides an effective imaging intrusion detection system. Figure 16.36 shows the system with a laser–illuminating source producing a fan shaped continuous sheet of light, a reflector, and a television receiver. In operation, the fan shaped beam is located at a perimeter or in front of the wall to be protected. The CCTV monitor presents the scene and a bright–line image of the laser–beam sheet of light. If an object or someone breaks any part of the beam, the television and detection electronics produce an alarm output.

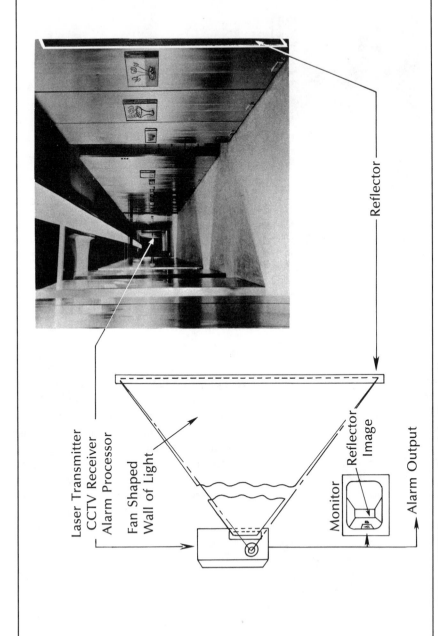

Figure 16.36. CCTV laser intrusion detection system

CCTV ACCESS CONTROL SYSTEM

The photo ID card has received widespread use, and provides a means for security personnel to admit or deny access to public, private, and government premises. CCTV provides two important features: 1) positive visual identification and 2) the guard can view (and/or a VCR can record) the person desiring access and his photo ID card simultaneously in real time. Since one guard can physically control only one access location at a time, a system permitting monitoring of more than one location by one guard is cost effective. The photo ID-CCTV access control system lets the security guard view more than one access location and therefore control many entrances. If an installation has only one access location, a CCTV system is still cost effective since it allows the security officer to perform other functions at the control console during slow periods of activity.

Several CCTV access control applications are listed below:

- Gates, turnstiles, or doors at outdoor perimeter access points.
- Main doors in lobbies, wide doors, or rear doors in buildings.
- Limited access areas inside a building (computer rooms, classified file rooms).
- Limited access areas such as outdoor storage depots or distribution facilities.

Figure 16.37 shows all of the parts of the television access control system required in the lobby and the remote guard location. For a CCTV access control system the television ID camera system is mounted in the lobby on the wall next to the access door. This way the face of the person desiring access may be viewed as well as the photograph of the person's face on a photo ID card. These two scenes (photo ID and person) are displayed on one television monitor simultaneously, side by side at the remote guard location.

A wide FOV camera system (See Figure 16.23) is mounted in a ceiling corner and views the entire lobby area to determine: 1) how many people are in the area, 2) that only one person after identification gains access, and 3) whether the person is carrying unauthorized packages.

In operation, the person desiring access enters the lobby. The guard views the person via the wide FOV camera picture. Alternatively, if the guard has other duties, the person presses an intercom or annunciator call button. The guard then switches to the access control video picture and compares the person's face to the photo ID card face. If the guard confirms a match, he or she presses the door release switch on the console releasing the access door strike. An open door status indicator light indicates an open door to the guard. After the person enters the secured area, a closed door indicator light indicates a secured mode again. The guard switches the video back to the wide FOV camera, thus completing the cycle. It is obvious that this system can be

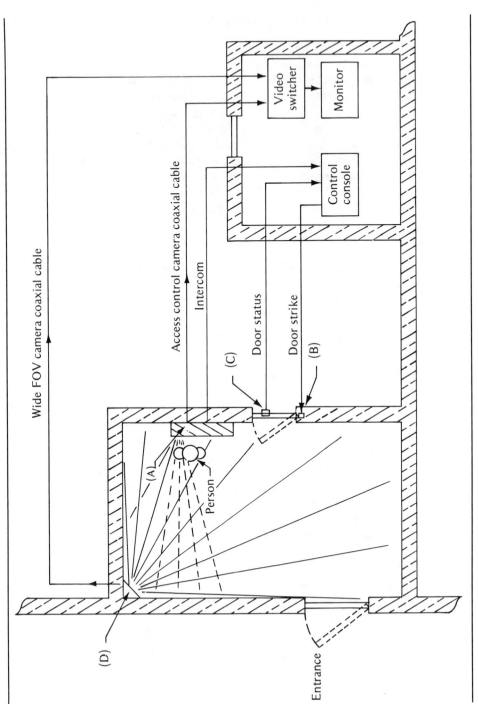

Figure 16.37. CCTV access control system

expanded to several access points, each with its own camera, so that one guard can monitor and control several access points. Since 100 percent television monitoring of the lobby is required to prevent tailgating, the wide FOV camera is needed.

The wall mounted television access control system contains a prealigned television camera, image splitting optics (see Figure 16.38), and lenses which *simultaneously* view the person desiring access and the photo ID card presented. It also contains a two-way intercom and annunciator switch.

Figure 16.38 shows the CCTV access to control guard console containing the television monitor and control functions just described. The video signal from the wide FOV system and the access control system in the lobby is alternately displayed via the built-in two position switcher.

Higher security can be achieved by combining the photo ID-CCTV access control system with an electronic ID card code reader. The electronic card reader (magnetic, capacitance, optical, etc.) is installed into the CCTV access control system so that the card is "read" while the photo on the card and the person's face is *simultaneously* displayed for the guard at the CCTV monitor. This dual system insures that a lost or stolen coded card is not used by the wrong person.

Many museum installations utilize the color photo ID badge system for access control into buildings as well as controlling passage of personnel within the building. A color photo ID card system utilizing the split image optics described in Figure 16.38 and a 1–inch color camera system is available. Utilizing the split image optics, only one television camera is required rather than two to simultaneously display on the color monitor the photo ID and photograph and the person's face. As with other CCTV systems, this color picture can be recorded on a VCR for later retrieval.

Another unique photo ID card access control system available uses a photo ID card having a photograph of an authorized card holder which is visible under ordinary illumination but also contains a second identical photograph of the user hidden from visibility (buried) inside the card. When the card is illuminated and viewed by a special lighting system and CCTV, both the visible and hidden photographs are clearly displayed on the television monitor. The availability of the visible and hidden photograph permit the guard to determine whether the visible photograph is authentic or counterfeit. Other information on the ID card includes: signature, personal printed data, and ID code number. The system combines high probability of identification with low probability of ID card counterfeiting.

CHECK LIST AND SUMMARY

The full potential of CCTV is only beginning to be utilized by the security industry. CCTV equipment has been highly developed technically and reliable

Figure 16.38. Top: Video access control camera and Bottom: console equipment

for many years. There are many areas in which CCTV systems can effect tremendous cost savings via reduction in the number of personnel required, and/or in significantly improved deployment of existing personnel.

CCTV should be a *part* of an integrated museum security system which includes surveillance, intrusion detection, and access control. The following list summarizes some of the questions which should be asked when designing a CCTV security system.

- Where should the camera be located so that the entire scene to be viewed is "seen" by the television camera?
- In what direction should the camera be pointed so that the sun, bright lights, or other variable lighting, have minimum effect on picture quality?
- Should the camera have a ⅔ inch or 1 inch diameter vidicon tube?
- What Field of View should the camera cover?
- Should a fixed focus (constant FOV) or zoom lens (variable FOV) be used and what focal length is best?
- Is there sufficient lighting available?
- Is daytime and/or nighttime operation required?
- Should the camera be mounted with brackets, recessed in the walls or ceiling (covert) or installed in a housing?
- Is a covert (hidden) camera and lens required?
- Should the camera voltage be 117 VAC, 24 VAC, or 12 VDC?
- Should it be powered via the coaxial cable?
- What is the distance between the camera and the monitor?
- What coaxial cable type should be used: RG 59, RG 11?
- Should wireless microwave or other wireless transmission be considered?
- What monitor screen size should be used?
- How should the monitor be connected and terminated?
- Is the monitor to be desk top or rack mounted?
- Should the video recorder use reel to reel or tape cassette?
- What is the maximum recording time on the reel or cassette?
- Is time-lapse mode necessary for extending record time?

Appendix 16.1

Glossary of CCTV Terms and References

GLOSSARY

Alarming sequential switcher. An automatic switcher which is activated by a variety of sensing devices including magnetic door or window locks and switches, pressure sensitive floor mats, window stripping, motion sensors. Once activated, the switcher connects the camera in the included area onto the monitor or to the recorder.

AM (amplitude modulation). The system of transmission based on varying the amplitude of the power output while the frequency remains the same.

AGC (automatic gain control). A circuit for automatically controlling amplifier gain in order to maintain a constant output voltage with a varying input voltage.

ALC (automatic light control). An electro-optical system which maintains near constant output levels when input light levels change over wide ranges. It is usually comprised of an optical attenuator (iris or filter) and an electrical servo system.

Aperture stop. An optical opening or hole which defines or limits the amount of light passing through a lens system. It takes the form of the front lens diameter in a pinhole lens, an iris diaphrahm, neutral density filter, spot filter.

Automatic iris. This device optically (by filters and mechanical iris) adjusts automatically to light level changes via the video signal from the television camera. Typical compensation ranges are 300,000 to 1. They are used on Newvicon, Silicon, SIT and ISIT cameras.

Balanced cable. Balanced cables consist of a pair of inner conductors, often twisted as in audio cable, with each insulated from the other having identical diameters. These are surrounded by additional insulation, a coaxial-type shield, and an outer insulative-protective coating. They offer many advantages for long cable runs, primarily in eliminating grounding or "hum" problems in long runs. The cables have an impedance of 124 ohms.

Bandpass. A specific range of frequencies that will be passed through a device.

Examples: An audio system will pass 20 Hz to 20 KHz. A video system will pass 30 Hz to 6 MHz.

Beta format. A ½-inch video cassette format found on all Sony VCR equipment. It is not compatible with VHS or other formats.

Bi-focal lens. A lens system having two different focal length lenses which image the same or two different scenes onto a single television camera. The two scenes appear as a split image on the monitor.

Bridging sequential switcher. A sequential switcher with separate outputs for two monitors, one for programmed sequence and the second for extended display of a single area.

Camera tube. An electron tube that converts an optical image into an electrical current by a scanning process. Also called a pickup tube and a television camera tube.

Camera format. Standard C mount television cameras are made with nominal ⅔-inch and 1-inch vidicon formats. The actual target area used (scanned) on the tubes are 8.8mm horizontal x 6.6mm vertical x 11mm diagonal for the ⅔-inch, and 12.8mm horizontal x 9.6mm vertical by 16mm diagonal for the 1 inch.

Cathode ray tube (CRT). The video display tube used in video monitors and receivers, radar displays and video computer terminals.

Charged coupled device (CCD). A solid state silicon imaging sensor in which the television scanning function is accomplished by moving the electrical video picture signal (charge) along paths on the silicon chip. It has no electron beam scanning like the vidicon tube and is therefore very small. It has lower resolution than a vidicon, and lower sensitivity than a standard silicon vidicon.

Charge injection device (CID). A solid state silicon imaging sensor similar to the CCD sensor, manufactured by General Electric Company. Readout of the signal is different from the CCD.

Charge transfer device (CTD). The generic name for CCD, CID and similar devices.

CCTV (closed circuit television). A distribution system which limits reception of an image to those receivers or monitors which are directly connected to the origination point by coaxial cable or microwave link.

Close-up lens. A low power accessory lens which permits focusing on objects closer to the lens than it has been designed for.

C mount. An industry standard for lens mounting. Has a one-inch diameter threaded barrel with 32 threads per inch. The focused image is located .69 inches behind the C mount mounting surface.

Coaxial cable. See *Balanced, Unbalanced Cables.* A type of cable capable of passing a wide range of frequencies with very low signal loss. It usually consists of a stranded metallic shield with a single wire accurately placed along the center of the shield and isolated from the shield with an insulator. Almost all CCTV coax cables have a 75 ohm impedance.

Composite video. The combined video picture signal, including vertical and horizontal blanking and synchronizing signals, with a one-volt amplitude.

CPS. Cycles per Second. See *Hertz.*

Depth of field. Depth of field of a lens is the area along the line of sight in which objects are in reasonable focus. Depth of field increases with smaller lens apertures (higher f/stop numbers), shorter focal lengths and greater distances from the lens.

Diopter. A term describing the power of a lens. It is the reciprocal of the focal length in meters. For example, a lens with a focal length of 25 cm has a power of 4 diopters.

Electronic focus. An electrical adjustment available on most television cameras, monitors and receivers for sharpening the picture image.

Electronic splitter (combiner). An electronic module which takes the video signals from two (or more) cameras and combines them so that a part of each appears on the final monitor picture. The part of each camera picture used is usually chosen via front panel controls.

Fiber optic bundle. This optical device is an assembly of many thousands of hair-like fibers, coherently assembled so that an image is transferred from one end of the bundle to the other.

Field of view (FOV). The field of view is the width and height of a scene to be monitored and is determined by the lens focal length, the lens-to-subject distance, and the camera format size.

F number (f/#). The speed of a lens is determined by the amount of light it transmits. This is the relationship between lens opening (controlled by the iris) and the focal length, and is expressed as a fraction referred to as f/number. Example: an f/4.0 lens is one having an aperture $\frac{1}{4}$ of the focal length. The markings (f/stops) on lenses are arbitrarily chosen ratios of aperture to focal length, such as f/1.0, 1.4, 2.0, 2.8, 4.0, 5.6, 8, 11, 16, 22. The smaller the f/stop number the faster the lens speed. The light passing through a lens varies as $(1/f\#)^2$. Therefore, an f/2 lens is four times as fast as an f/4 lens.

FM (frequency modulation). A system of signal transmission based on varying the frequency to transmit information rather than amplitude. FM has better signal to noise and noise immunity characteristics than AM.

Focal length (FL). The distance from the lens center to the focal plane (vidicon target) is the lens focal length and is expressed in inches or in millimeters.

Foot candle (FtCd). A unit of illuminance on a surface one square foot in area on which there is an incident light of one lumen. The illuminance of a surface placed one foot from a light source that has a luminous intensity of one candle.

Frame. The total picture area which is scanned while the picture signal is not blanked. One-thirtieth of a second (525 lines) in standard NTSC CCTV systems.

Front surface mirror. A mirror in which the reflective surface is on the front. All common glass mirrors have the reflective surface on the rear of the glass. A front surface mirror does not produce a "ghost" or secondary image as does a rear surface mirror. Since the reflecting coating on front surface mirrors is on the front, these mirrors should be handled carefully and not touched on the front surface.

HZ (hertz). Number of variations in a signal. Named after scientist Hertz. Formerly designated as cycles per second (CPS).

Homing sequential switcher. A switcher in which: 1) the outputs of multiple cameras can be switched sequentially onto a monitor: 2) one or more cameras can be bypassed (not displayed): or 3) any one of the cameras can be selected for continuous display on the monitor (homing). The lengths of time each camera output is displayed is independently selectable by the operator.

Horizontal resolution. The maximum number of individual picture elements that can be distinguished in a single horizontal scanning line. Also called horizontal definition. Five hundred lines typical with 4 MHz bandwidth.

Impedance. The input or output electrical characteristic of a system component (camera, etc.) that determines the type of transmission cable to be used. The cable used must have the same characteristic impedance as the component. Expressed in ohms. Video distribution has standardized on 75-ohm coaxial and 124-ohm balanced cable.

Interlace. The relationship between the two scanned fields in a television system. In a 2:1 interlaced system, the two fields are synchronized exactly. See *Random interlace* for unsynchronized fields.

Iris diaphragm. The iris is a device for mechanically closing the lens aperture, thus controlling the amount of light transmitted through a lens. In this way the iris adjusts the f/stop of a lens.

ISIT (intensified silicon intensified target). The ISIT tube is essentially the same as a SIT, the only difference being the use of double intensifier. This means that two intensifiers are stacked in series to yield a gain of about 2,000 over a standard vidicon. Typical sensitivity of an ISIT tube is about 1×10^{-6} foot candles of faceplate illumination.

Lens. A transparent optical component consisting of one or more pieces of glass with surfaces so curved (usually spherical) that they serve to converge or diverge the transmitted rays of an object, thus forming an image of that object onto a focal plane or target.

Lens speed. See *F/number.*

Line amplfier. A video amplifier used to amplify the camera video signal and compensate for the loss of signal level caused by the cable attenuation. It is put in series with the camera and monitor, at the camera or along the cable run.

Magnification. Magnification is usually expressed with a one-inch focal length lens as a reference. For example, a lens with a two-inch (50mm) focal length is said to have a magnification of 2.

Manual switcher. An electronic module which has multiple front panel switches to permit connecting one of a number of camera outputs into a single CCTV monitor or video tape recorder. The simplest is a passive switcher which contains no active (transistor or integrated circuits). The active switcher contains transistors and/or IC parts.

Monitor. A video display which shows the images detected and transmitted by a television camera or the face of a CRT.

Newvicon tube. Trade name of Matsushita. The Newvicon tube has a cadmium and zinc telluride target and provides sensitivity about 20 times that of a sulfide target. Spectral response is somewhat narrower than a silicon diode tube, 470 to 850 nm. The Newvicon operates very similar to the silicon tube, in that it uses a fixed target voltage and must use an auto iris lens system.

NTSC standard format. National Television Systems Committee. A committee that worked with the FCC in formulating standards for the present-day United States color television system. Uses 525 horizontal scan lines, 30 frames per second. Commonly used in the United States and Japan.

Optical splitter. An optical lens prism and/or mirror system which combines two or more scenes and images them onto one television or film camera. No electronics are used to combine the scenes.

PAL format. Phase Alternating Line. Uses 625 horizontal scan lines, 25 frames per second. Used in Western Europe, Australia, parts of Africa and the Middle East.

Pan-tilt mechanism. An electro-mechanical platform which has provisions to change the pointing direction of a camera and housing along a horizontal and vertical plane, from a remotely located controller.

Pinhole camera. An integral television or film camera having a small front lens to permit easy concealment. The lens and camera are a single unit.

Pinhole lens. A special lens designed to have a small (.1 inch to .25 inch) front lens diameter to permit its use in covert (hidden) camera applications.

Plumbicon. Trade name of N.V. Philips special tube. More sensitive than a

Vidicon. Used in some color video cameras and television X-ray inspection systems. Has very low picture lag particulary at low light levels.

Random interlace. The two scanned fields are not synchronized. See *Interlace.*

Raster. The geometrical pattern scanned on the camera or monitor tube by the electron beam. In standard CCTV, the first field is scanned from the top left corner of the tube to the lower right corner. The second field starts in the top left corner in between the first two lines of the first field.

Resolution. See *Horizontal* and *Vertical Resolution.*

SECAM. Sequential Color and Memory. 625 horizontal scan lines, 25 frames per second. Similar to PAL but differs greatly in method of producing color signals. SECAM is used in Saudi Arabia, USSR and France.

Signal to noise ratio. The ratio between the useful television picture signal and the scene, equipment, and interferring noise (snow). Mathematically: signal voltage / total noise voltage.

Silicon tube. The silicon target is made up of a mosaic of light sensitive silicon material, and depending on light source is between 10 and 50 times as sensitive as a sulfide vidicon. Other advantages are very broad spectral response 380-1100 nm, and high resistance to vidicon burn. The silicon tube does not permit automatic sensitivity control by means of signal electrode voltage regulation; therefore, an automatic iris must be used.

Slow scan television. An electronic video system which transmits single frames of television scenes from a standard CCTV camera via ordinary telephone or twisted pair lines. Each picture is stored in the form of picture elements — an array from 64 x 64 elements to 256 x 256 elements (or more). Every 8, 16, or 32 seconds, all the picture elements are transmitted and received, put into memory and displayed on a standard monitor. Since the signal bandwidth is from 300 Hz to 3000 Hz, the television pictures can be stored on an ordinary audio recorder. The picture is not realtime.

Switcher. See *Manual, Homing Sequential, Alarming, Looping.*

Target. The light sensitive material in the television camera pickup tube or silicon chip sensor. The standard vidicon tube target material is antimony trisulphide ($Sb_2 S_3$).

UHF (ultra high frequency). In television transmission, a term used to designate channels 14 through 83 (470 MHz to 890 MHz).

U-matic. A video cassette format offered by several manufacturers in which ¾-inch tape is used. Not compatible with VHS or Beta.

Unbalanced cable. The term "unbalanced" refers to the single-conductor shielded coaxial cable commonly used in television installations (RG-11/U and RG-59/U are of this type). It is manufactured in several impedances; however, for purposes of unbalanced video transmission, only the 75-ohm impedance is used. The shielding may be standard braid or double braid or solid aluminum. The dielectric used may be foam, solid plastic or even air.

VHF (very high frequency). In television transmission, a term used to designate channels 2 through 13 (54 MHz to 216 MHz).

VHS (Victor Home System). A ½-inch tape video cassette format in widespread use. Not compatible with Sony and U-Matic.

Vertical resolution. The number of horizontal lines that can be seen in the reproduced image of a television pattern. 350 lines maximum with the 525 NTSC system.

Video cassette recorder (VCR). A magnetic recorder which records live television pictures in black and white or color, with sound, onto a small cassette containing magnetic tape. Available systems can record continuously from ½ hour to 6 hours on one cassette. Time lapse recorders record up to 200 hours on one cassette. Standard formats are VHS, Beta, U-Matic, all incompatible.

Video tape recorder (VTR). A device which accepts signals from a video camera and a microphone and records images and sound on video magnetic tape in the form of a reel. It can then play back the recorded program for viewing on a television monitor or receiver.

Vidicon. Electron tube used to convert light to an electrical signal. The standard vidicon tube utilizes an antimony trisulfide ($Sb_2 S_3$) target and is the most widely used image tube for close circuit surveillance. The spectral response covers most of the visible light range and most closely approximates the human eye. A useful feature of the vidicon is the ability of the target voltage to be controlled to permit variation of sensitivity. The tube has a spectral sensitivity from 300 to 800 nm.

Vignetting. Vignetting refers to the loss of light through a lens system occurring at the edges due to lens design or obstruction. Lenses are usually designed to eliminate vignetting internal to the lens.

Zoom lens. A zoom lens is a variable focal length lens. The lens components in these assemblies are moved to change their relative physical positions, thereby varying the focal length and angle of view through a specified range of magnifications.

LIST OF REFERENCES

1. Electro-Optics Handbook, RCA, Harrison, NJ
2. Elevator CCTV Security — Elevator World March 1978, H. Kruegle
3. Which Video Switcher and Why, Security World, Part I, Feb, April 1978. S. Raia, R. Payne

4. Video Transmission Techniques, Dynair Inc., 1968

5. Secure Photo ID Card for Access Control Carnaham Conference On Crime Countermeasures 1978, H. Kruegle

6. Handbook of Loss Prevention and Crime Prevention, 1982, L. Fennelly Editor (CCTV Chapter H. Kruegle) Butterworth-Publisher.

7. The Basics of CCTV — Security Management, Jan. 1981, H. Kruegle

8. Innovative Banking: Security Problems and Solutions, Security World, Feb. 1977, H. Kruegle

9. Pinhole Camera Surveillance-Security Industry and Product News, April, May, June 1981, H. Kruegle

17. PHYSICAL SECURITY STANDARDS

Lawrence J. Fennelly
Louis A. Tyska

INTRODUCTION

The following standards are recommended as guidelines for establishing basic minimum security or for accessing your existing facility. Care should be taken when determining your individual security needs to integrate physical security standards as recommended, but only if your particular conditions require or permit them.

After physical and procedural security standards have been implemented, they do not become the be- all and end-all of security, thereby precluding any vulnerability to loss. These standards, however, are a measurement and a declaration by those of us responsible for the security of an area that these standards, when instituted, are the minimum security controls we will accept. "We," of course, refers to the management or supervisors responsible and accountable for the activities and assets at the facility secured.

This chapter was originally written for the U.S. Department of the Treasury. The booklet #72–56 provides recommendations for physical and procedural standards for security. These guidelines have been slightly modified to relate to the overall structure of this book.

PHYSICAL SECURITY STANDARDS

All museums should have a physical barrier against unauthorized access to the facility. Ideally, it should consist of a solid wall and apertures that can be securely closed and locked. In addition, fencing may be needed, as supplementary protection to prevent unauthorized persons and vehicles from entering on the property. An intrusion alarm system should also be considered for outside the facility, for example, on the grounds, rooftop, and other openings.

Buildings: General Standard

All buildings used to house art and associated support buildings should be constructed of materials that resist unlawful entry. The integrity of the structure must be maintained by periodic inspection and repair. Security protection should be provided for all doors and windows.

Recommended Specifications.

1. Equip all exterior doors and windows with double locks.
2. Protect all windows through which entry can be made from ground level by safety glass, wire mesh, or bars.
3. Similarly safeguard all glassed-in areas where documents are processed.
4. Construct all delivery and receiving doors of steel or other material that will prevent or deter unlawful entry and keep them closed and locked when not in use.
5. Where fencing is impractical or guards insufficient, equip the building with an intrusion detection or alarm system as required.
6. Inspections must insure that there are no avenues for surreptitious entry through floors, roofs, or adjacent buildings.

Fencing: General Standard

Where fencing is required, it should enclose an area around storage structures and support buildings. The fence line must be inspected regularly for integrity and any damage promptly repaired.

Recommended Specifications.

1. Install chain-link fencing with at least nine-gauge, 2-inch mesh at least 10 feet in height (not including a barbed-wire extension). If the level on which the fence is constructed is lower than the area outside of the

fence line, increase the height of the fence to provide a fence that is effectively 10-feet high at all points.

2. Top the fence with a 2-foot barbed-wire extension, consisting of three strands of barbed wire, properly spaced and at a 45-degree angle to the vertical.
3. Place fence posts on the inside of the fence and secure them in a cement foundation at least 2 feet deep.
4. Ensure that objects or persons cannot pass beneath the fencing by providing (a) cement aprons not less than 6 inches thick, (b) frame piping, or (c) U-shaped stakes driven approximately 2 feet into the ground.
5. Avoid any condition that compromises the fence line. Prohibit the placing of containers, vehicles, or any other item that may facilitate unlawful entry adjacent to the fence line.

Gates: General Standard

The number of gates in fences should be the minimum necessary for access. All fence gates should be at least as substantial as the fence. Gates through which vehicles or personnel enter or exit should be manned or under observation by management or security personnel.

Recommended Specifications.

1. Equip gates with a deadlocking bolt or a substantially equivalent type of lock that does not require use of a chain. All hardware connecting the lock to the gate should be strong enough to withstand constant use and attempts to defeat the locking device.
2. Construct swing-type gates so that they may be secured to the ground when closed.
3. Separate gates for personnel and vehicle traffic are desirable.

Gate Houses: General Standard

Operators of facilities handling a substantial volume of art should maintain a manned gate house at all vehicle entrances and exits during business hours.

Recommended Specifications.

1. Set the gate house back from the gate so that vehicles can be stopped and examined on the property.

2. Equip the gate house with a telephone and other communication systems.
3. Clear the area around the gate house of any encumbrances that restrict the guard's line of vision.
4. Post signs prominently on the exterior of all gate houses advising drivers and visitors about the conditions of entry. Include in conditions of entry a notice that all vehicles and personnel entering the area are subject to search.

Parking: General Standard

Private passenger vehicles should be prohibited from parking in areas nearby or immediately adjacent to buildings. Access to employee parking areas should be subject to security controls.

Recommended Specifications.

1. Locate parking areas outside of fenced operational areas, or at least a substantial distance from storage areas or buildings.
2. Require employees exiting to the parking area from the building to pass through an area under the supervision of management or security personnel. Require employees who wish to return to their private vehicles during working hours to notify management and/or security personnel.
3. Allow parking in employee parking areas by permit only. Maintain a record of each issued pemit, listing the vehicle registration number, model, color, and year. The permit should consist of a numbered decal, tag, sticker, or sign placed in a uniform location on each vehicle.
4. Issue to vendors and other visitors temporary parking permits that allow parking in a designated area under security controls.

Lighting: General Standards

Adequate lighting should be provided for the following areas:

1. Entrances, exits, and around gate houses
2. Along fence lines
3. Parking areas
4. General and yard lighting
5. Walkways
6. Building entrances

Recommended Specifications.

1. The Society of Illuminating Engineers recommend the following minimum light intensities measured at ground level:
   A. Active entrances and gate houses   5.0 footcandles
   Inactive entrances (normally locked or infrequently used   1.0 footcandles
   B. Fence line   0.2 to 0.5 footcandles
   C. General yard lighting   0.5 to 1.0 footcandles
   D. Walkways   1.0 footcandles
   E. Building entrances   2.0 footcandles
   F. Parking areas   1.0 to 2.0 footcandles
2. The selection of the right light source is essential to gain system effectiveness and energy efficiency and economy. Metal halide, high-pressure sodium, or mercury lamps should be used. Wattage of the lamp should be selected to provide the recommended footcandle values.
3. Fixtures with a light cutoff design should be selected, so as to produce minimum glare. Where necessary, fixtures should be of vandal-proof material to protect them against vandalism.
4. Location and height of poles should be selected to provide effective security lighting, while relating to the architectural design of the area.[1]

Locks, Locking Devices, and Key Control

General Standard. Locks or locking devices used on buildings, gates, and equipment should be so constructed as to provide positive protection against unauthorized entry. The issuance of all locks and keys should be controlled by management or security personnel.

Recommended Specifications.

1. Use only locks with (a) multiple pin tumblers, (b) deadlocking bolts, (c) interchangeable cores, (d) serial numbers, and (e) high security rating.
2. To facilitate detection of unauthorized locks, use only locks of standard manufacture displaying the owner's company name.
3. Number all keys and obtain a signature from the recipient when issued. Maintain a control file for all keys. Restrict the distribution of master keys to persons whose responsibilities require them to have one.

4. Safeguard all unissued or duplicate keys.
5. Limit the number of master and submaster keys that are to be issued.

Storage Areas

General Standard. Adequate space capable of being locked, sealed, or otherwise secured for storage of valuable pieces of art should have the following recommended specifications:

1. Construct special security rooms, cribs, or vaults that will resist forcible entry on all sides and from underneath and overhead.
2. Locate such special security areas, where possible, so that management and/or security personnel will be able to keep them under continuous observation. Otherwise, install an alarm system and provide for inspection at frequent intervals.
3. Release merchandise from such an area only in the presence of authorized supervisors and/or security personnel.
4. Log all movements of merchandise in or out of a special security area, showing date, time, condition of art upon receipt, name of truckman and company making the pickup, and registration number.
5. Draft security procedures for access and make sure that they are followed.

Personnel Screening

General Standard. Directors of art facilities should screen prospective employees before they are hired.

Recommended Specifications.

1. Require all personnel, including maintenance and clerical personnel, who will have access to art storage areas to submit a detailed employment application that contains a photograph of the applicant and lists residences and prior employment for the preceeding 10 years.
2. Obtain the following information:
   a. Verification of address and prior employment
   b. Credit record (get a list of the applicant's credit cards)

    c. Criminal record (if possible)

    d. Medical or hospital records

    e. List of savings and checking accounts

    f. Verification of references and information listed on the applicant's résumé

3. Conduct a thorough investigation of the applicant's background, concentrating on social standing and financial spending, as well as obtaining a list of all social, civic, fraternal, and religious organizations to which the applicant belongs.

4. Prepare proper documents for employees to read and sign that authorize you to have access to the above information.

Security Personnel

General Standard. Directors of art facilities should employ a security officer or assign a particular officer of the firm to be responsible for security.

Recommended Specifications.

1. Employ the number of guards required to provide adequate security for the size of the facility and the volume of cargo handled.

2. Train all company employee guard forces or insure that contract guard forces are trained.

3. Equip guard forces with uniforms that are complete, distinctive, and authoritative in appearance.

4. Provide firearms, vehicles, communications systems, and other equipment deemed necessary for the successful performance of the guard function.

5. Insist on physical fitness as a prime consideration in selecting a guard force. Require guards to undergo self-defense training similar to that of police agencies. Require a physical examination at least once a year.

6. Furnish each guard with a manual covering operating procedures and standards of conduct, and a clear statement of what management expects.

Security Education

General Standard. Management should institute a security awareness program for all employees.

Recommended Specifications.

1. Conduct a program of periodic security seminars for all employees involved in overall security.
   A. Instruct the staff as follows:
      1. Importance of key control
      2. Understanding their alarm systems
      3. The meaning of physical security
      4. Awareness of risk factors and vulnerabilities
   B. Instruct the guards as follows:
      1. Importance of physical security and controls
      2. How to physically test the alarm system
      3. Their role and authority, including basic law and report writing
      4. Basic knowledge of first aid, CPR, and medical transport procedures
2. Include in your security awareness program class lessons and handouts that fit into a professional binder. Employees with specific job descriptions should be properly trained in their respective fields.

Communications

General Standard. Adequate and reliable communications between members of the security force and the local police should be established.

Recommended Specifications.

1. Provide security personnel with a telephone at fixed posts and/or a two-way radio, intercom, or other type of equipment with the capability of voice communication within the facility.
2. Arrange an assured means (telephone, radio, or special alarm line) of summoning assistance from the local police.

Identification System

General Standard. All facilities should employ an identification card system to identify personnel authorized to enter.

Recommended Specifications.

1. Include on the ID card: (a) physical description or, preferably, a color photograph of the holder; (b) name and address; (c) Social

Security number; (d) date of birth; (e) employee's number, if any; (f) signature of holder; and (g) reasonable expiration date.

2. Laminate all cards to prevent alterations and assign each card a control number.
3. Recover ID cards from terminated employees as well as any keys they may have.
4. Require all employees to display their ID card to gain access to the facility. Preferably, an ID card should be displayed so that it is visible *at all times when the employee is within the facility.*

Independent Contractors

General Standard. The background and corporate structure of independent contractors providing janitorial service, refuse disposal, or other services should be verified. Access by independent contractors to the facility should be under security controls.

Recommended Specifications.

1. Periodically examine independent contractor vehicles that are parked in or near the facility.
2. Permit independent contractor employees to enter only areas necessary for them to perform their particular work, under the supervision of security and/or management personnel.
3. Require independent contractors to display identification similar to that required by the facility for its own employees.

Delivery Procedures

General Standard. Gate passes should be issued to truckmen and other carriers to control and identify persons who are authorized to enter a facility. Verification of the identity and authority of the carrier requesting delivery or receipt of materials should be made prior to releasing the material.

Recommended Specifications.

1. Require truckmen to submit proper personal identification (such as a driver's license or ID card) and a vehicle registration certificate before being issued a gate pass and being permitted to enter the facility; require them to surrender the gate pass before leaving the facility.

2. Seal containers and trailers and note the seal number on the gate pass before delivery is effected. Verify the seal number when the gate pass is surrendered at the gate.

3. Require the company name of all carriers to be clearly shown on all equipment. Do not accept temporary placards or cardboard signs as proper identification of equipment. Require carriers using leased equipment to submit the lease agreement for inspection and note the leasing company's name on the delivery order.

4. Release materials only to the carrier specified in the orders unless a release authorizing delivery to another carrier, signed by the original carrier, is presented and verified. Accept only original copies of the delivery or pickup orders.

5. Make sure that personnel processing prelodged delivery or pickup orders verify the identity of the truckman and the trucking company before releasing the pickup order. Limit access to areas where such documentation is processed or held to authorized personnel and rigorously safeguard all shipping documents from theft or unauthorized observation.

6. Conduct delivery and receiving operations at separate docks or doors, if possible.

7. Give guards assigned to the guard post a set of instructions of procedures to follow while assigned to this area.

NOTES

1. J. A. Buck, General Electric Company, Nela Park, Cleveland, OH 44112, September 1981.

18. The Security Survey

Lawrence J. Fennelly
Louis A. Tyska

CRIME RISK MANAGEMENT[1]

The crime prevention or loss prevention practitioner must possess a wide array of skills to be successful. New technologies and equipment in this developing field must be implemented, tested, evaluated, and modified as appropriate. The practitioner must operate as a manager, not necessarily of people, but of circumstances. This is accomplished by maintaining an up-to-date knowledge of the field and the tools necessary to reduce the opportunity for crime. Foremost among the skills needed is that of operationalizing the concept of crime risk management.

The ability to assess potential risks accurately is absolutely necessary for success in crime prevention. Concurrently, the capability to develop cost-effective crime risk management systems is crucial. If the decisionmaker, whether in the public or private sector, cannot perceive that benefits will accrue from acting to prevent a potential problem, no action will occur.

The concept of risk management is derived from the business world. Crime is categorized as a pure risk as contrasted to the dynamic risk assumed in business. A pure risk is one that can produce gain or profit. This is exemplified by investing in the stock market or in conducting a retail business in the hopes that customers will buy the goods offered for sale.

Crime prevention programming can be both general and comprehensive in nature; that is applicable to an individual, community, or an entire city. It can also be very specific and directed to one target. Crime risk management can be applied only if there is a central authority who is able to make tradeoff decisions, such as a business manager who wants to protect a potential target like a computer facility, a museum, an art gallery, or a library.

Crime analysis is one of the first tools to be applied in assessing risks. The basic investigative questions should be asked: What crimes are occurring? What are their locations (where)? What are the methods of commission (how)? This allows intelligent conjecture about potential crime in terms of frequency and also allows the client to begin to determine its level of vulnerability. It is the beginning phase of specific crime and target planning, allowing for awareness of the results of actions and indicating if crime displacement (by time, type, or location) is occurring.

When assessing vulnerability and the response to risk the client should consider the PML factors. PML stands for "Possible Maximum Loss" and "Probable Maximum Loss," which differ greatly. Possible maximum loss is the maximum loss that would be sustained if a given target or combination of targets were totally removed, destroyed, or both. In a retail store, for example, the possible maximum loss would be the store's entire stock. Probable maximum loss, on the other hand, refers to the amount of loss a target would be likely to sustain. This is an important distinction to consider when assigning priorities and determining cost–benefit ratios in order to make crime and loss prevention decisions.

After this process has been completed, the five principal crime management methods should be applied: (1) risk elimination or avoidance; (2) risk reduction; (3) risk spreading; (4) risk transfer; and (5) risk acceptance. A mixture of these methods is usually used to reduce criminal opportunity and the PML since no single method meets all needs.

Risk Avoidance:	Involves the removal of the target, such as dealing through direct deposit systems instead of handling cash and negotiable documents.
Risk Reduction:	This technique calls for minimizing the potential loss as much as possible. For example, not allowing over a set dollar amount to accumulate in a retail clerk's cash drawer before it is removed by the manager.
Risk Spreading:	The potential target(s) are spread over as large an area as possible in order to reduce the loss if a crime occurs. For example, precious gems may be kept in several small vaults in a jewelry store instead of one large vault.

Risk Transfer:	Perhaps the most overused method is the concept of transferring the risk to other parties, particularly insurance companies. Another example that combines risk reduction, spreading, and transfer would be that of depositing valuables in an insured safety deposit box at a bank.
Risk Acceptance:	There may be times when a risk must simply be accepted as such; this can be exemplified by the coin or art collector who refuses to be separated from the collection. Measures can be taken to reduce, spread, or even transfer part of the risk but some risk must be accepted by the act of displaying valuable articles.

These methods of crime risk management are critical to the crime prevention manager. Without them there is no systematic way of assessing the alternatives available when the vulnerability and criticality of a potential crime have been assessed.[2]

Identifying Risk

Risk analysis is invaluable to the security manager in establishing priorities for the protection of assets.

Below is a list of priority items of which you should be aware. Each item could very well be a chapter by itself.

- Theft from public and private collections
- Looting of religious items
- Vandalism to works on display
- Forgery and fraud
- Transportation of art
- Damage while in transit
- Changing climate
- Warehouse storage areas
- Insurance coverage and insurance fraud
- Title of ownership fraud
- Inventory control
- Internal theft
- Lack of trained guards
- Electronic security
- Environmental controls

Additional factors of which to be aware:

1. Fire, type of system, type of extinguishers.
2. Vandalism.
3. Guard training, CPR classes, updating knowledge of the law, review of emergency procedures, understanding alarm systems and who to notify for repairs, reviewing closing procedures.
4. Inventory control versus having no record at all of works of art. If works of art are recovered, ownership may be difficult to establish because of the lack of documentation, which could consist of photographs, identification marks, or a certificate of title.
5. Designing security, by working with architects to construct an area protected against fire and intrusion, and against sunlight, noise, humidity, and unsuitable temperatures. Keep in mind that few architects have designed a security system that houses valuable works of art. Your working objective is to strengthen and design adequate defensive measures.

CRIMINAL OPPORTUNITY

"Criminal opportunity can be lessened by improving security measures and by increasing the level of surveillance."[3]

Improving security measures means not only the installation and operation of sophisticated devices, but also the improved applications of devices that are currently installed.

Criminal opportunity can be lessened in several ways:

1. The environment can be designed so that the individual considering the criminal act feels that there is a good chance for him to be seen by someone who will take action on their own and/or call the police or security guard.
2. The target of the attack can be made to appear so formidable that the potential criminal does not believe his abilities will enable him to reach the "forbidden fruit."
3. If the potential criminal actually attempts to reach the goal, the probability of failure can be increased through the ready response of the police or security guard.

Reducing the opportunity for crime reduces the incidence of crime.

The greatest protection of assets is provided when a comprehensively designed security system integrally relates an appropriate mix of electronic, physical, and procedural security measures.

CRIME ANALYSIS

Although it is not necessary to be a statistician the more you know about and understand local crime problems, the better equipped you are to analyze the potential risk for losses from crime in surveying a business or a home.

Crime data collection is simply the gathering of raw data concerning reported crimes and known offenders. Generally, such information is obtained from crime reports, arrest reports, and police contact cards, although these are not the only sources of crime data.

The analysis process as applied to criminal activity is a specific step-by-step sequence of five interconnected functions:

1. Crime data collection
2. Crime data collation
3. Data analysis
4. Dissemination of analysis reports
5. Feedback and evaluation of crime data

This process gives you the risk factor upon which you set the degree of security required for the facility.

Crime Statistics[4]

Detailed information that pinpoints the types and locations of crime problems within a jurisdiction or an organization is the key to the design of a prevention program. Because burglary is becoming a crime of epidemic proportion in this country, the following outline of data elements relates directly to burglary. If, however, a jurisdiction or organization is also interested in robbery or other crime, similar types of data about those crimes will have to be assembled for the particular program design.

When to Collect Data and Why

Crime statistics must be gathered as a first step in designing a prevention program. In addition, they will have to be maintained throughout the program. In fact, they should be maintained on a daily basis and summarized monthly.

This information will serve as one of the "base lines" for designing, managing, and evaluating the program. The data will also provide useful details for inclusion in speeches, news stories, briefing memorandums, and so on.

What Data to Gather

The following kinds of data should be considered essential in the design of a burglary prevention program. How much data a particular organization will be able to gather will, of course, depend on their existing records. The *essential* elements include:

Location of occurrence.   Census tracts and exact locations of the crimes being analyzed should be gathered. This information will be valuable in identifying program target areas.

Date of occurrence.   The day, month, and year of incidents, or reporting dates if exact dates are not known, should be analyzed. These dates will indicate whether particular crimes are related to seasonal patterns, weekly community habits, or closed plant operations, which may enhance burglar opportunities. This information will be useful in formulating strategies to deal with the crime.

Time of occurrence.   The exact time of occurrence, when known (or morning, afternoon, or evening, when a range of time is given), should be analyzed. This information will be helpful to the security unit in terms of making personnel allocation plans, for example.

How entry was made.   Record what was done to get inside the facility. This might include whether force was used; if a door or window that had been left open was utilized; whether a lock and/or alarm system was defeated to gain entry, and so on. This data will be valuable in the formulation of public information and target-hardening strategies.

Type of property taken.   Information on the types of items taken, such as money or sound or office equipment, should be developed. Keep such accountings general in nature. This information will be helpful in the design of target-hardening strategies.

Property identification.   Record whether the property taken was identified with special markings. This will be valuable in terms of designing a program as well as evaluating its impact.

Dollar amount taken.   Record the total reported dollar loss of all items taken. This data can be used to help analyze the impact of your program; for example, dollar value loss before and after the implementation of a program.

How incident was reported.   Gather data on who detected and reported the crime, such as an employee, police, alarm, victim, and so on. This will be useful in designing a program; that is, crime-prevention programs are theoretically designed to "increase" citizen and employee participation and reporting — baseline statistics have to be developed to see if this actually happens.

In addition to the data noted above, there are various other items that may be useful in the design, monitoring, and evaluation of a program. However, they may be considered optional. Such elements include:

Point of entry.   Record where entry was made, such as door, window or air vent. When appropriate also note the location of the point of entry, such as rear door or side window.

Occupancy status.   Record whether premises were occupied when the reported crime occurred.

Instrument used to gain entry.   Data on the kind of tool or instrument used, such as screwdriver, pry bar, or saw, should be gathered.

Street and exterior lights.   For crimes occurring at night, note the existence of street and exterior lights.

Points of entry lighting.   For night crimes, record the existence of lights at point of entry.

Visibility at points of entry.   Record whether the point of entry was visible to patrolling units.

Alarm systems.   Record the existence of alarm systems.

Status of the alarm.   Record whether the alarm was activated, defeated, and so on.

When detected.   Record whether the crime was detected while in progress, on the day of occurrence, the next day, and so forth.

THE SECURITY SURVEY

Before making a security survey you should ask yourself, "Why am I doing this survey?" Has there been an attempted theft, a break into a complex, or an actual penetration into a particular area, with substantial losses as a result of this incident?

The security survey is described as "a critical onsite examination and analysis of an industrial plant, business or home, public or private institution to ascertain the present security status; to identify deficiencies or excesses; to determine the protection needed; and to make recommendations to improve the security."[5]

The survey is conducted to evaluate the facility's actual overall security and to identify vulnerabilities and deficiencies in security as well as risk-management principles. Thus the protection needed is defined so that, when and if the recommendations are implemented, criminal attack or opportunity will be reduced to a minimum.

> Crime Prevention is the anticipation, the recognition, and the appraisal of a crime risk and the initiation of some action to remove or reduce it.[6]

The definitions of the security survey and crime prevention go hand in hand. When conducting a security survey, don't be afraid to be critical of the site. Anticipate the deficiency and recognize your ability to make recommendations to improve the overall security. Make an appraisal of the protection that is needed, for your ultimate goal of adequate security will then be achieved (i.e., if the recipient follows your recommendations). Your recommendations must be not only sensible and practical, but also within the budgetary constraints of the facility. In addition to immediate recommendations, your report could also reflect long-range planning.

Communication

The first step in conducting a security survey is communicating with the recipient of the survey. This meeting will serve as a focal point for reviewing the risk factors and environmental and physiological security measures, as well as enabling you to learn about losses, crime patterns, fraud, internal theft, and larcenies that have occurred in the past.

Meeting with upper as well as middle management is important because they can provide valuable input into the design of your report. Remember that top management makes the decisions that will support, reinforce, and implement your recommendations for present and long-range changes in security. Obtaining support from top management is just like getting a commitment. After you have it, the rest is easy.

Sometimes you may find that in-house security personnel have a hard time in communicating to upper management that the security is poor and the defenses are weak. In this case you become the intermediary of middle management. Make sure your actions and recommendations support your communications.

You should meet with management at least twice, first to define the objectives, goals, and scope of the inspection and finally to describe the finished report in detail and go over your recommendations.

THE REPORT

If you have followed all of the security measures discussed in this chapter, in all probability your survey is complete; however, do keep in mind the following pitfalls:

1. Do not overexaggerate security conditions in your report. Management will see through this.
2. Do not inflate your report unnecessarily by adding maps and floor plans, thereby making it appear as if you are writing a book instead of a report. Such aids should be used only when a specific point has to be illustrated.
3. Do not repeat your statements over and over throughout the report.
4. Do not jump around in your report. Discuss your security plan logically, for example, perimeter protection, roof recommendations, second-floor coverage, and basement openings. Then place your security recommendations in order of the building floor plan as outlined, thereby allowing the recipient to follow in your footsteps systematically floor by floor.
5. Do not be afraid to be critical. This is your objective and what the recipient expects.

Survey Follow-up Evaluation

The final step is to evaluate the survey's effectiveness after the recipients have reviewed it and implemented the security changes you recommended. A natural question you may ask yourself is: "Why didn't they do this or that as compared to what they actually did?" In order to resolve any discrepancies between what you recommended and what was implemented, you should ask yourself the following questions:

1. Did you make your recommendations clear?
2. Did you identify the most important point and specific objective to be implemented?
3. Did you consider the overall physical structure of the site, keeping in mind that each building has its own personality and lifestyle?
4. Did you properly plan and communicate with management your overview of the site before leaving it?
5. Did you properly communicate in your report the vulnerabilities and specific needs of the site?

After you have followed the effective management guidelines in carrying out your security survey, you should inquire as to how well your ideas were accepted. This can be done in a very low-keyed way. After all, who is going to evaluate your work — if not you, then a thief?

PREPARING THE SECURITY SURVEY REPORT

I.   The Facility
- A.   Name and address of the facility
- B.   Location: city or town, zip code
  1. Proximity to other facilities
  2. Proximity to communities
  3. Telephone number
- C.   Physical nature of the facility and its surroundings
- D.   Function, number of departments within the facility
- E.   Staffing
  1. Nature and size of staff
  2. Hours
  3. Seasonal variations
  4. Number of people who have access (security officers, cleaners, etc.)
  5. Who does maintenance?
  6. Maintenance schedule
  7. Clearance level
- F.   Visitor access
  1. Visitor use characteristics
  2. Numbers of visitors
  3. House, type of weekend operation
  4. Seasonal variations
- G.   The climate
- H.   The law enforcement situation
  1. Type of jurisdiction
  2. Reaction times
  3. Distance from nearest fire station
  4. Law enforcement powers of security staff
- I.   Specific security problem of site
- J.   Area of highest dollar value identified

II.   Perimeter Security (External)

A. Fences and natural barriers
 1. Nature of fences and gates
 2. Gates (control, access, locks, etc.)
 3. Natural barriers
 4. Clear zones

B. The grounds (includes roads and parking areas)

C. Lighting
 1. Nature
 2. Location and areas of coverage
 3. Maintenance and testing
 4. Power supply and circuit reliability
 5. Tamper resistance
 6. Operation

D. Access control

E. Are there areas of cover for hiding and materials that would aid someone in gaining entry to the area?

F. Intrusion detection system
 1. Type of system
 2. Signal transmission mode
 3. Inspection, testing, and maintenance
 4. Power supply
 5. Tamper resistance
 6. Records of alarm incidents

G. Patrols
 1. Nature
 2. Frequency
 3. Seasonal variations

III. The Building

A. Perimeter security
 1. Doors
 2. Windows
 3. Other openings
 4. Walls
 5. Roofs
 6. Floors and basement

B. Interior security
 1. Connecting doors and pass-throughs
 2. Walls
 3. Ceilings

       4. Ductwork

       5. Storerooms and closets

       6. Vaults

       7. Storage cabinets

       8. Hiding places

       9. Restrooms

  C. Locks and related hardware, hinges, padlocks, and guard plates

  D. Lighting

       1. Security

       2. Emergency

       3. Lighting reliability, both interior and exterior

          a. Backup power

          b. Secure switches

          c. Maintenance

  E. Intrusion detection system

       1. Nature and area of coverage

       2. Location of controls

       3. Tamper resistance of wiring and components

       4. Alarm transmission mode

       5. Maintenance and testing

       6. Backup power

       7. Operating procedures and instructions

  F. Fire safety and control

       1. Detection systems (ask the same questions as asked above)

       2. Suppression mode(s)

       3. Housekeeping

       4. Evacuation

  G. Safes

IV. Procedures

  A. Key control (see separate checklist)

  B. Building opening, closing and search

  C. Housekeeping practices

  D. Employee control

       1. Screening and investigation

       2. Identification and pass control

       3. Package and material control

  E. Visitor control

        1. Control of visitors to areas limited only to the staff
        2. Passes
        3. Records or visits
        4. IDs for contractors, tradesmen, utility workers, etc.

  F. Visitor (public) surveillance and inspection

  G. Protection of administrative records

  H. Security of cash valuables
        1. On site
        2. In transit

  I. Control of access to restricted areas of facilities

  J. Property inventory and control

  K. Security communications
        1. Mode(s)
        2. Reliability
        3. Backup power and alternate modes of communication
        4. Employee operation
        5. Efficiency and speed

  L. Incident reporting
        1. Timeliness
        2. Accuracy

V. Emergency Action Plan and Contingency Plans
  A. Does it deal with all possible contingencies?
        1. Bomb threats and bombings
        2. Civil disturbances (riots, war, breach of peace)
        3. Natural catastrophes
        4. Vandalism
        5. Robbery and assault
        6. Burglary
        7. Fire
        8. Equipment failure
        9. Accidents with injury

  B. Does it provide for notification of the appropriate people in the correct sequence?

  C. Does it provide detailed reaction instructions or directions about how to obtain instructions?

  D. Does it provide for reporting of emergency incidents to the regional office and to the proper local authorities?

VI. Artifact Protection

A. Storerooms
1. Physical construction
2. Access control
3. Environmental control
4. Housekeeping practices
5. Storage cabinets and shelves
6. Inventory and material movement

B. Exhibits
1. Case construction
2. Lighting of cases and the gallery
3. Alarms
4. Surveillance by the staff
5. Inventory

C. Furnished rooms
1. Access control
    a. Physical
    b. Procedural
2. Alarms
3. Environmental controls
4. Housekeeping practices
5. Inventory

D. Artifact loan policies
1. Restrictions on recipient
2. Environmental control and protection requirements
3. Inventory
4. Shipping and receiving; packing
5. Insurance
6. Time limits
7. Usage limits

NOTES

1. *Training Manual.* Louisville, Ky.: National Crime Prevention Institute, Administration of Justice, University of Louisville.
2. Ibid.
3. *Establishing a Crime Prevention Bureau.* National Crime Prevention Institute, Administration of Justice, University of Louisville, LEAA Grant 72-DF-99-0009, p. 13.
4. Charles M. Girard, Ph.D., "Planning Management and Evaluation: Important Tools to the Crime Prevention and Security Officer," in *Crime Prevention and Loss Prevention Techniques,* ed. Lawrence J. Fennelly (Woburn, Mass.: Butterworth, 1982).
5. Raymond M. Moboisse, *Industrial Security for Strikes, Riots and Disasters* (Springfield, Ill.: Thomas, 1968), p. 13.
6. British Home Office, Crime Prevention Center, Stafford, England.

Appendix 18.1

Perimeter Protection

EXTERIOR PROTECTION

The purpose of a strong exterior perimeter is to reduce the risk of crime, defeating the criminal before he gets inside. Several years ago museums were being attacked from the skylight; entrance was gained and priceless art was stolen. A hole in the perimeter security was undetected by the administration of the museum but not by the thief.

There are many devices available to protect the perimeter, such as alarming the chain-link fence, enclosing it within barbed-wire fencing, or placing optic fiber underground, under water or within glass windows. These are not complex systems, but rather are considered basic coverage. In addition, there are aesthetic ways in which these security devices can be implemented.

The perimeter protection program is designed to:

1. Detect and verify any attempt at unauthorized entry.
2. Delay and slow down the individual while appropriate assistance is arriving.
3. Deter crime — preventing the individual access requires studying the overall environment. All sites have a personality; day, night, and weekend/night staff should be examined.
4. Deny entry — your final objective in preventing losses.

Emphasis on the environment of the site is important in order to construct the most effective security program.

Barriers*

Barriers can be used to create physical and psychological deterrents to accidental entry; to prevent deliberate unauthorized entry; to delay intrusion, making detection and apprehension by guards more likely; to make guards more effective; and to direct the flow of pedestrian and vehicular traffic.

There are two kinds of physical barriers — natural and structural. Natural barriers include rivers, marshes, or terrain difficult to negotiate by vehicle. Structural barriers include fences, walls, buildings, grills, bars, and gates. A barrier should be under physical or electronic surveillance to be fully effective.

---

*Guidelines for the Physical Security of Cargo, Department of Transportation (DOT p 5200.2), May 1972, Chapter IV, pp. 15-17.

The kind of barrier to use depends upon the size of the controlled area, the flow of traffic during the busiest and least busy periods, and the most prevalent local hazards.

The perimeter of a large controlled area may be a combination of natural and structural barriers. A limited area, however, generally has to be surrounded by a structural barrier.

Fencing. Fences should be of the chain link variety, with No. 9 gauge or heavier wire; they should be no less than 10 feet high, with mesh openings no larger than 2 inches per side and with a twisted, barbed selvage at the top. The fencing should be stretched taut and securely fastened to metal posts set in concrete. The bottom should be within 2 inches of hard ground or paving. On soft ground, the fencing should extend below the surface to compensate for shifting soil or sand. Culverts, troughs, or other openings larger than 96 square inches in area should be protected by fencing or iron grills to prevent unauthorized entry and yet allow proper drainage.

A top guard should be attached to perimeter fences and interior enclosures for greater security. A top guard is an overhang of barbed wire along the top of a barrier facing outward and upward at an angle of 45 degrees. The supporting arms, at least 2 feet long, are attached to the top of the fence posts. Four strands of standard barbed wire are tightly stretched between the supporting arms. Some fences have a double overhang, facing both outward and inward, which makes it more difficult to enter or leave the facility by scaling the fence.

The top guard can be firmly fixed or mounted on springs. The spring-type guard further increases the difficulty of scaling the fence. If a building less than three stories high forms part of the perimeter, a top guard should be used along the coping to deny access to the roof.

The fence line should be as straight as possible to provide ease of observation by the guard force. If practicable, fences should be located no closer than 50 feet to buildings or cargo in a controlled area. Twenty feet of clearance should be allowed between the perimeter barrier and exterior features, such as buildings or parking areas, which would offer concealment to a thief.

Fencing for limited areas should conform to the same specifications as for controlled areas, although it is recommended that the height be increased and that a top guard be used.

Exclusion areas should be located in secure buildings and consist of separate cribs, cages, or vaults. If fencing is used, it should be at least 10 feet high, extend to the ceiling, or be topped by a wire mesh roof, and be under observation by a guard.

If a wall serves as the barrier, or a part of it, it should be constructed to provide protection equal to that specified for each of the areas above. If it is less than the height specified, it should be topped with chain link fence and barbed wire to match the minimum requirements. If a fence connects with a building, it should extend within 2 inches of the wall of the building.

A body of water, whether it be a river, lake, or ocean, does not in itself constitute an adequate barrier. Additional measures, such as a fence, frequent security patrol, and floodlighting, usually are necessary.

To be effective, barriers have to be well maintained. Breaks or damage to the structure should be repaired as soon as they are discovered. Frequent inspection of the barriers must be made by the guard force to locate defects. In addition, the security officer should periodically tour the barriers, giving particular attention to cuts or openings in the barrier that may be camouflaged.

If the perimeter barrier encloses a large area, an interior all-weather road should be provided for guard force vehicles. The road should be in the clear zone and as close to the barrier as possible. Its use should be limited to guard and emergency vehicles.

Entrances. The number of gates and entrances to controlled areas should be limited to the minimum required for safe and efficient operation of the facility. A top guard, equal to that on the adjoining fence, should be attached to each gate. The bottom of the gate should be within 2 inches of hard ground or paving. Adequate lighting should be provided for fast, efficient inspection.

When gates or doors are not manned by guards, so that all those entering will be challenged, they should be securely locked, illuminated during hours of darkness, and periodically inspected by a roving guard.

Semiactive entrances, such as railroad siding gates or gates and doors used only during peak traffic-flow periods, should be locked except when actually in use. Keys to these entrances should be in the custody of the security officer or the chief of the guard force and should be strictly controlled. Periodic inspection should be made of these entrances.

Inactive entrances, which are used only occasionally, should also be kept locked. They are subject to the same key control and inspection as semiactive entrances.

Emergency exits should have alarmed break-out hardware installed on the inside.

Sidewalk elevators and other unusual entrances that provide access within controlled area barriers should be locked and patrolled.

Control signs stating the condition of entry to a facility or controlled area should be erected at all entrances. They should inform the entrant that he is subject to search of his person (subject to the extent the law allows), vehicle, or packages and of any prohibitions against packages, matches, smoking, or entry for other than business. The signs should be legible under normal conditions at least 50 feet from the point of entry.

To maintain the integrity of the barriers to controlled areas, guard control stations should be established at all entrances in service.

PERIMETER SECURITY CHECKLIST*

The checklist that follows may be used for many different types of facilities. It permits each facility manager to select those elements pertaining to his establishment and location in making his own security survey.

Barriers

1. Is the perimeter of the facility or activity defined by a fence or other type of physical barrier?

---

*Ibid., pp. 59-60.

2. If a fence or gate is used, does it meet the minimum specifications?
   a. Is the top guard strung with barbed wire and angled outward and up-ward at a 45° angle?
   b. Is it at least 10 feet in total height?
3. If building walls, floors, and roofs form a part of the perimeter barrier, do they provide security equivalent at least to that provided by a chain-link fence? Are all openings properly secured?
4. If a masonry wall or building forms a part of the perimeter barrier, does it meet minimum specifications of perimeter fencing?
5. If a river, lake, or other body of water forms any part of the perimeter bar-rier, are security measures equal to the deterrence of a 10-foot fence provided?
6. Are openings such as culverts, tunnels, manholes for sewers and utility ac-cess, and sidewalk elevators that permit access to the facility properly secured?
7. List number, location, and physical characteristics of perimeter entrances.
8. Are all portals in perimeter barriers guarded, secured, or under constant sur-veillance?
9. Are all perimeter entrances equipped with secure locking devices and are they always locked when not in active use?
10. Are gates and/or other perimeter entrances that are not in active use fre-quently inspected by guards or management personnel?
11. Is the security officer responsible for security of keys to perimeter entrances? If not, who is responsible?
12. Are keys to perimeter entrances issued to other than facility personnel, such as cleaning, trash removal, or vending-machine service personnel?
13. Are all normally used pedestrian and vehicle gates effectively and adequately lighted so as to ensure
    a. Proper identification of individuals and examination of credentials;
    b. That interiors of vehicles are clearly lighted; and
    c. That glare from luminaries is not in guard's eyes?
14. Are appropriate signs setting forth the provisions for entry conspicuously posted at all principal entrances?
15. Are clear zones maintained for the largest vehicles on both sides of the perimeter barrier? If clear zone requirements cannot be met, what additional security measures have been implemented?
16. Are automobiles permitted to park against or too close to perimeter barriers?
17. What is the frequency of checks made by maintenance crews on the condi-tion of perimeter barriers?
18. Do guards patrol perimeter areas?
19. Are reports of inadequate perimeter security immediately acted upon and the necessary repairs effected?
20. Are perimeters protected by intrusion alarm devices?
21. Does any new construction require installation of additional perimeter bar-riers or additional perimeter lighting?

Appendix 18-2

Lighting and Security

WHAT WOULD HAPPEN IF WE SHUT OFF ALL THE LIGHTS AT NIGHT? STOP AND THINK ABOUT IT! The results of such a foolish act would create an unsafe environment. Senior citizens would never go out and communities would have an immediate outbreak of thefts and vandalism. Commercial areas would be burglarized at an uncontrollable rate. Therefore lighting and security must go hand in hand.

Although the example just described may seem farfetched, in fact, the installation of improved lighting in a number of cities has resulted in the following:

1. A decrease in vandalism
2. A decrease in street crimes
3. A decrease in suspicious persons
4. A decrease in commercial burglaries
5. A general reduction in crime.

If the above principles are true, then you have no alternative but to take a hard look at your facility's lighting program.

THE LIGHTING SYSTEM*

At night, a protective lighting system enables your guard force to maintain a level of security approaching that observed during the day. Adequate lighting is relatively inexpensive. If it cannot be provided, management has to consider other more costly alternatives, such as additional guards, sentry-dog patrols, or expanded alarm systems.

The amount and intensity of light needed will vary from point to point within the facility. Designing a system for a large facility is a specialized task. Material is available from the manufacturers of lighting equipment that will assist management, but consultation with an expert in the field will save time and expense. It will undoubtedly produce a more satisfactory lighting system.

Protective lighting will permit guards to observe activities around or inside a facility. It is achieved by providing even light on areas bordering the facility, directing glaring light into the eyes of a potential intruder, and maintaining a low level of light on guard patrol.

---

*Guidelines for the Physical Security of Cargo, Department of Transportation (DOT P 5200.2), May 1972, Chapter IV, pp. 21-22.

Planning

When planning a protection lighting system, the creation of high contrast between an intruder and the background is a primary consideration. The ability of a guard to distinguish a darkly clothed man against a dark background improves significantly as the level of illumination is increased. predominantly dark, dirty surfaces require more light to facilitate observation than those of clean concrete or light-colored paint. This is also true inside buildings, where ceilings and walls redirect and diffuse light.

Generally, lighting should be directed downward and away from the structure or area to be protected, and away from the guards assigned to patrol the facility. It should create as few shadows as possible.

Units for lighting perimeter fences of controlled areas should be located within the protected area and above the fence. The light pattern on the ground should include an area both inside and outside the fence.

Movable lighting that can be controlled by the guards is recommended as part of the protective system for piers and docks. Lighting in these areas cannot be allowed to violate marine rules. The U.S. Coast Guard should be consulted to make sure that proposed lighting systems adjacent to navigable waters do not interfere with aids to navigation.

The lighting of open areas within a perimeter should be the same as the illumination required at the perimeter. Lighting units in outdoor storage areas should be so placed as to provide an even distribution of light in aisles and recesses to eliminate shadows where an intruder might be able to conceal himself.

Special Terms

Special terms used in describing lighting must be understood to discuss and develop a protection lighting system:

One *footcandle* is the amount of light on a surface 1 foot from the source of 1 candle power. The amount of light varies inversely as the square of the distance between the source and the surface; so the footcandles decrease rapidly as the distance is increased.

Horizontal illumination is the amount of light expressed in footcandles on a horizontal surface.

Vertical illumination is the amount of light expressed in footcandles on a vertical surface.

Continuous lighting (stationary luminary) is the most common protective lighting system. It consists of a series of fixed luminaries arranged to flood a given area continuously with overlapping cores of light.

Glare projection lighting provides a band of light with great angular dispersal. It directs the glare at an intruder while restricting the downward beam. It is a strong deterrent to a potential intruder and protects the guard by keeping him in comparative darkness. It should not be used if it would interfere with adjacent facilities.

Controlled lighting allows adjustment of the lighted strip to fit a particular need. If a highway, airport, or railroad adjoins the perimeter, this method will permit illumination of a narrow strip outside the fence and a wide strip inside the fence. The weakness of this method of lighting is that it often illuminates or silhouettes guards as they patrol their routes.

Standby lighting (stationary luminary) is similar to continuous lighting as described above. The luminaries, however, are not continously lit but are activated manually by the guard force or automatically by the alarm system only when required.

Movable lighting (stationary or portable) consists of manually operated movable searchlights that can be lighted during hours of darkness or only as needed. The system is a supplement to those described above.

Emergency lighting can duplicate any or all of the above systems. Its use is limited to emergencies that render the normal system inoperative. It needs an alternate power source such as installed or portable generators.

Power Sources

Normally, the primary power source for a transportation facility is the local public utility. The concern of the security force begins at the point at which power feeder lines enter the facility. Feeder lines should be located underground or, in the case of overhead wiring, inside the perimeter to minimize the possibility of vandalism to the lines.

An alternate source of power should be available to supply the system in the event of interruptions or failure. Standby gasoline-driven generators that start automatically upon the failure of the primary source will insure continuous light. They may, however, be inadequate for sustained operation. Generator or battery-powered portable or stationary lights should be available at key control points for use by the guards in case of a complete power failure that makes the secondary power supply inoperative.

Circuit Design

Both parallel and series circuits can be used to advantage in protective lighting systems. Circuits should be so arranged, however, that the failure of one lamp will not leave a large portion of the perimeter or a segment of a critical area in darkness.

The design should be simple and economical to maintain. It should require a minimum number of shutdowns for routine repair, cleaning, and lamp replacement. It should facilitate periodic inspections to replace or repair worn parts, tighten connections, check insulation, and clean, focus, and aim lights.

GENERAL TYPES OF LIGHTING SOURCES*

Listed below are the general lighting sources that are mostly used in providing indoor or outdoor lighting. Their characteristics are described and their lumen output is summarized in the chart at the end of this section. The lighting sources discussed are incandescent, mercury vapor, fluorescent, metal halide, and sodium vapor.

---

*National Crime Prevention Institute, Theory and Practice Manual, Administration of Justice, University of Louisville.

Incandescent. Incandescent lighting systems have low initial cost and provide good color rendition. Incandescent lamps are relatively short in rated life (500–4,000 hours), however, and low in lamp efficiency (17–23 lumens per watt) when compared to other lighting sources.

Mercury vapor. Mercury vapor lamps emit a purplish white color, caused by an electric current passing through a tube of conducting and luminous gas. This type of light is generally considered more efficient than the incandescent lamp and is also widespread in exterior lighting. Approximately 75 percent of all street lighting is mercury vapor. Because mercury lamps have a long life (24,000 + hours) and good lumen maintenance characteristics, they are widely used in applications where long burning hours are customary. Good color rendition is provided and the lumens per watt is 45–63.

Fluorescent. Provides good color rendition, high lamp efficiency (67–83 lumens per watt), and also long life (9,000–17,000 hours). Their long length, however, relative to their small diameter, causes luminaires to have very wide horizontal beam spreads. Fluorescent lamps are temperature sensitive, and low ambient temperatures can decrease the distances; thus these lamps are not desirable as flood-type lights.

Metal halide. Similar in physical appearance to mercury vapor, metal halide lighting provides a light source of higher luminous efficiency and better color rendition. The rated life of 6,000 hours is short when compared to the 24,000 + of mercury lamps. Used in applications where color rendition is of primary importance and generally where the burning hours per year are low. Rated at 85–95 lumens per watt.

High-pressure sodium vapor. A relatively new light source introduced in 1965, high-pressure sodium vapor is rapidly gaining acceptance for exterior lighting of parking areas, roadways and buildings, and industrial and commercial interior installations. Constructed on the same principle as mercury vapor lamps but emitting a golden white to light pink color. Provides high lumen efficiency (105–140) and relatively good color rendition. Lamp life expectancy is up to 24,000 hours. Maintenance of light output is good and averages about 90 percent throughout their rated life.

Low-pressure sodium vapor. Similar in principles of operation to other types of vapor lights, low-pressure sodium vapor provides a much higher ratio (135–180). Color produced is a golden yellow and is within a very narrow band of yellow wavelength. For this reason very poor color rendition is provided. LPSV lights have about 95 percent lumen maintenance throughout their rated life. The higher-wattage LPSV lamps increase to about 40 inches in length and thus reduce optical control. LPSV lamps normally restrike within a few seconds if there is a momentary power loss.

OPERATIONAL NEEDS

It must be stressed that recommendations for lighting should not, where possible, work contrary to operational needs. Furthermore, common sense is the key requirement in making any recommendations or suggestions as to type, number, and placement of lighting fixtures. For example, because operational management of a terminal has historically looked for additional space, it has often stacked containers three high directly in front of a "field" of light from a light fixture, thus rendering the light field ineffective. Other objects often create similar problems, such as debris, pallets, field cargo, or equipment, that is stacked and/or stored carelessly, preventing a proper field of light.

To avoid any misunderstandings about recommended locations for light fixtures, detailed diagrams should be drawn of the perimeter locations and structures showing exactly where lighting has been suggested.

When recommending where lighting should be located, much depends on the type of lighting fixture as well as the distance between placement of the fixture.

Importance must be placed upon the type and condition of interior as well as exterior lighting. The need for well-lighted loading platforms, clerical offices, and storage areas is just as critical as perimeter lighting.

When considering lighting for special areas, attention should be paid to the following locations:

1. Guard houses
2. Gates
3. Parking areas
4. Specific trouble areas in which known and repeated entries have been made

Under almost all circumstances, automatic timers or photoelectric cells should be used for outdoor lighting. Thus the responsibility for turning protective outdoor lighting systems on and off is removed from the individual employees.

A maintenance program planned to retain the protective lighting system as near to 100 percent effective as possible is always necessary. Occasionally, even highly efficient terminal operators become lax about replacing worn-out bulbs, fixtures, and other lighting materials. In addition, protection for the lighting fixtures should be provided. Bulbs, which are a favorite target for vandals, can be easily protected from damage by wire mesh or another kind of sturdy material that would not restrict the light beam.

Although the installation or upgrading of security or safety lighting will improve the effectiveness of your security system, it will not solve all of your security problems. You can, however, expect to improve greatly the ability of your security force and operational management to *see* what is under their control and supervision. Security or operational lighting is only one of the many tools a professional security manager can use in providing proper asset protection.

Good principles of protective lighting are achieved by having adequate light shine upon bordering areas, glaring light into the eyes of the intruder, and having no light on the guard or guards. In order to provide protective seeing, high brightness contrast between the intruder and background should be a primary consideration. It can be accomplished by using adequate light and painting surfaces with appropriate light colors. Two approaches to this problem can be used. The first method is to light the boundaries and approaches; the second method is to light the area and structures within the general boundaries of the terminal or property.

Lighting Checklist*

1. Is the perimeter of the installation protected by adequate lighting?
2. Are the cones of illumination from lamps directed downward and away from the facility itself and away from guard personnel?
3. Are lights mounted to provide a strip of light both inside and outside the fence?
4. Are lights checked for proper operation periodically and inoperative lamps replaced immediately?
5. Do light beams overlap to provide coverage in case a bulb burns out?
6. Is additional lighting provided at vulnerable or sensitive areas?
7. Are gate guard boxes provided with proper illumination?
8. Are light finishes or stripes used on lower parts of buildings and structures to aid guard observation?
9. Does the facility have a dependable auxiliary source of power?
10. Is there an alternate source of power for the lighting system independent of the plant lighting or power system?
11. Is the power supply for lights adequately protected? How?
12. Is the standby or emergency equipment tested periodically?
13. Is emergency equipment designed to go into operation automatically when needed?
14. Is wiring tested and inspected periodically to insure proper operation?
15. Are multiple circuits used? If so, are proper switching arrangements provided?
16. Is wiring for protective lighting securely mounted?
    a. Is it in tamper-resistant conduits?
    b. Is it mounted underground?
    c. If above ground, is it high enough to reduce possibility of tampering?
17. Are switches and controls properly located, controlled, and protected?
    a. Are they weatherproof and tamper resistant?
    b. Are they readily accessible to security personnel?
    c. Are they located so that they are inaccessible from outside the perimeter barrier?
    d. Is there a centrally located switch to control protective lighting? Is it vulnerable?
18. Is the lighting system designed and locations recorded so that repairs can be made rapidly in an emergency?
19. Is adequate lighting for guard use provided on indoor routes?
20. Are materials and equipment in shipping and storage areas properly arranged to permit adequate lighting?
21. If bodies of water form a part of the perimeter, does the lighting conform to other perimeter lighting standards?

---

*Department of Transportation, pp 60-61

Appendix 18-3

Locks and Key Control*

Attacks Against Locks

Although direct forcible assault is the method generally used to gain entry, more highly skilled burglars may concentrate on the lock. This may be their only practical means of ingress if the door and jamb are well-designed in security terms and essentially impervious to forcible attack.

Picking the lock or making a key by impression are the methods generally used. Both require a degree of expertise. In the former method, metal picks are used to align the levers or tumblers as an authorized key would, thus enabling the lock to operate. Making a key by taking impressions is a technique requiring even greater skill, since it is a delicate, painstaking operation requiring repeated trials.

Because both of these techniques are apt to take time, they are customarily used to attack those doors where the intruder feels he may work undisturbed and unobserved for adequate periods of time. The picked lock rarely shows any signs of illegal entry, and often the insurance is uncollectible.

Locks As Delaying Devices

The best defense against lock-picking and the making of keys by impression is the installation of special pick-resistant, impression-resistant lock cylinders. They are more expensive than standard cylinders but, in many applications, may well be worth the added cost. Generally speaking, in fact, locks are the cheapest security investment that can be made. Cost-cutting in their purchase is usually a poor economy, since a lock of poor quality is virtually useless and effectively — no lock at all.

The elementary but often overlooked fact of locking devices is that, in the first place, they are simply mechanisms that extend the door or window into the wall that holds them. If, therefore, the wall or the door itself is weak or easily detroyed, the lock cannot be effective.

In the second place, it must be recognized that any lock will eventually yield to an attack. They must be thought of only as delaying devices. But this delay is of primary importance. The longer an intruder is stalled in an exposed position while he works at gaining entry, the greater are the chances of discovery. Since many types of locks in general use today provide no appreciable delay to even the unskilled prowler, they have no place in security applications.

---

*Gion Green, *Introduction to Security,* 3rd edition (Woburn, Mass.: Butterworth, 1981), pp. 127-138.

Even the highest quality locking devices are only one part of door and entrance security. Locks, cylinders, door and frame construction, and key control are inseparable elements; all must be equally effective. If any one element is weak, the system breaks down.

Kinds of Locks

A brief review of the types of locks in general use, with notations of their characteristics, may serve to familiarize those as yet unacquainted with them with the variety available.

Warded Locks are those found generally in pre-war construction, in which the keyway is open and can be seen through. These are also recognized by the single plate which includes the doorknob and the keyway. The security value of these locks is nil.

Disc Tumbler Locks were designed for the use of the automobile industry and are in general use in car doors today. Because this lock is easy and cheap to manufacture, its use has expanded to other areas such as desks, files and padlocks. The life of these locks is limited because of their soft metal construction. Although these locks provide more security than warded locks, they cannot be considered as very effective. The delay afforded is, approximately, three minutes.

Pin Tumbler Locks are in wide use in industry as well as in residences. They can be recognized by the keyway, which is irregular in shape, and the key, which is grooved on both sides. Such locks can be master keyed in a number of ways, a feature which recommends them to a wide variety of industrial applications, although the delay factor is ten minutes or less.

Lever Locks are difficult to define in terms of security, since they vary greatly in their effectiveness. The best lever locks are used in safe deposit boxes and are, for all practical purposes, pick-proof. The least of these locks are used in desks, lockers and cabinets and are generally less secure than pin tumbler locks. The best of this variety are rarely used in common applications, such as doors, because they are bulky and expensive.

Combination Locks are difficult to defeat since they cannot be picked and few experts can so manipulate the device as to discover the combination. Most of these locks have three dials which must be aligned in the proper order before the lock will open. Some such locks may have four dials for greater security. Many also have the capability of changing the combination quickly.

Code-Operated Locks are combination-type locks in that no keys are used. They are opened by pressing a series of numbered buttons in the proper sequence. Some of them are equipped to alarm if the wrong sequence should be pressed. The combination of these locks can be changed readily. These are high security locking devices. Because this type of lock can be compromised by "tailgating" (more than one person entering on an authorized opening), it should never be used as a substitute for a guard or receptionist.

Virtually every lock manufacturer makes some kind of special high security lock which is operated by non-duplicable keys. A reliable locksmith or various manufacturers should be consulted in cases of such needs.

Card Operated Locks are electrical or, more usually, electromagnetic. Coded cards — either notched, embossed, or containing an embedded pattern of copper flecks — are used to operate such locks. These frequently are fitted with a recording device which registers time of use and identity of the user. The cards serving as keys may also serve as company ID cards. As with code-operated locks, tailgating can occur with this lock as well.

Electromagnetic Locks are devices holding a door closed by magnetism. These are electrical units consisting of the electromagnet and a metal holding plate. When the power is on and the door secured, they will resist a pressure of up to 1,000 pounds. A high frequency of mechanical failures with this type of lock can create problems. Inconvenienced employees will often block the door open or jam the door bolting mechanism so that the lock no longer operates. Quality equipment, preventive maintenance, frequent inspections, and quick response to problems will minimize these problems.

PADLOCKS

Padlocks should be hardened and strong enough to resist prying. The shackle should be close enough to the body to prevent the insertion of a tool to force it. No lock which will be used for security purposes should have less than five pins in the cylinder.

It is important to establish a procedure requiring that all padlocks be locked at all times even when they are not securing an area. This will prevent the possibility of the lock being replaced by another to which a thief has the key.

The hardware used in conjunction with the padlock is as important as the lock itself. It should be of hardened steel, without accessible screws or rivets, and should be bolted through the door to the inside, preferably through a backing plate. The bolt ends should be burred.

Locking Devices

In the previous list we have considered the types of locks that are generally available. It must be remembered, however, that locks must work in conjunction with other hardware which effect the actual closure. These devices may be fitted with locks of varying degrees of security, and themselves provide security to various levels. In a security locking system, both of these factors must be taken into consideration before determining which system will be most effective for specific needs.

Double Cylinder Locking Devices are installed in doors that must be secured from both sides. They require a key to open them from either side. Their most common application is in doors with glass panels which might otherwise be broken to allow an intruder to reach in and open the door from the other side. Such devices cannot be used in interior fire stairwell doors, since firemen break the glass to unlock the door from the inside in this case.

Emergency Exit Locking Devices are panic-bar installations allowing exit without use of a key. This device locks the door against entrance. Since such devices frequently provide an alarm feature that sounds when exit is made, they are fitted with a lock which allows exit without alarming when a key is used.

Recording Devices provide for a printout of door use by time of day and by the key used.

Vertical Throw Devices lock into the jamb vertically instead of the usual horizontal bolt. Some versions lock into both jamb and lintel. A variation of this device is the Police Lock, which consists of a bar angled to a well in the floor. The end of the bar contacting the door is curved so that when it is unlocked it will slide up the door, allowing it to open. When it is locked, it is secured to the door at one end and set in the floor at the other. A door locked in this manner is virtually impossible to force.

Electric Locking Devices are installed in the same manner as other locks. They are activated remotely by an electric current which releases the strike, permitting entrance. Many of these devices provide minimal security, since the engaging mechanisms frequently offers no security feature not offered by standard hardware. The electric feature provides a convenient method of opening the door. It does not, in itself, offer locking security. Since such doors are usually intended for remote operation, they should be fitted with a closing device.

Sequence Locking Devices are designed to insure that all doors covered by the system are locked. The doors must be closed and locked in a predetermined order. No door can be locked until its designated predecessor has been. Exit is made through the final door in the sequence, and entry can be made only through that same door.

Door Jambs

Since doors, when closed, are as a rule attached to the jamb, it is essential that the jamb be of as strong construction as the door or the lock. Aluminum jambs, for example, are frequently spread by a crowbar or an automobile jack. If they cannot resist such attack, the door can be opened easily. The locking bolt must be at least an inch into the jamb for security and to help prevent spreading. Cylinders should be flush or inset to prevent their being wrenched out or "popped."

Removable Cores

In facilities requiring that a number of keys be issued, the loss or theft of keys is an ever-present possibility. In such situations, it might be well to consider removable cores on all locks. These devices are made to be removed if necessary with a core key, allowing a new core to be inserted. Since the core is the lock, this has the effect of rekeying without the necessity of changing the entire device, as would be the case with fixed cylinder mechanisms.

Keying Systems

Keys are generally divided into change keys, submaster keys, master keys, and occasionally grand master keys.

1. *The change key* — a key to a single lock within a master-keyed system.
2. *The sub-master key* — a key that will open all the locks within a particular area or grouping in a given facility. In an office, a submaster might open all doors in the Accounting Department; in an industrial facility, it might open all locks in the loading dock area. Typically, such groupings concern themselves with a common function, or they may simply be located in the same area, even if they are not otherwise related.
3. *The master key* — where two or more sub-master systems exist, a master key system is established. Such a key would open any of the systems.
4. *The grand master key* — a key that will open everything in a system involving two or more master key groups. This system is relatively rare, but might be used by a multi-premise operation in which each location was master keyed while the grand master would function on any premise.

Obviously, master and sub-master keys must be treated with the greatest care. If a master key is lost, the entire system is threatened. Rekeying is the only really secure thing that can be considered, but the cost of such an effort can be enormous.

Master and grand master keys are normally machined to be very thin so that the use of each one is very limited. This is deemed to be a security measure, guarding against their extensive use in the event of loss or theft. This is a dubious proposition at best, since the loss of one of these keys effectively compromises the system and substantially reduces its security value. Even one or two ventures through the facility with such keys could do serious harm and, thin as they are, they might well stand up for that many uses. Unfortunately, when keys of such sensitivity are lost, rekeying is the only answer.

Any master key system is vulnerable. Beyond the danger of loss of the master itself and the subsequent staggering cost of rekeying — or, even more unfortunate, the use of such a key by enterprising criminals to loot the facility — there is the problem that it necessarily serves a lesser lock. Locks in such a system are neither pick-resistant nor resistant to making a key by impression.

On the other hand, relative security coupled with convenience may make such a system preferable in some applications where it would not be in others. Only the most careful evaluation of the particular circumstances of a given facility will determine the most efficient and most effective keying system.

Rekeying

In any sizable facility, rekeying can be very expensive, but there are methods to lessen the disruption and staggering cost that can be involved in rekeying. Outer or perimeter locks can be changed first, and the old locks moved to interior spaces requiring a lower level of security. After an evaluation, a determination of priorities can be made and rekeying can be accomplished over a period of time, rather than requiring one huge capital outlay at once.

Of prime importance is the securing of keys so that such problems do not arise.

KEY CONTROL

Every effort should be exerted to develop ways whereby keys remain in the hands of security personnel or management personnel. In those cases where this is not possible or practical, there must be a system of inventory and accountability. In any event, keys should be issued only to those demonstrably responsible persons who have compelling need for them. Though possession of keys is frequently a status symbol in many companies, management must never issue them on that basis.

Keys should never be issued on a long-term basis to outside janitorial personnel. The high employee turnover rate in this field would suggest that this could be a dangerous practice. Employees of this service should be admitted by guards or other building employees and issued interior keys which they must return before leaving the building.

By the same token, it is bad practice to issue entrance keys to tenants of an office building. If such is done, control of this vital security point is lost. A guard or building employee should control entry and exit before and after regular building hours. If keys must be issued to tenants, however, the lock cylinder in the entrance should be changed every few months and new keys issued to authorized tenants.

A careful, strictly supervised record of all keys issued must be maintained by the security department (See Figure 18.3-1). This record should indicate the name and department of the person to whom the key was issued, as well as the date of issue.

A key depository for securing keys during non-working hours should be centrally located, locked, and kept under the supervision of security personnel. Keys issued on a daily basis, or those issued for a specific one-time purpose, should be accounted for daily. Keys should be counted and signed for by the security supervisor at the beginning of each working day.

When a key is lost, the circumstances should be investigated and set forth in writing. In some instances, if the lost key provides access to sensitive areas, locks should be changed. All keys issued should be physically inspected periodically to ensure that they have not been lost, though unreported as such.

Master keys should be kept to a minimum. If possible, sub-masters should be used, and they should be issued only to a limited list of personnel especially selected by management. Careful records should be kept of such issuance. The list should be reviewed periodically to determine whether all those authorized should continue to hold such keys.

Before a decision can be reached with respect to the master and submaster key systems and how such keys should be issued, there must be a careful survey of existing and proposed security plans, along with a study of current and planned locking devices. Where security plans have been developed with operational needs of the facility in mind, the composition of the various keying systems can be readily developed.

KEY-CONTROL AND LOCK-SECURITY CHECKLIST*

1. Has a key-control officer been appointed?
2. Are locks and keys to all buildings and entrances supervised and controlled by the key-control officer?

---

*John E. Hunter, Physical Security Coordinator, U.S. National Park Service.

SECURITY DEPARTMENT KEY LOG

DATE	TIME OUT	NAME	DEPARTMENT	KEY SET NO.	SIGNATURE	RELEASING OFFICER	TIME IN	DATE	ACCEPTING OFFICER

Figure 18-3.1. Security department key log. A typical form used to record the issuance of keys.

3. Does the key-control officer have overall authority and responsibility for issuance and replacement of locks and keys?
4. What is the basis for the issuance of keys, especially master keys?
5. Are keys issued only to authorized personnel? Who determines who is authorized? Is the authorization in writing?
6. Are keys issued to other than installation personnel? If so, on what basis? Is it out of necessity or merely for convenience?
7. Are keys not in use secured in a locked, fireproof cabinet? Are these keys tagged and accounted for?
8. Is the key cabinet for duplicate keys regarded as an area of high security?
9. Is the key or combination to this cabinet maintained under appropriate security or secrecy? If the combination is recorded, is it secured?
10. Are the key locker and record files in order and current?
11. Are issued keys cross-referenced?
12. Are current records maintained indicating:
    a. Buildings and/or entrances for which keys are issued?
    b. Number and identification of keys issued?
    c. Location and number of master keys?
    d. Location and number of duplicate keys?
    e. Issue and turn-in of keys?
    f. Location of locks and keys held in reserve?
13. Is an audit ever made, asking holders actually to produce keys, to insure that they have not been loaned or lost?
14. Who is responsible for ascertaining the possession of keys?
15. Is a current key-control directive in effect?
16. Are inventories and inspections conducted by the key-control officer to insure compliance with directives? How often?
17. Are keys turned in during vacation periods?
18. Are keys turned in when employees resign, are transferred, or are fired?
19. Is the removal of keys from the premises prohibited when they are not needed elsewhere?
20. Are locks and combinations changed immediately upon loss or theft of keys or transfer or resignation of employees?
21. Are locks changed or rotated within the installation at least annually regardless of transfers or known violations of key security?
22. Are current records kept of combinations to safes and the dates when these combinations are changed? Are these records adequately protected?
23. Has a system been set up to provide submasters to supervisors and officials on a "need" basis, with facilities divided into different zones or areas?
24. If master keys are used, are they devoid of markings identifying them as master keys?
25. Are master keys controlled more closely than change keys?
26. Must all requests for reproduction or duplicaton of keys be approved by the key-control officer?
27. Are key holders ever allowed to duplicate keys? If so, under what circumstances?

28. Where the manufacturer's serial number on combination locks and padlocks might be visible to unauthorized persons, has this number been recorded and then obliterated?

29. Are locks on inactive gates and storage facilities under seal? Are seals checked regularly by supervisory or key-control personnel?

30. Are measures in effect to prevent the unauthorized removal of locks on open cabinets, gates, or buildings?

31. Are losses or thefts of keys and padlocks promptly reported by personnel and promptly investigated by key-control personnel?

32. If the building was recently constructed, did the contractor retain keys during the period when construction was being completed? Were locks changed since that time? Did the contractor relinquish all keys in his possession during construction after the building was completed?

33. If removable-core locks are in use, are unused cores and core change keys given maximum security against theft, loss, or inspection?

34. Are combination-lock, key, and key-control records safeguarded separately (i.e., in a separate safe or file) from keys, locks, cores, and other such hardware?

35. Are all locks of a type which offer adequate protection for the purpose for which they are used?

The above guidelines are recommended as a means of improving and eliminating poor key control.

Appendix 18-4

Files, Safes, and Vaults*

The final line of defense at any facility is in the high security storage areas where papers, records, plans, or cashable instruments, precious metals, or other especially valuable assets are protected. These security containers will be of size and quantity which the nature of the business dictates.

Every facility will have its own particular needs, but certain general observations apply. The choice of the proper security container for specific applications is influenced largely by the value and the vulnerability of the items to be stored in them. Irreplaceable papers or original documents may not have any intrinsic or marketable value, so they may not be a likely target for a thief, but since they do have great value to the owners, they must be protected against fire. On the other hand, uncut precious stones, or even recorded negotiable papers which can be replaced, may not be in danger from fire, but they would surely be attractive to a thief. They must therefore be protected from him.

In protecting property, it is essential to recognize that, generally speaking, protective containers are designed to secure against burglary *or* fire. Each type of equipment has a specialized function, and each type provides only minimal protection against the other risk. There are containers designed with a burglary-resistant chest within a fire-resistant container which are useful in many instances, but these, too, must be evaluated in terms of the mission.

Whatever the equipment, the staff must be educated and reminded of the different roles played by the two types of containers. It is all too common for company personnel to assume that the fire-resistant safe is also burglary-resistant, and vice versa.

FILES

Burglary-resistant files are secure against most surreptitious attacks. On the other hand, they can be pried open in less than half an hour if the burglar is permitted to work undisturbed and is not concerned with the noise created in the operation. Such files are suitable for non-negotiable papers or even proprietary information, since these items are normally only targeted by surreptitious assault.

Filing cabinets with a fire-rating of one hour, and further fitted with a combination lock, would probably be suited for all uses but the storage of government classified documents.**

---

*Gion Green, *Introduction to Security,* 3rd edition (Woburn, Mass.: Butterworth, 1981), pp. 138-139.
**Specifications of government requirements can be obtained from Industrial Security Manual for Safeguarding Government Classified Information available from the U.S. Government Printing Office.

SAFES

Safes are expensive, but if they are selected wisely, they can be one of the most important investments in security. It is to be emphasized that safes are not simply safes. They are each designed to perform a particular job to a particular level of protection. Two types of safes of most interest to the security professional are the record safe (fire-resistant) and the money safe (burglary-resistant). To use fire-resistant safes for the storage of valuables — an all too common practice — is to invite disaster. At the same time, it would be equally careless to use a burglary resistant safe for the storage of valuable papers or records, since, if a fire were to occur, the contents of such a safe would be reduced to ashes.

Safes are rated to describe the degree of protection they afford. Naturally, the more protection provided, the more expensive the safe will be. In selecting the best one for the requirements of the facility, a number of questions must be considered. How great is the threat of fire or burglary? What is the value of the safe's contents? How much protection time is required in the event of a fire or burglary attempt? Only then can a reasonable, permissible capital outlay for their protection be arrived at.

Record Safes

Fire resistant containers are classified according to the maximum internal temperature permitted after exposure to heat for varying periods. A record safe with a UL rating of 350-4 (formerly designated "A") can withstand exterior temperatures building to 2000°F for four hours without permitting the interior temperature to rise above 350°F.

The UL tests which result in the various classifications (See Table 18.4-1) are conducted in such a way as to simulate a major fire with its gradual build-up of heat to 2000°F including circumstances where the safe might fall several stories through the fire damaged building. Additionally, an explosion test simulates a cold safe dropping into a fire which has already reached 2000°F.

The actual procedure for the 350-4 rating involves the safe staying four hours in a furnace temperature that reaches 2000°F. The furnace is turned off after four hours but the safe remains inside until it is cool. The interior temperature must remain below 350°F during heating and cooling out period. This interior temperature is determined by sensors sealed inside the safe in six specified locations to provide a continuous record of the temperatures during the test. Papers are also placed in the safe to simulate records. The explosion impact test is conducted with another safe on the same model which is placed for one-half hour in a furnace preheated to 2000°F. If no explosion occurs, the furnace is set at 1550°F and raised to 1700°F over a half-hour period. After this hour in the explosion test, the safe is removed and dropped 30 feet onto rubble. The safe is then returned to the furnace and reheated for one hour at 1700°F. The furnace and safe are allowed to cool after which the papers inside must be legible and uncharred.

350-2 record safes protect against exposure up to 1850°F for two hours. The explosion/impact tests are conducted at slightly less time and heat.

350-1 gives one hour of protection up to 1700°F, and a slightly less vigorous explosion/impact test.

UL Record Safe Classifications

Classification	Temperature	Time	Impact	Old Label
350-4	2000°F	4 hrs.	yes	A
350-2	1850°F	2 hrs.	yes	B
350-1	1700°F	1 hr.	yes	C
350-1	1700°F	1 hr.	yes	A
(Insulated Record Container)				
350-1	1700°F	1 hr.	no	D
(Insulated Filing Device)				

UL Computer Media Storage Classification

150-4	2000°F	4 hrs.	yes
150-2	1850°F	2 hrs.	yes
150-1	1700°F	1 hr.	yes

UL Insulated Vault Door Classification

350-6	2150°F	6 hrs.	no
350-4	2000°F	4 hrs.	no
350-2	1850°F	2 hrs.	no
350-1	1700°F	1 hr.	no

Table 18.4-1   Fire Resistant Containers

Computer media storage classifications are for containers which do not allow the internal temperature to go above 150°F.

Insulated vault door classifications are much the same as for safes, except that they are not subject to an explosion/impact test.

UL testing for burglary-resistance in safes does not include the use of diamond core drills, thermic lance or other devices yet to be developed by the safecracker.

In some businesses, a combination consisting of a fire-resistant safe with a burglary-resistant safe welded inside may serve as a double protection for different assets, but in no event must the purposes of these two kinds of safes be confused if there is one of each on the premises. Most record safes have combination locks, relocking devices and hardened steel lockplates to provide a measure of burglar resistance. It must be re-emphasized that record safes are designed to protect documents and other similar flammables against destruction by fire. They provide only slight deterrence to the attack of even unskilled burglars. Similarly, the resistance provided by burglar-resistance is powerless to protect contents in a fire of any significance.

Money Safes

Burglary-resistant safes are nothing more than very heavy metal boxes which offer degrees of protection against various forms of attack. A safe with a UL rating of TL-15, for instance, weighs at least 750 pounds and its front face can resist attack by common hand and electric tools for at least fifteen minutes. Other safes will resist not only attack with tools but also attack with torches and explosives.

Since burglary-resistant safes have a limited holding capacity, it is always advisable to study the volume of the items to be secured. If the volume is sufficiently large, it might be advisable to consider the installation of a burglary-resistant vault which, although considerably more expensive, can have an enormous holding capacity.

UL Test Procedures for Money Safes*

To fully appreciate the significance of a UL label it is necessary to have a comprehensive understanding of UL test procedures, for few if any burglars have the skill and knowledge of UL's operators or work under such advantageous conditions. For example, when a manufacturer submits a safe which it is hoped will meet the requirements for a certain classification, UL testers proceed as follows:

1. First they study blueprints of the safe (which the manufacturer is required to submit) and determine which methods of attack might prove most successful. Knowing construction details, all material specifications, and the type, size and exact location of locking bars, relocking devices, protective drill-resistant plates, etc. gives the operators (there are always two working together) a tremendous advantage.

2. Once the operators determine a course of action, they attack the safe and, simultaneously, start a clock to determine elapsed net working time. "Net working time," as determined by UL, is the time the operators spend physically atacking the safe. All other activities, studying the blueprints, preparing for the test, taking safety precautions and dealing with causes of unexpected delays are not included in "net working time." Also, the operators may select a number of test procedures and attempt each attack for the full alloted time determined by the classification. For example, a TL-15 classified safe is required to resist burglarious attack with common tools and electric drills for 15 minutes (see Table 18.4-2). But UL operators might try drilling the lock mechanism for 15 minutes and then, perhaps, try forcing the bolt operating lever by punching, or forcing the handle to rotate with a large wrench for still another fifteen minute period. Therefore, these "cracksmen" might spend an hour or more violently attacking a safe that's designed to withstand such abuse for only a quarter of an hour. UL reasons, and rightly so, that a safe should withstand each method of attack for the full time — for who is to say which method the next burglar will try?

3. UL also has stricter definitions of "entry" (failure of the safe under test) than any burglar. Opening the door is the ideal way to burglarize a safe and that is, of course, considered "entry." But UL also says that the making of a 6 square inch hole through the door or front face of a TL-15 and TL-30 safe and a 2 square inch opening in the door or body of TRTL-30, TRTL-60 and

*Rosberg, Robert R., *Security Risk Management*. (Boston: Dorison House Publishers, 1980), pp. 65-76. Permission obtained from Publisher.

Table 18.4-2. Underwriters Laboratories Safe Classifications

Classification	Description	Construction	
TL-15	Tool Resistant	Weight:	At least 750 lbs. or anchored
		Body:	At least 1″ thick steel or equal
		Door:	At least 1½″ thick steel or equal
		Attack:	Door and front face must resist attack with common hand and electric tools for 15 minutes.
TL-30	Tool Resistant	Weight:	At least 750 lbs. or anchored
		Body:	At least 1″ thick steel or equal
		Door:	At least 1½″ thick steel or equal
		Attack:	Door and front face must resist attack with common hand and electric tools plus abrasive cutting wheels and power saws for 30 minutes.
TRTL-30 (meets UL Std. 687, 1972 ed. See note below)	Tool & Torch Resistant	Weight:	At least 750 lbs.
		Body:	At least 1″ thick steel with 3″ thick reinforced cladding or equal
		Door:	At least 1½″ thick steel or equal
		Attack:	Door and front face must resist attack with tools listed above and oxy-gas cutting or welding torches for 30 minutes.
TRTL-30X6	Tool & Torch Resistant	Weight:	At least 750 lbs.
		Attack:	Door and entire safe body must resist attack with tools listed above plus electric impact hammers and oxy-fuel gas cutting or welding torches for 30 minutes.
TXTL-60	Tool, Torch & Explosive Resistant	Weight:	At least 1000 lbs.
		Attack:	Door and entire safe body must resist attack with tools and torches listed above plus 8 oz. nitroglycerine or equal for 60 minutes.

Notes: All safes are required to have a UL listed combination lock.

Composite materials may be substituted for steel if attack resistance is equal or better.

Common hand and electric tools include chisels, punches, wrenches, screwdrivers, pliers, hammers and sledges, pry bars, ripping tools and electric hand drills not exceeding the ½″ chuck size.

As of January 31, 1980, UL stopped issuing the TRTL-30 label, replacing it with the TRTL-30X6 label which requires equal protection on all six sides of the safe. However, some manufacturers continue to produce safes meeting the requirements of the TRTL-30 label as specified in UL Std. 687, 1972 edition, to satisfy the demand for moderate protection against tool and torch attack at a reasonable price.

TXTL-60 safes are also considered "entry" and failure to pass the test. It would be frustrating indeed for any burglar to try to empty the contents of a safe through a 2 square inch opening (equal in area to a 1.6 inch diameter hole).

Thus, UL-rated safes are much tougher than the classification time allotments may indicate at first glance. Only a very skilled professional "cracksman" could "bust" a TRTL-30 safe in 30 minutes. In addition, it would take much more time breaking into the premises, hauling in and assembling the tools and oxyacetylene torch outfit, and, perhaps, stopping every so often to listen for a guard's steps and police sirens. The contents of this type of safe can be considered very well secured especially if it, and/or the premises, are properly alarmed.

Securing the Safe.

Whatever safe is selected must be securely fastened to the structure where it is located. Police reports are filled with cases where unattached safes, some as heavy as a ton, have been stolen in their entirety — safe and contents — to be worked on in uninterrupted concentration. A study of safe burglars in California showed that the largest group (37.3 percent) removed safes from the premises to be opened elsewhere.*

A convicted criminal recently told investigators how he and an accomplice had watched a supermarket to determine the cash flow and the manager's banking habits. They noted that he built up cash in a small, wheeled safe until Saturday morning, when he banked. Presumably, he felt secure in this practice, since he lived in an apartment above the store and perhaps felt that he was very much on top of the situation in every way. One Friday night, the thief and his friend rolled the safe into their station wagon. They pried it open at their leisure to get the $15,000 inside.

Pleased with their success, the thieves were even more pleased when they found that the manager replaced the stolen safe with one exactly like it and continued with the same banking routine. Two weeks later, our man went back alone and picked up another $12,000 in exactly the same way as before.

It is becoming a common practice to install the safe in a concrete floor where it offers great resistance to attack. In this kind of installation only the door and its combination are exposed. Since the door is the strongest part of a modern safe, the chances of successful robbery are considerably reduced.

VAULTS

Vaults are, essentially, enlarged safes. As such, they are subject to the same kinds of attack and must look at the same basic principles of protection as safes.

Since it would be prohibitively expensive to build a vault out of shaped and welded

---

*Dumbauld, J. and Porter, H., Safe Burglars, *Part II, A Study of Selected Offenders* (Sacramento: California Dept. of Justice, Division of Law Enforcement, 1971).

steel and special alloys, the construction, except for the door, is usually of high quality, reinforced concrete. There are many ways in which such a vault can be constructed, but however it is done, it will always be extremely heavy and, at best, a difficult architectural problem.

Typically, vaults are situated at or below ground level so they do not add to the stresses of the structure housing them. If a vault must be built on the upper stories of a building, it must be supported by independent members which do not provide support for other parts of the building. And, it must be strong enough to withstand the weight imposed upon it if the building should collapse from under it as the result of fire or explosion.

The doors of such vaults are normally 6" thick, and they may be as much as 24" in the largest installations. Since these doors present a formidable obstacle to any criminal, an attack will usually be directed at the walls, ceiling, or floor, which must match the strength of the door. As a rule, these surfaces should be twice as thick as the door and never less than 12".

If at all possible, a vault should be surrounded by narrow corridors which will permit inspection of the exterior, but which will be sufficiently confined to discourage the use of heavy drilling or cutting equipment by attackers. It is important that there be no power outlets anywhere in the vicinity of the vault.

Vault Classification and UL Test Procedures

For the past 60 years, Underwriters Laboratories has been testing vault doors to determine their fire resistance classification; that is, their ability to provide fire protection to contents for specific periods of time. Although, over the same period of time, UL had been testing safes for both their fire resistance and burglary resistance, this was not true of vault doors. There was no means available for determining the exact degree of burglary protection afforded by the vault door. In response to this problem, UL recently implemented a testing program to provide comparative standards for burglary resistant vault doors. The new standard is UL608, Tests for the Burglary Resistance of Vault Doors.

UL Classification

Like their ratings for money or burglary-resistant safes, the new UL classifications for burglary-resistant vault doors are based upon the length of time (elapsed) the doors will resist the efforts of skilled technicians, using tools and torches, to make a significant penetration (See Table 18.4-3). The three classifications are:

Class I — ½ hour
Class II — 1 hour
Class III — 2 hours

These classifications mean that the door will resist attempts at entry (using tools specified in the standard) for attack times varying from ½ hour to 2 hours. Entry is defined as opening the door or making a 96 square inch opening in the door or frame with the smallest dimension of the opening 6 inches or greater.

At the time of this writing ISO had not, as yet, compared their vault wall classification with the UL vault door ratings. Given below is a table providing a suggested comparison.

U.L. Performance Doors	Non-U.L. Steel Doors	Insurance Services Office (I.S.O.) Wall Specifications Effective October 30, 1974	I.S.O. Classification
	3½"	A. ½" Steel Lining*	
		B. 12" Reinforced Concrete	5R
Class II (1 Hour)		A or B	
	3½"	A. 1" Steel Lining*	
		B. ½" S.L. & 12" Reinforced Concrete	6R
		C. 18" Reinforced Concrete	
Class II (1 Hour)		A, B, or C	
	7"	A. 1" Steel Lining*	
		B. ½" S.L. & 12" Reinforced Concrete	9R
		C. 18" Reinforced Concrete	
Class III (2 Hour)		A, B, or C	
	9½"	A. 1½" Steel Lining*	
		B. 1" S.L. & 12" Reinforced Concrete	
		C. ½" S.L. & 18" Reinforced Concrete	
		D. 27" Reinforced Concrete or	10R
		18" Listed Reinforced concrete	
Class III (2 Hour)		A, B, C, or D	

*With fire resistive materials to meet local building codes

Table 18.4-3. Comparative Classifications for Security Vaults

UL Tests

The attack times for the UL tests are based on the time two UL technicians are actually working on the door. In other words, the considerable time spent in setting up, in determining how to actually attack the door, in studying the blueprints of the door supplied by the manufacturer and in regrouping after some unexpected interruption such as a tool failure is not counted into the attack time.

UL employs any or all of four methods of attack on the door using hand tools generally available to the burglar. The tools are common hand tools, picking tools, mechanical or portable electric tools, grinding points, carbide drills, pressure applying devices or mechanisms, abrasive cutting wheels, power saws, coring tools, roto hammers, fluxing rods and oxyacetylene cutting torches.

The four methods of attack are listed below:

1. *Combination Drifting and Drilling.* An attempt is made to knock off the com-

bination dial, punch or drill the spindle and then release the lock mechanism by means of picking tools.

2. *Lock Mechanism.* An attempt is made to penetrate through the door to the lock box, lug, carrying bar, or other parts of the mechanism, then release the boltwork by punching, prying, picking or cutting.

3. *Cutting an Opening.* An attempt is made to cut a 96 square inch opening entirely through the door.

4. *Cutting Locking Bolts.* An attempt is made to cut all or a sufficient number of bolts to permit the door to open.

The Class II performance vault door is positioned as superior to the 3½ inch steel door. A 6R classification when constructed with an 18 inch reinforced wall or equivalent as specified by the ISO effective 10/30/74.

The Class III performance vault door is positioned as superior to the 7 inch & 10 inch steel door. A 9R classification when constructed with a 18 inch reinforced wall or equivalent as specified by the ISO effective 10/30/74. A 10R with a 27 inch reinforced wall or equivalent.

All current steel doors still meet BPA & ISO regulations.

The above door classifications are recommended by Mosler as superior to existing ISO requirements.

The Class II door is recommended as a minimum door protection for financial safe deposit vault operations.

Vault Construction. Vaults are complete enclosures designed for the storage and protection of valuable records and merchandise including furs, jewelry, safe deposit boxes, currency, stocks, bonds, art, etc. Vaults are normally constructed at the site and so, unlike safes, they are permanently affixed and thus are an integral part of the building in which they are located. In theory, they should be built stronger than a safe since they will likely hold more valuables than the average safe.

The design of the vault and the types of materials used in its construction determine whether a vault is fire resistant or burglary resistant. Materials used include iron, steel, concrete, brick, tile and others which will resist burglary, fire, heat, explosion or the passage of water. Many modern vaults possess both fire and burglary resisting properties. This section will deal with the classification of burglary resistant vaults.

Classification of Bank Vaults. For bank vaults, ISO refers to the different categories as "classes." Vaults are rated from Class 1 to Class 10R, with Class 10R being the highest rated vault.

1. Vault walls of brick, concrete, stone, iron or steel; and an iron or steel door.

3. Vault walls of steel at least ¼ inch thick* or of 9 inches of reinforced concrete; and a steel door at least 1½ inches thick.

4. Vault walls with steel lining** at least ½ inch thick* and with fire resistant material to meet local building codes, and with a vault door (a) at least 2½ inches thick of metal including monolithic*** torch and drill resistant material used to protect the locking controls and (b) equipped with dual combination locks and at least a three-movement timelock.

5. Vault walls of steel at least ½ inch thick*; and (a) a round or square door with outer plate of solid cast-manganese steel 1½ inches thick, with return flanges 6 inches on edge, and the remaining 1½ inches of plate steel (this door no longer manufactured) or (b) a steel door(s) at least 3½ inches in thickness.

5R. Vault walls with steel lining** at least ½ inch thick and with fire resistant material to meet local building codes, and with a vault door (a) at least 3½ inches thick of metal including monolithic*** torch and drill resistant material used to protect the locking controls and (b) equipped with dual combination locks and at least a three-movement timelock.

6. Vault walls of steel at least 1 inch thick*, and steel door(s) at least 3½ inches in thickness, (no longer manufactured).

6R. Vault walls with steel lining** at least 1 inch thick* and with fire resistant material to meet local building codes, and with a vault door (a) at least 3½ inches thick of metal including monolithic*** torch and drill resistant material used to protect the locking controls and (b) equipped with dual combination locks and at least a three-movement timelock.

9. Vault walls of steel at least 1 inch thick*, and (a) a round or square door with outer plate of solid cast-manganese steel 2½ inches thick, with return flanges 6 inches on edge, and the remaining 2½ inches of plate steel (this door no longer manufactured) or (b) a steel door(s) at least 7 inches in thickness.

9R. Vault walls with steel lining** at least 1 inch thick* and with fire resistant material to meet local building codes, and with a vault door (a) at least 7 inches thick of metal including monolithic*** torch and drill resistant material used to protect the locking controls and (b) equipped with dual combination locks and at least a three-movement timelock.

10. Vault walls of steel at least 1½ inches thick* and (a) a round or square door with outer plate of solid cast-manganese steel 2½ inches thick, with return flanges 6 inches on edge, and the remaining 2½ inches of plate steel (this door no longer manufactured) or (b) a steel door(s) at least 9½ inches in thickness.

10R. Vault walls with steel lining** at least 1½ inches thick* and with fire resistant material to meet local building codes, and with a vault door (a) at least 9½ inches thick of metal including monolithic*** torch and drill resistant material used to protect the locking controls, and (b) equipped with dual combination locks and at least a three-movement timelock.

Bank Vault Classifications

The following are construction requirements that apply to the classifications given in Table 18.4-3.

Notes:
  *See Tables 18.4-4 and 18.4-5, Vault Wall Equivalency Tables.
  **Steel lining is to be fabricated of single or multiple plates with machined joints having an edge to edge fit with clearance not exceeding ⅛ inch to ensure security.
  ***The monolithic requirement became effective July 1, 1968.

* The word "walls" includes the roof and floor of the vault.
* Each vault door must be equipped with at least one combination lock subject to additional applicable specifications.
* The thickness of the vault door applies to the overall solid door exclusive of boltwork, and is not to include any decorative application on the vault door that may give it the appearance of being thicker than the overall solid thickness.
* Double doors (outer and inner) are each to be measured for the thickness exclusive of boltwork and the thicknesses are to be totaled to determine the combined thickness provided that the vault door is not less than one inch in solid thickness.

Vault Wall Equivalency Tables

The following Tables 18.4-4 and 18.4-5, are for converting walls to either a steel lining or a concrete or stone basis. Only the measurements set forth in the tables are to be used, as it is not permissible to interpolate the measurements.

Table 18.4-4

Non-Reinforced Concrete or Stone		Steel Lining
12 inches	=	¼ inch
18 inches	=	½ inch
27 inches	=	¾ inch
36 inches	=	1 inch
45 inches	=	1¼ inches
54 inches	=	1½ inches

Table 18.4-5

Reinforced Concrete or Stone		Steel Lining
12 inches	=	½ inch
18 inches	=	1 inch
27 inches	=	1½ inches

An exception in Table 18.4-5 is the use of a concrete reinforcing system listed by ISO in their Commercial Lines Manual. In this case, vault walls of listed reinforced concrete at least 18 inches thick are equivalent to steel 1½ inches thick. The following is an example intended to show how Tables 18.4-4 and 18.4-5 and the information in Classification of Bank Vaults, are used to determine the ISO classification for a particular vault.

Example: Classify a vault constructed of 18 inches of reinforced concrete with ½ inch steel lining and a steel door 9½ inches thick. From Table 18.4-5 we find that 18 inches of reinforced concrete is equivalent to 1 inch of steel lining. Adding this 1 inch of steel to the actual ½ inch steel lining gives the equivalent of 1½ inches of steel lining. From Table 18.4-3 we find that a vault with 1½ inches of steel lining and a 9½ inch steel door is given a 10 or 10R classification.

Classification of Mercantile Vaults

Burglary resistant vaults are rated by their ability to resist penetration or attack. The protection they afford is influenced by several factors. In the vault walls, which includes ceiling and floor, thickness, material used and type of reinforcing are important factors. In the door, the thickness of solid steel, the types of material used and the design of the locking and relocking mechanisms should be considered.

The entire vault structure is rated as a single unit. The door, walls, floor and ceiling of the vault must all carry the same classification. If any component carries a lower classification, then the entire unit will be rated at the lower classification. Openings into the vault structure must also comply with certain requirements.

Emergency vault ventilating devices, ducts for air conditioning and heating and openings for electrical conduits must be installed according to specific standards to be acceptable. UL listed emergency vault ventilators and vault ventilating ports must be used.

The scale for rating vaults has been established by the Insurance Services Office. ISO differentiated between those vaults used for mercantile application and those used in banks. For mercantile vaults ISO has four classifications as outlined in Figure 18.4-6.

Table 18.4-6. Classification of Mercantile Vaults

Vault Classification	Vault Construction	
	Doors	*Walls*
B (Burglar-Resistive Rating on a Fire-Resistive Vault)	Steel less than 1″ thick, or iron	Brick, concrete, stone, tile iron or steel
C (Burglar Resistive)	Steel at least 1″ thick	Steel at least ½″ thick; or reinforced concrete or stone at least 9″ thick; or non-reinforced concrete or stone at least 12″ thick
E (Burglar-Resistive)	Steel at least 1½″ thick	Same as for C
G (Burglar-Resistive)	One or more steel doors (one in front of the other) each at least 1½″ thick and aggregating at least 3″ thickness	Steel at least ½″ thick; or reinforced concrete or stone at least 12″ thick; or non-reinforced concrete or stone at least 18″ thick

Appendix 18.5

Intrusion Alarms

A physical security survey differs from an inspection in that a survey is a formal assessment of an installation activity. Each survey should include a study and analysis of all physical hardware and its operation.

An intrusion detection system should be used as a supplement to, but not a substitute for, the guard force of the facility. The alarm is intended to alert guards of an intrusion or attempted intrusion. How effective this combination of guards and alarm system is depends upon the response time of the guards as well as the quality and effectiveness of the alarm system. Before an intrusion detection system is installed a threat or risk analysis assessment should be made. Judging the extent of risk is the primary prerequisite for designing an effective security system. In drafting the design of an alarm system, however, it should be treated for what it actually is, an alert for well-trained security guard forces.

SYSTEMS

Alarm systems are devices made in numerous shapes and sizes, each with a specific purpose and installed in a specific way. In alarming a museum, library, art gallery, corporate office, or home that contains a considerable amount of art, the basic fact should be established that EVERY EXTERIOR DOOR, WINDOW, SKYLIGHT, OR OTHER OPENING MUST BE SECURED AND ALARMED; INTERIOR COVERAGE MUST ALSO BE PROVIDED, WHICH COULD CONSIST OF SPOT PROTECTION, OR COMPLETELY SATURATING THE INTERNAL STRUCTURE. Briefly, these systems consist of:

- Perimeter protection devices, magnetic contacts, switches, foil, break-glass detectors, pressure mats, and accessories.
- Space protection devices, photoelectric ultrasonic, microwave, passive infrared, audio detectors.
- Object protection, capacitance proximity detectors, pressure switches, vibration transducers, safe contacts.
- Audible annunciation, horns, sirens, bells, rotating beacon lights. (A silent on-site alarm may be preferred.)
- Alarm systems can send signals to either one or more of the following: central station, police connect, tape or digital dialer, proprietary or local.
- Control panel, with U.L. listing, custom made or computerized, AC or DC, with or without power backup, with or without high-security shunt keys.

These systems are affected by temperature changes, humidity, metal objects, animals, water movement, thin walls, heaters, the sun, ventilation ducts, and curtains.

ALARMS*

1. Is an alarm system used in the facility?
   a. Does the system indicate an alert only within the facility?
   b. Does it signal in a central station outside the facility?
   c. Is it connected to facility guard headquarters?
   d. Is it connected directly to an enforcement headquarters outside the facility proper? Is it a private protection service? Police station? Fire station?
2. Is there any inherent weakness in the system itself?
3. Is the system supported by properly trained, alert guards?
4. Is the alarm system for operating areas turned off during working hours?
5. Is the system tested prior to activating it for nonoperational periods?
6. Is the alarm system inspected regularly?
7. Is the system tamper resistant? Weatherproof?
8. Is an alternate alarm system provided for use in the event of power failure?
9. Is the emergency power source designed to cut in and operate automatically?
10. Is the alarm system properly maintained by trained personnel?
11. Are periodic tests conducted frequently to determine the adequacy of response to alarm signals?
12. Are records kept of all alarm signals received to include time, date, location, action taken, and cause for alarm?
13. Are the quality and effectiveness of the alarm system examined and any faults promptly corrected?
14. Are all motion-detection units and all areas that have magnetic contacts or switches walk tested?
15. Is the system experiencing false alarms and has the cause been determined?
16. How frequently is the system completely inspected? By whom? Is a report filed?
17. Can parts be obtained within 8 hours, thereby allowing for minimum down time?
18. Is more than one vendor capable of servicing the system?
19. Does the system have panic buttons and are they tested frequently?
20. Are all alarm keys accounted for?

Guidelines for the Physical Security of Cargo, Department of Transportation (DOT P 5200.2), May 1972, Chapter IV, pp. 61-62.

Appendix 18.6

Security Surveys for Libraries

The following five security points should be pertinent, in the ideal library. If they are not already part of your overall security program, they should be incorporated into it.

1.   A checkpoint system is essential, either a guard at each exit and/or an electronic monitoring device. A word about electronic devices: a great deal will depend upon the size of the library in question. Since most electronic systems require that a piece of special tape or metal plate be inserted inside each book, installing such a system can be very expensive if the library is large. For example, a library with three million books would cost (based on one estimate of 17 cents per book) over $500,000 in material alone, not even counting the cost of the labor, which would obviously be considerable. Since such a system is hardly foolproof, large libraries will probably not find this plan worthwhile, although small to medium-sized libraries might want to consider it. If you are experiencing losses, however, these checkpoint systems have proven effective and have reduced losses.

2.   It is also essential, in my view, that access to the books be restricted. There should be only one official stack entrance, and it should be monitored by a qualified person from the circulation desk.

3.   Close monitoring of all issued keys should be maintained. This would include (ideally) keeping key issuance to a *reasonable minimum,* and not issuing to anyone a key that grants access to a larger area than is needed, for example, if someone needs a key to a particular office, this person should be issued a key only for this area. Careful records should be kept as to who has what key at any given time. Keys should not be left around carelessly, that is, on a hook, in an unlocked office, or in an unlocked desk.
     Finally, every effort should be made to retrieve keys from employees or others who are leaving their jobs. In addition, there should be a regular changing (rekeying) of the locks periodically. The extent and frequency of this will, of course, depend on the individual library; I am well aware that, for a very large library, this can be a considerable expense, but I believe it to be well worthwhile and indeed essential.

4.   It is very important that the security department maintain a close and friendly relationship with the public services department of the library (circulation, library privileges, etc.), because all the points made above are dependent upon the goodwill of the majority of the library's staff and users. One can put in all the regulations and security systems in the world, but they will accomplish very little if they are railroaded through a sullen and resentful public. One

simply will not have, in that situation, the cooperation upon which any security system vitally depends. Even if something considered crucial from a security standpoint is axed or tabled by the library powers-that-be, it is usually best, having stated your case beforehand as reasonably and cogently as possible, to accept the final decision with good grace, thus preserving the atmosphere of goodwill that is so important for you in being heard in the future.

5. It is also always a good idea to educate the public about the security measures insofar as possible. This is especially true in an academic community where the Question of the Day is always "Why?" The process of patiently and fully educating the users of a library can become wearing sometimes, but it is ultimately far more effective in ensuring genuine cooperation than bulldozing a measure through by brute force or with a superficial show of power, for security then becomes "The Enemy."

Libraries historically underestimate their security needs and requirements. Two personal examples demonstrating this are as follows:

Several years ago while on vacation I visited the library of a famous resort area. I could not help but notice that the lock on the front door was the same type of lock that I have on my bedroom closet door.

While doing a security survey of a library located within a museum, the director argued for two hours concerning the need to follow all of my recommendations except for a fire alarm system, which he did not deem necessary. When he realized, however, that he had 30,000 first editions in his library and that a bad fire would eliminate his entire collection, he decided to put in a fire alarm system.

Although little has been published on library security as such, all that is necessary is to use the basic security principles for other structures and apply them to library security needs.

Libraries and archives require the additional precaution of carefully identifying readers, limiting access to rare material, plus keeping logs of those who have access as well as controlling material borrowed from the institution.*

Libraries have special needs; therefore, in conducting a survey of a library the following items should be looked into:

Repository Security Checklist**

1. Is there a repository security officer?
2. Is there a procedure to check all applicants' backgrounds before hiring?
3. Is the repository insured against theft by employees?
4. Is access to stack and storage areas on a need-to-go basis?
5. How many employees have master keys and combinations to vaults and other restricted areas?

*Excerpts from speech delivered to ASIS — 25th Annual Symposium, September 1979, entitled "Strengthening Security Systems," by Renata Rutledge.
**Timothy Walch, *Basic Manual Series Archives & Manuscripts: Security,* Society of American Archivists, Chicago, 1977, Permission to reproduce obtained.

6. Is an employee assigned to the reading room at all times?
7. Do employees recognize the seriousness of the theft problem and the need for vigilance in the reading room?
8. Have employees been instructed in the techniques of observation?
9. Have employees been told what to do if they witness a theft?
10. Has contact been made with the crime prevention unit of the appropriate law enforcement agency?
11. What type of personal identification is required of patrons?
12. Are patrons interviewed and oriented to collections prior to use of collections?
13. Has there been an effort to apprise patrons of the need for better security?
14. What are patrons allowed to bring into the reading room?
15. Is a secure place provided for those items not allowed in the reading room?
16. Do call slips include the signature of patrons? What other information is included? How long are call slips retained?
17. How much material are patrons allowed to have at any one time?
18. Are archival materials stacked on trucks near the patrons' seats or kept near the reference desk?
19. Has the reading room been arranged so that all patrons can be seen from the reference desk?
20. Do patrons have access to stack areas?
21. Are patrons allowed to use unprocessed collections?
22. Are patrons' belongings searched when they leave the reading room?
23. Do accession records provide sufficient detail to identify missing materials?
24. Are archival materials monetarily appraised as part of routine processing?
25. Are particularly valuable items placed in individual folders?
26. Are manuscripts marked as part of routine processing?
27. Do finding aids provide sufficient detail to identify missing materials?
28. Does the insurance policy cover the loss of individual manuscript items?
29. Does the insurance policy reflect the current market value of the collections?
30. What is the procedure for the return of archival materials to the shelves? Are folders and boxes checked before they are replaced?
31. Are document exhibit cases wired to the alarm system?
32. Are all exterior doors absolutely necessary?
33. Are there grills or screens on ground floor windows?
34. Are doors and windows wired to a security alarm?
35. If located in a library or building with easy access, does the repository have special locks and alarms to prevent illegal entry?
36. Is a security guard needed to patrol the repository after closing?
37. Are fire and alarm switch boxes always locked?
38. Are security alarms always secured, tamperproof, and away from the mainstream of traffic?
39. Does the repository have a vault or very secure storage area?
40. Is a master key system necessary?
41. Does the repository have special key signs to prevent addition, removal, or duplication of keys?
42. Is after-hours security lighting necessary?

43. Does the repository have a sprinkler system or other suitable fire suppression system?
44. Does the repository have adequate fire extinguishers in accessible locations?
45. Does the repository have a low temperature alarm in event of heat failure to prevent frozen pipes?
46. Are manuscripts and records stored in areas near water pipes or subject to flooding?
47. Does the repository have written procedures for fire alarms, drills, and evacuation?

19. Security Inspection and Evaluation

C. G. "Chuck" Coates

The main purpose of a security inspection and evaluation is to make a meaningful assessment of the existing organization security and to make reasonable recommendations to improve it to the desired level. It can also be used by planners to develop a good security package for any new or expanded facilities. The surveyor should prepare a suitable inspection and evaluation format and checklist to lead him systematically through the evaluation and give a guide to the eventual report.

The security of an organization includes the protection against theft, both internal and external, burglary, vandalism, fire and accident prevention, as well as planning for emergencies and disasters.

The inspection and evaluation of an organization should therefore take into consideration the risk assessment, an audit of the existing security by an on-site inspection, and by analyzing these factors prepare a report together with any recommendations to go forward to senior management for implementation. The recommendations and degree of security have to take into consideration what there is to protect and the risk to the building and contents. If there is very little to protect and no risk, then there are no reasons to make recommendations that are not cost effective.

The following is an example of a format that could be used as a primary checklist for the inspection and the basis for the report.

INTRODUCTION AND SUMMARY

Introduction

The introduction includes the purpose and objectives of the inspection, the scope or type of inspection, whether it is only a partial inspection or a complete inspection, and valuation. It should give a brief reason for the inspection and the authorization. The reason for an inspection could stem from problems, an update, or a series of thefts that have been recorded.

Location and Description

In this part the exact location of the establishment is given, including street address, lot number, and what is adjacent on all four sides. If it is located in a building and occupies only one floor or portion of same, the adjacent companies should be included. The area where the facility is located should state whether it is in a residential area, warehouse district, open country, etc.

The description given of the complex is only a general description, as it is described in more detail further on in the report.

Assessment of Existing Security

This should include date of last inspection and whether all recommendations were implemented. Then a description of the existing security, including guard force and special barriers, with a statement as to the present level and what level is required.

RISK ASSESSMENT

Type and Operation of Facility

In this part there is a complete description as to the type of operation, whether it is an oil refinery, oil company offices, retail warehouse, truck depot, museum, or whatever. It should also say whether the place is open and in operation for twenty-four hours a day or for just eight hours. The type of valuables or classified documents on location and any other information that can help to determine the degree of security required should be described here if the general public has access or if it is controlled access. The type of security will differ, depending on the function of the organization.

Responsible Security Authority and Responsibilities

This is to state the responsible security authority, where the position fits in the organization chart, and whether there are responsibilities other than security detailed in the job. It might be only a part-time job, with most of the time spent on other duties, depending on what value the organization puts on the security.

There may be a recommendation at this point that the responsible security authority should report high up in the organization or should be a full-time position. The person responsible for security should be at a proper level of management to be in a position to be informed on all programs, policies, and organizational objectives.

Threat Analysis

This is the portion of the inspection and report where the decision is made as to the degree of security that is necessary to protect building, assets, and personnel. It is imperative that a risk assessment be made prior to determining the degree and type of security required rather than fitting the risk to the security recommended. The formula normally used to assess the security risk is as follows:

Risk (Probability of occurrence) × Vulnerability (Degree of impact) = Criticality.

The above information can be obtained from previous occurrences or history, information obtained from local and national police forces, world trends, and discussions with employees.

Once this information has been gathered the next step is to set the objectives and scope of the survey. It is very important to include this information in your report so that management will know the reason for the recommendations. It must be decided by management what risk they are willing to take; however, it is the person doing the inspection who has set what is felt to be the security required and should state that in the report. It now comes down to a selling job which is within budgetary restraints.

ADMINISTRATIVE SECURITY

Security Organization

The security organization should be looked at with a positive approach, bearing in mind that security's purpose is to protect the company's assets and personnel with the least possible loss or interruption from illegal activities or undesirable influence so the company can continue its operation's profitability.

The main role of security is "prevention" or stopping an illegal act from occurring. A company that tolerates illegal acts does in fact encourage it. Therefore, all aspects of the security organization should be looked at from the administrative point of view and the following examined:

1. Security directives;
2. Security management and their job descriptions; and
3. An overview of the complete security staff in the form of an organization chart.

Any recommendations in this section should deal only with the managerial aspect and directive in regards to the security organization as the guard force is dealt with in full further on in the report.

Classified Document Security

The first consideration is, "Does the company have any classified material?" or "Should they have classified material?" If there is no classified material and no requirement the job is very easy; however, there may be some documents that should be classified and held in approved containers.

The consideration as to classification is, "What would the loss to the company or person be if the documents got into the wrong hands?" There are documents on personnel that could end up in blackmail or extortion or there could be a description of a valuable article or machine and a location which, if it got into the wrong hands, could prove embarrassing or lead to the easy theft of the article. The following should be taken into consideration when dealing with classified documents:

1. Are adequate containers used to protect the documents?
2. Are locking devices adequate?
3. If combination locks are used on containers, are the combinations changed
   a. every six months?
   b. when an employee leaves?
   c. are the combinations restricted to persons on a need-to-know basis?
4. If key padlocks are used, are they periodically changed or rotated and are the keys kept secured when the office is vacant?
5. If open shelf filing is used, are the following considered?
   a. Is the room secure?

    b.   Are the locks adequate?

    c.   Is there key control?

    d.   Is there a requirement for alarms?

    e.   Is access restricted?

    f.   Are employees given a records check and investigation before getting access to documents?

6. If cash and negotiable documents are handled, are adequate safes and vaults available and are they used?

7. Are classified documents left lying on desks and in baskets while not attended?

8. Are typewriter ribbons and carbons treated in the same manner as the classified documents and adequate protection afforded same?

9. Are classified documents and carbons thrown in with ordinary waste or are they properly destroyed by

    a.   burning?

    b.   shredding?

10. Is classified waste treated the same as the original documents when it comes to storage during quiet hours?

11. Is classified material transmitted in two sealed envelopes, the inner envelope suitably marked?

12. When mailing a classified document, is it registered?

13. If couriers are used, are they bonded?

14. Are classified documents suitably marked as such?

Inventory and Equipment Control

The organization that has a large inventory should have control of same, as a great amount of losses are attributed to employees. The cause is lack of proper inventory control or none at all. If there is a problem in this area some of the following might apply:

1. Is there control of inventory and equipment?

2. Is there a central storage area for tools and small machines?

3. Is there a "tool crib" system in effect?

4. Are small articles properly identified in event of loss or theft?

5. Are serial numbers recorded?

6. Are small articles locked in secure cabinets when not in use?

7. Is there a responsible person in charge of inventory?

8. Is there a periodic audit?

9. Are there removal slips used when articles are taken off property?

10. Is the security staff aware of the system and given authority to check and record removals?

11. Are the removal slips signed by persons in authority?
12. Are spot checks of persons and lunchboxes made?
13. Is there a policy in effect if articles are reported missing, or are they just written off?
14. Are unusual incidents reported and properly investigated?

If there are problems regarding equipment and inventory control and no effort is being made to correct them, then a number of recommendations can be submitted.

Shipping and Receiving

The following are some of the considerations to take into consideration when dealing with this area, as there are cases where goods disappear from the loading docks. It can happen where the shipper/receiver works in conjunction with drivers.

1. Are the shipping and receiving docks physically separated?
2. Are there a shipping clerk and a receiving clerk?

The above two may not be practical in a small organization, however, and have to be integrated.

3. Are loading docks fenced, giving only limited access when required?
4. Is the lighting adequate, particularly when material is left outside during the night?
5. Is access to areas restricted to authorized personnel only?
6. Are clerks given a background and indices check?
7. Is there a package and material control system in effect?
8. Is there a receipt system in effect?
9. Do security people make periodic checks of area during silent hours?
10. Are private vehicles allowed in compound?
11. Are materials allowed to pile up and not disseminated regularly?
12. Are losses investigated immediately?

The particulars regarding the access, perimeter barriers, locks, and key control are covered under Physical Security.

Vehicle Control

It must be kept in mind that vehicles make the best means of transportation for pilfered items, and when they are allowed in a protected area or near a facility there can be problems. It is therefore important that this area be carefully assessed, especially in large companies. The following are some of the things to look for:

1. Are there separate parking areas for
    a. company vehicles?
    b. visitors' vehicles?
    c. employees' vehicles?
2. Are the company vehicles parked within a fenced-in compound?
3. Are vehicles parked close to the fence where they can be used to assist in gaining entry?
4. Are vehicles parked near windows of the building?
5. Are employee vehicles parked within the compound?
6. Is there access control to company vehicle compound?
7. Are gates to company vehicle compound secured at night?
8. Are parking areas adequately lighted?
9. Is there indoor parking and if so are all safety regulations adhered to?
10. Are access points controlled by guard force?
11. Are company vehicles and delivery vehicles logged in, complete with manifest when applicable?
12. Are seals put on vehicles that are loaded and parked for a time in the compound?
13. Is access by personnel restricted according to the need to be into the vehicle compound?
14. If employee vehicles are parked in compound are stickers supplied and affixed for identification?
15. Is there a rail line into compound and is it secure when not in use?
16. Is there a requirement for CCTV?
17. If there is valuable cargo stored in compound overnight, can it be alarmed?
18. Is the area patrolled by the guard force?

There may be other areas that need to be covered; however, the size of the operation will determine to what extent the inspection will have to go.

Cleaning Staff

The cleaning staff can be one of the problem areas with regards to theft, vandalism, and pilferage. They are often working during the quiet hours when there are no other personnel in the building, and they are not supervised. The carts and garbage disposal units make ideal receptacles to put articles in and take past guards to the area where the garbage is picked up. Here are some of the things that can be looked for in this area:

1. Are the cleaning staff employees of company, and if so are they checked through police indices and given a background check before being hired?
2. If contract company is utilized are they
   a. Bonded?
   b. Are checks made on personnel, particularly supervisory persons?
   c. Are employees issued keys or must they pick them (e.g., from guard force) or do guard force open doors for them?
   d. Are they supervised as to movements by guard force?
   e. Are containers spot checked by guard force for pilferage?
3. Is the cleaning done at night and is there a possibility it can be done while employees are in the building?
4. Are cleaning staff identified by uniform or badges?
5. If employees are caught stealing are they charged in court or just let go?

Courier Service

When courier service is used, are the following taken into consideration:

1. Are they bonded?
2. Do they carry sufficient insurance to cover any article they carry?
3. Are employees bonded?
4. What are the types of vehicles used? They should be adequate for the type of goods they carry.
5. Are guards armed when carrying valuable cargo or money?

Personal Protection

This is a very challenging subject and differs depending on the vulnerability of the personnel. There should be a contingency plan in the event that there may be a requirement for one. The subject should be looked at from a risk point of view.

If large amounts of money or valuable materials with a high value on the illicit market are involved, there may be a requirement for protection of personnel who are dealing directly with the public, e.g., persons handling monies.

Visitor Control

The main thing to look for: Is there a requirement for control? Are there areas restricted to employees only both for reasons of company records and for safety reasons? If visitors are allowed access, the following should be considered:

1. Are they restricted to areas?
2. Are they registered in and out?
3. Are they issued identification badges?
4. Are they escorted?
5. Are they required to wear protective clothing?

Personnel Identification

The following should be taken into consideration depending on the size of the organization:

1. Are all employees issued company identification cards, and do the cards include:
   a. full name?
   b. date of birth?
   c. description?
   d. SIN number?
   e. photograph?
   f. company name and logo?
   g. any particulars as to where they may go in plant?
   h. occupation?
   i. signature?
   j. signature of signing authority?
2. Are access control badges worn on premises and are the following taken into consideration where required:
   a. color coded for access to areas?
   b. photographs?
   c. cards coded for protection?
   d. company logo on cards?
   e. cards changed on a regular basis (2 years to 3 years) or when description changes?

PERSONNEL SECURITY

Employee Selection

The problems of employee selection vary with the type of work they are going to be doing; however, there should be some form of continuity. If there is a chance that employees will have access to sensitive documents or valuable equipment or articles then they should be required to fill in a Personal History Form and have fingerprints taken. These should both be checked through local and national police if possible. There should be a background check made, in particular with references. It is essential, though, that there be a policy for the selection of all employees.

Employee Clearances

The first thing to establish is whether there is a requirement for a clearance program. If there is, are the following taken into consideration?

1. Personal History Form;
2. Fingerprints;
3. Indices check;
4. Background check with previous employers.

Security Orientation

There should be a policy that all new employees be given a security orientation lecture by the security staff, and then periodically the security staff should give talks to advise the staff of new procedures and rules. This could be done in conjunction with talks on fire prevention and contingencies.

Periodic Security Updating

There should be a policy that Personal History Forms be updated in the event of marriages, deaths, change of name, etc., of employees where required. This can be discussed with the employees at the time of their annual assessment. Obtain their feelings regarding security. The main thing is that the company have a policy.

Termination Procedures

Every company should have a policy for the termination of employees for whatever reason. Here are some of the things to take into consideration:

1. return of keys;
2. return of identification cards;
3. return of equipment and tools;
4. security debriefing when required.

PHYSICAL SECURITY

The physical security of the complex is the most important part of the inspection and evaluation and the lengthiest. It will take into consideration the total
physical aspects and description of the complex, note all the deficiencies, and
make recommendations to improve the security. The degree of security will
be in direct contrast with the risk assessment and the value and type of material that is to be protected. It will differ for valuable metals or articles and
for sensitive documents. The person doing the inspection and evaluation must
know the feelings of management, and if those feelings are negative, he may
have to do a selling job.

In some of the areas in this section there may be the requirement to call
in expert assistance as in the case of alarms, CCTV, lighting, or other areas,
or the recommendations may suggest that an expert evaluation be done in one
of these areas. The areas that should be inspected and evaluated will differ,
depending on the scope of the survey. It could mean inspecting the whole complex or just one room. The following are the areas of a complex that should
be covered in a complete inspection. There may be other areas not mentioned,
depending on the type of organization.

Physical Description of the Facility

This should be a complete description of the facility, including fences, location
of entrances and exits, windows, parking areas, and location of the different
operations of the business. It should indicate the type of construction of the
building, size, design, and any other pertinent information.

It is very important to have a complete set of plans, including site plans,
so that a more complete evaluation can be made and for location of the different areas identified. Photographs are also very valuable when describing the
building and areas. These should be overall photos covering as much area as
possible. These are valuable to the person the report is being sent to if he
is not on site. If there is more than one building all should be described and
marked as such on a site plan.

Perimeter Barriers

This will include a complete and thorough inspection of the complex, going
from the outside fence to the core of the building if a complete inspection
is being done. If the scope of the inspection is only one room, then the barriers
will only include that area; however, there should be some attention given to
the surrounding area in order to justify recommendations.

This is where photographs can be very helpful when describing the various types of fencing, doors, windows, walls, locks, etc. These, together with a complete description, will give the reader of the report as well as the person responsible for implementation of the recommendations a good idea of why they were made. All defects should be noted or a statement provided indicating that they are adequate. This is where experience pays off, both in security and a good knowledge of construction and the terminology used in the building trade. Plans or blueprints should be used to locate the doors, windows, etc., that are being described. This will give an exact location.

The inspection in this area must take everything regarding the building into consideration. It will be very time-consuming and must consider the risk factor as to what degree of security is required.

The definitions, terminology, and what to look for are a study in itself, and with experience a person can learn to know just what to look for. When making recommendations it is desirable to make them specific so that the person responsible for implementation will know exactly what is required. There are many firms and agencies that can supply specifications for doors, secure walls, windows, framing, locks, etc., as well as architects, fire, and police departments. A checklist for this section could be very lengthy depending on the scope of the inspection. The main points to consider, however, are whether the structure is adequate for the degree of security required and whether the construction is going as per the plans.

Key Control

The control of keys is a very important function in the security of any complex. There are a number of things that should be taken into consideration when dealing with the control of keys.

1. Has a key-control officer been appointed and does he/she have the authority and responsibility to go with the job?
2. Are keys issued only on a need-to-have basis?
3. Are complete records kept of the keys issued?
4. Are spare keys kept in a locked cabinet?
5. Are lost or stolen keys reported and locks changed when necessary?
6. Are only heavy-duty locks used?
7. When combination locks are in use, are combinations changed regularly and when employees leave?
8. Is reproduction of keys controlled and is there a registered key way?

Access Control

Access control could mean the difference between goods walking out the door or not. Tight control can mean dollars to a firm as well as the control of information and the money saved in goods not going out could pay for a good control system. There are different types of access control that can be used, such as

1. guard service;
2. access cards (computer);
3. keys; and
4. receptionists.

Any one or all could be used in any complex in the following locations:

1. gate entrance;
2. building entrance;
3. computer entrance;
4. stock rooms;
5. registries;
6. executive suites;
7. parking areas;
8. laboratories.

Once a decision has been made as to the type of access control to be used, consideration should be given to the use of identification badges. Different types can be used, including

1. badges with photographs;
2. color coded;
3. cards for contractors, etc.;
4. cards for visitors;
5. cards that are left on site;
6. cards that are taken home;
7. use of company identification cards only;
8. computer cards used as key control.

Once a decision is made on type of access required, then complete instructions should go out to the guard force as well as to all employees so they are familiar with the procedures as far as how the system works. There are a number of companies specializing in access control cards and systems. Once the decision has been made, everyone should be required to adhere to the regulations, with no exceptions.

Security Force

When looking at an existing guard force, the following should be taken into consideration:

1. Is it adequate for the protection that is required?
2. Are the guards uniformed?
3. Are instructions and post orders adequate and up to date?
4. Are they properly supervised?
5. Are they armed?
6. Are they licensed in accordance with local regulations?
7. Are they properly trained in
   a. first aid?
   b. fire prevention?
   c. safety?
   d. security?
8. Are they given an orientation course of the premises and made familiar with the regulations and orders before being put on post?
9. Are they required to operate control consoles and voice communications systems and have they been properly trained?
10. Do they also act as guides or as an information/receptionist?

If there is no guard force being employed at the time of inspection, the following should be taken into consideration:

1. Is there a requirement?
2. What type of force to recommend:
   a. in house?
   b. contract?
3. How many required which should include supervision?
4. To whom do they report?

When deciding on the type of security force required, consideration should be given to the pay, for it is stated, "Pay peanuts and you get monkeys."

Alarms

When looking at an existing alarm system, things to consider are whether it is adequate coverage for what it is to protect, and whether the type of alarms used is the proper type. This plus a walkthrough to see if they are all functioning is a necessary exercise. If there is a requirement for new or expanded alarms there should be a decision as to the type of alarms required:

1. contacts;
2. motion detectors;
3. tape;
4. floor mats;
5. break wire;
6. vibration detectors.

When a new alarm system is being considered, thought should be given as to whether it be a local system, in-house monitoring, or a central station. This will differ depending on location and the availability of a central monitoring company or police department that will monitor alarms. There may be a situation where there is a requirement for alarms; however, if there is no available response, then other considerations have to be made.

This is an area where the person doing the inspection can indicate the type of protection that is required and have a specialist set up the system, unless the person doing the inspection is able to assess the systems and do an inspection before take-over. There are a number of agencies and specialists in the field, and the cost will in most cases be justified by the end result. It must be remembered that alarms are only an extension of the guard service and only as good as the response available.

Closed-Circuit Television (CCTV)

Closed-circuit TV is another extension of a security guard's sight and is only as good as the response that can be obtained. It must be ascertained if the coverage by CCTV is going to do the desired job. There may be spots where CCTV in conjunction with motion detection and alarms will in fact do the desired job. The attention span for a person watching a monitor is approximately twenty minutes, and then any movement will be missed.

Once the decision has been made as to where CCTV is required, then expert consultation should be sought to complete the recommendation. There will be things such as lighting and lens selection that must be considered. If there is twenty-four-hour guard protection provided by only one guard during quiet hours, there must be another response available if that guard goes on patrol, for who is to monitor the system?

Lighting

Security lighting can perform a number of functions:

1. protection lighting;
2. as a physical barrier;
3. as a response mechanism;
4. as a detection mechanism.

Lighting is mostly a psychological barrier that can be used to dissuade vandals and lesser criminals; however, it may not have any impact on a determined would-be intruder. When taking lighting into consideration these elements must be considered:

1. background color of building;
2. local restraints;
3. obstructions that give shadows;
4. lighting from adjacent properties;
5. what the lighting provides;
6. environmental conditions (summer-winter).

Once you have assessed the existing lighting and taken the preceding into consideration then the type and level of lighting must be considered. This is an area where a consultant or lighting company can be of considerable help, for they know what the local regulations are and can adapt a system to them. Consideration should be given to the following as well:

1. turning on and off of lights and the system to be used;
2. maintenance, both emergency and preventive, which includes cleaning and replacing of bulbs when their suggested life is at approximately 80 percent.

When in doubt, check with a specialist.

Fire Prevention

There are a number of things that can be checked when doing an inspection, such as:

1. Is there an emergency organization?
2. Are they trained for emergency situations?
3. Are fire orders posted?
4. Are all exits properly marked and lighted?
5. Is there an approved fire alarm system?
6. Are fire extinguishers prominently displayed throughout the building and are they checked on a regular basis?
7. Are fire routes clearly marked and clear of obstructions?
8. Are emergency exits clear and are escape routes clear of obstructions such as boxes, snow, etc.?
9. Is there a fire suppression system?
10. Do all emergency doors open outward and are they equipped with appropriate hardware?
11. Is there life-saving equipment available and are the staff properly trained?
12. Are flammable materials properly stored?

There are other areas; however, should the persons doing the inspection not be completely familiar with all aspects of fire prevention, then they should consult with the local fire department and provincial or federal agents responsible. Normally, recommendations from these agencies give more clout and in some incidents are mandatory. Therefore, these agencies should always be contacted, and it is also recommended that the responsible person on site keep good liaison with them. Should there be new construction, these agencies should be called in to assist in the design stage.

Health and Safety

In most situations, the main thing to look for is whether there is a person responsible for health and safety within the corporation and on site. It should also be assessed whether there are regular inspections by authorities.

Auxiliary Power

The main question in this regard is whether there is auxiliary power or not and whether there is a requirement for same. If there is auxiliary power, are the following taken into consideration?

1. Is the unit adequate for the requirement?
2. Is it tested regularly?
3. Are the emergency lights connected to same?
4. Are sufficient lights throughout building connected to allow safe exit in event of a power failure?
5. Is the alarm system connected?
6. Is the fire emergency system connected?

Utilities

These will include hydroelectric power, telephone, water, gas, or oil supply and any other utilities that are supplied from off premises. This may be in the form of pipes, wire, storage tanks, etc.

The consideration here is to see if the hydro and telephone lines are located in such a manner that they cannot be tampered with and are also safe.

When it comes to gas or oil pipes, gauges, and valves, consideration should be given to securing them from tampering and accidents from vehicles, etc. This may require fencing or, in the case of new installations, locating in a safe and isolated area. In the case of storage tanks, the vents and filler pipes should be secured from vandalism and damage.

Security Containers

Security containers may be required for classified documents, cash, minerals, or other valuable materials. The size of the containers should fit what has to be stored. This could range all the way from a small wall safe to a large vault. There are government standards when it comes to fire rating for safes and vaults and for the degree of force required to open them. There are a number of accredited companies who will supply the information on the requirement for certain materials.

When a built-in vault is being recommended, then there should also be specifications regarding its construction. It should be properly reinforced and the door should be secure. There are also specifications for vents, hydro, etc. There may also be a requirement for alarms. This could include motion or vibration detection as well as contacts.

The following should be taken into consideration regarding padlocks and combinations:

1. Are padlocks adequate for what they are protecting?
2. Are they changed periodically?
3. Are combinations changed every six months or when employee leaves?
4. Are combination numbers given only to persons with a need to have?
5. Are combination numbers left on calendars, calendar pads, etc.?

Intransit Security of Classified Documents and Valuable Materials

The following should be considered when dealing with this type of security:

Documents.

1. Are classified documents securely sealed in two envelopes?
2. The outer envelope should have no indication of classification.
3. Is this type of mail registered when sent through post office?
4. If courier service is used, is it a bonded carrier and are all employees bonded?
5. When large shipments of documents are transported are they under escort?

Valuables.

1. Are valuables enclosed in secure containers?
2. Are bonded carriers used?

3. Are articles insured?
4. Are trained persons used to pack materials?
5. Are inventories and invoices completed and enclosed in cartons as well as copies retained?
6. Are all articles properly identified and photographed when this appears practical?
7. Are signatures obtained?
8. Are containers void of any indication of contents?
9. Are employees of couriers properly identified and bonded?
10. When necessary, are shipments escorted?

Consideration also has to be given to the value or classification of the material being shipped and how it is shipped.

Classified Waste Disposal

It must be remembered with classified waste that it be given the same protection as if it were not waste. This includes carbon paper, the new typewriter ribbons that are only typed on once, and any other material that has a classification. Work plans and design drawings could also be classed in this department. There should be special containers used, and such materials should not be thrown in with regular waste or regular waste thrown in with it. Classified waste should be destroyed in one of the following ways:

1. pulping;
2. shredding;
3. burning.

While it is being destroyed there should be a person classified to the level of the material supervising until it is fully destroyed.

COMMUNICATIONS AND E.D.P. SECURITY

This is a portion of the inspection where normally the person only has the expertise to do the physical security of the area in order properly to secure same. When it comes to the security of the information and the electronic security, assistance of a specialist familiar with all the software and hardware and lines is required.

CONTINGENCY PLANNING

Things to consider when dealing with this part of the inspection:

1. Are there contingency plans for the following:
   a. fire?
   b. explosion?
   c. bombs and bomb threats?
   d. accidents?
   e. power failures?
   f. riots, demonstrations, and sit-ins?
   g. floods?
   h. earthquakes?
   i. civil disturbances and strikes?
   j. kidnapping and extortion?
   k. robberies?
2. Are these plans reviewed regularly and revised when necessary?
3. Is there an emergency organization, is it trained, and are regular practices conducted and list kept up to date?
4. Is there a government organization available for direction and guidance and is it used?
5. In the event of an emergency or disaster are there arrangements for off-site storage of valuable equipment and documents?

THE INSPECTION REPORT

The report is the most important part of the inspection because the writer must convince management that there are deficiencies and that the recommendations will help to protect the assets whether they be information or property. It is for this reason that the report must be clear and concise and the recommendations be practical and still give the desired protection.

The report should be classified and go to the person who originated or authorized the inspection. Should the report get into the wrong hands, there could be the possibility of the premises being compromised. The appendices at the end of the report should include such items as

1. a summary of recommendations;
2. plans and blueprints;
3. specifications for specific items;
4. photographs.

CONCLUSION

The main objectives in doing an inspection and evaluation are to indicate the weaknesses in security and to make recommendations to bring it to the level required. Then management has to be convinced there is a weakness and that there is a requirement to improve it. This can be done by meeting with management, putting forward your proposals, explaining them, and answering any questions dealing with the evaluation.

20. Transportation of Cultural Art Objects

Saul L. Chafin

PROBLEMS IN TRANSPORTING ART

Preservation of the art while it is in transit is your greatest problem. When you are moving artwork out of a relatively stabilized environment, such as a museum, whether you are moving it across the country or only across the street, it is more subject to theft or damage than otherwise. And protecting the objects while they are in transit is, of course, very important.

Hence to avoid moving a work of art other than by road has some advantages: Road shipment takes longer than flying and consequently there are more chances of damaging the art object. In addition, more security arrangements have to be undertaken, such as coordination with the various police departments on the route of the shipment.

We must consider, however, whether we are transporting a single painting or 40 crates of art that are part of an exhibition?

As a security manager in charge of an art shipment, there are several questions that you must answer:

1. What does the shipment consist of?
2. What is the total value of the shipment?
3. What is the method of transportation?
4. Was or is the shipment professionally packed?
5. Who packed the shipment?

INSURANCE COVERAGE

Have insurance arrangements been made to cover:

1. The permanent collection, including long-term loans.
2. Temporary loans, including transportation to and from the museum and domestic traveling exhibitions.
3. Legal or bailee liability.
4. Foreign exhibitions, including transportation to and from the United States as well as transit between both foreign and domestic exhibition sites.[1]

THE SECURITY ASSIGNMENTS

Whether a shipment is slated for intrastate or interstate delivery, the importance of good security personnel and equipment cannot be overemphasized.

Unmarked security vehicles, well maintained and fitted with two-way radio systems, are best suited for transport assignments. Citizen band radio systems might also be included as a backup. In *no* event should anyone other than security personnel have access to the security radio system or frequency. One way to overcome this and provide additional security would be to assign a portable radio to an armed security officer who rides "shot gun" in the truck. This is not to imply that the security officer should have this type of weapon in the cab. All communications between security personnel should be coded and kept to an absolute minimum. Since there is always the possibility of vehicle maintenance problems, a backup truck and driver might be something to think about in advance. If a breakdown occurred, the shipment could be transferred and the transport continued. Valuable art should never be left for any length of time of the side of the road.

TANDEM VEHICLE ARRANGEMENT

A convoy of vehicles may stand out unless the cars and trucks are switched from time to time. To remain as unobtrusive as possible, the security car drivers may want to sandwich the van, precede it for a distance, then tail it, reverting back and forth depending on the road conditions. A problem that security drivers may have to overcome is driving for long periods of time without rest. Many truck drivers are used to long road trips, driving as long as 12 to 16 hours straight. Such a long continuous drive can be taxing for the inexperienced driver. Security officers have seldom been called upon to sit behind the wheel of a vehicle committed to steady driving. In fact, they are better suited for surveillance of the vehicle, motionless or not, and on the look out for suspicious persons or other potential hazards.

Hijacking probably comes to mind as the first possibility for cargo loss during one of these transports. In addition to picking the most desirable route, the security representative is advised to check with local and state law enforcement officials to learn of any recent intelligence on truck hijackings. It is debatable whether the pending transport should be announced to anyone. Sometimes, the less advertised, the better. Moving art interstate is a matter requiring serious thought and preparation. An outside agency, such as the FBI in all probability would be able to offer valuable assistance.

SECURITY FUNCTION IN OVERSEAS SHIPMENT

Usually, a museum hires a "broker" to arrange the shipment with a professional mover. With the museum as a client, the firm makes the necessary global contacts to arrange for and coordinate the shipment. This may involve such things as contacting airports, museums, transport companies, the embassy, and local and federal police officials in the country from which the shipment is coming or going.

Literally the middleman, the broker firm saves a lot of work for the security director. However, there are some important things that must be done by security. First and foremost, all security personnel accompanying the shipment must have passports and any other official papers needed to prove identity and authorization for the art transport. In this age of airline hijackings and international terrorism it is helpful if someone in the security force has connections with the international law enforcement network. In the event the natural flow of transport were to go astray, predesignated personnel should be prepared to remain with the shipment at all times.

Large shipments of valuable art may have to be shipped separately for insurance purposes. In this case a duplication of personnel would be required, particularly if the cargo were shipped simultaneously.

In addition to the overseas transportation, which is usually by air freight, once the cargo has arrived at the initial destination further travel by motor carrier is necessary. In that event, the same precautions as for interstate or intrastate shipment should prevail.

One rule of thumb is that security personnel must remain with the art until it has arrived safely at its destination.

THE TRANSPORTATION COMPANY

As a general rule, the transport firm should be a reputable, licensed moving company, preferably with past experience in the handling of valuable art. Museum and fine art staffs are usually acquainted with those companies that can be relied upon. Any questions regarding the company's business practices should be clarified immediately, before bid procedures have been completed. To avoid misunderstandings, it is suggested that key personnel from the transport company, the museum (i.e., conservation personnel and registrars), and security arrange to meet to discuss and plan the entire shipment. Each representative can then communicate any concern he or she might have. It would be ideal to have the same key personnel involved in the planning phase participate in the actual art shipment. The overall goals should be to utilize the necessary resources to ensure an efficient and safe transport, to have open communication by all parties involved, and to develop a true sense of the mission to be completed.

PACKING

Under the watchful eye of a conservator, curator, or courier, the cargo is carefully wrapped and packed. In some instances, special crates designed to protect the objects from shifting or damage due to environmental changes are built to specifications. The crates are sealed, well marked, and recorded. After packing and before loading takes place, the security director should apply a special mark to the sealed crate. This is addressed in more detail later in the chapter. Being on hand during the packing phase helps to ensure the integrity of the shipment.

Moving art *is no* simple matter. It is a joint venture by many members of the art facility. Failure to involve essential personnel could result in losses or damages. The following example explains why.

SHIPMENT OF CANVAS PAINTINGS DURING THE WINTER

In 1960 the Dutch authorities lent Canada a very valuable collection of paintings and drawings by Van Gogh. It was intended to circulate this extensive exhibition through several large cities, extending into the winter period of that year. Thus, at the end of December, it was to travel from Ottawa to Winnipeg (in the interior of the country), a distance of approximately 3000 kilometers, with outside temperatures as low as -30°C and correspondingly dry atmospheres. Some of the paintings were wax-relined, but most were not; these were, therefore, in the moisture-sensitive category, whence great attention had to be paid to conditions of relative humidity in transit. Likewise the prints and drawings required protection to avoid desiccation. While these works of art had been shipped mainly by air from Holland in light containers it was considered essential to repack the entire exhibition for winter travel. Consultations were arranged with the scientific staff, the packaging and handling staff and officials of the National Railroad system to ensure that maximum safety would result. Cases were constructed of top-quality white pine, painted on the outside and carefully lined with a fibre-board material (compressed de-fibred wood pulp) to serve as a heating-insulating and moisture-retentive envelope to surround the painting and graphic art works. All construction materials had been stored inside the National Gallery at the conditions prevailing there; that is, at a relative humidity of 48 percent and a temperature of 21°C. Under such conditions the equilibrium moisture content (oven-dry basis) for the wood is 10 percent and that of the fibre-board is approximately 8 percent. The works themselves were prepacked in draft paper to afford additional protection.[2]

Technology has changed since the above was written in 1963. However, we mentioned this example in order to give you an idea of the complicated problems involved in such a program as transportation of art.

COSTS FOR TRANSPORTATION – A BREAKDOWN

- Number of transport vans
- Number of security escort vehicles
- Specifications to transporter
- Export packing required
- Registrars, conservators, museum staff, and security coverage
- Insurance coverage
- Special packaging materials

As part of your overall planning and budgeting all of these factors must be taken into consideration.

LOADING THE TRUCK

Reputable moving firms provide their personnel with a manual that instructs them in the proper way to load a truck. Much of this instruction is common sense. For example, one person holds a painting with both hands while someone else clears a pathway and opens doors, versus having one person hold a painting by the frame with one hand and open several sets of doors with the other. When large, heavy crates must be moved, two or more persons may have to lift and carry the crates while the same pathway and clearing and door opening procedure is conducted by still another person.

The golden rule of "Never Touch the Surface or Back of a Painting" applies at all times. This also means that one painting or object should never be permitted to rest against another. In packing, every effort should be made to ensure that this rule is not violated. Since a frame can be highly valued as well as valuable, special consideration must be given to the preservation of its condition. Therefore stacking of frames should be avoided at all costs.

TIPS ON LOADING

1. When loading a truck, one man should stay inside. His main function is to receive the art object and place and secure it before transit. He can signal when he is ready for the next object.
2. Vehicles should *never* be overloaded. Crates or paintings should not extend beyond the back end. Remember, the truck's rear doors must be secured and sealed.
3. Works of art should never be dragged, pulled, or slid across any type of surface, whether it is smooth or rough. Some truck rear compartments are built with specially cushioned wood floors and walls. Proper handling requires carrying, lifting, and the use of dollies. Due consideration must be given to having an adequate number of trained workers on hand before the loading process starts.
4. If possible, the rear of the trucks should have stabilizers. Ropes, straps, and dollies must not come into contact with the surface or sides of framed paintings not being transported in crates. However, there is little or no reason to ship any painting or work of art without a crate.
5. Avoid stacking works of art on top of each other. Try not to place large or heavy paintings directly against each other.
6. The largest art object should be placed in the rear of the truck closest to the cab, leaving space for the smaller objects nearer the tailgate. Alternate the paintings vertically or horizontally and secure them to prevent shifting while in transit.

STOPPING EN ROUTE

Some art transports cover such long distances that it becomes necessary to stop overnight for a well-deserved rest. In most instances, arrangements for overnight accommodations will have been covered during the planning phase. Since our emphasis throughout this chapter is on the safe and secure transport of art, it holds that there can be no breach of security while people rest. Therefore continued surveillance of the art van is absolutely necessary. If more than one van is used, it is suggested that they be parked back to back so that the rears (doors already secured and sealed) of both vehicles touch. This would make it almost humanly impossible to get between the vans to tamper with the locks. In addition to these precautions, the security director should assign personnel to watch the cargo in shifts of two, if possible. Throughout the night, there can be a tradeoff of duties every couple of hours with fresh personnel taking over the surveillance responsibility. When and where possible, depending on the value or political nature of the art, an advance security team should be sent to watch the cargo while the main security force sleeps. An alternative plan, if you do not have the manpower, is to hire a reliable contracted guard agency to stand by at a prearranged location to watch all vehicles while your main security force rests.

CARGO THEFT

During rest stops, everyone should keep their conversations with strangers to a minimum. As stressed earlier, it is important to remain as inconspicuous as possible. Indeed, the entire operation may be more secure it if remains generally unknown. There is a readily available market for valuable art and it might prove difficult to characterize a potential thief who might be listening. There is no definite or exacting profile that might serve us here.

Some small losses in the industry are considered part of the price of doing business. This does not hold true for the theft of art valued at hundreds or even millions of dollars. As stated by Lou Tyska, CPP, in his article, in *Security Management Magazine* (ASIS). "Such thefts are not accidents nor unavoidable, they are premeditated, well organized and are permitted."[3]

The small losses receive little or no media attention, nor would there be much interest in the investigation. However, the theft of any well-known piece of art gets immediate attention in the news and any number of law enforcement agencies may be called upon to assist in its recovery.

This may be as good a time as any to stress the importance of developing a training program for investigators that deals specifically with the loss and recovery of art. So few police investigators have any knowledge or direct experience in art investigations. Personal experience has shown that an appreciation of antiques can be a step in the right direction. An investigator with this leaning or with an appreciation of art would probably be best suited for the training. Every metropolitan city in this country should have at least one police investigator trained in this area.

ARRIVAL OF THE ART SHIPMENT

A designated secure area should be cleared for the incoming shipment. Here an inventory can be taken at the time of arrival. Earlier it was mentioned that the security representative may want to affix some special marking on a crate; these areas can be checked at this point without too much difficulty.

An indelible marking placed strategically on the crate will respond to infrared or black light and confirm that the shipment, at least from an exterior viewpoint, is in order. This marking should be known only to security personnel. On a recent overseas shipment, every crate was marked in an inconspicuous place, but recorded mentally by the security officer in charge. In this instance, a date of birth was used. Upon arrival at a holding place, the security officer checked each crate with a black light to account for the shipment. Next there was a complete inventory of the crates' contents by a courier. The initial marking of the crates took place in Europe and both museum and security officials on that end were impressed with this type of technology. One mentioned he would surely recommend this procedure for future shipments.

One person should be assigned to direct the unloading operation. A prior meeting with the facility staff would have covered the expected time of arrival of the art, number of units (crates) to be off-loaded, type of equipment needed to assist in the off-loading, and other concerns critical to the removal and temporary storage of the shipment. The facility supervisor should directly supervise the removal of all art objects from the truck and into the holding area.

Upon discovering a broken or damaged object and before any moving takes place, the supervisor should call upon the expert services of the conservator. The responsibility for safeguarding the art object at this point would then rest on the shoulders of someone knowledgeable about the protection and preservation of art. Another important reason for closer scrutiny of the art object while it is still on the truck is for insurance purposes. Any liability to the company is easier to clarify at this time.

TIPS ON UNLOADING

1. Regardless of its size, one object should be carried at a time. Here, too, both hands should be used and the object should be firmly gripped.
2. Know exactly where the storage area is so that the object can be placed there. A mixup could be disastrous.
3. Never rush the removal operation. Ensure that adequate number(s) of personnel are on hand to lift bulky or otherwise heavy loads.
4. To prevent tripping, try to arrange the body positions and weight distribution so that no one has to walk backwards.
5. If storage is temporary, make sure adequate security measures are in force until the art can be placed in a more secure environment.
6. Be careful not to place art objects in with other crates in an area normally used for shipping and receiving.

IN REVIEW

As stated in the book, *Cargo Theft and Organized Crime:*[4] "Under modern legal definitions, rare is the shipment that is not of an interstate character and the theft of which would not fall within the investigative jurisdiction of the FBI." It goes on to say, "its (the FBI) investigative jurisdiction over thefts of property and valuables involved in interstate and foreign commerce relates to the following offenses."

1. Obtaining by theft or embezzlement or by fraud or deception any goods or chattels that are moving as — or constitute a part of — an interstate or foreign shipment.
2. Buying, receiving, or possessing such goods or chattels, knowing that they were stolen, embezzled, or obtained by fraud or deception.
3. Embezzling of certain monies of any corporation engaged in interstate or foreign commerce as a common carrier by employees or officers of the corporation.
4. Unlawfully breaking the seal or lock of — or entering with the intent to commit larceny — any railroad car, truck, aircraft, vessel, or other vehicle containing interstate or foreign shipments.

The complexities of preventing the theft of art, safeguarding it during transportation, and protecting it for perpetuity is a monumental job, to say the least. Any art loss should be looked upon as significant since replacement, especially if it is one of a kind, may well be impossible. A serious problem facing the investigator when tracing leads and following up other information is the difficulty of identifying the recovered artifact. In many cases of recovery, art identification is based upon an ability to associate it with a specific owner. Unlike some items bearing serial numbers, art is not as easily catalogued, and therefore computerization and retrieval of stolen art information is not an easy science.

It is therefore essential that investigators taking reports in stolen art direct their questioning of victims along these lines. Are there photographs — color is best — available that can depict the art, showing whether it is three dimensional, sculpture, or painting? How fragile is the object and where would it most likely be sold? Since some art is signed and/or dated, with either mark thus becoming a means for identification, an investigator would certainly be wise to ask about these markings. Museums can sometimes provide answers to the investigator. It has happened that a museum official has known where in the world the market currently is for a stolen object. A stolen French painting, for example, may leave the Boston or New York area, travel to South America, only to end up in Switzerland. Usually a museum or private donor will have a photograph of the art object. However, there are some things, such as coins and ceramics, for which ownership or origin is hard to determine. To mark either of them, especially coins, would just about destroy them. Even a numismatist may be of little help in identifying ownership of old rare coins.

Again, to stress the importance of art, let us examine the importance of protecting and preserving objects d'art. A Rembrandt in the possession of a museum in the United States is classified as property of the museum, which becomes its sole owner. This art form becomes part of this country and its culture. Should something happen to the painting, such as theft or vandalism, it is governed by local statute making it a felony in each instance where the larceny value is more than $100 (in Massachusetts). Because there are no specific criminal statutes dealing with the theft of cultural art objects, most cases of this type may take their place among the investigative priorities of officers assigned to the crimes against property section. Probably as important as recovery is the prosecution of offenders. Such prosecutions may be the only deterrent known beyond good protection devices and other security programs.

Much emphasis has been placed on paintings and their related value. Too little has been said about the frames that encase these precious paintings. Although usually a frame does not exceed the value of a painting, nonetheless some frames are highly valued. An example is a frame personally selected by the artist. The wood or other material used, as well as the design of the frame, adds to its importance. Some encasements are an art form in themselves and have been made by the artist. According to one museum official, there is a frame around a famous portrait valued in excess of $100,000. This is strong reason why much caution should be exercised in crating and otherwise protecting the entire painting during transportation.

CONCLUSION

Art, like music, is an international language. Although it is understood and appreciated worldwide, there are times when art, especially during shipments, should be accompanied by experts not only knowledgeable about its esthetic qualities, but also capable of articulating its educational value in whatever language is spoken in the country to which the art is being shipped. Linguistics must be considered during the planning phase and appropriate consideration given to anticipating what problems could arise if someone is not familiar with the native tongue of the country being visited.

NOTES

1. *The Fine Art of Insuring Fine Art*, Washington, D.C.: Huntington T. Block Insurance.
2. Nathan Stolow. "Some Studies on the Protection of Works of Art During Travel." In *Recent Advances in Conservation*, edited by G. T. Thomson. London: Butterworths, 1963.
3. Lou Tyska. "Confusion, Conspiracy, and *the Common Denominator in Cargo Theft, Security Management,* January 1975.
4. *Cargo Theft and Organized Crime.* Washington, D.C.: LEAA, Department of Transportation, 5200.6, October 1972.

VI. THE SECURITY FORCE

21. The Guard Force

Joseph G. Wyllie

INTRODUCTION

From 1975 to 1980, the uniformed security guard industry in the United States has flourished. Various industries throughout the United States have engaged the services of private security firms or in-house security guard forces on a full time basis.

A close look at the existing situation in the United States today readily indicates the vital need for security guards. The most recent statistics on record with many large metropolitan police departments and the FBI show a definite increase in crime of all types throughout this country. Due to inadequate police protection in large as well as small cities, private concerns are turning to security guards as a deterrent to major crime.

It is a known fact that private security guards, both contract and in-house, outnumber municipal police in this country and, in some cities, they outnumber them by as much as two to one. In 1973, money spent for security guards and investigative services in the United States amounted to $2.5 billion. The *New York Times* estimated that in 1979, this amount has risen to $12 billion.

In 1973, in-house guard forces amounted to approximately 65 percent of the total force of security guards. In 1979, however, the growth of contract security guards has increased over this six year period to approximately 50 percent in-house and fifty percent contract.

It is not the intent of this chapter to supply arguments pro and con about the benefits of the in-house guards as compared to the contract guards. Various discussions and studies have been presented to support both sides and an analysis of many of these show the following main arguments. Cost is a factor for both in-house and contract guard forces. The old adage, "you get what you pay for," may still be the solution to this ongoing argument. Administration of both in-house and contract guards has merits on both sides. Neither of the two can function without this strong administrative capability. Unionization is another argument that has been bandied back and forth for years. The majority of in-house guard forces is unionized. In recent years, there have been increased efforts by a number of private guard unions to move into the contract guard arena. Eventually, arguments in this area between in-house and contract will negate each other.

Objectivity has arguments on both sides. For example, contract guards do not establish close relationships with employees, since the guards are not employees of the client. On the other hand, in-house guards are considered of higher quality due to higher pay and better fringe benefits, and consequently possess company loyalty which is a plus factor.

There is no doubt that a number of companies presently using in-house security guards, are taking a close look at existing costs with the future possibility of converting to contract guards. With the present economic situation in the United States, the future of increasing in-house guard forces is hazy. The salary increases and the fringe benefit packages negotiated at union contract renewals are being filtered down to the in-house security guard forces. This is increasing the hourly rate costs for in-house guards. In some firms, it is becoming prohibitive to continue with an in-house force that is so expensive.

Due to the confidentiality of the security programs in various large corporations employing in-house guards, there is little information available. There are several large in-house guard forces that in actuality are police departments. Two well-regarded in-house guard forces with 150 to 200 man units are Ford Motors in Detroit and Grumman Aerospace, Bethpage, New York.

There is a wealth of information available regarding the private security contract guards. All available records show that the big three in the United States are Pinkerton's, Inc., founded in 1850, the oldest and largest with 40,000 employees. Next in size is Burn's International Security Services, Inc., with 38,000 employees and then the Wackenhut Corp. with 20,000 employees. The balance of the contract guard firms are made up of several substantial firms such as Guardsmark, Globe Security Systems, and Wells Fargo. Then there are some medium-sized firms as well as thousands of local guard companies. It has been estimated that there are between 5,000 and 6,000 local guard companies throughout the United States.

OPERATIONS OF A GUARD FORCE

The basic mission of a guard force is to protect all property within the limits of the client's facility boundaries and to protect employees and other persons on the client's property. This type of service offered by a guard agency must start with the basic requirements. The firm's concept of service must be one of integrity and professionalism, implemented by people with years of experience and expertise in their particular field of security. A guard agency may have assignments that range from protection of a nuclear power plant to actual guarding of the Alaska pipeline. The agency may supply a single guard for a small business or the total security force for NASA's Kennedy Space Center. No matter what the size, the commitment to the concept of service remains the same. The total dedication to the job at hand is the paramount issue.

Today's demands for facility security are complex and diverse. Meeting such demands often requires expertise from the guard agency. The varied requirements of highly sophisticated clients, with far-flung operating facilities, calls for a highly professional approach to begin to meet some of the client's security problems. Guard clients today could be anyone from the government of an emerging nation concerned with the development of its internal security capability to a giant petro-chemical complex or a nuclear power generating facility.

The watchman service of thirty years ago has evolved into the modern "system approach" to total security. The "system approach" requires, first, an in-depth analysis of the client's situation and requirements. This assessment of the client's needs is vital to the development of a plan of action for a total security concept.

In the case of a small guard job, such analysis and planning will be brief yet thorough. As larger clients present more detailed requirements, the procedure grows accordingly. And, as occurs frequently in the large agencies, due to worldwide activities, the resolution of extremely complicated and diverse security situations for giant business, industrial or government facilities at home or abroad results in major analytical and planning procedures for the guard agency management.

The complexities of modern times have enlarged the realm of security to include a number of additional services to the basic guard force. The uniformed guard, armed or unarmed, continues to be fundamental to most programs involving security. The large security agencies have operations that include subsidiary and affiliate companies in many countries throughout the world. Through these operations, the security firms have the capability of serving not only international areas, but clients whose operations include foreign investment or international travel.

Whatever the special requirements, the agency must have the resources to provide security in the broadest context of the security profession. As government, business and various professions see more clearly the impact of total security planning on efficiency, cost control, and bottom line earnings, it becomes more apparent to them that the cost of security services is, in fact, a sound investment accompanied by a very satisfactory return.

Today's guard agency must have the ability and flexibility to develop a plan of action completely compatible with the client's requirements. The modern concept of operations places great emphasis on local in-depth supervision of the security force, backed up by area, district, and regional, and eventually corporate management committed to excellence in the fulfillment of the program. New developments and philosophies in physical security guard services have emphasized the need for progressive and sophisticated training of security officers. It now requires classroom training, the production of training manuals and audio-visual training aids for use in the field.

The challenges of the future are only beginning to take shape. Whatever their eventual definition, the problem-solving ability of skilled individuals and organizations will be crucial for survival in tomorrow's business and industrial world. Although the security programming has become highly diversified, the basic uniformed guard service is still the backbone of the large security corporations. The guard will be no less important in the future, but will have increasingly greater responsibility and training. The fundamental job of the security guard as stated earlier is basically the same as it has always been. But the methods of doing this effectively have changed with the times.

LIABILITIES CONNECTED WITH GUARD FORCE

There are various legal aspects of industrial security and plant protection that must be fully understood by the security guard.

A guard force is not engaged in law enforcement as such and, therefore, the guard is not a law enforcement officer, like a police officer or sheriff. The guards are engaged in the protection of goods being produced and services. The plant management makes the rules regarding the conduct of persons engaged in production. The final end is a smooth flow of production, not law enforcement.

Rules and regulations do not have the force of law. An employee cannot be deprived of his freedom because he has broken a rule or regulation to help production. The most that can be done is to dismiss the employee. Violation of law by someone working in the plant presents the same situation as if he had broken the law elsewhere. The case is under the jurisdiction of law enforcement agencies local, state or federal. The work performed by a security guard is not related to police work. Execution of the job and training are different. The security guard must leave law enforcement to the responsible agency.

There are special situations, however, in which a security guard may make arrests. A security guard, peace officer or any other person may arrest an offender without a warrant where the offense is committed in his presence, within his view if the offense is a felony or an offense against public peace. A felony is ordinarily an offense punishable by confinement in a penitentiary for a period of more than one year. Arrests such as this should be made only with the consent of a superior, except in an emergency situation, and only on company property. False arrests and searches can result in civil and criminal law suits. A security guard has no authority in a civil case and if required to testify in any civil case relating to his duties, the security guard should report the facts to the supervisor of the force and in turn demand a subpoena in order to testify.

Before making the arrest, the security guard should be sure that the law has actually been violated, that the violation is a crime, and that he has information in his possession beyond a reasonable doubt to prove that the person committed the crime. No arrest is legal until after the actual violation of the law. No person may be arrested on a charge of suspicion. The arrest is made by actual restraint of the person or by the guard saying, "You are under arrest." Actual touching of the person is unnecessary. It is enough if the person submits to the guard's custody. The guard has no authority beyond the company property line other than that of a *private citizen*. No person is to be transported as a prisoner off company property by a security guard. The guard must notify the local law enforcement agency and turn the prisoner over to them on company property. Crimes that may occur on company premises include murder, arson, assault, burglary, larceny, intoxication, violation of sabotage and espionage laws.

When a crime is committed on company property, it is imperative that the guard on duty take prompt measures to afford protection of the crime scene. In the event of a serious crime, the security guards will not investigate the area. The guard should refrain from touching any evidence in the crime scene area and should prevent unauthorized persons from handling such evidence. The nature of the crime and the type of evidence in the area requires that the security guard be extremely careful in moving about so as not to obliterate or otherwise destroy crime evidence. The security guards will isolate the area and avenue of entry or escape believed to be used. No one should be allowed to enter or leave the area pending the arrival of representatives of a law enforcement agency having primary investigative jurisdiction. The guard should then obtain the names and addresses of any possible witnesses to be furnished to the law enforcement agency.

GUARD TRAINING

In view of the demands of industry for fully trained security guards, a new phase has come into view. To give the training required for the basic guard who could be working on a one-man site up to the basic guard working at a nuclear power plant, a new look has been given to guard training.

Training today must be organized so as to provide the initial or basic training as well as the follow-up programs necessary to maintain the quality standards for the personnel. Most professional security agencies have, at least, a basic security officers program. These programs can run as long as twenty-four hours and cover subjects ranging from laws of arrest to weapons safety. The present system is attempting to package the training in a practical delivery system and to keep quality high in terms of testing.

Many of the basic training courses are tailored to individual client needs. Of recent years a number of states have mandated requirements for security officers and most states have mandated requirements for weapons training.

Another offshoot of the training for guards has been the pre-departure screening services required at all airports across the United States. In screening carry-on baggage with an X-ray machine, the ability to detect the outline, shape or form of a weapon or an explosive device is critical. The Federal Aviation Agency (FAA) has mandated a training program that must be uniformly given to every screener at every airport in the country. In addition, audio-visual training programs have been prepared in cooperation with the FAA. Besides instruction in the techniques of "reading" the outlines of X-ray screens, the course offers new pointers in the use of magnetometers, both the walk-through models and the hand held "wands."

Training is a major responsibility and a supervisor must be able to provide training to all appropriate personnel. At least three situations exist in which training must be given:

1. Orientation of new security officers.
2. Instruction in the use of weapons, procedures, or equipment.
3. Retraining.

Since security personnel are charged with the protection of life and property, they must be highly trained to insure accomplishment of duties, whatever they may be. There is no room for partially trained security officers. An untrained person is a liability — a threat to security. More than most people, security personnel must know instantly what actions are appropriate in response to any situation. These instant responses result from TRAINING and EX-PERIENCE.

All security personnel should receive an orientation program which provides them with an understanding of their duties and responsibilities, as well as orienting them to the overall security mission. This initial training is supplemented by classroom work and continuing on-the-job training as well as any specific client training requirements.

There will be, however, certain other areas which will require special attention, and it will be up to the supervisor to determine what these areas are, and what additional training emphasis is required. There are certain symptoms which indicate the need for training such as:

- waste of materials
- low morale
- high accident rate
- lack of cooperation
- poor paperwork
- high absenteeism and tardiness
- incomplete patrols
- improper uniform appearance
- client complaints.

If any areas requiring special attention are discovered, the office manager should be informed of your findings. This information will serve as an alert to the problem, which can then be corrected.

Keys to Training

New personnel must be told from the beginning that their jobs are important to the overall security mission and therefore, they must effectively accomplish their task. The security of expensive equipment and material, as well as the client's personnel is a job that calls for well-trained security forces, and your interest is a major part of providing a well-trained force.

Employees that have been on the security force for a number of years should be treated a little differently. Sometimes the "old hand" thinks he/she knows all there is to know about the job and there isn't any reason for more training. You might approach this person by indicating that chances for promotion and higher pay will improve as job performance improves. In addition, over the years new equipment and techniques evolve which must be explained to all personnel associated with such developments.

If you are called upon to train personnel, you should be familiar with several keys to training. Before beginning the training process, you must create ways to prepare your trainees to receive the information. Don't forget the trainee's point of view. Approach your training with these thoughts in mind:

1. Stress how the information will be used. The trainee wants to know right away how this new information will apply and how it will be used in daily activities. Take the time to explain carefully just where the information you are about to give fits into the trainee's job.
2. Get the trainee to *participate*. Don't simply hand out manuals or workbooks and give lectures. Force the trainee to make an effort, bringing him/her into the training. Encourage questions and take the time to answer them. Create an atmosphere in which the trainee feels

free to ask questions and to state thoughts on the material you are presenting.

3. Give the trainee *time to digest* the information you are presenting. Don't cram everything into one session. Divide the training into digestible portions and make sure that the trainee has "eaten" each one before you move on to the next.

4. Assist the trainee to see what is important. Within every job there are certain key points at which a mistake could ruin the entire operation. Emphasize what is important so the employee will know what to look out for.

5. Guide the trainee to insure understanding of the importance of what is taught. When an employee understands why a whole procedure is important, a vital step is rarely omitted along the way. If the trainee learns without understanding the entire process, the person may not even know when something is omitted.

6. Instill in your personnel the desire to learn. Each security officer must feel that the instruction he/she is about to receive is related *directly* to job performance and therefore, the instruction is important.

SECURITY AWARENESS FOR GUARDS

The security guard of the 1980's is a far cry from the night watchman of the previous decades. To be an effective guard force in today's competitive market requires a training program that can guarantee a guard who can make a judgment based on existing conditions that, in some cases, could save a multibillion dollar facility from total destruction.

As shown earlier in this chapter, the federal government has mandated the general criteria for security personnel. These standards establish requirements for the selection, training, equipping, testing and qualifications of individuals who will be responsible for protecting special nuclear materials, nuclear facilities and nuclear shipments.

A close look at the mental qualifications mandated for guards under 10 CFR 73.55 will give an indication of the security awareness required for guards in today's competitive market. "Individuals whose security tasks and job duties are directly associated with the effective implementation of the licensee physical security and contingency plans shall demonstrate the following: mental alertness and the capability to exercise good judgment, implement instructions, assimilate assigned security tasks, and possess the acuity of senses and ability of expression sufficient to permit accurate communication by written, spoken, audible, visible or other signals required by assigned job duties."

In the past, the security guard was principally concerned with protection of the site or facility. The post orders mainly were concerned with alerting the fire department in case of fire or explosion. If there was a break-in or intrusion by an individual or group, the local police were to be called. For any other problem occurring during the tour of duty, an up-to-date alert list was available for phone calls to the client for decisions not to be handled by the guard force.

With the advent of the terrorist actions throughout the world, the security guard now has an awareness of security that was never considered until the early 1970's. It is a known fact that a successful act of sabotage against a nuclear power plant could result in serious and disastrous consequences to the health and safety of the public. The mission of the security guard has been changed to one of vital importance to the overall health and safety of the public.

Security personnel are responsible for the protection of special nuclear material on sites and in transit and for the protection of the facility or shipment vehicles against industrial sabotage. They must be required to meet minimum criteria to assure that they will effectively perform their assigned security related job duties.

The new security awareness for guards in our nuclear-oriented society has made a radical change in their basic mission. The guard's duties will shift from those of a patrolman to the operation of sophisticated equipment. At the same time, the guard will remain ready for immediate deployment as part of a coordinated armed response unit.

In the future, capable, confident guards will have increasingly greater responsibility and awareness and will need professional training for their work with electronics and other new security requirements. Obviously, it takes more than a snappy uniform and a shiny badge to make a security guard. The guard of the 1980's will be a unique individual, highly trained, specializing in a type of physical security that was unknown ten years ago.

To be competitive in the security guard market of the future, the security firm must be ready to meet the challenges with new concepts, bold innovations and unrelenting insistence on high standards.

REPORT WRITING

Very few people like paperwork, yet it seems that the occupation does not exist where paperwork is not required. For the security officer, the paperwork is in the form of reports. There are four basic reasons for completing so many reports.

1. *To inform.* Written communications reduce the chances of misunderstandings or errors. Verbal communications, however, are highly prone to misunderstandings, errors in reproduction, and can be easily ignored.

2. *To record.* Never trust memory. No memory is perfect. Exact amounts, costs, dates, times, and similar data are easily forgotten unless recorded.

3. *To demonstrate alertness.* By recording incidents, the security officer makes his supervisor and client aware of the job he is doing. It is very easy for people to get the impression that security officers do little but stand around. One way of avoiding this type of image is to conscientiously document all incidents.

4. *To protect yourself.* There may come a time when it becomes necessary for a security officer to prove he has witnessed an event, accomplished a certain action or notified the proper authorities of an incident. The reports he writes will accomplish all four of these goals.

The report should be clear and concise. A good report answers five basic questions:

1. *What?* The report must state what happened as accurately as possible.

2. *Where?* The exact location of an occurrence can have great bearing in establishing guilt, innocence or liability.

3. *Who?* When writing a report, the officer should answer as many who's as possible; for example, who did it and who was notified?

4. *When?* The "when" of an incident may establish an alibi, or help to prevent damage, theft or injury.

5. *Why?* The "why" involves judgment and opinion and may not be easily proven, but it may be very important in judgment of guilt or liability.

In addition to answering these questions, there are simple guidelines to follow when preparing a report to assure that the final result is clearly written and well organized.

1. Use simple language which anyone can understand. When using technical words and phrases, be sure the meaning is clear. Avoid using slang terms or words that have multiple meanings.

2. Be sure that you use the proper spellings and addresses of the individuals involved in the report.

3. Prepare the report in such a manner that the happenings are in logical sequence and, when possible, show the approximate time of the occurrence.

4. Do not ramble. It is preferable to use short paragraphs, with each covering one particular point.

5. Do not use vague descriptions. Write only specific observations.
6. When descriptions of individuals are obtained, list all the usual manners of description such as height, weight, color of hair, etc., but also include unusual details such as presence of a mustache, sideburns, eyeglasses, and any peculiarities of walk or speech. Notice and report all information possible on types and color of dress.
7. Avoid contradictory statements which would tend to discredit the overall information.
8. Facts, not fiction, are important. If you include your opinion, label it as your opinion, not as a fact.

Any problem, from a missing light bulb to a major safety hazard, should be reported. The security officer should continue to provide written reports on any incident until appropriate action is taken to correct the situation. In this way, he will demonstrate his own importance to the client.

SAFETY

Accident prevention is said to be everybody's job, but, as "everybody's job," no one does too much about it. It does, however, fall well within the domain of security personnel. It is the security officer's responsibility to observe all unsafe conditions and to warn people of potential hazards. It is also his responsibility to report any violations of safety rules and to set a good example by his own behavior.

Far too many accidents happen due to unsafe conditions which were not noted, reported, or corrected. After finding an unsafe condition, the officer must do one of two things: correct the condition or report it to someone who can make the correction. If a storm blows a power line down, the security officer should report it. If, on the other hand, he finds a bag of oil rags in the corner, he would simply place them in a metal covered container and report it later. Safety is purely a matter of common sense. Corrective action should be taken when possible, or the proper authority should be called to handle the situation.

It is important that the security officer undertake the sometimes thankless task of safety. It is important both to the client he is protecting from damage claims and to the people he is protecting from injuries due to careless safety practices.

Safety Checklist

1. Are the floors kept clean and free of dirt and debris?
2. Are rough, splintered, uneven or other floor defects repaired or the hazards suitably marked?

3. Are non-skid waxes used to polish floors?
4. During bad weather, are storm mats placed near entrances and floors mopped frequently?
5. Are stairways equipped with handrails?
6. Are steps equipped with handrails?
7. Are stairways well lighted?
8. Are electric fan or heater extension cords tripping hazards?
9. Are cords of electric fans or heaters disconnected from the power source when not in use and at the end of each working day?
10. Are electric fans or heaters adequately grounded?
11. Are cigarette or cigar stubs placed in suitable ashtrays or containers?
12. Are grounds free of debris, etc.?
13. Are sufficient containers provided for trash, ashes, etc.?
14. Are floors free of oil spills, grease or other substances which create a slipping hazard?
15. Are windows clean?
16. Is broken glass in evidence?
17. Are the aisles clearly defined and free of obstruction?
18. Is material neatly stacked and readily reached?
19. Does piled material project into aisles or passageways?
20. Are tools left on overhead ledges or platforms?
21. Is the lighting adequate?
22. Are materials stored under or piled against buildings, doors, exits or stairways?
23. Are walks kept clear of obstructions, slipping and tripping hazards, broken glass, snow and ice?

BOMB THREATS

Bomb threats are a serious concern to all security personnel. Fortunately, most bomb threats turn out to be false alarms, but the next encounter with such a threat may turn out to be real so none should be taken lightly. All bomb threats should be treated with quick, calm, steady professional action.

Normally, local police authorities will be notified by client management when a bomb threat occurs. Upon receiving a bomb threat, a security officer's first duty is to notify the client immediately and to take the action he orders. If ordered to call the police, he should do so and then evacuate anyone in or near the facility. The handling of bombs and bomb disposal are police duties. The security force's job is to assist the police in finding the bomb and in evacuation proceedings.

The security officer should *NOT* attempt to examine a bomb, regardless of any previous experiece he may have had in the world of explosives. Many bombs are extremely complicated and designed to explode when any attempt is made for deactivation. Only trained demolitions experts are qualified to safely handle a bomb.

Bomb Search

The number of locations where a bomb may be hidden are innumerable, and only the most obvious places can be searched in a reasonable amount of time. However, most facilities have areas which are generally more vulnerable than others and should be checked first. The following thoughts should be kept in mind when searching for a bomb:

1. Do not touch anything that does not have to be disturbed. If lights are off, do not turn them on. If fuse panels are turned off, do not activate them. These may be wired to detonate explosives.
2. Most bombs which have actually been found were of the time-mechanism variety. The timing devices are usually cheap alarm clocks which can be heard ticking at surprising distances. Be on the alert for ticking sounds.
3. Bombs found in searches were usually found near an exit. Look closely in areas near doorways.
4. Be alert for objects which look out of place, or are of unusual size or shape.
5. Thoroughly check any areas which are accessible to the public. Rest rooms and janitors' closets are frequently used as hiding places.
6. A bomb search should be conducted for a period of twenty to thirty minutes. This should provide ample time for a reasonable search, without creating unnecessary danger to the searchers.
7. A methodical search technique is necessary to ensure that no areas are overlooked. An orderly investigation of all rooms within the facility is mandatory. It is wise to prepare a checklist of places to be searched in advance so that a thorough search can be conducted.
8. As you search, be alert to:
    *   freshly plastered or painted places
    *   disturbed dirt in potted plants
    *   pictures or other hanging objects not straight
    *   ceiling tiles that have been disturbed
    *   torn furniture coverings
    *   broken cabinets or objects recently moved
    *   trash cans, air conditioning ducts, water fountains
    *   elevator shafts, phone booths.

Precautions

A security officer can assist police by observing the following precautions:

Don't:
- Touch a bomb.
- Smoke in the immediate vicinity of a suspected bomb.
- Expose the bomb to sun. Direct rays of the sun or light of any kind may cause detonation.
- Accept identification makeup as legitimate. Don't take for granted the identification markings on packages and boxes as they may have been forged. Keep in mind that bombs are usually camouflaged in order to throw the recipient off guard. Don't take for granted that the package is bona fide because of its having been sent through the mail. Many bombs are forwarded in this manner. Others are sent through express agencies, while some are delivered by individual messengers.
- Take for granted that it is a high explosive bomb. Be prepared in the event that it is of the incendiary type. Have sand and extinguishers on hand.
- Use two-way radios as transmitting could detonate a bomb.
- Have unnecessary personnel in the immediate area of the suspected bomb or explosive.

Do:
- Evacuate the building or area around the suspected bomb, only if the client orders it. In large cities, this function is usually performed by the fire department. Only vital and necessary personnel should be allowed within 100 yards of the package.
- Remove all valuable equipment, important files, computer tapes etc. at least 100 yards away from the package.
- Open all windows and doors in the immediate vicinity of the suspected device. This allows the blast to escape, thereby reducing pressure on the walls and interiors. It will also reduce window breakage and the hazards caused by flying glass and debris.
- Shut off all power services to the area *immediately*. This reduces the possibility of gas explosion or electrical fires.

Types of Explosives

Blasting Caps or Detonators are:
- Metallic cylinders approximately 2 inches long, 3/16 inches in diameter closed at one end (may be larger or smaller).

- Partially filled with a small amount of relatively easily fired or detonated compound.
- When fired, the resultant shock or blow is sufficient to detonate explosives.
- *Very* dangerous to handle, as they can be detonated by heat, friction, or a relatively slight blow.

Nitroglycerin is:
- Colorless to yellow liquid with a heavy, oily consistency.
- Highly dangerous — extremely sensitive to heat, flame, shock or friction.

Dynamite is:
- High explosive, usually cylinderical in shape, size: 1-1/4 inches diameter and approximately 8 inches long, (may be up to 12 inches diameter, and 30 inches long).
- Outer wrapper often covered in parafin and *usually* marked "DANGEROUS — HIGH EXPLOSIVE."
- Shock sensitive — needs a blasting cap for detonation.

FIRE PROTECTION

Of the many jobs a security officer performs, one of the most important is that of fire protection. To do the job effectively, he must be familiar with fire fighting equipment and know how and when to use it.

Fire is comprised of three elements: heat, fuel and oxygen. Remove any one of these three and the fire will go out.

If a fire should break out the following directions will most effectively safeguard persons and property against harm and damage.

1. Call the fire department first.
2. Direct all employees out of the burning building and keep them out after evacuation.
3. Notify and enlist the help of the company fire brigade if one exists.
4. Check and close fire doors.
5. Shut off machinery, power and gas.
6. Check to see if gate valves are in working condition, if a sprinkler system exists.
7. Now and only now, attempt to control the fire by means of an extinguisher.
8. Post someone to direct the firefighters to the fire.
9. Remove motor vehicles from the area.

10.   Once the fire has been contained, keep a close watch on the area to see that the fire does not start again.

11.   Be sure all extinguishers used are immediately recharged.

12.   Complete a written report covering all of the information about the fire.

FIRE PREVENTION

The best way to fight a fire is to prevent a fire from starting. Following is a list of things that you should be alert for while on patrol to eliminate sources of fire and obstructions that might lead to fire spreading.

1.   Look for violations of no-smoking regulations.

2.   Investigate any unusual odors, especially smoke and gas. Don't be satisfied until you have found the cause and action has been taken.

3.   Check for obstructed passageways and fire doors.

4.   Look for obstructions in front of fire-alarm boxes, extinguishers and fire hydrants.

5.   On every patrol, check all gas or electric heaters, coal and kerosene stoves to see that they do not overheat.

6.   Check to see that boxes, rubbish or hazardous materials are not left close to stoves, boilers, steam or smoke pipes.

7.   Check to see that all gas or electric appliances not in use are disconnected.

8.   Check to see that all discarded and disposable materials have been placed in their proper containers.

EMERGENCY MEDICAL ASSISTANCE

It is possible that a security officer will be present when someone needs medical assistance. The first reaction should be to summon help. If this is not possible, the officer should be prepared to assist the victim. Guards should be trained in emergency medical assistance (EMA) procedures in the event a severe accident occurs. Someone's life may depend on his knowledge of EMA.

At the Scene

People at the scene of an accident will be excited. A security officer must remain calm, dealing with the most serious injury or condition first. The most urgent medical emergencies which require prompt action to save a life are:

severe bleeding, stoppage of breathing, and poisoning. Shock may accompany any of these, depressing the body functions and keeping the heart, lungs and other organs from functioning normally.

What To Do First

1. Don't move the injured person, unless it is absolutely necessary to save him from danger. If he has been injured internally, or if his spine is broken, unnecessary movement may kill or cripple him.
2. Act fast if the victim is bleeding severely, if he has swallowed poison, or if he has stopped breathing because of drowning, gas poisoning or electric shock. Every second counts. A person may, for example, die within three minutes of the time breathing stops, unless given artificial respiration.
3. Because life-and-death emergencies are rare, in most cases a guard can start EMA with these steps: Keep the patient lying down quietly. If he has vomited and there is no danger that his neck is broken, turn his head to one side to prevent choking. Keep him warm with blankets or coats, but don't overheat him or apply external heat.
4. Summon medical help. The doctor should be told the nature of the emergency, and asked what should be done pending his arrival.
5. Examine the patient gently. Cut clothing, if necessary, to avoid movement or added pain. Don't pull clothing away from burns.
6. Reassure the patient, and try to remain calm. Calmness will convince him that everything is under control.
7. Always be prepared to treat shock.
8. Do not force fluids on an unconscious or semiconscious person. Fluids may enter his windpipe and cause strangulation. Do not try to arouse an unconscious person by slapping, shaking or shouting. Do not give alcohol to any victim.
9. Following any incident where EMA would be rendered, a detailed written report should be made covering all of the circumstances. Be sure to include the treatment given.

CONTROLLING BLEEDING

The adult human body contains approximately six quarts of blood. Although an adult can readily withstand the loss of a pint, the amount usually taken for transfusion purposes, that same loss by a child may have disastrous results. In an adult, lack of consciousness may occur from the rapid loss of as little as a quart of blood. Because a victim can bleed to death in a very short period of time, immediate stoppage of any large, rapid loss of blood is necessary.

Direct Pressure

The preferred method for control of severe bleeding is direct pressure by pressing a hand over a dressing. This method prevents loss of blood from the body without interfering with normal circulation.

Apply direct pressure by placing the palm of the hand on a dressing directly over the entire area of an open wound on any surface part of the body. In the absence of compresses, the fingers or bare hand may be used, but only until a compress can be obtained and applied.

Do not disturb blood clots after they have formed within the cloth. If blood soaks through the entire compress without clotting, do not remove, but add additional layers of padding and continue direct hand pressure, even more firmly.

On most parts of the body, a pressure bandage can be placed to hold pads of cloth over a wound. Properly applied, the bandage will free the hands for another EMA.

To apply the bandage, place and hold the center directly over the pad on the wound. Maintain a steady pull on the bandage to keep the pad firmly in place while wrapping the ends around the body part. Finish by tying a knot over the pad.

Elevation

If there is no evidence of a fracture, a severely bleeding hand, arm or leg should be elevated above the level of the victim's heart. Once elevated, the force of gravity will reduce blood pressure at the site of the wound and slow the loss of blood. Elevation is used in addition to direct pressure.

The combination of pressure and elevation will stop severe bleeding in most cases, however, there are times when additional techniques are required. One additional technique is pressure on the supplying artery.

Pressure on the Supplying Artery

If severe bleeding from an open wound of the arm or leg does not stop after the application of direct pressure plus elevation, the use of pressure points may be required. Use of the pressure point technique temporarily compresses the main artery which supplies blood to the affected limb against the underlying bone and tissues.

If the use of a pressure point is necessary, do not substitute its use for direct pressure and elevation, but use the pressure point in addition to those techniques. Do not use a pressure point in conjunction with direct pressure any longer than necessary to stop the bleeding. However, if bleeding recurs, reapply pressure at a pressure point.

Pressure Point: Open Arm Wound

Apply pressure over the brachial artery, forcing it against the arm bone. The pressure point is located on the inside of the arm in the groove between the biceps and the triceps, about midway between the armpit and the elbow.

To apply pressure on the brachial artery, grasp the middle of the victim's upper arm, your thumb on the outside of the victim's arm and your other fingers on the inside. Press your fingers toward your thumb to create an inward force from opposite sides of the arm. The inward pressure holds and closes the artery by compressing it against the arm bone.

Pressure Point: Open Leg Wound

Apply pressure on the femoral artery by forcing the artery against the pelvic bone. The pressure point is located on the front center part of the diagonally slanted "hinge" of the leg, in the crease of the groin area, where the artery crosses the pelvic bone on its way to the leg.

To apply pressure to the femoral artery, position the victim flat on his back, if possible, and place the heel of your hand directly over the pressure point. Then lean forward over your straightened arm to apply the small amount of pressure needed to close the artery. To prevent arm tension and muscular strain, keep your arm straight while applying the technique.

CALL FOR ASSISTANCE

Whenever possible, get medical assistance as soon as you have made the victim comfortable and are sure the person's life is not in immediate danger. Often you can do more harm than good if you don't summon proper help immediately.

If in doubt as to a victim's well-being, keep the person quiet, preferably lying down and covered. Sometimes a concussion victim will appear perfectly normal and insist upon returning to work only to collapse later. In any case, do not allow the victim to move around. Remember, your greatest contribution to a victim's well-being may be to restrain efforts to move the person in a mistaken belief that such efforts are helpful. It is usually best to let the victim remain calm and relaxed before transporting to the medical station. Obtain professional help whenever possible.

REPORTING A MEDICAL CASE

When reporting a medical case, the following information must be given clearly so that the necessary equipment and medical assistance can reach the victim in the shortest possible time:

- Exact location and phone number from which you are reporting
- Type of injury, if evident
- Seriousness of injury
- Number of persons involved
- Visible symptoms, such as heavy bleeding, poison stains, etc.
- Cause of injury, if known, so that adequate personnel may be sent to the area to handle such dangerous conditions as leaking gas, flowing chemicals, etc.

GUARD SUPERVISION

In every business organization, different management levels exist that are responsible for various tasks. At the top of the structure are people who must decide the organizational goals and policies. At the opposite end of the operational spectrum are those who are immediately responsible for the accomplishment of established goals. Between top management and these workers are the people who must explain management's objectives to all employees. These people give guidance and leadership. They represent top management to the workers by setting standards, developing work schedules, training employees, and exercising necessary controls to insure quality performance. A guard supervisor is one of these important people.

The Supervisor

A supervisor, the person in the middle, is the key to success. The greater his ability to carry out his responsibilities, the more efficiently the company will operate.

In addition to job skills, a modern supervisor must be familiar with up-to-date personnel practices and the legal requirements that affect the jobs of his personnel. He must also know how to deal with the day-to-day problems of a security department.

A supervisor's job is one of the most important in business today. As the person responsible for getting the work done, the supervisor must be well versed in modern management practices. The following sayings may seem trite, but they hold a great deal of truth:

"A good supervisor is someone who can step on your toes without messing up your shine."

"Leaders have two important characteristics: first, they are going somewhere; second, they are able to persuade other people to go with them."

"A good boss is someone who takes a little more than his share of the blame and a little less than his share of the credit."

"The goal of criticism is to leave the person with the impression that he has been helped."

"Good supervision is the art of getting average people to do superior work."

One of the most important things a supervisor can do to get the best results from his people is to let them know they have his full support. He can reinforce this knowledge by giving the employees the necessary authority to do their jobs, and by seeing that this authority is respected. He should step in to share responsibilities and, if things go wrong, he should help to clear up the problem without condemnation. As happens on occasion, a good worker may run into controversy. When this occurs, it is comforting for him to know that he has a boss who will stand by him. This does not mean insisting someone is right when clearly he is not, but rather it is accepting some of the responsibility for a poor plan and helping someone to carry the blame. All these steps will demonstrate a supervisor's support of his crew, and people support a leader who supports them.

Another important trait of a good supervisor is his willingness to accept suggestions from his workers. In fact, he encourages such comments. It is natural for people to offer suggestions. A supervisor who makes it clear that he is not interested in such input cuts off an important flow of communication between himself and his staff. Once the employees realize their supervisor is not interested in their ideas, maybe even resents them, they will not take the time to devise a better system of doing things.

Making the mistake of ignoring the thoughts and ideas of another person will hinder working relationships within the company. One person cannot think of everything. Those employees most knowledgeable in a specific area could be of assistance and should not be overlooked. The people who handle the day-to-day situations are in the best position to suggest changes in the organization's policies and operations.

The best way to get more suggestions from the staff is to simply ask for them. Whenever a problem arises, the supervisor should discuss the situation with the people involved to further encourage input. By offering them the chance to do some of the thinking, the manager is openly demonstrating his interest in their ideas. Most employees would love to do some brainwork.

Effective Listening

Success in management depends on your ability to problem solve. Most problems must be solved with people, usually people who have highly individual points of view. And in working with people, no tool will take you further than skilled and effective listening.

When talking with someone who has an opposing point of view to your own, don't jump on this person the minute he takes a breath. Listen to the other's point of view closely and sympathetically. Listen with an open mind. Put the person at ease by listening attentively to what they have to say. Some good points may be uncovered that you had not considered!

A few basic principles should be considered to become an effective listener. The most important of these principles is that listening is an active process. A good listener's mind is alert; his face and posture should reflect this attitude. Also by questions and comments, the listener encourages the speaker to express his ideas fully. Another principle involves the ability to understand what the speaker is saying. What is his point of reference? Also you must be able to evaluate a statement; pull fact out of pure fancy. The next involves imaginative understanding of the other's point of view. This is the essential point. As psychologist Carl Rogers has explained: "If you really understand another person, . . . enter his private world and see the way life appears to him, . . . you run the risk of being changed yourself. You might see it his way; you might find yourself influenced in your attitudes or your personality."

Rate yourself on the following listener's checklist. When taking part in an interview or group conference, do you:

1. Prepare yourself physically by sitting facing the speaker, and making sure that you can hear?
2. Watch the speaker as well as listen?
3. Decide from the speaker's appearance and delivery whether or not what he has to say is worthwhile?
4. Listen primarily for ideas and underlying feelings?
5. Determine your own bias, if any, and try to allow for it?
6. Keep your mind on what the speaker is saying?
7. Interrupt immediately when you hear a statement you feel is wrong?
8. Make sure before answering that you've taken in the other's point of view?
9. Try to have the last word?
10. Make a conscious effort to evaluate the logic and credibility of what you hear?

Think about it!

Keep Communications Open

While not every idea submitted will be a workable one, no suggestion deserves the fifteen-second brush-off. The supervisor must be appreciative of all suggestions submitted to him, regardless of its caliber. Each and every idea merits consideration. The employee should be thanked for his time and interest and encouraged to keep trying, on the premise that the next idea could be a winner. To use an old saying, "if at first, you don't succeed . . . "

Leadership

The guard supervisor sets the example of professional quality for his staff. The subordinates are a mirror of the management. If a guard appears sloppy, unshaven, in need of a haircut and a shoeshine, his supervisor probably needs to take a good look at his own appearance. If a guard speaks sharply to the client's customers or employees, it may be a reflection of the man who is in charge. Perhaps the supervisor should pay careful attention to his own manner. The guard force reflects the company's image and the supervisor should ensure that the proper appearance is being projected.

Techniques for Setting the Example
1. Be physically fit, well-groomed and correctly dressed.
2. Master your emotions. Erratic behavior, ranging from anger to depression, is non-effective.
3. Maintain an optimistic outlook. Excel in difficult situations by learning to capitalize on your own capabilities.
4. Conduct yourself so that your own personal habits are not open to censure.
5. Exercise initiative and promote the spirit of initiative in your subordinates.
6. Be loyal to those with whom you work and those who work with you. Loyalty is a two-way street.
7. Avoid playing favorites.
8. Be morally courageous. Establish principles and stand by them.
9. Share hardships with your people to demonstrate your willingness to assume your share of the difficulties.

The Professional Security Supervisor

Today's security work requires a man with an exceptionally high degree of skill, training, and information. The person who demonstrates these qualities is recognized by others as a professional. He exudes the confidence and skill to make it possible for the rest of the community to have faith in his ability to act in their interest. The security officer who meets these standards is a professional in the fullest meaning of the word, and is respected as such.

The term "professional person" generally connotes lawyers, doctors, or perhaps teachers or accountants. These people are characterized by:

Education. By virtue of having completed certain education programs and having passed official examinations, professional people are recognized as possessing distinctive kinds and amounts of knowledge and skill. These are types of knowledge and skill in which the average citizen feels deficient, and therefoie, turns to professionally-trained people for help, in the form of advice or other services.

Standards of Performance. A professional person is expected to be dedicated to high ideals. He is assumed to operate under a superior code of ethics. To this end, the professional organizations establish standards of ethical performance, as well as standards of competence. Professional people take pride in these standards and expect members of their profession to meet them. Because of the continuous flow of social and economic changes in our world, training and the improvement of standards is a continuing problem for every security authority.

It is the understanding of fundamental principles which distinguishes the competent professional person from the mere technician. This is as true in security work as it is in medicine, law, and other professional fields.

A security supervisor is personally judged by the general public. The client, as well, looks upon him as his contact with the organization and will measure the company by what he sees in the supervisor. The security personnel, as well, look to the supervisor to set an example. As in other areas, therefore, the leader must maintain a professional code of ethics. Professionalism is vital to any pcsition of authority and this fact is no less true for the security supervisor.

Train Personnel Effectively

The responsibilities of a guard supervisor include providing sound, effective training to his staff. An understanding of every operational requirement of the security officers will give the supervisor more awareness of the difficult facets of their work, areas where he may be able to offer assistance when and where it is needed.

The supervisor can facilitate this aspect of his job by determining the duties of each security officer and establishing a master training plan that will teach the new employees their respective tasks. This plan will also serve as refresher training for other personnel who have been on the force for a long period of time.

Treat Employees Courteously

Mutual respect is essential to an efficient working relationship. Employees should not be treated as natural enemies nor should they be made to feel inferior. A superior must in turn report to his bosses and he should treat his staff in the same courteous manner he expects from *his* superiors.

"Consideration" is a key word. A demand should be accompanied by an explanation. Advance notice of any situations that might alter an employee's plans, such as overtime, post reassignments, or special orders, is a simple courtesy that will prevent unnecessary ill will. Reprimands or criticisms made in private, away from the watchful eyes of one's peers, precludes humiliation of a staff member.

Develop Loyalty

An effective supervisor is loyal to the employees, the company, and the client. Constant criticism of the company and management is destructive to employee morale. While criticism is a necessary and unavoidable part of any activity, it must be offered constructively to resolve a problem, improve a system, lower costs, and other worthwhile purposes. Criticism for the sake of criticism has no worth and no place in business.

A responsible supervisor does not indulge or pass on gossip or rumors about other employees. A supervisor who is loyal to the personnel is usually repaid with loyalty from the unit.

When You Must Criticize

"To err is mortal; to forgive, divine." The supervisor is sitting on the semicolon of this statement. Not only must he recognize errors, see that they are corrected, and discourage further mistakes, but he is also expected to maintain his composure while doing so.

It is a fact of life that most people resent being told that they have done something wrong, especially if the person who does the criticizing is tactless and forceful. Harsh criticism can hurt a person's morale, damage the ego, and create lasting antagonisms. When faced with the job of criticizing an employee, the supervisor should try to follow these seven simple rules:

1. *Be sure of the facts.* Ask the right people the right questions, and do so objectively. Only when you are sufficiently satisfied that an error has been made should you call in the employee. If being criticized for something you *did* can cause resentment, being criticized for something you *didn't* do will really breed antagonism.
2. If the mistake is important and has upset you, *cool off before you talk to the employee.* When you are angry, you are more likely to say something personal. Avoid personal criticism; address your comments to correcting the mistake, not to punishing the security officer.

3. *Discuss the situation in private.* Nothing embarasses a person more than being reprimanded before one's peers or, worse yet, one's subordinates. Take time to move away from inquisitive eyes and ears. Your criticism will be better and lasting resentment may be avoided.

4. *Ask questions first — don't accuse.* This fits in neatly with the "Be sure of your facts" rule. Don't come into the discussion with your mind made up. Ask for the employee's side of the story. Everyone appreciates being heard, especially when a mistake has been made.

5. *Before you criticize,* let your worker know that you appreciate some of the good work produced. Medicine is easier to swallow if you mix it with sugar!

6. When the situation dictates that an oral reprimand be given, *explain to the employee the reasoning behind your actions.* An employee deserves to know why there is criticism and how this will affect the future. For example, if a security officer is being criticized for the first tardiness, the officer should not be made to feel that the job is in jeopardy. However, if the reprimand is for continual absences or latenesses, and the job *is* on the line, the employee should know this as well.

7. If at all possible, *leave a good impression* with your employee at the end of the discussion. This does not mean you should make light of mistakes. Rather, it will remove some of the tension and embarassment if, when the employee returns to work, you pat the person on the back or say something like, "At least we know you're human."

These seven rules will help the supervisor to deal tactfully with the situation when he *must* criticize. He should remember that "the goal of criticism is to leave the person with the feeling of having been helped."

Personal Counseling

Every supervisor must be prepared to discuss an employee's personal problems when asked to do so, but only to the extent that the individual desires, and within limits carefully set by the supervisor.

The biggest problem for the manager, in a counseling situation, is to steer a proper course between practical and constructive advice, and particularly to stay clear of "amateur psychiatry." When an employee seeks personal counseling from him, the supervisor should consider these guidelines:

1. *Watch your general attitude.* Always show a continuing sincere interest in your people as individuals with homes and families and not simply as subordinates. If there is sickness at home, remember to ask

about progress. If someone's daughter is graduating from high school, show some interest in that also.

2. *Make yourself available.* If someone indicates that he wants to talk to you about a matter that has come up, answer by saying that if it is important to the employee, you'll be glad to take whatever time is necessary. The employee will probably be glad to have the interview after hours, when nobody else is around. In any case, it is obvious that you should make it possible to have the employee talk to you in private. Have the meeting as soon as possible after the request.

3. *Some meetings you will have to initiate.* This can occur, for example, when a usually competent and reliable person shows a marked falling off in interest or quality of work, or is unusually tardy or frequently absent, all indicating that some personal situation is interfering with efficiency. Don't keep putting the meeting off . . . it will never be any easier than at the present moment.

4. *Be as prepared as possible.* If you have initiated the meeting, be sure of your facts with specific examples of the kinds of behavior that are giving you concern. If the employee has asked for the meeting, refresh your memory about any personal situations that may previously have come to light about the employee.

5. *Put the employee at ease.* You will already have achieved part of this by arranging for a private meeting. Maybe a cup of coffee or a soft drink is indicated.

6. *Be a good listener.* Whether the problem is real or imagined, give the employee a chance to explain the situation without interruption.

7. *Be wary of advice on personal matters.* On emotional and personal problems, your best contribution will be to serve as a sounding board. You can, of course, give advice on any company policy that may be involved, avenues of financial assistance available through the company, and other matters where you are sure of your ground. But with a personal problem, your main function as a counselor should be to help the individual recognize what the problem is, and to explore possible alternate solutions, with final decisions left to the individual. Always remember, when you are dealing with personal and emotional problems, you will rarely be in possession of enough facts to take the responsibility for recommending specific solutions.

8. *Avoid assuming the psychiatrist's function.* If you have reason to believe that the employee has more than the normal kinds of anxiety, suggest professional counsel.*

---

*Excerpts taken from "How To Communicate Better With Workers" by Carl Heyel.

22. Job Descriptions for Security Supervisors and Security Officers

Lawrence J. Fennelly

INTRODUCTION

Security for an art facility or library in which personnel are assigned to a variety of posts is a complex task, and for this reason a precise job description for each position is a valuable asset to your overall operation. In the pre-employment screening it provides a method of determining whether or not an applicant's qualifications match the job requirements.

Currently, many security positions do not have adequate job descriptions or post orders established as part of their daily operations. The preparation of high-quality job descriptions is a critical step in personnel selection, assignment, and training, for without them the employer, employee, and persons responsible for developing training programs are at a tremendous disadvantage.[1]

SECURITY SUPERVISOR

Guidelines for Job Description

Under the general direction of the security manager or chief administrator supervises an operational component of the security services branch consisting of a museum, gallery, support element, or a part thereof; provides safety and information for the visiting public and employees; provides protection for the collections and security for the corporation assets; provides safety information and a controlled environment for the visiting public, and performs other related duties.

Duties.

1. Administers and supervises an operational component of the security services branch consisting of a museum, gallery, support element, or a part thereof, and comprising up to 100 security officers (number immaterial; may also include indirect supervision of contracted security guards, elevator operators, cloakroom attendants, and parking lot attendants).

    -   Reviews reports from other security supervisors in order to accommodate new situations, alleviate problems, and establish a more effective and efficient security system. Implements necessary follow-up procedures when indicated by the guards' reports.
    -   Issues special equipment (radios, flashlights, keys, etc.) and the corresponding instructions, written and verbal, concerning their proper use, protection, and return.
    -   Makes inspection tours to all areas of responsibility on both a scheduled and random basis to observe and appraise work performance of officers on duty and to verify that the procedures as established in setting up the security system are being adhered to.
    -   Obtains written and oral reports on security incidents or on recommendations from the security officer; reviews and replies to these reports, and where appropriate or necessary, forwards these reports to the security manager along with corresponding comments or observations.
    -   Responds to requests for assistance when extra help is required (e.g., a sudden large influx of visitors or a VIP visit; such requests may be from museum or gallery curators or from other security officers).
    -   Coordinates, maintains, and reviews the design, use, and control of special registers and lockup systems for lost and found property, keys, visitors, passes, etc.
    -   Deploys security officers to various posts on special assignments, and also plans the rest and lunch relief periods of these officers.
    -   Coordinates the collection, tabulation, and charting of visitor count figures.
    -   Ensures that all security officers are properly dressed and equipped in a professional manner in keeping with the museum or gallery environment and image.

- Issues clear and concise instructions to security officers and ensures that these instructions are carried out in a manner conducive to good security and good public relations.
- Counsels security officers for failure to comply with written and verbal instructions and regulations and recommends to the security manager the appropriate action if such is required.
- Provides evaluation reports on all security officers, on a biannual basis.
- Acts as a training coordinator within the department for the purposes of providing on-the-job training on a continuing basis, orientation and indoctrination for a new or recently transferred-in security officer, and advises on extra training requirements available from within or from other institutions.
- Prepares attendance records for the security component, bearing in mind hours worked, absences, shift premiums, overtime, etc., for pay and cost recovery programs.
- Makes, in the absence of the security manager or his deputy, immediate decisions on:

  Use of overtime, replacements, changes in assignments, and suspension of a security officer if the action of this officer precludes his continuing on shift.

  Preparing shift schedules, or amendments, giving due consideration to available human resources, museum–gallery policy, public hours, visiting patterns, vacation leave, holidays, and the appropriate union agreement.

2. Provides protection for the collections and security for the corporation assets:
- Briefs security officers on special events, exhibitions, or situations that require additional security coverage (gold case, new temporary exhibitions, traveling criminal notice, etc.).
- Responds immediately and in a knowledgeable manner to requests for assistance from security, maintenance, or museum–gallery personnel concerning serious security problems or violations, damage to works of art, theft of artifacts, and failure of building utilities or environmental controls.
- Acts, under the authority of the director and/or trustees and when they are present, as an area or floor fire emergency officer (these decisions could involve calling the police and/or fire department, evacuating and readmitting museum personnel and the public, bomb searches, etc.).
- Acts as the functional coordinator in the complex artifact alarm system to enable curators to change or work on artifacts or works of art (this requires a certain amount of technical knowledge to be able to disconnect, connect, balance, and test the system).

- Plans and develops communications systems procedures, including procedures for quick response to alarms (fire, theft, illegal entry into controlled areas, unauthorized touching of exhibits, or removal of exhibits).
- Plans and develops procedures for special events and exhibits, taking into account management policies, available resources, public desires, security procedures, and unusual threat situations (some exhibits, such as those depicting nudity or warfare, may be construed to have political or moral implications by certain individuals or groups).
- Conducts physical security surveys within all relevant areas of concern in order to determine if in fact a particular area is secure (such a survey is a comprehensive written report, utilizing many other personnel with specialized training, and provides definite recommendations and conclusions).
- Conducts investigations of suspected or actual complaints, incidents, or security violations: conducts preliminary investigations of crimes by interviewing employees, security officers, and in some cases the public and various police or guard company officers, and preparing the necessary reports.
- Affects an arrest when someone is found committing an offense on the corporation's property (also acts on behalf of the corporation in laying out information and lodging complaints with the local police as well as giving evidence).

3. Provides safety, information, and a controlled environment for the visiting public:
   - Provides recommendations to corporate management on methods of improving the museum–gallery environment in order to make it safe for the visiting public (recommendations necessary on a day-to-day basis as exhibits change frequently).
   - Replies to and investigates complaints received from the public to the satisfaction of both the corporation and the complainant.
   - Provides for the maintenance of a quiet, secure, and proper atmosphere conducive to study and contemplation in public exhibition areas.
   - Controls disruptive visitors in a firm, professional, and diplomatic manner.
   - Ensures that the first aid room is adequately supplied in accordance with directives, that the room is cleaned on a regular basis, and that all security officers are trained in accordance with standards that have been established.

4. Performs other related duties such as attending meetings as the museum–gallery security representative, studying incidents to detect

trends, performing as a training instructor in the support force on a rotational basis (this necessitates that each supervisor have the ability to complete research projects, prepare lesson plans, and lecture to large classes, with limited supervision), conducting surveys or investigations of areas of concern to the corporation as a whole and providing appropriate recommendations and conclusions (i.e., shipments of high value, collections via air, rail, transport), and becoming fully conversant with the duties and responsibilities of the security manager in order to be able to assume this responsibility in the absence of the security manager.

Summary of the Roles of the Supervisor

I. ADMINISTRATIVE RESPONSIBILITIES
   a. Plan
      - Implement portions of plan
      - Issue schedules
      - Determine workloads
      - Provide instructions
      - Sell ideas to supervisors
   b. Organize
      - Responsibilities understood
      - Job descriptions
      - Lines of authority defined
      - Delegation
      - Key link in chain of command
   c. Control
      - Enforce rules
      - Set standards
      - Maintain physical facilities
   d. Direct
      - Personnel
      - Office procedures
      - Analyze and improve procedures
      - Interpret policy
      - Evaluate personnel
      - Maintain follow-up schedules to see that procedures are improved
      - Make decisions
   e. Coordinate
      - Activities with other units
      - Between management and nonmanagement

II. HUMAN RELATIONS RESPONSIBILITIES
    a. Communicate
    b. Motivate
- Supervision
- Training programs
- Communications
- Understand human relations

    c. Behavior control or discipline
    d. Complaints and grievances
    e. Catalyst or agent for change
- Work methods
- Behavior
- Attitude

III. TRAINING AND DEVELOPMENT RESPONSIBILITIES
    a. Philosophy
    b. Development of supervisor
    c. Develop staff
    d. Evaluate staff
    e. Promote staff

Specifications

Skill and Knowledge.

Basic knowledge. The position of security supervisor requires a thorough knowledge of the principles of protecting material, buildings, information, and people against harm, loss, or damage and in particular a detailed knowledge of the security policies, regulations, and procedures applicable to the museum.

The job requires a significant amount of recent experience, preferably as a supervisor in related fields such as security, police work, fire department, safety, or intelligence; or an equivalent combination of training and related experience. Each security supervisor must also have the ability, interest, and motivation to complete other courses offered by the corporation and outside institutions (community college, universities, and private agencies such as the International Association Chiefs of Police.)

The daily tasks require writing comprehensive investigative or survey reports to recommend and support changes within the security or administrative systems of the museum. Such reports should be extensive enough to include suggestions about other or better uses of human or material resources.

The security supervisor must understand that as the threats to the collections change or vary, so also must the security system protecting the collections change; consequently, education, which is the continuing acquisition of knowledge, must be an ongoing experience. The supervisor is also required to instruct and train new officers both as part of the basic course and as part of the continuing on-the-job training.

Comprehension and judgment. The work requires a thorough understanding of pertinent orders and instructions, i.e., museum regulations, radio/telephone procedures, offenses under relevant statutes, powers of arrest, security techniques, pyschology of crowds and small groups, post orders, fire orders, emergency orders, and fire departments directives, so that immediate action, based on sufficient knowledge, can be taken in a variety of possible emergencies. (Note: at times during public hours the supervisor will be the responsible building authority and the chief building fire emergency officer as required under regulations. The supervisor's decisions could result in building evacuation for fires, bomb threats, or other emergency situations.)

The degree of comprehension and judgment required in this work must be viewed in light of the fact that, on certain occasions, time and circumstances will not permit referral to higher authority and that any delay in the decision-making process could mean irreplaceable losses and/or panic by the public. Because of the consequences of error and time delay, a good deal of latitude in judging how to solve problems must be allowed the supervisor as no two emergencies or incidents are similar.

Specific vocational training. In order to qualify for employment as a security supervisor, a great deal of experience and training is required. It is necessary to acquire such training through institutions; federal, provincial, or regional law enforcement training centers; or fire departments, in courses ranging from a few weeks to several months. Special vocational training, on a part-time basis, at institutes such as local colleges is definitely encouraged and, when possible, sponsored by the corporation. Because of the nature of the supervisor's responsibilities the training required for such special duties as physical security surveys, investigations, etc., must be acquired through international, national, or provincial agencies and departments.

On-the-job Training. Because of the constantly changing technology, which results in changes in the security systems of the museum or gallery, on-the-job training is a continuous process for personnel at the management level; this training is often handled by companies or agencies.

Effort.

Mental effort. The complicated mix of communications, alarm systems (including intrusion, motion, and touch sensors), museum personnel, the public, and the extremely high value of the collections requires the highest level of attention and precise mental and sensory coordination. Because of the length of each shift (with only two short rest breaks and a one-half hour lunch period) mental fatigue resulting from the sustained periods of concentration and the constant attention to details (artifacts and people) must be expected.

Operational fatigue is also likely, considering that the supervisor is in charge of six to thirty security officers as well as monitoring and supervising the operation of a complex mechanical security system.

Physical effort. The work requires moderate physical effort, as the supervisor is either checking various posts, systems, and areas on a patrol basis or standing while lecturing to a class. Two short rest breaks and a lunch break are permitted. Occasionally, the duties require the supervisor to climb stairs or ladders, or to handle lightweight objects such as fire-fighting equipment or fragile artifacts. (All supervisors are rotated through all shifts and duties, thus disrupting their personal living habits.)

Responsibility.

Resources or services. Each security supervisor is a major part of the total security system designed to protect the buildings, material, people, and the collections. The collections are nonrenewable resources and therefore must be given the greatest protection possible as they are important to the world as well as to various ethnic groups. They may also be on temporary loan from other governments, museums, or individuals. The security supervisor must be capable of making correct "on-the-spot decisions," especially when considering the value of the assets involved and the degree of international, national, or corporate embarrassment that might result from a careless decision. For example, an error in judgment could result in valuable assets being threatened by theft, vandalism, or other overt attacks.

Safety of others. Special care is required to prevent injury and distress not only to personnel employed by the corporation but also to the thousands of visitors to the museum or galleries each year. Frequently museum or gallery visitors are large numbers of children or groups of elderly or infirm people. The security supervisor must be trained to implement preventive security and safety measures, which have been carefully worked out and recommended in comprehensive surveys and analytic reports prepared by the supervisors.

Working Conditions.

Environment. Occasionally, the supervisor may be exposed to extreme heat or extreme cold (exterior patrols) or noise (hundreds of children). It is also necessary for the supervisor to wear communications equipment in order to keep in touch with all the security posts.

Hazards. Sometimes the supervisor may be exposed to hazards because of the need for vehicular or foot exterior patrols in high-crime areas, or because of the nature of some of the collections. These injuries could be minor, such as cuts or sunburn, but occasionally they could be serious enough to result in lost time from work. This kind of injury might be a fracture, severe bruising, etc., resulting from an accident, inside or outside of the museum, or from a confrontation with someone while protecting museum assets. If an injury like this does occur, a report must be filled out.

Supervision Duties. A supervisor is in charge of six to thirty security officers, giving them work assignments and arranging their shift schedules, instructing new employees, coordinating a work group involved with many facets of the security system, assessing the performance of security officers, and reporting serious grievances and disciplinary proposals to higher authority (duties may include indirect supervision of contract security guards, elevator operators, cloakroom attendants, and parking lot attendants).

Contacts. The work requires frequent contact (weekly) with middle-management officers in other agencies and with police and fire departments. This contact may be made in the course of conducting fire and emergency orders and planning for the future (i.e., test evacuations). There is daily contact with museum–gallery personnel at the senior- and middle-management levels while carrying out routine duties.

SECURITY OFFICER

Guidelines for Job Description

Under the general supervision of the duty supervisor, performs the duties of a security officer by acting as the museum contact with the public in the museum, providing protection for the collection, providing safety to the employees and visiting public, providing security for the corporation's assets, and carrying out other related duties.

Duties.

1. Represents the museum or gallery and acts as control officer for the public visiting the museum:
   - Maintains a quiet, secure, and proper atmosphere conducive to study and contemplation in public exhibition areas that require this kind of atmosphere.

- Relates to and effectively controls disruptive public visitors in a firm and diplomatic manner (note that this is normally the only direct contact the visiting public has with a member of the museum or gallery staff).

2. Protects the collection, which includes priceless, irreplaceable treasures, and also international collections borrowed for special exhibitions, etc.:
  - Monitors and responds to the artifact alarm and signal system (point and area sensors, etc.).
  - Remains informed about the movement of exhibitions and artifacts within the premises.
  - Maintains surveillance of the visiting public in order to identify individuals who might vandalize or steal exhibits.
  - Ensures that directives and instructions for visitors in the building are strictly adhered to, for instance, concerning smoking, eating, and carrying of items dangerous to exhibits, etc.
  - Affects an arrest of a person found committing an offense, restrains a person from causing further injury or damage, and requests police assistance as required.
  - Handles and protects artifacts and works of art in the appropriate manner when required or on own initiative in emergency situations.

3. Performs the following duties related to the safety of the visiting public and special guests (who may include international VIPs, large numbers of children, or groups of elderly or handicapped persons) and museum personnel:
  - Provides first aid in cases of accidents or illness, summons a doctor or ambulance, and calls for police support as required.
  - Acts in a calm and decisive manner as area fire emergency officer in the evacuation of the public and museum personnel from the premises during fire alarms or bomb threat emergencies.
  - Applies courteous and firm crowd control and assistance to the public while they are visiting the exhibitions.
  - Communicates to the supervisor in report form all public safety hazards (torn or loose carpets, sharp objects, unsteady exhibits, poor lighting conditions, unattended maintenance tools or ladders, blocked stairwells and emergency exit doors) that might cause danger to the public or personnel while on the premises.
  - Regulates the flow of visitors in the building or specific areas of the exhibitions.

4. Maintains the physical security of the assets of the corporation (assets include offices, public buildings, warehouses, equipment vehicles, etc.):

- Monitors and responds either as the security control center operator or as the security officer on patrol, to the security communication system (base radio, two-way radio, emergency phones), fire and security alarm systems (intrusion, space and point protection alarms, smoke, heat and pull station alarms), and CCTV surveillance systems, etc.
- Controls and verifies by an access control system the movement of personnel and visiting public, vehicles, and materials in and out of restricted areas.
- Carries out scheduled and random security patrols and inspections in all areas with particular emphasis on high-risk areas.
- Determines on each patrol that there are no situations or materials that would endanger public, property, or the collections (i.e., fire, broken water pipes, escaping gas, radiation leaks, environmental control, defective safety lights) in such areas as offices, washrooms, galleries, laboratories, workshops, or behind false exhibition walls, and, if problems are found, takes prompt corrective action to rectify these problems.
- Responds to a fire alert situation by searching to detect the location of whatever caused the alarm to sound and fighting the fire with available fire-fighting equipment.
- Searches buildings systematically after public hours to ensure that no unauthorized persons have remained behind and to secure all points of access.
- Resolves and takes corrective action on all incidents that have a bearing on the security, safety, and protection of buildings and their contents, submits reports and makes appropriate recommendations in writing to the supervisor (such reports may be reviewed by senior management).
- Searches and identifies suspect items during bomb threats.

5. Other duties: performs other security and administrative duties, for example:
   - Relieves fellow officers of various duties during their rest periods as required.
   - Initiates emergency response procedures upon receipt of alarm or telephone information.
   - Completes reports, charts, graphs, and other statistical information (i.e., visitor count) as required for managerial planning.
   - Maintains local records on personnel information (leave application, etc.), equipment control systems, supply requisitions, and key control records.
   - Performs special duties as required during visits of VIPs and special functions.

Summary of the Functions of Security Guards

1. Prevention
    Prevent crimes
    Patrol designated areas
    Make patrol tours

2. Protection
    Protect life and property
    Observe conditions and exits
    Provide access control

3. Enforcement
    Apprehend violators
    Enforce rules and regulations of employer
    Vehicle control

4. Detection
    Monitor alarms (burglary, fire, video)
    Make watch tours
    Respond to alarms

5. Investigation
    Recover stolen property
    Investigate losses

6. Emergency Services
    First aid
    Handle bomb threats
    Control fires
    Handle disturbances

7. Reporting
    Report to supervisor
    Assist police with reports
    Appear in court

8. Inspections
    Fire, safety, and security checks
    Check equipment
    Enforce parcel restrictions

9. General Services
    Identification services
    Visitor control
    Give information

10. Other Duties as Assigned

Specifications

Skill and Knowledge.

Basic knowledge. The work requires the successful completion of an extensive two-week (eighty-hour) training course that includes first aid, fire and emergency procedures, protection of evidence, security techniques and systems, human relations, and criminal law. Each security officer must have the ability to complete this initial course as well as the ability, interest, and motivation to complete other courses given by the corporation, government departments, or community colleges.

In addition, a one- or two-week orientation course is given at the museum or gallery. This course, most of which is given in a classroom, is designed to enable security officers to respond to the public with accurate general information about the exhibitions and the museum, to appreciate the relative sensitivity of certain exhibits, to learn about historical security and safety problems, and know about the total security program in the institution.

The daily tasks involve maintaining security records, writing reports or memoranda on work performed, accidents, or incidents, which may on occasion be forwarded to senior management of the corporation, and the maintaining of security registries as part of a complete security system (i.e., a registry of lost and found items, visitors register, key registers, etc.). Such reports or memoranda may include recommendations for better methods and procedures to achieve the required objectives. This degree of motivation, as well as the ability to work with others, is an important ingredient that should be evident in the initial training course.

Comprehension and judgment. The work requires the ability to understand pertinent orders and instructions thoroughly — regulations, radio/telephone procedures, offenses under relevant federal statutes, powers of arrest, security techniques, psychology of crowds and small groups, post orders, fire orders, emergency orders, and fire commissioner directives — so that immediate action, based on in-depth knowledge, can be taken in a variety of possible emergencies. This ability is critical because on certain occasions time and circumstances will not permit referral to higher authority and a delay in action could result in irreplaceable losses ranging from thousands to millions of dollars or possibly in death from fire or smoke in the case of a building emergency. Because of the consequences of an error in judgment or delay in action (picture slashing), some latitude for judgment in interpreting instructions and solving problems must be allowed the security officer, for no two emergencies, accidents, or incidents (false fire alarm) are similar and because supervisory personnel are not always present in the building.

Specific vocational training. Vocational training, on a part-time basis, is definitely encouraged — to the extent that there is an ongoing liaison with the law and security coordinator. A number of specific skills are required in the security services, and this kind of training is both a motivating factor for the security officers and a financial and security benefit for the museums. A certain amount of experience and training is required to qualify for employment. In Canada, for example, adequate training in security can only be acquired in the government or in certain community colleges.

On-the-job training. Because of constantly changing technology and necessary alterations in the security systems of the museums, on-the-job training is important not only at the time of initial employment, but also as an ongoing task for qualified personnel at the supervisory or management levels. The requirement to rotate personnel after certain periods necessitates that on-the-job training be available and that the individual have sufficient ability to absorb the level and amount of information involved.

Effort.

Mental effort. Because of the complicated mix of communications systems, alarm systems (including motion and touch sensors), museum personnel, the public, and the extremely high value of the collections, the work requires the highest level of attention and precise mental and sensory coordination. Because of the length of each shift (two short rest breaks and one-half hour lunch period allowed per shift), mental fatigue resulting from the sustained period of concentration and the constant attention to details (artifacts and people) is to be expected. Operator fatigue is also a factor when monitoring the security equipment control console.

Physical effort. A security officer, regardless of whether on post or patrol, stands or walks continually throughout the entire shift, relieved only by two short breaks and a half-hour lunch period. All security officers are rotated through all shifts and duties, disrupting their personal living habits.

Responsibility.

Resources or services. Each security officer is a significant part of the total security system designed to protect the buildings, material, people, and the collections. The collections are nonrenewable resources, and therefore must be protected accordingly as they are important to the world as well as to various ethnic groups. Because the security officer must work under a situation of limited supervision and make "on-the-spot decisions," it is imperative that the officer be explicit and correct at all times. Possible errors in judgment could embarrass the museum (storehouse full of collections that are looted or burned) and the corporation (painting on loan that is damaged) or could result in a situation where the public is not given the necessary degree of protection it expects while visiting a museum (an uncontrolled number of elderly persons or wheelchair patrons that are allowed above ground level of the museum or gallery).

Safety of others. Special care is required to prevent injury and distress not only to personnel employed by the corporation but also to the thousands of visitors to the museum each year. The security officer must be trained to prevent accidents and injuries by recommending changes in security procedures and to assist injured or distressed people when called upon to do so. When injuries occur to the public, embarrassment to the corporation usually occurs only if the security officer has not efficiently and effectively handled the situation.

NOTES

1. National Advisory Committee on Criminal Justice Standards and Goals, *Private Security,* Report of the Task Force on Private Security, LEAA, Washington, D.C., 1976.

23. Developing Policies and Procedures

Lawrence J. Fennelly

INTRODUCTION

This chapter mainly consists of a set of working guidelines that can be used in any facility. They can be part of your policy and procedure manuals. Established policies can aid the professional security manager in controlling spending, establishing rules and regulations, establishing codes for dress and conduct, and determining guidelines for departmental promotions and hiring of personnel. It is a good security practice to follow procedures because they can establish security guidelines and standards; advise staff in the event of accidents, fires, burglaries, theft patrol, and disasters; and develop and implement long-range planning and predict your existing risks and vulnerabilities.

Management must have the ability to motivate its employees. This motivation can be turned into a strong security asset for community involvement, thereby increasing employee morale.

This chapter is divided into two parts. The first section addresses everyday procedures and objectives, whereas the second section gives a specific direction to guards that allows them a greater understanding of their duties and responsibilities.

MAJOR DUTIES AND RESPONSIBILITIES

The primary objective of the security department is to provide a high level of safety, security, and service for all members of the art facility, their visitors, and their guests. To accomplish this goal the responsibilities of the security department will include:

1. The prevention and control of crime.
2. The protection of life and the safeguarding of property.
3. The investigation of crime, the apprehension of criminal offenders, and the recovery of stolen property.
4. The preservation of the peace and the resolution of conflict.
5. The immediate response to all emergencies and to all persons in need of aid or assistance.
6. The performance of such other services required by the members of the community.
7. The advancement of a cooperative relationship with all members of the community.
8. The adherence to all museum policies and department rules and procedures.
9. The accomplishment of all department purposes and objectives within the framework of the law and the constitutional guarantees of all persons.

Required Conduct

The following provisions are applicable to all members of the security department:

Reporting for duty. All members shall report for duty at the time and place required by the instructions of their supervisors. They shall be properly uniformed and equipped and ready to assume their duties immediately. Upon returning to duty after an absence, they shall inform themselves of any new orders, instructions, or other important matters relative to their assignment. While on duty they shall avoid any activities not directly related to their responsibilities.

Courtesy. All members shall be courteous and considerate at all times to the public, to their supervisors and command officers, and to their fellow employees. They shall be tactful in the performance of their duties and exercise the utmost patience and discretion, even in the face of extreme provocation.

Identification. All members shall carry or wear appropriate identification while on duty, to indicate that they are members of the security department. All members shall properly identify themselves to any person requesting this information while they are on duty except when the withholding of such information is necessary for the performance of police duties or when authorized by proper authority.

Address and telephone. All members of the security department shall have a telephone in their place of residence or a telephone where they may be reached and shall report any change of address or telephone number to their supervisor or other appropriate person within the department.

Submitting reports. All members shall promptly and accurately complete and submit all department reports and forms as required.

Truthfulness. All members shall truthfully state the facts in all reports and before any judicial proceeding, official investigation, or department inquiry.

Conformance to laws. All members shall obey all laws of the United States and of any state or local jurisdiction in which they are present.

Physical fitness. All members shall maintain good physical fitness and mental alertness, to a degree sufficient to perform their duties, and shall report for a physical examination, at the expense of the department, when so directed by the security manager.

Personal appearance. All members shall be neat and well groomed. All articles of uniform and equipment shall conform to departmental regulations and shall be kept presentable and in good order at all times. The operational manager may prescribe other types of clothing when necessary to meet particular objectives. Office employees wearing civilian attire shall conform to general standards for office personnel.

Dissemination of information. All members shall treat the official business of the department as confidential and such information shall be disseminated only to those for whom it is intended in accordance with established procedures. Access to departmental files, records, and reports shall be limited to those employees authorized by the operational manager.

Departmental communications. All members shall transmit communications promptly, accurately, and completely, to other members of the department as required, and shall immediately inform their superior officer of any matter of importance coming to their attention during their tour of duty, or otherwise. They shall call to the attention of their relieving officers any information regarding unresolved problems or problems that may arise during the next tour of duty.

Civil disputes. All members shall take a neutral position in any dispute of a civil nature, acting only to prevent or control a breach of the peace.

Mutual protection.   All members shall come to the immediate aid, assistance, or protection of other members of the department who, in the performance of their duties, require such aid and assistance.

Duty beyond specific assignment.   All members are employed to provide security, safety, and service in all areas, not merely for their particular place of assignment. It is expected that all serious matters, particularly those that involve the protection of persons and property, will receive immediate and appropriate attention.

Prohibited Conduct

The following acts by any member of the security department are prohibited or restricted:

Unbecoming conduct.   Any specific type of conduct, on or off duty, that reflects discredit upon the art facility and upon the department and its members.

Neglect of duty.   Being absent from assigned duty without leave, failure to fulfill specific assignment, or failure to take suitable and appropriate action when any crime, disorder, or other incident requires attention.

Insubordination.   Failure or deliberate refusal to obey a lawful order from a superior officer.

Unnecessary force.   The use of more physical force than that which is reasonably necessary to accomplish a lawful purpose.

Use of alcohol.   The use of intoxicating beverages while on duty. The use of intoxicating beverages while off duty to the extent that it renders a member unfit to report for the next tour of duty or impairs their duty performance.

Possession and use of drugs.   The personal possession or use of controlled substances or narcotics except when prescribed by a reputable physician for a legitimate medical purpose.

Sleeping on duty.   All members shall remain awake at all times while on duty.

Improper associations.   Voluntarily establishing or maintaining relationships with persons engaged in unlawful activity, except in the official performance of duty with the prior knowledge of the security manager.

Gifts, gratuities, or rewards.   Soliciting or accepting any gift or reward for the purpose of affecting the performance or nonperformance of an official duty, except as specifically authorized by the security manager. Soliciting, collecting, or receiving money or anything of value while on duty, or in uniform, for any charitable organization, gift, testimonial, or other such purpose without the approval of the security manager.

Abuse of position.   Using official position or department identification for personal or financial gain or for avoiding the consequences of illegal acts.

Feigning illness.   Making a false report of illness or injury or feigning illness, or otherwise deceiving or attempting to deceive any superior officer as to the condition of health.

Processing property or evidence.   Converting to personal use, tampering with, or destroying any evidence or other property received or being held for safekeeping in connection with departmental responsibilities.

Abuse or misuse of department property or equipment.   Negligently abusing, misusing, damaging or losing department property or equipment.

Misuse of firearms.   Using or handling firearms in a careless or imprudent manner, while on duty, in violation or disregard of department procedures.

Arrest, search, or seizure.   Making an arrest, search, or seizure that is not in accordance with law and department policy and procedures.

Withholding police information.   Unjustifiably and deliberately withholding security information from superior officers and other members of the department.

Assault on member.   Applying for a court process for a person accused of an assault and battery committed on a member while on duty without first reporting the circumstances to the supervisor and seeking his permission to make such application.

Violation of rules.   Committing or omitting any act that constitutes a violation of any of the rules and procedures of the department.

Orders

An order is a command or instruction, written or oral, given by a superior officer. All lawful orders shall be carried out fully, promptly, and in the manner prescribed. This will include orders relayed from a superior officer by an officer of the same or lesser rank.

General order.   A general order is an order in writing, issued by the operations manager outlining a policy or course of action, permanent in nature and affecting the entire department. A general order may amend, supersede, or rescind any previous order and remains in full effect until amended or canceled by the operations manager.

Special orders.   A special order is a temporary written order, issued by the operations manager, outlining instructions for a particular situation and is automatically canceled when its objective is achieved.

Unlawful orders.   Members shall not obey any order that would require the commission of an unlawful act. If in doubt as to the legality of the order, members shall request clarification of the order or a conference with higher authority. Obedience to an unlawful order is never a defense for an unlawful action but the responsibility and justification for refusal to act rests with the employee.

Unjust or improper orders.   When an order appears to be unjust or improper, the member to whom the order is given shall respectfully notify the superior officer of the impropriety of the order. If the order is not corrected, the order shall be carried out and a subsequent report made to the security manager through the chain of command, giving the circumstances and the reasons for questioning the order and requesting clarification of department policy.

Conflicting orders.   When an order given by a superior officer conflicts with any previous departmental order, the member to whom the order is given will respectfully call attention to such conflict. If the conflicting order is not altered or retracted, the order will be obeyed but the action taken will be the responsibility of the superior officer. The member obeying such an order will not be held responsible for the disobedience of a previous order. It should later be reported to the security manager for clarification.

Instructions from radio dispatcher.   All messages transmitted over the security department's radio system shall be clear, concise, and as complete as possible. No member shall disobey or refuse to take cognizance of any communication transmitted by the radio dispatcher, unless directed to do so by a superior officer.

Department Property and Equipment

All property and equipment issued or assigned to members shall remain the property of the department. All members shall maintain department property and equipment in good condition.

Damaged or inoperative property and equipment. Members shall immediately report to their commanding officer any loss or damage to departmental property or equipment assigned to them. This report will include any defects or hazardous condition of such property or equipment.

Surrender of department property. Members shall surrender all departmental property or equipment in their possession upon termination of service, or when otherwise ordered to do so.

Department of motor vehicles. All members are required to have a valid driver's license. They shall operate department vehicles in a careful and prudent manner and shall be knowledgeable of and obey all laws, rules, and regulations pertaining to such operation. Loss or suspension of driver's license shall be reported to the supervisor immediately.

Department radio equipment. All members of the department are to use radio equipment in the most efficient manner so that they can rapidly respond to incidents occurring anywhere in their area and effectively perform their duties. They must use all radio equipment in accordance with the rules and regulations of the Federal Communications Commission, which provides heavy fines and imprisonment for willfully damaging radio equipment; transmitting irrelevant, profane, obscene, or indecent radio communications; willfully or maliciously interfering with radio communications; or issuing false or deceptive radio communications or signals.

All department radio equipment, including hand-held mobile radios, should be used for security business only. All radio equipment issued to members during their tour of duty will be their personal responsibility and they will be held accountable for any unjustifiable loss of or damage to such equipment.

PERSONS AUTHORIZED TO DIRECT SECURITY PERSONNEL

Purpose

The purpose of this policy is to clarify who is permitted to direct or order security personnel.

Policy

Guard supervisors are the only persons who are permitted to direct security personnel.

Guards and supervisors will be responsive to requests by all employees and managers at the museum, but shall not take orders from nonsecurity persons.

Guards and supervisors should exercise common sense in responding to requests from nonsecurity persons and act in the best interests of security at the museum.

Talking with the Public

Purpose. The purpose of this procedure is to review the mission of security and to evaluate the need to deal effectively with the public. The main purpose is to protect the museum and its contents from harm. Guards cannot perform effectively if they are talking to visitors. By the very nature of the work, however, guards must be friendly to visitors at all times.

Requests for Information. Guards frequently are asked about art or the museum. When this occurs, they should give a brief answer if possible and refer the visitor to an information booth. Guards should not enter into conversations regarding art. Directions should be brief and courteous.

Questions regarding Security or Incidents. When a visitor asks a question about security, a security procedure, or a security system, the guard should reply that guards are not permitted to discuss security at any time. If the visitor persists in seeking an answer to a question about the museum's security, the guard must be polite but firm in refusing to answer.

Frequently the press and the public are curious about incidents such as thefts from a museum. Incidents should never be discussed with anyone — on or off duty — or in the presence of other employees or visitors.

Questions from the Press. No member of the security force is authorized to discuss any matter with the press. All questions from the press are to be referred to the public relations office.

This policy is not intended to keep the press from having access to information. The purpose of the policy is to ensure that information is given out in a fair and impartial manner.

A security guard is a representative of the museum, and therefore information released to the press or printed in the press as a result of a guard's comments can be considered prejudicial in matters where a fair and impartial trial is sought for a theft or other criminal act committed in the museum. The public relations office is better equipped to provide information in a manner that will not be considered unfair to someone who may ultimately be arrested and prosecuted.

In addition, it is useful to remember that the less the public knows about the museum's security systems, procedures, and staffing, the less potential thieves will know. A security system is compromised when everyone knows how it works. Every detail of the overall security operation is part of a master plan that should not be compromised.

Arguing with the Public. Some members of the public will not agree with a guard's instructions. If asked to check a briefcase, for example, they may wish to argue with the guard and offer several reasons why these instructions should be changed.

Very little, if anything, is accomplished by arguing with the public on matters of policy. Guards should be polite but firm in carrying out their duties. The person who may wish to argue should be told that there is no argument possible about policy matters and the conversation should be ended. If anyone persists in arguing about the issue, a supervisor should be contacted immediately and the supervisor allowed to handle the situation.

> **Security Guard Courtesy.** Nothing does more to up-grade the public image of the department or to enlist the public cooperation than does police courtesy. Police courtesy is neither subservience nor courtesy in the Chesterfieldian sense. We must be firm but in a courteous, considerate and respectful way.
>
> Police courtesy is courtesy in a broader sense — in the sense of human kindness; respect for the rights of the individual, including an individual in police custody; avoiding rough talk and provocative actions and gestures; allowing the other fellow to save face; friendliness, helpfulness, tact, and understanding.[1]
>
> O. W. Wilson, *On This We Stand,* 1963

O. W. Wilson is probably the foremost police administrator in this century. What he said about police courtesy is true for security guard courtesy as well. Most of the contact guards have with employees and visitors is in the capacity of rendering assistance. Part of the time, at least, guards interact with other people in a restrictive capacity. They tell people not to violate gallery rules; they enforce museum rules and regulations; and they inspect incoming and outgoing packages. The manner in which guards deal with the employees and visitors at the museum has a great impact on how they are viewed in the eyes of these individuals.

Every man or woman is entitled to respect and dignity. Every person, to some extent, resents being told to do something he does not want to do or being told not to do something he is intent upon doing. As the group of people who must enforce the rules, guards have one strike against them from the beginning, for they are the symbol of the authority that the employee, visitor, or student resents when a rule must be enforced. So guards must work extra hard to enforce the rules in a firm but courteous manner.

Tact and politeness are the basic elements of good public relations. Guards must work to develop the skills of dealing with other people in a tactful and polite manner. The old adage that you can catch more flies with honey than with vinegar is true.

A basic fact of life is that people, on the whole, react favorably to ordinary courtesies. If a sincere concern for the problems and feelings of others is expressed, in time, this concern will be returned.

Self-discipline is needed on the part of the security guard to avoid tendencies toward sarcasm, vulgarity, or rudeness. Guards should never allow themselves to lose their temper. They should never let the opinions and prejudices of the person with whom they are dealing get the better of them. Every person should be treated with the respect and dignity they deserve.

The Golden Rule — "Do unto others as you would have them do unto you" — is easily applied to security guard behavior. Guards should create a friendly atmosphere by appearing friendly, smiling and exchanging words of courtesy with other persons.

Guards should be patient with people, taking time to help them and letting them feel at home. Visitors should be made to feel welcome.

Using the title "Sir," "Miss," or "Madam" is helpful. It will cement a strong image of courtesy and concern for the dignity of others and let others see the guard as a professional.

The better guards get along with their co-workers, other employees, and visitors, the easier the job becomes. Courtesy is contagious.

Leaving a Post

Purpose. The purpose of this policy is to establish guidelines for permitting a guard to leave his post to perform emergency duties.

General Information. This policy is established to provide guidelines and not to give hard and fast rules. Each guard should use his discretion as to when he is justified in leaving a post unattended. Guards are never justified in leaving a post without first notifying their supervisor unless the delay caused by their notification would endanger life or property. Guards are never justified in leaving a post except for a bona fide emergency or unless they become seriously ill or injured.

Emergencies. Guards should be careful not to be drawn from their post by a diversion caused to permit access by persons seeking to enter the facility illegally. They should be sure that an emergency exists before leaving a post. They may accept the word of an employee that an emergency exists.

Before leaving a post a guard should notify the security office if possible, and attempt to use an employee to watch the post while the guard is responding to the emergency. If possible, an employee who the guard recognizes should be told that an emergency requires the guard's presence elsewhere and the guard should instruct the employee to remain at the post and attempt to limit access to employees only.

Only the guard closest to an emergency should leave his post and respond unless he knows that the guards farther away are needed.

Guards on post are permitted to leave their post to investigate the ringing of fire bells, calls for help, or other bona fide indications that assistance is needed.

What a Guard is Supposed to do on Post in a Gallery

Purpose. The purpose of this policy is to define what a guard is supposed to do on post or gallery patrol during hours when the galleries are occupied by visitors or contractors.

General Information. Security guards must be familiar with the general policies of the department, museum policy regarding access control and parcel control, all training materials, and information provided at roll calls and on the announcement clip board.

Once given an assignment a guard must thoroughly familiarize himself with the post or patrol area, being sure that he fully understands its territory and special problems.

It is not possible for a guard to perform well if he does not know the area in which he is to work.

Policy. Guards are responsible for the protection of the museum's assets, employees, and visitors. A guard should prevent theft, vandalism, fire, accidents, and other disasters. He should do whatever is necessary to abate conditions that will result in one of the above adverse situations.

In addition to the above situations; a guard is responsible for assisting visitors. Guards should provide friendly assistance with simple directions but should *not* engage in discussions of art, policy, security, or any other matters. Directions should be simple.

Guards should remain alert on their post or patrol. Posts are relatively fixed assignments where the guard remains in one spot. Patrols are posts that cover larger areas where the guard may roam looking for problems.

Considerable benefit is gained simply from the guard's presence. Criminals will not act in the presence of an alert guard. Therefore it is essential that guards be alert and move quickly on patrols. A large area should be covered in a short time. Patrol patterns should not be predictable. Guards should double back and move at random.

EVERY corner of every gallery on a patrol area should be covered completely every few minutes. Small galleries should be entered.

The first patrol of every shift is the most important. Guards should examine every piece of art to make sure that all items are present and accounted for. Guards should look for paintings that have been removed and where no art removal notices have been posted. Art is to be examined for vandalism and damage. Guards are to look for improper display procedures such as missing or inadequate hardware on picture frames, etc., and report such conditions to their supervisor immediately.

Throughout the shift, each patrol should recheck for missing or damaged art.

At the end of each shift another thorough check is to be made of all art in the area.

Guards should avoid being distracted by visitors and other guards. They should not congregate at the borders of other posts or patrol areas and talk with other guards. They should make their presence known to visitors. If a suspicious visitor is observed, the guard should use subtle means to let the visitor know that he is being observed.

Areas for Special Attention.   Doors to closets in the patrol area should be locked. Guards should know the locations of all fire extinguishers. The closest fire exit should be known to the guard. Knowing the locations of all light switches is another important factor.

Areas used for art storage should be frequently checked to make sure they are locked.

Visitor conduct should be a matter of concern. Children or adults who are disorderly should be quieted. No smoking is permitted in any gallery area. Food is prohibited as well.

Guards should prevent visitors from touching items in the collection. A guard may inform "touchers" that, even on dry hands, the oils combine with pollution in the air and cause paint and pigments to deteriorate. This is true for statues and decorative arts as well.

Guards should be alert for visitors carrying parcels too large to be permitted in the gallery. If someone is seen with a large parcel, a guard shouldn't be shy about politely challenging him. If he does not have a parcel permit for an oversize bag or briefcase, this person should be asked to go immediately to the front desk area and check the item. Umbrellas are not permitted in the museum, although employees who have office areas in the gallery areas are permitted to pass through the museum with umbrellas. Other employees may not enter the gallery areas with umbrellas.

Persons with cameras must have a camera permit. Camera bags are permitted if the size is reasonable and a permit is issued.

Lost and found items should be picked up and turned over to a supervisor and a report should be filed.

Conducting a Patrol. Guards patrol galleries and nonpublic areas before, during, and after museum hours. It is essential that patrols be conducted properly.

What to Look For. Guards should be alert to intrusions, rule violators (smokers, touchers, vandals, etc.), security breaches (unlocked doors, lock and hardware malfunctions, safety and fire hazards, damaged and missing art work, improperly displayed items, and other matters concerning safety and security).

If employees and contractors are in the facility, guards must be alert to conditions that affect the safety of objects such as smoking or food in the galleries, use of saws and other tools in the proximity of paintings, the unauthorized handling of art, or the intentional or unintentional abuse of art by employees or contractors.

Patrols While the Museum Is Open. Patrols during museum hours are an essential part of the guard's security profile. A guard assigned to a patrol or a post that covers more than one gallery should be visible at all times.

Patrols should move briskly from place to place in order to maximize the appearance that there are more guards in the galleries than there actually are.

Immediately upon arrival at a patrol area, a guard should walk the route and check the art to become familiar with the paintings that have been removed or added. *Each item should be examined for vandalism and its condition noted mentally.*

Guards should be alert to the fact that a theft will almost always occur at the same time as a distraction or disturbance occurs.

Night patrols should be conducted with a flashlight and radio. All areas should be searched early in the shift and throughout the night.

Electrical appliances should be checked to make sure that they are turned off. Doors should be checked on every patrol. Water leaks and hazards should be noted immediately.

Stairs and never elevators should be used in conducting patrols. Patrols should be thorough. They are the first line of defense against fire and intrusion.

Conducting the Safe Patrol. The purpose of this policy is to provide procedures that will help to assure the safety of the security guard while conducting outside patrols.

A guard conducting a patrol of the exterior of the museum facilities should make sure that he has all necessary equipment before beginning the patrol. A radio and all necessary keys are items that should remain with the guard at all times on any patrol. Outside patrols during the night also require a flashlight since observation under objects or bushes is often necessary.

Should the guard encounter suspicious people on the museum property, he should observe them from a distance to ascertain if they are simply walking across the property or if they in some way threaten the security of the facilities. As soon as the suspect is observed, the guard should immediately notify the guard base by radio of the situation and the fact that surveillance is being conducted. If the person or persons linger in the area, the supervisor should decide if the services of police are required. It is not wise to approach suspects alone at night without assistance and the request for assistance from the police is justified if proper discretion is used.

Upon the arrival of the police, the security guard must explain the actions of the suspects that he considers suspicious. The police will ask the suspects to give a good account of their actions.

Grooming and Appearance for Security Personnel

It is important that security guards be neat and clean in appearance and convey a professional demeanor at all times. Guards are highly visible in uniform and are often the first persons that visitors and employees see when they enter the building each day. First impressions are important and therefore guards must always try to appear at their best. A favorable image is a major asset to any security guard.

Each member of the force is expected to maintain a high standard of personal hygiene and uniform appearance. Guards are expected to wear a neat, clean, and pressed uniform, and black lace shoes that are shined to a luster. A clean, pressed shirt is a necessity. Mustaches are to be neatly trimmed. Hair shall be worn neatly trimmed. Length of hair is not an issue as long as it is neat in appearance.

All issued uniform insignia are to be worn in the appropriate manner. No unauthorized lapel pins or decorations are to be worn.

A guard's appearance speaks for itself. Every visitor should be greeted with a smile. A guard is a professional and should look like one!

What to do When Informed of a Fire or Evacuation

Purpose.   The purpose of this policy is to advise all guards as to what to do when a fire is discovered or an evacuation is ordered.

General Information.   Whenever a fire is discovered a guard should call the fire and police departments by radio or phone. The guard should assess the situation and try to provide these departments with enough information to decide if an evacuation is necessary. For example, if the guard smells smoke but finds no other evidence of fire an investigation by supervisors should be made before an evacuation is ordered. If the guard sees flame or thick smoke, the supervisor may suggest an evacuation.

Evacuation. Only the director or high ranking official of the museum, chief of police, chief of the fire department, or their assistants can order an evacuation. An evacuation can be ordered by a *steady ringing of fire alarm bells or a steady sounding of alarm horns.*

If guards are told by horns, bells, or radio to evacuate their area, they should immediately move through their gallery telling people to evacuate the museum immediately. They should avoid creating panic.

All areas are to be searched and elderly, handicapped, or very young persons assisted. Special attention is to be paid to school groups.

Checking Patrol Areas. Guards should check their area and report dangerous conditions to the director as quickly as possible.

Unless fire conditions warrant it, guards are not to evacuate the museum until so instructed. Guards are to make sure everyone has been evacuated before leaving their post.

Parcel Control. Guards must pay special attention to outgoing parcels during an evacuation. As long as conditions permit, parcel control will remain tight. No work of art is to leave the building.

Evacuation Instructions.

1. Secure all art and valuables when conditions permit.
2. Close the door when leaving but don't lock it.
3. Walk to the nearest exit or stairwell.
4. Do not use elevators.
5. Exit via nearest exit.
6. Leave all parcels or packages, artwork, etc., BEHIND.
7. Employees should cross the street from the exit used and wait for signal to return, which will be given by guards.

Never call the security office to verify an evacuation alarm. Evacuate the museum and ask questions later.

Fire Prevention and Protection. The single most devastating threat to a museum is fire. Security guards must be responsive to the problem of fire prevention and must know what fire is and how it is caused in order to understand how it is prevented. The elements of fire are:

1. Fire is a chemical reaction (rapid oxidation that creates heat).
2. An oxidizing agent, combustible material, and ignition source must be present for combustion to take place.
3. Combustible material must be heated to its ignition temperature before it will burn.

4. Combustion will continue until one of the above elements (oxidizing agent, combustible material, or heat) is removed.

Classes of Fire. It is important to know the classes of fire a security guard might confront. They are:

Class A. Fires involving ordinary combustible materials (such as wood, cloth, and paper) where extinguishment is most readily secured by the cooling effects of certain dry chemicals that retard combustion.

Class B. Fires involving flammable or combustible liquids, flammable gases, greases, and similar materials where extinguishment is most readily secured by excluding air — the oxidizing agent.

Class C. Fires involving energized electrical equipment where safety to the firefighters requires the use of nonconductive extinguishing agents. Note: water conducts electricity, so if water is used on an electrical fire, the firefighter may be electrocuted. When the electricity is turned off, the use of extinguishing agents effective against Class A and Class B fires may be indicated.

Class D. Fires involving certain combustible metals such as magnesium, titanium, zirconium, sodium, etc., requiring a heat-absorbing extinguishing agent not reactive with the burning.

Fire Extinguishers. Property owners provide portable fire extinguishers as their first line of defense against accidental fires. Frequently, fire extinguishers can be used to put out a fire before it becomes too large to handle or before it triggers an automatic water sprinkling system with the resulting water damage.

Most fire extinguishers manufactured today utilize a series of markings recommended by the National Fire Protection Association, thus allowing users to quickly identify the class of fire the extinguisher can be used on effectively. This code is as follows:

Extinguisher	Color	Symbol	Letter	Letter color
Class A	Green	Triangle	A	White
Class B	Red	Square	B	White
Class C	Blue	Circle	C	White
Class D	Yellow	Star	D	White

If an extinguisher is useful against more than one class of fire, it should carry a marking symbol designating each class of fire against which it is effective on it. It is important to know the different classes of fires because some portable fire extinguishers are of primary value for only one class of fire and some are suitable for two or three classes of fire, however, none is suitable for all four classes.

Evacuation and Reporting Procedure. The most important thing a guard can do (besides preventing fires in the first place) is to turn in an alarm and evacuate the people promptly. The procedure is as follows:

1. Turn in the alarm. Know the location of all alarm boxes and how they work. Know the location of all telephones. The nearest phone may be needed in a big hurry and it must be one that works. Know the location of all fire extinguishers, what types of fires they can be used on, how they operate, and how to use them. But remember first of all, when there is a fire, *TURN IN THE ALARM!*
2. Protect the lives of any persons who might be affected by the fire. Know the location of all aisles and where they go so people can be directed into a safer area. Know the location of all exits so that if an evacuation becomes necessary, it can be directed safely.
3. Have someone meet the fire department at the entrance of the museum and direct them to the correct location of the fire.

Suspicious Packages

Just as any professional strives for perfection in a product he produces, so does the professional terrorist strive for perfection in the bombs he produces. With the twentieth-century technology we enjoy today, the possible variations in bombs used by "professionals" is limitless. Years ago, mention of the word bomb brought to mind visions of a black ball with a smoking fuse. Today, however, bombs can be a sophisticated piece of electronic equipment to a truck load of chemicals all the way to a primitive fuse parked in front of a building. Security personnel should always keep in mind that a bomb can look like almost anything. For this reason, the following material has been prepared to help the museum security guard perform his duties more safely and effectively.

What Is a "Suspicious Package"? To the trained security guard a broad range of items could fall into this category. Depending upon the skill and knowledge of explosive devices, almost anything could raise the suspicions of a guard and justify further investigation. Since anything could look like a bomb, anything could appear suspicious to a guard. But how does a guard tell what objects should merit further investigation? How does a guard decide what is *really* suspicious? The following examples can help in recognizing a suspicious package or object:

1. The package or object is labeled "BOMB," "DANGER," "DO NOT OPEN," or in some other way that may be intended to inspire curiosity or fear.
2. The object or package fits the description of an object or package described in a threat.
3. The object or package is alien to the area or premises; it "does not belong."
4. The origin of the package is questionable or cannot be readily determined.
5. The physical characteristics of the package are suspicious in size, shape, weight, smell, or in some other way. (Example: a package or object making an audible noise such as a time bomb.)

Handling of Suspicious Packages.

1. Don't touch, tilt, or tamper with an explosive or suspected explosive device in any manner.
2. Don't take for granted the markings on a package; they may be forged or altered to camouflage the device and throw a person off guard.
3. Don't submerge a suspected explosive device in water. If it is electrical, water will complete the circuit and cause a detonation.
4. Don't bring a suspicious package into or near a building.
5. Don't cut a string or unlatch a box or package because of the possibility of a pressure release device.
6. *Don't use a radio or allow anyone else to use a radio transmitter near the package.*
7. Don't underestimate time delay or evacuation time or distance.
8. Don't underestimate the size of a package, as a very small amount of explosive, properly compounded, can be very dangerous.
9. Don't tell unauthorized persons of the presence of a suspicious device or object unless necessary to protect them. Treat all bomb threats and searches as VERY CONFIDENTIAL and discuss such matters — even after they are over — only with authorized personnel.
10. Don't be a hero with a suspected bomb. One heroic but foolish act can cost someone their life.

Intelligence Information

Whenever there is a bomb threat, contact with an explosive device or even a suspected explosive device, or other security problem of this nature, an investigation will be conducted. It is the duty of every security guard to preserve and protect all information relating to the incident. The following information should be sought:

1. Where did the object under question come from?
2. When was it first observed?
3. Who first observed it?
4. Why was it suspected of being a bomb?
5. Are there any more such devices nearby?
6. Has the object been moved or disturbed?
7. If so, how and by whom?
8. Are there witnesses to what happened? Who?
9. What other details would the investigator want to know?

Discovery of a Bomb or Implementation of a Bomb Search. The following procedures are to be followed after a bomb has been discovered:

1. Determining, by the proper authority, whether an evacuation is in order.
2. Securing the building.
3. Establishing a command center in the security office.
4. Broadcasting instructions to security guards on post.
5. Establishing a search.
6. Notifying assisting personnel and wardens.
7. Proper recording of areas "cleared" or declared safe by searchers.

The proper duties of specific guards on post, on patrol, on break, or at control are outlined next for this procedure.

Techniques of a Bomb Search. Although the emergency evacuation and bomb search plan calls for the actual search to be made by persons other than security guards, thus leaving guards available for other duties, from time to time guards will be called upon to conduct or supervise a bomb search. The technique to be followed is as outlined:

1. Look around before entering a room. Take a few seconds to look for trip wires or other "booby-traps."
2. Listen for unusual audible sounds before doing anything. Listen for timing devices, etc.

3. Divide a room into sections by height. Assign areas: each guard or searcher is to search only the area assigned. For example, searcher number 1 will check everything from the floor to the selected search height. Searcher number 2 will check everything from the search height to the ceiling, etc. After the room has been searched, the room can be re-divided and re-searched as time and manpower permit. On a second search, the searchers should switch areas so that each area is searched by a different guard or searcher.

Lockers and public parcel check areas will be checked first. Special care will be taken to search galleries and storage areas with great speed and care. Nothing should be taken for granted. Waste receptacles, toilet stalls, and underneath sinks in restrooms are ideal places to hide bombs, as are stairwells. As soon as a guard discovers a suspicious parcel, he should consider all unattended parcels as suspicious; the guard should move away from the parcels and call for help.

Guidelines for Handling the Theft of Art Objects

Purpose.   The purpose of this procedure is to address the theft of art objects, whether definitely established or strongly suspected. The goal in such a situation is to move quickly and effectively against the thief while releasing innocent visitors without excessive delays.

General Information.   Specific duties and procedures are to be followed when there is a strong possibility that the theft of an art object has occurred during the hours that the museum is open to the public. An immediate alert shall be broadcast and each security guard, depending upon his assignment at that time, shall be responsible for performing specific duties. It is incumbent upon each security guard to be fully aware of the duties and responsibilities of his assigned post upon the broadcast of a theft alert.

Immediate notification of concerned personnel and deployment of all available security guards to meet the emergency situation are essential, in a manner that will not create panic among the museum visitors. An emergency situation does not justify a lower degree of courtesy toward any person.

Some indications that the theft of an art object may have occurred are as follows:

- Observation of the theft taking place.
- Smashed glass in a display case.
- Painting cut from its frame.

- Someone observed carrying or concealing a suspicious object, or possibly a large bulge showing under their coat.
- An art object missing from its normal location without a "temporary art removal" card by a duly authorized staff member put in its place.

Gallery Guard's Duties. If a gallery guard determines that the theft of an art object has possibly occurred, he shall immediately:

- Notify his supervisor and, if possible, identify the art object.
- Inform other security guards via telephone.
- Ensure that a security guard is posted at each exit on that floor even if it means pulling guards off other posts.
- Quickly begin to screen all persons in an attempt to locate the missing art object and the possible thief.
- Check persons leaving the building.

Security Control Guard's Duties. If a security guard is notified that the theft of an art object has probably occurred, the guard assigned to the specific area shall immediately:

- Communicate the following message: "Secure the Premises."
- Notify the director, associate director, and operations manager.
- Ensure that a security supervisor is dispatched to make an immediate preliminary investigation to determine what is missing and the circumstances of the theft.

Security Supervisor's Duties. Upon notification that the theft of an art object(s) has probably occurred, the most available security guard shall ensure that all exits from the museum are under observation. Visitors will be allowed to leave the museum only through the main entrance, after it has been determined that they are not carrying or concealing any object of the approximate size or shape of the missing art object.

After Museum Hours. When the theft or possible theft of art is discovered after hours, the director, associate director, or operations manager will be notified. There should be no delay in making this notification as the suspected loss of art is a matter of the highest priority.

While awaiting their arrival, guards should seal all entrances, check all doors and windows, prevent all outgoing shipments, and gather information regarding the situation.

Avoid touching the walls or floors or other objects near the crime scene and keep all persons, including guards, away to protect any evidence.

Closing or Locking of Doors — Searching Procedures. Guards at the main desk must be prepared to close and lock doors on the command of the director of security. If this course of action is taken, guards will permit visitors and employees to leave when it is apparent they are not carrying the missing object.

If such an action is taken, a guard will remain outside the doors to inform visitors who want to enter the museum that the museum is closed temporarily and will reopen soon.

When doors are secured or under observation a systematic search will be made of all areas of the museum. If any visitor objects to having his parcels searched, this person shall be held for the police.

Cancellation of Alert. The alert shall be cancelled only upon direction of the director of security. Upon notification of the cancellation of the alert, all security guards shall return to their assigned duties and the museum can resume normal operations.

Modified Alert. When it is discovered that an art object is missing from its normal location and it is likely that the object has been improperly removed by a staff member, a modified alert may be instituted by the director of security.

During a modified alert, each museum exit shall be manned by a security officer and the exit door shall be observed but not locked. Persons obviously not carrying anything capable of concealing the missing object will be allowed to leave the museum. Camera cases, large handbags, and other articles large enough to conceal the missing object shall be searched thoroughly.

Staff members normally authorized to remove art objects from display shall be questioned as to whether they know the location of the object. Staff offices, conservation rooms, storage areas, and the photo laboratory shall be immediately checked, in an attempt to locate the missing object.

After Museum Hours. There should be no delay in making the proper notification as the suspected loss of art is a matter of the highest priority.

Guards should seal all entrances, check all doors and windows, *prevent all outgoing shipments*, and gather information regarding the situation. AVOID TOUCHING THE WALLS OR FLOORS OR OTHER OBJECTS NEAR THE CRIME SCENE AND KEEP ALL PERSONS, INCLUDING GUARDS, AWAY TO PROTECT ANY EVIDENCE.

Handling of Art Objects by Guards

Policy. No guard shall handle or move art objects except when:

1.   The art object is in *immediate* danger.

2. Verbal instructions have been obtained from a curator, assistant curator, or associate curator in order to save the object.
3. Moving the art object has been authorized by the director of the museum.

In addition to the persons named, no one besides the director of security may authorize the handling of art.

Calling the Police or Fire Department

It may be necessary to call the police or fire department for assistance from time to time. The policy for calling the fire department should be: they are to be called for *every* fire regardless of the size. The police are to be called when necessary to protect lives and property, to arrest offenders, or to assist with investigations of crimes. A guard should always seek the advice of a supervisor when calling the police or fire authorities but may make the decision to call for such assistance if conditions warrant it.

If a guard calls the police or fire authorities, he should speak clearly and calmly in a normal tone of voice. He should give his name, title (security guard), and the name of the institution. He should tell the dispatcher who answers the call what the emergency is. "I need the police." "I need the fire department." The guard should explain the nature of the incident and give details as required by the situation. It if is a fire, he should explain the location of the fire, *which entrance the firemen should respond to,* the type of fire, whether any people are trapped or injured, etc. He should remain on the line as long as the dispatcher needs him.

Upon receiving a call for assistance, the dispatcher will record the basic information and then have the guard wait on the line while dispatching the emergency equipment or police personnel. The dispatcher will then return to the phone and take other necessary information that he will relay to the responding personnel.

A guard should remain cool and calm. After giving all the information needed, he should perform his other tasks. He should remember that the responding police or fire officials cannot give help if they do not have all the necessary and accurate information.

Responding to Alarms. The museum has a variety of alarm devices that detect intruders, fire, or smoke, and problems with certain equipment on mechanical systems. Some of these alarms are audible in the galleries, whereas others are silent in the galleries, sounding only on the monitoring devices located in security control or the panel room. Guards are responsible for responding to alarms, whether they actually hear the alarm or whether they are dispatched to investigate an alarm.

The guard nearest the alarm or the area where the alarm has been activated should make an immediate, initial investigation and report back to a supervisor. If assistance is needed the guard should immediately request help from a supervisor. If no problem is discovered (i.e., fire, smoke, or an intruder), a supervisor will reset the alarm or instruct the guard to do so.

An alarm has sounded for a particular reason, and it is the guard's responsibility to investigate to determine why it has sounded and report his findings as soon as possible.

Handling of Decorative Arts

Decorative arts are the furniture and other objects on display in the museum that are not generally referred to as paintings, drawings, etc. Chairs, desks, vases, snuff boxes, and statues can be classified as decorative arts.

Often, because the homes of guards are full of "decorative arts," guards tend to underestimate the importance of these objects. Furniture often is thought of as merely furniture.

It is important to remember that these pieces have been selected for display in the museum because of their importance and value. They deserve the same respect and careful handling as any other piece of art and they deserve protection and careful observation because of potential damage to them. Often the members of the public tend to forget the value and importance of these pieces.

Guards have to be especially alert to people handling objects in the gallery. Frequently, visitors tend to pull out drawers of desks and other pieces to see the furniture construction. This is not permitted. Another area of concern that requires a protective eye is the metal hardware on these rare pieces. Guards should be alert to the theft of the hardware. It is not unlikely for a thief to steal a piece of hardware literally a screw at a time! He removes the first screw, then returns for the second screw, etc., until all the hardware is removed.

Another concern regarding decorative arts not displayed in cases is the hazard involving contact with objects such as a fire hose, which can actually smash a valuable piece. In a museum fire, more damage can be done by a fire hose being dragged through the gallery than by the fire itself. Guards should be alert to this problem and assist when necessary.

Above all, the number-one rule for guards and visitors to remember is — NEVER touch an art object in any way.

Visitor Sign-in Procedures

Purpose. The purpose of this order is to establish a policy that will ensure that all visitors to the facility are properly signed in and accounted for.

Visitors.   A visitor is a nonemployee who enters a nonpublic area of the facility such as an office area. For the purpose of this order the term visitor does not refer to a patron who enters during regular museum hours to view the exhibits.

Policy.   All visitors must be signed in and announced by the on-duty guard. All visitors must be under the control of a responsible employee. Visitors may be admitted to the facility during the following hours:

> Monday-Friday, 9:00 A.M. to 5:00 P.M.
> Saturday during hours the museum is open.
> Sunday during hours the museum is open.
> Holidays during hours the museum is open.

Visitors may not be admitted to the facility at other times without authority of a department head or higher authority.

When a department head or higher authority authorizes entry to a visitor beyond the hours noted above, the director of security, associate director of security, or operations manager will be immediately notified. Such entry should be logged at the security desk.

Visitors must be escorted in the following circumstances:

1. When they carry a parcel that would not normally be permitted in a gallery.
2. When they enter a storage room, conservation work area, or other areas where they could damage art or objects lying about.
3. When they enter the museum beyond the normal hours noted above.

Sign-in Sheet.   The name of the person who authorizes entry when the guard announces the arrival of the visitor shall be entered under the column, "Person Authorizing Entry." The name of the person being visited shall also be entered in the appropriate space. The visitor is required to sign in when entry permission is granted.

Searches.   All visitors are subject to search of incoming and outgoing parcels. A visitor who refuses a search shall be detained and a supervisor immediately summoned.

Guard Responsibility.   It is the guard's responsibility to make sure that every visitor is announced, that only authorized visitors are permitted to enter, and that all spaces on the sign-in sheet are legibly and accurately entered.

Identification.   A visitor may be asked to show identification such as a company ID or driver's permit when the guard deems it appropriate.

Challenging Unescorted Visitors. Visitors should be challenged by guards when observed unescorted in sensitive areas such as the galleries before museum hours.

Packages and Parcels Leaving the Museum by any Exit

Purpose. The purpose of this policy is to establish that employees leaving the premises with a package or parcel must make the item available for inspection.

Policy. It is the policy of the museum that employees leaving the premises with parcels, briefcases, packages, and other hand-carried items larger than an average-sized woman's purse must make these items available for inspection by security personnel. This policy will be in effect *at all exits and at all times of day and night.*

In addition, any employee bringing a parcel, including lunches purchased outside the building, into the museum during hours that the museum is open to the public must use the main entrance. If there is a need to carry the parcel into a public area of the museum during open hours, a pass for this purpose must be obtained at the front desk and affixed to the package. Failure to comply with this policy will be recorded and could result in disciplinary action.

Handling of Juveniles

Children are a welcome part of the museum community. The museum staff should invite children to visit the galleries and become involved in the appreciation of fine art.

Children also pose a unique security and safety problem. Guards should protect the museum from the children and the children from hazards within the museum.

Visits to the museum are educational in nature, and every effort should be made to encourage museum visits by children.

When it becomes necessary to be firm with a child or to enforce a rule, the guard should be polite and friendly. A child should never be embarrassed in front of his peers. A guard should avoid interrupting tours and lectures to correct a child, except, of course, in the case of major infractions of the rules.

Guards are an important part of the child management process. They should be firm but polite and considerate at the same time.

Handling of Mentally Disturbed Persons

From time to time, mentally disturbed persons may appear at an entrance to the museum and attempt to gain entry. A security guard may be called upon to handle this situation or a situation involving a mentally disturbed person already in the building.

A mentally disturbed person is considered a sick person and cannot be arrested for simply being mentally disturbed; however, this person can be apprehended for an act he commits that violates the law. For purposes of this guide, a mentally disturbed person is defined as: "One who, by his irregular actions, is a danger to himself or to others." Certain guidelines are given to distinguish this type of person from a normal offender. A mentally disturbed person may be depressed, angry, or have a persecution complex. He may have grandiose ideas about himself or believe he is someone else. He may feel that others are watching him or talking about him or he may imagine impossible kinds of body ailments, for example, that his stomach has disappeared or that his heart has stopped. He may talk of suicide or make requests that are impossible to meet. It is not difficult, after talking with a mentally disturbed person for any length of time, to suspect that a mental condition exists.

If a guard suspects that a person in the museum facilities is mentally disturbed, even if the person has not shown evidence of violence, *a supervisor must be called.*

The three primary objectives of a guard in dealing with a mentally disturbed person are: to protect the public, to protect himself, and to treat the person as if he were handling a sick person. The general principles a guard should follow in handling a mentally ill person are as listed below:

1. The guard should look over the situation carefully but remain constantly alert. He should not drop his guard.
2. The guard should remain calm, patient, and gentle. A conversational tone of voice is usually best.
3. The contact should be kept as dignified as the situation will allow. First names should be avoided unless the person is well known to the guard.
4. The guard should not talk about the person in the person's presence, or act as if the ill person were not present.
5. The guard should try to be as sincere as possible. Deceit will only magnify the situation or make it worse.
6. The security officer should not abuse or threaten the person. The subject is usually frightened and may turn on the guard if he feels that the guard is against him.
7. The guard should avoid exciting the subject. A crowd, if it has gathered, should be dispersed quietly. Spectators should be avoided.
8. If restraint is needed, assistance should be sought. A mentally ill person often has superhuman strength.
9. When restraining a mentally ill person, it is best to remember that the person is not to blame for his resistance. He must often be protected from himself as his struggling may cause him to be injured.

The guard should call for assistance as soon as he suspects that the person he is dealing with is mentally ill or unbalanced.

Since a number of major acts of vandalism to art have involved mentally disturbed people, every effort should be made to separate the suspect from the works of art.

Handling of Intoxicated Persons

Intoxicated employees on the museum's property should be handled differently from intoxicated persons on the property who are not employees. Employees, as long as they pose no threat to anyone, should be allowed to go on their way without obstruction. However, guards should attempt to quiet disorderly employees, and assistance from security supervisors should be sought as soon as possible.

Visitors who are intoxicated and disorderly should be asked to leave the museum and a supervisor should be notified. If they are incapable of leaving the museum on their own and there is no responsible person available to take custody of them, the decision whether to seek police assistance or not should be made by the supervisor. An arrest will not be made, but arrangements should be made with the police to remove the person to a location where he can receive treatment.

A guard who finds a derelict intoxicated on the grounds should not hesitate to ask this person to leave the museum property. If he refuses, the guard should notify a supervisor that there is an intoxicated person on the grounds who should be removed.

Guards should use extreme caution in dealing with intoxicated persons who are not conscious. Every effort should be made to ascertain if the person is actually intoxicated or ill. Even obviously drunk persons like derelicts can be injured in addition to being intoxicated, and for this reason care should be taken to avoid aggravating these injuries while moving the subject.

A report should be filed whenever action is taken regarding an intoxicated person.

Handling of Disorderly Persons

One of the most difficult tasks of a security guard is the handling of disorderly persons. The unarmed guard must use extreme caution in confronting any potentially dangerous person. Assistance should be summoned at the earliest sign of disruption and guards should not hesitate to request assistance from supervisors.

In confronting a disorderly person, the guard would be wise to remain at a cautious distance just out of sudden reach from the person. The guard should retain a solid stance at a 45-degree angle to the disorderly person with his balance firmly established.

The guard should avoid an attitude of belligerance, which might further provoke the person, but be firm and calm. It is often possible to reduce the tenseness of the situation by inspiring a relaxed attitude and retaining a low-key profile. Sometimes it is helpful for the guard to address the offender as "sir," "friend," "pal," or by some other greeting that conveys to the offender that the guard's attitude is casual and friendly rather than angry or excited. "Relax, my friend; what seems to be the problem?" is the kind of greeting that promotes an atmosphere of cooperation to an obviously disorderly person. The guard should offer to assist the person with his problem — at least until backup help arrives.

The guard should try to determine the cause of the problem and find out what is upsetting the person. He should ascertain if this person's anger is directed toward an employee of the institution itself or whether the person is upset by other matters or individuals.

When assistance arrives, guards should position themselves in the best location for self-defense against the possibility that the person may become violent. The guards should still attempt to resolve the problem peacefully, but if this is impossible, more firmness and control by the guards may be required. The disorderly person should be asked to leave the museum if he has no business at the museum. He should be told that he will be arrested if he refuses to leave, and a supervisor should decide whether or not the police should be called.

Handling of Demonstrators

The purpose of this policy is to discuss the problem of dealing with peaceful and militant demonstrators at the museum.

One of the duties and responsibilities of the security guard is the protection of individual rights. Freedom of speech and assembly are two fundamental rights granted to all Americans by the Constitution. Peaceful picketing and demonstrating are included in the rights of all citizens. Thus the security guard has the right and duty to regulate the actions of people for the protection of everyone. But these responsibilities are not always well defined and therefore the guard must use his discretion in dealing with such situations. He must act to protect individual rights and often these rights come into conflict. A person's right to demonstrate or picket may interfere with other's rights to move freely into or out of the museum. It is in these situations that the security guard faces the difficult decision as to what course of action he should follow.

The actions of security guards are critically watched during demonstrations. Therefore guards must act with restraint and maintain discipline when dealing with situations where the actions of others are regulated.

There are two types of demonstrations; one is peaceful and the other is militant. Peaceful demonstrations are often protected by the U.S. Constitution. Guards must act prudently in dealing with these situations and follow the instructions of their supervisors in handling them fairly. Guards should remember that the demonstrator is generally only someone who is exercising his rights to correct what he feels to be an unjust situation. The fact that the museum has been chosen as the target of a demonstration should not be taken personally by the guards. Action — i.e., peaceful action — against the museum or another target is not action directed against the security guard.

If guards are called upon to break up a demonstration on museum property such as a sit-in, they should, after proper warning, firmly but nonviolently use the *minimum amount of force necessary* to carry out these orders. Guards should maintain a quiet and unaggressive profile in dealing with demonstrators. The attitude of the demonstrators is that they have a job to do, which is to carry out a peaceful demonstration against the museum. The guards' attitude should be that they have a job to do which is *to protect the rights of everyone involved in a peaceful manner.*

The second type of demonstration is militant or violent. Often individuals in a larger peaceful group will attempt to use a peaceful demonstration to elicit violent reactions from guards, hoping to make them become frustrated or violent.

Violent situations will result in a request for help from the police department. Guards will never handle a violent situation entirely by themselves as they are not equipped to do so.

One tactic of militant demonstrators in trying to force the guard's hand and create violence is "baiting." Some individuals will try to reduce a guard to their level by name-calling, racial slurs, or attacks upon standards. Guards should maintain their cool and self-control so as not to be reduced to the level of such demonstrators.

Another tactic of demonstrators is to attempt to force a guard's hand by making a guard break from his disciplined ranks and attack the demonstrating group. Rocks may be thrown and other acts of minor violence may be directed against the guards. Guards should remember that these tactics are designed to make them disobey their supervisors and lose their control. Guards shouldn't fall for them.

Guards should remember that in demonstrations maintaining their discipline is essential. The orders of the supervisors should be followed while they keep a calm and cool profile. Guards should never resort to unnecessary force and they shouldn't take verbal attacks upon them or the museum personally.

Enforcement of Rules

The museum, through the director's office, has established rules and regulations designed to protect the collections, the visitors, and the financial interests of the museum. For the most part, guards are the ones who must enforce these rules.

Rules are not laws. Laws are regulations that have been passed by governmental bodies. Museum rules do not have the force of law.

Examples of the rules are "No Smoking in the Galleries," "No Disorderly Conduct in the Galleries," "You must pay something to get in except on Thursdays," and "All parcels must be checked in the coatroom or a locker if the guard says so."

Can a visitor be arrested and punished for failing to abide by a rule? The answer is "No." If a rule also is a law, then of course an arrest, trial, and punishment may follow, but generally the only penalty that can be imposed for failure to abide by a rule is ejection from the museum.

It is an important concept for a guard to understand that a rule-breaker cannot be arrested. Nor can he be manhandled, physically abused, handcuffed, punched, or even unnecessarily detained. A guard who "arrests" a rule-breaker can himself be arrested for assault or false imprisonment and false arrest.

When a guard enforces a rule he must take great care to do so in a fair and impartial manner. When a guard tells a violator to stop breaking the rules and the rule-breaker refuses to listen to him, what can be done? To protect the guard, a supervisor should be called. If the violator attempts to leave, the guard need only step in his way. The guard should take a defensive posture and not be the aggressor. He should simply stand in the violator's way. The instant the violator lays hands on the guard he has committed an assault and the guard may then detain the violator, using the minimum amount of force necessary. *Of course, if a rule violator wants to leave, the best thing to do is let him go!*

A guard on a night patrol who encounters a burglar or a guard in a gallery who encounters a vandal or thief need not take such a defensive profile. A law has been broken and, unlike a rule infraction, the guard may immediately take action to stop the violation, *using the minimum amount of force necessary* to detain the violator for the police.

Enforcement of both rules and laws requires fair and impartial action. A rule, to be legal, must be equally applied to everyone. A man carrying a purse or bag is subject to the same rules as a woman carrying a purse or bag. If the woman does not have to check her purse, neither does the man. The fact that the man has pockets in which to carry his wallet and keys is irrelevant in the eyes of the law.

Guards must be aware of the above information. Civil penalties can be imposed on them for failure to enforce rules and laws in a fair and equitable manner.

Use of Handcuffs and Restraining Devices

Security has issued handcuffs for use by guards and supervisors. It is essential that personnel who have been issued handcuffs fully understand their function and use as well as the legal ramifications of their use.

Handcuffs are a temporary restraining device for controlling a person arrested by a law enforcement officer or security guard. Handcuffs may never be used on a person who is not under arrest. To restrain a person with handcuffs or in any other way constitutes an arrest, and *if an arrest is not justified, the person causing the arrest is subject to prosecution under the law.*

Security guards must also recognize that handcuffs are not toys and are considered offensive by many persons. All personnel are to wear their handcuffs on the belt strap provided. The handcuffs are to be concealed by a suitcoat or uniform coat at all times when out of the area of security control.

If an arrest is made, however, the use of handcuffs is always legally justified. The decision to use handcuffs is left up to the arresting guard or his supervisor. But if handcuffs are used, they must be used properly. They must never be tightened to the point of causing excessive pain to the arrested person and they should be double locked to make sure that the arrested person does not himself tighten the devices and harm himself.

Each member of the security force who is issued handcuffs should also be issued the FBI Bulletin entitled: "Temporary Restraining Devices," which is prepared by the FBI Academy, Quantico, Virginia. This bulletin outlines the proper use of handcuffs. In addition, personnel should be issued the FBI Manual entitled: "Defensive Tactics," which carefully explains handcuffing procedures and methods. All personnel should familiarize themselves with this material.

NOTE

1. O. W. Wilson, *Police Administration,* 2nd Ed. New York: McGraw-Hill, 1963.

Appendix 23.1

Post Orders
C. G. "Chuck" Coates

The most important document for a company or organization with an in-house or contract guard force is a clear, concise, up-to-date, and complete set of post orders for the following reasons:

1. These orders are expressing the policy of the particular company or organization with respect to the duties or functions that management expect of the guards.
2. The orders are a summary of the duties required of the guard at a particular post.
3. The orders should avoid a great deal of word-of-mouth and on-the-job training and instructions. There should be some oral instructions and on-the-job training. This means a new guard should be able in an emergency to handle most situations that might arise with only limited instructions.

The post orders should be written with the following in mind.

1. Each order should deal with only one subject. This will allow for easy revision or cancellation when required and easily located through a complete index.
2. The order should be as brief and clear as possible.
3. The order should be written in the simplest language possible. This is to say that it should be written in basic English/French that can be understood by a person with only secondary education. If three readers cannot agree on the clear meaning of a passage, sentence, or instruction, then it is badly written for order purposes.
4. Orders should be indexed in detail and cross-referenced where possible.
5. A copy of all pertinent orders should be available at each guard post and be kept up to date and in good order. If there are more than one post in a building or agency, then there should be a complete set of post orders for all posts and should be available for the supervisor of the guard staff.
6. The drafter or originator of orders should keep a master copy from which additions, deletions, and amendments are made.
7. Loose-leaf folders or books where pages can be removed and replaced with amended pages.

Orders for guards are normally divided into three categories as follows:

1. *Permanent Orders.* These orders are set out in a manual that sets the standard procedures and instructions for all guards irrespective of building or location for the company or agency. They also set out the deportment, dress, and conduct required of all the guards employed.

2. *Post orders.* These are specific orders that pertain to one post, and deal with routine duties and prescribed courses of action for the guard at that post.

3. *Special instructions.* These are special instructions for a specific event or orders of a temporary nature. They should be issued in memorandum form and have a cancellation date if at all possible. These instructions should be kept up to date and cancelled orders should either be destroyed or returned to the originator on cancellation date or when special event is completed. These special instructions should be kept to a minimum.

POST ORDER FORMAT

The layout for the orders should be simple and be standardized for all Posts. The following are some of the standards that should be utilized:

1. Capitalize all headings in bold print and underline.
2. Use short, concise sentences.
3. Amend pages when required.
4. Change any phone numbers and reporting personnel immediately.
5. Have complete index preferably at front of orders.

The following is a sample layout for guidance only and headings can be added, deleted, or changed depending on circumstances and requirements:

The first page should contain the following information:

POST ORDERS
FOR
(NAME OF BUILDING)
(ADDRESS OF BUILDING)
COMPANY OR AGENCY
POST
(This should indicate location)

Signing Authorities
Position

Place & Date

Index

A complete and concise index, together with cross-references where required.

Emergency Phone Numbers

These should include the following:

- POLICE: having local authority
- FIRE:
- AMBULANCE:
- HOSPITAL:
- MAINTENANCE:
- HEATING:
- ELECTRICAL:
- ALARM COMPANY:
- ELEVATOR: trouble
- DEPARTMENTAL or COMPANY REPRESENTATIVES: to be contacted in event of emergency

These numbers should be both office and home phone numbers.

1. Introduction

These orders should be read in conjunction with permanent orders, and where there is a conflict, "permanent orders" will take precedence. The guard should familiarize himself with all orders and instructions.

2. Hours of Duty

This should give hours of duty for each guard at this post. Example:

```
2400-0800   1 guard
0800-1600   1 guard
1600-2400   2 guards (guard number 2 to patrol and
            supervise cleaning staff)
```

Guard should report at least 10 minutes prior to commencement of shift for any instructions or information from outgoing guard.

3. Location of Post

This should give an exact location of the post if it is static or indicate, if roving, what the tour is to entail.

4. Duties of Guard

This should give the guard a brief description of the duties that are expected of him at this post, making only brief reference to patrols, etc., which are to be covered under separate heading.

5. Reporting

If the guard has to report by phone at intervals, these should be laid out and he should have the telephone number to report to.

6. Patrols

This should give the times patrols are to be made, or, if staggered, how may per shift, the route, and the location of punch stations if applicable. There should also be a paragraph listing what the guard should look for while on patrol, and reporting procedures. See Appendix A for a plan of the building with location of key punches clearly marked by number if possible.

7. Locking and Unlocking Doors

This should include a complete list of doors and when they should be locked and when unlocked.

8. Keys

This should list the general instructions for the guard regarding keys at the post. See Appendix C concerning keys and instructions for each key.

9. Cleaning Staff

This should give the hours the cleaning is done, the name of the company and contact at the company should there be a problem, including office and home telephone number. Also included here should be any area where the cleaning staff are restricted and if they have to be under escort.

10. Building Passes

Permanent Pass. Should give a short description and, if more than one, list the restrictions for each.

Temporary pass. Give description and when applicable.

See Appendix D for photostatic copy, together with list and sample of authorized signatures for signing authorities.

11. Access Control

This will give instructions to guard on who is to be allowed into building and when. It should also include

1. whether or not employees have to show passes;
2. when employees are required to sign in and out if this is applicable;
3. description of form to use for signing in both visitors and employees working after hours.

12. Visitors

This should be a specific instruction of what procedure to follow regarding visitors, e.g., free entry, signing in, escorts.

13. Fire

List specific instructions of what the guard's duties are and who to be contacted. This may include designated employees as well as fire and police department.

14. Bomb Threat or Threatening Phone Calls

List instructions for guard as well as any pertinent material which can be included under Appendix E, e.g., reporting forms, phone instructions.

15. Injury to Personnel

List instructions for guard in event of injury to employees.

16. Electrical Power Failure

Instructions on what to do in event of failure including contacts and whether there is auxiliary power, plus any instructions.

17. Heat Loss or Other Emergencies

Instructions for guard and contacts.

18. Lost and Found

Instructions to the guard for the disposition of lost and found articles.

19. Removal of Material, Equipment by Employees

This should give instructions to guard who notices employees or other persons removing equipment or material from building and whether they require written authority.

20. Reports and Reporting Procedures

This instruction should advise guard when reports are to be submitted and a short description of form. Copy of report form should be included under Appendix F.

21. Telephones

This instruction should indicate to guard how the phone should be answered, e.g., "Good morning.   Department Security Desk."

22. Parking

If there is parking on the premises, instructions concerning illegal parking, etc.

23. Accidents

Instructions should be given in the event of an accident, e.g., whom to notify, phone numbers.

24. Press, Radio, Photographers

In the event of the above having access to the premises, instructions should be given as to whom to contact, etc.

25. Notebooks

Instructions for filling out of notebooks and disposition of same.

26. Peddlers and Canvassers

Instruction re: above.

27. Telegrams, Newspapers and Messengers

Instructions should be given for both working hours and after hours on the above.

28. Designated Authorities

In cases not covered in these orders, the guard should be instructed to obtain authorization from a designated authority.

Appendices

A. Plans of building with patrols and clock punch station locations.
B. Plans of building with door locations marked.
C. List of keys and specific instructions.
D. Permanent and temporary passes and signing authorities.
E. Bomb threats.
F. Reporting form.

SAMPLE OF POST ORDERS

1. Introduction

These orders are to be read in conjunction with permanent orders and "Guidelines for Security Guards." The Security Guard is to familiarize him/herself with all orders and instructions.

2. Hours of Duty

The following are the hours of duty for the main door post:

2400-0800   1 Guard
0800-1600   1 Guard
1600-2400   2 Guards
#1 Guard — Main Door Post
#2 Guard — Patrol and Supervisor

The guards should report ten minutes prior to shift so that they can be briefed.

3. Location of Post

The guard designated for the main door post is to be situated at the desk located at the main entrance of the museum located at the Regina Street entrance. The guard will remain at this post unless otherwise relieved.

Guard #2 in the 1600-2400 hour shift will assist the guard on the main door post until 1730 hours, at which time he will do a patrol of the building, checking for staff and unlocking doors listed in Appendix B for the cleaning staff. He will then patrol the building on a continuous basis until the cleaning is completed, checking the rooms and locking same when cleaning is completed.

Patrols will be conducted as per paragraph 6.

When not on patrol, this guard will relieve and assist the main door post guard.

4. Duties of Guard

The duties of the guard at the main door post are as follows:

2400-0800 hours:
    a. Control access to building and insure that only authorized persons enter the building;
    b. Insure that persons authorized to enter building sign in and out on appropriate forms;
    c. Insure that no articles or artifacts leave the building without pass signed by authorized person;
    d. Insure that front door is locked at all times;
    e. Complete patrols as indicated in paragraph 6;
    f. Will unlock front door at 0700 and control entry of staff ensuring that they are properly identified; and
    g. All staff entering or leaving prior to 0700 hours will sign in on appropriate forms.

0800-1600 hours:
    a. Will control entry of staff, ensuring that they are properly identified;
    b. Sign in visitors and ensure that they are escorted if going into restricted areas;
    c. Ensure that any contractors, term employees, etc., are properly identified, signed in, and escorted where required;
    d. Ensure that alarms are in proper mode as per direction;
    e. When museum is open to the general public, ensure doors are unlocked at the required time (see schedule) and there is no obstruction to the normal flow of traffic;
    f. Take an accurate count of all visitors, noting same on sheets supplied on the hour;
    g. Ensuring that no visitors take parcels, umbrellas, etc., into the galleries;
    h. Ensure that persons are wearing footwear while in museum.
    i. In the case of baby carriages or strollers, the persons are to be instructed

on the care to be taken while in the museum and supply a pass indicating they have been given these instructions;

j. Answer any inquiries regarding museum and direct persons to areas of galleries;

k. Ensure that all articles going out of museum are properly identified and have a property pass if museum property;

l. Familiarize him/herself with the museum and be able to answer questions or direct persons to the proper person; and

m. Familiarize him/herself with all memos and instructions and ensure they are followed.

1600–2400 hours: Guard #1

a. This guard is to be familiar with all duties pertaining to the other shifts both for public hours and closed hours of museum;

b. At closing time is to control entry to museum and both the main doors when the museum has been cleared;

c. After closing time is to ensure that only authorized persons enter building after being properly identified;

d. Ensure that all persons entering or leaving building after 1800 hours sign in or out;

e. Ensure that all cleaning staff sign in when reporting;

f. Ensure that all patrols are made by Guard #2;

g. Familiarize him/herself with all other orders and instructions;

1600–2400 hours: Guard #2

a. Will familiarize him/herself with all orders and instructions dealing with Guard #1 and relieve him/her for lunch breaks;

b. Assist Guard #1 until closing time;

c. At closing time of the museum will do a complete patrol of the museum building ensuring that all visitors to galleries have left and noting staff members still in building. During this patrol he will check for any fire hazards, machines running, kettles plugged in, etc., and report same on form provided;

d. At 1800 hours when the cleaning staff commence cleaning this guard will open the doors required and check offices and labs for any irregularities or articles left out that should be under lock and key. He/she will report same on form provided. This guard will do a continuous patrol during the time the cleaning staff are in the building and check on the following:

i. Ensure that cleaning staff do not handle articles they shouldn't;

ii. Ensure they only have access to the areas required;

iii. Check to see that nothing goes out with the garbage;

iv. Ensure that cleaning staff do not smoke in restricted areas; and

v. When rooms are cleaned, lights are to be turned off and doors locked.

e. At 2100 hours a complete patrol is to be made of building, ensuring all cleaning staff have finished; lock doors, turn off lights, and check for any fire or safety hazards; and

    f. Conducts other patrols.

In addition to the preceding duties all guards are to familiarize themselves completely with all other orders and instructions, in particular:

    i.   Fire orders;
    ii.   Contingency plans;
    iii. Guard deportment and dress;
    iv. Bomb threats.

While patrolling the building guards are to familiarize themselves with the location of the following:

    i.   Emergency exits;
    ii.   Fire extinguishers and hoses;
    iii.   All offices;
    iv.   Laboratories;
    v.   Heating plant;
    vi.   Water shut-offs;
    vii. Electrical panels.

5. Reporting

All guards will report to the control center at least fifteen minutes before their shift starts so that they can be briefed. Should a guard not be able to report for duty because of sickness, etc., he is to contact the control center at least three hours prior to shift schedule.

6. Patrols

Patrols of the building will be made at the following times:

- 0100
- 0300
- 0500
- 0630
- 1700 — Closing time
- 1800 — Unlocking doors
- 2100 — Locking doors
- 2300

During days when the museum is closed, additional patrols will be made at the following times:

- 0900
- 1100
- 1300
- 1500

While on patrol the guard is to look for the following and report defects on form provided:

a. Any burnt-out lights;
b. Machines left running;
c. Hotplates or kettles plugged in;
d. Any fire hazards;
e. Garbage boxes or other obstructions left in hallways, offices, etc.;
f. Ensure all emergency routes are clear;
g. Any safety hazards such as torn rugs, staircase trim loose or broken, etc.;
h. Water leaks;
i. Broken pipes, and
j. Any other deficiency that could be a hazard for fire or safety or could if left cause more damage.

7. Locking and Unlocking Doors

This should list all the doors that are to be locked or unlocked and time. The remainder of the post order can follow the post order format, which is self-explanatory for these paragraphs. There may be the necessity to add or delete paragraphs depending on the nature or particular requirement of the museum. The main thing is that the guard be given as much information as possible in order to carry out the job.

The problem now is ensuring that all guards read and understand these orders.

24. The Museum Guard Pocket Manual:*

Steven R. Keller

One of the most basic problems in any security operation is that of training all of the security personnel in their duties. Too often, training is the forgotten element in the development of a strong and effective force. When training is provided it rarely can provide the security guard with all of the information he will need to do his job. Usually, the more important policies and procedures are covered and the less critical duties are left for the guard to learn in "On-Job Training."

My experience has been that even with a strong training program, a large number of relatively important duties which should be performed by a guard "fall through the cracks." There is just too much for a guard to learn in a one-week training program. New guards are especially vulnerable to the problem of not knowing all of the facets of their job.

In a museum environment, guards often perform duties which might otherwise be performed by nonsecurity personnel. The rigid temperature and humidity demands require that alert guards constantly report conditions adverse to the safety of the art. The large number of square feet devoted to a relatively low volume of art in storage or on display means that guards have more space to patrol, more doors to check, and more things to find that "went wrong" than they would in other environments.

---

*THE WAY TO KEEP THOSE SMALL BUT IMPORTANT DETAILS FROM "FALLING THROUGH THE CRACKS"

After years of frustration at finding tasks undone, doors unchecked, lights left burning, and hazards undetected, it became apparent to me that the only solution to resolving the problem was to prepare a policy and procedure manual. The high turnover in our operation necessitated something which detailed for the guard exactly what he is supposed to do in each of several posts to which he could be assigned.

First, I prepared a large-format (8½-by-11-inch) manual on policies and procedures. This "Operations and Training Manual" was issued to all guards and contained a series of about fifty "General Orders." Each general order outlined a policy so that, in theory, the force could function in my absence and be guided by my written desires on any of a number of probable situations which could occur. Part two of that manual contained all of the training materials and bulletins that each guard receives in his "Basic" and "Roll Call" training sessions.

It soon became apparent that this format was not the cure-all I thought it would be. It was usually in a locker when it was needed most. I decided that a small format pocket manual containing specific instructions for manning each of our specific posts would be the answer to our needs. In addition, the pocket manual would contain other information that the guard needs at his fingertips while on post. And finally, some of the more important "General Orders" outlining policies of a broad nature could be added to the end of the manual. As it turns out, this pocket manual has indeed been the answer to our problem of providing all guards with the information they need to keep those details which prove to be so important and troublesome from "falling through the cracks."

FORMAT

First, it was necessary to establish a format for the manual. A "Pocket Manual" should, obviously, fit in the pocket. So we examined both the men's and women's guard uniforms to determine the size limitations. Samples were obtained and "comfort surveys" were conducted to determine whether the particular binders being tested would be functional. There is no sense in buying a pocket manual binder that is so uncomfortable that guards will "forget" to carry it each day.

Ultimately, we selected a loose-leaf-style vinyl plastic binder with six rings. The binder spine is relatively flexible providing comfort when carried in the breast pocket. (Incidentally, our women's guard uniform did not have an inside breast pocket and these had to be added by our tailor.)

The color of the binder, blue, was selected for its attractiveness and compatability with our uniform color and gold foil embossing was used to provide an attractive cover title and our department's logotype. The size selected was the 5-inch-by-7¼-inch-by-¾-inch-thick binder to accommodate a page size of 3¾ by 6¾ inches. We can accommodate approximately 90 sheets of paper or 180 pages of print since most pages have information printed on both sides. In addition, we accommodate several index stock section dividers and five blank sheets at the end for use by the guard as notebook paper is needed. The capacity is sufficient.

STYLE

Prior to beginning our project, we selected, with the assistance of our publications department, a logotype which would be used exclusively by the security department on all of its printed materials. The logotype provides a professional appearance and serves visually to identify specific sections and documents within the manual.

The manual is printed on white paper for all sections dealing with normal day-to-day operation and supplements listing post duties for special exhibitions are printed on colored paper to provide quick visual reference, especially for new guards, who are interested only in their own special section and not in the sections directed to guards in general.

With the help of the publications department, we established a reduction ratio so that our departmental secretary could type the material on a standard typewriter and the printer could reduce it slightly to fit the reduced page size. Care should be taken to develop a reduction ratio which does not reduce the size of the print so much that the manual is difficult to read. Museums often have a number of older individuals on their guard staffs and readability is important. It is also a principle of adult education that when directing a written document to the typical audience found on the museum security force, small print is less likely to be read than larger print. My point is to take care in selecting a reduction ratio which suits your needs but is not too small to be practical.

CONTENT

Establishing what you want to print in your pocket manual is the most difficult task of all. With the loose-leaf format, changes can be made easily, but from a cost standpoint, you will want to limit your changes as much as possible. In order to make sure that I included all important elements in my first printing, I worked on each post for a day as if I were a new guard assigned without orientation. I knew that it was my job to turn on the lights at opening of the museum — but I didn't know where to find the panel box or light switches. I knew that I needed a key ring but I didn't know which one con-

---

TO: All Security Personnel

FROM: Steve Keller
           Director of Security

This manual is the result of many weeks of hard work by the members of the Training Office. For years, members of the force have been placed on post without the benefit of detailed instructions regarding light operations, key and equipment requirements, etc. Today, we are pleased to present this pocket manual.

This manual will be expanded over the next several months. You will be given updates and revisions as they are issued and you will be expected to make changes in your manual immediately.

You will note that post number designations have changed in some areas to streamline the production of maps and floor plans and to enable new guards to learn the post numbers more quickly.

We have added other information which should assist you in aiding the public. Please carry this manual with you at all times when on duty. It is no longer necessary to carry a notebook unless you want to because we have added pages in this manual for the taking of notes.

There will without doubt be several changes which will have to be made since we cannot be sure that such a massive job as this can be accomplished without some error. Therefore, we will be making revisions soon based upon your input. Pass any changes you deem appropriate on to me or to the Training Coordinator.

Because this manual contains information regarding some of our posts and patrols and other specialized information for night personnel and panel operators, please protect your copy.

Figure 24.1. Letter of introduction

---

tained the keys I would need. After taking careful notes on "everything I always wanted to know about being a guard on post" I prepared a list of elements each post instruction sheet should contain. I knew that directional material, administrative information, phone numbers, etc., were all essential so I decided to prepare a draft keeping this in mind.

First, I prepared a letter introducing the new manual to members of the force (Figure 24.1). I reminded them that although they, as experienced guards, did not need the information contained in the manual as much as the newly hired guards would need it, a number of new duties and assignments were placed in the manual after my observation and after consulting with them during my "stint" as a guard. I asked them to review carefully the accuracy of items in the manual and make notes with pencil where they noted inaccuracies. I explained that after about six months of use, we might reprint the manual with their corrections and additions.

TABLE OF CONTENTS

I. GENERAL INFORMATION
   A. Sick and Vacation Policies
   B. Personnel Policies
   C. Museum Hours
   D. Security Force Hours

II. LOCATIONS AND POINTS OF INTEREST

III. POST PROCEDURES

IV. MAPS OF THE GALLERIES SHOWING
   A. Points of Interest
   B. Public Facilities

V. MAPS OF THE FACILITY SHOWING
   A. Security Posts

VI. POLICIES
   A. Parcel Policy
   B. School of Art Faculty Parcel Policy
   C. Clearing Procedures at Closing
   D. Fire and Evacuation Policy
   E. Personal Appearance Policy
   F. Procedure for Handling Art Theft
   G. ID Cards—Access Hours

VII. PHONE NUMBERS

VIII. NOTES AND PERSONAL CALENDAR

Figure 24.2. Table of contents. Note that not all policy orders are placed in a "pocket manual." Only the most important or most "troublesome" were included.

Next, I added a Table of Contents (Figure 24.2). It should be noted that although there are "sections," there are no page numbers. This permits the addition or deletion of pages without the need for reprinting the entire manual.

The first major section is "General Information" (Figure 24.3). A summary is presented in an easy-to-read format telling guards what they are to do if they want to call in sick, who they are to call if they expect to be late for work, how they are to go about requesting vacation time, etc. Information regarding holidays and a reference to our more detailed general order on personnel policies is also included.

The next major section of the "Pocket Manual" is a section dealing with the hours each part of our museum is open to the public (Figure 24.4). First, the general museum hours for each day of the week are included. Then we note the exact opening and closing time for the museum store, the libraries,

---

GENERAL POLICIES

Requesting Sick Leave

Call Security Control 555-1234 *at least* two (2) hours before starting
time.

Requesting Vacation or Bonus Holidays

Make request *in person* to Operations Manager or your supervisor.

Place your name in vacation book. Have your leave entry signed
by your supervisor or Operations Manager.

Vacation is not considered to be approved unless entered in leave
book and approved by supervisor or Operations Manager.

Holidays

Time off for holidays is not automatic for guards. Guards are paid
holiday pay when they work. Be sure you are off before you take off.

Personnel Policies

Each full time employee is issued a personnel manual and Security
Operations and Training Manual. Part time employees may consult the
office copy in the Security Office.

Figure 24.3. General information

---

study rooms, and public accommodations such as dining facilities and the facilities dedicated to the needs of our museum members.

A section is included which deals with the hours of the security force
(Figure 24.5). Exact roll-call reporting times are noted for each day of the
week, for holidays, and for special events. Also included are the exact gallery
opening times and closing times and a summary of guard lunch and coffee-
break times for each shift.

Another problem was solved by adding a section dealing with major
points of interest in the museum (Figure 24.6). Some facilities such as the
women's board room might not be too familiar to the new guard, so each
major facility is listed and brief location information is provided which allows
guards to locate the facility, auditorium, etc., on the map of the galleries.
Since smoking is limited to only two public areas of the facility, it is a good
idea to list smoking areas as well as specific facilities. Public telephones and
restrooms (including those restrooms with handicapped facilities) should be
included.

The meat and potatoes of the manual is the section dealing with post procedures (Figures 24.7 and 24.8). In order to illustrate the format established

HOURS

1. MUSEUM
    Monday, Tuesday, Wednesday, Friday—
    10:30 a.m. to 4:30 p.m.
    Thursday—10:30 a.m. to 8:00 p.m.
    Saturday—10:00 a.m. to 5:00 p.m.
    Sunday & Holidays—12:00 p.m. to 5:00 p.m.

2. MUSEUM STORE
    Monday, Tuesday, Wednesday, Friday—
    10:30 a.m. to 4:45 p.m.
    Thursday—10:30 a.m. to 8:00 p.m.
    Saturday—10:00 a.m. to 5:15 p.m.
    Sunday & Holidays—12:00 p.m. to 5:15 p.m.

3. RYERSON LIBRARY & BURNHAM LIBRARY OF ARCHITECTURE
    South side of Grand Staircase
    Monday thru Saturday—10:30 a.m. to 4:30 p.m.
    Open to members, faculty, employees, others by appointment.

4. GLORE PRINT ROOM
    Gallery 107—Michigan Avenue
    Monday thru Friday—1:00 p.m. to 4:30 p.m.
    Open to members, employees, students and faculty of col-
    leges, universities, others by appointment.

5. DINING ROOM
    2nd Floor East Entry
    11:00 a.m. to 2:30 p.m.

6. OUTDOOR RESTAURANT
    Ground Floor East Entry, McKinlock Court
    11:00 a.m. to 3:00 p.m.—Summer season, weather permitting.

7. CAFETERIA
    Ground floor East Entry
    Monday, Tuesday, Wednesday, Friday—
    11:00 a.m. to 4:00 p.m.
    Thursday—11:00 a.m. to 7:00 p.m.
    Saturday—11:00 a.m. to 4:00 p.m.
    Sunday & Holidays—12:00 p.m. to 4:00 p.m.

8. MEMBER'S LOUNGE
    2nd Floor East Entry at entrance to Dining Room
    Monday, Tuesday, Wednesday, Friday—
    10:30 a.m. to 4:00 p.m.
    Thursday—10:30 a.m. to 7:00 p.m.
    Saturday—10:00 a.m. to 4:00 p.m.
    Sunday & Holidays—12:00 p.m. to 4:00 p.m.

Figure 24.4.   Hours museum open to public

HOURS OF THE SECURITY FORCE (DAY SHIFT)

MONDAY, TUESDAY, WEDNESDAY, FRIDAY
Roll Call 10:00 a.m.
Museum opens 10:30 a.m.
Galleries close 4:30 p.m.*

THURSDAY
Roll Call 10:00 a.m.
Museum opens 10:30 a.m.
Galleries close 8:00 p.m.

SATURDAY
Roll Call 9:30 a.m.
Museum opens 10:00 a.m.
Galleries close 5:00 p.m.*

SUNDAY & HOLIDAYS
Roll Call 11:30 a.m.
Museum opens 12:00 p.m.
Galleries close 5:00 p.m.*

*Museum Store and Michigan Avenue door
close 15 minutes later than Galleries.

LUNCH AND BREAKTIME

MONDAY, TUESDAY, WEDNESDAY, FRIDAY
Half hour lunch—20 minute break

THURSDAY
Half hour lunch—20 minute break
Half hour dinner—20 minute break

SATURDAY
20 minute break—half hour lunch—20 minute
break

SUNDAY
Half hour break

HOURS OF THE SECURITY FORCE (NIGHT SHIFT)

EVENING SHIFT
Roll Call—4:15 p.m.
On post—4:30 p.m.
Off duty—When relieved by next shift

BREAKS AND DINNER
When received

MIDNIGHT SHIFT
Roll Call—None
Dressed and at Security Control—12:00 midnight
Off duty—When relieved

BREAKS AND DINNER
When relieved

HOURS FOR SPECIAL EVENTS AND EXHIBITIONS
Will be announced

Figure 24.5. Security force hours

LOCATIONS—POINTS OF INTEREST

1. WOMEN'S BOARD ROOM
   Located Off Of Gallery 26

2. TRUSTEE'S ROOM & TRUSTEE'S ANNEX
   3rd Floor, East Entry via Elevators

3. DUTCH ROOM (DINING ROOM 1)
   Dining Rooms 2 & 3
   Ground Floor East Entry

4. SCHOOL OF ART
   Jackson & Columbus
   From East Entry, Pass Through Chicago Gallery

5. GOODMAN THEATRE
   Monroe & Columbus

6. COLUMBUS DRIVE AUDITORIUM
   Main Floor East Entry—In The Lobby

7. SMOKING AREAS
   A. Ground Floor Michigan Avenue (Lacy Armour Gallery)
   B. East Entry Dining Areas
   C. Offices & Staff Lounge (Ferguson Wing Employees Only)

8. FULLERTON HALL
   Michigan Avenue, North Side of Grand Staircase

9. MORTON LECTURE HALL
   Ground Floor Michigan Avenue; Lacy Armour Gallery

10. PRICE AUDITORIUM
    Ground Floor Michigan Avenue Near Junior Museum

11. PUBLIC TELEPHONES
    A. Ground Floor East Entry, Cafeteria Area
    B. Ground Floor Michigan Avenue Down East Stairs
    C. Checkroom Michigan Avenue
    D. Goodman Theatre Lobby

12. RESTROOMS
    A. Ground Floor East Entry, Cafeteria Area
    B. Ground Floor Michigan Avenue
    C. American Wing Gallery 32

13. FERGUSON WING—FERGUSON DESK
    Off Limts To General Public Unless They Have An
    Appointment. Located On North Side of Oriental Galleries.
    Ferguson Desk Refers To Desk Occupied By Receptionist
    Outside Personnel Department Office.

14. LOST AND FOUND
    Contact the Security Office—Extension 3560; 3561

15. THORNE MINIATURE ROOMS
    American Wing

Figure 24.6. Major points of interest

POST 3 — PRINTS AND DRAWINGS

Gallery Names
Gallery 107   — Marjorie Kovler
Gallery 108   — Tiffany Blake and Potter Palmer
Gallery 108A — Buckingham
Gallery 109   — Thomas E. Donnelly
Gallery 109A — Helen Regenstein

Primary Responsibility — To prevent the theft of art; to patrol all galleries.
Secondary Responsibility — To assist tourists, to assist in emergencies.

Post 3 Is Responsible For Obtaining The Following Equipment Before
Taking Post:
1. Radio With Fresh Battery
2. Key Ring #24
3. Post Inspection Report

Post Duties — Opening/Closing
1. **Turn off lights in south part of Glore Print Room — Monday thru Friday.**
2. **Turn off light on south wall in Gallery 106.**
3. **Turn on/off lights in Glore Print Room — Saturday and Sunday.**

Special Information
Fire Extinguishers — Located In Closet In Gallery 107;
Also East End of Print Room.
Fire Alarm Box — Located In Closet In Gallery 107;
Also End of Print Room:
Note: The Glore Print Study Room is open to members only. Visitors
who inquire about entering should be directed to the Information
Booth, Michigan Avenue of Lobby.

Figure 24.7. Post orders: Post #3. The same format is followed for each post.

for this section, I have included some sample "Post Procedures" using the
general format we actually use in our manual although the post are non-exist-
ent. You should remember when you prepare a manual that nothing should
be placed in your pocket manual that you wouldn't mind seeing printed in
the newspaper. Copies of your manual will, on occasion, be lost. Use the
examples I have provided as samples even though the posts are imaginary.
    Another important part of our manual is a map of the galleries. Our
manual contains two complete sets of maps. The first set shows all gallery
names or numbers, locations of facilities, and public accommodations such
as restrooms and wheelchair ramps. The second set excludes nonessential information and is printed in two colors. The map itself is printed in black ink.
Each security post (Post 1 through Post 30) is indicated in red ink. A line
is drawn on the map into each gallery where a specific post or patrol extends.
A notation is made at the begining of this section that only regular posts for
uniformed guards are shown. Nonuniformed, supervisory, undercover, special-
event, and roving patrols are not shown. It is important that anyone finding

POST 8

Gallery Name: Lacy Armour Gallery

Primary Responsibility: To prevent theft of art; to patrol gallery.

Secondary Responsibility: To assist tourists; to assist in emergencies.

Post 8 Is Responsible For Obtaining The Following Equipment Before Taking Post:

1. Radio With Fresh Battery
2. Key Ring #25
3. Post Inspection Report

Post Duties — Opening/Closing

1. Turn on top two (2) lights located in box in Gallery #2; then turn on lights on the opposite wall.
2. Turn on alarm located thru double wooden doors. Alarm must be on in the morning.
3. Turn lights on located near men's washroom.

SPECIAL INFORMATION

Public Phone: Located South Side of Grand Staircase, Lobby Of Women's and Men's Washroom.

Public Restrooms: Located North Side Of Grand Staircase.

Smoking Area: Located In Lacy Armour Gallery.

Fire Extinguishers: "ABC" Type Located Thru Double Wooden Doors; Also "ABC" Type Located In Touch Of Art Gallery.

Fire Alarm Box: Located Thru Double Wooden Doors; Also Located In Touch Of Art Gallery.

Note: Old Employee Lounge Off Lacy Armour Gallery Will Be Converted To Photography Department Office Area. During Renovation, Keep Public Out.

You Are Also Responsible For Patrolling Hallways By Touch Gallery (Also Called Tactile Gallery). Check Rooms In This Area With Card Readers To Be Sure They Are Secure.

You Are Primary Back-up To Junior Museum In A Fire. In A Fire Or Fire Alarm, Go Immediately To The Junior Museum To Assist With Evacuation Of Children If Necessary.

Figure 24.8. Post orders: Post #8. Note that special emergency duties are spelled out as needed, when guards are to check special doors, windows, etc. Guards use a preprinted "Gallery Inspection Sheet" to inspect their area and art in their area each shift. The "Gallery Inspection Sheet" provides a checklist of general items to be checked or dealt with while the "Pocket Manual" deals with specific post problems and duties

Purpose

The purpose of this order is to establish a procedure to insure that:

1. No visitors or unauthorized employees stay behind after closing.
2. The art work is inspected for condition.
3. All existing hazards are discovered prior to closing each day.
4. The Museum remains open and then closes on a uniform schedule each day.

Clearing Procedure at Closing Time

A thorough and comprehensive search of the Museum shall be made at closing time on each day that the Museum is open to the public and following each special event when the galleries are open to the persons attending the special event. All possible hiding places in the Museum shall be inspected to insure that no unauthorized persons remain in these areas after the Museum is closed. Each Security Supervisor shall have specific areas of responsibility in the clearing procedures.

Main Floor Supervisor's Duties

On days that the Museum is open to the public, the Floor Supervisor shall be responsible for the following duties at the times indicated. For special events, the duties shall remain essentially the same, but the times will be dictated by the closing time for the special event.

Thirty minutes prior to closing the Floor Supervisor will obtain the necessary keys for closing the Museum and recovering the donations and respond to Post #1.

Security Supervisors

Supervisors will insure that no attempt is made to close galleries until 15 minutes prior to closing.

Fifteen minutes prior to closing the Supervisors will insure that all guards in his/her area make the first announcement, "The galleries will close in 10 minutes."

Ten minutes before closing of the Museum the Supervisors will assure that guards begin to check all closets and other doors in their area to assure that they are secure. The second announcement will be made, "The galleries close in 5 minutes."

Five minutes prior to Museum closing the guard will announce that doors close in five minutes and all galleries are now closed. Lights may be flashed and visitors may be told they must leave.

Lights will remain on at all times except when flashed. They may be flashed at one minute intervals until all visitors are out of the gallery.

During the last 5 minutes the Supervisors will insure that guards check every gallery looking for:

1. unlocked doors
2. condition of art work
3. visitors hiding in galleries
4. lost property
5. visitors hiding in elevators and rest rooms

Figure 24.9. Clearing procedures at closing time

Supervisors will report to the Floor Supervisor when their areas are clear.

Supervisors will insure that guards continue to check and recheck galleries until all duties have been performed and that guards do not congregate waiting for relief.

Store Detail

The Museum Store shall remain open 15 minutes past closing time, Post #1 and #2 will remain open to accommodate visitors wishing to shop in the store.

Ground Floor Detail

The guard assigned to the Ground Floor will clear the lower level 10 minutes before closing.

Night Shift Supervisors Duties

As soon as the Museum is declared secure, the night shift supervisor will dispatch one guard to immediately check the Second Floor area for trespassers. This guard will check each work of art. The lights shall remain on during this search if necessary.

One guard will be dispatched to conduct a search for trespassers in the American Wing.

When both searches are complete, The Second Floor Guard will search the non-gallery areas west of Gunsaulus Hall such as but not necessarily limited to:

1. elevators
2. stairways
3. staff lounges
4. hallways and basement areas

This guard will check the South fire exit door to Morton Wing and report to Control when the door is certified as being secure in the night mode.

When completed this guard will check non-gallery areas such as but not limited to:

1. elevators
2. stairways
3. dining areas
4. The Trading Room wheelchair ramp
5. The Women's Board Room

This guard will check the door leading from Gallery 64 to the North Wing and will report by radio that this door is secure when it is verified as such.

He shall certify by radio that the door leading from the gallery to the wheelchair ramp is locked.

He shall insure that all folding doors in the Dining Rooms 1, 2, 3 and the cafeteria are open and shall certify by radio that this has been done.

Supervisors Responsibility

The Control Supervisor shall make a note on the shift report the time the above verifications are made and insure that guards do in fact check these critical points.

Figure 24.9. Continued

Closing Procedures and Schedule

15 Minutes Before Closing.   Announcement only – "The galleries close in 10 minutes."

10 Minutes Prior to Closing.   Guards begin to check closets and doors in their area.

Announcement "The galleries close in 5 minutes."

5 Minutes Before Closing.   Announce that the museum is closed. All visitors must leave.

Flash the lights but don't leave them off.

Guards check every gallery for people.

When the last person is out of your gallery, check every gallery for:

   1. Collection condition
   2. Environmental conditions
   3. Lost Property
   4. Visitor hiding
   5. Unlocked doors
   6. Visitors in rest rooms, elevators, etc.

Remember, you get paid 15 minutes past closing time. Don't run out at closing time until your work is done right.

Figure 24.9.   Continued

a lost copy of this manual understand that your assets are protected by far more than those few uniformed posts on the map.

   The next section to the manual is entitled "Some of the Most Used Policies and Procedures." This section contains general policies and orders that a guard might find useful while on post. A sample of one type of policy is included for format purposes (Figures 24.9 and 24.10). Other policies which are often included in such manuals are policies dealing with "What to do if . . ." an evacuation occurs, you think you have discovered a missing work of art, etc. Policies dealing with access and parcel control and admissions procedures are also helpful.

   Also included in the pocket manual is a list of most-used phone numbers in the facility including the phone number for each security department post or office and the general emergency number for the complex (Figure 24.11).

   On the reverse side of that page, we have included a list of bell codes for our building's coded fire alarms system so that guards have at their disposal the means of determining the exact location of a fire should the coded bells ring (Figure 24.12).

   The final section of the manual is a series of blank sheets of paper. Guards have always been required to carry a notebook in which to note suspicious occurrences, locks needing service, and other problems encountered. This manual now eliminates the need for guards to carry a separate notebook.

Purpose

The purpose of this policy is to establish standards of personal appearance.

General Information

All security personnel are expected to maintain a high standard of personal appearance and hygiene. It is the responsibility of each individual to maintain the standards set forth in this order. It is the responsibility of each shift supervisor to set a proper example and to inspect his guards to insure conformance with this order and to take corrective action when the standards are not met. Without a high standard of hygiene and appearance, we cannot be recognized as a professional security operation.

Personal Appearance

The face will be kept clean and shaven. Mustaches and beards are to be neatly trimmed.

Hair length is not important as long as it is neatly combed or brushed at all times.

Security guards will be clean and sanitary at all times and will wear a clean, well-pressed uniform when reporting to duty.

Uniform Care

Uniform insignias, accessories, and equipment for the performance of assigned duties are issued to each member of the Force, and it is the responsibility of each member to maintain the issued materials in a serviceable condition.

Shoes are to be kept in good repair and well shined.

Wearing of Uniform

Each guard or supervisor will wear the uniform in accordance with these instructions:

- A. **Jacket:** To be fully buttoned and worn at all times.
- B. **Footwear:** Low quarter black laced shoes, highly shined, to be worn with black socks.
- C. **Skirts:** Gray; length shall be at the discretion of the guard so long as it is approximately one inch above or one inch below the knee.
- D. **Trousers:** Gray; to be worn so that the cuff is one inch above the point where the heel joins the shoe.
- E. **Shirts:** White; will be clean and unwrinkled when reporting for duty; long or short sleeve is optional under jacket. Shirt must be buttoned at all times.

Wearing of Insignias and Accessories

The following insignia or accessories shall be worn as set forth below:

Figure 24.10. Personal appearance

A. **ID Card:** To be worn on the left lapel of the jacket.
B. **Nameplate:** To be worn centered on the area just above the pocket of the jacket (Supervisor only)
C. **Baton:** To be carried in its proper holster and attached to the belt securely on all patrols (night shifts only)
D. **Pistol:** To be worn when on post and secured to the belt and only when issued in accordance with official policy.
E. **Insignia:** Will be provided by the Security Department and be worn on the left pocket of the jacket.

Uniform Issuance

All items of uniform and equipment provided by the Institute shall be issued by the Operations Manager or assigned supervisor and a record kept on permanent file in a secure location. Each item of equipment received will be signed for.

Return of Equipment and Uniforms

Upon separation from the Force, members will return all Institute-provided items of uniform and equipment in a clean, pressed or otherwise serviceable condition.

Responsibility for Issued Items

The member to whom a piece of equipment or uniform is assigned is responsible for the proper upkeep of the equipment, and, considering normal wear and tear, shall be responsible for replacement if damaged or misplace.

Additional Uniform Components

The Director of Security may authorize members to wear other insignia or equipment as he deems appropriate.

Hair

Guards must be alert to the serious hazard long hair and beards cause to the guard when attacked by an assailant and set their hair length accordingly.

Figure 24.10. Continued

SPECIAL EXHIBITIONS

Major special exhibitions requiring the hiring of a large number of part time or temporary guards often call for the printing of a supplement dealing with special crowd-control and security assignments for the exhibit. Since reporting hours and museum hours often change during such events, hours of operation and special admissions policies can be outlined.

PHONE NUMBERS

POST	LOCATIONS	NUMBERS
EMERGENCY	MONROE DOCK	3900
#1	MICHIGAN ENTRANCE	3585
#4	GALLERY 103 (WALL) & 119	3572 – 3575
#6	MONROE DOCK	3507
SECURITY CONTROL	MONROE DOCK	3507 – 3588
#9	JR. MUSEUM STORE	3522
#11	GALLERY 106A – CLOSET	3568
#12	GALLERY 212 NORTH CLOSET	3562
#13	GALLERY 219A CLOSET	3562
#14	GALLERY 225 CLOSET	3568
#15	GALLERY 219A CLOSET	3562
#16	GALLERY 228 SE CORNER	3568
#17	GALLERY 26 UNDER STAIRS	3576
#18	GALLERY 37 ON WALL	3576
#19	GALLERY 37 ON WALL	3576
#20	GALLERY 37 ON WALL	3576
#22	GOODMAN OFFICE DOCK	3564
#25	COLUMBUS EAST ENTRANCE	3563
2ND FL. BALCONY EAST	GALLERY 238 NORTH CLOSET	3569
FOOD SERVICE	EAST ENTRANCE LOWER LEVEL	3530
GOODMAN THEATRE	GOODMAN THEATRE LOBBY	3584
MORTON 1ST FLOOR	GALLERY 111 SW (ON WALL)	3572
PANEL ROOM	2ND FLOOR BALCONY MUSEUM	3590
PHYSICAL PLANT	FERGUSON WING 1ST FLOOR	3595
OPERATIONS MANAGER	MONROE DOCK	3904
SECURITY OFFICE	FERGUSON WING 1ST FLOOR	3560 – 3561
THORNE ROOMS	AMERICAN WING	3640
WHEELCHAIR RAMP	EAST ENTRY – CHICAGO GALLERY	3918

Figure 24.11. Phone numbers

COST

The initial cost of such a program, excluding the time you must devote to its research, is high. It is not unusual for a pocket manual in the format described to cost $10 each in quantities of 250 manuals. Remember that once purchased, the manual binders can be used for many years. Extra units should be purchased initially since minimum orders for binders are often in units of 100. The cost of the binder is by far the most expensive part of the project. Printing is second and typesetting is third. There are several things that should be done, however, since their cost is minimal and their benefit quite important.

INTERNAL FIRE ALARM SYSTEM
WEST MUSEUM AND AMERICAN WING

Pulling down the lever on any of the following fire alarm boxes will sound gongs simultaneous-ly throughout the West Museum and the American Wing, annuciating the coded number of the box activated. The coded gongs will sound four (4) times. For example: When Box #2-4 is activated in Gallery 228 the bells will ring: ** _ ****; ** _ ****; ** _ ****; ** _ ****.

ALARM		BOX LOCATION
		Ground Floor
Box No.	1	Boiler Room
	2	Gallery 26 Guards' Station
	3	Furniture Storage Corridor, South of (new) Photography Gallery
	4	Gallery 36
	5	Morton Lecture Hall, Rear Closet
	6	Gallery 4, Rear, Art Rental and Sales
	7	Storage Room, West of Women's Washroom, Main Building
	8	Morton Wing Corridor Outside Lacy Armour Gallery
	9	Closet Between Galleries 41 and 42
		First Floor
	10	Emergency Evacuation (40 Strokes)
	1-1	Museum Store
	1-2	East End Gunsaulus Hall, South Closet
	1-3	Gallery 112, Closet
	1-4	Gallery 109, Off Michigan Avenue Entrance
	1-5	Gallery 105, By Freight Elevator
		Second Floor
	2-1	Gallery 217A, Closet
	2-2	Gallery 208A, Closet
	2-3	Gallery 229, Stairs to Skylight
	2-4	Gallery 228
		Fourth Floor
	4-1	Above Gallery 201 in Attic
		Ferguson Wing Basement
	5-1	Corridor by Carpenter Shop Entrance
	5-2	Mechanical Equipment Room, Across from Paint Shop
	5-3	Pressure Reduction Room, South End
		Ground Floor
	5-4	Shipping Room, North End
	5-5	Corridor, South End
		First Floor
	5-6	Corridor by South Stairs
		Second Floor
	5-7	Corridor by Registrar's Office
		Third Floor
	5-8	Corridor by North Stairs
		Penthouse
	5-9	Elevator Room

EMERGENCY EVACUATION ALARM

The emergency evacuation alarm will sound forty (40) strokes to distinguish it from the ten (10) stroke opening and closing bells. All non-security and non-emergency personnel must then evacuate the building immediately in accordance with the evacuation procedures.

April, 1980   Director of Security

Figure 24.12. Fire alarm bell-codes

First, I suggest using an IBM changeable-font typewriter to type the material. This eliminates the need for expensive typesetting, and delays when changes need to be made or supplements added. Buy a typestyle font for the typestyle you find attractive and readable and retain it for this project so that all future type matches your initial product.

Second, have your printer die cut the page edges so that they are rounded. This makes for a more attractive manual and pages don't seem to get dog-eared so easily.

Third, when you order the product from your printer, have him assemble the pages and band each manual in a paper band after punching the holes. This way you do not have to assemble the manuals yourself, a time-consuming job.

Finally, take a little time doing your manual. Someone once said, "If it's worth doing, it's worth doing well." A professional and attractive product will carry more respect from your guards and your management. Your manual will speak for your security department on many occasions.

25. Guidelines for Guard Training

Lawrence J. Fennelly

The purpose of training guards is to provide them with the necessary skills and knowledge to perform their job in a professional manner. The training curriculum that follows was assembled from a variety of sources; such as leading museums that have in-service training, in addition to a sample syllabus. I believe that, based on the following information, you will be able to select and prepare a minimum, middle, and maximum level of training for your security personnel.

TRAINING DEFINED[1]

As stated earlier, the training function means different things to different people; it is widely misunderstood. Certainly there is a question of definition, and a typical dictionary definition *(Webster's)* tells us little when it describes training in this manner:

> training. *Noun.* Act, process, or method of one who trains; state of being trained. *Adjective.* That trains; used in or for training; as, a *training* ship for sailors.

Even aside from its obvious circularity, what does this explanation really explain? Is it any wonder there is confusion?

A more workable definition might be the following:

Training is an educational, informative, skill development process that brings about anticipated performance through a change in comprehension and behavior.

Basically there are three things that management wants the employees to know. It is important for them to understand

1. *What* management wants them to do.
2. *Why* management wants them to do it.
3. *How* management wants it done.

"POP" Formula: Policy, Objective, Procedure

Interestingly enough, the *what, why* and *how* are related to *policy, objectives,* and *procedures.* From this correlation the author has developed the POP Training Formula as the basic building block for job training.

The area of the Why/Objective in Figure 25.1 deserves special attention. Too frequently the training process overlooks the necessity of informing employees *why* this should be done, *why* that should be done, etc. When employees are informed as to the why's, their performance will improve. This point cannot be overstressed.

MEETING ORGANIZATIONAL NEEDS[2]

The types of training programs are limited only by organizational needs. True, much material is available at local universities and community colleges, and

Figure 25.1. The "POP" formula for training (Source: Sennewald, *Effective Security Management,* Butterworth Publishers, 1981)

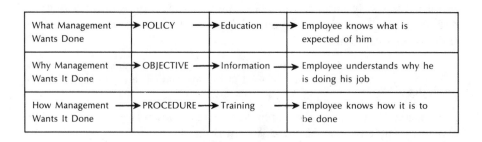

What Management Wants Done → POLICY → Education →	Employee knows what is expected of him
Why Management Wants It Done → OBJECTIVE → Information →	Employee understands why he is doing his job
How Management Wants It Done → PROCEDURE → Training →	Employee knows how it is to be done

security personnel should be encouraged to further their education at such institutions. Specific organizational needs, however, usually must be met through "in-house" education.

Organizational needs come down to people needs. Security management had a need to communicate the reasons for and details of a major reorganization. Security management also recognized the daily operating problems connected with poor interpersonal communication skills between security people themselves and between nonsecurity people and security. Therefore a second need was addressed in the program. The remainder of the agenda was the result of a survey (made in advance by the training officer) of the employees' stated needs. Thus, training objectives are identified and material designed to achieve those objectives. Too many training programs are the master works of art of training personnel or management, but they miss the mark of satisfying what employees want and need.

Security Training Manual

A security training manual or handbook is an absolute essential, and it must be updated on a regular basis. The subject matter should include pertinent company policies, departmental policies, job descriptions, emergency phone numbers, and a great many procedural instructions for specific incidents, such as telephone bomb threat or facility black-out. In some organizations the manual is deemed sacred and consequently most employees are not allowed to touch it — a foolish attitude. The manual should be put in the hands of all regular security personnel.

SAMPLE SYLLABUS FOR SECURITY OFFICERS

A. Orientation Session

Objective. To provide an opportunity for the security officers to become acquainted with the course and its scope; the basic expectations of your department; and the lines of internal authority and communication.

Content.
1. Familiarization with the Museum:
    - Location of classrooms, washroom, and cafeteria.
    - Explanation of rules and regulations of the museum.
2. Course Purpose and Goals:
    - To stress the importance of group interaction for effective learning.

- To point out that as professional security officers the course will be not "taught" exclusively by the instructors, but rather the instructor will act as a leader for a group learning experience, drawing on the wealth of experience possessed by the students in the class.

3. Purposes: Museums and Museum Security:
   - To review the actual goals of museums and the security function as related to museums.
   - To point out the security services function as security officers and their relationship to the visiting public and museum staff.
   - To review types of problems encountered with security officers in the last five years.
   - To outline possibilities in career advancement in museum security fields.

4. Work Conditions and Administration:
   - To review the museum guidelines regarding work conditions and expectations.
   - To assist the security officers in understanding the collective agreement.
   - To impart an understanding of the basic rules governing employees.
   - To review paperwork required by guards by personnel from security office.
   - To impart knowledge of the procedures used to:
     1. Requisition clothing
     2. Request a check advance
     3. Request a cash advance

5. Dress, Deportment, and Motivation:
   - To stress the public relations aspect of proper dress.
   - To analyze the significance of "body language" and attitude when dealing with the public.
   - To discuss the profession of security, its disadvantages as well as its advantages.
   - The problems of motivation in the security field.

6. Post Orders:
   - To review the need for stated policy and the compilation of information into post orders.
   - To review the importance of post orders as the authority of the security officer.
   - To review what should be included in post orders.
   - To review the structure of post orders.

7. Communications:
   - To review the radio telecommunication procedures used within the museum.

- To state the proper use and answering format of telephones within the museum.
- To advise the security officers of the proper grievance procedures and use of chain of command.

B. Human Relations Session

Objective. To analyze the human relation problems encountered by museum security officers and to impart the knowledge and human relations skills necessary to deal with the various types of persons encountered in museums.

Content.
1. *Relating to Museum Visitors and Staff:*
   - To discuss the attitudes of the visiting public to security in general and security officers specifically.
   - To impart the knowledge of the correct procedures to be followed in dealing with museum workers, contract workers, and the visiting public, with reference to policies specifying the official language to be used.
2. *Handling Juveniles and Handicapped Persons:*
   - To provide an understanding of the special problems in relating to juveniles and the legal protection given them.
   - To provide an understanding of the problems encountered by mentally and physically handicapped persons and how a security officer can effectively assist them.
3. *Crowd Control: Strikes, Protests, and Riots:*
   - To analyze the function and responsibilities of security officers during strikes and protests.
   - To discuss the proper attitudes and procedures used in dealing with civil disturbances.

C. Enforcement Session

Objective. To ensure that the security officers in the museum have an understanding of the legal authority they have to carry out their duties and the correct procedures to follow when an offense has been committed.

Content.
1. *Criminal Code and Other Statutes:*
   - To investigate the recognition of a crime when it has been committed and the identification of the specific offense with reference to museum security.

2. *Parking and Traffic Control*
   - To give an understanding of the regulations relating to traffic control.
   - To give instruction in the basic skills used in traffic control.
3. *Enforcing Museum Rules and Regulations (Security and Safety)*
   - To cover the basic fire and safety regulations and the correct procedures to follow if a potential hazard is discovered.
   - To review the general security regulations relating to all of the staff, and the correct procedure to follow if a breach of security relations is discovered.
4. *Investigative Techniques:*
   - To analyze the procedures to be followed to protect the scene of a crime, and things to look for when it has been determined that a crime has been committed.
   - To impart knowledge about the basic techniques used in carrying out an effective investigation.

D. Emergency Services Session

Objective. To provide an understanding of the accepted procedures to be followed in the event of an emergency situation. To look into the methods of preventing potential emergency situations from escalating.

Content.
1. *Emergency First Aid and Resusitation Review:*
   - To give a very basic review of emergency first aid procedures.
2. *Fire Fighting and Fire Control Systems:*
   - To review the emergency procedures to be followed if a fire is discovered.
   - A review of the types and applications of the various fire extinguishers and fire control systems found in the museum.
3. *Alarms and Alarm Responses*
   - To give an understanding of the different types of alarms and applications of these alarms used by the security department.
   - To review the proper response techniques to alarms, and the proper attitudes toward alarm systems.
4. *Police and Security Relations:*
   - To investigate the concept of "preventive security" as opposed to the police function in society.
   - To point out the responsibilities the police and security personnel have to each other and how each can best assist the other.

5. *Museum Environmental Problems:*
   - To point out the various environmental threats and problems involved in protecting artifacts and other museum assets.
   - To advise the correct emergency procedures to be taken in order to protect artifacts from damage.

E. Prevention and Protection Session

Objective. To investigate the various techniques available to security systems to protect assets and prevent damage and/or theft of these assets.

Content.
1. *Patrolling:*
   - To review the importance of physical security patrols needed to back up the alarm system.
   - To impart knowledge about the components of a good patrol and the techniques involved.
2. *Personnel and Access Control*
   - To supply information about the various methods employed to control the movement of persons within the context of the museum.
   - To discuss the various types of access control and the hardware used to limit access.
   - To review the aspects of using IDs and passes as an aid to security.

F. Special Problems Session

Objective. To supply knowledge about the accepted procedures to follow in the event that various problems that may be encountered by security officers occur.

Content.
1. *VIP Protection/Escorts in Museums:*
   - To analyze the threat to VIPs who visit museums and galleries.
   - To discuss the procedures to follow, and the possible problems encountered, for VIP visits.
2. *Vandalism/Arson:*
   - To investigate the reasons that motivate vandals and arsonists.
   - To review the protection that can be used against these threats.

3. *Drugs/Alcohol Abuse:*
   - To discuss the problems of alcohol and drug abuse, with special mention of their abuse by shift workers.
   - To provide understanding of the assistance available to employees who have drug-related problems.
4. *Burglary, Theft, Robbery, and Shoplifting:*
   - To review the definition of each of these offences and discuss the possibility of these offences being committed within the museum.
   - To discuss ways of protecting the museum against these threats.
5. *Sabotage, Espionage, and Terrorism:*
   - To supply knowledge about the increasing threat from these actions.
   - To discuss the accepted procedures for counteracting these threats, as well as their definitions and sources.
6. *Bombs, Bomb Threats, and Searches:*
   - To impart knowledge about the accepted procedures to use in dealing with a bomb threat.
   - To review the procedure to follow in searching for a bomb.

CURRICULUMS

In Chapter 27 Keith W. Forbes outlined a 240-hour training program; however, not everyone can attend such a program. Samples of a variety of curriculums follow. The curriculums listed in this chapter as well as in Chapter 27 can serve as a guide for any library or art facility.

Curriculum Suggested for Managers

- First-line supervisor management skills
- Management by objectives
- Creative problem solving
- Communication skills
- Delegation of authority
- Leadership and management styles
- Time management
- Motivating subordinates
- Planning and decisionmaking
- Written communication
- Dealing with difficult people
- Managing the professional practice
- Effective styles of leadership

- Dealing with stress
- The meaning of organization development
- Career development: A framework for managing human resources
- Team building and development
- Labor relations

Outline for Management Training

- Writing skills
- Communication for results
- Personnel evaluation as a tool of management
- Principles of human relations
- The organization and the people it serves
- Reading development
- Records — a tool of management
- Responsibilities of management
- Social order and social change
- Oral presentation
- Planning and control through management by objectives
- Styles of leadership
- Processes of management:
  1. Planning
  2. Organizing
  3. Directing people
  4. Controlling budget
  5. Evaluation

Specific Training Required if Managers Have Police Powers

- Probable cause
- Affidavits and complaints
- Investigative detentions
- Search of a person
- Search of a premise
- Search of motor vehicles
- Confessions
- Eyewitness identifications
- Electronic interception
- Civil liability
- Informants
- Entrapment
- Exclusionary rule

Training for Security Officers with the Authority to Carry Weapons

- Defensive tactics
- Handcuffing
- Revolver familiarization and requalification
- Use of club and baton

Training Program for Guards

- Chain of command
- Review of equipment
- Introduction to security covering what to check and how to check
- Alarm — fire and intrusion, how to respond
- Rights and authority to make an arrest
- Guards — limitation and liability
- Public relations
  1. Dealing with the public
  2. Handicapped visitors
  3. Crowd control procedures
  4. Relationship with outside agencies
- Bomb threat procedures
- Communications
  1. Report writing
  2. Daily log
  3. Use of two-way radios
- Uniforms
- First aid
  1. Basic first aid (certification program)
  2. Recertification of first aid
  3. CPR
  4. EMT
- Clearing and closing procedures
- Procedures for special events
- Tour Guides and the role of the security guard
- Procedure to report missing works, damages, or unusual occurrences
- Card access control and key control
- Fire and evacuation procedures
- Use of department manuals
- Determining who is a suspicious person
- Lost and found property policy
- Halon — what it is and how it works

Two sample outlines for a five-day guard training program follow:

Sample A.

- Security and the supervisor
- Museum public relations
- Human relations
- Work conditions and the administration
- Communication skills
- Investigation techniques
- Prevention versus apprehension
- Legal authority and limitations
- Criminal code and other statutes
- Bomb threats and procedures
- Security survey and inspections
- Emergency procedures
- Procedures for fires and explosions
- Fire prevention
- Fire and safety inspection
- Procedures for strikes, riots, and protest demonstrations
- Alarms and response
- Supervisory patrols
- Supervisory theory and skills

Sample B.

- Museums and museum security
- Post orders
- Security: Preparation for a career
- Communication
- Relating to visitors and museum staff
- Relating to juveniles, handicapped, and mentally disturbed persons
- Crowd control, riots, and protests
- Criminal code and other statutes
- Parking and traffic control
- Enforcing safety and security regulations
- Investigation and preservation of evidence
- First aid and CPR
- Alcohol and drug abuse
- Alarms and alarm response
- Police and security relations
- Environmental problems
- Card access control

- Patrolling procedures
- Physical security
- Writing reports
- VIP protection and escorts in museums
- Vandalism and arson
- Burglary, theft, robbery, and shoplifting (store)
- Fire-fighting and fire control systems
- Bombs, bomb threats, and bomb searches
- Sabotage, espionage, and terrorism
- Course examination

Crime Prevention Training Curriculum

1. History and Principles of Crime Prevention
2. Introduction to Security
   A. Security barriers: The three lines of defense
   B. Applying the concepts of risk management.
3. Security Lighting
   A. General description of outside security lighting
   B. Types of lighting equipment
   C. Automatic lighting controls
4. Safes
   A. Description of the various safes
   B. Purpose of each safe
5. Intrusion Alarm Systems
   A. Introduction to intrusion detection system
   B. Reducing and causes of false alarms
   C. Controls, circuiting, transmission, sensing devices, central station, and U.L.
6. Locks
   A. Introduction to lock terminology and mechanical security
   B. Door hinges and window locks
   C. Key control
   D. Glossary of terms
7. Fire Alarm Systems
   A. Introduction to various types of detection equipment
   B. Description and purpose of Halon
   C. Fire extinguishers and their purpose.
8. Security Survey
   A. How to make a security survey and how to understand its principles
   B. Reviewing police responsibility

C. Identifying vulnerabilities
9. Risk Management Principles
10. Obtaining Community Support
11. Reducing Criminal Opportunity
12. Designing Security with Architects
13. Physical Security
14. Building and Fire Codes

CONCLUSION

Museum training should include more than physical protection, first aid, CPR, and fire safety. It should include a basic understanding of what is ART; which is, after all, what the employee is being called upon to protect. This can be accomplished with the help of the conservation department.

An effective security training program should also include other museum employees, that is, secretaries, janitors, curatorial staff, and administrative personnel, thereby making security everyone's responsibility. There is an art to selling security and after you have acquired it, you have reached an effective level in the STATE OF THE ART IN MUSEUM SECURITY.

NOTES

1. Charles A. Sennewald, *Effective Security Management,* (Woburn, Mass.: Butterworths, 1978) pp. 89-90.
2. Ibid p. 95

26. Motivating Security Personnel

Osborne Frazier

We must readily accept the view that modern security is no longer associated with hiring a retired or semiretired individual to turn the lights on at dusk and lock a few doors. Today's complex societal problems coupled with a spiraling crime rate dictate that businesses, public institutions, and facilities must turn to the security professional for the required protection of persons and property. Effective security is preventing a loss as opposed to rendering a reaction to a loss. Law enforcement officials are quick to note the important role that security professionals play in reducing crime. The field of security is currently one of the more rapidly expanding industries in the nation.

THE SECURITY DIRECTOR

We should also realize that not everyone can become a true security professional and that there are in fact far too many individuals currently employed in the field who are little more than ineffective lukewarm bodies who fail to apply themsleves during instances that dictate effective and decisive action. Others are often portrayed as "social guards" as opposed to security guards or officers. In view of this analysis, the security director, if he is to effectuate his charge effectively and efficiently, must first emphasize a tight screening process for new hires and provide a concentrated, in-depth, and ongoing training program.

The basic aptitudes and necessary qualities for becoming an effective security officer should be sought in applicants. What are the outstanding characteristics of the applicant's previous record? Is he or she dependable? Does the applicant require close and constant supervision? What is the record with respect to arrivals and departures (tardiness or abandoning the post prior to the authorized time)? Does the applicant possess the ability to think quickly? Is he or she appropriately inquisitive? An effort should also be made to hire physically capable individuals who can enhance the organization's ability to respond with a physical presence when needed. All of these factors form the nucleus of a high-caliber guard force.

You will find that a well-trained, informed, handsome (well-groomed), physically capable, and self-respecting guard organization tends to be somewhat self-motivating in that the individual members strive toward professionalism in executing their duties. The basic idea is to develop a high level of pride and competence within the ranks. Generally, competence and pride tend to be synonymous within the field of security. Invariably, employees from all walks of life enjoy the feeling of "belonging" to a worthwhile organization, and their level of productivity is reflected accordingly. Statistics indicate that additional remuneration alone is not the cure-all for higher motivation and productivity. Rather, the financial reward must be coupled with a strong sense of job satisfaction, security, and the notion that the employee is engaged in worthwhile and meaningful assignments that contribute to the overall success of the program.

With respect to individual work assignments, it is important that security officers be told why their assignments are structured as they are, and what problems their assignments are designed to abate. The officers will then understand the exact correlation of their importance to the overall departmental or organizational objective. Their desire to fulfill their work assignment will be enhanced, and their work will be performed with enthusiasm and an eagerness to do the job better. Generally, this kind of treatment results in constructive suggestions by the officers, improved attention to detail, improved attendance, and ultimately more solid and motivated employees.

GOOD COMMUNICATION

While the foregoing paragraph is not intended to oversimplify the important and sometimes difficult task of motivating security personnel, it goes without saying that the role of the security director is paramount in achieving this end. The director of security must strive to be an effective communicator both up and down the organizational ladder. Good communication between the security director and other department officials within the organizational structure must be established and maintained. The objectives of the security division should be explicitly communicated to all sectors of the organization by the security director so that the needless risk of confrontation with security officers by either staff members or visitors may be reduced.

If a confrontation does occur, however, while a security officer is properly engaged in discharging his duties, strong support for this officer should be shown by the security director as well as the other administrators in the organization. If an officer cannot be supported because of improper action taken by that officer, the facts in the case, coupled with the reason/s why support could not be given, should be communicated immediately to the officer involved. All other officers within the command should also be given this information as soon as reasonably possible; preferably at roll call and then at the monthly security staff meeting. The matter should be utilized at the monthly meeting as an additional training tool, serving to define the role of the security officer further. This would be conducive to keeping motivation and morale within the ranks high. Under no circumstances should the security director or his immediate administrative team sit idly by and permit rumors or the thoughts of a disgruntled officer to permeate throughout the ranks of the security force. Immediate steps should be taken to squelch all rumors and to put the potentially disgruntled officer back on track.

As previously stated, good communication in every form (staff conferences, written directives, etc.) is essential. Additionally, it is crucial that the security administrative personnel who report directly to the director of security fully support and understand the director's philosophy as it reflects the direction and philosophy set by the organizational heirarchy. If a weakness exists within the security supervisory ranks with respect to support for organizational programs and/or a limited understanding of such programs, a serious breakdown in overall effectiveness and motivation within the ranks is imminent. Again, constant and effective communication is vital.

In keeping with the theme of communication with the objective of motivating security employees, each employee's performance evaluation should be utilized constructively in order to motivate the officers to strive toward excellence. The officers should be evaluated quarterly or at least half yearly. And the director of security or his designee should seize this opportunity to talk with each officer individually. Inasmuch as many security officers feel that they are at the low end of the totem pole within the overall scheme of things, the evaluation, if handled properly in a relaxed setting, can do much toward motivating the individual. When an individual cannot measure up to the department's standards, the evaluation process then acts as an effective and well-documented means of terminating the employee's services.

The following lists suggest some categories that the evaluation process should address. Each officer should be informed of his strengths as well as his weaknesses. These strengths should not be played down but should be tactfully highlighted by the director, showing the officer that he is cared for. In this way the security director can convey to the officer that, based upon the officer's demonstrated abilities (strengths), the director is confident that the weaknesses will be overcome. Whenever an officer shows a weakness the security director should specify what it is and outline measures for the officer to follow to correct this deficiency. Rather that terminating the officer, a close and sincere follow-up of this remedial program should be conducted with the objective of further development and motivation of the officer.

Categories

1. *KNOWLEDGE OF WORK*
   - Lacks sufficient knowledge for satisfactory performance.
   - Has most required knowledge but lacks depth or breadth.
   - Possesses adequate knowledge for good work performance.
   - Work reflects comprehensive and suitable knowledge.
   - Has exceptionally commanding knowledge and insight into work.
2. *PRODUCTIVITY*
   - Useful output or volume of work is generally inadequate.
   - Somewhat slow or erratic in production of useful work.
   - Volume of useful output wholly adequate.
   - Consistently produces superior volume of useful work.
   - Work output is phenomenal.
3. *ACCURACY*
   - Error of commission or ommission, or lack of precision, is frequent or serious.
   - Work is sometimes imprecise, incomplete, incorrect, or superficial.
   - Careful, conscientious, work meets position demands for accuracy.
   - Excells in thoroughness and accuracy. Makes a minimum of errors in commission or omission.
   - Invariably turns out work outstanding in accuracy or completeness.
4. *INITIATIVE*
   - Does not take independent action.
   - Sometimes overlooks need for action or seeks guidance or approval unnecessary before action.
   - Acts on his own in unusual activities; is quite adequate.
   - Sees opportunities and acts promptly and independently in new or unforeseen situations.

- Invariably sees opportunities and acts promptly and independently even in the most difficult or important situations.

5. *RESOURCEFULNESS*
   - Goes strictly "by the book." Does not produce ideas or adaptations.
   - Prefers conventional solutions to problems but occasionally displays inventiveness.
   - His work reflects the imagination required.
   - Highly adept at finding solutions to the most difficult problems with exceptional success.

6. *DEPENDABILITY*
   - Fails to follow instructions, observe commitments, or complete work on time.
   - Needs an undue amount of supervision to comply with instructions and to meet deadlines and commitments.
   - Conscientious and steady worker. Complies with commitments, meets deadlines, and produces useful work with normal supervision.
   - Conscientious and reliable worker. Completes each task and meets deadlines and commitments with a minimum of supervision.
   - Regardless of own inconvenience, invariably meets the most difficult commitments and deadlines. Certain to follow through even in absence of instructions.

7. *DECISIVENESS*
   - Either cannot make up his mind or he vacillates.
   - Slow at making decisions unless pushed or jumps too hastily to conclusions.
   - Makes sound decisions with reasonable promptness.
   - Makes sound decisions in a very timely or confident fashion.
   - Is decisive even under acute pressure; is outstanding in speed or success.

.8 *ANALYTICAL ABILITY*
   - Generally misjudges or fails to realize causes or significance of problems, facts, or events.
   - Tends to accept statements or events with little critical thought or frequently fails to interpret or interrelate them adequately.
   - Generally identifies the facts or underlying events, ideas, or problems and interprets them with reasonable accuracy.
   - Thoughtfully and successfully examines the essential elements of problem situations and reaches valid conclusions.
   - Exceptionally effective in reaching the heart of a difficult problem, evaluating its elements and their interrelationships and true significance.

9. *ABILITY TO ANTICIPATE*
    - Shortsighted. Tries to solve today's problem without regard to other problems or tomorrow's needs.
    - Sometimes compartmentalizes problems; does not perceive relationships to other events and later eventualities. Occasionally caught off base.
    - Farsighted. Usually chooses course of action that has broad and lasting utility.
    - Nearly always shapes actions to future developments as well as to present problems.
    - Exceptionally sensitive to ultimate consequences of action. Invariably examines particular item as part of the total stream of events. Entire decisionmaking is integrated.

10. *JUDGMENT*
    - Judgment unreliable. Overlooks pertinent considerations or has little sense of proportion.
    - Judgment adequate if clear-cut precedents exist; lacks practicality, wisdom, or sensitivity in new situations.
    - Exercises good judgment in normal activities. Carefully considers facts and possible courses of action.
    - Nearly always displays good judgment in meeting both normal and unusual situations.
    - Displays excellent judgment, timing, and insight, even in the most difficult and sensitive situations. Judgment unimpaired by work pressures.

11. *PERSPECTIVE*
    - Has a poor understanding of the tools of his job.
    - Fair understanding of the principal objectives of his job but poorly oriented in some respects.
    - Good knowledge of objectives and of his part in achieving them.
    - Well informed, with very good insights, knows what he is doing and why.
    - Remarkable grasp of relationship of his job to total picture and of currents that might affect this relationship.

12. *ATTITUDE TOWARD JOB*
    - Indifferent attitude. Shows little interest in his work.
    - Makes an effort but has little real enthusiasm for the job.
    - Has an interest in the work and helps out on other tasks when asked.
    - Displays keen interest in the job. Works extra hours on own initiative. Offers to assist in other duties.
    - Exceptionally high degree of interest, willingness, and dedication. His job invariably comes first.

13. *ACCEPTANCE OF RESPONSIBILITY*
   - Generally seeks to avoid responsibility for past or future actions.
   - Sometimes reluctant to acknowledge or accept responsibility and then only within well-defined limits.
   - Generally acknowledges or accepts responsibility willingly.
   - Displays well above average sense of responsibility for past or future actions including those of his subordinates.
   - Invariably regards himself as fully accountable for his actions and those of his subordinates, if any.

14. *WRITTEN COMMUNICATION*
   - Does not get ideas across clearly on paper.
   - Writing often lacks clarity, brevity, or effectiveness.
   - Writing is understandable, to the point, and acceptably organized; composition requires little editing.
   - Composition has all the qualities of excellence: clarity, precision, conciseness, good organization, persuasiveness, and style.

15. *ORAL COMMUNICATION*
   - Has great difficulty in conveying ideas orally.
   - Effectiveness of oral communication sometimes lessened by defects such as wordiness, imprecision, poor grammar, or rambling.
   - Gets ideas across clearly in oral communication.
   - Speaks well. Is convincing and to the point.
   - Outstandingly articulate in choice of words, clarity, conciseness, and persuasiveness. Holds listeners interest even under adverse conditions.

16. *ADAPTABILITY*
   - Resists change or new approaches or is upset by new or different environmental situations.
   - Adjustments to change or new approaches in work are somewhat hampered by old habits or fixed ideas; or adjusts with difficulty to new environment.
   - Accepts change, new approaches, and new ideas in work and works well with them. Adjusts to new environment reasonably soon.
   - Receptive to new approaches and ideas in work. Applies them readily and effectively. Quickly adapts to new or different environment.
   - Immediately grasps new approaches, ideas. Exceptionally able to blend old and new, and adapt own interest and enthusiasms. Takes difficult environmental situations in stride.

17. *OFFICIAL REPRESENTATION*
   - Makes a poor impression as a representative of the department.

- Does not make the contacts he should or sometimes is rather ineffective in contacts.
- Does his part in mixing with the public and represents the department effectively.
- Has wide range of useful contacts and is effective at using them and at promoting the interest of the department.
- Makes excellent use, for the department, of extraordinary range of contacts.

Personal Qualities

1. *APPEARANCE*
   Does he dress neatly and make a good appearance?
   > Unsuited
   > Deficient
   > Satisfactory
   > Excellent
   > Outstanding
2. *ALERTNESS*
   Does he understand complex and difficult questions, or is he slow and confused by details? Do you have to repeat and explain?
   > Unsuited
   > Deficient
   > Satisfactory
   > Excellent
   > Outstanding
3. *TEMPERAMENT*
   Is he poised, friendly, and free from bias? Does he take offense easily; become angry, tactless, or excited?
   > Unsuited
   > Deficient
   > Satisfactory
   > Excellent
   > Outstanding
4. *SECURITY INTEREST*
   Is he enthusiastic? Does he consider policing a long-term career? Does he strive for self-improvement?
   > Unsuited
   > Deficient
   > Satisfactory
   > Excellent
   > Outstanding

5. *ATTENDANCE*
   Is he frequently absent? Does he report for duty on time? Does he leave early?
   Unsuited
   Deficient
   Satisfactory
   Excellent
   Outstanding

6. *EFFECTIVENESS WITH OTHERS*
   Consider the degree to which the officer maintains cooperative and professional relations with others and is effective in accomplishing objectives.

DESIRABILITY RATING

Evaluation

- Do not want him in my command.
- Do not mind having him in my command.
- Happy to have him in my command.
- Prefer him to most personnel.
- Highest and most desirable type of personnel.

With respect to supervisory staff it is recommended that all awards, promotions, and salary increases, and so on, be tied into how well subordinates are utilized to accomplish organizational objectives, and the extent to which help is provided by supervisors for their subordinates' development. Next are several basic areas that examine the pitfalls of supervision. If these pitfalls are not avoided, they tend to negate cooperation within the ranks.

* *Trying to be liked rather than respected.*
  - Don't accept favors from subordinates.
  - Don't grant special favors for purposes of trying to be liked.
  - Don't aim for popular decisions.
  - Don't be soft about discipline.
  - Don't party or socialize with subordinates.
  - Have a sense of humor.
* *Failure to ask subordinates for their input.*
  - Make them feel that a problem is also their problem.
  - Encourage individual thinking.
  - Facilitate a mechanism that would make it easy for them to communicate their ideas to you.
  - Follow through on their ideas.

* *Failure to develop a sense of responsibility in subordinates.*
  * Encourage dialogue.
  * Encourage cross training whereby a subordinate can learn his superior's job.
  * When delegating responsibility, also give authority.
  * Hold subordinates accountable.
* *Emphasizing rules rather than skill.*
  * Give a person assignment to do — and let him do it.
* *Failure to keep criticism constructive.*
  * Control your temper.
  * Allow a subordinate to retain his dignity.
  * Suggest specific steps to prevent recurrence of a mistake.
  * Be a good listener.
* *Failure to pay attention to employee gripes and complaints.*
  * Make it easy for subordinates to come to you.
  * Maintain an OPEN DOOR policy.
  * Eliminate red tape.
  * Assist a subordinate in voicing his own complaint.
  * Always grant a hearing.
  * Practice patience.
  * Ask a complainer what he wants you to do.
  * Don't render a hasty or biased judgment.
  * Get all the facts.
  * Let the complainer know what your decision is.
  * Double check your results.
  * Be concerned.
* *Failure to keep subordinates informed.*
  * Let subordinates know where they stand with you.
  * Praise subordinates properly.
  * Let subordinates know as early as possible of any changes that will affect them.
  * Let them know of changes that will not affect them, about which they may worry.

ATTENDANCE

In addition to the pitfalls of supervision just mentioned, it is recommended that an awards program be established within the command. The objective would be to promote "espirt de corps" among the officers of the command that may engender a spirit of dedication and achievement in the field of security. Good attendance by all officers must be considered paramount. Not only does poor attendance affect the efficiency and morale of the department, but it also increases the costs of the overall operation. Generally, when absences run high there are several key officers who are constantly asked to work double shifts. Even though the officer is asked to perform extra hours at a premium rate of overtime pay, his morale is eventually affected as the solid team approach is diminished. In addition, even though the officer may not refuse the overtime assignment, there are periods when he would much rather be engaged in other activities or be with his family. The officer soon tends to lose respect for the effectiveness of the leadership, and he himself may become an absentee problem. A lax absenteeism policy will invariably affect the security command adversely. Listed below are several areas in which the security supervisor can have a positive impact and simultaneously motivate the individual if handled properly.

- Insist on prompt notification when someone must be absent unexpectedly.
- Insist on prior discussions about necessary absences for personal reasons, rather than explanations after the fact. In any event, require real explanations rather than "phony" excuses.
- What is the "Blue Monday" situation in your command? Maintain a running record of absences on Monday or the day after each holiday and compare it with absences on the best-attendance day. The difference is a good indicator of "phony" absenteeism.
- Avoid crises caused by unexpected absences by having standard operating procedures and standard backup procedures; who is to be kept informed of what details, who is to pinch hit for whom, etc.
- Maintain good command and individual officer absence records. Scrutinize them periodically to identify the abusers.
- Have heart to heart discussions with the individuals who cause most of your absentee problems. Ascertain whether or not they have personal problems for which counsel by you or someone else from the personnel or medical department can help.
- Develop facts and figures on actual costs of absenteeism within the command, related as well as direct costs. Drive home the seriousness of the problem.
- Know the officers within your command. Without prying, show an interest in their personal lives. Encourage after-hour discussion of problems that affect attendance, productivity, and morale.

EVALUATION PROCESS

The evaluation process can have an impact if it is properly administered. All supervisory positions should be filled with people who can fulfill the many responsibilities of the position, that is, leadership. The evaluation process is one of the most important functions of supervision. A guard has a right to know what is expected of him, where he stands in the department, and how to improve his performance. It is a time for credit to be given, bad habits to be stated, and a method for improvement explained. For supervisors who have been doing their job, this will be merely an extension of their daily work. For others, however, it is a time to evaluate their own effectiveness and get squared away with the people they supervise.

A few words of caution:

1. Beware of the "halo effect"; that is, being overly impressed by a recent act or unusual incident that unduly influences your evaluation positively or negatively.
2. Do not display an attitude that demeans the evaluation process. Be positive and act like a supervisor. If you do not, the process will be negative for everyone concerned.
3. Let each person know how improvement can be shown and how you will keep track of his progress.
4. For the unusual person who may demonstrate a negative posture in the conference, do not buy this attitude. Let this person know the importance of being a professional and proceed. In rare cases, another conference time may be arranged.
5. Keep evaluations confidential. Do not give out copies. Explain that the guard may review the evaluation at any reasonable time by contacting the director of operations.
6. Review all evaluations to be certain standard treatment is being given. We all have our strengths and weaknesses. Be fair, but be firm.

SELF-ESTEEM

Next are ten ways that will inspire motivation and enhance self-esteem:

1. Stroking or giving a pat on the back after a specific task has been completed.
2. Creating special assignments that need to be done; for example, checking all aspects of the fire and instrusion alarm monthly.
3. Rotating guard assignments.
4. Having the staff write their job descriptions for you. Maybe some of the things they are doing they should not be doing. After reviewing the report acknowledge their good work.
5. Delegating authority.

6. Not being afraid of being truthful. For example, when conversing with a guard, do not be afraid to say you were wrong and the guard was right.
7. Using employee recommendations. For example, when the guards make a recommendation do not be afraid to follow through with it and make sure they receive the credit.
8. Asking for employee recommendations and suggestions.
9. Knowing the employees' names; properly addressing them ("Good morning, Stephen") and even smiling once in a while.
10. Showing concern and compassion for the problems of your employees. When was the last time you asked them about a sick member of their family in a way in which you showed you really cared.

STROKING

To further understand the principle of "How to Motivate Your Security Personnel," first you must understand some basic definitions in psychology.

Motivation	— Inner influence on behavior as represented by physiological condition, interests, attitudes, and aspirations.
Motivational Hierarchy	— A hierarchy of needs which human beings presumably fill successively in the order of lowest to highest. The five levels are physiological needs, safety, love and belonging, self-esteem, and self-actualization.
Motivational Sequence	— A series of related events involved in motivation, namely, need, drive, incentive, and reinforcement.
Personality	— The most characteristic integration of an individual's structures, modes of behavior, interests, attitudes, capacities, abilities, and aptitudes — the whole person as others know him or her.
Psychology	— The science of behavior experience: the science of the adjustments of organisms to their environment.

When was the last time you (the security manager) told one of your guards that he or she was doing a great job and that you appreciated all the small things that he or she did that were not unnoticed. Although some people call it *stroking,* or patting the employee on the back, "What is wrong with it?" Look at the above definitions again and list how you motivate your personnel by "stroking."

STEPS TO MOTIVATE GUARDS IN AN ART FACILITY

1. Identify and determine the shape and attitude of your staff's behavior.
2. Identify and determine dissatisfaction, problems, gripes, and complaints and handle them in such a way as to motivate your staff.
3. Identify sensitive situations, problem employees, and union problems.
4. After the above has been accomplished, a form of effective communication with the staff should be developed. This can be done by:
    *   Monthly or semimonthly staff meetings.
    *   Daily reports written and signed by the supervisor indicating that some type of action has been implemented.

27. Vicarious Liability of Security Administrators For The Actions of Their Guards

Keith W. Forbes

Picture yourself as the director of security and safety for a large metropolitan museum which is operated through county government funding. One day you are notified by the deputy director that a lawsuit has been brought against the museum. The suit is for $1.5 million. The plaintiff in the suit is alleging that she was mentally and physically abused by one of the museum's security guards while she was visiting the museum.

You contact the shift supervisor who was working on the day the purported incident took place. He tells you that he is not aware of such an incident since none of the security officers assigned to work that particular day either told him of a negative citizen contact or submitted a written report.

The guard named in the suit has several valid citizen complaints on file. He has been disciplined several times during the last three-year period for unnecessary use of physical force against a patron, displaying an aggressive, threatening behavior, under the influence of an unknown substance which caused him to fall asleep while on duty, and lying to a supervisor.

You are probably asking yourself, why wasn't this guard terminated? It is extremely difficult to terminate a civil-service employee even when you have the appropriate documentation to prove that the employee is negligent. This is a good example of this. If the guard had not been a civil servant I can assure you he would have been terminated as a result of the first incident.

Whatever your title may be — Director of Security, Security Manager, Chief of Security — you are responsible for the recruitment, selection, hiring, training, and, if necessary, disciplining and/or termination of your security employees, unless of course you are in a civil-service system, when some of these areas are not within your area of authority. All of us who are security administrators must be increasingly knowledgeable and concerned regarding a concept that is relatively new to us. This concept is vicarious liability.

Vicarious liability is a legal concept that has caused police administrators much concern, especially during the last few years. This concept is now starting to cause security administrators the same concern.

VICARIOUS LIABILITY

Vicarious liability is a legal concept formally called the Doctrine of Respondeat Superior. Respondeat Superior means the employer is liable for the wrongs committed by an employee where the employee has acted within the scope of his employment.

Although individual employees are also liable for the wrongs they may commit, the law provides for judgment against employees to be paid for by public entity. The exceptions to this law, however, concern false arrest and false imprisonment. All payments are for personal damages only. The pertinent laws concerning vicarious liability may be found in your state's government codes and within certain court decisions. These code sections will cover the following areas: injuries by employees within scope of employment — immunity of employee; exemplary damages; public employee liability for injuries generally; discretionary acts; execution or enforcement of laws — exception and request for defense by public entity — payment of judgment, compromise, or settlement.

Injuries by Employees within Scope of Employment; Immunity of Employees

This section imposes upon public entities vicarious liability for the wrongful acts and omissions of their employees. It is necessary in every case to identify the particular employee upon whose act the liability of the public entity is to be predicated. All that is necessary is to show that an employee of a public entity wrongfully inflicted the injury in the scope of his employment under circumstances where he would be personally liable.

Exemplary Damages

A public entity is not liable for damages imposed primarily for the sake of example and by way of punishing the defendant.

Public Employee Liability for Injuries Generally

A public employee is liable for injury caused by his act or omission to the same extent as a private person except as otherwise provided by law.

Discretionary Acts

A public employee is not liable for an injury resulting from his act or omission where the act or omission was the result of the discretion vested in him, whether or not such discretion be abused. This is followed except as otherwise provided by law.

Execution or Enforcement of Laws; Exception

A public employee is not liable for his act or omission if he exercises due care in the execution or enforcement of any law. Nothing in this area exonerates a public employee from liability for false arrest or false imprisonment.

Request for Defense by Public Entity; Payment of Judgment, Compromise, or Settlement

This section requires public entities to pay claims and judgments against public employees that arise out of their public employment where the public entity has been tendered the defense. This, usually, will not authorize a public entity to pay such part of a claim or judgment as is for punitive or exemplary damages.

Vicarious liability suits are dependent on the employment relationship. In other words, the employee must have acted in the scope of his employment during the time his conduct caused the plaintiff's injury.

In all instances, the plaintiff has the burden of proof.

AREAS OF VICARIOUS LIABILITY

Vicarious liability deals with five specific areas. These are negligent hiring, negligent retention, negligent assignment, negligent supervision, and negligent training.

Negligent Hiring

Under the theory of negligent hiring, an employer's liability is direct because of his own negligence in hiring the employee. To state a cause of action for negligent hiring, the grieving party must allege (1) the existence of an employment relationship which is usually undisputed; (2) that the employee was unfit for the position occupied; (3) that the employer had knowledge, either actual or constructive, of the employee's incompetence at the time he was hired; and (4) that the employer was guilty of negligence or intentional misconduct of the employee at the time in question thereby causing the grieving party's injuries.

In other words, for the liability to be attached to the act of hiring, the grieving party must show that the employee was incompetent and that the employer knew or should have known of the employee's incompetence. The last element in the grieving party's suit against the employer is proof of the employee's negligence or intentional misconduct. This part of the case is not dissimilar from an ordinary suit against an employee except in one major respect. This distinction lies in the admissibility of certain evidence, namely evidence of past acts of negligence or misconduct to prove negligence or misconduct at the time in question.

Negligent Retention

Where the employee was competent at the time of employment the appointing power may escape liability for negligent employment. But where, during the period of employment, the employee demonstrates that he is no longer capable of occupying his position without creating an unreasonable risk of harm to the public at large and the appointing power fails to take affirmative action to discharge the employee or remove him to a less sensitive position, the appointing power may be held personally liable under the theory of negligent retention.

Incompetence or unfitness to hold a particular position is established in much the same manner as with negligent hiring; i.e., carelessness, recklessness, physical or mental defect, a propensity for violence or maliciousness, or the habitual use of drugs or intoxicating liquor. In this kind of situation, the employing agency is likely to be besieged by requests for discovery of information heretofore thought to be confidential. Notwithstanding the claim of confidentiality, the general rule would appear to be that any material in the possession of the employing agency that bears on the employee's performance is discoverable in a suit for negligent retention.

Negligent Assignment

Whereas the theories of negligent hiring and retention allege that the employee is unfit or incompetent to be employed, the theory of negligent assignment tends to focus upon the particular task the employee has been assigned. The elements of the grieving party's case are essentially the same as in negligent hiring or negligent retention, with one exception. Rather than alleging that the employee is incompetent or unfit to hold a particular position, the grieving party is asserting that the employee is unfit or incompetent when it comes to performing certain tasks associated with this position.

Negligent Supervision

A superior officer who is given a supervisory duty and fails to perform it, or does so negligently, may suffer liability for his negligent conduct or negligent omission. He is not liable directly for the misconduct of his subordinate under the Doctrine of Respondeat Superior. As a security administrator he is not vicariously liable for the acts of a subordinate employee unless he (1) participates in, (2) directs, or (3) authorizes or ratifies the misconduct of the subordinate. The administrator, however, may be personally liable under the Doctrine of Proximate Cause if his negligent supervision involves a breach of duty. Negligence in supervision imposes the same liability as if he had personally participated in the actual wrongdoing.

Negligent Training

Most courts recognize that employing agencies and security administrators have a duty to train officers they employ. Administrators have been held liable where there had been a negligent breach of his duty which proximately causes an injury to the grieving party. The negligent failure to train involves a breach of executive duty and imposes the same liability as if the administrator had participated in the actual wrong. Generally a security adminstrator is not vicariously liable for the acts of a subordinate officer unless he participates in, directs, authorizes, or ratifies the misconduct of the employee.

A security administrator in private industry, who contracts with a security vendor for security personnel, is not immune from civil liability, regardless of how the contract is written.

If the contracting party is a city or county, which has some form of civil-service system, it becomes critical to any discussion of personal liability for negligent hiring, retention, or assignment, to determine where the power to hire or discharge lies since it is the holder of the power upon whom liability will rest.

In the case of hiring, the civil-service commission is normally charged with the responsibility of certifying a list of eligible candidates for employment from which the security administrator is allowed to hire. The security administrator is then charged with the responsibility of doing a background investigation prior to hiring the candidate. If the investigation reveals adverse information regarding the candidate and the security administrator still hires him, the security administrator will be personally liable. On the other hand, if the security administrator refuses to hire the candidate and the candidate appeals to the commission and is subsequently successful, the security administrator will be absolved of any liability for negligently hiring the candidate.

Where the security administrator is made aware of an employee who is no longer competent, the normal course of action is to discharge the individual. This would eliminate any further basis of liability. The order to discharge would relieve the security administrator of any personal liability, notwithstanding the fact that the commission subsequently orders the discharged employee reinstated.

Should the civil-service commission not sustain the security administrator in his/her efforts to discharge an employee based upon its finding the facts of the case to be untrue it will order the employee reinstated. Should the commission find the facts of the case to be true but the punishment too harsh or severe it again may order the employee reinstated.

If the security administrator has attempted to discharge an employee for incompetence in a given area and he/she is not sustained by the commission because of the severity of the punishment, due care should be taken in reassigning this employee.

Incompetence in a given area may be temporary and corrected with further training.

In a situation wherein the security administrator has attempted to discharge a security guard for past violent misconduct involving the use of a weapon and the guard is reinstated by the civil-service commission, the security administrator should use due care to assign the guard to duties in which he/she will be alertly supervised and will normally have little occasion to use his/her weapon.

Many states have statutes which attempt to protect the decision of public employees made in the course and scope of their employment. This should provide some encouragement to the security administrator whenever he uses his discretion in the assignment of any employee. Failure to exercise such discretion may unnecessarily expose the security administrator to liability for negligent assignment.

Vicarious liability is an area of law that the security administrator must always be concerned about, more so if his staff is comprised of armed security guards. He should not be lulled into a false sense of security, though, if he does not have armed officers. There have been numerous court cases involving vicarious liability when the security guard was not armed.

SECURITY GUARD QUALIFICATIONS

A security administrator can do several things to decrease the possibility of vicarious liability.

Hiring Standards

The security administrator should establish and maintain strict hiring standards. These standards cannot be discriminatory in the areas of race, sex, and/or creed, and they should be written and filed. These standards are as follows:

1. You may require that the security guard applicant can read, write, and speak the English language and you can give a basic test to insure this.
2. If you are hiring the guard in an armed capacity you can require that he meets the state/county/municipal licensing requirements, whichever the case may be.
3. If the assignment is one of high trust or security you can require that the applicant has not been convicted of a felony and/or major misdemeanor thefts.
4. If the applicant is going to be required to drive a company vehicle you can require that he possess a valid state driver's license and have a safe driving record.
5. You can require that the applicant is not currently addicted or habituated to illegal or dangerous drugs.
6. You can require the applicant to submit to a polygraph examination.
7. You can require the applicant to be in good physical condition; i.e., vision standards corrected and uncorrected, standard height/weight relationship, free of physical and mental defects which would keep the applicant from doing the job.
8. You would also want to check the applicant's previous employment record.

Preemployment Background Investigation

In order to insure that the applicant meets the hiring standards you are going to have to conduct a preemployment background investigation on him/her. In doing this you will have to contact the following:

1. State Criminal Index Information.
2. State Department of Motor Vehicles.
3. Local law enforcement agency.
4. Previous employers.

You will also have to send the applicant for a complete medical examination to insure that he/she also fits the physical requirements of the position.

Training

A good, in-depth, preservice and in-service training program can and will diminish the possibility of vicarious liability. As security administrators many of us think that we know what a good training program consists of. This is not always true. What we must always take into consideration is the type of assignment the security guard is filling. If the security guard is armed, then your training program should be more extensive. There usually are state-mandated training requirements for armed security guards. Many states, counties, and municipalities have mandated licensing requirements for security guards, whether they be armed or unarmed.

When developing a training program for security guards the following questions must be resolved.

1. Are the guards armed, unarmed, or a combination of both?
2. Are there state-, county-, or municipality-mandated training requirements, and if so, what are they?
3. Is there to be preservice as well as in-service training or only in-service training?
4. What will the training cost?
5. What will it consist of?
6. Where will it be given?
7. When will it be given?
8. Are there qualified instructors to do the training or must instructors be trained?

Armed vs. Unarmed Security Guard Training. Training for an armed security guard is going to be significantly different in several areas from training for an unarmed security guard, particularly if there are state, county, or municipal training requirements. These mandated training requirements are in the area of weapon familiarization, weapon use, and knowledge of state statutes or county or municipal ordinances which deal with dangerous weapons, specifically handguns, and laws of arrest, search, and seizure. Proof of completion of training is always required prior to the licensing agency authorizing the guard to carry a weapon.

Preservice Training.   Preservice training can be very costly. Many new armed security guard applicants must be trained to meet the mandated training requirements.

There are three sources for this training that I am aware of. One of these is private security training organizations. This type of organization charges a set fee for an eight-hour minimum through a forty-hour maximum training program. This program usually consists of weapons familiarization (orientation, firing, and maintaining the weapon), laws of arrest, search, and seizure, and laws that pertain to the carrying and use of a weapon. If the training program is eight hours or less in duration, the applicant is usually told, after the program is completed, to go to one of the local gun clubs in order to familiarize himself with and fire his weapon. The eight-hour class consists basically of lecture material.

The instructors for these classes are usually full-time police officers who are moonlighting on their days off, ex-military personnel, and/or individuals who possess a state specialized teaching credential.

The second source for this training is large national and/or international security firms. Most of these major firms have their own in-house, preservice training programs that are tailored to meet their specific needs. They only train their own employees.

The third source is the community colleges. There are numerous community colleges throughout the nation that now offer security guard academies. The duration of this training is from forty hours to two hundred hours. The cost is set by the community college and usually averages between $35 and $45 per student. The subject matter meets the state-local training requirements.

In the recent past I was the director of security for one of the major museums in the United States. This museum was a county facility, supported by a county budget, and many of its employees were county civil-service employees.

The security staff was composed of thirty-eight armed security officers and thirty-four unarmed security attendants. The armed security officers have full police powers while on duty. They receive this authority from the state penal code.

There are four other county departments in this county that also have armed security officers who have the same status as the museum security officers.

The only preparation these officers had was forty hours of training through the county sheriff's department. This training fulfilled the mandated training requirements and allowed the officers to be armed. Each department also had an in-service training program but these were, for the most part, ineffective.

Due to the increasing potential of vicarious liability, particularly in the area of training, I and the other county departments' security directors approached one of our local community colleges and proposed the establishment of a security officer academy. The school administration was delighted and agreed.

We worked closely with the school curriculum committees in developing what we considered to be an outstanding training program which was tailored to our particular needs and fully complied with the state-mandated training requirements. We also agreed that anyone could attend this program. It was not limited to county security officers. This made the program particularly attractive to several security specialist firms, which now send all their new employees to this training. There have been several individuals in each class who have taken the training with the idea of going to work for a private security firm as an armed guard.

The training is 240 hours in duration. It costs the student or employer $42.50. This includes all handout material. The students or employers are required to furnish all of their own equipment and uniforms including the following:

1. Pistol/revolver and ammunition.
2. Sam Brown belt and holster, handcuff case, keeper straps, ammunition holder, baton holder.
3. Handcuffs.
4. Baton PR-24.
5. Sweat outfit.
6. Gym shorts.
7. Tennis shoes.
8. Khaki shirt and trousers.
9. Smooth-leather black lace shoes or Wellington boots.

The curriculum consists of classroom lectures, practical application, and physical fitness. The curriculum includes the following subjects: orientation, departmental policies and procedures, county security system, cadet counseling and motivation, ethics, discretionary decision-making, United States Constitution, physical fitness, the security officer, security philosophy, criminal law, use of force, security concepts, search and seizure, weapon familiarization, physical security, laws of arrest, evidence firearms safety, physical evidence handling, range training, probable cause, field note-taking, the court system, defensive tactics, weapon retention, first aid, state vehicle code, investigative techniques, county ordinances, state penal code, criminal procedures, basic writing skills, VIP protection, baton PR-24 training, childbirth, CPR, security on premises, security objectives, preventative enforcement, report forms, court testimony, report-writing, revolutionary ideology, the terrorist, terrorism today, mentally ill persons, handcuffing techniques, the bomb, bomb threat, search techniques and evaluation procedures, interview and interrogation, the emergency now, evacuation procedures, burglary, robbery, disturbances, the Four Cs of response, the hostage situation, officer attitude and demeanor, mob psychology, crowd-control measures, crowd-control practical application, weaponless defense, traffic control, and radio communication.

There are written examinations covering each phase of training as well as a written examination which covers the state-mandated training courses. The student must pass the state-mandated training course with a 70 percent score and he/she must maintain an overall 75 percent grade point average. Should the student fail the state-mandated training course, he/she is terminated. If he/she fails to maintain an overall 75 percent grade point average, he/she is also terminated. If the student successfully completes the course, he/she is awarded a Certificate of Completion.

Although the cost of preservice training is minimal in one sense, it is costly in another. The cost of the course is minimal, but if you employ the individual, issue equipment and uniforms, and then send him/her to the preservice training, the cost is exorbitant. The time the employee spends in the preservice training is nonproductive as far as the work relationship is concerned. If he/she does not successfully complete the training, then you do not get any return for the money invested.

The security administrator may require, as a condition for employment, that the prospective security guard purchase his/her own equipment and uniform and enroll in and complete the course. Upon successful completion of the course there would be an agreement to hire the individual and reimburse for the cost of the equipment and uniform and the registration fee. In order to protect both parties, this agreement would have to be in writing. This would also mean that a background investigation would have to be completed prior to the individual's purchasing equipment and a uniform and enrolling in the class. You would not agree to hire an individual if he/she did not meet all the licensing requirements.

Preservice training for unarmed security guards is not cost productive and should not be considered.

In-Service Training. In-service training for security guards should be continuous, consistent, and kept simple. In-service training can be costly depending on how elaborate it is. A good security administrator will develop a program wherein the cost is minimized and the training is maximized.

If a security guard is working a stationary post, it is relatively easy to orient him/her to the duties and responsibilities of that post, especially if it is to be a permanent assignment. A good security administrator knows, though, that assigning a guard to a permanent stationary post can be counter-productive since the guard can become sedentary in the manner he/she carries out the duties and responsibilities of the post.

Training should be approached with the idea that each guard should be thoroughly familiar with the duties and responsibilities of every post. In addition, the guard should be trained in emergency and disaster procedures; i.e., fires, earthquakes, floods, hurricanes, tornadoes, bomb threats, evacuation procedures, reporting, report-writing, public relations, telephone demeanor, etc.

The training can consist of formal lectures, roll-call briefings, role-playing situations, films, slides, question-and-answer sessions, etc.

Once the training program has been developed, instructors must be selected. The partial success of any training program lies with the instructor. A good instructor should possess a combination of the following characteristics and skills.

1. The desire and interest to be an instructor.
2. A genuine interest in people.
3. Knowledge of the subject matter or the ability to gain the knowledge.
4. Good verbal and written communication skills.
5. A friendly and inquiring attitude.
6. Patience.

Many security administrators will delegate the authority for training to a supervisor primarily because one of a supervisor's responsibility is to train subordinates. I would caution you if you do this. If the supervisor does not possess the previously enumerated characteristics and skills, there is a high probability that the in-service training program will not be one of substance and therefore will not be successful.

CONCLUSION

The intent of this chapter was to increase the awareness of security administrators to the potential for vicarious liability suits. Nine out of ten vicarious liability suits would be unnecessary and unsuccessful if the security administrator would take the necessary time to deal properly with and avoid the five specific areas of vicarious liability; i.e., negligent hiring, negligent retention, negligent assignment, negligent supervision, and negligent training. Of these five areas, negligent training is the one area where the security administrator is most susceptible. The cost of a good preservice training program for armed guards and a good, in-depth, consistent, continuous in-service training program for all guards produces benefits that far surpass the disastrous effects of a successful vicarious liability suit.

VII. ART THEFT AND INVESTIGATION

28. Interpol Symposium on Thefts of Works of Art and Cultural Property

The I.C.P.O.-INTERPOL's First International Symposium on Thefts of Works of Art and Cultural Property opened at the Organization's Headquarters at 9:30 A.M. on June 14, 1977.

The SECRETARY GENERAL welcomed the participants, observers, and experts and indicated in his opening address that thefts of works of art and cultural property were of considerable concern to the police throughout the world. He recalled that INTERPOL had been one of the first to recognize the problem and to work toward a solution. As early as 1959, the General Secretariat had made a study of the protection of museums against theft; since that time, the Organization had been providing assistance in recovering stolen property, in conducting investigations, and in arresting offenders.

It was then decided that a representative of the General Secretariat should chair the Symposium, and the draft agenda was adopted unanimously.

This chapter is based upon the minutes from the *First International Symposium on Thefts of Works of Art and Cultural Property* held in Saint-Cloud, France, June 14-16, 1977. The symposium was sponsored by International Criminal Police Organization–Interpol, Paris. The minutes are reprinted here with permission of the United States Department of Justice, National Central Bureau–Interpol, Washington, D.C.

STUDY OF THE THEFTS THEMSELVES

Types of Objects Stolen; Places Where
These Thefts Are Committed; Volume of Such Thefts

The term "cultural property" is defined in Article 1 of the Convention on the Means of Prohibiting and Preventing the Illicit Import, Export and Transfer of Ownership of Cultural Property (Cf. Appendix 28.1) adopted by the UNESCO General Conference in Paris on November 14, 1970. The Symposium's participants sought to determine those types of objects most often stolen.

In the PHILIPPINES, there are very diverse types of cultural property. Recent archaeological digs indicate that the islands were inhabited as far back as 500,000 years ago. The Islamic and Christian religions have left very important cultural remains on the islands, whose coastlines facilitate smuggling operations. Local police and National Research Bureau records indicate that statues, several hundred manuscripts, Ming vases, and other antiques have been stolen.

In INDIA, about 75 percent of such thefts involve property stolen from temples. Medals, jewelry, sculpted or engraved bricks and tiles, statues, porticos, etc., have been stolen. Items seized by the customs authorities have included paintings, sculptures, miniatures, clocks, porcelain objects, coins, and rare manuscripts.

In ITALY, thefts of paintings are predominant, followed by thefts of sculptures, objects from archaeological digs, coins, etc. The thefts occur most often from churches, followed by private homes, local and national museums and archaeological digs. Statistically, such thefts increased in number each year until 1975, when there were 758 thefts involving 17,313 objects; the comparable figures for 1976 showed a drop (557 and 6,794, respectively).

In PORTUGAL, thefts of works of art and cultural property have not assumed alarming proportions over the past three years. The few thefts from museums and public places which have occurred were due in each case to inadequate security measures. One noteworthy case involved an Angolan statue stolen from a Lisbon museum; one part of it was later recovered in Amsterdam, the other in Brussels.

In FRANCE, the number of stolen paintings (oils, gouaches, watercolors, drawings, pastels) recorded in selected past years has increased as follows:

- 1,261 works stolen in 1970;
- 2,712 works stolen in 1972;
- 3,750 works stolen in 1975;
- 3,040 works stolen in 1976.

A French Delegate also mentioned several thefts of well-known paintings committed since 1961, the most recent being the theft of 118 Picasso paintings from the Papal Palace in Avignon on December 30, 1975. In 1976, the French authorities recorded 389 thefts from churches (as opposed to 227 in 1970), 166 thefts from castles, country houses, etc. (112 in 1970), 124 thefts from museums (37 in 1970), and 256 thefts from art galleries (69 in 1973).

In SPAIN, many thefts are committed from churches and various other places of worship in isolated areas. A Spanish Delegate described the theft of an altar-piece and of books of engravings. Thefts are also committed from public archives and libraries.

In GREECE, thefts of Byzantine-era religious works are most prevalent. Tourists have been known to steal small items, paintings, and rare books from places where it is difficult to ensure security.

In the NETHERLANDS, thefts are committed mostly from private homes and museums, particularly since September 1973. A Netherlands Delegate reported that porcelain items had been stolen from Delft Museum in April 1975; in the eighteen months prior to the Symposium, there had been fifty-seven thefts from public buildings. There had been 900 thefts from private homes in 1976 and 300 during the first five months of 1977. He pointed out that churches in the Netherlands were more austere and had fewer works of art on display than churches in certain other countries.

In INDONESIA, many antiquities are stolen, particularly items from unlawful digs.

In CANADA, there have been many thefts from public archives and libraries; in some cases, pages have been cut out of rare books or very old illustrated collections. A Canadian Delegate said that it was difficult to ensure continuous surveillance and to detect thefts in establishments open to the public twenty-four hours a day, seven days a week.

In the UNITED KINGDOM, the Metropolitan Police's special Art and Antique Squad (covering the London area) recorded 890 cases in 1975, 1,039 cases in 1976, and 822 cases for the first five months of 1977, involving losses of about 2,500,000 pounds sterling.

In UPPER VOLTA, cultural property (masks, altar-pieces) is stolen from shrines, sanctuaries, and royal tombs.

An IRAQI Delegate pointed out that considerable cultural property had been discovered in Iraq during digs made in the nineteenth and twentieth-century colonial period; he read out a list of such objects currently in the possession of museums in other countries.

The UPPER VOLTA, LIBYAN, and SYRIAN Delegates reported similar situations as far as their countries were concerned (cf. also section VI-b).

Consequences of the Thefts

The consequences of such thefts are felt to be primarily of a cultural nature, in that places of worship and archaeological sites are robbed and objects of very great value are damaged.

Moreover, organizing exhibitions of works of art and cultural property becomes complicated because of the dangers involved, and exhibitors are sometimes reluctant to put such items on display, thus contributing to scientific as well as cultural deprivation.

Criminologically, the profits to be made on the fraudulent market in works of art entice criminals to expand their operations, thus creating new problems for the police. Private individuals or groups and public authorities in possession of works of art are consequently forced to spend large amounts of money for security purposes. Moreover, legitimate art dealers and museum curators find themselves in a very embarrassing situation upon learning that they might be in possession of works of art of dubious origins.

The Symposium placed considerable emphasis on the need to make national authorities and international organizations aware of the magnitude of the problem.

Modus Operandi — Thieves

In FRANCE, there are a number of offenders specializing in thefts of works of art who have contacts among secondhand and antique dealers. The offenders in question may specialize in such thefts for only limited periods of time. In addition, there are other offenders who, while habitually committing other offences, may decide to burgle churches or museums. Moreover, some thieves commit burglaries with the intention of stealing whatever they might find on the premises, and this stolen property may well include works of art. Generally, the modi operandi are those normally used in cases of theft. Recently, however, the use of violence has been noted (this observation was confirmed by several delegations). There are no indications that commissioned thefts are committed by highly structured and organized gangs. There was one case in which an antique dealer masterminded a theft committed by a team of secondhand dealers and gypsies; another case involved someone who photographed works of art to be stolen for specific individuals on request.

In CANADA, professional offenders from organized crime circles have begun to take an interest in stealing works of art.

In INDONESIA, the usual modi operandi (breaking and entering, etc.) are followed. Private residences are often burgled during their occupants' absence, especially during vacation periods. Occasional use of violence has been noted. Such offenses are usually committed by specialists who know the value of the property in question.

In INDIA, there have been commissioned thefts, carried out after the prospective purchaser has chosen the items on the basis of photographs. Some thieves are more interested in the value of the metal in the objects stolen; copper, for example, is very highly prized in India. There have also been cases where monuments have been dismembered; sometimes the stolen parts are replaced by copies. This happens especially with statues from which the heads are stolen.

In ITALY, there are very few offenders who really specialize in the theft of works of art and cultural property. On the other hand, there are many thieves who steal whatever they might find of interest on the premises and, because of their ignorance of the true value of such objects, they take few if any precautions against damaging them; very often such items do indeed suffer damage.

In BELGIUM, thefts committed for the purpose of stealing anything of value found on the premises occur mostly at weekend or holiday homes, etc.

In UPPER VOLTA, thefts of cultural property (masks, altar-pieces) are committed mainly by foreigners; nationals of Upper Volta generally refrain from stealing sacred objects. Complaints of theft are rarely lodged with the authorities; such thefts are discovered most often during customs checks at ports and airports.

In PORTUGAL, there was a case in which thieves attacked a museum guard and stole a precious eighteenth-century crown. In another case, thieves broke through a museum wall.

In SPAIN, such offenses are often committed by gypsies who, because of their nomadic way of life, have a thorough knowledge of the countryside and the churches, castles, and country houses containing works of art. They usually operate by breaking and entering or by scaling walls and seem to be well equipped to commit these offenses. They are sometimes granted access to such premises by domestic employees. In several cases, paintings were cut from their frames and stolen.

In GREECE, thefts of religious works of art are committed by offenders acting alone.

In IRAQ, some thefts of works of art have reportedly been committed by specialists.

RECEIVING AND TRAFFICKING — DESTINATION OF THE STOLEN ARTICLES

Receivers: The Illicit Market

In BELGUIM, there are three categories of receivers: (1) receivers specializing in works of art of great value; (2) professional dealers such as antique and secondhand dealers who specialize in disposing of low- and medium-value works of art in local markets where there is little effective sales control; (3) amateurs, who usually operate in the same markets as the professional dealers in category 2.

In ITALY, art thieves do not normally operate directly on behalf of receivers but they are aware of the market situation and of where stolen works of art can be trafficked, either in Italy or abroad. The thieves sometimes put only a few of the stolen items on the illicit market, keeping the rest of them temporarily hidden away.

In the PHILIPPINES, many stolen works of art have been found in antique shops.

Mr. Jean CAILLEUX, President of C.I.N.O.A. (International Confederation of Art Dealers), who had been invited to attend the Symposium in his expert capacity, stressed how difficult it was for professional art dealers to check on the origins of works of art, of which there were so many. He also spoke of the problems encountered when stolen works of art changed hands several times and were finally found in the possession of persons who had purchased them in good faith. He pointed out, however, that whether the purchasers were art dealers, musuem curators, art collectors, or simply lovers of good art, it would be unwise for them not to question the origin of each work of art, especially when the price asked for it seemed too low. He further noted that art dealers in some countries (for example, France, Italy, and Belgium) were obliged by law to verify the identity of each person from whom they intended to buy any work of art.

However, a French Delegate pointed out that, in practice, this obligation was sometimes overlooked or only partially complied with.

In SPAIN, every art dealer has to keep a record of every transaction involving a work of art; within forty-eight hours, he must record the transaction number and a description of each work of art in a ledger. A Spanish Delegate said he felt it would be useful to record more information, especially concerning the persons involved in the transaction — for example, the identity information appearing in their passports, etc. He also pointed out that, because the supply of works of art and antiques was limited, dealers who wanted to build up their stocks were sometimes prepared to buy such property from persons who did not always offer the desired guarantees. Moreover, buyers with sufficient funds available often paid too little attention to determining the origins of paintings offered to them. Finally, the gypsies mentioned earlier often had contacts with certain unscrupulous middlemen, and some thieves themselves became antique dealers and were thus in a very good position to sell the stolen works of art.

In the NETHERLANDS, it has been noted that a gang specializing in stealing antiques takes the stolen articles to salesrooms very soon after the thefts are committed, this has proved a very effective way of disposing of the stolen property.

In INDONESIA, stolen objects from archaeological digs are sold to collectors, but also to persons who consider them to be good-luck charms. Fraudulent transactions involving such objects are extremely difficult to investigate since they usually take place between antique dealers and clients who know one another.

An Observer from the INTERNATIONAL COUNCIL OF MUSEUMS (ICOM) pointed out that thieves could refrain from disposing of the stolen goods until the time limit for prosecution (which varied from country to country) had expired.

The SENEGALESE Delegate brought up the important topic of "certificates of authenticity" accompanying certain paintings.

Mr. CAILLEUX replied that his was one of the thornier problems confronting the art world. The current trend was for art dealers to offer certificates of authenticity in place of their own professional guarantees; this practice enabled responsibility to be transferred elsewhere.

It was reported that, in 1970, ICOM had devised a twenty-point "Ethical Acquisition Code" for museums, including:

1. *Ethical rules,* particularly stressing that no acquisition should be made without full documentation of the object's origins. This guideline had been adopted immediately by national museums but its adoption by other museums was taking longer, because they were independently operated.

2. *Practical proposals for museums' professional staffs:* Museum professionals were usually well placed to determine whether or not the items had been stolen. In addition, ICOM stressed the need for more cooperation among the various countries in defining what constituted their respective cultural property and in restoring stolen items to their rightful owners, even if no requests to that effect had been made by the victims.

Several delegations indicated that it was extremely difficult to dispose of stolen works of art that were world-famous.

The ITALIAN Delegate said that thieves often stole such works of art with a view to obtaining a ransom.

In FRANCE, receivers reportedly pay theives about 10 percent of the true value of works of art of medium importance, especially paintings and tapestries; then, through unscrupulous intermediaries, they get in touch with buyers and offer them the works in question at more or less normal prices, while being willing always to lower the prices to help entice the clients to buy the items. Also, stolen works of art can change hands several times, thus obscuring the fact that they are stolen, so that the final purchasers have no reason to suspect anything.

International Traffic

In view of the large number of stolen works of art that are not subsequently recovered, it is difficult to establish precisely how great the international trafficking volume is or what the trafficking trends are. However, most of the participants considered that many stolen works of art and items of cultural property are disposed of in countries other than those in which they are stolen.

Thieves and traffickers are obviously well advised to put as much distance as possible between the victims and the prospective buyers; moreover, there are countries where the demand for works of art is high because of the financial resources of the inhabitants and the traditional importance of certain art markets; and there are of course numerous less economically developed countries with considerable cultural wealth (paintings, statues, religious objects, antiques, etc.) which constantly tempt traffickers.

The ITALIAN Delegate reported that it was mainly works of medium value which were fraudulently exported from Italy to countries where prospective buyers were numerous, such as the United Kingdom, Federal Germany, Switzerland, and the United States. Organized crime rings with international operations involving other types of offenses had become interested in trafficking in stolen works of art as soon as it was realized that this could be profitable. Specialized thieves had then begun to avail themselves of these established connections, and individual offenders had begun to do likewise around 1975.

In the UNITED STATES, art markets are quite flourishing businesses; this fact naturally leads to the smuggling of stolen works of art into the country.

In IRAQ, it is believed that professionals control the trafficking of works of art to other countries.

In INDONESIA, there is an undercurrent of fraudulent exportation that is very difficult to check. The items are smuggled out of the country by post, in accompanied luggage, and sometimes even in diplomatic bags.

In UPPER VOLTA, tribal masks and objects from sanctuaries and tombs are stolen for export.

A FRENCH Delegate cited several cases in which works of art had been exported almost immediately after they had been stolen. He confirmed that in certain countries, there was considerable demand for specific types of objects, especially from archaeological digs and places of worship.

In the PHILIPPINES, the authorities believe that many items of cultural property are fraudulently exported from the country.

The Observor from the CUSTOMS COOPERATION COUNCIL and several Delegates pointed out that the volume of international trade and the openness of many national borders made international traffic in such items much easier.

ACTION OF THE POLICE AND THE MEANS AT THEIR DISPOSAL AT NATIONAL LEVEL

Creation of Special Departments or National Offices

Because the UNITED KINGDOM is one of the world's major art markets, New Scotland Yard set up an Art and Antique Squad in 1960. Originally functioning with only one officer, it now has a staff of fourteen police officers and three civilians. New Scotland Yard's jurisdiction extends only over the London area, but the Squad works closely with other police forces throughout the country; it has also had considerable success in working with police forces abroad. In 1976, thirty-one people were arrested and about 250,000 pounds' worth of stolen cultural property was recovered. In the first five months of 1977, twenty-two arrests were made and works of art worth a total of about 100,000 pounds were recovered.

In FRANCE, an *Office Central pour la Répression du Vol d'Oeuvres et d'Objets d'Art* (Central Bureau to combat thefts of works of art) was set up at the Ministry of the Interior in 1975. Its staff currently consists of thirty officers. In collaboration with other government departments *(Secrétariat d'Etat à la Culture, Direction Centrale de la Sécurité Publique, Direction de la Gendarmerie),* it studies measures for protecting works of art against theft. It is responsible for initiating and coordinating investigations of thefts of works of art and prosecution of the offenders throughout the national territory. Through INTERPOL, it has searches for stolen works of art and their thieves made in other countries.

In ITALY, three departments *(Pubblica Sicurezza, Guardia di Finanza* and *Carabinieri)* work together on cases involving stolen works of art. Since early 1975 there has been a special national police squad of sixty specialists attached to the Ministry of Cultural Property working in cooperation with various experts. The *Guardia di Finanza* ensures liaison with the customs service, and the Italian INTERPOL National Central Bureau, which has had a special file on stolen works of art since 1970, is responsible for relations with services in other countries.

In INDIA, thefts of works of art were not a serious problem prior to 1972. Toward the end of 1973, the authorities became aware of the need to set up a special service in each state and a central office at national level.

In INDONESIA, there is a special department for protection of the country's historical and archaeological heritage.

In the UNITED STATES, there is a highly specialized service in New York, but it has only a small staff. In cooperation with other police forces and art experts, it assists with investigations.

In PORTUGAL, there is no national office or department specializing in cases involving thefts of works of art. The most important cases are handled by the squad dealing with aggravated theft. However, a bill is currently under study regarding the reorganization of the criminal investigation department; in the new system, the INTERPOL National Central Bureau would be responsible for centralizing information on stolen works of art.

In SPAIN, there is a small national service that keeps a special file and circulates information about stolen works of art.

In DENMARK, a special group of police, customs, and museum officials is currently being set up to deal with the problem.

In SENEGAL, no such special department or service has been set up;

however, the holding of an African Arts Festival there, scheduled for the near future, may raise security problems that will induce the Senegalese authorities to give more serious consideration to the matter.

The other countries represented at the Symposium currently have no such special departments or services; cases involving stolen works of art and cultural property are handled by police officers who usually deal with thefts and burglaries. In all cases where it is indispensable, police officers request assistance from art experts. It is also very common for them to work closely with officials of the appropriate government ministries and museums in their respective countries. In all the countries in question, the INTERPOL National Central Bureaus are alerted to cases of major importance likely to have international ramifications; in such cases, the NCBs act as centralizing agencies.

As INDIAN and UNITED KINGDOM Delegates pointed out, training police officers to handle cases involving stolen works of art and cultural property, is not designed to make real art experts of them.

Generally speaking, it seems that special departments or services are set up in countries directly concerned with thefts of works of art and cultural property, especially those in which there are active markets in such articles.

An observer from ICOM reported the existence of a major documentation center in Paris, which could be used by interested police services and by the INTERPOL General Secretariat.

Centralization of Information

In CANADA, electronic data processing has been used since 1975 for classifying and storing data on collections of works of art. The system can of course be consulted by interested police services in Canada and access to the data could be granted to services outside Canada, which would be of great help. To accomplish this, compatible systems would have to be set up and appropriate security precautions taken, since the possibility of certain criminals acquiring access to the system should not be ruled out; maximum precautions would therefore have to be taken.

In SPAIN, there is a file on works of art (paintings, sculptures reredos, religious objects, and various items such as furniture, lamps, etc.). Data on stolen property that is subsequently recovered are also kept on file.

In the UNITED KINGDOM, there used to be manual files like those maintained by many police forces, but they proved to be unwieldly for investigation purposes. Moreover, investigations were hindered by the fact that many of the stolen items were not adequately identified òr described; often the victims themselves were unable to provide essential details. In 1974, an electronic data processing system was set up; it currently contains data on about 7,000 stolen works of art. In 1976, the computer was consulted 1,400 times, resulting in 275 identifications. In this computerized system, the subject of each painting is recorded as a series of letters and numbers. Two major precautions are taken to prevent unauthorized access to the data: (1) the code used is secret; (2) access to the computer is announced beforehand by telephone. To obtain data to be fed into the computer, a nine-point reporting form is supplied to all police forces in the United Kingdom.

An OBSERVER from ICOM stressed the need for the various computerized systems to be compatible, pointing out that such compatibility did not always exist within a given country, let alone internationally. Moreover, it would be desirable for the police to have unimpeded access to computers used to record data about collections of works of art. Referring to a meeting, held in Spain in October 1976, of the special UNESCO commission on museum collection inventories, the ICOM Observer expressed the desire that INTERPOL should participate in such activities in the future.

A FRENCH Delegate reported that the *Office Central* used the national police computer, which stored information on all stolen property, including stolen works of art. There was also a two-part manual file: one part contained identity information on various persons (victims, artists, art dealers), the other technical data about the objects themselves and the thefts.

A poll of the delegates revealed that, in each country represented — even those with no special services or departments — there were centralized files, either manual or computerized, in which information on stolen works of art was recorded, together with data on other stolen property.

Methods of Identifying Objects

Mr. CAILLEUX stressed the importance — for art experts as well as the police — of having detailed descriptions of stolen works of art. Often the victims themselves are unable to supply the necessary details, and the inventories drawn up for some museums, churches, and public monuments often do not contain adequate descriptions of the inventoried items. In other cases, investigators fail to ask the appropriate questions to obtain the information they need. Consequently, many stolen property notices are much too vague to permit positive identification. For this reason, in recent years some professional bodies have been forced to sort through the notices supplied by the police and to publicize only those thefts where there is sufficient information for positive identification of the stolen property.

The most practical way of identifying works of art is through photographs; all possessors of valuable works of art are therefore strongly advised to take the precaution of having photographs of them taken, even if only with ordinary cameras.

Photographs, however, cannot replace normal descriptions; they can only complement them. The materials used, the technique, the size, and other specific details should also be known; many works of art, moreover, have "special features" which should also be pointed out. Describing sculptures involves even greater problems than those encountered in the case of paintings.

For practical purposes, different types of objects should be classified in different categories. The French National Association of Antique Dealers, for example, uses a classification system with the following categories: silver, gold, jewelry; autographs, documents, books, manuscripts; bronzes; drawings, engravings, paintings, etc.; furniture; objects from archaeological digs; clocks and watches; sculptures; tapestries and carpets.

Circulation of lists of objects and their corresponding file cards bearing easily codable data on each object might well be a good idea. Some art documentation centers systematically file information on all such objects; for paintings, this might include such indications as subject painted widthwise (or lengthwise), country scene with river, mountain scene, religious subject with two figures, etc.

Also according to Mr. CAILLEUX, the descriptions intended for police use — which may be based on descriptions prepared by museums — should contain only the information necessary for identifying the work in question and should not contain extraneous information (for example, information of interest primarily to art historians.)

It is noteworthy that insurance companies are tending more and more to require that their clients provide them with precise descriptions of works of art to be insured. Their associations are reported to be contemplating recommending to their members not to pay an insurance compensation in connection with works of art without first obtaining from the insured owner a full description and a photograph of the work in question.

Mr. CAILLEUX concluded his remarks by noting that police departments and services could count on obtaining whatever cooperation they needed from professional art dealers and experts in compiling art work descriptions in connection with investigations and recovery of stolen works of art and cultural property.

A BELGIAN Delegate then advocated that data should be circulated systematically, and agreed that better descriptions should be given of the works in question. He belived that a certain standardization could be achieved, which would make notices of stolen works of art and cultural property understood and interpreted in the same way by all concerned.

INDIA's 1972 law on works of art and cultural property has spurred development of an improved method for photographing such items.

A FRENCH Delegate reported that, in France, the police often received reports of thefts of objects of dubious artistic value. He believed it would be a good idea to *screen such reports* and only send the professional associations information on particularly serious cases. The main thing was to have *very* precise *identifying descriptions* of allegedly stolen works of art, especially when *measures* of conservation (such as seizure, etc.) had to be taken in connection with them. Moreover, such information should be made available *as soon as possible* after the theft occurred.

In TUNISIA, descriptions of stolen property are usually quite precise. The police computer has proved to be of great help in filling and storing pertinent data.

In SPAIN, the collected data on stolen property sometimes prove to be insufficient, and it would be helpful if photographs of the items in question were available more often.

The ITALIAN Delegate felt that the most important element was the speed with which the police took action. Information reaching the police was sometimes sketchy but nonetheless required that immediate action be taken. The INTERPOL National Central Bureau in Rome had a manual file on stolen property and thieves; information was circulated immediately, using the national police computer. To ensure accuracy in the identification of stolen works of art, assistance was required from experts at the Ministry of Cultural Property. The existence of special services had resulted in more effective and rapid police intervention, which was most useful when measures of conservation had to be taken.

The latter point was also stressed by several other delegates.

An INDIAN Delegate said that, in his opinion, the main problem was that of identifying stolen objects and adequate identifying details had to be obtained from the victims themselves. Stolen objects should be so conclusively identified that the courts would be convinced that the objects recovered were indeed those reported stolen. Objects of value should therefore be marked (for example, with indelible ink) at points on the objects known only to their owners. In 1975, the theft of a life-sized bronze statue of a human figure had been reported to the police, but the description given had been so vague as to make police enquiries difficult; however, it had been learned from a confidential source that the whites of the statue's eyes were silver-gilt, and the police had been able to positively identify the stolen statue.

Circulation of Information on Stolen Works of Art

In INDIA, the Central Investigation Bureau publishes a monthly bulletin on stolen works of art and circulates it to all border posts, to the Department of Archaeology, and to all police services. If necessary the mass media are used. When stolen works of art are recovered and returned to their owners, cancellation notices are published in the monthly bulletin.

In the UNITED KINGDOM, as many police departments and cultural bodies as possible are advised of major art thefts. For thefts of works of lesser historical and cultural value, Scotland Yard publishes a monthly summary and circulates it to police stations in the London area and to the dealers' association, the auctioneers' association, the British Museum, and the airport and seaport police. The information is also given to various publications, together with the telephone number of the police. If necessary, it is broadcast on radio and television. Cancellations are a problem because the services concerned are not always informed when stolen articles are recovered, or are informed only after considerable time has elapsed. Scotland Yard periodically sends a form letter out to the notified services to ask them if the stolen property has been found.

In FEDERAL GERMANY, police forces and art dealers are informed of thefts of works of art through notices in the daily bulletin published by the criminal investigation department and in a special arts magazine.

In the NETHERLANDS, notices of stolen works of art are circulated by telex and, together with photographs of the works, are published in the police gazette. Such notices are published in newspapers only upon request by the victims, who are responsible for paying the costs involved.

In INDONESIA, the police receiving the theft complaint first conduct a local investigation; if this proves fruitless, they then contact the Department of History and Archaeology to obtain photographs and further information about the stolen work. This information is then circulated to the appropriate services, including the customs service. Such thefts are often reported in the newspapers, with follow-up items when the stolen property is recovered.

In CANADA, such notices are published in professional journals. In addition, stolen works of art are recorded in a two-part register; part one contains information on such thefts occurring before 1975 and part two details thefts that have occurred since that time. Cancellation notices are also noted in the register.

In TUNISIA, the mass media are used only in certain specific cases. The Ministry of the Interior and the customs service are informed of such thefts.

In ITALY, the regional services report theft data to a central service. Police and customs services and museums are kept informed through a computer-based system of daily publications. The Italian Delegate stressed the importance of circulating cancellation notices without delay, especially because of the problems that might arise if the police were to take action in connection with a stolen work of art which had already been recovered.

A Delegate from UPPER VOLTA reported that, in his country, notices concerning stolen works of art and cultural property were circulated with the help of the news services.

Collection and Circulation of Information on Thieves, Receivers, and Traffickers

In the PHILIPPINES, the Central Investigation Bureau has a file on art thieves and traffickers. Investigators and magistrates may avail themselves of the bureau's services for general information that might be of use to them in their investigations. A computerized system is currently being introduced.

In the NETHERLANDS, local police departments are responsible for maintaining files on art thieves; the country's central file contains information on recidivists.

In INDIA, such information is computerized. Data on persons implicated in cases involving thefts of cultural property are circulated to all the services concerned, including the Department of Archaeology. This list is consulted by the Department when issuing antique dealer licenses.

In the UNITED KINGDOM, Scotland Yard maintains a file, in cooperation with the airport and seaport police, in which the movements of certain types of art dealers are recorded. There is also a special file on door-to-door salesmen.

In FRANCE, there is no national-level file specifically on art thieves; however, the *Office Central* keeps the names of art smugglers and traffickers on file. A French Delegate felt that it would be extremely valuable if a list of habitual thieves could be drawn up; this would be of considerable interest to several countries.

In SPAIN, there is a special national-level file on art thieves and data pertaining to such offenders is sent to all the police departments throughout the country. For particularly interesting art thefts a report is drawn up, giving the names of the offenders and the suspected whereabouts, their modus operandi, the motor vehicles used, etc.

In INDONESIA, there is a file on habitual thieves, receivers, and traffickers.

In GREECE, a central service maintains a file on arrested or convicted individuals and on all persons who have violated the laws on trafficking in works of art. Details of the offenders' modi operandi are circulated to all the appropriate police services.

In FRANCE, the *Office Central* has sent out a circular asking local services to furnish information (including photographs and fingerprints) on persons engaging in stealing and trafficking in cultural property. The collected information will be used for publishing general warning notices.

Cooperation with Customs Services

In the UNITED STATES, the customs services are particularly aware of the problems of illegal traffic in works of art; they regularly exchange pertinent information with the other United States and foreign services concerned. Federal laws and customs regulations will soon be amended to facilitate development of international cooperation, which is indispensable. It is essential to exchange information on suspected offenders and photographs of the suspects and the stolen items, and to provide full information on smuggling operations across United States borders. Some cultural property can be prohibited from entry into the United States if there is an agreement with the country of origin (for example, prohibited importation of ivory from certain African countries). A federal law specifically prohibits the importation of South American pre-Columbian works into the United States without official authorization; this law has proved an effective customs law-enforcement instrument.

In GREECE, the police cooperate closely with the customs services, to which bulletins on suspects are regularly circulated.

In INDONESIA, works of art cannot be exported without authorization from the Government's Archaeological Service. Cooperation with the customs services is excellent.

In the PHILIPPINES, the customs services watch out for illegal exportation of cultural property.

In INDIA, such cooperation is also excellent, especially with the Department of Archaeology. An archeologist is stationed at every port of entry to check works of art being exported. Under Indian law, committees stationed at border posts may grant authorization to export various items, such as those less than 100 years old (less than seventy-five years old in the case of manuscripts) and not considered to be antiquities.

The Delegates at the Symposium agreed that, overall, cooperation between the police and the customs services was satisfactory as far as the circulation of information was concerned (cf. also General Secretariat circular No. 602/RELCO/950 of December 18, 1975, on police/customs cooperation).

Cooperation with Public Bodies;
Cooperation with the Professions Concerned

An ICOM OBSERVER expressed satisfaction with the excellent cooperative working relationship which his council enjoyed with INTERPOL and with police services in general.

The UNESCO OBSERVER stressed the importance of developing cooperative working relationships with various services, for it was essential that pertinent information be circulated satisfactorily to all concerned. She reported that UNESCO received information from various sources: a UNESCO national commission was attached to the Ministry of Cultural Affairs or similar government department in each member state. UNESCO also received official government reports.

In LIBYA, cooperation is developing satisfactorily.

In INDONESIA, cooperation with the Ministry of Finance and Trade is very good.

In FRANCE, cooperation with museums is called for in the directive which created the *Office Central;* it would be desirable for similar cooperation to develop between the police and the professional art world, on a reciprocal basis.

In the UNITED KINGDOM, there is very good cooperation with sales-rooms, museums, and galleries, whose security directors are often former policemen. In addition, specialized police officers take brief training courses at certain galleries, thus affording them the opportunity to make very useful contacts among art experts.

In SPAIN, the Madrid and Barcelona art dealers' associations are furnished with information on thefts of cultural property.

In FEDERAL GERMANY and in the UNITED KINGDOM art galleries report suspect items to the police.

In the PHILIPPINES, the police have a very close working relationship with religious authorities in cases involving theft of religious art objects.

Mr. CAILLEUX pointed out that professional art dealers could cooperate with the police, notably by making their technical expertise available to them. Art dealers also assisted in circulating information about thefts of works of art and cultural property, either through their various publications or through telephone "hot-line" alert systems organized among themselves.

INTERNATIONAL COOPERATION

Role of the I.C.P.O.-INTERPOL General Secretariat

The CHAIRMAN outlined the procedures for international cooperation through INTERPOL. He reminded the meeting that the General Secretariat had recently sent out a list of persons arrested for theft of cultural property and asked if the list was in fact useful to the various police services.

A CANADIAN Delegate said that the list was useful, but asked that future lists of this type be as selective as possible. The BELGIAN, NETHERLANDS, and FRENCH Delegates seconded the request.

The UNITED KINGDOM and SPANISH Delegates drew attention to the necessity of knowing the legal outcome of cases involving offenders arrested for such offences.

The CHAIRMAN suggested to the Delegates that the following proposal be submitted to the forthcoming General Assembly: "The First International Symposium on Thefts of Works of Art and Cultural Property expressed the wish that the INTERPOL General Secretariat study the possibility of pub-lishing a guide for use by police officers when collecting precise identifying descriptive data on stolen works of art and cultural property, particularly from the victims of such thefts. The symposium also felt that it would be useful to revise the AR 1 reporting form to include more detailed guidelines for iden-tifying and describing such objects."

The delegates unanimously accepted this proposal.

The BELGIAN Delegate suggested that the General Secretariat should also continue to organize working meetings of investigators from different countries handling the same cases, such as the meeting that had been held in connection with investigations into a gang of criminals specializing in stealing works of art from churches and castles in France, Belgium, Luxembourg, and Federal Germany.

The CHAIRMAN said that the General Secretariat was quite prepared to organize such meetings whenever the National Central Bureaus requested them.

PREVENTION

Security Measures

In CANADA, electronic security systems are used and have proved very effective and relatively economical, in comparison to the cost of using guards. Television cameras that automatically adjust to the light conditions are used in museums; they are hooked up to videotape recorders in some cases. They can be programmed to scan a given area and can be used either automatically or manually, for either continuous surveillance or spot-checks, and can operate at various speeds. Through such systems, excellent evidence can be obtained for presentation in court. Visible cameras are used as deterrents while other cameras are used at entrances to aid in identifying persons entering the premises (through electronic reading of special entry cards). Guards are employed both as guides and as security agents responsible for apprehending offenders in cases of irregularity.

In INDIA, modern security devices are considered valuable for museums, but, for security at various sites and monuments, different measures are needed. Mainly traditional crime prevention measures are taken, coupled with attempts to increase personnel strength (police and security guards) — there are about 400 monuments to protect. The results of following this policy seem to be good, since the number of thefts has decreased annually since 1974, when there were 584: in 1975 there were 462 and in 1976, 381.

In ITALY, a "Security Commission" has been set up in accordance with a Ministry of Cultural Property directive of January 3, 1976. The Commission is responsible for working in close cooperation with UNESCO, ICOM, and other specialized bodies, to draw up a program for fighting vandalism and thefts of works of art and cultural property. The Commission's membership includes senior officials of the Italian Police, the Ministries of Cultural Property and Justice, and the Italian universities, as well as technical experts. It has decided to undertake national and international projects and plans to study protection techniques, security guard training, public awareness programs, and coordination of police and Ministry of Cultural Property action taken to identify and recover stolen works of art. Because of better security organization, the number of thefts from national museums has dropped.

In the NETHERLANDS, the government has not yet issued any general directives on prevention, but a committee within the Ministry of Cultural Affairs, Recreation and Social Welfare is currently studying the matter. Meanwhile, progress is being made in developing security measures for protecting private residences. The independent museums in the country use various security systems, but attempts are currently being made to ensure greater standardization.

In the UNITED KINGDOM, security is sometimes compromised by the costs of the systems used and by public indifference. The police are well aware of the fact that art thefts must be prevented and that protection measures must be studied on the basis of experience acquired in handling actual cases. Police crime prevention officers offer free advice to art dealers and individual owners of works of art.

In CANADA, an effective and inexpensive program entitled "Operation Identification" has been inaugurated to prevent thefts from private residences. Under this program, private citizens and dealers are encouraged to mark their possessions with an identifying number, using an electric engraving pencil available from the police stations; they are encouraged to mark not only their works of art, but all their valuable property. The numbers used may be either their social security numbers or their motor vehicle registration numbers. These are then registered with the police and stored in the police computer data bank. In addition, an "Operation Identification" sticker is affixed to the door of every house and shop participating in the program. This essentially dissuasive program also enables the police easily to identify the owners of recovered stolen property. This system is based on the one instituted in Monterey, California, United States, in 1963. In addition, the Canadian police conduct other theft prevention programs, such as in Ottawa, where there is a special theft prevention police service.

In ITALY, the Ministries of the Interior and National Education have organized a traveling exhibition, using a van containing samples of all the known antitheft devices available on the international market. This program requires the services of only three police officers.

In FRANCE, guards as well as electronic security systems are used in the museums under the direction of the Ministry of Cultural Affairs. A program for ensuring at least minimal protection of churches in the countryside is also under way. Some works of art have been relocated to more secure places, but the authorities in charge of the project feel that such operations should be limited so as not to compromise the artistic value of certain collections. The *Office Central* is currently responsible for prevention programs and for offering technical advice.

A SPANISH Delegate reported that there was a considerable amount of clandestine marine prospecting off the Spanish coast, which was giving cause for alarm, and asked if other delegates at the Symposium had had any experience of this problem.

In CANADA, this has been a problem for several years, but some pertinent laws have been enacted there. Under those laws, for example, the deep-sea divers who salvaged a major portion of the treasure from an abandoned French frigate shipwrecked off Luisbourg were obliged to declare their find and pay a very high precentage of its value in taxes to the Canadian government.

The UNESCO OBSERVER said that the Council of Europe was studying legislation on the matter in member countries and was preparing a formal recommendation that such laws be revised and updated. She also pointed out that the problem was not one of the concern only to countries with sea coasts; for example, there was intensive underwater prospecting in the lakes in Austria.

Inventories

In SPAIN, the inventory situation is good for the national museums and fair for private collections; until quite recently, it was very bad for church-owned property, but at an episcopal conference held recently in Madrid it was decided to make local priests responsible for safeguarding church property, for preparing inventories of such property, and for protecting it from unauthorized disposal. Such property is being entrusted more and more to museums, where it is better protected.

In BELGIUM, the authorities are concerned about just how much publicity should be given to such inventories. In Brabant-Wallon, an inventory has been drawn up of works of art located on public property and some people feel that this should be published in order to make the general public more aware of such works; on the other hand, there are those who feel that publishing it would be a dangerous thing to do, especially since it could serve to provide valuable information for potential thieves.

A CANADIAN Delegate felt that inventories could be used not only for general information, but also for scientific research purposes. In North America, there were collections from all parts of the world and about 70 percent of the items in them had not been inventoried and sometimes not even photographed. Drawing up inventories of such collections would be a very long and difficult task if done by conventional procedures; increasing use was therefore being made of electronic data processing techniques. The National Inventory Programme in particular made use of such techniques in maintaining a computer-based data bank of the information appearing in museum records. The program's objectives were to facilitate exchanges of information and to encourage standardization of cataloguing procedures and terminology throughout the country. By the end of 1976, thirty-five museums had been participating in the program, data on more than 350,000 objects and samples had been computerized, and a network of twelve computer terminals had been set up throughout Canada.

In INDONESIA, a new 1977 inventory has been drawn up to replace those prepared in 1913–14 and 1932; the new inventory lists only the immovable cultural property located in the country's twenty-six provinces. It is in fact very difficult to make inventories of movable cultural property, much of which is in private ownership, but it has been attempted in Bali, Java, and Jakarta provinces. Local police forces are responsible for making inventories of the works of art located within their respective areas of jurisdiction.

In ITALY, the "Central Cataloguing Institute" has done quite satisfactory work. The main problem is the nearly overwhelming abundance of items involved; currently, the Institute prepares about 10,000 inventory cards per year. The items at certain archaeological excavations have not yet been catalogued.

In LIBYA, similar work has been begun, but a shortage of technicians and experts is causing problems.

In INDIA, the inventorying program is closely linked to the enactment of related legislation. The work of inventorying objects of historical importance is the responsibility of the Department of Archaeology, while the local authorities are in charge of inventorying other items of cultural property. Many statues have already been inventoried, but this type of work requires considerable time.

Legislation

An ICOM Publication* on pertinent national laws was distributed to the delegates.

In INDIA, there are laws to protect archaeological sites, to govern the import and export of antiquities and chance discoveries at archaeological excavations, and to protect wildlife.

The TUNISIAN Delegates felt that legislation in certain countries should be modified to take account of trends in the situation with regard to thefts of works of art and cultural property and trafficking in such objects.

The CHAIRMAN pointed out that, with that objective in mind,

---

*The Protection of Cultural Property: Handbook of National Legislations, by Bonnie Burnham. International Council of Museums, 1974. It also contains the texts of relevant international conventions and recommendations. Copies can be obtained from the International Council of Museums (ICOM), Maison de l'UNESCO, 1 rue Miollis, 75732 Paris Cedex 15, France.

INTERPOL's 40th General Assembly had adopted a resolution on the subject at its session in Ottawa in 1971 (cf. Appendix 4).

An INDONESIAN Delegate felt that the legal penalties for such offenses were not heavy enough to be truly deterrent and cultural wealth was therefore still endangered. Several other delegates were of the same opinion. An INDIAN Delegate particularly stressed the fact that the police could take more effective action if the penalties provided by law were greater.

The UNESCO OBSERVER, speaking about the November 14, 1970, "Convention on the Means of Prohibiting and Preventing the Illicit Import, Export and Transfer of Ownership of Cultural Property,"* said that some countries had expressed doubts about the convention's effectiveness. She recognized that there were many practical difficulties causing ratification delays, especially difficulties in harmonizing national legislations, but pointed out that the convention had at first seemed to some to be too ambitious and to others, not ambitious enough, and that it was the basis for many measures currently being applied. The UNESCO Observer further reported that the dangers menacing cultural riches were now more clearly understood than they had been in 1970.

The CHAIRMAN pointed out that the UNESCO Convention of 1970 was a very useful instrument and as many countries as possible should ratify it; such ratification did of course mean that countries had to bring their national laws into line with the provisions of the convention.

Education and Consciousness-raising of the Public

Do the police participate in public-awareness campaigns and school programmes and take an interest in the tourist factor (as in vandalism at tourist sites)?

The UNESCO OBSERVER believed that the police could play a major part in this respect. They should have brochures distributed to tourists, either at airports or at travel agencies or immediately upon their arrival, in order to draw their attention to various legal provisions with regard to stealing and damaging cultural property.

The UNITED KINGDOM Delegate felt that every visitor to a foreign country should realize that he was subject to the laws of the country visited, regardless of the nature of the items stolen.

In FRANCE, the public authorities have conducted a theft prevention campaign during which brochures were distributed and use was made of the press, radio, and television. Similar campaigns have also been conducted in

---

* At May 31, 1977, thirty-three states had "deposited an instrument of ratification, acceptance or accession" (cf. Appendix 3).

CANADA, and, on occasion, security personnel from museums have taken part in school programs on respecting and safeguarding works of art.

In INDIA, two "national crime prevention weeks" were organized in 1972 and 1975. The general public actively participated in the programs and seemed to understand that it is up to them to report to the appropriate authorities every act of vandalism or theft which they witness. The authorities have also tried to make students proud of the cultural property forming part of their national heritage. Films designed to arouse students' awareness of the country's archaeological riches were shown at 200 camps, where they were called upon to help perform maintenance work on some monuments.

The TUNISIAN Delegate said he had found the UNESCO Observer's suggestion about distributing warning brochures to tourists most interesting, since tourists committed many thefts from archaeological sites.

The ITALIAN Delegate felt that modern society was losing respect for culture, with market values becoming more important than artistic values. He thought that works of art damaged through theft should be shown on television in order to make the public more aware of the seriousness of the problem.

In the PHILIPPINES, public awareness programs have been conducted, particularly in schools, but it has been noticed that such programs could "backfire" by supplying valuable information to potential offenders. It seems, however, that tourists who acquire items of cultural property rarely steal such items themselves or engage in acts of vandalism; they buy items from middlemen interested only in making a profit.

A SPANISH Delegate pointed out that the press could be of great service in searches for stolen objects, but the negative aspects must also be recognized and attempts made to correct them.

MISCELLANEOUS

Insurance — Ransoms — Transactions

The UNESCO OBSERVER reported that the insurance companies had formally adopted a policy under which no ransom should ever be paid.

In the NETHERLANDS, insurance compensation may only be paid if the thieves are arrested.

A FRENCH Delegate expressed the opinion that the payment of ransoms by insurance companies would only encourage such thefts. Most of the delegates shared this view.

Returning Stolen Property to its Rightful Owner

Copies of a General Secretariat document considering the problem solely from the legal standpoint (cf. Appendix 5) were distributed to the delegates.

In FRANCE, cultural property is classed as specially protected property, and, if it is stolen, there is no time limit for returning it to its rightful owner.

A UNITED STATES Delegate said that there was a special treaty between the UNITED STATES and MEXICO for restoring stolen works of art to their rightful owners.

An ICOM OBSERVER reported that some museums had willingly returned to their rightful owners some works of art that they had acquired in good faith before learning that they had originally been stolen.

The ITALIAN Delegate felt that differences in national laws made it difficult to officially seize and return stolen works of art to their rightful owners. Nonetheless, the Italian authorities' requests to the authorities in other countries for seizure of stolen works of art had generally yielded satisfactory results when the requests had been supported by precise legal arguments and by proof that the works in question had indeed been stolen.

In INDIA, a stolen item of cultural property is always considered to be a stolen item that must be returned to its rightful owner, no matter what the good faith of the person in whose possession it is discovered. However, such persons are entitled to compensation, although this is relatively small even when the stolen item is of considerable value. An Indian Delegate described the difficulties encountered in connection with attempts to have stolen property returned from other countries.

The CHAIRMAN recalled that the resolution adopted by the General Assembly in Ottawa in 1971 recommended that I.C.P.O.-INTERPOL affiliated countries should, as far as possible, facilitate the return to their country of origin of any works of art found in fraudulent circumstances in another country (cf. Appendix 4).

The CHAIRMAN declared the First International Symposium on Thefts of Works of Art and Cultural Property closed at 1 P.M. on June 16, 1977.

Appendix 28.1

Convention on the Means of Prohibiting and Preventing the Illicit Import, Export, and Transfer of Ownership of Cultural Property (Paris, November 14, 1970)

ARTICLE 1

For the purposes of this Convention, the term "cultural property" means property which, on religious or secular grounds, is specifically designated by each State as being of importance for archaeology, prehistory, history, literature, art, or science and which belongs to the following categories:

(a) Rare collections and specimens of fauna, flora, minerals, and anatomy, and objects of palaeontological interest;

(b) property relating to history, including the history of science and technology and military and social history, to the life of national leaders, thinkers, scientists, and artists, and to events of national importance;

(c) products of archaeological excavations (including regular and clandestine) or of archaeological discoveries;

(d) elements of artistic or historical monuments or archaeological sites which have been dismembered;

(e) antiquities more than one hundred years old, such as inscriptions, coins, and engraved seals;

(f) objects of ethnological interest;

(g) property of artistic interest, such as:

    (i) pictures, paintings, and drawings produced entirely by hand on any support and in any material (excluding industrial designs and manufactured articles decorated by hand);

    (ii) original works of statuary art and sculpture in any material;

    (iii) original engravings, prints, and lithographs;

    (iv) original artistic assemblages and montages in any material;

(h) rare manuscripts and incunabula, old books, documents, and publications of special interest (historical, artistic, scientific, literary, etc.), singly or in collections;

(i) postage, revenue and similar stamps, singly or in collections;

(j) archives, including sound, photographic, and cinematographic archives;

(k) articles of furniture more than one hundred years old and old musical instruments.

29. Reporting Stolen Works of Art

Donna Carlson

Some weeks ago a young lady showed me a photograph of a large bas-relief that hangs in the lobby of a building in the Wall Street area of Manhattan. Her employer wanted a similar work for his office. She had been to the building where the work hung and despite numerous inquiries could not find anyone there who knew the name of the artist who had done the work. Perhaps the architect had commissioned it. She wanted to know if I could identify the artist from a Polaroid photo she had taken. While she was talking, I thought what if that work was stolen. There are security personnel in that building. But who knows what it is that hangs in the lobby where they stand each day. Are there any documents that accurately describe that work? Probably not. This is not, alas, uncommon. No one notices what they have until it is gone and then they rack their brain to recall some description of it. Still they want someone to do something.

It is not my intention here to launch into a presentation of statistics; that the theft of works of fine art, collectibles, and other items of personal property is on the increase is not controverted. There is confusion only as to the volume of crime in these areas. Documentation of this sort is, in my opinion, solely useful to those who must demonstrate the need for the assignment of personnel and the budgeting of such staff. It is disappointing that public attention focuses on this problem only when an item stolen is reported in the media, often with an attendant flash and flare that exaggerates the actual situation. Government budgets, at the federal, state, and local levels, are almost nonexistent for providing specially trained and competent personnel to deal with this area of crime. Statistics can be useful as a wedge in bringing attention and, hopefully, some relief to this problem. It is difficult, of course, when funds of every institution and government agency are limited, to determine priorities but the theft of works of fine art definitely has no priority in this country. European countries have treated the loss of personal property with more concern. We have no agency to compare with the Art and Antiques Squad of New Scotland Yard, for example. It is distressing to note that in the entire United States there are only a few law enforcement people who have developed an expertise in the area of losses of fine art, with or without the encouragement and support of their respective agencies.

Appreciation of any of the fine arts demands what might be called "connoisseurship." It is virtually impossible for the security officer, for example, to determine with confidence the difference between an engraving and a lithograph — which are only two of the many types of printing processes available to the graphic artist. For the description, evaluation, and identification of artwork, the law enforcement complex must rely on members of the art community for their knowledge and expertise. This is to some degree desireable. Dealers and scholars become specialists in the same way we now accept that most doctors in the medical profession are specialists. Taking some courses in art history may whet the appetite for lovely things but it does not equal connoisseurship.

"After it's gone" is too late to prepare for the eventuality that the property or work of art may someday be "gone." Here are some suggestions of things that I believe should be done in order to be prepared. Because my area of knowledge is in the fine arts, the examples I have given are from that field. If you are in the security force of an institution that is not involved with the fine arts, you must make some adjustments to ascertain which ideas may be applicable to your current situation.

It is unfortunately true that often, when some incident of theft or vandalism occurs, there is no procedure for dealing with it. So much attention is given to providing security that once something happens to penetrate that security, there is no agreement between the security staff and the administrative staff as to a procedural plan of action. For example, a painting is stolen from a museum. This is not the time to have hurried telephone calls between the staff and the board of directors to discuss whether or not to release the story to the newspapers. In the past, more than now, museums often wanted no publicity of losses because they felt it was a public embarrassment and, further, because they suffered such stinging criticism from their own contributors and supporters. There must be some agreement between the security department and the administrative staff before the occurence of such an event so that things can proceed judiciously. Of course, there is always flexibility in any arrangement that an institution makes to deal with certain incidents but there should be some general guidelines. Sometimes this means having a discussion at administrative staff meetings and with the board of directors so that everyone is on notice.

The reason why I urge this settlement of procedural policies beforehand is that it eliminates needless delay in getting all available help in the possible recovery of the work. It also alleviates a great deal of the emotional distress that thefts elicit.

What are you securing? What are the individual items for which you are now responsible? Every fine arts institution, including museums, keeps some record of each object in its possession. Even the Smithsonian is currently making a heroic attempt to get all of its vast collection of objects numbered and described with the help of a computer. Endless fossils, bones, feathers, stones, books, kitchen utensils, and models as well as all of the great works of art in its collection will soon be accounted for, thus completing an indexing of its entire holdings, which number several million.

I have, however, seen curatorial file cards that are woefully inadequate in providing helpful data for someone who wants to recognize a particular item. If you are searching for a person, the more detailed the description, the greater are the chances that someone will be able to recognize and identify that person. The same is true for items of personal property. It is, of course, much more difficult to make a specific statement about a SONY color television because it is massproduced. This has led to the idea of engraving such items with various numbers, "fingerprinting" them as it were. In fine arts, however, there is not the same degree of mass production. Accurate, detailed descriptions are not just helpful; they are of paramount importance. If you cannot describe the work, no one can help you find it. I cannot tell you how many times I have received a telephone call or a letter reporting the loss of a "Landscape" approximately 16" x 24". This information is virtually useless.

Assuming again that I am discussing a public collection, items are very often marked with an accession number. Marking works that are difficult to distinguish because of multiplicity and similarity, such as television sets or items of china, may be useful. However, if we are discussing works of fine art such as paintings, drawings, graphics, or sculpture, such markings are not particularly helpful and in no way supplant the need for an accurate description. Because they are original works of art, they can be distinguished by noting their individual characteristics. "Fingerprinting" a painting is a waste of time.

So what information do you need for original works of art? I suggest that you check the data kept on the objects under your jurisdiction to see if you have the following facts:

1. *Name of the artist:* Give the artist's full name and the year of his life, if possible. This immediately lets someone know if the work is

an old master or a contemporary work. If there is no artist, you can still help determine an object by giving the name of its designer or the name of the factory that produced it. Many items of silver are identified by the designer, such as John Storr silver. Corning Glass or Limoges porcelain provides instant data on the maker — the artist. If the work is a primitive work, the identification should be made by the name of the tribe, for example, Benin bronze, or by the culture or geographical area from which it originated — Egyptian, Amlash, and so forth.

2. *Title of the work*. If the title is given in French or Italian is there also an English translation? Not all of us are fluent in French! If there is no known title for the work, I suggest that you give it a title that would be appropriate, such as "Portrait of an Elderly Woman" or "Two Men Fishing." Even objects can be given a short descriptive entry, such as "Carriage Clock," "Card Tray," or "Female Fertility Image." With these two entries, name of the artist and title of the work, there is already a good feeling for the general nature of the work being reported.

3. *Medium*. What is it made of? For works of fine art, the medium is extremely important. Is the painting an oil on canvas, oil on wood panel, gesso on cardboard, or gouache on paper? Is the drawing made with crayon, ink, wash, pencil, or chalk? Graphics is a general term; a good description should instead provide the specific printing technique used, engraving, lithograph, silkscreen, etching, and so on. If the work is a stone sculpture identify the type of stone used, for example, Vermont grey marble or rose quartz. The type of stone often indicates a color as well. If the work is a bronze, also note the color of the patina because the color of the corrosion, resulting from natural or artificial oxidation, is the color one sees. One is misled if one has a mental image of a shiny brass-colored work. Many works are a combination of materials, for example, a primitive mask may be made of carved wood with a bone and shell inlay. Modern works use all types of contemporary materials, including steel, acrylic, plastic, ceramic, and various found objects.

4. *Dimensions*. If the item is two-dimensional, it is common in the art community to give the dimensions so that height precedes width. The dimensions provided should be the dimensions of the actual work — not the image seen after matting, as in graphics, or the size of the work after framing. Try to help someone see the work itself and not the frame. Additional and separate notations can be made for special frames but they should never be confused with the description of the work they frame. By reading the dimensions of a work one can instantly know if the work is a horizontal or a vertical composition. Giving the dimensions in this order requires some attention to detail.

It is a bit difficult to get used to since we are accustomed to giving paper dimensions or photographic dimensions in the reverse way. An 8½" x 11" photographs means a photograph 8½" wide by 11" high. If the work is a graphic that you are describing for security purposes, the entry should be made 11" x 8½". If the item is three-dimensional, the depth is given last. The proper progression for dimensional information is height, width and depth. Since there is an international confusion between measurement systems at this time, it is useful to give all dimensions in inches as well as centimeters, if centimeters are the appropriate measuring units for the work being described.

The weight of sculpture is sometimes given. In the case of large works, it indicates if the work is hollow-cast. This information may be of special interest to the security personnel who must consider how such a work could have been transported out of the building. In giving the measurements of sculpture, provide accurate data on the sculpture, not its base. Details about the base can be added as supplemental information. Keep in mind the fact that the work may be separated from its base in the same way that a painting or print is frequently removed from its frame.

Many items of china and silver give the diameter of the work, indicating whether this measurement was taken at the fullest point, at the base, or at the rim or lip. All of the measurements given for objects that lend themselves to being confused with many other similar objects are extremely helpful because, by measurement alone, you can help eliminate the confusion. For example, there are many items of Chinese Ming porcelain. Even with a photograph you would be hard pressed to know if you were looking for a small mustard jar or a large mustard jar. In this instance, dimensional information may be the critical factor in identification.

5. *Edition:* This is a specific area of required information for works produced in editions, such as sculpture and prints. Let us suppose that an artist makes a form and then makes twelve castings of that form. This means that the work was produced in an edition of twelve. It is the practice for each work to bear a number showing the sequence in which it was cast from the form. For example, a work by the famous English sculptor Henry Moore may be stolen. It is not enough to know the name of the artist, the title of the work, the medium and its dimensions. It is also important to know which cast is missing — number one of the twelve casts or perhaps number twelve of the twelve casts. These numbers usually appear directly on the sculpture in the following manner — 1/12, 2/12. . . 12/12, the latter number being the number of the total edition. We refer to this number as the size of the edition.

While the matter of the edition number may not be so important if there are only twelve items, consider the case of a graphic work that is produced in an edition of 500! The edition number is then critical. You are not looking for all 500 items but rather only a particular work from the 500. This number usually appears in the lower left- or right-hand corner of each graphic work of art. Some old master prints have no numbers and were printed several times, for the plate with the image on it was not destroyed as is the custom today. In these instances you need a scholar to determine which edition of the work it is. The problem of multiple editions of the same image is not just a historic problem. Some modern artists are putting out their graphic work in large editions and sometimes in multiple editions. Salvadore Dali graphic works are impossibly difficult for this reason. He publishes not only one large edition in Europe but also other editions for distribution in the United States. Several editions may exist, each numbered 1/500. The only difference may be in the type of paper used for the individual editions. If you want to indicate exactly which print you are looking for, in this case you need even more than the particular edition number that appears on the work. Try to encourage the curatorial staff to ascertain all of this technical but necessary data.

6. *Other data including description.* Take note of any other details that would help identify the item. If the work is signed and dated, how is it signed and where does the signature appear on the work? Are there other labels or stamps or accession numbers on the item and where are they located?

Describe the work. Even though you may have the title and the size of the work, it does not tell you what you would see if you had the work before you. If it is the "Landscape" that I referred to earlier, which is so often lost, what do you see when you look at the work? Perhaps trees in full foliage to the left, a small thatched cottage in the center with two peasants on a bench outside; clouds drifting across a grey-blue sky that takes up about two-thirds of the height of the canvas; cows grazing in a sun-lit meadow to the right. This is only a verbal picture showing the kind of descriptive data that you can provide. There are now a few agencies attempting to keep information in archival form or on the computer. Photographic retrieval in these situations is slower than verbal and written data. Someone can give such information quickly over the telephone.

Recently, the general term "Landscape" has been supplanted with the proverbial title "Abstract" or "Composition." Again, describe what you see. . . two black triangular forms intersected with three red and yellow striped rods against a pale pink background spattered with fine blue dots.

Some artists painted several versions of the same scene. A careful description noting small details can provide an easy method of distinguishing the particular work. Edward Hicks, for example, did a number of paintings called "The Peaceable Kingdom." The paintings are similar in that they all show a combination of animals and figures in a forest setting. But the works are similar — not alike! By carefully noting the position of the animals, color of apparel of the figures, gestures, season, time of day, and so on, the exact work in question can be described accurately. Of course, since some of the paintings may be of different sizes, the dimensions of the work would be of help in differentiating the missing version from the others.

Some note should be made as to the condition of the work, such as slight foxing in the lower left corner of a drawing or upholstery repair in the center cushion for a couch. For items of silver noting the hallmark is very important, as silver is often identified by its hallmark. Reference to color is always helpful. . . blond girl in blue dress, and so on. Sometimes what is known as a provenance may be available, which is a history of prior ownership of the work referring to previous owners, collectors, auction sale of the work, and so forth. This information is useful to the professional dealer or scholar, who will appreciate having it if he is assisting you.

7. *Photograph.* When I was taking an art class in high school the teacher once asked us to describe a tree to someone as if that person were blind and had never seen a tree! You immediately come to realize how useful an image is. While the specialist may be able to imagine the work clearly from the data given, it is not so helpful to the less knowledgeable person who is often the very police officer or insurance investigator whose help you now need.

Again, try to plan ahead. If the archive of information on works is maintained on fiche film or with negatives alone, it will take time to have photographs printed for distribution if you should need them. Review your situation ahead of time so that you will not suddenly find yourself in a situation where you cannot provide the authorities concerned with photographs for several days or, worse still, not at all. I sometimes feel that one of the great curses of the modern world is the Polaroid camera. It certainly serves well in providing an easy way to document the possessions of the individual homeowner. But, unfortunately, the pictures are generally of such poor quality that they do not reproduce well and lack clear detail. It is not sufficient to have the "Landscape" accompanied by a blurry Polaroid photograph that shows no details. In this instance, a good description is better than a poor photograph.

Good black and white glossy photographs are excellent, although for certain objects of art color may play a more important role. For example, color might be extremely helpful in the identification of rugs and china. Some-one should consider whether a photograph of some unique detail of the work would be especially useful if any problem arose and identification became necessary. For rugs would a photo of some portion of the border provide a simple and expedient way of identifying that particular rug?

The accumulation of this data bank, to borrow a computer term, must be the job primarily of the people with knowledge and the ability to gather the facts. How the information is kept, where and who has access to it, should be mutually resolved between the administrative staff and the security staff. I believe that the security officer can assist the institution by asking to review the data on hand. See if you would be able to proceed on the basis of the data provided for the item if an emergency were to arise. Suppose you have an entry card showing an accession number, Benin Female Figure, approxi-mately 5" high, wood, with no photograph or additional descriptive detail. You can see that more data would, if a theft were to occur, be needed. The curators see the items so often that they "know" them and brief entries are sufficient for their purposes. But you are in a position to understand what type of information would help the law enforcement community proceed with dispatch should that particular item be stolen. There is no substitute for the usefulness of this detailed and time-consuming labor of documentation. "After it's gone" is too late!

It is not that you want the staff to spend hours updating and reviewing all of this data in anticipation of a future event. It is simply realistic to expect to have detailed information readily available. There must be an accurate accounting of items as well as of funds. Bookkeepers do a better job of accounting for each penny than do many institutions of the works in their collections. This information can be useful in the event that any work is damaged or lost in transit and negotiations with the insurance company become necessary. It is difficult legally to repossess a work if you lack suf-ficient substantiating documentation to show that *that* particular work did, in fact, belong to you.

I have, of course, been discussing these problems only with respect to fine arts institutions. But I hope that I have stimulated you to think about what it is that is within your security area. Are the carpets in the director's office valuable? Who owns them? A general survey of the premises may be worthwhile. Documentation is an important security tool; it is a way of being prepared.

WHAT DO YOU DO "AFTER IT'S GONE?"

Here's an opportunity to take advantage of all the previous work. Of course, you have to notify the key people including various law enforcement agencies.

I assume that you have their names and addresses readily available. The insurance company should be notified either by the security department or someone in the administrative staff. This should be done promptly as the insurance company often wants to participate in the investigation. If you have a chain of calls laid out beforehand, you can save a lot of time. Unfortunately, as I said earlier, there are very few law enforcement people who specialize in the fine arts. We are lucky in New York City to have an agent in the U.S. Customs Service, an FBI agent, and one New York City police officer, all of whom have developed expertise in the handling of fine art thefts and frauds. Knowing who in the law enforcement community can be of assistance to you is your professional concern. You should have on hand, for example, the name of the special agent in your nearest FBI branch.

Works of fine art are either recovered through normal police procedures, usually in a relatively short time, or else they surface sometime in the future — perhaps years. If no one knows that a work is lost, how can someone find it! Since most art works eventually reenter the art market, it is important that the professional art community be alerted for its protection and for your benefit. Even works stolen "to order" will eventually reenter the market. For this reason, masterpieces will eventually be recovered; they will be noticed and recognized. Minor works are much more difficult to recover.

It is useful to prepare a notice of the loss as soon as possible. The focus of the law enforcement and security personnel is often on the technologies available to them, staffing procedures, and so on. When a crime occurs, scrupulous details are recorded as to the manner in which the crime was committed. I frequently receive detailed reports on the manner of entry, and so forth, only to reach the end of the report to find my old friend "Landscape." Newspaper stories give breathless accounts of forced entry and vans vanishing into the night but fail to give their readers any information about what was taken. These same readers might, if given some details, be able to help.

The question of value is controversial. Sometimes it is the focus of a news item. The majority of the evaluations provided in the material that I receive are inaccurate or outdated. A work is not found because it has an exact value. Some idea of value is important, however, if you want the FBI or U.S. Customs to be involved since both of them have jurisdictional limitations based on value. If there is a problem about value, consult a specialist. Unless there is a question of federal jurisdiction, in my opinion a value given on any published notice of loss does not help in the recovery.

This raises the question of the offering of rewards for the recovery of a work or for information leading to its recovery. This is a matter for the insurance company; there are arguments pro and con. Whatever decision is made should be made promptly. The preparation and circulation of a notice of a theft should not be held up because of a debate on whether or not a reward should be offered.

Generally speaking, law enforcement departments prepare inadequate notices of loss. They often fail to provide data of the most obvious kind, including a complete mailing address with the zip code or a complete telephone number with the area code. It is not a good notice if someone who has some information is in any way stymied in trying to get that information back to you. I have received notices from police departments that have only the banner heading of the department on them. No street address at all; no phone number!

Once a flyer or another type of announcement describing the stolen item has been prepared, where do you send it? Begin with the obvious — the law enforcement people who are assisting you. This assumes that the institution has, in fact, decided to publicize its loss. It is the position of the Art Dealers Association of America that public information on art thefts is the most useful aid to recovery. The distribution of such information may also be a deterrent to crime. For example, some of the crimes committed in public institutions are "in-house" thefts. If the staff knows that the policy is to distribute such information quickly, they may think twice before stealing something.

After a notice of loss has been made up, it is useful to alert dealers in the immediate area who buy and sell items of the type taken. If a Faberge enamel piece was taken, for example, find out who buys and sells works of Faberge in a 100-mile radius. The advantage to having a separate list of the dealers within your geographic area is that you can prepare a simple alert bulletin and distribute it within hours of the loss. These lists of appropriate dealers should be prepared in advance so that you are not in a position of making many inquiries "After it's gone."

For wider circulation of the loss, send a notice to any relevant publications. If it is an important rug, for example, notify HALI, the International Journal on Carpets and Textiles, P.O. Box 4312, Philadelphia, Pa. 19118 (215)843-3090. HALI is the most prestigious periodical on carpets to which every major dealer and collector subscribes. Some publications will publish a notice of loss as a public service and others will not. If the magazine does not publish this information as a public service, consider placing an advertisement. My point is that if you should wish to publish a notice, you should have on hand a list of the appropriate publications. The curatorial staff can be very helpful in providing the names and addresses of the periodicals that they consult in their areas of speciality.

In addition, there are professional organizations that focus on almost every type and category of object — Oriental works of art, guns, or snuff bottles. Some of these associations are willing to forward information to their members. Others will not do this but will probably provide you with a list of their members. You can then mail your notice directly to them.

Since my expertise is in the fine and decorative arts, I can offer some suggestions for notification in this broad field.

Notices of thefts of important items of furniture, china, glass, and Oriental works of art should be sent to The National Antique and Art Dealers Association of America, 59 East 57th Street, New York, N.Y. 10022 (212) 355-0636. Its membership comprises the leading antique dealers in the United States.

Information about stolen fine arts, decorative arts, antiquities, ethnographic objects, and Oriental art can be directed to "The Stolen Art Alert," which is published ten times a year. It is sold by subscription only. You may get additional information by writing to IFAR, 46 East 70th Street, New York, N.Y. 10021 (212) 879-1780.

Antiques and other collectibles that are missing can be reported to "Maine Antique Digest," one of the leading publications on antiques. It is a publication to which most antique dealers subscribe, and any notice that appears there receives a great deal of professional attention. Your bulletin or letter should be addressed to Mr. Samuel Pennington, Maine Antique Digest, Box 358, Waldoboro, Maine 04572 (207) 832-7534.

Notices of stolen drawings should be directed to The Drawing Society, 500 Park Avenue, New York, N.Y. 10022 (212) 688-7630. Information on missing or stolen prints should be sent to Print Collector's Newsletter, 16 East 82nd Street, New York, N.Y. 10028 (212) 628-2654. Thefts of archaeological items should be reported to "Classical Archaeology" magazine, Indiana University, 422 N. Indiana Avenue, Bloomington, Indiana 47401, attention Ms. Karen D. Vitelli. Notices of stolen sculpture should be directed to The National Sculpture Society, 15 East 26th Street, New York, N.Y. 10010 (212) 889-6960.

This is only an indication of the types of specialized associations at your disposal. If you are responsible for a mineral collection, I don't know which periodicals or associations are appropriate but I am sure they exist. It will be for you to determine.

Theft Notice Service of the Art Dealers Association of America: Since 1963 the ADAA has distributed information on art thefts and frauds. We have what we believe to be the largest archive of this information. In order to assist in the recovery of stolen property, we publish and distribute monthly notices of stolen and missing works of art. These notices are sent to an extensive mailing list of more than 1,000, including:

- Dealers, in the United States and abroad
- Museums, in the United States and abroad
- Major auction houses, in the United States and abroad
- Law enforcement personnel, including police departments, FBI, and U.S. Customs offices in the major cities
- Foreign law enforcement agencies — INTERPOL, Scotland Yard, French police, etc.

- Professional art organizations, associations, and societies in the United States and abroad
- Leading art magazines and publications in the United States and abroad

On August 13, 1979, ADAA received a Certificate of Appreciation from the U.S. Custom Service in acknowledgement of our work. It reads in part: "The efficient cataloguing and timely dissemination of stolen art notices from both domestic and foreign police agencies has been most welcomed. . . . Your pro-law enforcement attitude and swift cooperation with this Service's investigation of international art thefts and frauds is greatly appreciated by this office."

All information is filed in alphabetical order, by artist, with some categorical listings. Our files are constantly consulted by various police departments, insurance companies, and so on.

Please note that our primary areas of concern are the fine arts — painting, drawing, sculpture, and graphics. Our Theft Notice Service is a public service and is absolutely free. Should your institution suffer the loss of a work of fine art, send your fully detailed and informative notice to Art Dealers Association of America, Inc., 575 Madison Avenue, New York, N.Y. 10022 (212) 940-8590.

Whether or not the work taken from your institution is a work of fine art, on the basis of your preparedness you can quickly provide clear and useful information to the media, law enforcement agencies, associations, and publications that can assist in the recovery of the work..."after it's gone."

30. Art Theft Investigation

Leonard Poteshman

INTRODUCTION

Crimes involving art, until recently, have been limited to isolated incidents that were perpetuated more through fictionalized novels than reality. Today, the use of a scenario based on a clever, sophisticated art theft can easily contain the necessary elements for a successful TV drama. In the past, publicity regarding real art crimes evoked more curiosity than concern. The last decade and a half has seen an expansion of the world art market, manifested by an ever-enlarging purchasing public, making these crimes a growing concern of the art community and law enforcement agencies.

The unprecedented buying of art will attract not only the common burglar, but the more sophisticated criminal as well. Any criminally inclined individual with a little knowledge of current events will soon realize that the risk of being apprehended in an art crime is slight, and even if he is caught, he faces a relatively light sentence compared to the tremendous potential for profit.

Art crimes are like a double-edged sword; police agencies are poorly equipped to handle this new form of crime. Many art collectors in the community are acknowledged leaders of society. When they become victims of art crimes, their demand for positive action carries considerable weight.

Museums are highly vulnerable targets. Supported by private and public funds, museums have been entrusted with the preservation of our cultural heritage. Thefts from these repositories represent a financial and cultural loss to the community or, in some cases, the nation.

According to a recent survey of museums in the United States conducted by the International Foundation for Art Research, of 243 responses about 75 percent had suffered thefts in the last five years. Though the percentage is great, the author has been informed that many thefts of smaller, less expensive items go unreported, indicating that many museums would rather sustain the loss and avoid publicity that may encourage more thefts. Also art pieces from private collections might be loaned less freely, with the museum's security undermined. Thomas McShane, Senior Art Thefts Investigator for the FBI, commenting on the seriousness of art crimes, states, "The increase is to an extent where art thefts are now second only to narcotic activity."

In France, works of art are being stolen at the rate of one an hour. As a result, the French Ministry of the Interior has instituted a forty-five-man art theft squad. Other European countries are beginning to respond to this problem.

The necessity that individuals specializing in art theft investigations undergo specific training becomes apparent as a consequence of the plundering of archaeological sites and the accelerated thefts from museums and private collections. The present preparation of individuals is insufficient.

Although technology of antiintrusion devices has reached a high level of sophistication, and the art of theft prevention is of concern to those responsible for museum function, the burglary investigator assigned to a case involving a stolen art work is frequently ineffective.

If, for example, a Miro lithograph is stolen:

1. Does the investigator know the difference between a lithograph and an etching?
2. Would a conventional burglary report form be used?
3. Who would be contacted for effective dissemination of information?
4. What about the preservation of the art piece in the event of recovery?
5. How would an art work be marked as it is transferred through a number of individuals?
6. Would a recovered work be secured in an evidence locker, where it may remain up to a year or more?
7. Would the work sustain damage due to police evidence/property storage procedures?

The purpose of this chapter is not to make the investigator an art expert — that would be presumptuous. It is hoped that the following information on investigation, interrogation, and art techniques will sensitize the investigator to the peculiarities of art crimes investigation. It is also understood that the investigator is not an art curator, and that priorities as to human safety must take precedent over other considerations.

THE INVESTIGATOR

Webster defines the word investigate as "to follow up or make research by patent inquiry and observation and examination of facts" and the word investigator as "noun: one who investigates." Although the definition is fundamentally sound, the skills and knowledge that distinguish the competent investigator are more complex.

Although conclusions can be the result of an individual's using good judgment, with an observation of things and people, the effort alone is not necessarily an investigation, nor is the person with an inquiring mind necessarily a skilled investigator. Besides intelligence and inquisitiveness, intangibles like native ability and sensitivity are essential.

The investigator must be imaginative, with the capability to create mental scenarios with variations and to think like an offender, but still arrive at dependable conclusions based on objectivity, relevance, thoroughness, and accuracy.

Understanding people and their environment is a prerequisite for the investigator in facilitating rapport with individuals being interviewed. The knack of being able to get along with others encourages confidence and trust.

Commitment or promises should never be made that cannot be fulfilled, nor should the integrity of the investigator be compromised. People, regardless of their social status, will detect insincerity and dishonesty, thus hampering the interview from which meaningful facts can be derived.

Temptation and its consequences, be they physical, emotional, or material, which can alter the facts, are always present. Taking no action or altering a conclusion that would undermine a direction of investigation, thus proving it wrong, will require strong integrity.

It would therefore appear that an individual with these attributes is most unusual, and rather difficult to find. However, many can meet these requirements and are capable of doing a remarkable job in the face of seemingly insurmountable obstacles.

EVIDENCE

The investigator, from the beginning, is unaware of which fragments of evidence will be used in the legal proceeding, so such findings must be handled in a manner where each is as important as the next.

Since evidence is anything that relates to the crime, nothing is considered insignificant. The awareness as to what constitutes evidence, together with the preservation and collection of that evidence, can determine the outcome of the case. Bungling by improper care can mean an irrevocable loss.

Physical evidence found at the location of the crime is often sufficient in constructing the manner in which the act was committed, as well as in identifying the culprit. A tool mark left at the entry way, a thread of cloth, finger- or footprints, etc., can be traced to an individual who was present at the scene.

Evidence is classified in two categories: fixed and movable. Fixed is that which in the retaining has to be recorded in another mode. With latent fingerprints, as with tool marks or various markings, photographing and/or lifting the impression is necessary for its retention. Evidence less difficult to handle and not requiring reproduction methods because of its transportability is considered movable evidence.

In addition to the handling, preservation, and identification of evidence, a "chain of custody" must be maintained. From a legal standpoint, any evidence in court must be accounted for at every moment, from the time it was discovered to the court presentation.

Evidence must be accountable by receipt when transfer of possession is made. Time, date, and place are noted, together with the name of the individual taking possession. If the investigator gives the evidence to an officer whose intent is to deliver it to the crime lab for analysis, the purpose of the transfer should be noted. When the case eventually goes to court, all persons involved in the chain of custody will have to testify that they possessed or had the evidence placed in a locked compartment to which they alone had access, and that in no way was it altered or contaminated. If it cannot be accounted for, even for a moment, it may be rendered inadmissible.

The investigator should begin a log, indicating pertinent information up to his arrival, time of discovery of the crime, by whom, and names and addresses of persons seen at or adjacent to the scene.

Those individuals will then be questioned as to the exact location and the approximate time of the offense, but no attempt will be made to conduct an interrogation at this period. An effort should be made to keep witnesses from discussing the incident until each is questioned thoroughly. If several witnesses are involved, an appropriate number of officers should be assigned to take statements.

Unfortunately, as is often the case, the interval between the discovery of the crime and the arrival of the investigator is long. With the theft of an art piece as with other crimes, the victim or museum personnel will sometimes unintentionally disturb the scene of the crime, and evidence can be lost forever.

In a case of vandalism of several paintings in a major museum, the custodian had vacuumed the floor beneath the paintings before the arrival of the investigator, thus eradicating evidence that might have been essential to the case. All personnel working in the confines of the museum, whether security guards, curators, or maintenance workers, should be aware of the hands-off policy of the area near the location of the crime.

Had a theft really occurred?

As absurd as it may sound, although the credibility of the victim is beyond reproach, ascertaining whether a crime had indeed occurred should be of primary consideration. Curators are usually given responsibility for their displays and thus are knowledgeable as to their inventory. In larger museums the situation is compounded; a plethora of art works requires inventory systems not available. Pieces can be misplaced, and works not located in a given place are assumed missing or stolen. A major museum reported four paintings missing, and notices were sent to agencies throughout the country reporting the loss. Embarrassingly, the paintings were located in a secluded area of the building, and the notices had to be retracted.

Many museums are now using computer systems which keep a perpetual inventory of the collection and its location.

MUSEUM SEARCH

Past experience has shown that a majority of museum thefts are personnel related. If the loss had been noticed soon after the occurrence, the thief may have secreted the objects within the building, waiting for a propitious moment to remove his cache from the premises.

A potential criminal, knowledgeable as to the nooks and crannies of the museum, can go one step further; a work of art can be removed from its last known area and hidden in a location infrequently visited, with the intention of its never being removed from the facility. Through an anonymous call to the office of the director, a ransom for the return of the work could be initiated.

A thorough search of the facility should be the first line of action. Personnel knowledgeable in the physical layout of the building should be consulted. Engineers with architectural plans, electricians, plumbers, and custodians who utilize crawl spaces and other out-of-the-way places can be of invaluable assistance.

PHYSICAL EVIDENCE

As previously indicated, a hands-off policy of the immediate area of the crime must be established by cordoning off the perimeter to prevent the disruption or loss of evidence. Members of the crime lab from the local police agency should be dispatched. Although most museums and exhibition halls hang paintings on textured walls which prevent the lifting of latent prints, smooth surfaces like nearby frames or wood trim should not be overlooked. Dust or microscopic fragments that are near the area should be photographed with a direct and raking light together with a ruler laid within the photo frame in order to document the size.

The theft of some valuable art objects had recently occurred at a warehouse where the burglar or burglars, in order to cover up possible prints, threw paint over the forced entry way. In their haste, one walked through the paint that had splattered on the ground, leaving footprints. Using the ruler next to the print provided the size of the shoe, together with the pattern and characteristic wear. All were retained on film for future reference.

Information regarding the art pieces in question can be obtained from the museum's registrar. The Office of the Registrar is usually the hub of information as to physical characteristics, i.e., medium, size, name of work, artist, etc., that would be pertinent to the crime report that will be made. Photos of the stolen objects are invaluable in the distribution of information, but unfortunately experience has shown that museums as a rule have not kept up with the documenting of their ever-increasing inventory. If the stolen object is a major work, or one that may be on loan from a private collector, chances are photos and information pertaining to the work are available.

For distribution to the news media and agencies specializing in art crimes, 5-x-7-inch black and white glossies are sufficient. If colored prints or transparencies are the only photos available, the police department's criminal lab photo section can reproduce them in black and white.

REPORT TAKING

Conventionally, the police agency taking a theft report utilizes a burglary form which is supposedly adaptable to all situations. Though information includes time, place, names of victims, officers involved, and other data pertinent to the case, art pieces and their specifics are frequently glossed over. Technicalities as to the medium of the work, color, size, name of artist, etc., can be hidden within the report so as to make it inaccessible for distribution. Figure 30.1 is a sample of an art theft form.

The form, as indicated, can be used as an art theft or recovery report. A file number can be substituted for the URN (Uniform Report Number), dependent upon the specific term used by the agency. The CLASSIFICATION line will indicate the type of incident leading to the use of the form; i.e., burglary, robbery, fencing confiscation, etc. Line three, indicating number of pieces involved, will be accompanied by a similar quantity of descriptive pages.

URN NUMBER_____Date_____Page_____of_____

CLASSIFICATION _____
....

Victim's Name _____

If victim is a business, list its name _____

Victim: Museum____Gallery____Dealer____Collector____Auctioneer____Other_____

Home Address_____

Business Address _____

Check day phone: Home phone _____ ☐   Business phone _____ ☐

....

INSURED? Yes_____ No_____ Insurance Company _____

Agent _____ Policy #_____ Phone _____
....

Reporting Agency _____ Phone _____

Address _____

Investigator _____ Agency File Number _____
....

Number of thefts in this report? _____ List appropriate totals below:

Paintings____Drawings____Prints____Sculptures____Antiques____Other _____

_____
....

AUTHORIZATION TO REPORT LOSS TO STOLEN ART FILE: Experience has proven that stolen
art objects are likely to leave the jurisdiction from which they were taken. It is conceivable
that this information may be input into non-law enforcement computer files funded by nonprofit organizations to increase awareness among museums, galleries, and collectors in regards
your theft, thus enhancing the chances of recovery. If you desire information concerning your
loss to be made available to these organizations, please sign the authorization below.

Only information pertaining to the description of the property will be released. Personal data
will remain confidential.

VICTIM'S SIGNATURE AUTHORIZATION _____ Date _____
....

By Deputy _____ Employee #_____ Unit of Assignment _____
....

(This report may also be used to report recovered property when attempting to locate the
origin of theft and/or the owner.)

Figure 30.1. Sample art theft form

URN_____Date_____Page_____of_____

CLASSIFICATION _____ ( ) STOLEN   ( ) RECOVERED

                                                    PHOTOS ATTACHED   ( ) YES   ( ) NO

(CHECK APPROPRIATE DATA, ONE ART OBJECT PER SHEET)

1. PAINTING
   ( ) a. OIL
   ( ) b. WATERCOLOR
   ( ) c. GOUCHE
   ( ) d. TEMPERA
   ( ) e. ACRYLIC
   ( ) f. COLLAGE
   ( ) g. MONTAGE
   ( ) h. MIXED MEDIUM
   ( ) i. OTHER (Describe)
         _____

2. DRAWING
   ( ) a. PEN & INK
   ( ) b. CRAYON
   ( ) c. PENCIL
   ( ) d. PASTEL
   ( ) e. CHARCOAL
   ( ) f. COLLAGE
   ( ) g. MIXED
   ( ) h. OTHER (Describe)
         _____

3. *PRINT
   ( ) a. ETCHING
   ( ) b. ENGRAVING
   ( ) c. LITHOGRAPH
   ( ) d. LINOCUT
   ( ) e. SILKSCREEN
   ( ) f. BATIK
   ( ) g. WOODCUT
   ( ) h. AQUATINT
   ( ) i. OTHER (Describe)
         _____

 *Edition Number _____/_____
(E.G., 1/100 – IF APPLICABLE)

4. SUPPORT
   ( ) a. CANVAS
   ( ) b. COMPOSITION
   ( ) c. PAPER
   ( ) d. WOOD
   ( ) e. OTHER (Describe)
         _____

5. *SCULPTURE
   ( ) a. BRONZE
   ( ) b. WOOD
   ( ) c. MARBLE
   ( ) d. STONE
   ( ) e. STEEL
   ( ) f. FIBERGLASS
   ( ) g. CLAY
   ( ) h. PLASTER
   ( ) i. MIXED
   ( ) j. OTHER (Describe)
         _____

6. *PHOTOGRAPHY
   ( ) a. BLACK & WHITE
   ( ) b. COLOR
   ( ) c. SEPIA
   ( ) d. TINT
         _____

7. FINISH (Photograph)
   ( ) a. MATTE
   ( ) b. GLOSSY

8. SUBJECT OF WORK
   ( ) a. LANDSCAPE
   ( ) b. SEASCAPE
   ( ) c. CITYSCAPE
   ( ) d. INTERIOR
   ( ) e. PORTRAIT
   ( ) f. FIGURE STUDY
   ( ) g. RELIGIOUS
   ( ) h. STILL LIFE
   ( ) i. ABSTRACT
   ( ) j. ANIMAL
   ( ) k. OTHER (Describe)
         _____

9. FABRICATION
   ( ) a. CARVED
   ( ) b. CASTING
   ( ) c. WELDED
   ( ) d. OTHER (Describe)
         _____

10. OTHER
   ( ) a. TAPESTRY
   ( ) b. GLASS
   ( ) c. STAINED GLASS
   ( ) d. MOSAIC
   ( ) e. CARVED IVORY
   ( ) f. OTHER (Describe)
         _____

11. SCHOOL OF ART
   ( ) a. REALISM
   ( ) b. EXPRESSIONISM
   ( ) c. IMPRESSIONISM
   ( ) d. ABSTRACT
   ( ) e. SURREALISM
   ( ) f. OTHER (Describe)
         _____

VALUE:

ARTIST _____ TITLE _____ COUNTRY _____
IS WORK SIGNED? ( ) YES; LOCATION _____ ( ) NO
IS WORK DATED? ( ) YES; LOCATION _____ ( ) NO
DIMENSIONS ____ IF SCULPTURE, APPROX. WEIGHT _____ BASED? ( ) YES ( ) NO
DESCRIPTION & DOMINANT COLORS OF WORK _____
_____
_____

Figure 30.2. Art theft data sheet

The authorization paragraph should be shown to the victim and, if necessary, explained in detail.

The bottom of the first page is self-explanatory, and although questions as to whether the victim is insured, is not usually of concern to police agencies, the information may be of help in furthering the investigation. In the private sector of art collecting, fraudulent claims are becoming epidemic, and assessing whether the loss is indeed truthful or contrived for insurance purposes may have to be considered.

The second page, the art theft data sheet (Figure 30.2), is structured to accommodate issues dealing with this specific type of crime. As indicated, each sheet will give information for one art object only.

Besides basic categories of art — i.e., Painting, Drawing, Sculpture, etc. — the subject matter and materials used are included.

Assuming a painting by Dutch artist Justus Van Huysum had been stolen, the investigator will question the victim, using the general categories:

- "Was it a painting?" 1
- Victim: "Yes"
- "What kind?"
- Victim: "An oil painting" (a)
- "What was it painted on?" 4
- Victim: "Wood" (d)
- "What subject did the painting depict?" 8
- Victim: "Still life" (h)

Obviously, the general categories 2, 3, 5, 6, 7, 9, and 10 would not pertain to this specific theft report page, but category 11 would.

- "What school of art?" 11
- Victim: "Realism" (a)

The bottom of the art theft data sheet is self-explanatory, but some of the questions might be unanswerable. On this particular theft sheet, the author filled it in as indicated below with the assistance of the victim's recollection and photos that were fortunately available.

ARTIST Justus Van Huysum TITLE Still life with flowers COUNTRY Dutch
IS WORK SIGNED? (X) YES; LOCATION Lower right hand corner ( ) NO
IS WORK DATED? ( ) YES; LOCATION _____ (X) NO
DIMENSIONS 11 ¾" x 9½"
IF SCULPTURE, APPROX. WEIGHT _____ BASED? ( ) YES ( ) NO
DESCRIPTION & DOMINANT COLORS OF WORK Multi-color
Includes insects and dew drops on flowers in basket on corner of table.
Background color a warm, off black.

The rectangular box at the lower right-hand corner of the sheet will indicate the value of the work, not necessarily realistic. The value may have been hiked by the victim for insurance purposes. On this particular form, the value was placed at $65,000.

The EDITION NUMBER just above the VALUE box is preceded by an asterisk, relating to general categories: 3. PRINT, 5. SCULPTURE, and 6. PHOTOGRAPHY.

Since the edition number on a multiple work of art is perhaps the best way of identifying a stolen piece, a short background leading to the purpose of numbering follows.

The whole idea of limiting editions of prints and numbering them came into usage as recently as the 1920s. Certainly in the early days of printmaking the thought never occurred to the artist or buyer that a print would be made in a limited edition. If an artist had a "best seller," he continued to produce it until it wore out. Dürer could pay for his travel among the Flemish by selling his woodcuts as he went, and no one questioned what the size of the edition was. By the Eighteenth century, the economics of printmaking was clearly evident to the artist, such as Giovanni Battista Piranesi (Italian, 1720–1776), whose etchings yielded 4,000 impressions per plate.

The fact that early works were plentiful has also led to the very reason that they were not prized, but discarded, and therefore became rare. The desire for rarity and uniqueness spread simultaneously with the emergence of the private collector.

Today, each portion of a limited edition, each numbered section of the whole, should be of equal value and quality, since numbering does not necessarily follow the succession of pulling impressions. The one exception to this is dry-point, which wears out quickly after a few impressions. The quality difference is apparent. The artist usually restricts the size of the dry-point edition to under twenty prints.

Editions are limited not only in the issuance of prints, sculpture, and photography, but multiples. Multiples are a recent invention and are usually three dimensional and most often made of fabric or plastic. They are usually classified as prints because they involve silk-screen (serigraph) techniques. The size of the edition and number are usually written in the lower left-hand margin of the print or multiple and on the base of the sculpture.

An A.P. (artist's proof) is frequently substituted for the edition number. A.P./50 indicates an artist's proof, pulled from an edition totaling 50. Artist's proofs should be limited to around six pulls, since its original purpose is for the artist's personal collection or distribution. Many contemporary print artists like Dali, Miro, and Chagall permit dozens of artist's proofs to be pulled. Complete documentation of a given work should disclose the total number of prints produced and not solely the size of the numbered edition.

The art theft data sheet is patterned after the Federal Bureau of Investigation's Stolen Art Data Sheet (FD-531). The general categories and subclassifications are identical. The art theft data sheet, with the information included for dissemination, can also be sent to the National Stolen Art File of the FBI and put into their computer bank without transcribing. The differences are that the FBI's sheet does not contain an edition number classification ("Is work dated?") or a notation for a sculpture's weight or whether it is based.

DISTRIBUTION OF INFORMATION

If the investigator is not from the local police agency, a follow-up as to whether they had been notified by museum officials is essential. Frequently because of the police department's workload and limited personnel, a theft report is taken over the phone with a promise of sending a detective unit to the location as soon as one is available. You, the investigator on the scene, determining that physical evidence may have been left behind, might suggest that the police department send someone from their crime lab to retrieve the evidence. Because of a breached display case, and the possibility of latent prints on the glass, a print man would be required. Footprints, abrasions, or flakes of paint might require photographers. The breaking of a glass case may have injured a suspect, leaving spots of blood at the scene. The police agency should be made aware of any physical evidence on their first telephone contact, thus expediting the examination of the evidence by lab technicians.

If the value of an object is $50,000 or more, the Federal Bureau of Investigation is always called into the case. Since stolen art is frequently transported across state lines, making it a federal case, an art piece stolen with a value in excess of $5,000 warrants a call to the local FBI office. The National Stolen Art File (NSAF) of the FBI, a recently instituted system, is accessible to INTERPOL, which has a similar computer art file. Notices of theft of a major art piece can be distributed throughout the world in a matter of days. Agents taking the report should be informed of the compatibility of the art theft form with that of the NSAF. Further information regarding the file can be obtained from the FBI in Washington, D.C.

Assuming the victim consents to the distribution of the report to stolen art files as indicated on the first page of the art theft data sheet, notifying the news media should also be approved by the victim. Information disseminated to the media most certainly will require the value of the object stolen. The consensus among some museums as well as private collectors is that publicity of an art theft encourages future thefts.

Two nonprofit organizations, both located in New York City, have had success in recovering stolen art through their monthly publication, which is distributed throughout the United States. The Art Dealers Association of America (ADAA) has a membership of around 150 dealers whose concern is the ever-increasing incidents of art thefts. The ADAA's address is 575 Madison Avenue, New York, NY 10022. A copy of the art theft data sheet, together with available photos, should be sent to this organization at the above address. The phone number is (212) 940-8590.

The International Foundation for Art Research (IFAR) publishes a monthly magazine called *Stolen Art Alert,* which has international distribution to its subscribers. Along with notices of stolen art, articles regarding fraudulent art, which has become epidemic in proportion and theft recoveries, fill their format. Information should be addressed to International Foundation for Art Research, 46 East 70th Street, New York, NY 10021. The phone number is (212) 879-1780. Submitting of art crimes notices to both ADAA and IFAR does not require being a subscriber.

INTERROGATION

Interrogation is an art unto itself. There is no formula to guide one to a successful encounter with those being interrogated. Knowledge and experience are undoubtedly necessary adjutants, but these alone are not enough. Whether it be called intuition, hunch, or insight, that unknown factor distinguishes the competent interrogator.

The dialogue that ensues between the investigator and the subject is frequently very personal, requiring an understanding of people, their attitudes, prejudices, and psychological characteristics. A knowledge of human behavior instills a sureness permitting flexibility and adaptability with the subject, thus generating confidence. Being interviewed in itself is a disconcerting experience and, together with a lack of rapport with the investigator, much information that would ordinarily be free-flowing might not be revealed. To this extent, it requires that the interrogator know himself.

SUBJECTS INTERROGATED

Whether the subject be the victim, witness, informer, suspect, or accused, any of these may be cooperative or uncooperative, with the reasons for their reactions being variable. Listed are but a few factors that can be encountered in a subject being interrogated:

- Impudent or cocky
- Introverted or shy
- Fearful of possible incrimination
- Fearful of recrimination by fellow employees
- The neurotic
- The liar
- The antisocial
- The antiestablishment
- The person not wanting to get involved

With the individual willing to talk, the investigator is confronted with the problem extracting information pertinent to the case which can be checked for accuracy and authenticity. As for the individual who is unwilling to talk, the problem is to convert the person into a willing subject. The problem with the individual who is unable to talk is to find the reason for the reticence or inability and overcome that reason. The fearful may be induced to give information upon assurance that no harm will come to them. The introverted type will be encouraged to talk through a gradual acquaintance and development of rapport with the investigator.

A classification according to age and sex can also be of consequence to the investigator. Bear in mind that all information, no matter what group, will require verification.

Children

Boys and girls from ages seven to ten observe and retain information that adults would ordinarily overlook. The investigator should be aware that children are greatly influenced by gossip, rumor, and overheard conversation. They may have been cautioned by parents or others not to relate certain incidents or to repeat what is told them. Children are imaginative and can color incidents beyond recognition. Care should be taken not to influence children through leading questions, nor should they be made to believe that a certain answer is wanted by the investigator. In spite of the admonitions listed, valid information is obtainable through proper interrogation.

Boys. Adolescent boys can be accurate observers about many things, especially those material and mechanical. Dress and personal descriptions of adults can be flawed unless attention is directed to the person for a specific reason. Their descriptions are usually objective and not colored.

Girls. Adolescent girls tend to be more aware of neighborhood dress, hairstyle, and personal concerns. They are often emotional, which can color their feelings about persons, objects, or incidents. Fabrication and exaggeration are not unusual. However, through careful questioning the skilled interviewer can obtain relevant information, particularly on incidents that have personally affected them.

Young Adults

Generally speaking, young adults, whether married or single, are poor observers. Concerned with their own social and economical problems, their observation is often introspective. However, if observations are made, they are usually reliable.

Mature Adults

The best and most reliable information is obtained from this group, providing they are sound of principle and moderated in their ideas and acts.

Old Men and Women

The very old tend to be similar to children in their accuracy to observe, but are easily influenced by suggestion and imagination. Although information relayed to the investigator may be accurate, the senile or presenile, due to their short memory, may make the information unreliable.

Museum Personnel

In interrogating members of the museum staff, the investigator frequently encounters the introverted individual. A slow approach is usually best, allowing the subject to get acquainted not through intimidation, but confidence and diplomacy.

Interviewing a curator of European art will be different from an interview with a custodian. Each requires an adaptability to the background of the subject. Individuals from all walks of life are more inclined to communicate on their own social level. Museum staff members as a rule are dedicated, sensitive people whose life evolves around their chosen profession. An interrogation not handled tactfully can be construed as an accusation. The investigator should be sensitive to the art world and its distinctions. Nothing turns off the curator, conservator, or collector faster than a negative remark about the work in question. "I have a kid at home who can paint as well as that Picasso," and "you mean to tell me that it's worth $75,000?" Prejudgment has no place in interrogation.

PLACE OF INTERROGATION

The location in which the interrogation is to be held can determine the success of the interview. Often, due to circumstances beyond the investigator's control, the interrogation is held in a location familiar to the subject. Familiar territory like the office, workshop, or home of the subject places the investigator at a disadvantage. The optimum location should be the investigator's office or the police station, where the subject would feel less secure, thereby reducing the possibility of contrived answers. Windows and lights should be in back of the investigator, with the subject facing the source. The room must be as free from distraction as possible. Provocative wall hangings and desk objects are to be avoided. Major changes in the arrangement of the room are not necessary, but the objective is to have as little distraction as possible.

PRELIMINARIES

Although the preliminaries may start with several persons in attendance, the interrogation should be a two-person dialogue; the investigator and the subject. Acknowledging the need for information that may determine the outcome of the case, rapport between the subject and the investigator is essential. The subject is under no legal obligation to provide information.

Objectivity and an attitude of impartiality and fairness toward the subject are the building blocks on which to conduct an investigation. Negative attitudes like personal prejudices, overpatronizing, self-degradation, loss of temper, aggression, or impatience can inhibit the subject from volunteering information.

When "breaking the ice" at the beginning of the interview, avoid comments or jokes that contain innuendo that might be distasteful to the subjects. Be pleasant, radiating confidence in a professional manner, never letting the subject control the interrogation. There is never a need to intimidate or embarrass. Flaunting your intelligence and talking down to the individual can only create resentment, minimizing the effectiveness of the interview.

Learn what the subject's relationship is to the case, and to others involved. Comments of others, including those of the news media, can influence one's statements; the investigator must distinguish firsthand knowledge from opinions of others.

RECORDING INTERROGATION

Since information is the purpose of the interrogation, the need for recording the interview is essential. In an emergent situation, mental notes may be considered, but at the first opportunity information should be transcribed. If recording devices are used, permission should be obtained from the interviewee if the tape is to be used in court as evidence.

The use of a notebook during the course of investigation should make the subject feel he has given permission to record the statements. Jotting down pertinent information is less likely to cause discomfort to the suspect. Important information given spontaneously should be noted after a few additional comments. The subject will try to interpret your notetaking, which might dictate the continuum of future information. After the subject departs, the notes should be elaborated as closely to the verbal dialogue as possible.

Obviously, the tape recorder is valuable in the transcription. Records of the interview, if used within the limits of the law, can be used as court evidence to trap subjects in lies, and possibly to implicate others.

METHODS

There are two methods in the approach to interrogation: the Narrative and the Question and Answer. Both methods will probably be used in an interview. Assuming the subject is willing to discuss his relationship to the incident, the narration approach uninterrupted by the investigator should be used. Physiological reactions, as well as verbal statements, should be noted. An occasional word or two from the investigator can control the pertinence of the interview. Showing respect and gratitude for the narration encourages the subject to follow through with information. In a situation where the subject, a suspect in the crime, is interrogated, the same approach would be used. A statement that might appear inconsequential at the moment can be important when additional information is compiled.

At the completion of the narrative, questioning of the subject can clarify or help in elaborating a point. The investigator must compile sufficient information regarding the crime in order to ask pertinent questions and to know whether the answers are true or false. Ask one question, and wait for a response before proceeding to the next. They should not be leading questions.

Because of nervousness on the part of the subject, contradictions are not unusual and shouldn't be construed as an indication of guilt. Diplomacy in permitting the subject to "save face" will gain respect for the investigator.

If the answer is yes or no, the subject should be asked to elaborate. Intimidation should be avoided. The investigator, having done his homework, proceeds with the interrogation that is well planned, based on knowledge, not bluff.

BODY LANGUAGE

Although visual indicators of tension are apparent, they do not necessarily mean guilt or involvement in the crime, but the investigator should be aware that within limits there is less control of reasoning and caution on the part of the subject. Symptoms like sweating, flushed skin, erratic breathing, and fidgeting should be noted. If the elbows are hanging loose, the subject is relaxed; but, if held close to the sides tensely, the matter in question is affecting the subject strongy. Continual swallowing, lip licking, and a desire for excessive amounts of water also indicate nervousness. The use of straight-back chair without arms is suggested. An awareness to these physical reactions should be mentioned to the subject, pointing out they show an unwarranted tension, while pretending a lack of knowledge or innocence of the crime.

If the subject tries to justify a particular action, go along with the explanation. Through sympathy, kindness, or even flattery, the investigator can lessen the degree of caution, making the subject vulnerable to jolting questions and other traps. Avoid excessiveness in any ploy; confidence and free-flowing information are obtained when the interrogator comes across as an individual reacting to answers in a genuine way.

JOLTING QUESTIONS

Unsuspecting, spontaneous questions thrown at the suspect "out of the blue" can be very informative as to the reaction and response time. When other approaches have come to an impasse, this method of "shooting in the dark" can evoke some pertinent information. The subject can be in a situation where there was no preparation for this type of attack. A question can be hurled at the unsuspecting subject during a dialogue totally irrelevant to the investigation. The investigator should take care that the intentions are not telegraphed.

The methods and techniques set forth are not totally inclusive, so variations and other approaches are as extensive as the imagination of the investigator. They can be applied to the suspect as well as witness or informant. The investigator will have to rely on memory when information cannot be recorded during the interview. Presence of mind and sincerity of purpose in a legal and proper way must be constant during the interaction with the subject. Objectivity, lack of bias, and control of the situation should be a conscious effort. A good investigation is the preliminary to a successful interrogation. Force, violence, and intimidation are admissions of inadequacy on the part of the investigator.

UNDERCOVER OPERATIONS

One of the oldest forms of investigation is undercover work. Throughout history, agents had to assimilate themselves into situations in order to acquire information or to disrupt the plans of their adversary. It requires the ability to be accepted into the confidence and good graces of the person being investigated. The involvement can be anything from telephone conversation to living with that person.

The ability of a competent investigator does not assure that the individual will be a good undercover agent. A talent for acting not only can determine the success of the operation but the safety of the investigator partaking in the ruse. The capacity to leave the real self and assume a fictitious character so completely as to "live and think" the character is necessary; otherwise one might reveal a contradiction in the role being played.

Personal habits of speech and physical action are developed after years of living, so unceasing mental awareness is required, often modifying one's character in order to fit into a situation.

With art crimes, the problem might be even more complex. The undercover investigator may have to deal with people who are versed in art history and the techniques of art. To infiltrate a group, whether as a prospective buyer of stolen art or a liaison for a fictitious purchaser, awareness of the complexity of the art field is important. If the agent is not aware of the language of art, the chance of an incorrect statement during dialogue with the suspect is possible. A rule not to be forgotten is: if you are not sure of a line of conversation, it's better not to fake a response. It would be prudent to back away from an answer as skillfully as possible.

If a situation arises that might compromise the investigation, an offensive technique gives the undercover agent control of the conversation. The author, during an undercover operation, acting as an appraiser of stolen pre-Columbian artifacts, was informed by the suspects that the pieces were tested and proven authentic with the use of the Radio Carbon 14 Dating Test. Not being knowledgeable as to the capacity of the testing equipment, the author informed the suspects that he was not interested in any alleged test and his interest was to assess the pieces as to their authenticity using his own methods. Afterwards it was made apparent that the suspects were checking the legitimacy of the "appraiser" through a ploy that may have aborted the undercover operation. The Carbon 14 Test is used specifically on organic materials. The pre-Columbian stolen artifacts were made of clay, a non-organic substance.

Working undercover as an intermediary for a "potential buyer" does not necessarily require a knowledge of the arts. Professing ignorance in a dialogue of technical reference would be permissible. Trying to bluff one's way into the confidence of the subject whose expertise can detect a lack of knowledge is a no-win situation. The undercover agent, once establishing credentials or references, must be prepared to prove his adopted character.

Distinctive from the conventional undercover operation, where background and names of friends are sometimes used as references, the art crimes undercover agent does best to keep anonymity a conscious effort. Participants in the field of art are adept at obtaining information on people in this specialized work. If you say you are John Smith, a conservator from Detroit, Michigan, a question might be asked concerning where and with whom you had studied. In a protracted investigation where an identity is required, careful preparation through contact with agencies or individuals whom the suspect might check out should be arranged before the need arises. If a background city is selected by the agent, questions about the city and its localities will require proper answers. Use places or situations that you are adequately familiar with.

Having taken on a new identity, the undercover investigator must leave behind all credentials or personal identification that might reveal an impostor. Anticipating any extended operation, fictitious identification cards should replace those that are ordinarily carried.

Bogus business cards should not have an address but a phone number that is valid and should be directed to a person or persons aware of the operation who can respond accordingly. A good method is to have calls received on a phone tape machine, on which all calls are recorded. The prerecorded tape might begin: "Hello, this is John Smith, art dealer. Unfortunately, I'm not available at present. Please leave your name, phone number, and message after hearing the signal. I'll return your call as soon as I can. Thank you." Beep. This method will give credibility to your position. It will also permit you to respond at your convenience or have the call monitored by an associate without compromising your identity.

POLICE AGENCIES

Although law enforcement is notified immediately after the commission of a crime, the likelihood of having members of the police infiltrate the world of a suspect as an undercover agent at the preliminary stages of the investigation is unrealistic. You, as a contracted private investigator, will find that when sufficient evidence is obtained that can lead to the apprehension and prosecution of the suspect the police will have to become involved. The question is, which police agency? Local law enforcement most certainly will be notified, and in the case where the value of the art work stolen exceeds $5,000 or if the offense is a violation of federal law, i.e., interstate transportation of stolen property, etc., the Federal Bureau of Investigation will be notified.

It is likely that once the police are involved, the continuance of the investigation will be under their control from that point on. Requirement of constitutional due process as to reading of the rights to the suspect before being taken into custody and prosecution is the responsibility of law enforcement.

The following summarizes the points of awareness for the undercover investigator:

1. Any interaction due to the complexities of individuals or situations makes predicting the outcome of any operation impossible.
2. The agent should anticipate unforeseen events and be inventive and flexible in adjusting preplanned scenarios.
3. The new identity required for the role must feel comfortable and unalien.
4. The role is not spontaneously adapted but should be developed through practice.

5. Don't assume your bluffing abilities will get you through a technical dialogue with credibility. Most art crimes suspects are knowledgeable and hypersuspicious toward unknown individuals entering their space.
6. If your undercover role is alien to your background, don't permit lack of knowledge or ego to propel you into a position of compromise.
7. Know the law. Infractions as to search and seizure, coercion, entrapment, wiretapping, etc., have overturned many prosecutable cases.
8. The investigator is as bound by the law as is the perpetrator of a crime. Violations are subject to civil or criminal charges.

In the event an undercover operation must be aborted, the objectives in order of priority are:

1. The safe and immediate withdrawal of the agent.
2. Notify the law enforcement agency that was originally called when the crime occurred as to the chain of events leading to the termination.
3. Salvage as much of the accumulated data as possible.

A CRASH COURSE IN ART: DEFINITION, MEDIA, AND TECHNIQUES

The ability to communicate with the victim of an art theft requires some knowledge of the materials and language commonplace in the art world. We all know the difference between painting and sculpture, but both art forms have subclassifications. Frequently the victim is so distraught over the loss of valuable art that pertinent facts used to identify missing works would be omitted in the crime report. You as an investigator should be aware that incomplete information is almost as useless as no information. Questions such as those found on the art theft form should be considered when interviewing the victim.

Classification: Two Dimensional, Three Dimensional

When discussing two-dimensional art, height and width are used. Describing the size of a 24" (inch) x (by) 18" painting, the first dimension is always the height. Most paintings and graphics require some form of framing, but the size of the work excludes the size of the frame. Frames come in various widths and are interchangeable. Two-dimensional works are designed to be viewed on a vertical surface.

Three-dimensional art is generally thought of as sculpture, with the third dimension indicating depth. When describing a size, as with two-dimensional art, the first size is the height, the second is width, and the third indicates depth.

As with so many other things, there are exceptions to this rule. Frequently our contemporary artist will mix media, or might have dimensional objects stuck on paint surfaces or painting on sculpture. A new classification is often encountered and that would be called mixed media.

Defining the Materials of the Work

The medium (singular) or media (plural) indicates the material used in the art work. When we talk about what the art piece is classified as, it is said to be of this or that medium. For example, all paintings of Rembrandt are in the oil medium. Rembrandt is equally as well known as a graphic or paint artist. His etchings are said to be in the print medium. Michelangelo carved in marble; the medium is stone. If you get a frantic call from a victim stating that his Remington was stolen, you'll want to know whether it was an oil painting (medium) or bronze (medium) — or perhaps the victim was a gun collector!

The painters of the Renaissance had but a handful of materials with which to be creative. A few basic materials were and still are the foundation of all visual arts, and they are pigments. Pigment is nothing more than color in a powdered state.

Another Definition of Vehicle

Powdered pigment mixed with linseed oil, which in this case is the vehicle, creates an oil medium for painting. Using other vehicles like acrylic, water-soluble glue, or any other kind of media that would bind the powdered pigment, identifies the two-dimensional art work. Even egg mixed with powdered pigment will produce an egg tempera medium. Although egg tempera is used by notable artists today like Andrew Wyeth, the medium pre-dates oil and many works exist in a well-preserved state that was created back in the fourteenth century.

With the powdered pigment mixed with a selected vehicle, the next step for the artist is to have a surface on which to paint. This is called the support. Until the twentieth century, certain media were used on specific supports. For example, the temperas that preceded the advent of oil painting were applied to wood panels. No great collection of old master paintings is complete without some examples of twelfth- to fifteenth-century medieval and Byzantine art. The Madonna and Child motif not only used the pigment that was available to the artist, but gold leaf and semiprecious jewels that were pulverized and mixed with either egg or another adhesive vehicle. Oil paintings that had their origin around the beginning of the fifteenth century are generally executed on canvas, though earlier tempera with oils were painted on panels. Noting that the format for many religious works of ancient masters was circular, tops of seasoned wine barrels made an ideal support. Contemporary artists used just about any surface on which to paint. Composition board, metal, glass, and paper are frequently employed as a ground.

Techniques: Brush, Trowel, or Splatter

The tools of the painter are numerous. Preceding the twentieth century, the brush was the primary tool for applying paint to a two-dimensional surface. Oils as well as acrylics are frequently identified through the brush strokes that are left on the paint surface. Often with earlier paintings, a glazing technique was used. By the use of large amounts of turpentine and linseed oil for oils, or water with acrylics, a thin wash or glaze is obtained, leaving no brush marks, but by and large a combination of techniques are used.

Another technique popular with modern painters is pallette knife. In order to achieve a thicker and more textured surface, a small offset knife with a triangular blade is used to apply paint directly to the painted surface. Artists like Jackson Pollack discarded these approaches to painting in their later works and just poured or dribbled paint onto a canvas.

PRINTS: ARE THEY FOR REAL?

One classification of visual arts that is distinctive from those mentioned previously and perhaps will be encountered by the investigator oftener than all the others combined is prints.

Prints are an "in" medium now, from a collector's point of view, since many are within the affordable price range of the middle-class income group. Unfortunately, due to the difficulty of identifying a legitimate original, the market is open season for the crooked dealer and not too honest collector as well. Experience shows that the investigator involved with stolen or fraudulent prints has little knowledge of prints or how they are made. The proliferation of bogus lithographs and etchings being manufactured and sold to the unwary collector is so great that many dealers and auction houses whose reputation is beyond question won't handle works of artists like Chagall, Dali, Miro, and even Norman Rockwell unless accompanied with documentation.

There are several techniques that come under the category of prints, and they have one thing in common: all are created to make editions other than the original art work. This statement seems somewhat contradictory, but the editions taken or pulled from the original art are also considered original, provided specific steps are adhered to.

Original prints are each made by the artist himself. The image to be created is inscribed in or upon a plate, woodblock, stone, or other flat material for the purpose of producing more than one original work of graphic art. Each impression is made directly from the original art work.

A limited edition of originals is produced. Each is inspected, signed, and numbered by the artist and must be as fine as the others to be accepted for the artist's signature, thus guaranteeing authenticity and originality. If the signature was included in the picture itself and comes out printed, it is referred to as "signed in the stone."

The quantity of the edition should be indicated on the print by the artist. Most artists number their prints in pencil in the lower left-hand corner. If the edition number is indicated as 123/250 it means the edition's total is 250 and this particular print is number 123. Except for some types of intaglios, the quality of the print, regardless of the edition number, should remain unchanged.

An A/P, where an edition number should be indicated, means "artist's proof." A/Ps are not included in the number series, should be limited to approximately six prints or pulls, and the intent is to permit the artist to make corrections of color or minor design changes before proceeding with the edition run.

A Little About Printmaking

There are three ways to treat a surface so that a greasy ink, deposited on that surface, will reproduce an identical pattern over and over. These groups are known as RELIEF, LITHOGRAPHIC, and INTAGLIO PROCESSES. Each requires special tools, presses, and inks, though they can be interchangeable or combined.

Wood Cut

The oldest of the relief processes is the wood cut. The technique was used for printing textiles over 1,000 years ago. In Europe, the printing of pictures began around A.D. 1400.

Besides the use of wood on which the artist cuts his design, flat surfaces of metal and plastic can be employed. As children, many of us used a linoleum block or even a potato to print designs for greeting cards that we proudly presented to our parents on Christmas. It was an assignment in our grammar-school art class, showing us how easy a creative undertaking can be reproduced over and over.

Small knives or gouges are used to cut away the lines that have been drawn on the flat surface. The area of the material not cut away will be that which picks up the ink from the roller. A sheet of paper is laid down on the inked surface, and by rubbing the back, which can be accomplished with a press or the back of a spoon, the ink is transferred to the paper.

If more than one color is used in the final print, each color will require another wood block. Since half tones or shadings are not a characteristic of block prints, the artist can only simulate them through fine lines or cross-hatching.

Lithographic Print

Invented a little before 1800, the technique is basically quite simple; when a flat, clean surface is given a slight texture and water is poured over it, a thin film of the water will remain. If the surface has a greasy spot, it will tend to resist water, as, for example, when you wax your car and, as frequently happens, it rains the following day. You will notice the water beads up due to the characteristics of the waxy surface.

As for a lithographic print, a roller charged with greasy ink is passed over the wet surface. The ink will adhere to the greasy areas but not the area that remains wet. If a piece of dampened paper is laid upon the inked surface, the ink will adhere to the paper. The original greasy area will remain on the plate or stone, so that the process of dampening its surface, inking, and printing can be repeated hundreds of times without having to repeat the original image again. The mark or the image can be made with a grease pencil, crayon, or lithographic stick; all three have the waxy property that will repel water. The color desired in the print is as diversified as the color of ink used. Each color will require a separate plate or stone so that for a full-color lithograph the artist can use ten or more plates or stones. The finished print moves through a sequential series of presses and pulls; each color must follow the dictates of the artist. For example, if two colors were interchanged, the completed print would appear different.

Since each edition requires inking, pressing, and pulling of the print, the edition is considered an original. The prints are usually made by a print master but rightfully viewed by the artist who approves the pull by signing and numbering the print (edition and number).

If the artist decides he has a potentially salable print, he may make or have made 200 of them and then destroy the image on the stone to insure the collector that his original litho print has no more than 199 others like it. Determining the number of prints pulled is not limited to the editions. There are also prints pulled, signed by the artist, which are marked A/P. The artist's proof is made before sequential numbering begins. Frequently artist's proofs are not registered, thus defeating the purpose of the limited editions.

Lithographs are printed in a press especially designed to rub the back of the paper as it lies on the inked plate or stone. The stone lies on a traveling bed that moves on rollers. After it is inked, the dampened paper is laid upon it. On top of the paper is placed a sheet of thin, shiny cardboard. The bed with the stone, paper, and board is then passed under a rounded edge which squeezes the cardboard and paper against the stone. As mentioned previously, each color employed by the artist requires a separate stone.

The Intaglio Process

A scratch or gouge mark on the surface of a highly polished plate will hold printer's ink and can be printed. Although half tone or shading is impossible with intaglios, lines or incisions can be made so close together that the appearance of half tones can be created. Frequently ink rubbed onto the plate, which should be wiped clean from the surface, is left on areas to simulate shading. These techniques, though interesting, are still considered a line cut.

A copper plate is usually used in the making of three types of intaglios.

Dry Point. A metal or diamond-point tool is dragged along the smooth plate, creating a rough ridge of metal on either side of the scratch. In early editions, the burr can sometimes be seen as an uninked impression on either side of the inked line. The burr wears down rapidly in the course of the printing.

Engraving. The technique uses a V-shaped steel tool called a graver or burin. It is pushed along the surface of the plate; unlike dry point, it gouges out a shaving as it travels along the plate. Early engravers would let the fine burr wear away through use, but more recently the engraver will scrape away the burr before printing.

Etching. Of the three intaglio processes, the etching technique is possibly most often encountered by the investigator. As the name implies, the lines on the metal plate are eroded or etched by putting the plate into an acid bath. Before this step is done, the polished plate is covered with a specially prepared ground, the principal component being wax. The grounded plate is blackened with smoke, and the artist scratches his design on the blackened surface with an etching needle or some other pointed instrument. It is not necessary for the etcher to dig into the plate, but enough pressure is applied to expose the metal, so that the nitric acid "bites" into the plate. The longer the plate remains in the acid bath, the deeper the lines and thus the darker the ink impression.

The three intaglio processes are sometimes used in combination with one another. An artist may feel that, after a plate has been etched, finer lines would enhance the print through the use of engraving or dry point.

Distinguishing between dry point and engraving is difficult to the untrained eye, although the distinction between these processes and that of the etching technique is easier.

With engraving and dry point, the technique using the tools mentioned produces a line that feathers to a point, whereas the etching line ends rather bluntly, since the process is one of erosion. Through a strong magnifying glass, the sides of the etched line look crumbled compared to the smoothness of the engraved or dry point line.

Serigraph (Silk Screen)

A distinctive subclassification of prints which has gained much popularity in the last couple of decades is serigraphy. It is nothing more than a silk-screen process, created around 1930 as an efficient way to produce multiple copies for commercial purposes. The Chinese used a similar technique over a thousand years ago by creating a stencil, cutting out designs from paper, and then lining it with silk to hold the design together. By rubbing ink over the stencil, the paper would act as a blockout, letting the ink come through the cut-out area.

Today silk or synthetic cloth is stretched over a wood frame using an emulsion as the block-out. The ink is then squeezed onto the paper. Each color requires a separate screen. By using transparent colors, one color overlaid onto another, a third color is produced; e.g., yellow over red will produce an orange hue.

Sculpture

Although bronze and marble have been equated with fine sculpture for hundreds of years, with the advent of plastic technology in the last two decades the diversity of materials used in dimensional art today is virtually unlimited. Frequently one encounters a variety of materials in modern sculpture. Art pieces made from materials like crushed auto-body parts or wire strung on wood are not uncommon. Welded metal sculpture like Calder's stabiles are frequently used to complement new building structures. Contemporary sculptors often use combinations of material to create statements of our times. These are called assemblages.

As with the graphic medium, dimensional art is sometimes made in multiples. Bronze is a metal particularly adaptable to duplicating, and artists like Auguste Rodin and Henry Moore have their pieces represented throughout the world because of the medium's capability.

Simply stated, the artist usually creates the original sculpture in clay, from which an agar or rubber mold is made. The clay is removed and the mold cleaned, and melted wax is poured into it. The hardened wax is removed, leaving the mold intact for additional wax casts. The wax is then covered with a plasterlike material which is capable of withstanding high temperatures. The next step is the melting out of the wax, leaving the mold hollow with the exact impression of the original piece. This technique is called the lost-wax process. Molten bronze is then poured into the mold and permitted to cool and harden. The mold is then broken away, leaving the bronze ready for chasing (finishing) and patination (coloring).

Sculpture is usually signed on the base, and with bronze castings the name of the foundry is also inscribed.

CONCLUSION

Past experience indicates that art theft recovery falls into specific time frames. If the art is to be recovered, assuming it is not a contracted theft, destined for a specific buyer, or where a ransom or finder's fee is the intent of the theft, the criminal is most vulnerable within the first few weeks after the crime was committed. It is important that the investigation begin immediately.

Art crimes research organizations, law enforcement agencies, (including the FBI and United States Customs), and galleries dealing in similar works should be alerted. Telephonic communication to local galleries should precede the distribution of information, as noted in this chapter.

Private galleries are concerned with problems of art theft and have been helpful in the recovery of stolen pieces. Burglars, inexperienced in fencing stolen art, will at times attempt to sell the work to a local gallery. Recently a thief took a small sculpture from an art establishment and tried fencing the piece to another gallery several blocks away. Fortunately, the owner of the work noticed the loss soon after the act and immediately began telephoning galleries in the area. A prospective buyer, aware that the sculpture presented for sale was stolen, notified the police, who subsequently apprehended the criminal.

With crime accelerating at an unprecedented rate, law enforcement personnel are overworked, requiring that specific crimes be given priority. Theft reports are frequently taken over the phone, and days might pass before police investigators can get physically involved. Relying only on the local police to disseminate information to other agencies quickly may waste valuable time.

After the optimum period of recovery (two to four weeks) has lapsed, the possibility of the stolen art's surfacing in the area from which the theft took place is diminished. It is likely that the work has left the area and perhaps the country.

The more significant the stolen art is, the more likely it is that professional art thieves were involved.

Many third world nations with little or no diplomatic ties with the United States become repositories until a final destination is found for the work. Recently an important Dutch painting stolen from a West Coast museum was seen in a small central African Nation. At this time, the possibility of its return is remote.

Again, it is essential that investigation and dissemination of information not be delayed.

At the present time, the United States has no global legislation concerning the prevention, protection, import, or export of cultural property, and the theft of such property is treated with no special sanctions under the National Stolen Property Act. Although the FBI is the governmental agency most concerned with this problem, several other agencies are indirectly involved.

The United States Customs works in close collaboration with the State Department and Interpol, investigating claims from here and abroad on illegal art moving internationally. Their roles have never been particularly active but might be expected to expand in the years to come.

Bibliography
John E. Hunter

BIBLIOGRAPHY TABLE OF CONTENTS

Introduction
Part 1: Access Controls
Part 2: Alarm Equipment and Systems
    A. General Works
    B. Interior Intrusion Detection
    C. Exterior Intrusion Detection
    D. Alarm Signal Communication and Monitoring
    E. Proprietary and Computer-Based Systems (including Energy Management Systems)
    F. False Alarm Problems and Solutions
    G. Electronic Article Surveillance and Metal Detection
Part 3: Archives and Library Security
Part 4: Cargo and Transportation Security
Part 5: Closed Circuit Television and Film Camera Surveillance
Part 6: Communications
Part 7: Computer, EDP, and Data Security
Part 8: Guards, Guarding, and Private Security
    A. General
    B. Guard Training
    C. Guard Dogs
    D. Weapons
Part 9: Insurance
Part 10: Internal Theft and Pilferage
Part 11: Legal Aspects of Security
Part 12: Locks, Keys, and Key Control

Part 13:   Museum, Historic House, and Archive (Specific) Security
    A.   General
    B.   Art Theft, Smuggling, Fraud, and Forgery
    C.   Building Planning and Design for Security
    D.   Security for Exhibits and Period Rooms
    E.   Marking and Photographing Objects for Identification
Part 14:   Physical and Structural Security
Part 15:   Public Relations and Information Aspects of Security
Part 16:   Safety in the Museum
Part 17:   Security Lighting
Part 18:   Security Surveys and Audits
Part 19:   Security Planning and Design
Part 20:   Security Administration and Risk Management
Part 21:   Security Codes and Standards
    A.   Security and Other Standards of Underwriters Laboratories, Inc.
    B.   U.S. Department of Justice Standards
Part 22:   Miscellaneous Security Subjects
    A.   General Works
    B.   Criminal Investigations
    C.   Robbery
    D.   Safes and Vaults
Part 23:   Fire Protection – General
    A.   General Works
    B.   Fire Prevention
    C.   Fire Detection
    D.   Fire Suppression
    E.   Emergency Exits and Evacuation
Part 24:   Fire Protection for Museums, Historic Houses, and Archives
Part 25:   Fire Codes and Standards
    A.   Codes and Standards of the National Fire Protection Association (NFPA)
    B.   Fire Protection Standards of Safety of Underwriters Laboratories, Inc.
Part 26:   Emergency and Disaster Preparedness – General
Part 27:   Emergency and Disaster Preparedness for Museums, Historic Houses,
    and Archives
Part 28:   Natural Disasters
    A.   General Works
    B.   Earthquakes
    C.   Floods
    D.   Tornadoes, Hurricanes, and Other Wind Storms
Part 29:   Salvage and Recovery of Damaged Buildings and Collections
Part 30:   Bombings and Terrorism
Part 31:   Vandalism, Violence, and Civil Disorder
Part 32:   Useful Addresses
    A.   Sources for Useful Periodicals
    B.   Sources for Useful Books and Monographs
    C.   Other Useful Addresses

INTRODUCTION AND PREFACE

The purpose of this bibliography is to provide useful references on the several topics that must be considered when developing emergency preparedness plans for a museum, historic site, or archives. No attempt was made to include all known works. In some instances, where other bibliographies on certain of the specialized topics of concern exist, reference to them was made. Works of transitory or marginal value and works that contained obsolete information were excluded insofar as they could be recognized.

Most of the entries in this bibliography have been annotated. Where a work was not available to the compiler for review and an abstract of it could not be obtained from another source, the notation "Not available for review." was entered. It is hoped that future editions (if any) of this bibliography will be more fully annotated. Annotations for some works were taken from ART AND ARCHEOLOGY TECHNICAL ABSTRACTS and from bibliographies published by the New York State Historical Association, the American Association for State and Local History, the Minnesota Historical Society, the Society of American Archivists, the International Council of Museums, and others. The work of the compilers of these bibliographies is gratefully acknowledged.

Users of this bibliography are encouraged to inform its compiler of any works not listed that should be listed in future editions or supplements. When providing information about such works, it would help if a copy of the work itself could be furnished. Otherwise, full bibliographic data and, if possible, an abstract should be furnished. All assistance will be gratefully acknowledged and appreciated.

Time did not permit the compilation of a list of sources and a guide to the periodicals cited. Anyone unable to locate a particular work may contact the compiler for assistance. Please note that some cited works may be out of print or the name of a journal may have changed. It is hoped that any future editions of this bibliography will contain a list of sources.

The compiler welcomes any criticism, friendly or otherwise, of this work. Especially welcome would be suggestions as to how the scope of the work can be improved (broadened or limited) in order to make it more useful to the majority of persons working in museums, historic sites, archives, and libraries.

PART 1: ACCESS CONTROLS

"Access Controls: A Basic Part of Your Growth Plan." SECURITY DISTRIBUTING AND MARKETING, Vol. 11, No. 6 (June 1981), pp. 26–34.

Austin, Brian B. "Controlling Physical Access from a Central Location." SECURITY MANAGEMENT, Vol. 25, No. 7 (July 1981), pp. 86–88, 91–93, 95–97, 99–101.

Bajackson, Richard A. "Before You Buy Computer-Based Access Control. . ." SECURITY WORLD, Vol. 18, No. 9 (September 1981), pp. 60–64, 66, 92, 96, 98, 100, 102, 104, 106, 109.

Bean, Charles H., and James A. Prell. "Personnel Access Control — Criteria and testing." SECURITY MANAGEMENT, Vol. 22, No. 6 (June 1978), pp. 6–8, 45–47. Biblio.

Byers, Charles M. "Designing an Effective Access Control System." SECURITY INDUSTRY AND PRODUCT NEWS, Vol. 9, No. 8 (August 1980), pp. 24–25.

"Cost-Effective Access Control." SECURITY WORLD, Vol. 16, No. 6 (June 1979), pp. 26–27.

Darrow, Richard (interview). "How Access Security Pays Off for Business." SECURITY WORLD, Vol. 15, No. 7 (July 1978), pp. 36–38.

Davis, Jim. "Ultimate Security in Personal Identification." SECURITY WORLD, Vol. 12, No. 8 (September 1975), pp. 30–31.

de Bruyne, P. "Developments in Signature Verification." SECURITY MANAGEMENT, Vol 22, No. 6 (June 1978), pp. 58–61. Biblio.

Godding, Don. "Card Access Control Systems: A Modern Approach to Improving Building Security." TECHNOLOGY AND CONSERVATION (Spring 1980), pp. 44–46.

Hoffman, Terry W. "ABCs of Access Controls." SECURITY MANAGEMENT, Vol. 24, No. 11 (November 1980), pp. 80–84, 86.

"Laser Card Encoding." SECURITY INDUSTRY AND PRODUCT NEWS, Vol. 10, No. 7 (July 1981), pp. 24, 33.

Mendelson, Fred S. "The Great (photo-identification) Card Game." SECURITY MANAGEMENT, Vol. 21, No. 1 (March 1977), pp. 6–7.

Miller, Floyd G. "Practical Solutions to Entrance Security for Large Area, Multiple Buildings." SECURITY WORLD, Vol. 11, Nos. 9 and 10 (October and November 1974), pp. 16–20 (Oct.) and 36–37, 43 (Nov.).

Osborne, W. E. "Access Through the Locking Barrier." SECURITY WORLD, Vol. 15, No. 7 (July 1978), pp. 35, 50.

"Photo ID Cards Close Security Loopholes." SECURITY INDUSTRY AND PRODUCT NEWS, Vol. 6, No. 4 (August 1977), pp. 30–32, 37.

Post, Deborah Cromer. "The Technology of Access Control." SECURITY WORLD, Vol. 17, No. 10 (October 1980), pp. 22–24.

Powell, Greg E. "Identification Cards: How to Select Them." SECURITY WORLD, Vol. 12, Nos 2 and 4 (February and April 1975), pp. 22–23 (Feb.) and 38–39, 41 (Apr.).

Pulcini, John V. "Cost Effectiveness in Access Control." SECURITY MANAGEMENT, Vol. 20, No. 5 (November 1976), pp. 21–23.

Rose, Richard N. "Access Screening" (use of X-Ray devices). SECURITY INDUSTRY AND PRODUCT NEWS, Vol. 9, No. 4 (April 1980), pp. 22–23, 34.

Rubin, Xavier. "Planning Your Controlled Access System." SECURITY WORLD, Vol. 12, No. 8 (September 1975), pp. 18–19, 48–50.

Rush, Steven M., and William A. Warren. "Asset Management Through Access Control." SECURITY WORLD, Vol. 17, No. 10 (October 1980), pp. 26–29.

Sassover, Nate. "Security Is 140,000,000 Private Codes." SECURITY WORLD, Vol. 12, No. 8 (September 1975), pp. 22–23, 51.

"Security World Equipment Focus: Access Controls." SECURITY WORLD, Vol. 18, No. 6 (June 1981), pp. 30–32.

Thorsen, June Elizabeth. "Has 'Absolute Identity' Come of Age?" SECURITY WORLD, Vol. 15, No. 7 (July 1978), pp. 32–33.

Warfel, George H. "Automated Identification Methods." SECURITY MANAGEMENT, Vol. 22, No. 6 (June 1978), pp. 14–16, 36–37.

– – –"Signature Dynamics for Access Control." SECURITY MANAGEMENT, Vol. 4, No. 7 (July 1980), pp. 46-50. Biblio.

Watson, Perry. "Card Control System Rounds Out Security." SECURITY WORLD, Vol. 12, No. 8 (September 1975), pp. 26–27.

PART 2: ALARM EQUIPMENT AND SYSTEMS

A. General Works

Ahern, John J. "Will Your Security Plan Be Left Powerless?" SECURITY MANAGEMENT, Vol. 23, No. 2 (February 1979), pp. 12–13, 16.

"Alarm System Standards and Goals." SIGNAL (3rd Quarter 1976), pp. 36, 38, 40, 42.

ASIS Private Security Services Council. "Alarms — Their History and Terminology." SECURITY MANAGEMENT, Vol. 24, No. 6 (June 1980), pp. 32–41.

Astor, Saul, "Should Management Invest in Electronic Security." SECURITY WORLD, Vol. 11, No. 1 (January 1974), pp. 30–33.

Barnard, Paul D. "An Evaluation System for New Equipment." SECURITY MANAGEMENT, Vol. 24, No. 9 (September 1980), pp. 155–168.

Barnard, Robert L. "Designing Your Intrusion Detection System." SECURITY WORLD, Vol. 15, Nos. 1 and 4 (January and April 1978), pp. 24–25, 75 (Jan.) and 34–35, 87 (Apr.).

— — —"Guidelines for Designing an Effective Intrusion Detection System." SECURITY WORLD, Vol. 13, No. 6 (June 1976), pp. 54–57.

— — —INTRUSION DETECTION SYSTEMS: PRINCIPLES OF OPERATION AND APPLICATIONS. Woburn, Ma: Butterworth Publishers. 1981. 339 pp., illus., biblio.

Brann, Donald R. HOW TO INSTALL PROTECTIVE ALARM DEVICES. New York: Directions Simplified Inc. 1972. 130 pp.

Brualdi, U.J. "Guidelines for Buying Alarm Systems." HISTORY NEWS, Vol. 31, No. 9 (September 1976), p. 166.

BUILDING SECURITY SYSTEMS: APPLICATIONS AND FUNCTIONS. Minneapolis: Commercial Division, Honeywell, Inc. 1969. 85 pp. Form No. 74–2800 (1–69) D.L./D.E.L.

Burgener, R. C., and D. Ensminger. DEVELOPMENT OF AN IMPROVEMENT OF INTRUSION ALARM SYSTEM, PHASE 2: COMPONENT EVALUATION, ENVIRONMENT AND DESIGN RULES. Research Report. Columbus, OH: Battelle Memorial Institute. 1971.

BURGLAR-INTRUDER ALARMS: BASIC AND INSTALLATION INSTRUCTIONS. Des Plaines, IL: Locksmith Ledger Division, Nickerson and Collins Publishing Co. 1972. 127 pp., illus., glossary, paper. Stock No. TB-510.

Capel, Vivian. BURGLAR ALARM SYSTEMS. Woburn, MA: Butterworth Publishers. 1979. 151 pp., illus., paper. Newnes Technical Books Series.

Carlton, Stephen A. "New Insight into the Protection Fields — A Systems Approach." SECURITY MANAGEMENT, Vol. 22, No. 5 (May 1978), pp. 26, 30, 38. Biblio.

Chleboun, T. P. COMMERCIAL ALARM SYSTEMS: THEIR EFFECTIVENESS AND LIMITATIONS. Washington, DC: National Bureau of Standards, U.S. Department of Commerce. 1973. National Technical Information Service Doc. No. PB-220223.

Chleboun, T. P., and K. M. Duvall. EVALUATION OF SMALL BUSINESS AND RESIDENTIAL ALARM SYSTEMS. 2 Volumes. Mountain View, CA: GTE Sylvania, Inc., for The National Institute of Law Enforcement and Criminal Justice. June 1972. 295 pp., biblio. National Technical Information Service Doc. No. PB 214-795.

Cole, Richard B. PROTECT YOUR PROPERTY: THE APPLICATION OF BURGLAR ALARM HARDWARE. Springfield, IL: Charles C. Thomas. 1971. 180 pp., illus., biblio.

CONSIDERATIONS WHEN LOOKING FOR A BURGLAR ALARM SYSTEM. Washington, DC: National Burglar and Fire Alarm Association. 1980. 10 pp.

Cunningham, John E. BUILDING AND INSTALLING ELECTRONIC INTRUSION SYSTEMS. Woburn, MA: Butterworth Publishers. 1978. 128 pp.

— — —SECURITY ELECTRONICS. Woburn, MA: Butterworth Publishers. 1977. 192 pp., illus.

Fuss, Eugene L. "Handbook of Modern Alarm Systems." SECURITY WORLD, Vol. 11, Nos. 6, 8, and 9 (June, September, and October 1974).

– – –"Security Equipment and Technology" column. In issues of SECURITY WORLD as follows:

"Magnetic Door Contacts." Vol. 11, No. 10 (November 1974), p. 69.

"Pressure Floor Mats." Vol. 11, No. 11 (December 1974), pp. 24, 64.

"Trip Wires and Vibration Contacts." Vol. 12, No. 1 (January 1975), p. 41.

"Photoelectric Beams." Vol. 12, No. 2 (February 1975), pp. 21, 46.

"Modulated Photoelectric Beams." Vol. 12, No. 3 (March 1975), pp. 42, 44.

"Laser-Type Beam Devices." Vol. 12, No. 3 (March 1975), p. 44.

"Audio Detection Systems." Vol. 12, No. 4 (April 1975), pp. 44–45.

"Vibration Detectors." Vol. 12, No. 5 (May 1975), pp. 40, 61.

"Capacitance Detection Devices." Vol. 12, No. 6 (June 1975), pp. 42, 48.

"Ultrasonics: How the Doppler Effect Works." Vol. 12, No. 7 (July 1975), pp. 20, 134–135.

"Microwave Motion Detectors." Vol. 12, No. 8 (September 1975), pp. 33, 52.

"Infrared 'Body Heat' Motion Detection." Vol. 12, No. 9 (October 1975), pp. 38, 103.

Kelley, R. D. MODEL PHYSICAL SECURITY SYSTEM COMBINING HUMAN AND ELECTRONIC RESOURCES. AFIT-CI-76-9. Air Force Institute of Technology, Wright-Patterson AFB, Ohio. 1976. National Technical Information Service Doc. No. AD-AO25-386.

KINKS AND HINTS FOR THE ALARM INSTALLER (compiled from SECURITY DISTRI-BUTING AND MARKETING magazine). Woburn, MA: Butterworth Publishers. 1979. 94 pp., paper.

Kmet, Mary Alice. "The Proof Is in the Planning." SECURITY MANAGEMENT, Vol. 24, No. 7 (July 1980), pp. 69–71.

"Microwave Intrusion Detection: What It Is and When to Use It." SECURITY INDUSTRY AND PRODUCT NEWS, Vol. 8, No. 3 (March 1979), p. 28.

Nuclear Systems Division. INTRUSION DETECTION SYSTEMS HANDBOOK. 2 volumes. SAND76-0554. Albuquerque, NM: Sandia Laboratories. 1976 updated through July 1980.

Phillips, Patrick E. "Designing a Dependable Detection System." SPECIFYING ENGINEER (May 1977), pp. 94–99.

PROCEEDINGS OF THE 1970 CARNAHAN CONFERENCE ON ELECTRONIC CRIME COUNTERMEASURES, 16–18 April, 1970. PB-190 589. Lexington, KY: University of Kentucky. 1970. 245 pp., illus.

PROCEEDINGS OF THE 1971 CARNAHAN CONFERENCE ON ELECTRONIC CRIME COUNTERMEASURES, 22–24 April, 1971. PB-198 324. Lexington, KY: University of Kentucky. 1971. 159 pp., illus.

PROCEEDINGS OF THE 1973 CARNAHAN CONFERENCE ON ELECTRONIC CRIME COUNTERMEASURES, 25–27 April, 1973. PB-220 223. Lexington, KY: University of Kentucky. 1973. 177 pp., illus.

Roth, Steven I. "Stop Thief! Electronic Security Systems Help Curb Crimes Against Property." LAW ENFORCEMENT COMMUNICATIONS, Vol. 4, No. 5 (October 1977), pp. 28–29, 42–43.

Ruyle, Robert. "SDM Equipment Analysis: Microwave Motion Detection." SECURITY DISTRI-BUTING AND MARKETING, Vol. 11, No. 9 (September 1981), pp. 48–52.

Sands, Leo G. ELECTRONIC SECURITY SYSTEMS. Indianapolis, IN: Theodore Audel and Co. 1973. 281 pp.

"Security Roundup: Guide to Manufacturers and Suppliers of Products and Systems for Protecting Facilities from Intrusion, Vandalism, and Theft." TECHNOLOGY AND CONSERVATION (Winter 1979), pp. 38, 41.

Shanahan, James C. "The Basics of Security Alarm Systems." SECURITY MANAGEMENT, Vol. 24, No. 8 (August 1980), pp. 110–113, 115–116, 118.

Sher, A. H., Gerald N. Stenbakken, and the Law Enforcement Standards Laboratory. SELECTION AND APPLICATION GUIDE TO COMMERCIAL INTRUSION ALARM SYSTEMS. Washington, DC: National Bureau of Standards, U.S. Department of Commerce. 40 pp. U.S. Govt. Printing Office Stock No. 003–003–02098–2.

Swearer, Harvey. INSTALLING AND SERVICING ELECTRONIC PROTECTIVE SYSTEMS. Blue Ridge Summit, PA: Tab Books. 1972. 256 pp., illus., paper.

Thorsen, June-Elizabeth. "Dictionary of Anti-Intrusion Devices for Architects and Builders." SECURITY WORLD, Vol. 10, No. 10 (November 1973), pp. 30–33, 35.

– – –"Security Applications, Needs and Trends." SECURITY WORLD, Vol. 10, No. 9 (October 1973), pp. 18–19, 48–50.

– – –"Security Devices, Systems, and Electronic Technology." SECURITY WORLD, Vol. 10, No. 9 (October 1973), pp. 20–21, 50, 52–53, 57.

– – –"Technology, Application, and the Marketplace – An Overview." SECURITY WORLD, Vol. 10, No. 9 (October 1973), pp. 16–17, 48.

Trimmer, William. UNDERSTANDING AND SERVICING ALARM SYSTEMS. Woburn, MA: Butterworth Publishers. 1981. 277 pp.

"User's Guide to Anti-Intrusion Hardware." SECURITY WORLD, Vol. 12, No. 11 (December 1975), pp. 12–21, 23–24.

Weber, Thad L. ALARM SYSTEMS AND THEFT PREVENTION. Woburn, MA: Butterworth Publishers, 1973. 385 pp., index.

Wels, Byron G. FIRE AND THEFT SECURITY SYSTEMS, 2nd ed. Blue Ridge Summit, PA: Tab Books. 1976. 192 pp., illus.

Whitehurst, Susan A. "Survey of Product Reliability." SECURITY DISTRIBUTING AND MARKETING, Vol. 11, No. 5 (May 1981), pp. 24–34.

Williams, James D. "Intrusion Detection System Planning." SECURITY MANAGEMENT, Vol. 25, No. 8 (August 1981), pp. 74–77, 79–82.

B. Interior Intrusion Detection

Barnard, Robert L. "Performance Standards for Ultrasonic and Microwave Motion Detectors." SIGNAL (3rd Quarter 1975), pp. 28–36, 38, 40, 42. 13 figures, 6 tables.

Berman, Herbert L. "Principles of Passive Infrared Detection." SECURITY MANAGEMENT, Vol. 25, No. 8 (August 1981), pp. 88–90.

Fraden, Roger. "Ultrasonics Provide Cost-Effective Security." SECURITY DISTRIBUTING AND MARKETING, Vol. 9, No. 6 (June 1979).

Garrett, William C. INFRARED MOTION SENSOR EVALUATION. Fort Belvoir, VA: MERADCOM, U.S. Army. March 1978.

Hackett, Kenneth R. "Ultrasonics: Tips and Techniques." SECURITY INDUSTRY AND PRODUCT NEWS, Vol. 7, No. 4 (April 1978), pp. 16–18, 32.

Luks, Henry J. "Audio Discrimination – Fact or Fiction?" SECURITY DISTRIBUTING AND MARKETING, Vol. 7, No. 4 (April 1977).

Malec, Michael J., and Larry A. Thomas. "IR Catches 'Em Coming and Going." SECURITY WORLD, Vol. 16, No. 8 (August 1979), pp. 30-31, 54, 56.

Moore, Michael H. "Audio — Can You Afford to be Without It?" SECURITY DISTRIBUTING AND MARKETING, Vol. 7, No. 4 (April 1977).

NILECJ STANDARD FOR CAPACITANCE SENSING UNITS FOR INTRUSION ALARM SYSTEMS. NILECJ-STD-0312.00. Preliminary Draft. Washington, DC: Law Enforcement Standards Program, U.S. Department of Justice. July 1976. 31 pp., illus.

NILECJ STANDARD FOR MAGNETIC SWITCHES FOR BURGLAR ALARM SYSTEMS. NILECJ-STD-0301.00. Washington, DC: Law Enforcement Standards Program, U.S. Department of Justice. March 1974. 20 pp., illus., biblio.

NILECJ STANDARD FOR MECHANICAL CONTACT VIBRATION SENSORS FOR BURGLAR ALARM SYSTEMS. NILECJ-STD-0312.00. Preliminary Draft. Washington, DC: Law Enforcement Standards Program, U.S. Department of Justice. April 1976. 15 pp., illus., biblio.

NILECJ STANDARD FOR MECHANICALLY ACTUATED SWITCHES FOR BURGLAR ALARM SYSTEMS. NILECJ-STD-0302.00. Washington, DC: Law Enforcement Standards Program, U.S. Department of Justice. May 1974. 14 pp., illus., biblio.

NILECJ STANDARD FOR MERCURY SWITCHES FOR BURGLAR ALARM SYSTEMS. NILECJ-STD-0303.00. Washington DC: Law Enforcement Standards Program, U.S. Department of Justice. May 1974. 13 pp., illus., biblio.

NILECJ STANDARD FOR SOUND UNITS FOR INTRUSION ALARM SYSTEMS. NILECJ-STD-0308.00. Washington, DC: Law Enforcement Standards Program, U.S. Department of Justice. March 1977. 14 pp.

NILECJ STANDARD FOR ULTRASONIC MOTION DETECTORS FOR BURGLAR ALARM SYSTEMS. NILECJ-STD-0309.00. Preliminary Draft. Washington, DC: Law Enforcement Standards Program, U.S. Department of Justice. November 1975. 29 pp., illus., biblio.

Nothaft, Eugene M. "Methods for Evaluating Passive Infrared Detectors." ALARM SIGNAL (July-August 1981), pp. 6, 11, 12, 14.

Olmstead, Joe, Jr., and Graham Piggott. "Shock Detection: A New, Old Security Device." ALARM SIGNAL (March-April 1980), pp. 42, 44, 48.

Osborne, W. E. "All on the Same Wavelength." SECURITY WORLD, Vol. 15, No. 2 (January 1978), pp. 32-33.

Prell, J. A. INTERIOR INTRUSION ALARM SYSTEMS. NUREG-0320. Washington DC: Office of Standards Development, U.S. Nuclear Regulatory Commission. February 1978. 41 pp., biblio.

"Protecting Space by Detectors and Sensors: Part 1, The Detection Factor; Part 2, Space Protection Detectors; Part 3, Devices Against Intrusion." SECURITY WORLD, Vol. 15, No. 12 (December 1978), pp. 28-32.

"Protecting Space by Detectors and Sensors: Part IV, Other Types of Anti-Intrusion Detection." SECURITY WORLD, Vol. 16, No. 1 (January 1979), pp. 62-64.

"Reaping Protection Rewards from Audio Alarms and Invisible Beams." SECURITY WORLD, Vol. 16, No. 1 (January 1979), pp. 20, 21, 66-68, 70-73.

Reed, Philip L. "So You Need a Warehouse Alarm." SECURITY WORLD, Vol. 13, No. 10 (October 1976), pp. 26-27.

Reiss, Martin H. "Selecting Intrusion Devices for Your School." SECURITY WORLD, Vol. 11, No. 2 (Feburary 1974), pp. 24, 25, 27.

Ruyle, Robert. "SDM Equipment Analysis: Ultrasonic Motion Detection." SECURITY DISTRI-BUTING AND MARKETING, Vol. 11, No. 10 (October 1981), pp. 50-52.

Sabatino, Leonard N. "The Rebirth of the Audio Alarm System." SECURITY MANAGEMENT, Vol. 24, No. 12 (December 1980), pp. 37-39.

Schwarz, Frank. DESIGN AND APPLICATION OF A WIDE FIELD PASSIVE IR INTRUSION DETECTOR. Washington, DC: National Bureau of Standards, U.S. Department of Commerce. 1973. National Technical Information Service Doc. No. PB-22-223.

"Security World Equipment Focus: Space Protection." SECURITY WORLD, Vol. 18, No. 10 (October 1981), pp. 26-28.

"Sound Off on Sonics: A Dealer Dialog Report." SECURITY DISTRIBUTING AND MARKETING, Vol. 11, No. 8 (August 1981), pp. 65-66, 102.

Stenbakken, Gerard N. TEST METHOD FOR THE EVALUATION OF METALLIC WINDOW FOIL FOR INTRUSION ALARM SYSTEMS. NBS Special Publication 480-34. Washington, DC: National Bureau of Standards, U.S. Department of Commerce. August 1978. 5 pp., illus.

"Surveillance and Motion Detection in a Single Package." SECURITY WORLD, Vol. 18, No. 8 (August 1981), pp. 44-45.

C. Exterior Intrusion Detection

Agranoff, Michael A. "An Evaluation of Perimeter Protection Systems Available." SECURITY MANAGEMENT, Vol. 21, No. 5 (September 1977), pp. 60, 62-63.

Barnard, Robert L. "When Security Covers the Expanded Picture . . ." SECURITY WORLD, Vol. 14, No. 9 (September 1977), pp. 34-35, 59-61, 71.

"Buried Seismic System with Audio Listen-In Feature." SECURITY DISTRIBUTING AND MARKETING, Vol. 7, No. 4 (April 1977).

Carpency, Frank M. "Perimeter Protection: Foundation of Construction Site Security." SECU-RITY MANAGEMENT, Vol. 24, No. 2 (February 1980), pp. 74-79.

Finkelstein, A. B. "Watch Your Step!" SECURITY WORLD, Vol. 13, No. 6 (June 1976), pp. 24-25.

Fite, Robert A. COMMERCIAL PERIMETER SENSOR EVALUATION. Report 2209. Fort Belvoir, VA: MERADCOM, U.S. Army. May 1977.

Fuss, Eugene L. "Security Equipment and Technology" column. In issues of SECURITY WORLD as follows:

"Photoelectric Devices." Vol. 13, No. 6 (June 1976), 40.

"Capacitance Devices." Vol. 13, No. 8 (August 1976), pp. 38, 125, 127.

"Taut-Wire Devices." Vol. 13, No. 11 (November 1976), pp. 49-50.

Geiszler, T. D. "A New Method of Outdoor Perimeter Protection." SECURITY WORLD, Vol. 12, No. 10 (November 1975), pp. 40-41.

Hansen, R. W. "Perimeter Intrusion Detection." SECURITY INDUSTRY AND PRODUCT NEWS, Vol. 10, No. 6 (June 1981), pp. 28-29, 46-48.

Harman, R. K. "Developments in Perimeter Surveillance and Intrusion Detection." SECURITY MANAGEMENT, Vol. 22, No. 10 (October 1978), pp. 10, 13.

"KEEP OUT Is Not Enough." SECURITY WORLD, Vol. 13, No. 6 (June 1976), pp. 30-32.

Osborne, W. E. "Long-Range Infra-Red Intruder Alarm Resists Fault Triggering." ELEC-TRONICS. 1972.

"Redefining Perimeter Protection." SECURITY WORLD, Vol. 17, No. 7 (July 1980), pp. 24–28.

Siatt, Wayne. "Security World Equipment Focus: Perimeter Protection." SECURITY WORLD, Vol. 18, No. 9 (September 1981), pp. 44–48.

D. Alarm Signal Communication and Monitoring

Allen, George R. "Designing a Dual Tone Multi-Frequency Security System." SECURITY DISTRIBUTING AND MARKETING, Vol. 11, No. 5 (May 1981), pp. 46–48.

Baker, Hugh M. "The Economics of Multiplexing." SECURITY DISTRIBUTING AND MARKETING, Vol. 8, No. 5 (May 1978).

– – –"Multiplex: What's Happened to It?" SECURITY DISTRIBUTING AND MARKETING, Vol. 6, No. 2 (February 1976).

Barget, R. J. (ed). "Multiplexing: What Where Is It? Where Is It Going?" SECURITY DISTRIBUTING AND MARKETING, Vol. 6, No. 2 (February 1976).

Bell, Everett. "Digital Is More Than Alarm Reporting." SECURITY DISTRIBUTING AND MARKETING, Vol. 8, No. 2 (February 1978).

– – –"Listening In Makes the Difference." SECURITY DISTRIBUTING AND MARKETING, Vol. 7, No. 4 (April 1977).

Boggs, William. "Automating the Digital Communicator: Going the Microcomputer Route." ALARM SIGNAL (September–October 1980), pp. 16, 18.

– – –"Automating the Digital Communicator: Using an Existing Computer." ALARM SIGNAL (September–October 1980), pp. 17, 20.

Day, Donald F. "Multiplexing and the Polling Computer." SECURITY DISTRIBUTING AND MARKETING, Vol. 6, No. 2 (February 1976).

"Digital Communications Comes of Age." SECURITY DISTRIBUTING AND MARKETING. Vol. 8, No. 2 (February 1978).

Facility Protection Department. SAFEGUARDS CONTROL AND COMMUNICATIONS SYSTEMS HANDBOOK. SAND78-1785. Albuquerque, NM: Sandia Laboratories. May 1979. 124 pp.

Fuss, Eugene L. "Alarm Line Supervision – The Weak Link." SECURITY MANAGEMENT, Vol. 23, No. 7 (July 1979), pp. 40–44.

King, Claude. "Basic Considerations for Multiplexing Systems." SECURITY DISTRIBUTING AND MARKETING, Vol. 6, No. 2 (February 1976).

LeNay, Tom W. "Line Integrity for McCulloh Circuits." SIGNAL (2nd Quarter 1975), pp. 30–34, 36–37.

– – –"New Concepts in Multiplex Security." SECURITY DISTRIBUTING AND MARKETING, Vol. 8, No. 5 (May 1978).

Morgan, Jack B. "Remote Multiplexing Techniques." SECURITY DISTRIBUTING AND MARKETING, Vol. 8, No. 5 (May 1978).

Post, Deborah Cromer. "Capitalizing on Central Station Protection." SECURITY WORLD, Vol. 17, No. 1 (January 1980), pp. 34–36.

Schnabolk, Charles. "Transmitting the Alarm Signal." SECURITY MANAGEMENT, Vol. 23, No. 12 (December 1979), pp. 70–76 and Vol. 24, No. 1 (January 1980), pp. 58–63.

Stevens, Terry. "Is Wireless in Your Future?" SIGNAL (1st Quarter 1977), pp. 22, 24, 26, 28.

Vail, Kit, "Multiplex: Is It for You Yet?" SECURITY DISTRIBUTING AND MARKETING, Vol. 6, No. 2 (February 1976).

Williamson, William W. "Switch Line Systems for Central Station Signaling." SECURITY DISTRIBUTING AND MARKETING, Vol. 2, No. 8 (February 1978).

Wood, Nat. "Security With No 'Strings' Attached" (wireless alarms). SECURITY WORLD, Vol. 16, No. 4 (April 1979), pp. 22, 23, 74, 77, 78, 80.

Zatz, Saul. "An Introduction to Integrated Circuits for the Industrial Security Professional." SECURITY MANAGEMENT, Vol. 21, Nos 1 and 2 (March and May 1977), pp. 60–66 (Mar.) and 60–65 (May).

E. Proprietary and Computer-Based Systems (including Energy Management Systems)

"Computing Search Pays Off for Central Stations." SECURITY DISTRIBUTING AND MARKETING, Vol. 6, No. 10 (October 1976).

Daly, Glenn. "Microprocessor-Based System Helps Tighten Security, Lower Cost." SECURITY WORLD, Vol. 16, No. 11 (November 1979), pp. 24–26.

Duffy, Michael. "A Look at Proprietary Alarm Systems." SECURITY MANAGEMENT, Vol. 23, No. 12 (December 1979), pp. 32, 34–35.

Federal Supply Service, Standardization Division. INTERIM FEDERAL SPECIFICATION W-A--00450B (GSA-FSS): ALARM SYSTEMS, INTERIOR, SECURITY COMPONENTS FOR. Washington, DC: General Services Administration. February 16, 1973.

Glicksman, Mark. "Human Engineering for the Security Control Center." SECURITY MANAGEMENT, Vol. 25, No. 3 (March 1981), pp. 24, 26–30.

James, Pamela, "Security on a Chip." SECURITY MANAGEMENT, Vol. 24, No. 9 (September 1980), pp. 81–82, 84.

Keener, George. "Small Computer Boosts Surveillance Security." SECURITY WORLD, Vol. 11, No. 4 (April 1974), pp. 22–23, 56.

Longworth, Roy. "Computers as an Aid to Security Efforts." SECURITY MANAGEMENT, Vol. 21, No. 3 (July 1977), pp. 59–60.

McGinty, William. "About the Secureness of Your Security." SECURITY WORLD, Vol. 15, No. 4 (April 1978), pp. 23, 88–89, 94–95.

Meiners, Frank J. "One-Stop Shop for Electronic Physical Security, Energy Management Needs." SECURITY WORLD, Vol. 16, No. 2 (February 1979), pp. 24–27.

Post, Deborah Cromer. "Combining Building Controls." SECURITY WORLD, Vol. 17, No. 4 (April 1980), pp. 30–33.

"Proprietary System Provides Security and Energy Management at California College." SECURITY DISTRIBUTING AND MARKETING, Vol. 6, No. 10 (October 1976).

Siatt, Wayne, "Doubled Systems Promise Documented Savings." SECURITY WORLD, Vol. 17, No. 1 (January 1980), pp. 30–32.

— — —"Security/Fire/Energy Management: Integrating Systems for Maximum Performance." SECURITY WORLD, Vol. 18, No. 8 (August 1981), pp. 64–69.

Stossell, George F. "Smart' Security." SECURITY WORLD, Vol. 16, No. 6 (June 1979), pp. 24–25, 128.

Wilson, Stanley, Jr. "Distributed Processing with Microprocessors in Security Equipment." SECURITY DISTRIBUTING AND MARKETING, Vol. 6, No. 10 (October 1976).

F. False Alarm Problems and Solutions

Beerman, Bernard. "False Alarms and the Law." SIGNAL (1st Quarter 1979), pp. 46–48, 50, 52, 54, 57.

Berlin, Robert J. "Alarm Industry in Evolution: Reducing False Alarms." SIGNAL (1st Quarter 1977), pp. 52, 54.

Bozeat, N., M. A. Johnson, R. F. Penn, and M. A. Sinclair. SOME ERGONOMIC AND OTHER ASPECTS OF FALSE ALARM CALLS FROM INTRUDER ALARM SYSTEMS. Proceedings of the Sixth Congress of the International Ergonomics Society and Technical Program of the 20th Annual Meeting of the Human Factors Society, Leicester, U.K.: Loughborough University of Technology, 1976.

Darling, Don D. "According to Rigid Government Standards . . ." SECURITY WORLD, Vol. 11, No. 11 (December 1974), p. 42

– – –"Equipment to Reduce False Alarms." SECURITY WORLD, Vol. 13, No. 8 (August 1976), pp. 40, 127.

"False Alarm Prevention: The Advantages of Zoning." ALARM SIGNAL (September–October 1980), pp. 24, 28.

"False Alarm Prevention: Installation Planning and Procedures." ALARM SIGNAL (July–August 1980), pp. 11, 12, 14.

Kellem, Carl. "Legislation vs. the False Alarm Problem." SECURITY DISTRIBUTING AND MARKETING, Vol. 8, No. 1 (January 1978).

National Burglar and Fire Alarm Association. "25 Ways to Cry Wolf." SECURITY MANAGEMENT, Vol. 23, No. 12 (December 1979), pp. 12–13.

"Pinpointing the Culprits Behind False Alarms." SIGNAL (2nd quarter 1979), pp. 8–10, 12.

"Running a Few Tests Can Head Off False Alarms." SIGNAL (4th Quarter 1979), pp. 14–15.

Smith, Ray T. "You Cannot Always Blame the Equipment for False Alarms." SECURITY WORLD, Vol. 13, No. 4 (April 1976), pp. 47–48.

"Teach Your Subscribers False Alarm Prevention." ALARM SIGNAL (March–April 1981), pp. 14, 17–19, 28.

"A Trained Staff Will Prevent False Alarms." ALARM SIGNAL (May–June 1980), pp. 11, 12, 14.

G. Electronic Article Surveillance and Metal Detection

Association of Research Libraries. THEFT DETECTION AND PREVENTION. Kit 37. Washington, DC: Systems and Procedures Exchange Center. October 1977.

Cooper, Harrison R., Bill H. Lane, and Frances E. Rutherford. "Metal Detectors Come of Age." SECURITY MANAGEMENT, Vol. 20, No. 5 (November 1976), pp. 24–26, 28.

"The Differences Between a Systems Approach and a Methods Approach." SECURITY MANAGEMENT, Vol. 25, No. 5 (May 1981), pp. 120–123, 125.

Harbin, George. "Electronic Article Surveillance – It's Inevitable." SECURITY MANAGEMENT, Vol. 21, No. 3 (July 1977), pp. 14–15, 18.

James, Pamela. "Love/Hate and Lots of Hassles, But . . ." SECURITY MANAGEMENT, Vol. 25, No. 2 (February 1981), pp. 24–25, 27–28, 45–46.

Knight, Nancy H. THEFT DETECTION SYSTEMS FOR LIBRARIES. Library Technology Reports 12. Chicago, IL: American Library Association. November 1976. Pp. 575–691.

NILECJ STANDARD FOR HAND-HELD METAL DETECTORS FOR USE IN WEAPONS DETECTION. NILECJ-STD-0602.00. Washington, DC: Law Enforcement Standards Program, U.S. Department of Justice. October 1974. 9 pp.

NILECJ STANDARD FOR WALK-THROUGH METAL DETECTORS FOR USE IN WEAPONS DETECTION. NILECJ-STD-0601.00. Washington, DC: Law Enforcement Standards Program, U.S. Department of Justice. June 1974. 20 pp., illus.

TESTS OF HAND-HELD METAL WEAPONS DETECTORS. LESP-RPT-0603.00. Washington, DC: Law Enforcement Standards Program, U.S. Department of Justice. March 1977. 10 pp.

Wallach, Charles, and Roy Ricci. "Technical Notebook: Security Metal Detection Systems." SECURITY MANAGEMENT, Vol. 21, No. 3 (July 1977), pp. 61-66.

PART 3: ARCHIVES AND LIBRARY SECURITY

Brand, M. "Security of Academic Library Buildings." LIBRARY AND ARCHIVAL SECURITY, No. 3 (Spring 1980), pp. 39-47.

Brook, Philip R. "Library Design for Today's User." CANADIAN ARCHITECT (January 1978), pp. 30-35.

Casterline, Gail Farr. ARCHIVES AND MANUSCRIPTS: EXHIBITS. Chicago, IL: Society of American Archivists. 1980. 70 pp.

Cronon, M. J. "Workshop Approach to Library Security." LIBRARY AND ARCHIVAL SECURITY, No. 3 (Spring 1980), pp. 49-56.

Hellmuth, Obata, and Kasselbaum. LIBRARIES. St. Louis, MO. 1975

Johnson, Edward M. (ed.) PROTECTING THE LIBRARY AND ITS RESOURCES: A GUIDE TO PHYSICAL PROTECTION AND INSURANCE. Chicago, IL: American Library Association. 1963.

Ladenson, Alex. "Library Security and the Law." COLLEGE AND RESEARCH LIBRARIES, No. 38 (1977), pp. 109-118.

MARKING MANUSCRIPTS. Preservation Leaflet No. 4. Washington, DC: The Library of Congress. 1977.

Mason, Philip P. "Archival Security: New Solutions to an Old Problem." AMERICAN ARCHIVIST, Vol. 38 (October 1975), pp. 477-492.

McCarthy, J., and E. Perica. "Burglary: A Rising Problem in Library Security." UNABASHED LIBRARIAN, No. 37 (1980), pp. 19-20.

Metcalf, Keyes D. PLANNING ACADEMIC AND RESEARCH LIBRARY BUILDINGS. New York: McGraw-Hill. 1965.

Mitchell, Thornton W. (ed.). NORTON ON ARCHIVES: THE WRITINGS OF MARGARET CROSS NORTON ON ARCHIVAL AND RECORDS MANAGEMENT. (See Chapter 10 on protection of archives.) Carbondale, IL: Southern Illinois University Press. 1975. 288 pp.

Piez, Gladys T. "Insurance and the Protection of Library Resources." BULLETIN of the American Library Association (May 1962), pp. 421-424.

Rhoads, James B. "Alienation and Thievery: Archival Problems." AMERICAN ARCHIVIST, Vol. 29 (April 1966), pp. 197-208.

Sager, Don. "Protecting the Library After Hours." LIBRARY JOURNAL, Vol. 94, No. 18 (October 15, 1969), pp. 3609-3614. Illus., biblio.

"Securing the Back Door." AMERICAN LIBRARIES, Vol. 12 (May 1981), pp. 278-279.

SECURITY PROBLEMS IN ARCHIVES. Kit No. 2. Chicago, IL: Society of American Archivists. 1979.

Surridge, O. "Thief Detection Equipment." LIBRARY ASSOCIATION RECORD, Vol. 82 (July 1980), p. 324.

Trezza, Alphonse F. LIBRARY BUILDINGS: INNOVATION FOR CHANGING NEEDS. Chicago, IL: American Library Association. 1972.

Tuttle, J. A. "Security and Safety: UW, Madison Takes Steps to Solve Memorial Library Problem." WINCONSIN LIBRARY BULLETIN, Vol. 76 (May–June 1980), pp. 135–136 + .

Walch, Timothy. ARCHIVES AND MANUSCRIPTS: SECURITY. Chicago, IL: Society of American Archivists. 1977. 30 pp.

– – –"Common Sense Security for Museum Libraries." CURATOR, Vol. 12, No. 3 (September 1979), pp. 217–223. Biblio.

PART 4: CARGO AND TRANSPORTATION SECURITY

American Trucking Association Security Council. "Controlling Cargo Thefts." SECURITY INDUSTRY AND PRODUCT NEWS, Vol. 9, No. 1 (January 1980), pp. 20–22, 30, 32.

Arkin, Joseph. "Handling Problems of Incoming Freight." SECURITY MANAGEMENT, Vol. 20, No. 4 (September 1976), pp. 8–10.

Bray, Samuel E., and Robert Hurley. FREIGHT SECURITY MANUAL. Los Angeles: Security World Publishing Co. 1970.

CARGO LOSS PREVENTION RECOMMENDATIONS. Zurich: International Union of Marine Insurance. 1970.

CARGO THEFT AND ORGANIZED CRIME: A DESKBOOK FOR MANAGEMENT AND LAW ENFORCEMENT. Washington, DC: Department of Transportation and Justice. October 1972. 78 pp.

Darling, Don D. "Making Big Problems Out of Little Ones." SECURITY WORLD, Vol. 12, No. 8 (September 1975), p. 39.

Di Domenico, Joseph M. "How Secure Is Your Distribution Center?" SECURITY WORLD, Vol. 15, No. 11 (November 1978), pp. 24, 25, 50.

Dudley, Dorothy H., and Irma B. Wilkinson. MUSEUM REGISTRATION METHODS (includes chapters on packing and shipping, importing and exporting, and insurance). Washington, DC: American Association of Museums. 1979. 437 pp., illus., biblio.

Frier, John P. "How Much Light for the Shipping Dock?" SECURITY WORLD, Vol. 15, No. 11 (November 1978), pp. 26–27, 43.

GUIDELINES FOR THE PHYSICAL SECURITY OF CARGO. Washington, DC: U.S. Department of Transportation. May 1972. DOT P 5000.2.

Hebda, Joseph B. "Shipping Vehicle Entry and exit: An Overview." SECURITY WORLD, Vol. 15, No. 11 (November 1978), pp. 22–23, 58.

Hurley, John E. "Cutting Cargo Losses in Port." SECURITY MANAGEMENT, Vol. 22, No. 1 (January 1978), pp. 6–8.

Jorgensen, Ronald E. "Shipping and Receiving – Weak Link in the Cargo Security Chain." SECURITY MANAGEMENT, Vol. 22, No. 1 (January 1978), pp. 10, 13–15.

Little, David B. "Safeguarding Works of Art: Transportation, Records and Insurance." Technical Leaflet No. 9 from HISTORY NEWS, Vol. 18, No. 7 (May 1963).

Lucas, Walter A. "Protection of High Value Cargo." SECURITY MANAGEMENT, Vol. 21, No. 6 (November 1977), pp. 9–10.

Pizer, Harry. "Transporting Art Objects." ASSETS PROTECTION, Vol. 1, No. 2 (Summer 1975), pp. 33–34.

Putnam, Ronald R. "For Safe Transport, Try Discreet Packaging." SECURITY MANAGEMENT, Vol. 24, No. 9 (September 1980), pp. 8–10.

Siatt, Wayne. "Securing a Shipping Dock." SECURITY WORLD, Vol. 18, No. 5 (May 1981), pp. 26–28.

PART 5: CLOSED CIRCUIT TELEVISION AND FILM CAMERA SURVEILLANCE

Carroll, John M. "3 Missions for CCTV in Physical Security: Detection, Surveillance, Access Control." SECURITY WORLD, Vol. 16, No. 2 (February 1979), pp. 48–49. Biblio.

Cochran, H. A. "Lighting for Closed-Circuit TV Surveillance." LIGHTING DESIGN AND APPLICATION, Vol. 4, No. 3 (1974), pp. 47–49.

"Concealed Camera Systems." LAW ENFORCEMENT COMMUNICATIONS, Vol. 4, No. 1 (February 1977), pp. 21–22.

"Coverage at Low Light Levels." SECURITY DISTRIBUTING AND MARKETING, Vol. 9, No. 10 (October 1979).

Crowther, Charles. "Better Cameras or More Light?" SECURITY WORLD, Vol. 13, No. 11 (November 1976), pp. 32–33.

Dale, John. "Preventive Maintenance: The Best Prescription for Videotapes." SECURITY INDUSTRY AND PRODUCT NEWS, Vol. 10, No. 2 (February 1981), pp. 11, 24.

Glicksman, Mark. "Lighting Requirements for CCTV." SECURITY MANAGEMENT, Vol. 25, No. 1 (January 1981), pp. 81–86.

"A Glossary of Video Terms." SECURITY MANAGEMENT, Vol. 23, No. 9 (September 1979), p. 132.

Grover, Charles. PHOTOGRAPHIC TERMS AND DEFINITIONS. LESP–RPT–0307.00. Washington, DC: Law Enforcement Standards Program, U.S. Department of Justice. October 1975. 52 pp.

Horn, Donald N. "To Watch a Thief." SECURITY INDUSTRY AND PRODUCT NEWS, Vol. 7, Nos. 7 and 8 (July and August 1978), pp. 22 and 24 (July) and 20, 22, and 37 (August).

Kmet, Mary Alice. "Play It Again, Sam." SECURITY MANAGEMENT, Vol. 24, No. 10 (October 1980), pp. 8–9, 11–12.

Kravontka, Stanley J. "CCTV Systems Design for School Security." SECURITY WORLD, Vol. 11, No. 2 (February 1974), pp. 22, 23, 48, 49.

Kruegle, Herman. "The Basics of CCTV." SECURITY MANAGEMENT, Vol. 25, No. 1 (January 1981), pp. 45, 48, 50–54, 57–63.

– – –"Pinhole Camera Surveillance." SECURITY INDUSTRY AND PRODUCT NEWS, Vol. 10, Nos. 4, 5, and 6 (April, May, and June 1981), pp. 22–25 (April), 24, 46–47 (May), and 24–27, 46 (June).

– – –"Understanding CCTV Lenses and Accessories." SECURITY INDUSTRY AND PRODUCT NEWS. Vol. 7, Nos. 2–5 (February–May 1978), pp. 22–23 (Feb.), 20–22 (Mar.), 20, 22, 24 (Apr.), and 30, 32, 34 (May).

Kuhns, Roger. "Photographic Identification." SECURITY MANAGEMENT, Vol. 21, No. 1 (March 1977), pp. 8–10, 12–13.

Mick, Peter R. "Crime Time Television: Digital Video Analyzers — A New Dimension in CCTV Security Systems." SECURITY INDUSTRY AND PRODUCT NEWS, Vol. 9, No. 1 (January 1980), pp. 24–28.

Palm, Noel. "Multi-Camera Set-Up Enhances Time Lapse VTR Systems." SECURITY WORLD, Vol. 16, No. 1 (January 1979), pp. 32–33.

Pergola, Paola Della. "L'Impianto Televiso a Circuita Chioso della Galleria Borghese." MUSEI E GALLERIE D'ITALIA (Rome), Vol. 13, No. 36 (1968).

Peterson. H. E., and D. J. Dugas. "The Relative Importance of Contrast and Motion in Visual Detection." HUMAN FACTORS, Vol. 14, No. 3 (1972), pp. 207–216.

Raia, Salvatore L., and Raymond W. Payne. "For the User: Which Video Switcher . . . and Why?" SECURITY WORLD, Vol. 15, No. 2 (February 1978), pp. 30–32, 47.

— — —"For the User: Completing the Look at Video Switchers." SECURITY WORLD, Vol. 15, No. 4 (April 1978), pp. 36–37, 70–71.

Richmond, Joseph C. IMAGE QUALITY OF MONOCHROME TELEVISION CAMERAS. NBS Special Publication 480-25. Washington, DC: National Bureau of Standards, U.S. Department of Commerce. October 1977. 7 pp., illus.

— — —A SIMPLE TEST FOR EVALUATING THE SPECTRAL RESPONSIVITY OF MONOCHROME TELEVISION CAMERAS. LESP-RPT-0310.00. Washington, DC: Law Enforcement Standards Program, U.S. Department of Justice. February 1977. 24 pp., illus.

Rosenbaum, Richard W. "Convenience Magic for VTR in Security." SECURITY WORLD, Vol. 15, No. 6 (June 1978), pp. 30, 51, 57.

Ruyle, Robert. "SDM Equipment Analysis: CCTV Scanner Repair." SECURITY DISTRIBUTING AND MARKETING, Vol. 11, No. 4 (April 1981), pp. 44–46.

Schwartz, Allen E. "Management Guide to Closed Circuit Television Security Systems." SECURITY INDUSTRY AND PRODUCT NEWS, Vol. 5, No. 1 (February 1976), pp. 18–21.

"The Security Side of Film and Tape: Two Case Histories." SECURITY WORLD, Vol. 15, No. 6 (June 1978), pp. 18–19, 48–49.

"Security World Equipment Focus: CCTV Systems." SECURITY WORLD, Vol. 18, No. 2 (February 1981), pp. 32–36.

SELECTION AND APPLICATION GUIDE TO FIXED SURVEILLANCE CAMERAS. NILECJ–Guide-0301.00. Washington, DC: Law Enforcement Assistance Administration, U.S. Department of Justice. December 1974. 24 pp., illus.

"The 'Small Security' Solution." SECURITY WORLD, Vol. 13, No. 4 (April 1976), p. 25.

"Surveillance Equipment: Its Functions and Uses." SECURITY WORLD, Vol. 12, Nos. 2 and 5 (February and May 1975), pp. 15, 16, 43, 67 (Feb.) and 28–30 (May).

Tanaka, James. "Selecting CCTV Lenses." SECURITY WORLD, Vol. 17, No. 6 (June 1980), pp. 36–38.

Tickner, A. H., and E. C. Poulton. "Monitoring up to 16 Synthetic Television Pictures Showing a Great Deal of Movement." ERGONOMICS, Vol. 16, No. 4 (1973), pp. 381–401. Medical Research Council, Cambridge, England.

"TV 'Stills' Verify Alarm Events." SECURITY WORLD, Vol. 16, No. 2 (February 1979), pp. 46–47.

Tiefer, George. "Warehouse Security — Conscious and Innovative." SECURITY INDUSTRY AND PRODUCT NEWS. Vol. 6, No. 1 (February 1977), pp. 21–23.

Venus Scientific. "Low Light Level TV Cameras and Their Use in Security Systems" SECURITY INDUSTRY AND PRODUCT NEWS, Vol. 6, No. 1 (February 1977), pp. 24, 29.

Yaggi, Lawrence M., Jr. "CCTV as a Multi-Building Access Control System." SECURITY MANAGEMENT, Vol. 21, No. 5 (September 1977), pp. 40–42,

Yonemura, Gary T. IMAGE QUALITY CRITERION FOR THE IDENTIFICATION OF FACES. LESP-RPT-0303.00. Washington, DC: Law Enforcement Standards Program, U.S. Department of Justice. May 1974. 20 pp., illus., biblio.

PART 6: COMMUNICATIONS

Greene, Frank M. TECHNICAL TERMS AND DEFINITIONS USED WITH LAW ENFORCE-MENT COMMUNICATIONS EQUIPMENT. LESP-RPT-0203.00. Washington, DC: Law Enforcement Standards Program, U.S. Department of Justice. June 1973. 139 pp.

Jesch, R. L., and I. S. Berry. BATTERIES USED WITH LAW ENFORCEMENT COM-MUNICATIONS EQUIPMENT: COMPARISON AND PERFORMANCE CHARACTER-ISTICS. LESP-RPT-0201.00. Washington, DC: Law Enforcement Standards Program, U.S. Department of Justice. May 1972. 37 pp., illus., biblio.

Jickling, R. M., and J. F. Shafer. REPEATERS FOR LAW ENFORCEMENT COMMUNICA-TION SYSTEMS. LESP-RPT-0206.00. Washington, DC: Law Enforcement Standards Program, U.S. Department of Justice. October 1974. 14 pp., illus., biblio.

Martenson, Nils. "Radio Detectors and Guard Communications Systems." In PROCEEDINGS OF THE FIRST INTERNATIONAL ELECTRONIC CRIME COUNTERMEASURES CON-FERENCE. Edinburgh, Scotland. 1973.

NIJ and NILECJ STANDARDS. The following 13 publications are standards of the National Institute of Justice, U.S. Department of Justice (formerly National Institute of Law Enforcement and Criminal Justice). All are published by the Justice Department in Washington, DC. Publication numbers, titles, and dates of publication are given.

NILECJ-STD-0201.00. FIXED AND BASE STATION FM TRANSMITTERS. September 1974. 16 pp., illus., biblio.

NILECJ-STD-0202.00. MOBILE FM TRANSMITTERS. October 1974. 18 pp., illus., biblio.

NIJ-STD-0204.01. FIXED AND BASE STATION ANTENNAS. April 1981. 19 pp., illus.

NILECJ-STD-0205.00. MOBILE ANTENNAS. May 1974. 9 pp., illus., biblio.

NILECJ-STD-0206.00. FIXED AND BASE STATION FM RECEIVERS. September 1975. 13 pp., illus., biblio.

NILECJ-STD-0207.00. MOBILE FM RECEIVERS. June 1975. 14 pp., illus., biblio.

NILECJ-STD-0209.00. PERSONAL FM TRANSCEIVERS. December 1978. 28 pp., illus., biblio.

NILECJ-STD-0211.00. BATTERIES FOR PERSONAL/PORTABLE TRANSCEIVERS. June 1975. 9 pp., illus.

NILECJ-STD-0212.00. RF COXIAL CABLE ASSEMBLIES FOR MOBILE TRANS-CEIVERS. September 1975. 5 pp., illus., biblio.

NILECJ-STD-0213.00 FM REPEATER SYSTEMS. November 1977. 12 pp., biblio.

NILECJ-STD-0214.00. BODY-WORN FM TRANSMITTERS. December 1978. 15 pp., illus., biblio.

NIJ-STD-0217.00. MICROPHONE CABLE ASSEMBLIES FOR MOBILE FM TRANS-CEIVERS. August 1980. 6 pp., illus., biblio.

NIJ-STD-0219.00. CONTINUOUS SIGNAL-CONTROLLED SELECTIVE SIGNALING. August 1980. 20 pp., illus., biblio.

Scott, Winston W., Jr. BATTERIES USED WITH LAW ENFORCEMENT COMMUNICA-
TIONS EQUIPMENT: CHARGERS AND CHARGING TECHNIQUES. LESP-RPT-0202.00.
Washington, DC: Law Enforcement Standards Program, U.S. Department of Justice. June 1973.
43 pp., illus., biblio.

– – –COMMUNICATION SYSTEMS GUIDE. NBS Special Publication 480-12. Washington,
DC: National Bureau of Standards, U.S. Department of Commerce. January 1979. 32 pp.,
illus., biblio.

Scotti, Anthony J., and Robert Hibner. "Radio Frequencies for Security Uses." SECURITY
MANAGEMENT, Vol. 24, No. 9 (September 1980), pp. 68, 70–71.

"Security Communications: What Fiberoptics Has to Offer." SECURITY MANAGEMENT,
Vol. 23, No. 4 (April 1979), pp. 18–20.

Sugar, George R. VOICE PRIVACY EQUIPMENT FOR LAW ENFORCEMENT COM-
MUNICATION SYSTEMS. LESP-RPT-0204.00. Washington, DC: Law Enforcement Standards
Program, U.S. Department of Justice. May 1974. 22 pp., biblio.

PART 7: COMPUTER, EDP, AND DATA SECURITY

Aaron, Harold R., and Robert P. Campbell. "Managing the Corporate Computer Security Problem." SECURITY MANAGEMENT, Vol. 21, No. 6 (November 1977), pp. 14–17.

Bequai, August. COMPUTER CRIME. Woburn, MA: Butterworth Publishers. 1978. 224 pp.

Carroll, John M. COMPUTER SECURITY. Woburn, MA: Butterworth Publishers. 400 pp.

"Computer Coverage" (controlling access). SECURITY WORLD, Vol. 17, No. 1 (January 1980),
pp. 44–47.

"Controls and Audits for an Inventory System." ASSETS PROTECTION. Vol. 3, No. 3 (Fall
1978), pp. 13–15.

GUIDELINES FOR AUTOMATIC DATA PROCESSING PHYSICAL SECURITY AND RISK
MANAGEMENT. FIPS Publication 31. Washington, DC: National Bureau of Standards, U.S.
Department of Commerce. June 1974.

Hemphill, C. F., Jr., and J. Hemphill. SECURITY PROCEDURES FOR COMPUTER
SYSTEMS. Homewood, IL: Dow Jones-Irwin. 1973.

Hoyt, Douglas B. COMPUTER SECURITY HANDBOOK. New York: Macmillan Publishing
Co., 1973.

Hsiao, David K., Douglas S. Kerr, and Stuart E. Madnick. COMPUTER SECURITY. Woburn,
MA: Butterworth Publishers. 1979. 293 pp.

Jacobson, Robert V. "Seven Fallacies Confuse Computer Fire Safety." SECURITY MANAGE-
MENT, Vol. 23, No. 8 (August 1979), pp. 60–63. Biblio.

Paird, Lindsay L., Jr. "Auditing (Around) the Computer Center." SECURITY MANAGEMENT,
Vol. 20, No. 4 (September 1976), pp. 52–54, 56–58, 60–62.

"Protecting Computer Hardware." SECURITY WORLD, Vol. 17, No. 9 (September 1980), pp.
22–26.

Sapse, Anne-Marie, Peter Shenkin, and Marcel Sapse. COMPUTER APPLICATIONS IN THE
PRIVATE SECURITY BUSINESS. Woburn, MA: Butterworth Publishers. 1980. 139 pp.

Schweitzer, James A. MANAGING INFORMATION SECURITY: A PROGRAM FOR THE
ELECTRONIC AGE. Woburn, MA: Butterworth Publishers. 1982.

– – –"Personal Computing and Data Security." SECURITY WORLD, Vol. 17, No. 6 (June
1980), pp. 30–35.

"A Step-by-Step Approach to Computer Security." SECURITY WORLD, Vol. 16, No. 9 (September 1979), pp. 18-30. A series of articles by different authors.

Wagner, Charles R. THE CPA AND COMPUTER FRAUD. Woburn, MA: Butterworth Publishers. 1979. 176 pp.

Walker, Bruce J., and Ian F. Blake. COMPUTER SECURITY AND PROTECTION STRUCTURES. Woburn, MA: Butterworth Publishers. 1977. 142 pp.

PART 8: GUARDS, GUARDING, AND PRIVATE SECURITY

A. General Works

Astor, Saul. "Contract Guards: The Facts as I See Them." SECURITY WORLD, Vol. 12, No. 7 (July–August 1975), pp. 18-19, 123-125, 127.

Bernstein, Ira H. "One Way to Screen Security Guards." SECURITY MANAGEMENT, Vol. 25, No. 9 (September 1981), pp. 35-38.

Brock, Randolph D, III. "So — What Do You Want from a Guard Company?" SECURITY WORLD, Vol. 14, No. 8 (August 1977), pp. 31, 118-122.

Butler, William G. "Asking the Right Questions." SECURITY MANAGEMENT, Vol. 25, No. 3 (March 1981), pp. 50-54, 56.

Chamberlain, Charles S. "A Short History of Private Security." ASSETS PROTECTION, Vol. 4, No. 3 (July–August 1979), pp. 35-38. Biblio.

Cohen, Joseph. "Choosing Contract or Proprietary Security." SECURITY MANAGEMENT, Vol. 23, No. 10 (October 1979), pp. 26-28, 30.

— — —"Contract Security or Proprietary Security." ASSETS PROTECTION, Vol. 4, No. 1 (March–April 1979), pp. 31-33.

Colglazier, Charles W. "Financial Considerations in Security: A Guard Service Study." SECURITY MANAGEMENT, Vol. 22, Nos. 1-3 (January–March 1978), pp. 30-31 (Jan.), 14-16 (Feb.), and 14 (March).

Covington, Stuart. "How to Select a Supervisor." SECURITY MANAGEMENT, Vol. 24, No. 10 (October 1980), pp. 16, 18.

Cunbow, Thomas L. "Getting Off on the Right Foot with a Contract Guard Service." SECURITY MANAGEMENT, Vol. 22, No. 11 (November 1978), pp. 14, 17.

Daly, James W. "Security Supervision: What Does It Require?" SECURITY INDUSTRY AND PRODUCT NEWS, Vol. 4, No. 4 (July–August 1975), p. 8.

Darling, Don D. "I Wasn't Asleep, I was Praying." SECURITY WORLD, Vol. 15, No. 2 (February 1978), pp. 52-53.

Doughty, Norman E. "Which Guard Service to Use? It's Simple Arithmetic." SECURITY MANAGEMENT, Vol. 22, No. 11 (November 1978), pp. 18-20.

Dunker, Ralph R. "Contract Guard Users Tell Why." SECURITY MANAGEMENT, Vol. 22, No. 7 (July 1978), pp. 14, 16.

Gibbs-Smith, Charles H. THE ART OF OBSERVATION: A BOOKLET FOR MUSEUM WARDERS. London: Victoria and Albert Museum. 1971. 16 pp.

Gossin, Francis. "A Security Chief Comments on Guards." MUSEUM NEWS, Vol. 50, No. 5 (January 1972), pp. 30-31.

"Guarding Upgraded." SECURITY WORLD, Vol. 17, No. 1 (January 1980), pp. 48-50.

Hall, R., P. Benner, J. Caldwell, W. Hanna, D. Solomonson, and W. Weaver. SECURITY PERSONNEL PERFORMANCE MEASUREMENT SYSTEM. 2 vols. Santa Barbara, CA: Mission Research Corp. 1979.

Hoffman, Bernhard. "Good Morale from a Sense of Purpose." SECURITY MANAGEMENT, Vol. 24, No. 6 (June 1980), pp. 19–21, 24, 27.

Jones, D. L. "Those Dangerous 'Regular Rounds'." SECURITY WORLD, Vol. 14, No. 6 (June 1977), pp. 38–39, 44.

Kakalik, James S., and Sorrell Wildhorn. THE PRIVATE POLICE, SECURITY AND DANGER. New York: Crane Russak & Co. 1977.

Kingwell, Robert G. "Labor Relations and Your Guard Force." SECURITY MANAGEMENT, Vol. 25, No. 7 (July 1981), pp. 28–29, 31.

Kmet, Mary Alice. "Placing Employees for Best Results." SECURITY MANAGEMENT, Vol. 23, No. 3 (March 1979), pp. 6–8, 10, 13, 26.

Lang, James C. "Don't Call Him a 'Guard' Unless That's All He Does." SECURITY INDUSTRY AND PRODUCT NEWS, Vol. 8, No. 6 (June 1979), pp. 24–25.

Law Enforcement/Private Security Relationship Committee, Private Security Advisory Council, LEAA. "LEAA Private Security Codes of Ethics." SIGNAL (1st Quarter 1977), pp. 16, 18, 20.

Lipman, Ira A. "Cracking Crime by Guarding the Guards." SECURITY INDUSTRY AND PRODUCT NEWS, Vol. 6, No. 4 (August 1977), p. 26.

Lipson, Milton. ON GUARD, THE BUSINESS OF PRIVATE SECURITY. New York: The New York Times Book Co. 1975.

Mackie, R. M. (ed.) VIGILANCE: THEORY, OPERATIONAL PERFORMANCE, AND PHYSIOLOGICAL CORRELATES. New York: Plenum Press. 1977.

McElroy, Daniel E. "Private and Public Security: A Professional Alliance." SECURITY WORLD, Vol. 16, No. 8 (August 1979), pp. 34–35.

Melnicoe, William, and Jan C. Mennig. ELEMENTS OF POLICE SUPERVISION. Beverly Hills, CA: Glencoe Press. 1970.

Miller, James C., and Robert R. Mackie. VIGILANCE RESEARCH AND NUCLEAR SECURITY: CRITICAL REVIEW AND POTENTIAL APPLICATIONS TO SECURITY GUARD PERFORMANCE. NBS-GCR-80-201. Prepared for National Bureau of Standards, U.S. Department of Commerce, Washington, D.C., by Human Factors Research, Inc., Goleta, California. June 1980. 285 pp., biblio.

Montgomery, John M. "Employee Suitability Screening." ASSETS PROTECTION, Vol. 5, No. 3 (May–June 1980), pp. 35–38.

Minion, Ronald R. "Motivating Security Guards." SECURITY WORLD, Vol. 14, No. 6 (June 1977), pp. 10, 12, 14, 32, 56.

National Advisory Committee on Criminal Justice Standards and Goals. PRIVATE SECURITY: REPORT OF THE TASK FORCE ON PRIVATE SECURITY. Washington, DC: U.S. Department of Justice. 1976. 580 pp.

"National Research Efforts on Private Security." SECURITY MANAGEMENT, Vol. 21, No. 5 (September 1977), pp. 44–46.

Nelson, Francis B., Jr. "Factors Affecting the Relationship Between Public Police and Private Police." SECURITY MANAGEMENT, Vol. 20, No. 6 (January 1977), pp. 22–23, 15.

Newby, Carl G. "Guard Regulation." SECURITY MANAGEMENT, Vol. 25, No. 5 (May 1981), pp. 30–34, 36–37.

Norwood, Francis W. "Licensing, Standards, and Certification in the Private Security Sector." SECURITY MANAGEMENT, Vol. 20, No. 5 (November 1976), pp. 34-36.

Pizer, Harry. "Preparing for Strikes." ASSETS PROTECTION, Vol. 2, No. 1 (Winter 1976), p. 30.

Private Security Advisory Council. SCOPE OF LEGAL AUTHORITY OF PRIVATE SECURITY PERSONNEL. Washington, DC: Law Enforcement Assistance Administration, U.S. Department of Justice. 1977. Also published by the National Burglar and Fire Alarm Association, Washington, DC.

Private Security Task Force. STANDARDS AND GOALS FOR PRIVATE SECURITY. Washington, DC: Law Enforcement Assistance Administration, U.S. Department of Justice. 1977.

"The Pros and Cons of Proprietary and Contract Security Forces." SECURITY WORLD, Vol. 18, No. 7 (July 1981), pp. 32-35.

Reddin, Thomas. "Law Enforcement Turned Civilian: A New Look at Guard Forces." SECURITY WORLD, Vol. 12, No. 6 (June 1975), pp. 18-19.

Sathre, Ronald R. "Fitting the Form to the Need." SECURITY MANAGEMENT, Vol. 25, No. 7 (July 1981), pp. 50-54.

Schurr, Robert. "The Guard Force — Direct Hire or Contract." SECURITY MANAGEMENT, Vol. 19, No. 6 (January 1976), pp. 42-43.

— — — "Pre-Employment Interview and Investigation of Security Officers." SECURITY MANAGEMENT, Vol. 20, No. 4 (September 1976), pp. 12, 14, 15.

"Security World Survey: Contract/Proprietary Guards: How They Suit User's Needs." SECURITY WORLD, Vol. 18, No. 7 (July 1981), pp. 21-30.

Sheley, Joseph F., and Douglas D. Dodd. "Private Security Officers as Imitators of the Police." SECURITY WORLD, Vol. 16, No. 8 (August 1977), pp. 33-34.

Shirar, Gerard. "You Can Motivate Your Nighttime Guards." SECURITY MANAGEMENT, Vol. 22, No. 12 (December 1978), pp. 32-35.

Slutzky, Kenneth B. "Defining the 'Right Person' for That Security Job." SECURITY WORLD, Vol. 14, No. 8 (August 1977), pp. 29, 99-103.

— — — "Upgrading Security Forces." SECURITY MANAGEMENT, Vol. 21, No. 3 (July 1977), pp. 40-41, 42, 44.

Spain, Norman M., and Gary Lee Elkin. "Private Security Versus Law Enforcement: There Is a Difference." SECURITY WORLD, Vol. 16, No. 8 (August 1979), pp. 32, 38, 40.

Steeno, David L. "Hiring Security Personnel: The Employment Interview." SECURITY WORLD, Vol. 17, No. 1 (January 1980), pp. 56-57, 76, 78, 80.

Strobl, Walter, HANDBOOK FOR INDUSTRIAL/COMMERCIAL SECURITY FORCES. Knoxville, TN: Training Consultants, Inc. 1977. 232 pp.

Stroh, C. M. VIGILANCE: THE PROBLEM OF SUSTAINED ATTENTION. New York: Pergamon Press. 1971.

Swartz, John L. "Security Activity Reports — Indexes to Performance." SECURITY MANAGEMENT, Vol. 23, No. 10 (October 1979), pp. 74-75.

"Tackling Scheduling and Deployment Problems." SECURITY MANAGEMENT, Vol. 22, No. 5 (May 1978), pp. 24-25.

Tucker, Partricia G. "Big A Versus Little P." SECURITY MANAGEMENT, Vol. 23, No. 6 (June 1979), pp. 48-49, 51-52, 54.

Van Meter, Clifford W. "The Private Security Task Force — Review and Preview." SECURITY MANAGEMENT, Vol. 20, No. 3 (July 1976), pp. 26–29.

Walker, Don. "Technical Notebook: Loss, Offense, and Incident Reporting." SECURITY MANAGEMENT, Vol. 21, No. 5 (September 1977), pp. 82–89.

Wathen, Thomas W. SECURITY SUBJECTS: AN OFFICER'S GUIDE TO PLANT PROTECTION. Springfield, IL: Charles C. Thomas. 1972. 172 pp.

Williams, Mason. THE LAW ENFORCEMENT BOOK OF WEAPONS, AMMUNITION AND TRAINING PROCEDURES. Springfield, IL: Charles C. Thomas. 1977.

Wolfe, Howard A. "Security Attire." SECURITY MANAGEMENT, Vol. 24, No. 5 (May 1980), pp. 6–7.

B. Guard Training

"The Advantages of AV for Training." SECURITY MANAGEMENT, Vol. 24, No. 5 (May 1980), pp. 10–12, 14–15. Biblio.

Clark, Lawrence F. "Security Education — For All Employees." SECURITY MANAGEMENT, Vol. 22, No. 3 (March 1978), pp. 44–46, 48.

Cunbow, Thomas L. "Training an In-House Security Force." SECURITY MANAGEMENT, Vol. 22, No. 3 (March 1978), pp. 50–53.

Didcot, Don. "Quarterbacking the Teaching Process." ASSETS PROTECTION, Vol. 2, No. 4 (Winter 1977), pp. 20–21.

– – –"Selecting Media for Training." ASSETS PROTECTION, Vol. 3, No. 1 (Spring 1978), pp. 17–19.

– – –"Training or Instruction." ASSETS PROTECTION, Vol. 2, No. 3 (Fall 1977), pp. 25–26.

Fee, Dwight. "Training Programs, Methods, Topics and Standards for Uniformed, Non-Supervisory Security Personnel." SECURITY MANAGEMENT, Vol. 20, No. 5 (November 1976), pp. 30–32.

GUARD SUPERVISOR TRAINING. Knoxville, TN: Training Consultants, Inc. 1975. 103 pp.

Higgins, Clay E. "The Security Director as Trainer." SECURITY MANAGEMENT. Vol. 24, No. 5 (May 1980), pp. 77–81.

– – –"Security Training: The Security Director's Role." Presented at Public Utilities Program at the American Society for Industrial Security's Annual Seminar, New Orleans, LA, August 31–September 3, 1981. 13 pp. (Released by Stone and Webster Engineering Corp., Boston, Massachusetts.)

Lukins, Richard A. "Security Training for the Guard Force." SECURITY MANAGEMENT, Vol. 29, No. 2 (May 1976), pp. 32–35.

Porter, Raymond H. "Teaching Security and Safety with Audio/Visual Equipment." SECURITY INDUSTRY AND PRODUCT NEWS, Vol. 8, No. 3 (March 1979), pp. 22–25.

SECURITY OFFICER TRAINING MANUAL. Knoxville, TN: Training Consultants, Inc. 1975. 103 pp.

Security Services Branch. GUARD SUPERVISOR TRAINING, 1971. 88 pp. From Department of Supply and Services, Place du Portage Phase 3, 11 Laurier Street, Hull, Quebec, Canada.

– – –PROTECTIVE SECURITY GUARD TRAINING COURSE. n.d. 300 pp. For source, see previous citation.

Shaw, Paul D. "Security Training." ASSETS PROTECTION, Vol. 2, No. 3 (Fall 1977), pp. 24–25.

Training Division, Federal Protective Service. BASIC TRAINING COURSE INSTRUCTOR'S GUIDE. Washington, DC: U.S. General Services Administration, n.d. 250 pp.

C. Guard Dogs

Blakley, Andrew M. "Guard Dogs as a Security Aid: A Case Study." SECURITY MANAGE-MENT, Vol. 21, No. 2 (May 1977), pp. 23-25.

"Increasing Museum Security with Canine Teams." SECURITY INDUSTRY AND PRODUCT NEWS, Vol. 9, No. 10 (October 1980), pp. 24-26, 33. Biblio.

Pellant, Leland T. "Are Museums Going to the Dogs?" WESTERN MUSEUMS QUARTERLY, Vol. 2, No. 4 (June 1964), pp. 19-22.

D. Weapons

Goldberg, Melvin S. "To Arm or Not to Arm." SECURITY MANAGEMENT, Vol. 24, No. 5 (May 1980), pp. 84-87.

Gross, Philip J. "Memo to Management — Subject: Issuance of Weapons to Security Personnel." SECURITY MANAGEMENT, Vol. 21, No. 3 (July 1977), pp. 50-52.

Nikoden, Joseph, Jr. "Firearms: Guidelines on Training and Ranges." SECURITY WORLD, Vol. 15, Nos. 4, 6, and 8 (April, June, August 1978), pp. 20-21, 90-91 (April), 22-24 (June), and 74-79 (August).

PART 9: INSURANCE

Babcock, Phillip H. "Insurance: Alternatives to Certificates." MUSEUM NEWS, Vol. 57, No. 5 (May-June 1979), pp. 56-57.

Babcock, Phillip H., and Marr T. Haack. "Plain-English Collections Insurance." MUSEUM NEWS, Vol. 59, No 7 (July-August 1981), pp. 22-25.

DuBose, Beverly M., Jr. "Insuring Against Loss." Technical Leaflet No. 5 from HISTORY NEWS, Vol. 24, No. 5 (May 1969).

Gale, Cynthia. "Insuring Valuable Documents." SECURITY MANAGEMENT, Vol. 25, No. 8 (August 1981), pp 113-114.

Gross, Philip J. "Memo to Management — Subject: Security, Insurance and the Bottom Line." SECURITY MANAGEMENT, Vol. 21, No. 1 (March 1977), pp. 25-26.

Kmet, Mary Alice, "Reducing Risk Through Crime Insurance." SECURITY MANAGEMENT, Vol. 24, Nos. 1 and 2 (January and February 1980), pp. 10-11, 13-15 (Jan.) and 61-64, 66-67 (Feb.).

Lawton, J. B., and Huntington T. Block. "Museum Insurance." CURATOR, Vol. 9, No. 4 (December 1966), pp. 288-297.

Mills, Paul Chadbourne. "Insurance: Are Fine Arts Premiums Out of Line?" MUSEUM NEWS, Vol. 57, No. 5 (May-June 1979), pp. 54-55.

OCCUPANCY BULLETIN: LIBRARIES. New York: American Insurance Association. 1971.

Pfeffer, Irving. "Strategies for Insurance Cost Reduction in Museums." RISK MANAGEMENT MANUAL. New York: Association of Art Museum Directors. pp. 107-124.

Singer, Dorothea M. INSURANCE FOR LIBRARIES, A MANUAL FOR LIBRARIANS. Chicago: American Library Association, 1946.

PART 10: INTERNAL THEFT AND PILFERAGE

Barefoot, J. Kirk. EMPLOYEE THEFT INVESTIGATION. Woburn, MA: Butterworth Publishers. 1979. 232 pp.

Bologna, Jack. "Creating the Right Motivational Environment for Good Internal Controls." ASSETS PROTECTION, Vol. 5, No. 2 (March–April 1980), pp. 46–48.

– – –"A New Look at the Internal Theft Prevention Process." ASSETS PROTECTION, Vol. 5, No. 5 (September–October 1980), pp. 32–33.

– – –"Why Employees Steal – CPAs and DPers Views." SECURITY MANAGEMENT, Vol. 24, No. 9 (September 1980), pp. 112–113.

Carson, Charles R. MANAGING EMPLOYEE HONESTY, Woburn, MA: Butterworth Publishers. 1977. 230 pp.

Cary, Fred W. "Property Pass Systems – A Deterrant to Internal Theft." SECURITY MANAGE-MENT, Vol. 19, No. 5 (November 1975), pp. 18–19.

Clark, John P., and Richard C. Hollinger. "Theft by Employees." SECURITY MANAGEMENT, Vol. 24, No. 9 (September 1980), pp. 106–108, 110.

Cressey, Donald R. "Why Employees Steal." SECURITY WORLD, Vol. 17, No. 10 (October 1980), pp. 30, 32, 34, 36.

Curtis, Bob. HOW TO KEEP YOUR EMPLOYEES HONEST. Woburn, MA: Butterworth Publishers. 1979. 228 pp.

Durang, Charles, "How to Prevent the 'Inside Job'." SECURITY MANAGEMENT, Vol. 22, No. 4 (April 1978), pp. 6–7.

Ellis, Ernest W. "Risk Management and Fraud." ASSETS PROTECTION, Vol. 2, No. 1 (Winter 1976), pp. 26–29.

Fisher, Richard P. "Inside or Outside: They're Not on Your Side." SECURITY MANAGEMENT, Vol. 25, No. 8 (August 1981), pp. 40, 42–45, 66, 68, 73.

"415 Basic Ways to Steal: Reducing Employee Dishonesty." SECURITY INDUSTRY AND PRODUCT NEWS, Vol. 9, No. 7 (July 1980), pp. 30, 34–35.

Fuss, Eugene L. "Looking Out for #1: Employee Theft." SECURITY WORLD, Vol. 16, No. 6 (June 1979), pp. 28–30, 32, 34, 36.

Goldsmith, Reginald. "Recognizing the Employee Thief." SECURITY MANAGEMENT, Vol. 23, No. 8 (August 1979), pp. 53–54.

– – –"When there's Money to Burn ... Hints to Management on Recognizing the Employee Thief." SECURITY WORLD, Vol. 15, No. 9 (September 1978), pp. 28–29.

Gross, Philip J. "Paper Ripoffs: The Basics of Fraud." ASSETS PROTECTION, Vol. 3, No. 3 (Fall 1978), pp. 10–12.

– – –"Prosecution of Employees." ASSETS PROTECTION, Vol. 6, No. 3 (May–June 1981), pp. 30–32.

Hernon, Frederick E. "The Security and Internal Control Survey." SECURITY MANAGEMENT, Vol. 20, No. 4 (September 1976), pp. 26–28, 30.

Hertzoff, Ira. "Acceptance Sampling: An Analytic Tool for Security." ASSETS PROTECTION, Vol. 3, No. 4 (Winter 1978), pp. 19–32. Biblio.

– – –"Accountability, Controls, and Audit." ASSETS PROTECTION, Vol. 3, No. 3 (Fall 1978), pp. 29–35.

– – –"Risk Analysis Applications in the Design of Secure Systems." ASSETS PROTECTION, Vol. 4, No. 1 (March–April 1979), pp. 16–21. Biblio.

Hill, Ivan. "Common Sense and Everyday Ethics." SECURITY MANAGEMENT, Vol. 25, No. 7 (July 1981), pp. 123–128, 130–132.

Hollinger, Richard C., and John P. Clark. "Organizational Control and Employee Theft." ASSETS PROTECTION, Vol. 5, No. 5 (September–October 1980), pp. 34–40.

Lafferty, Fred B. "Why Not a Prosecution Policy?" SECURITY MANAGEMENT, Vol. 25, No. 12 (December 1981), pp. 49–50.

Lapides, G. A. "Exit Interviews as a Loss Prevention Technique." SECURITY MANAGEMENT, Vol. 23, No. 5 (May 1979), pp. 36–37.

Leininger, Sheryl (ed.) INTERNAL THEFT: INVESTIGATION AND CONTROL, AN ANTHOLOGY. Woburn, MA: Butterworth Publishers 1975. 273 pp.

Milne, Robert F. "Investigative Accounting." ASSETS PROTECTION, Vol. 5, No. 2 (March–April 1980), pp 23–24. Biblio.

Morneau, Robert H., Jr. "Indentifying Factors of Loss: A Quantitative Approach." ASSETS PROTECTION, Vol. 5, No. 1 (January–February 1980), pp. 22–24.

Putnam, Ronald R. "Psychological Deterrents to Employee Dishonesty." ASSETS PROTECTION, Vol. 6, No. 4 (July–August 1981), pp. 30–37.

Rosenbuam, Richard W. "Can We Predict Employee Theft?" SECURITY WORLD, Vol. 12, No. 9 (October 1975), pp. 26–27, 104, 106–108.

Sawyer, Lawrence, Albert A. Murphy, and Michael Crossley. "Management Fraud: The Insidious Specter." ASSETS PROTECTION, Vol. 4, No. 2 (May–June 1979), pp. 13–20.

Wallach, Charles. "New Technologies to Stop Industrial Pilferage." ASSETS PROTECTION, Vol. 2, No. 4 (Winter 1977), pp. 22–36.

PART 11: LEGAL ASPECTS OF SECURITY

Bassiouni, M. Cherif. CITIZENS ARREST. Springfield, IL: Charles C. Thomas. 1977.

Cammage, Allen Z., and Charles F. Hemphill, Jr. BASIC CRIMINAL LAW. New York: McGraw-Hill. 1974.

Darling, Don B. "Limiting Your Liability." SECURITY WORLD, Vol. 12, No. 4 (April 1975), pp. 18, 116.

– – –"Who Is Your Alarm System Really Protecting?" SECURITY WORLD, Vol. 13, No. 6 (June 1976), pp. 46, 48.

Ellis, Bill. "Proof of Loss in Fidelity Bond Claims." SECURITY WORLD, Vol. 15, No. 5 (May 1978), pp. 22–23.

Meisel, George. "The Professional Liability of Architects and Engineers." FIRE JOURNAL, Vol. 66, No. 4 (July 1972), p. 14.

Salit, Robert-Ian. "Private Security and Your Local Prosecutor." SECURITY MANAGEMENT, Vol. 22, No. 2 (February 1978), p. 39.

Steeno, David. L. "Be Sure Your Security Is Legally Secure." SECURITY WORLD, Vol. 18, No. 6 (June 1981), pp. 34–36.

PART 12: LOCKS, KEYS, AND KEY CONTROL

Crichton, Whitcomb. PRACTICAL COURSE IN MODERN LOCKSMITHING. Woburn, MA: Butterworth Publishers. 1979, 222 pp., illus.

Dickie, Robert. "Locks: A Basic Element of Security." SECURITY REGISTER, Vol. 1, No. 1 (January–February 1974), pp. 15–22, 57, illus.

"Door and Window Locks." CONSUMER REPORTS, Vol. 44, No. 3 (March 1979), pp. 132–141, illus.

"Door Locks." CONSUMER REPORTS, Vol. 36, No. 2 (February 1971), pp. 93–103, illus.

"Exit Control Locks Protect Milwaukee Art Center." SECURITY INDUSTRY AND PRODUCT NEWS, Vol. 5, No. 4 (August 1976), pp. 37, 44, illus.

Freimuth, K. C. LOCK SECURITY. Santa Cruz, CA: Davis Publications, Inc. n.d. 13 pp., illus.

Harter, M. Earl. "High Security Locks and Key Control." SECURITY MANAGEMENT, Vol. 24, No. 6 (June 1980), pp. 55–62, illus.

Holcomb, Robert C. "Key Control." ASSETS PROTECTION, Vol. 6, No. 4 (July–August 1981), pp. 46–47.

– – –"Key Control: Turning the Lock Against Unwanted Entry." SECURITY INDUSTRY AND PRODUCT NEWS, Vol. 10, No. 2, (February 1981), pp. 14–15.

Mackersie, A. J. "Improving Entrance Security Without Chains." SECURITY MANAGEMENT, Vol. 23, No. 6 (June 1979), pp. 60, 62–63.

McInerney, William D. "Give Your Locks Something to Hold Onto!" SECURITY WORLD, Vol. 13, No. 6 (June 1976), pp. 26–27.

– – –THE USE OF LOCKS IN PHYSICAL CRIME PREVENTION. Louisville, KY: National Crime Prevention Institute. 1976. 34 pp., illus.

Peyronnet, Jacques. "Locks vs. Burglars." SECURITY INDUSTRY AND PRODUCT NEWS, Vol. 7, Nos. 5 and 6 (May and June 1978), pp. 20, 25 (May) and 23, 25 (June).

Rhodes, Richard C. "Technical Notebook: Lock Security." SECURITY MANAGEMENT, Vol. 22, Nos. 23 and 24 (March and April 1978), pp. 64–69 (Mar.) and 42–45 (Apr.).

Robinson, Robert L. COMPLETE COURSE IN PROFESSIONAL LOCKSMITHING. Woburn, MA: Butterworth Publishers. 1973. 392 pp.

– – –"Masterkeying: The Decision to Masterkey." SECURITY WORLD, Vol. 11, Nos. 7 and 9 (July–August and October 1974), pp. 20–22, 25–28 (Jul.–Aug.) and 50–52, 54 (Oct.). Illus.

Roper, C. A. THE COMPLETE HANDBOOK OF LOCKS AND LOCKSMITHING. Blue Ridge Summit, PA: Tab Books. 1976. 390 pp., illus.

Tobias, Marc Weber. LOCKS, SAFES, AND SECURITY: A HANDBOOK FOR LAW ENFORCEMENT PERSONNEL. Springfield, IL: Charles C. Thomas. 1971. 338 pp., illus., biblio.

Toepfer, Edwin F. "The Doors That Locks Must Go On." SECURITY WORLD, Vol. 11, No. 10 (November 1974), p. 22.

– – –"Lock Security: Cylinders, Keys and Keying." SECURITY WORLD, July–August, September, and October 1965.

———"A New Building Look at Locks and Keys." SECURITY WORLD, Vol. 11, No. 10 (November 1974), pp. 20–21.

PART 13: MUSEUM, HISTORIC HOUSE, AND ARCHIVES (SPECIFIC) SECURITY

A. General Works

"Aesthetics in Museum Secrity." SECURITY WORLD, Vol. 16, No. 10 (October 1979), p. 29.

Alsford, Dennis B. AN APPROACH TO MUSEUM SECURITY. Ottawa, Ontario: Canadian Museums Association. 1975. 12 pp., illus.

Bauer, W. P. "Moderne Einbruchsicherungen im Wiener Völkerkundemuseum" (Modern burglary protection in the Vienna Ethnology Museum). MUSEUMKUNDE, Vol. 32, No. 2 (1963). Berlin.

Baxi, Smita J. "Security in Museums." In MUSEUM WORK. Bangkok, Thailand: National Museum. 1974.

———"Security Problems in Indian Museums." INDIAN NATIONAL COMMITTEE FOR ICOM NEWSLETTER, Vol. 1, No. 2 (1973). New Delhi.

Boothe, Kenneth. "Old North Church on the Terrorist List." SECURITY WORLD, Vol. 14, No. 10 (October 1977), pp. 30–31, 100. Illus.

Bostick, William A. THE GUARDING OF CULTURAL PROPERTY. Paris: UNESCO. 1977. 40 pp., illus.

———"What is the State of Museum Security?" MUSEUM NEWS, Vol. 46, No. 5 (January 1968), pp. 13–19.

Burcaw, G. Ellis. "Security" in INTRODUCTION TO MUSEOLOGY. Moscow: University of Idaho Press. 1973, pp. 84–88.

Chapman, Joseph, "Concepts in Achieving Security for Your Collections." PROCEEDINGS of the 18th Annual Conference of the Mountain-Plains Museums Association, September 15-17, 1971. pp. 26–68.

———"Stepping Up Security." MUSEUM NEWS, Vol. 44, No. 3 (November 1965), pp. 18–21.

———"Your Security Questions Answered." MUSEUM NEWS, Vol. 50, No. 5 (January 1972), pp. 22–25.

Coleman, C. William. "A Look at IAMSO" (International Association of Museum Security Officers). ASSETS PROTECTION, Vol. 1, No. 1 (Spring 1975), pp. 63–64.

Comité Technique Consultatif de la Sécurité. PRÉVENTION ET SÉCURITÉ DANS LES MUSÉES. Paris, France: Direction des Musees de France. 1977. 191 pp.

COMMISSION DE SÉCURITÉ DES MUSÉES CONTRE LE VOL: DISPOSITIFS ANTIVOL. RAPPORT DU GROUPE DE TRAVAIL. Brussels, Belgium. 1972 (Commission for Security of Museums Against Theft: Anti-Theft Devices. Report of the Working Group.)

Dikshit, K. N. "Museums, Monuments, and Security." JOURNAL OF INDIAN MUSEUMS (New Delhi), Vol. 27–28 (1971).

Dudley, Dorothy H., Irma B. Wilkinson, and others. MUSEUM REGISTRATION METHODS. Washington, DC: American Association of Museums. 1979. 3rd edition. 437 pp., illus., biblio. Includes chapters on loans, packing and shipping, importing and exporting, insurance, computers, and building planning among others.

"Electronic 'Eyes' and 'Ears' Always Alert for Around-the-Clock Protection of Museum/Historic Site." TECHNOLOGY AND CONSERVATION (Winter 1976), pp. 7, 11.

FINAL ACT OF THE INTER-GOVERNMENTAL CONFERENCE ON THE PROTECTION OF CULTURAL PROPERTY IN THE EVENT OF ARMED CONFLICT, The Hague, 1954. Paris: UNESCO. 1954. 83 pp. Text in English, French, Spanish, and Russian.

Foramitti, Hans. MESURES DE SÉCURITÉ ET D'URGENCE POUR LA PROTECTION DES BIENS CULTURELS (Security and Emergency Measures for the Protection of Cultural Property). Rome: Centre International d'Etudes Pour la Conservation et la Restauration des Biens Culturels. 1972. 47 pp.

Force, Roland W. "Museum Collection — Access, Use, and Control." CURATOR, Vol. 18, No. 4 (December 1975), pp. 249-255.

Francis, Frank. "Security." MUSEUMS JOURNAL, Vol. 63, No. 1-2 (June-September 1963), pp. 28-31.

Fuss. Eugene. "Security in Cultural Institutions: Advances in Electronic Protection Techniques." TECHNOLOGY AND CONSERVATION (Winter 1979), pp. 34-37. Illus.

Gorr, Louis F. "A Museum Management Bibliography." MUSEUM NEWS, Vol. 58, Nos. 5 and 6 (May-June and July-August 1980), pp. 71+ (May-June) and 67-77 (Jul.-Aug.).

Grossman, Albert J. "Television: Museum Watchdog." MUSEUM NEWS, Vol. 44, No. 3 (November 1965), pp. 22-24.

Heinonen, Jorma. "Museoiden Murtosuojaus." SUOMEN MUSEOLIITON JULKAISUJA (Helsinki, Finland), No. 10A (1972).

Hilpert, Bruce. "Constructing Doorway Barriers for Period Rooms." HISTORY NEWS, Vol. 34, No. 4 (April 1980), p. 45.

Howard, Richard F. MUSEUM SECURITY. Washington, DC: American Association of Museums. 1958. 12 pp.

Hunter, John E. "An Intimate Relationship" (museum security in the National Park Service). SECURITY MANAGEMENT, Vol. 25, No. 5 (May 1981), pp. 43-44, 46, 48-49.

———SECURITY FOR MUSEUMS AND HISTORIC HOUSES: AN ANNOTATED BIBLIOGRAPHY. Technical Leaflet No. 83. Nashville, TN: American Association for State and Local History. May 1975, 8 pp.

INTERNATIONAL SYMPOSIUM ON THE PROBLEMS OF SECURITY IN MUSEUMS, St. Maximin, 28 May-1 June, 1973. Paris: International Council of Museums. 1973. 43 pp., biblio.

Ivins, William M. HOW PRINTS LOOK. Boston: Beacon Press. 1958.

James, Pamela. "Subtle Solutions Span the Centuries" (security at Colonial Williamsburg). SECURITY MANAGEMENT, Vol. 25, No. 12 (December 1981), pp. 14-18, 51. Illus.

———"Telling Crime to Take a Hike" (NPS crime prevention measures). SECURITY MANAGEMENT, Vol. 25, No. 5 (May 1981), pp. 38-42.

Jedrzejewska, Hanna. "Zagadnienia Techniczne w Muzealnictwie" (Technical Problems in Museums). BIBLIOTEKA MUZEALNICTWA I OCHRONY ZABYTKOW, Vol. 32, Series B (1972), pp. 1-209. In Polish.

Jha, R. C., M. S. Bandyopadhya, and A. R. Muralidhar. "Thefts from Indian Museums." JOURNAL OF INDIAN MUSEUMS (New Delhi), Vol. 25-26 (1969-1970.)

Johansen, Robert, BRAND OG TYVERISIKRING (Report on Fire and Burglary Security). Copenhagen, Denmark: Lokalmuseumstilsyn. April 1975.

Johnson, E. Verner, and Joanne C. Horgan. MUSEUM COLLECTION STORAGE. Paris: UNESCO. 1979. 56 pp., illus., biblio. Technical Handbooks for Museums and Monuments Series No. 2.

Karl, H. "Sicherung von Museen Gegen Raub, Einbruch and Diebstahl" (Protection of Museums Against Robbery, Burglary, and Larceny). MUSEUMKUNDE (Berlin), No. 1 (1962).

Keck, Caroline K. HANDBOOK ON THE CARE OF PAINTINGS. Nashville: Watson-Guptill, 1976.

− − −"Security Depends on People." CURATOR, Vol. 10, No. 1 (1967), pp. 54-59.

Keck, Caroline K., Huntington T. Block, Joseph M. Chapman, John B. Lawton, and Nathan Stolow. A PRIMER ON MUSEUM SECURITY, Cooperstown, NY: New York State Historical Association. 1966. 85 pp., paper.

"Keeping the National Symbol of a Safe New Land Safe" (security systems at the Statue of Liberty). TECHNOLOGY AND CONSERVATION, Summer 1978, pp. 10, 12.

Kelly, Francis. ART RESTORATION. New York: McGraw-Hill, 1972.

Koppatz, Jurgen. "Alarmanlagen in Museen" (Alarm Systems in Museums). INFORMATION FÜR DIE MUSEEN IN DER DDR, Vol. 2, No. 2 (1970), pp. 6-8,

Lampart, Thomas. "Europe's Museums Teach Security." SECURITY WORLD, Vol. 13, No. 9 (September 1976), pp. 26-30.

Lapaire, Claude. "Sicherung der Museen Gegen Diebstahl und Feuer" (Protection of Museums Against Theft and Fire). INFORMATION VMS/AMS (Zurich), No. 5 (1970).

Leblanc, R. "Thief-Proofing Our Art Museums." UNESCO COURIER, No. 18 (1965), pp. 4-6, 10.

Leo, Jack. "A Basic Security Checklist for the Small Museum." NEWSLETTER of the Mountain-Plains Museums Association, Nos. 1-2. (1978), pp. 3-5.

− − −"How to Secure Your Museum: A Basic Checklist." HISTORY NEWS, Vol. 35, No. 6 (June 1980), pp. 10-12.

Lewis, Ralph H. MANUAL FOR MUSEUMS. Washington, DC: National Park Service. 1976. 412 pp., illus., biblio. Includes several sections on historic house, museum, and exhibits security.

Mankad, B. L. "Security and Some Other Urgent Problems Before Our Small Museums." STUDIES IN MUSEOLOGY (Baroda, India), Vol. 5 (1969).

Mannings, J. "Security of Museums and Art Galleries." MUSEUMS JOURNAL, Vol. 70, No. 1 (June 1970), pp. 7-9.

Matteson, Sally. "A Masterpiece of Museum Security." SECURITY WORLD, Vol. 16, No. 10 (October 1979), pp. 18-19, 21.

McKenna, George A. "Security and the Spirit of Cooperation." MUSEUM NEWS, Vol. 58, No. 2 (November–December 1979), pp. 7-9.

McQuarrie, Robert J. "Security." MUSEUM NEWS, Vol. 49, No. 7 (March 1971), pp. 25-27.

Michaels, A. F. "Security and the Museum." MUSEUM NEWS, Vol. 43, No. 3 (November 1964), pp. 11-16.

MUSEUMS AND THE THEFT OF WORKS OF ART. Entire issue of UNESCO MUSEUM, Vol. 26, No. 1 (1974), 64 pp. Includes the following articles:
  Michael Clamen. "Museums and the Theft of Works of Art."
  Guy Rosolato. "Psychoanalytic Notes on the Theft and Defacement of Works of Art."
  William A. Bostick. "The Ethics of Museum Acquisition."
  Goerges Sportouch. "Museum Attendants."
  Norman Pedgen. "An International Meeting on Museum Security."
  Andre Noblecourt. "The Need for a Systematic Approach to the Protection of Museums."
  Norman Pedgen. "A Comparison of National Laws Protecting Cultural Property (with a selective bibliography)."

Netherlands National Museum Soceity. BRANDVEILIGHEIDSZORG. Dutch National Committee of ICOM. 1956.

Noblecourt, Andre F. "The Protection of Museums Against Theft." UNESCO MUSEUM, Vol. 17, No. 4 (1964), pp. 184–196, 211–232. English and French. Illus.

O'Rourke, William J. "Magnetometers for Museum Theft Control." CURATOR, Vol. 16, No. 1 (1973), pp. 56–58.

Pakalik, Michael J. "Security and Protection in a Museum." CURATOR, Vol. 1, No. 4 (1958), pp. 89–93.

Probst, Tom. "Electronic Eyes and Ears on Guard." MUSEUM NEWS, Vol. 44, No. 3 (November 1965), pp. 11–16.

"The Protection of the King Tut Treasures." SECURITY INDUSTRY AND PRODUCT NEWS, Vol. 8, No. 9 (September 1979), p. 32.

RECOMMENDATIONS CONCERNING THE PRESERVATION OF CULTURAL PROPER-TY ENDANGERED BY PUBLIC OR PRIVATE WORKS. Adopted by the General Conference of UNESCO at its Fifteenth Session, Paris, 19 November, 1968. Paris, France: UNESCO. 1968. 26 pp. Text in English, French, Spanish, and Russian.

RECOMMENDATIONS FOR THE PROTECTION OF MOVABLE CULTURAL PROPER-TY. Adopted by the General Conference of UNESCO at its Twentieth Session, Paris, 28 November 1978. Paris, France: UNESCO. 1978. 39 pp. Text in English, French, Spanish, and Russian.

"Religious Observance" (historic church security). LAW ENFORCEMENT COMMUNICA-TIONS, Vol. 3, No. 5 (October 1976), pp. 17–18.

Richoux, Jeanette, Jill Serota-Braden, and Nancy Demyttenaere. "A Policy for Collections Ac-cess." MUSEUM NEWS, Vol. 59, No. 7 (July–August 1981), pp. 43–47.

Rutledge, Renata. "Strengthening Museum Security." SECURITY WORLD, Vol. 16, No. 10 (October 1979), pp. 25–26.

Schroder, G. H. H. MUSEUMBEVEILIGING. Netherlands Museum Soceity. 1974.

Schwarz, Frank. "Security" in THE CARE OF HISTORICAL COLLECTIONS: A CONSER-VATOR HANDBOOK FOR THE NON-SPECIALIST by Per E. Guldbeck. Nashville, TN: American Association for State and Local History. 1972.

– – –Special security supplement of ARTS REVIEW, Vol. 21, No. 18. London.

Schwippert, G. A., and P. H. Ong. SAFEGUARDING MUSEUMS AGAINST BURGLARY, THEFT AND DAMAGE TO THEIR COLLECTIONS. Delft, Netherlands: Central Laboratory. 1973. Report No. 73/108.

– – –TUSSENTIJDS   RAPPORT: ONDERZOEK   BEVEILIGINGSSYSTEM   EN TECHNIEKEN TEN BEHOEVE VAN MUSEA (Interim Report: Inquiry into Security Systems and Security Techniques for Museums). Delft, Netherlands: Central Laboratory TNO. 1972

"Security: The Schroder Report." ICOM NEWS, Vol. 28, No. 4 (1975), pp. 141–147.

Spet, Jiri. "K Soucasnému Stavu Ochrany a Bezpecnosti Sbirek v Museich." MUZEJNI A VLASTIVEDNÉ PRACE (Prague), Vol. 8, No. 1–4 (1970).

Stredl, Frantisek. "Electrická Poziarna Signalizácia, Automaticky Strazca Poziarnej Bezpectnosti" (Electrical Firefighting Signalling System, Automatic Protection for Fire Security). MÚZEUM (Bratislava), Vol. 18, No. 2 (1973).

– – –"Revizia Electrickych Silovych Zriadení a Bleskozvodov" (Revision of Electrical Power Equip-ment and Lightning Rods). MÚSEUM (Bratislava), Vol. 19, No. 1 (1974).

Stickland, Robert L. "An Inexpensive Alarm System for the Small Museum." MUSEUM NEWS, Vol. 43, No. 10 (June 1965), pp. 24–26. Illus.

Synk, J. A. "Art and Artifact Theft: How to Protect the Past." TECHNOLOGY AND CON-SERVATION, Vol. 1, No. 1 (Spring 1976), pp. 20–22.

Tillotson, Robert G., and the International Committee for Museum Security. MUSEUM SECURITY. Paris, France: International Council of Museums. 1977. 243 pp., illus., biblio. English and French.

"U.S. Museums Tightening Security to Check Thefts." NEW YORK TIMES, May 24, 1972.

Ward, Ralph V. "The Museum Security Officer." SECURITY MANAGEMENT (March 1976), pp. 30–33.

Ward, Ralph V. and James P. O'Connell. "Federal Funds for Museum Security." SECURITY MANAGEMENT, Vol. 21, No 2 (May 1977), pp. 44–46.

Weldon, Stephen. "Winterthur: Security in a Decorative Arts Museum." MUSEUM NEWS. Vol. 50, No. 5 (January 1972), pp. 36–37. Illus.

Williams, R. "The Management of Risk Associated with the Property of Museums." MUSEUMS JOURNAL, Vol. 77, No. 2 (September 1977), pp. 59–60.

B. Art Theft, Smuggling, Fraud, and Forgery

Adams, Laurie. ART COP: ROBERT VOLPE, ART CRIME DETECTIVE. New York: Dodd, Mead, and Company. 1974. 240 pp., illus.

Amram, Phillip W. "The Georgia O'Keefe Case: New Questions About Stolen Art." MUSEUM NEWS, Vol. 57, No. 3 (January–February 1979), pp. 49–51, 71–72.

– – – "The Georgia O'Keefe Case: Act II." MUSEUM NEWS, Vol. 58, No. 1 (September–October 1979), pp. 47–49.

Baynes-Cope, D., "Museum Frauds and Forgeries – Intentional and Unintentional." MEDICO-LEGAL JOURNAL, Vol. 43, Part 1 (1975).

Burnham, Bonnie. THE ART CRISIS. New York: St. Martin's Press. 1975.

– – – ART THEFT: ITS SCOPE, ITS IMPACT, AND ITS CONTROL. New York: International Foundation for Art Research. 1978. 205 pp.

– – – HANDBOOK OF NATIONAL LEGISLATIONS. Paris: International Council of Museums. 1974. 206 pp., biblio.

CONCLUSIONS OF THE MEETING OF INTERNATIONAL, INTERGOVERNMENTAL AND NON-GOVERNMENTAL ORGANIZATIONS, ORGANIZED BY UNESCO AND THE BELGIAN NATIONAL COMMISSION FOR UNESCO, TO MAKE A PRELIMINARY STUDY OF THE PROBLEMS OF RISKS INCURRED BY WORKS OF ART AND THE COVERAGE OF THESE RISKS, 13–15 September 1972, Brussels. Paris, France: UNESCO. 1972. Document No. SHC/72/Conf. 44/9.

DeBroglie, A., and P. Levantal. "Alerte aux Vols" (Theft Alert). CONNAISSANCE DES ARTS (Paris), No. 240 (February 1972).

DeSanto, Joseph A., and Thomas Kissane. "Appreciation Aids Investigation." SECURITY MANAGEMENT, Vol. 24, No. 9 (September 1980), pp. 126–128, 130.

Duffy, Robert E. ART LAW: REPRESENTING ARTISTS, DEALERS, AND COLLECTORS. New York: Practicing Law Institute. 1977. 542 pp.

Esterow, Milton. THE ART STEALERS. New York: Macmillan. 1973.

"Experts Probe Solutions to Art Thefts." SECURITY MANAGEMENT, Vol. 23, No. 10 (October 1979), p. 25.

Foramitti, Hans. "A Modern Approach to the Prevention of Thefts of Works of Art." ICOM NEWS, Vol. 24, No. 4 (December 1971), pp. 72–73.

Gore, Allen. STOLEN ART ALERT. Vol. 1, No. 11 (November 1980).

Green, Timothy. "Trafficking in Treasure." Chapter 6 in THE SMUGGLING BUSINESS. New York: Crescent Books. 1977. pp. 94–111.

Gupte, Pranay. "The Big Business of Art Theft." PORTFOLIO, Vol. 1, No. 1 (April–May 1979), p. 66.

Keller, Steven, R. "Protecting the Corporate Art Collection." SECURITY MANAGEMENT, Vol. 25, No 9 (September 1981), pp. 81–83.

Mason, Donald L. "Art Theft Investigations." FBI LAW ENFORCEMENT BULLETIN, January 1979. 5 pp., illus.

Mason, Donald L. THE FINE ART OF ART SECURITY. New York: Van Nostrand Reinhold. 1979. 96 pp., illus.

McAlee, James R. "The *McLain* Decision: A New Legal Wrinkle for Museums." MUSEUM NEWS, Vol. 57, No. 6 (July–August 1979), pp. 37-41.

McLeave, Hugh. ROGUES IN THE GALLERY: THE MODERN PLAGUE OF ART THEFTS. Boston: David R. Godeine. 1981. 278 pp., illus.

Meyer, Karl E. THE PLUNDERED PAST. New York; Atheneum. 1977.

Raguideau, Gilbert B. "Recent French Experience in Reducing Theft of Art Objects." CURATOR, Vol. 23, No. 3 (September 1980), pp. 195–208.

Reit, Seymour V. THE DAY THEY STOLE THE MONA LISA. New York: Summit Books. 1981. 254 pp., illus.

Shapiro, Michael, and Bev Montgomery. "Stolen Art." THE COLLECTOR-INVESTOR, (November 1981), pp. 18, 20–23.

Shirar, Gerard. PROTECTING WORKS OF ART. Washington, DC: American Society for Industrial Security. 1978. 221 pp., illus., biblio.

" 'Snap Judgements' Prevent Art Theft and Forgery" (photographing paintings). LAW ENFORCEMENT COMMUNICATIONS, Vol. 3, No. 1 (February 1976), p. 17. Illus.

C. Building Planning and Design in Museum Security

Bhowmik, Kamal S. "Design of A Museum Building and Preservation." In CONSERVATION IN THE TROPICS. 1974. pp. 74–80.

Harrison, Raymond O. THE TECHNICAL REQUIREMENTS OF A SMALL MUSEUM. Technical Paper No. 1. Ottawa, Ontario: Canadian Museums Association. 1969. 27 pp.

MUSEUM ARCHITECTURE. Entire issue of UNESCO MUSEUM, Vol. 26, No. 3/4 (1974). pp. 125–280. Illus., plans, biblio.

"Programming for Museums." UNESCO MUSEUM, Vol. 31, No. 2 (1979), pp. 70–144. Illus.

D. Security for Exhibits and Period Rooms

Alderson, William T., and Shirley P. Low. "The Interpreter and Security," Chapter 9 in INTERPRETATION OF HISTORIC SITES. Nashville, TN: American Association for State and Local History. 1976, pp. 132–145, illus.

Bergmann, Eugene. "Exhibits: A Production Checklist." CURATOR, Vol. 19, No. 2 (June 1976), pp. 157–161.

Blair, C. Dean. PROTECTING YOUR EXHIBITS: SECURITY METHODS AND DEVICES. Technical Leaflet No. 99. Nashville, TN: American Association for State and Local History. September 1977. 8 pp., illus.

Carroll, Richard S. "A Low-Cost System of Protecting Paintings." MUSEUM NEWS, Vol. 41, No. 10 (June 1963), pp. 27–29, illus.

Gebhardt, Keith, and Milton Thompson. "Open Major Exhibits or 'To Glass or Not to Glass?'." Midwest Museums Conference QUARTERLY, Vol. 29, No. 4 (Fall 1969), pp. 7–12.

Klotz, Rolf-Michael. "Design a Better Idea: Playboy's Answer to Securing Art on Exhibit." SECURITY MANAGEMENT, Vol. 25, No. 9 (September 1981), pp. 76–78, 80.

"New Jewel Cases in the Ashmolean Museum." MUSEUMS JOURNAL, Vol. 54 (1955), p. 269.

Stolow, Nathan. CONSERVATION STANDARDS FOR WORKS OF ART IN TRANSIT AND ON EXHIBITION. Museums and Monuments Series No. 17. Paris, France: UNESCO. 1979. 129 pp., illus.

– – –"The Technical Organization of an International Art Exhibition." UNESCO MUSEUM, Vol. 21, No. 3 (1968).

Tyler, Barbara. "Silent Security: Protection of Museum Objects on Display." Canadian Museums Association GAZETTE, Vol. 5, No. 1 (February–March 1971), pp. 3–10. Biblio. French and English.

E. Marking and Photographing Objects for Identification

Baer, Alan J. " 'Fingerprinting' of Works of Art: An Identification Technique for Theft Prevention/Recovery." TECHNOLOGY AND CONSERVATION (Winter 1976), pp. 20, 21, 31. Illus.

"Keeping Household Possessions in the Picture." LAW ENFORCEMENT COMMUNICATIONS, Vol. 3, No. 1 (February 1976), p. 16.

Kissane, Thomas. "Protecting Works of Art from Theft and Fraud." SECURITY MANAGEMENT, Vol. 21, No. 2 (May 1977), pp. 6–9.

Pink, Marilyn. HOW TO CATALOGUE WORKS OF ART. Los Angeles: Museums Systems. 1972.

PART 14: PHYSCIAL AND STRUCTURAL SECURITY

"Barrier-Free Design vs. Security" (access for the handicapped). SECURITY MANAGEMENT, Vol. 25, No. 4 (April 1981), pp. 43–45.

Cosher, Howard. "Elevators 'React' and Prevent in Building's Security System." SECURITY WORLD, Vol. 16, No. 3 (March 1979), pp. 23–24.

Gambino, Henry J., Jr. "Security You Can See Through." SECURITY DISTRIBUTING AND MARKETING, September 1975.

Martin, Robert W. "Transparent Bullet-Resisting Glazing Material." U.S. GLASS, METAL AND GLAZING, July 1971.

Moore, Raymond T. BARRIER PENETRATION TESTS. NBS Technical Note 837. Washington, DC: National Bureau of Standards, U.S. Department of Commerce. June 1974. 191 pp., illus.

– – –PENETRATION RESISTANCE TESTS OF REINFORCED CONCRETE BARRIERS. NBSIR 73-101. Washington, DC: National Bureau of Standards, U.S. Department of Commerce. 1973.

– – –PENETRATION TESTS ON J-SIIDS BARRIERS. NBSIR 73-223. Washington, DC: National Bureau of Standards, U.S. Department of Commerce. 1973.

NILECJ STANDARD FOR PHYSICAL SECURITY OF DOOR ASSEMBLIES AND COMPONENTS. NILECJ-STD-0306.00. Washington, DC: Law Enforcement Standards Program, U.S. Department of Justice. May 1976. 30 pp., illus.

PHYSICAL SECURITY. Field Manual 19-30. Washington, DC: U.S. Department of the Army. 1971. (Updated periodically)

Schultz, Donald. PRINCIPLES OF PHYSICAL SECURITY. Houston: Gulf Publishing Co. 1978. 169 pp.

"Security Glazing: Effectiveness Is a Physical Force Barrier." SECURITY INDUSTRY AND PRODUCT NEWS, Vol. 9, No. 7 (July 1980), pp. 16, 40–41.

Strobl, Walter M. CRIME PREVENTION THROUGH PHYSICAL SECURITY. New York: Marcel Dekker. 1978.

– – –HANDBOOK: PRINCIPLES OF PHYSICAL SECURITY. Knoxville, TN: Training, Consultants, Inc. 1977. 225 pp.

Stroik, John S. TERMS AND DEFINITIONS FOR DOOR AND WINDOW SECURITY. NPS Special Publication 480-22. Washington, DC: National Bureau of Standards, U.S. Department of Commerce. May 1977. 13 pp.

PART 15: PUBLIC RELATIONS AND INFORMATION ASPECTS OF SECURITY

Bernstein, Alan Bart. "Security and Public Relations: Crisis Reporting." SECURITY WORLD, Vol. 18, No. 1 (January 1981), pp. 34–36, 38.

Blinn, Edward G. "Learn How the Media Works." In THE PUBLICITY PROCESS, James W. Schwartz, editor. Ames: Iowa State University Press. 1970. pp. 128–137.

Leiding, O. LAYMAN'S GUIDE TO SUCCESSFUL PUBLICITY. Ayer Press. 1979.

Lerbinger, O., and N. Sperber. "Communicator-in-Chief" in KEY TO THE EXECUTIVE HEAD. Reading, MA: Addison-Wesley Publishing Co. 1975. pp. 41–48.

Naval Training Publication Detachment and others. JOURNALIST 2 and 3. Washington, DC: U.S. Department of the Navy.

PUBLIC MEDIA MANUAL. Austin, TX: Texas Association of Museums.

Siller, B., T. White, and H. Terkel. TELEVISION AND RADIO NEWS. New York: Macmillan. 1960.

Warren, C. MODERN NEWS REPORTING. Educational Manual MB420, rev. ed., Reprinted for U.S. Armed Forces Institute. Madison, WI: Harper & Brothers. 1951.

Weiner, R. "Clipping Bureaus." In PROFESSIONAL'S GUIDE TO PUBLIC RELATIONS SERVICES. Englewood Cliffs, NJ: Prentice-Hall. 1968. pp. 15–45.

PART 16: SAFETY IN THE MUSEUM

Amoroso, Louis J. "Where Do We Stand with OSHA?" SECURITY WORLD, Vol. 14, No. 7 (July 1977), pp. 14–15, 58–59.

Congress of the United States. OCCUPATIONAL SAFETY AND HEALTH ACT. Washington, DC: U.S. Government Printing Office. 1970, with revisions.

INDUSTRIAL SAFETY AND FIRE PREVENTION. London: T. Bell & Son. 1973.

King, R. W., and J. Magid. INDUSTRIAL HAZARD AND SAFETY HANDBOOK. Woburn, MA: Butterworth Publishers. 1979. 842 pp.

Loyd, E. R. "Safety and Security Must Go Hand-in-Hand." SECURITY MANAGEMENT, Vol. 22, No. 11 (November 1978), p. 21.

Robert, L., and A. Denis Peraldi. "Some Reflections Concerning Vigilance and Occupational Accidents." ARCH. MAL. PROF. MED. TRAV. SECUR. SOC. (France), Vol. 28, Nos. 1–2 (1977), pp. 149–150.

Thorsen, June-Elizabeth. "Security and the OSHAct Puzzle." SECURITY WORLD, Vol. 14, No. 7 (July 1977), pp. 22–23, 25.

Torrington, Arthur E. "The Security/Safety Merger." SECURITY WORLD, Vol. 12, Nos. 1 and 3 (January and March 1975), pp. 36+ (Jan.) and 28–29, 52–53 (Mar.).

PART 17: SECURITY LIGHTING

Colbeck, J. P. "Security Lighting — First Line of Night Defense." ELECTRICAL REVIEW, No. 194 (1974), pp. 41–43.

Cox, K.T.O. "Value for Money — Exterior Lighting." LIGHTING RESEARCH AND TECHNOLOGY, Vol. 4, No. 4 (1972), pp. 236–242.

Dorsey, R. T., and H. R. Blackwell. "A Performance-Oriented Approach to Lighting Specifications." LIGHTING DESIGN AND APPLICATIONS, Vol. 5, No. 5 (1975), pp. 13–27.

Illuminating Engineering Society. AMERICAN NATIONAL STANDARD PRACTICE FOR PROTECTIVE LIGHTING. ANSI A85.1 1965 (R1970). New York: American National Standards Institute. 1970. 20 pp.

Jennings, R.E. "Exterior Security Fence Lighting." LIGHTING DESIGN AND APPLICATION, Vol. 4, No. 4 (1974), pp. 35–37.

LaGuisa, F. F. "Facade Lighting for Nighttime Security Surveillance." LIGHTING DESIGN AND APPLICATION, Vol. 4, No. 4 (1974), pp. 23–25.

Lewis, Robert A. "Better Security Through LPS Lighting." SECURITY MANAGEMENT, Vol. 22, No. 4 (April 1978), p. 8.

Lewis, Robert. "More Security, Less Cost." SECURITY WORLD, Vol. 15, No. 5 (May 1978), pp. 27–29.

Lyons, S. "Lighting — A Vital Security Aid." ELECTRICAL REVIEW, Vol. 198, No. 7 (1976), pp. 37–38.

– – – "Lighting for Night Security of Industrial and Commerical Premises." LIGHT & LIGHTING, Vol. 64, No. 4 (1971), pp. 149–153.

Meguire, Patrick G., Joel J. Kramer, and Addie Stewart. SECURITY LIGHTING FOR NUCLEAR WEAPONS STORAGE SITES: A LITERATURE REVIEW AND BIBLIOGRAPHY. NBS Special Publication 480-27. Washington, DC: National Bureau of Standards, U.S. Department of Commerce. November 1977. 31 pp., biblio.

Oppen, Larry. "Security Lighting from a Distributor's Viewpoint." SECURITY WORLD, Vol. 15, No. 5 (May 1978), pp. 20–21.

"Save on Lighting Without Sacrificing Security." SECURITY MANAGEMENT, Vol. 23, No. 9 (September 1979), pp. 127, 130–131.

Thorsen, June-Elizabeth. "Considering the Source." SECURITY WORLD, Vol. 15, No. 5 (May 1978), pp. 24–25, 44, 50.

PART 18: SECURITY SURVEYS AND AUDITS

Fennelly, Lawrence J. "Security Surveys." ASSETS PROTECTION, Vol. 4, No. 3 (July–August 1979), pp. 19-34.

Gigliotti, Richard J., Ronald C. Jason, and Nancy J. Cogan. "What Is Your Level of Physical Security?" SECURITY MANAGEMENT, Vol. 24, No. 8 (August 1980), pp. 46, 48, 50.

Girard, Charles M. "Planning Management and Evaluation: Important Tools to the Crime Prevention and Security Officer." In CRIME PREVENTION AND LOSS PREVENTION TECHNIQUES, Lawrence J. Fennelly, editor. Woburn, MA: Butterworth Publishers, 1982.

James, Pamela. "Casing the Joint: For Security Surveys, Think Like A Thief." SECURITY MANAGEMENT, Vol. 25, No. 3 (March 1981), pp. 38-40, 42, 44-45.

Kingsbury, Arthur A. INTRODUCTION TO SECURITY AND CRIME PREVENTION SURVEYS. Springfield, IL: Charles C. Thomas. 1973. 364 pp.

Krohne, Stephen A. "Efficiency Evaluations Can Improve Communciation." SECURITY MANAGEMENT, Vol. 25, No. 3 (March 1981), pp. 93-96.

Nagle, Thomas B. "Working Smarter, Not Harder." SECURITY MANAGEMENT, Vol. 24, No. 10 (October 1980), pp. 37-38, 40-43.

Post, Richard S. DETERMINING SECURITY NEEDS. Madison, WI: Oak Security Publications. 1973. 263 pp.

Ursic, Henry S., and Leroy E. Pagano. "Do-It-Yourself Security Evaluation Checklist." SECURITY WORLD, Vol. 11, No. 7 (July–August 1974), pp. 38-41.

PART 19: SECURITY PLANNING AND DESIGN

Bailey, Dustin L. "Nuclear Security: A Systematic Approach." SECURITY MANAGEMENT, Vol. 25, No. 6 (June 1981), pp. 44, 45, 48-51, 53-54.

Callahan, Keith L., and Calvin H. Maledy. "A Cookbook for Defense in Depth: Security Department Policies and Procedures Manual – Typical Table of Contents." SECURITY WORLD, Vol. 16, No. 2 (February 1979), pp. 28-29.

Carlton, Stephen A. "The Future of Systems Thinking in the Protection Field." SECURITY MANAGEMENT, Vol. 22, No. 6 (June 1978), pp. 28-29, 32.

– – –"New Insight Into the Protection Fields – A Systems Approach." SECURITY MANAGEMENT, Vol. 22, No. 5 (May 1978), pp. 26, 30.

Carter, Roy. "Writing the Corporate Security Manual." SECURITY MANAGEMENT, Vol. 25, No. 5 (May 1981), p. 119.

"Consultants Consider Designing for Security." SECURITY WORLD, Vol. 17, No. 6 (June 1980), pp. 44-47.

Darling, Don D. "Guidelines for a Security Consultant." SECURITY WORLD, Vol. 13, No. 4 (April 1976), pp. 34, 63.

de Laval, Nancy Dunn. "Security Engineering: A New Discipline." ASSETS PROTECTION, Vol. 5, No. 4 (July–August 1980), pp. 30-32.

Fennelly, Lawrence J. "Crime Prevention and the Architects." ASSETS PROTECTION, Vol. 4, No. 2 (May–June 1979), pp. 30-36. Biblio.

Finkelstein, A. B. "Principles of the Security System Concept." SECURITY WORLD, Vol. 13, No 9 (September 1976), pp. 20-23.

Gale, Richard B. DESIGNING FOR SECURITY. West Caldwell, NJ: Loss Prevention Diagnostics, Inc. n.d. 6 pp.

Healy, Richard J. DESIGN FOR SECURITY. New York: John Wiley and Sons. 1968. 309 pp.

Hopf, Peter S. HANDBOOK OF BUILDING SECURITY PLANNING AND DESIGN. New York: McGraw-Hill Book Co. 30 chapters (by contributing authors), 2 appendices, illus., approx. 700 pages.

Hughes, Margaret. "High-Rise Safety and Security in Action." SECURITY WORLD, Vol. 12, Nos. 3–6 (March–June 1975). In four parts.

Jeffery, C. R. CRIME PREVENTION THROUGH ENVIRONMENTAL DESIGN. Beverly Hills, CA: Sage Publications. 1971. 290 pp.

Kelly, Robert E. "Should You Have an Internal Consultant?" HARVARD BUSINESS REVIEW, (November–December 1979).

Kmet, Mary Alice. "How to Choose and Use Consultants." SECURITY MANAGEMENT, Vol. 24, No. 9 (September 1980), pp. 150–151, 153.

Mandelbaum, Albert J. FUNDAMENTALS OF PROTECTIVE SYSTEMS: PLANNING, EVALUATION, SELECTION. Springfield, IL: Charles C. Thomas. 1973. 272 pp.

Murphy, Ralph. "Design for Physical Security." SECURITY MANAGEMENT, Vol. 20, No. 2 (May 1976), pp. 12, 14.

Murphy, Ralph, and William Norman. "Physical Security: Chance – Choice – Change." SECURITY MANAGEMENT, Vol. 20, No. 2 (May 1976), pp. 8, 10.

Newman, Oscar. ARCHITECTURAL DESIGN FOR CRIME PREVENTION. Washington, DC: U.S. Government Printing Office. 1971.

– – –DEFENSIBLE SPACE – CRIME PREVENTION THROUGH URBAN DESIGN. New York: Macmillan. 1972. 264 pp.

Post, Deborah Cromer. "Specifying a Security System." SECURITY WORLD, Vol. 18, No. 2 (February 1981), pp. 29–31.

Reynolds, S. Wesley. "Security Consultants – How and When to Use Them." SECURITY MANAGEMENT, Vol. 22, No. 7 (July 1978), pp. 18–20.

Robertson, Elizabeth, and John V. Fechter. DIRECTORY OF SECURITY CONSULTANTS. LESP-RPT-0309.00. Washington, DC: Law Enforcement Standards Program, U.S. Department of Justice. October 1975. 59 pp.

Sandia Laboratories. A SYSTEMATIC APPROACH TO THE CONCEPTUAL DESIGN OF PHYSICAL PROTECTION SYSTEMS FOR NUCLEAR FACILITIES. NCP/DO789-01 UC-15. Washington, DC: U.S. Department of Energy. May 1978. Available from Government Printing Office as Stock No. 061-000-00060-7.

Siatt, Wayne. "Designing for Security." SECURITY WORLD, Vol. 17, No. 4 (April 1980), pp. 22–28.

– – –"Nuclear Plant Security Needs: A Systems Approach." SECURITY WORLD, Vol. 18, No. 6 (June 1981), pp. 24–29.

Strobl, Walter M. "Planned Security for High-Rise Buildings." SECURITY WORLD, (reprint, n.d.), pp. 32, 34, 36–37.

Wood, Nat. " 'Built-in' Security." SECURITY WORLD, Vol. 16, No. 6 (June 1979), pp. 28–30, 32, 34, 36.

Wright, K. G. COST-EFFECTIVE SECURITY. New York: McGraw-Hill Book Co. 1972. 244 pp.

PART 20: SECURITY ADMINISTRATION AND RISK MANAGEMENT

Allen, C. James. "Job Analysis Defines Security Tasks." SECURITY MANAGEMENT, Vol. 24, No. 2 (February 1980), pp. 36, 38.

Allen, Tom C. (ed.) RISK MANAGEMENT METHODOLOGY. An anthology of articles reprinted from THE JOURNAL OF COMMERCE.

Barefoot, J. Kirk. "A Broader View of Risk Management." SECURITY MANAGEMENT, Vol. 25, No. 6 (June 1981), pp. 61-62.

Barrus, Walter R., and Monroe J. Paxman. "Management Style as a Crime Deterrent." SECURI-TY WORLD, Vol. 15, No. 1 (January 1978), pp. 28-29, 75.

Barry, Robert L. "Loss Prevention for the Loss Preventors." SECURITY MANAGEMENT, Vol. 23, No. 3 (March 1979), pp. 22-24, 26.

Bornhofen, Frederick A. "Where Security Fits In: Behavioral Guideline on What Is — and Is Not — Expected from a Security Department." SECURITY WORLD, Vol. 15, No. 8 (August 1978), pp. 92-93.

Burton, Gene E. "Communicating for Results." SECURITY MANAGEMENT, Vol. 22, No. 2 (February 1978), pp. 22-25.

Byrne, John M. "Something Extra — Prescription for Selling Security to Management." SECURI-TY WORLD, Vol. 12, No. 6 (June 1975), pp. 16-17, 52, 54-55.

Carroll, John M. "How Cost-Effective Is Your Security?" SECURITY WORLD, Vol. 14, No. 11 (November 1977), pp. 24-25, 54-55.

Criscuoli, Ernest J., Jr. "Delegation: A Management Tool." SECURITY MANAGEMENT, Vol. 21, No. 1 (March 1977), pp. 41-43.

Currier-Briggs, Noel. SECURITY: ATTITUDES AND TECHNIQUES FOR MANAGEMENT. London: Hutchinson & Co. 1968.

Drucker, Peter F. MANAGEMENT — TASKS, RESPONSIBILITIES, PRACTICES. New York: Harper & Row Publishers. 1974.

Fay, John "The Security Director as Leader." SECURITY MANAGEMENT, Vol. 25, No. 7 (July 1981), pp. 104, 106.

— — —"The Security Manager as Counselor." SECURITY MANAGEMENT, Vol. 25, No. 8 (August 1981), pp. 147-149.

Finneran, Eugene. SECURITY SUPERVISION: A HANDBOOK FOR SUPERVISORS AND MANAGERS. Woburn, MA: Butterworth Publishers. 1981. 280 pp.

Gigliotti, Richard J. "The Fine Art of Justification." SECURITY MANAGEMENT, Vol. 24, No. 11 (November 1980), pp. 30, 31, 34.

Gross, Philip J. "Security Management." ASSETS PROTECTION, Vol. 2, No. 2 (Spring 1977), pp. 20-23. Biblio.

Guy, Edward T., John J. Merrigan, Jr., and John A Wanat. FORMS FOR SAFETY AND SECURITY MANAGEMENT. Woburn, MA: Butterworth Publishers. 1980. 448 pp.

Healy, Richard J., and Timothy J. Walsh. "Translating Security into Business Terminology." SECURITY MANAGEMENT, Vol. 23, No. 6 (June 1979), pp. 30-32, 34.

Hemphill, Charles F., Jr. MANAGEMENT'S ROLE IN LOSS PREVENTION. New York: American Management Association. 1976.

Kingsbury, Arthur A. SECURITY ADMINISTRATION — AN INTRODUCTION. Springfield, IL: Charles C. Thomas. 1973 (2nd ed.). 368 pp.

McCauley, R. Paul. "Adapting Contemporary Business Concepts to Security." SECURITY MANAGEMENT, Vol. 22, No. 1 (January 1978), pp. 40-42, 44.

Morneau, R. H., Jr., and G. E. Morneau. SECURITY ADMINISTRATION: A QUANTITATIVE HANDBOOK. Woburn, MA: Butterworth Publishers. 1982.

Post, Richard D. "What Is Security?" In OPTIMUM SECURITY THROUGH RISK MANAGEMENT. Gaithersburg, MD: International Association of Chiefs of Police. 1973, pp. Al-1.

Post, Richard S., Arthur A. Kingsbury, and Charles L. Buckley, Jr. SECURITY ADMINISTRATION, Springfield, IL: Charles C. Thomas, 1975. 351 pp., glossary, appendices.

Price, Stanley. "Justifying Your Budget." SECURITY MANAGEMENT, Vol. 25, No. 10 (October 1981), pp. 39-41.

Prohaska, C., and W. Taylor. "Minimizing Losses in a Hostile Environment: The Cost of Defending One's Castle." JOURNAL OF RISK AND INSURANCE, Vol. 40, No. 3 (September 1973).

Reeser, Clayton, and Marvin Loper. MANAGEMENT, THE KEY TO ORGANIZATIONAL EFFECTIVENESS. Glenview, IL: Scott Foresman & Co. 1978.

"Risk Management." SECURITY MANAGEMENT, Vol. 21, No. 2 (May 1977), pp. 16-19, 21.

Rosberg, Robert R. SECURITY RISK MANAGEMENT. Woburn, MA: Butterworth Publishers. 1980. 192 pp.

Rosberg, Robert R. (ed.) A PRACTITIONERS GUIDE FOR SECURITY RISK MANAGEMENT. Boston: Dorison House Publishers. 1980. 192 pp., illus., glossary.

Sasser, W. Earl, Jr., and Frank S. Leonard. "Let First-Level Supervisors Do Their Job." HARVARD BUSINESS REVIEW, (March–April 1980).

Schweig, Barry B. "Decision-Matrix: A Risk Management Aid." ASSETS PROTECTION, Vol. 5, No. 1 (January–February 1980), p. 29.

Schweitzer, James A. "A Policy Structure Gives the Basis for an Effective Security Program." SECURITY MANAGEMENT, Vol. 24, No. 12 (December 1980), pp. 18, 21-22, 25.

Sennewald, Charles. EFFECTIVE SECURITY MANAGEMENT. Woburn, MA: Butterworth Publishers. 1978, 273 pp.

Siatt, Wayne. "Blending Basic Elements for Budget Solutions." SECURITY WORLD, Vol. 18, No. 12 (December 1981), pp. 21-26.

– – –"Risk Management: Balancing Threats and Protection." SECURITY WORLD, Vol. 18, No. 4 (April 1981), pp. 30-33.

– – –"Selling Security Inside." SECURITY WORLD, Vol. 17, No. 2 (February 1980), pp. 18-21.

Smith, Robert. "Evaluations Can Ease Security Staff Management." SECURITY WORLD, Vol. 18, No. 9 (September 1981), pp. 36-41.

Sopsic, John P. "Memo to Management — Subject: Security in Its Proper Management Perspective." SECURITY MANAGEMENT, Vol. 21, No. 2 (May 1977), p. 66.

Ursic, Henry S., and Leroy E. Pagano. SECURITY MANAGEMENT SYSTEMS. Springfield, IL: Charles C. Thomas. 1974. 372 pp.

Wanat, John, Edward Guy, and John Merrigan, Jr. SUPERVISORY TECHNIQUES FOR THE SECURITY PROFESSIONAL. Woburn, MA: Butterworth Publishers. 1981. 145 pp.

Weber, Howard T. "Implementing A Practical Risk Management Program." SECURITY MANAGEMENT, Vol. 24, No. 7 (July 1980), pp. 18-22.

"Zero Budgeting Lends Strength to Security Operations." SECURITY WORLD, Vol. 17, No. 2 (February 1980), pp. 27-30.

PART 21: SECURITY CODES AND STANDARDS

A. Security and Other Standards of Underwriters Laboratories, Inc.

The Safety Standards of UL have been drawn up to provide specifications and requirements for the construction and performance under test and in actual use of systems, devices, materials, and appliances submitted to UL. Generally, the standards are most useful to equipment manufacturers who must meet them in order for their equipment to be UL Listed and to systems installers who must meet them in order for their systems to be Certificated by UL. Systems employing UL Listed equipment may qualify the owner for a discount on his insurance. The UL Standards may be useful to equipment owners and operators who wish to inspect or test their equipment to determine if it in fact meets UL Standards before it is placed into service.

The following UL Safety Standards are among those of potential use to museums, historic houses, and archives. Other standards may be useful to such users in specific cases; a catalog of standards is available from UL on request. All UL Standards are revised periodically and only the latest editions should be used or cited in specifications.

UL No.	Title
44	Rubber-Insulated Wires and Cables
83	Thermoplastic-Insulated Wires
140	Relocking Devices
294	Access Control System Units
365	Police Station Connected Burglar Alarm Units and Systems
437	Key Locks
464	Audible Signal Appliances
609	Local Burglar Alarm Units and Systems
611	Central-Station Burglar-Alarm Units and Systems
634	Connectors and Switches for Use With Burglar Alarm Systems
636	Holdup Alarm Units and Systems
639	Intrusion-Detection Units
681	Installation and Classification of Mercantile and Bank Burglar Alarm Systems
687	Burglary Resistant Safes
752	Bullet-Resisting Equipment
768	Combination Locks
771	Night Depositories
786	Key-Locked Safes (Class KL)
887	Delayed-Action Timelocks
904	Vehicle Alarm Systems and Units
972	Burglary Resisting Glazing Material
983	Surveillance Cameras
1034	Burglary-Resistant Electric Door Strikes
1037	Antitheft Alarms and Devices
1076	Proprietary Burglar Alarm System Units

B. U.S. Department of Justice Standards

The Department of Justice promulgates standards for a variety of security and law enforcement equipment under the aegis of the Technology Assessment Program. The research and publication activities of this program are carried out by the Law Enforcement Standards Laboratory located at the National Bureau of Standards. Earlier standards were published by the National Institute of Law Enforcement and Criminal Justice or NILECJ. In the last two years, such standards have been published by the National Institute of Justice, successor to NILECJ.

Because NILECJ and NIJ standards cover such a broad variety of equipment, it was decided to list them throughout this bibliography under the various subjects headings for user convenience. Most of the standards will be found in Parts 2, 5, and 6, although a few are in other parts. The reader also should note that the Department of Justice publishes various reports and monographs under the Law Enforcement Standards Program; these reports do not carry the authority of standards but usually discuss how standards are developed or explain them for the layman. These publications also are scattered throughout this bibliography.

A catalog of currently available NILECJ and NIJ Standards and other publications of the Law Enforcement Standards Program is available upon request from the Department of Justice.

PART 22: MISCELLANEOUS SECURITY SUBJECTS

A. General Works

Astor, Saul D. LOSS PREVENTION CONTROLS AND CONCEPTS. Woburn, MA: Butterworth Publishers. 1978. 273 pp.

Berger, David L. INDUSTRIAL SECURITY. Woburn, MA: Butterworth Publishers. 1979. 360 pp.

"Burglary — A White Paper." SECURITY WORLD, Vol. 11, No. 10 (November 1974), pp. 11, 29.

Cole, Richard B. PROTECTION MANAGEMENT AND CRIME PREVENTION. Cincinnati: Anderson Publishing Co. 1974. 225 pp.

Curtis, Bob. SECURITY CONTROL: EXTERNAL THEFT. New York: Chain Store Age Books. 1971. 372 pp., appendices.

Fennelly, Lawrence J. THE HANDBOOK OF LOSS PREVENTION AND CRIME PREVENTION. Woburn, MA: Butterworth Publishers. 1982.

Ferry, John, Marjorie Kravitz, and Ollie Smith (compilers). PUBLICATIONS OF THE NATIONAL INSTITUTE OF LAW ENFORCEMENT AND CRIMINAL JUSTICE: A COMPREHENSIVE BIBLIOGRAPHY. Washington, DC: National Criminal Justice Reference Service, U.S. Department of Justice. February 1978. 230 pp., cross-referenced. (New editions published periodically.)

Fisher, James A. SECURITY FOR BUSINESS AND INDUSTRY. Englewood Cliffs, NJ: Prentice-Hall. 1979.

Green, Gion. INTRODUCTION TO SECURITY, 3rd edition. Woburn, MA: Butterworth Publishers. 1981. 416 pp.

HANDBOOK OF INDUSTRIAL LOSS PREVENTION. New York: McGraw-Hill Book Co.

Healy, Richard J., and Timothy J. Walsh. INDUSTRIAL SECURITY MANAGEMENT: A COST-EFFECTIVE APPROACH. New York: American Management Association. 1971. 274 pp.

Hemphill, Charles E. SECURITY FOR BUSINESS AND INDUSTRY. Homewood, IL: Dow Jones-Irwin. 1971. 328 pp.

Higgins, Joe. "Common Sense — That's What Crime Prevention Is All About." SECURITY MANAGEMENT, Vol. 21, No. 6 (November 1977), pp. 20–25.

Kramer, Joel J. (ed.) THE ROLE OF BEHAVIORAL SCIENCE IN PHYSICAL SECURI-
TY, Proceedings of the First Annual Symposium, April 29–30, 1976. NBS Special Publication
480–24. Washington, DC: National Bureau of Standards, U.S. Department of Commerce.
November 1977. 118 pp.

– – –THE ROLE OF BEHAVIORAL SCIENCE IN PHYSICAL SECURITY, Proceedings
of the Second Annual Symposium, March 23–24, 1977. NBS Special Publication 480–32.
Washington, DC: National Bureau of Standards, U.S. Department of Justice. June 1978. 90 pp.

– – –THE ROLE OF BEHAVIORAL SCIENCE IN PHYSICAL SECURITY, Proceedings
of the Third Annual Symposium, May 2–4, 1978. NBS Special Publication 480–38. Washington,
DC: National Bureau of Standards, U.S. Department of Commerce. December 1979. 107 pp.

Lapinsky, George M., and Ann Ramey-Smith (eds.) THE ROLE OF BEHAVIORAL SCIENCE
IN PHYSICAL SECURITY, Proceedings of the Fourth Annual Symposium, July 25–26, 1979.
NBSIR 81-2207 (R). Washington, DC: National Bureau of Standards, U.S. Department of Com-
merce. February 1981. 93 pp.

Lipman, Ira A. HOW TO PROTECT YOURSELF FROM CRIME. New York: Atheneum.
1975.

Lipman, Mark. STEALING. New York: Harpers Magazine Press. 1973.

Matteson, Sally. "Security Retrofit and Review Survey." SECURITY WORLD, Vol. 18, No.
2 (February 1981), pp. 20–27.

Meyer, Marshall M., and John P. Hill. "Prevention: Security's Future Role." SECURITY IN-
DUSTRY AND PRODUCT NEWS, Vol. 10, No. 8 (August 1981). pp. 24–26.

Moolman, V. PRACTICAL WAYS TO PREVENT BURGLARY AND ILLEGAL ENTRY.
New York: Cornerstone Library, Inc. 1970. 192 pp.

Oliver, Eric, and John Wilson. PRACTICAL SECURITY IN COMMERCE AND INDUSTRY,
3rd edition. Woburn, MA: Butterworth Publishers. 1978. 522 pp.

Rosberg, Robert P. GAME OF THIEVES. Woburn, MA: Butterworth Publishers. 1980. 288 pp.

Russell, A. Lewis. CORPORATE AND INDUSTRIAL SECURITY. Woburn, MA: Butterworth,
Publishers. 1980. 288 pp.

San Luis, ed. OFFICE AND OFFICE BUILDING SECURITY. Woburn, MA: Butterworth
Publishers. 1973, 304 pp.

Strauss, Sheryl (ed.) SECURITY PROBLEMS IN A MODERN SOCIETY. Woburn, MA: Butterworth Publishers. 1980. 314 pp.

Strobl, Walter M. SECURITY. New York: Industrial Press. 1973, 280 pp., illus., biblio.

Walsh, Timothy J., and Richard J. Healy. "A Glossary of Common Security Terms." SECURI-
TY WORLD, Vol. 11, No. 10 (November 1974), pp. 26–28.

– – –PROTECTION OF ASSETS MANUAL, 4 vols. Santa Monica, CA: The Merritt Co.
1974 with monthly updates.

Woodruff, Ronald S. INDUSTRIAL SECURITY TECHNIQUES. Columbus, OH: Merrill
Publishers. 1974.

B. Criminal Investigations

Blackwell, Gene. THE PRIVATE INVESTIGATOR. Woburn, MA: Butterworth Publishers.
1979. 241 pp.

Carroll, John M. CONFIDENTIAL INFORMATION SOURCES: PUBLIC AND PRIVATE.
Woburn, MA: Butterworth Publishers. 1975. 352 pp.

Dienstein, William. TECHNIQUES FOR THE CRIME INVESTIGATION. Springfield, IL: Charles C. Thomas. 1959.

Fuqua, Paul, and Jerry V. Wilson. SECURITY INVESTIGATOR'S HANDBOOK. Woburn, MA: Butterworth Publishers. 1979. 232 pp.

Lazo, Douglas T. "Videotaping for Security Investigators." SECURITY MANAGEMENT, Vol. 22, No. 5 (May 1978). pp. 20–22.

Schultz, Donald O. CRIMINAL INVESTIGATION TECHNIQUES. Woburn, MA: Butterworth Publishers. 1978. 229 pp., illus.

Sennewald, Charles A. THE PROCESS OF INVESTIGATION: CONCEPTS AND STRATEGIES FOR THE SECURITY PROFESSIONAL. Woburn, MA: Butterworth Publishers. 1981. 225 pp.

Weston, Paul B., and Kenneth M. Wells. CRIMINAL INVESTIGATIONS – BASIC PROCEDURES. Englewood Cliffs, NJ: Prentice-Hall. 1979.

C. Robbery

Hemphill, Charles F., Jr. "Prompter Card: What to Do in a Robbery." SECURITY WORLD, Vol. 14, No. 5 (May 1977), p. 34.

International Association for Hospital Security. "Key Points for Positive 'ID'." SECURITY WORLD, Vol. 13, No. 9 (September 1976), pp. 24–25.

McCormick, Mona. ROBBERY PREVENTION: WHAT THE LITERATURE REVEALS: A LITERATURE REVIEW AND ANNOTATED BIBLIOGRAPHY WITH A LIST OF INFORMATION SOURCES. La Jolla, CA: Western Behavioral Sciences Institute. 1974. 75 pp.

D. Safes and Vaults

Murray, Robert S. "How Secure Is Your Safe? What to Look For." SECURITY MANAGEMENT, Vol. 23, No. 12 (December 1979), pp. 50–52.

Post, Deborah Cromer. "Security World Equipment Focus: Safes and Vaults." SECURITY WORLD, Vol. 18, No. 4 (April 1981), pp. 26–29.

Tobias, Marc Weber. LOCKS, SAFES, AND SECURITY: A HANDBOOK FOR LAW ENFORCEMENT PERSONNEL. Springfield, IL: Charles C. Thomas. 1971. 338 pp., illus.

PART 23: FIRE PROTECTION – GENERAL

A. General Works

Amoroso, Louis J. "Where Is Your Company in a Fire Emergency?" SECURITY WORLD, Vol. 12, No. 3 (March 1975), pp. 20, 21, 46–48, 51.

"Analyzing Arson After the Fact." SECURITY WORLD, Vol. 17, No. 3 (March 1980), pp. 30–33.

ARSON. Norwood, MA: Factory Mutual Engineering Corporation. 1977.

Bahme, Charles W. FIRE OFFICER'S GUIDE TO DISASTER CONTROL. Boston: National Fire Protection Association. 1978. 404 pp., illus., biblio.

– – –FIRE OFFICER'S GUIDE TO EMERGENCY ACTION. Boston: National Fire Protection Association. 1976.

Benjamin, I. A., F. Fung, and L. Roth. CONTROL OF SMOKE MOVEMENT IN BUILDINGS: A REVIEW. NBSIR 77-1209. Washington, DC: National Bureau of Standards, U.S. Department of Commerce. July 1977. 39 pp., biblio.

Brannigan, Francis L. BUILDING CONSTRUCTION FOR THE FIRE SERVICE. Boston: National Fire Protection Association. 1971.

Bugbee, Percy. PRINCIPLES OF FIRE PROTECTION. Boston: National Fire Protection Association. 1978. 339 pp., illus.

Cohn, Bert M. "Fire Safety in Recycled Buildings: Establishing the Level of Protection Equivalent to Code Requirements." TECHNOLOGY AND CONSERVATION (Summer 1980), pp. 40–45.

Colburn, Robert E. FIRE PROTECTION AND SUPPRESSION. New York: McGraw-Hill Book Co. 1975. 342 pp. illus.

Cosher, Howard. "Elevators 'React and Prevent' in Building's Security System." SECURITY WORLD, Vol. 16, No. 3 (March 1979), pp. 23–24.

Di Rezze, Nello. "Keep Fire Systems Functioning." SECURITY WORLD, Vol. 18, No. 5 (May 1981), pp. 50–51.

Doyle, Bob. "Fire Scene Investigation." SECURITY MANAGEMENT, Vol. 24, No. 9 (September 1980), pp. 56–58.

Egan, M. David. CONCEPTS IN BUILDING FIRESAFETY. New York: John Wiley and Sons. 1978.

– – –FIRE PROTECTION AND LIFE SAFETY. 3 vols. Clemson, SC: Clemson University College of Architecture. 1975.

Factory Mutual System. "Battling Incendiary Fires." SECURITY MANAGEMENT, Vol. 22, No. 6 (June 1978), pp 22–25.

"Fire Blanket A Reality." SECURITY INDUSTRY AND PRODUCT NEWS, Vol. 9, No. 10 (October 1980), pp. 21, 35.

"Fire Safety Means Using the Right Equipment." SECURITY WORLD, Vol. 18, No. 5 (May 1981), pp. 44–46.

FIRE SAFETY REFERENCE 1977. Washington, DC: Fire Prevention and Control Administration, U.S. Department of Commerce. 1977. 3 pp. This bibliography appears annually; see later editions as well.

Fuss. Eugene. "High-Rise Fire Management System." SECURITY WORLD, Vol. 13, No. 5 (May 1976), p. 34.

Gately, Glenn S. "The Security Manager Faces Arson." SECURITY MANAGEMENT, Vol. 24, No. 9 (September 1980), pp. 50–52, 55.

"In Fire Protection, Decisions Matter Most." SECURITY WORLD, Vol. 17, No. 1 (January 1980), pp. 38–43.

Jacobson, Robert V. "Seven Fallacies Confuse Computer Fire Safety." SECURITY MANAGEMENT, Vol. 23, No. 8 (August 1979), pp. 60–63.

Jarvey, Donald, J. "Involving the Whole Team in Fire Fighting." SECURITY MANAGEMENT, Vol. 22, No. 3 (March 1978), pp. 6–9.

Jensen, Rolf (ed.). FIRE PROTECTION FOR THE DESIGN PROFESSIONAL. Boston: Cahners Books. 1975. 197 pp., illus.

Koegler, Charles. "High-Rise Fire Traps." SECURITY MANAGEMENT, Vol. 24, No. 7 (July 1980), pp. 13, 14, 16.

Langdon-Thomas, G. J. FIRE SAFETY IN BUILDINGS. New York: St. Martin's Press. 1973.

Lefer, H. "Where There's Fire There's Smoke." PROGRESSIVE ARCHITECTURE (September 1976), pp 58-63.

Lerup, Lars. LEARNING FROM FIRE: A FIRE PROTECTION PRIMER FOR ARCHITECTS. Berkeley: University of California Press. 1977.

Levin, Bernard. "Psychological Characteristics of Firesetters." FIRE JOURNAL, Vol. 70, No. 2 (March 1976), pp. 36-41.

Lucht, David A. "Basic Considerations: How Safe Is Safe?" SPECIFYING ENGINEER, Vol. 29, No. 5 (May 1978), pp. 66-69.

Lyons, Paul R. FIRE IN AMERICA! Boston: National Fire Protection Association. 1976.

Maatman, Gerald L. "The Consultant's Role in Fire Protection." FIRE JOURNAL, Vol. 64, No. 2 (March 1970). NFPA reprint No. FJ70-10.

Maher, Kathleen, "A New Idea in Fire Blankets." SECURITY WORLD, Vol. 18, No. 1 (January 1981), p. 33.

Marchant, E. W. (ed.) A COMPLETE GUIDE TO FIRE AND BUILDINGS. New York: Barnes and Noble Books. 1973.

McKinnon, Gordon P. (ed.) FIRE PROTECTION HANDBOOK, 14th edition. Boston: National Fire Protection Association. 1976. 1296 pp., 790 illus. and diagrams, 6 appendices. NFPA Publ. No FPH1476.

Melinek, S. J. METHODS OF DETERMINING THE OPTIMUM LEVEL OF SAFETY EXPENDITURE. Boreham Wood, U.K.: Fire Research Station, Building Research Establishment. October 1974.

Morris, John. "Current Fire Protection Topics." PROFESSIONAL SAFETY (February 1975), pp. 38-43.

"The Need for Greater Security Against Arson." FIRE PREVENTION (London: Fire Protection Association). No. 125 (June 1978), pp. 20-23.

Patton, Richard. "The Life Safety System." FIRE JOURNAL, Vol. 65, No. 1 (January 1971), pp. 48-52.

Planer, Robert G. FIRE LOSS CONTROL: A MANAGEMENT GUIDE. Woburn, MA: Butterworth Publishers. 1979. 250 pp.

Post, Deborah Cromer. "Technology: First Line Defense Against Fire." SECURITY WORLD, Vol. 17, No. 3 (March 1980), p. 24.

PROTECTION AGAINST INCENDIARY FIRES. Norwood, MA: Factory Mutual Engineering Corporation. 1977.

PROTECTION OF ELECTRONIC COMPUTER/DATA PROCESSING EQUIPMENT. Boston: National Fire Protection Association. 1972.

THE SYSTEMS APPROACH TO FIRE PROTECTION (A compilation of articles from FIRE JOURNAL and FIRE TECHNOLOGY). Boston: National Fire Protection Association. 1975. 75 pp.

Thompson, Robert J. "The Decision Tree for Fire Safety Systems Analysis: What Is It and How to Use It." FIRE JOURNAL (July, September, and November 1975).

WAS IT ARSON? New York: General Adjustment Bureau. 1975.

Wilson, Rexford. "The L-Curve: Evaluating Fire Protection Tradeoffs." SPECIFYING ENGINEER (May 1977), pp. 110-113.

B. Fire Prevention

Bhatnagar, Vijay Mohan. FIRE RETARDANT FORMULATION HANDBOOK. Westport, CT: Technomic. 1972. 245 pp.

Black, Douglas. "Fire Prevention, Security and Safety: Building It In." SECURITY MANAGE-MENT, Vol. 21, No. 2 (May 1977), pp. 39, 41–42.

FIRE RESISTANCE DESIGN MANUAL. Evanston, IL: Gypsum Association. 1975. 104 pp.

Harp, Dale W. "Intumescent Paints: A Useful Component of Fire Protection Plans." TECHNOLOGY AND CONSERVATION (Spring 1981), pp. 30–31.

Underdown, G.W. PRACTICAL FIRE PRECAUTIONS, 2nd edition. Woburn, MA: Butterworth Publishers. 1979. 546 pp., illus.

Whitman, Lawrence E. FIRE PREVENTION. Woburn, MA: Butterworth Publishers. 1979. 315 pp.

C. Fire Detection

Ahern, John J. "Will Your Security Plan Be Left Powerless." SECURITY MANAGEMENT, Vol. 23, No. 2 (February 1979), pp. 12–13, 16.

Bright, Richard G. A NEW TEST METHOD FOR AUTOMATIC FIRE DETECTION DEVICES. Washington, DC: National Bureau of Standards, U.S. Department of Commerce. December 1976. 23 pp.

Bukowski, Richard W., and Richard G. Bright. RESULTS OF FULL-SCALE FIRE TESTS WITH PHOTOELECTRIC SMOKE DETECTORS. Interagency Report NBSIR 75-700. Washington, DC: National Bureau of Standards, U.S. Department of Commerce. September 1975. National Technical Information Service Stock No. COM–75–11280.

Bukowski, Richard W., Richard L. P. Custer, and Richard G. Bright. FIRE ALARM AND COMMUNICATIONS SYSTEMS. NBS Technical Note 964. Washington, DC: National Bureau of Standards, U.S. Department of Commerce. April 1978, 43 pp., illus.

Cholin, Roger R. "Reappraising Early Warning Detection." FIRE JOURNAL, Vol. 69, No. 2 (March 1975). NFPA Reprint FJ75–1, 3 pp.

Christian, W. J., and P. M. Dubivsky. "Basic Information on Fire Detection Devices." SECURITY WORLD, Vol. 11, No. 3 (March 1974), pp. 71–73.

Custer, Richard L. P., and Richard G. Bright. FIRE DETECTION: THE STATE-OF-THE-ART. NBS Technical Note 839. Washington, DC: National Bureau of Standards, U.S. Department of Commerce. June 1974. 110 pp., illus., biblio.

Egesdal, S.E. "The Basics of Fire Alarm Systems." SECURITY MANAGEMENT, Vol. 24, No. 7 (July 1980), pp. 58–61.

Fuss, Eugene. "Security Equipment and Technology: Fire Detection and Alarm Sensors." SECU-RITY WORLD, Vol. 13, Nos. 2 and 3 (February and March 1976), pp. 38 (Feb.) and 36, 56 (Mar.)

– – –"Security Equipment and Technology: High-Rise Fire Management System." SECURITY WORLD, Vol. 13, No. 5 (May 1976), p. 34.

Gorman, Robert. "Smoke Detectors: How to Choose and How to Use Them." POPULAR SCIENCE, Vol. 213, No. 4 (October 1978), pp. 50, 52, 54, 58, 60. Illus.

Greer, William. "Remote Smoke Alarms Sharply Reduce Fire Losses." SIGNAL, (4th Quarter 1978), pp. 24–26, 30.

Harris, King. "Are Municipal Smoke Detector Codes Adequate?" ALARM SIGNAL (July–August 1981), pp. 36, 38.

HONEYWELL FIRE & SECURITY PLANNING GUIDE. Minneappolis, MN: Honeywell, Inc. 1977. 26 pp.

Lein, H. "Automatic Fire Detection Devices and Their Operating Principles." FIRE ENGINEERING (June 1975), pp. 38–42.

Longworth, Roy. "Brownout Conditions and Building Fire Alarm Systems." SECURITY WORLD, Vol. 11, No. 3 (March 1974), pp. 25, 50.

Matteson, Sally A. "Smoke Detectors Complete Industrial Fire Protection Circle." SECURITY WORLD, Vol. 16, No. 3 (March 1979), pp. 16–19.

Meiners, Frank J. "Energy Cut-Back: How Will It Affect Your Fire Alarms?" SECURITY WORLD, Vol. 11, No. 3 (March 1974), pp. 24, 46–50.

Mniszewski, K. R., T. E. Waterman, and S. W. Harpe. DETECTOR DIRECTORY. Washington, DC: IIT Research Institute for the National Fire Data Center, U.S. Fire Administration, Federal Emergency Management Administration. December 1978.

Pasek, Frank. "Your Smoke Detectors Are Where?" SECURITY WORLD, Vol. 14, No. 3 (March 1977), pp. 30–31.

Phillips, Patrick E. "Designing a Dependable Detection System." SPECIFYING ENGINEER (May 1977), pp. 94–99.

Post, Deborah Cromer. "Security World Equipment Focus: Fire Protection Systems." SECURITY WORLD, Vol. 18, No. 3 (March 1981), pp. 30–32.

Post, Deborah Cromer. "Technology: First Line Defense Against Fire." SECURITY WORLD, Vol. 17, No. 3 (March 1980), pp. 24–26, 29.

Rajan, K. S., and others. NEW CONCEPTS OF FIRE DETECTION. Washington, DC: IIT Research Institute for the National Fire Data Center, U.S. Fire Administration, Federal Emergency Management Administration. December 1978.

Ruyle, Robert. "SDM Equipment Analysis: Fire Protection Equipment." SECURITY DISTRIBUTING AND MARKETING, Vol. 11, No. 3 (March 1981), pp. 38–42.

Schmidt, William A. "Smoke Detection: Part of A Complete Building System." SPECIFYING ENGINEER (May 1979), pp. 58–62.

Schmied, Ernest. "Plan Ahead for Power Supply Problems." BUILDINGS, May 1972. 4 pp. Reprinted by Defense Civil Preparedness Agency, January 1973.

Shanahan, James C. "Back-Up Power Supply Codes Being Reappraised." SECURITY WORLD, Vol. 11, No. 3 (March 1974), pp. 25, 50.

SMOKE AND OTHER PRODUCTS OF COMBUSTION. A compilation of articles from FIRE JOURNAL and FIRE TECHNOLOGY. Boston: National Fire Protection Association. 1976. 97 pp. NFPA Publication No. SPP-41.

SMOKE DETECTOR RESOURCE CATALOG. Volume 1 of a series. Washington, DC: National Fire Prevention and Control Administration, U.S. Department of Commerce. June 1977. 39 pp.

SMOKE DETECTORS AND LEGISLATION. Volume 4 of a series. Washington, DC: National Fire Prevention and Control Administration, U.S. Department of Commerce, September 1977. 60 pp.

SMOKE DETECTORS: MOVING THE PUBLIC. Volume 2 of a series. Washington, DC: National Fire Prevention and Control Administration, U.S. Department of Commerce. June 1977. 30 pp.

SMOKE DETECTOR TECHNOLOGY. Volume 3 of a series. Washington, DC: National Fire Prevention and Control Administration, U.S. Department of Commerce. July 1977. 22 pp.

SMOKE DETECTOR TRAINING. Volume 5 of a series. Washington, DC: National Fire Prevention and Control Administration, U.S. Department of Commerce. 1978. 42 pp.

Waterman, T. E., K. R. Mniszewski, and D. J. Spadoni. COST/BENEFIT ANALYSIS OF FIRE DETECTORS. Washington, DC: IIT Research Institute for the National Fire Data Center, U.S. Fire Administration, Federal Emergency Management Administration. September 1978.

Whitehurst, Susan A. "Update on Fire Protection." SECURITY DISTRIBUTING AND MARKETING, Vol. 10, No. 3 (March 1980).

D. Fire Suppression

Bahme, Charles. FIRE OFFICER'S GUIDE TO EXTINGUISHING SYSTEMS. Boston: National Fire Protection Association. 1970 (reprint 1977). 104 pp., illus.

Bryan, John L. AUTOMATIC SPRINKLER AND STANDPIPE SYSTEMS. Boston: National Fire Protection Association. 1976. 402 pp., illus., biblio.

Crosby, George, Jr., and Daniel J. Mackay, Jr. "Testing Halon 1301 System Design." FIRE JOURNAL, Vol. 71, No. 5 (1977), pp. 74+.

"Equipment for Detection and Warning of Fire and Fighting Fires." Fire Protection Design Guide No. 6 in the Series FIRE AND THE ARCHITECT. London: Fire Protection Association.

FIRE PROTECTION BY HALONS. A compilation of articles from FIRE JOURNAL and FIRE TECHNOLOGY. Boston: National Fire Protection Association. 1975. 87 pp. NFPA Publication No. SPP-26.

Ford, Charles L. "Halon 1301 Fire-Extinguishing Agent: Properties and Applications." FIRE JOURNAL, Vol. 64, No. 6 (November 1970), p. 36.

– – –"Halon 1301 Update: Research, Application, New Standard." SPECIFYING ENGINEER (May 1977).

Goldman, Jeff. "Selecting a Fire Extinguisher." SECURITY INDUSTRY AND PRODUCT NEWS, Vol. 4, No. 6 (November–December 1975), pp. 26, 28.

"Halogenated Extinguishing Agents." NFPA Quarterly, Vol. 48, No. 2 (October 1954).

Hammack, James M. "Talking Extinguishing Equipment: The Halons." FIRE JOURNAL, Vol. 64, No. 3 (May 1970). NFPA Reprint No. FJ70-27.

Jensen, Rolf. "Twenty-One Ways to Better Sprinkler System Design." FIRE JOURNAL, Vol. 68, No. 1 (January 1974), p. 47.

Merdinyan, Philip H. "A Fully Approved On-Off Sprinkler." FIRE JOURNAL, Vol. 67, No. 1 (January 1973), pp. 11–15.

Nash, P., and R. A. Young. AUTOMATIC SPRINKLER SYSTEMS FOR FIRE PROTECTION. London: Victor Green Publications. 1978.

Northey, J. "Halon Extinguishing Agents." FIRE PREVENTION, No. 122 (December 1977), pp. 22–24.

Organic Chemistry Department. DUPONT HALON 1301 FIRE EXTINGUISHANT. Bulletin B-29C. Wilmington, DE: E. I. DuPont de Nemours & Co. 1972. 15 pp.

Organic Chemistry Department. THERMODYNAMIC PROPERTIES OF DUPONT HALON 1301 FIRE EXTINGUISHANT. Bulletin T-1301, Wilmington, DE: E. I. DuPont de Nemours & Co.

Organic Chemistry Department. TOXICOLOGY OF DUPONT HALON 1301 FIRE EXTIN-GUISHANT. Bulletin S-35A. Wilmington, DE: E. I. DuPont de Nemours & Co. 1971. 14 pp., biblio.

Organic Chemistry Department. TRANSFER AND HANDLING OF DUPONT HALON 1301 FIRE EXTINGUISHANT. Bulletin FE-2. Wilmington, DE: E. I. DuPont de Nemours & Co.

"Sprinkler Systems: Still a Cost-Effective Fire Fighter." SECURITY WORLD, Vol. 18, No. 8 (August 1981), pp. 54–61.

Wood, Jack A. "Stop-and-Go Sprinklers." FIRE JOURNAL, Vol. 61, No. 6 (November 1967), pp. 86–88.

"Zoned Halon System Overcomes First-Cost Hurdle." ARCHITECTURAL RECORD, Vol. 162, No. 6 (Mid-October 1977), pp. 12–13.

E. Emergency Exits and Evacuation

Cathey, B. H. "A Technique for Analyzing Building Evacuation Plans and Facility Designs." JOURNAL of the American Society of Safety Engineers, August 1974, pp. 26–28.

Holcomb, Robert C. "Emergency Exit Doors." ASSETS PROTECTION, Vol. 6, No. 5 (September–October 1981), pp. 30, 33.

– – – "Emergency Exit Doors." SECURITY INDUSTRY AND PRODUCT NEWS, Vol. 10, No. 5 (May 1981), pp. 14, 44.

Levin, B. M. (ed.) FIRE AND LIFE SAFETY FOR THE HANDICAPPED. Reports of the Conference on Fire Safety for the Handicapped held at the National Bureau of Standards, November 26–29, 1979, and Workshops on Life Safety for the Handicapped held in Washington, DC, and Sacramento, CA, August and September 1979. Washington, DC: National Bureau of Standards, U.S. Department of Commerce. July 1980. 144 pp.

Melinek, S. J., and R. Baldwin. EVACUATION OF BUILDINGS: SOME EFFECTS OF CHANGES IN PERFORMANCE STANDARDS. Boreham Wood, U.K.: Fire Research Station, Building Research Establishment. October 1975.

Melinek, S. J., and S. Booth. AN ANALYSIS OF EVACUATION TIMES AND THE MOVE-MENT OF CROWDS IN BUILDINGS. Boreham Wood. U.K.: Fire Research Station, Building Research Establishment. October 1975.

PEOPLE CARE DURING A FIRE EMERGENCY: PSYCHOLOGICAL ASPECTS. Boston: Society of Fire Protection Engineers. 1975.

Rubin, Arthur I., and Arthur Cohen. OCCUPANT BEHAVIOR IN BUILDING FIRES. NBS Technical Note 818. Washington, DC: National Bureau of Standards, U.S. Department of Commerce. February 1974. 28 pp., biblio.

Scott, Donald, THE PSYCHOLOGY OF FIRE. New York: Charles Scribner's Sons. 1974.

Spehler, R., and W. Peissard. "The Evacuation of Premises." THE ARCHITECT (September 1972), pp. 80–81.

Stahl, Fred I., and John Archea. AN ASSESSMENT OF THE TECHNICAL LITERATURE ON EMERGENCY EGRESS FROM BUILDINGS. NBSIR 77-1313. Washington, DC: National Bureau of Standards, U.S. Department of Commerce. October 1977. 62 pp., biblio.

Stevens, R. E. "Movement of People." FIRE JOURNAL, Vol. 63, No. 1 (January 1969), pp. 27–29.

Wadey, W. J. "Principles and Means of Escape in Case of Fire." THE BUILDER (August 8, 1965), p. 788.

"Woman Discovered Dead in Boston Library" (because of faulty fire door). LIBRARY JOURNAL, Vol. 102, No. 18 (October 15, 1977), p. 2106.

Wood, P. G. THE BEHAVIOR OF PEOPLE IN FIRES. United Kingdom: Department of the Environment and Fire Officers' Committee, Joint Fire Research Organization. November 1972.

PART 24: FIRE PROTECTION FOR MUSEUMS, HISTORIC HOUSES, AND ARCHIVES

Advisory Committee on the Protection of Archives and Records Centers. PROTECTING FEDERAL RECORDS CENTERS AND ARCHIVES FROM FIRE. Washington, DC: General Services Administration. April 1977. 202 pp., illus., biblio.

Beers, R. J. "High-Expansion Foam Fire Control for Records Storage." FIRE TECHNOLOGY (May 1966).

Bertschinger, Susan. "Protecting Ontario's Historic Buildings Against the Threat of Fire." Canadian Museums Association GAZETTE, Vol. 9, No. 3 (Summer 1976), pp. 14–18.

Brewer, Norval L. "Fire Destroys Aerospace Museum." FIRE ENGINEERING, Vol. 131, No. 6 (June 1978), pp. 24–25.

Chapman, Joseph M. "Fire." MUSEUM NEWS, Vol. 50, No. 5 (January 1972), pp. 32–35.

Chergotis, Nick. "Never Again! One Records Fire Is Too Many." SECURITY MANAGEMENT, Vol. 23, No. 11 (November 1979), pp. 39–40.

Chicarello, Peter J., J. M. Troupe, and R. K. Dean. FIRE TESTS IN MOBILE STORAGE SYSTEMS FOR ARCHIVAL STORAGE. Technical Report No. J.I. 3A3N4.RR. Norwood, MA: Factory Mutual Engineering Corp. June 1978.

Corbett, Dennis F. "Halon 1301: A Fire Suppressant That Respects Rare Books." HARVARD MAGAZINE, Vol. 78, No. 9 (May 1976), p. 12.

Dowling, John H., and Charles Burton Ford. "Halon 1301 Total Flooding System for Winterthur Museum." FIRE JOURNAL, Vol. 63, No. 6 (November 1969), p. 10. NFPA Reprint No. FJ69–17.

FIRE SAFETY SELF-INSPECTION FORM FOR MUSEUMS. Boston: National Fire Protection Association. 1976. 8 pp.

Fischer, Walter R. "Fire Safety Systems: Protecting Our Treasures from Threat of Fire." TECHNOLOGY AND CONSERVATION (Fall 1976), pp. 14–17.

Ford, Charles L. "Winterthur Revisited." FIRE JOURNAL, Vol. 69, No. 1 (January 1975), pp. 81–82.

Genov, P. "Merki za Protivopozarha Zascita na Muzeite i Pametnicite na Kulturata" (Methods of Safeguarding Museums and Monuments of Culture from Fire). MUZEU U NAMEMNUCU NA KUPMURAMA (Rumania), Vol. 8, No. 3 (1968), pp. 52–53.

Gondos, Victor, Jr. "Records and Fire Protection." AMERICAN ARCHIVIST, Vol. 14, No. 2 (April 1951), pp. 155–159.

Habersaat, René. "Lutte Contre l'Incendie dans les Musées" (Fighting Fires in the Museum). INFORMATION VMS/AMS (Zurich), No. 5 (1970).

Harvey, Bruce K. "Fire Hazards in Libraries." LIBRARY SECURITY NEWSLETTER, Vol. 1, No. 1 (January 1975).

Haure, René. "La Prévention de l'Incendie dans les Musées" (Prevention of Fires in Museums). MUSÉES ET COLLECTIONS PUBLIQUES DE FRANCE (Paris), Vol. 120, No. 4 (1972).

Hemphill, C. F. "Lessons of A Fire." LIBRARY JOURNAL, 87 (1962), pp. 1094–1095.

Hunter, John E. EMERGENCY PREPAREDNESS: AN ANNOTATED BIBLIOGRAPHY. Technical Leaflet No. 114. Nashville, TN: American Association for State and Local History. April 1979. 12 pp.

Jenkins, Joseph F. (ed.) PROTECTING OUR HERITAGE: A DISCOURSE ON FIRE PROTEC-TION AND PREVENTION IN HISTORIC BUILDINGS AND LANDMARKS. Boston: National Fire Protection Association. 1970. 39 pp., illus.

Kennedy, J. "Library Arson." LIBRARY SECURITY NEWSLETTER, Vol. 2 (Spring 1976), pp. 1-3.

Lynes, Russell. "How the Museum of Modern Art Survived the Fire." SMITHSONIAN, Vol. 4, No. 2 (May 1973), pp. 58-67. Illus.

Metcalf, Keyes D. "The Design of Book Stacks and the Preservation of Books." RESTAURATOR, Vol. 1, No. 2 (1969), pp. 115-125.

Mittelgluck, E. L. "Case Study in Library Arson." LIBRARY SECURITY NEWSLETTER, Vol. 2 (Spring 1976).

Morris, John. "Is Your Library Safe from Fire." AMERICAN SCHOOL AND UNIVERSITY, 52 (April 1980), pp. 60-63.

— — —MANAGING THE LIBRARY FIRE RISK. Berkeley: Office of Risk Management and Safety, University of California. 1979 (2nd edition). 147 pp., illus., biblio.

Neilson, George. "New Fire Protection for High Value Areas." DUPONT MAGAZINE, Vol. 65, No. 1 (1971), pp. 6-9.

Newman, R. Murray. RECORD STORAGE FIRE TESTS. Norwood, MA: Factory Mutual Engineering Corp. December 1974.

Peissard, W. G. "Les Tresors Partent . . . en Fumee" (Treasures Gone Up . . . in Smoke). INFORMATION VMS/AMS (Zurich), No. 12 (1974).

Probst, Tom. "Fire Detection — Fire Protection." MUSEUM NEWS, Vol. 44, No. 9 (May 1966), pp. 11-17.

— — —Protection of Museum Collections. Boston: National Fire Protection Association. 1974.

"Protecting Historical Buildings from Fire." ENVIRONMENTAL DESIGN (Winter 1969/70). Industrial Publications, Inc. 3 pp.

PROTECTING OUR HERITAGE FOR FUTURE GENERATIONS. A special seminar presented under the auspices of the NFPA Committee on Libraries, Museums and Historic Buildings at the NFPA Annual Meeting at Toronto, Ontario, on May 20, 1970. Boston: National Fire Protec-tion Association. 1970. 24 pp. NFPA Stock No. MP70-1.

Rudie, Gunnar. "Erfaringer fra en Museumsbrann" (Experiences Gained from a Fire Incident Within the Museum Premises). MUSEUMSNYTT (Oslo), No. 1-2 (1966).

Schur, Susan E. "Fire Protection at Mount Vernon: Incorporating Modern Fire Safety Systems into an Historic Site." TECHNOLOGY AND CONSERVATION (Winter 1980), pp. 18-25. Illus.

"A Sensing Approach Smokes Out Possible Threats to Historic Structures." TECHNOLOGY AND CONSERVATION (Summer 1981), pp. 9, 10, 12, 13.

"Silent Sentinals in Museum/Archives Extinguish Possibility of Fire Damage." TECHNOLOGY AND CONSERVATION (Winter 1979), pp. 14, 16.

Stender, Walter W., and Evans Walker. "The National Personnel Records Center Fire: A Study in Disaster." AMERICAN ARCHIVIST, Vo. 37, No. 4 (October 1974), pp. 521-549.

Stolow, Nathan. "Emergency, Fire-Protection, Security Systems." In MAN AND HIS WORLD, Expo 67, Montreal.

Swartzburg, S. G. "Fire Safety Self-Inspection Form for Libraries." In PRESERVING LIBRARY MATERIALS. Metuchen, NJ: Scarecrow Press. 1980. pp. 129–135.

Swayne, Leo H. "Fire Protection at the National Archives Building." FIRE JOURNAL, Vol. 69, No. 1 (January 1975).

Tiszkus, Alphonse T., and E. G. Dressler. "Fire Protection Planning for Cultural Institutions: Blending Risk Management, Loss Prevention, and Physical Safeguards." TECHNOLOGY AND CONSERVATION (Summer 1980), pp. 18–23.

Tomokichi, Iwasaki. "Scientific Preservation Methods for Cultural Properties: II: Precautions for Fire." MUSEUM (Tokyo), No. 138 (1962), pp. 28–30.

Trelles, Oscar M. "Protection of Libraries." LAW LIBRARY JOURNAL, Vol. 66, No. 3 (August 1973), pp. 241–258.

"Warehoused Antiques Get Fire Safety." SECURITY WORLD, Vol. 14, No. 3 (March 1977), p. 21.

Wilson, Rexford. "The New York Museum Fire." QUARTERLY of the National Fire Protection Association, 52 (July 1958), pp. 67–77.

Windeler, Peter. "Fire: Endangers the Past — for the Future." MUSEUMS JOURNAL, Vol. 70, No. 2 (September 1970), pp. 72–74.

Yates, Rob, and others. "Engineering Library Survives" and other accounts of the University of Toronto Fire. TOIKE OIKE, Vol. 80, No. 7 (February 17, 1977). A special issue of the University of Toronto Undergraduate Engineering Society newspaper.

Yee, Roger. "Smoke Gets in your Van Eycks." PROGRESSIVE ARCHITECTURE (March 1975), 4 pp.

PART 25: FIRE CODES AND STANDARDS

A. Codes and Standards of the National Fire Protection Association (NFPA)

NFPA publishes a wide variety of codes and standards. The codes are compiled into a multivolume work entitled THE NATIONAL FIRE CODE. The 1981 edition of NFC consists of 16 volumes plus two supplementary volumes (stock numbers FC–Set and FC–S81, respectively).

The codes also are available as separately published hard-bound books and paper-bound booklets for those users who do not need the entire NFC. Below are listed the separate codes that museums, historic houses, and archives will find most useful. Dates of publication are given. In all cases, the dates are those of the latest editions available as of November 1981. These publications may be purchased using their code numbers except for the handbooks that have separate stock numbers.

Code No.	Date	Title
10	1981	Portable Fire Extinguishers
12A	1980	Halon 1301 Fire Extinguishing Systems
12B	1980	Halon 1211 Fire Extinguishing Systems
13	1980	Installation of Sprinkler Systems
13A	1981	Care and Maintenance of Sprinkler Systems
14	1980	Standpipe and Hose Systems
40	1974	Cellulose Nitrate Motion Picture Film

45	1975	Fire Protection for Laboratories Using Chemicals
49	1975	Hazardous Chemicals Data
57	1973	Standard of Fumigation
70	1981	National Electrical Code
SPP–6c	1981	National Electrical Code Handbook
71	1977	Central Station Signaling Systems
72A	1979	Local Protective Signaling Systems
72B	1979	Auxiliary Protective Signaling Systems
72C	1975	Remote Station Protective Signaling Systems
72D	1979	Proprietary Protective Signaling Systems
72E	1978	Automatic Fire Detectors
75	1981	Protection of Electronic Computer/Data Processing Equipment
80	1981	Fire Doors and Windows
101	1981	Life Safety Code
101 HB81	1981	Life Safety Code Handbook
231	1980	Indoor General Storage
232	1980	Protection of Records
232AM	1980	Archives and Record Centers
910	1980	Protection of Libraries and Library Collections
911	1980	Protection of Museums and Museum Collections

B. Fire Protection Standards of Safety of Underwriters Laboratories, Inc.

The Safety Standards of UL have been drawn up to provide specifications and requirements for the construction and performance under test and in actual use of systems, devices, materials, and appliances submitted to UL. Generally, the standards are most useful to equipment manufacturers who must meet them in order for their equipment to be UL Listed and to systems installers who must meet them in order for their systems to be certified by UL. Systems employing UL Listed equipment may qualify the owner for a discount on his insurance. The UL Standards may be useful to equipment owners and operators who wish to inspect or test their equipment to determine if it in fact meets UL Standards before it is placed into service.

The following UL Safety Standards are among those of potential use to museums, historic houses, and archives. Other standards may be useful to such users in specific cases; a catalog of standards is available from UL on request. All standards are revised periodically and only the latest editions should be used or cited in specifications.

UL No.	Title
38	Manually actuated Signaling Boxes for Use with Fire Protective Signaling Systems
72	Tests for Fire Resistance of Record Protection Equipment
167	Smoke Detectors, Combustion Products Type, for Fire Protective Signaling Systems
168	Smoke Detectors, Photoelectric Type, for Fire Protective Signaling Systems
217	Single and Multiple Station Smoke Detectors
228	Electromagnetic and Electromechanical Door Holder-Releases and Combination Door Closer-Holders
305	Panic Hardware
521	Fire Detection Thermostats
539	Single and Multiple Station Heat Detectors

680   Emergency Vault Ventilators and Vault-Ventilating Ports
827   Central-Stations for Watchmen, Fire-Alarm, and Supervisory Services
864   Control Units for Fire-Protective Signaling Systems
924   Emergency Lighting and Power Equipment
1093   Halogenated Agent Fire Extinguishers

PART 26: EMERGENCY AND DISASTER PREPAREDNESS – GENERAL

American Red Cross. ADVANCED FIRST AID AND EMERGENCY CARE. Garden City, NY: Doubleday. 1973.

American Society of Corporate Secretaries, Inc. CONTINUITY OF CORPORATE MANAGE-MENT IN EVENT OF MAJOR DISASTER. Washington, DC: Office of Civil Defense, Department of Defense. December 1970. 56 pp., biblio.

Bologna, Jack. "Disaster/Recovery Planning: A Qualitative Approach." ASSETS PROTECTION, Vol. 6, No. 4 (July–August 1981), pp. 25–29.

Callahan, Keith L., and Calvin H. Maledy. "Security Organizations: A Cookbook for Defense in Depth." SECURITY WORLD, Vol. 16, No. 2 (February 1979), pp. 28–29.

Catherwood, Dwight W., and Leonard I. Krauss. "Systems Contingency Planning." SECURITY INDUSTRY AND PRODUCT NEWS, Vol. 8, No. 7 (July 1979), pp. 20, 24, 37.

Chenault, William W. THE CONSIDERATION OF MULTIPLE HAZARDS IN CIVIL DEFENSE PLANNING AND ORGANIZATIONAL DEVELOPMENT. McLean, VA: Human Sciences Research, Inc. January 1972.

CIVIL DEFENSE PRINCIPLES OF WARNING. Publication No. CPG 1-14. Washington, DC: Defense Civil Preparedness Agency. June 1977. 14 pp.

Couch, Virgil L. "Blueprint for Industrial Disaster Readiness." ENVIRONMENTAL CONTROL AND SAFETY MANAGEMENT (February 1971), pp. 33–36. Biblio.

Cox, David L. "Training for Facility Self-Protection." SECURITY MANAGEMENT, Vol. 23, No. 3 (March 1979), pp. 33, 36–38.

Davis, John E. "Disaster Management – A Dual Responsibility." SECURITY MANAGEMENT (October–November 1972). Reprinted by Defense Civil Preparedness Agency. 2 pp.

DISASTER OPERATIONS: A HANDBOOK FOR LOCAL GOVERNMENTS. Publication No. CPG 1-6. Washington, DC: Defense Civil Preparedness Agency. July 1972.

DISASTER PLANNING GUIDE FOR BUSINESS AND INDUSTRY. Publication No. CPG-25. Washington, DC: Defense Civil Preparedness Agency. May 1974. 54 pp.

DISASTER RESPONSE AND RECOVERY PROGRAM GUIDE. Washington, DC: Federal Emergency Management Agency. February 1980. 28 pp.

Dynes, Russell R., and E. L. Quarantelli. THE ROLE OF LOCAL CIVIL DEFENSE IN DISASTER PLANNING. Columbus: The Disaster Research Center, Ohio State University. 1975.

Gay, William G., and William W. Chenault. IMPROVING YOUR COMMUNITY'S EMERGENCY RESPONSE: AN INTRODUCTION TO DISASTER PLANNING. Publication No. MP-67. Washington, DC: Defense Civil Preparedness Agency. November 1973. 121 pp.

Gervasio, Louis. "Emergency Planning: Getting Down to Basics." SECURITY INDUSTRY AND PRODUCT NEWS, Vol. 7, No. 1 (January 1978), pp. 24, 26.

Healy, Richard J. EMERGENCY AND DISASTER PLANNING. New York: John Wiley and Sons. 1969. 290 pp.

INTRODUCTION TO CIVIL PREPAREDNESS. Publication No. CPG 1-1. Washington, DC: Defense Civil Preparedness Agency. July 1975. 28 pp.

Isaacson, Gerald. "Disaster Recovery Planning." SECURITY INDUSTRY AND PRODUCT NEWS, Vol. 9, No. 7 (July 1980), pp. 23, 41.

Kreps, Gary A., Russell R. Dynes, and E. L. Quarantelli. A PERSPECTIVE ON DISASTER RESEARCH PLANNING. Columbus: The Disaster Research Center, Ohio State University. June 1972. Published as Defense Civil Preparedness Agency Report No. TR-77.

LOCAL GOVERNMENT EMERGENCY PLANNING. Publication No. CPG 1-8. Washington, DC: Federal Emergency Management Agency. July 1978. 101 pp.

Macy, John W., Jr. A NEW IMPETUS! EMERGENCY MANAGEMENT FOR ATTACK PREPAREDNESS. Washington, DC: Federal Emergency Management Agency. June 1980. 10 pp.

Manning, Diana H. Disaster Technology: AN ANNOTATED BIBLIOGRAPHY. New York: Pergamon Press. 1976. 282 pp.

Martincic, Joseph A. "A Disaster Recovery Plan." JOURNAL OF SYSTEMS MANAGEMENT (February 1976), pp. 40-42.

Quarantelli, E. L. AN ANNOTATED BIBLIOGRAPHY ON DISASTER AND DISASTER PLANNING. Columbus: The Disaster Research Center, Ohio State University. 1976.

Tucker, Patricia G. "CPR Is Good for Business." SECURITY MANAGEMENT, Vol. 23, No. 1 (January 1979), p. 13.

Webre, A. L., and P. H. Liss. THE AGE OF CATACLYSM. New York: G. P. Putnam's Sons for Berkeley Publishing Corp. 1974.

Yee, Elbert. " 'Pearl Harbor' Facing U.S. Industries?" SECURITY WORLD, Vol. 15, No. 2 (January 1978), pp. 34-35.

PART 27: EMERGENCY AND DISASTER PREPAREDNESS FOR MUSEUMS, HISTORIC HOUSES, AND ARCHIVES

Association of Records Executives and Administrators. PROTECTION OF VITAL RECORDS. Washington, DC: Office of Civil Defense. July 1966. 24 pp., biblio.

Bohem, Hilda. DISASTER PREVENTION AND DISASTER PREPAREDNESS. Berkeley: Office of the Assistant Vice President for Library Plans and Policies, Systemwide Library Administration, University of California. April 1978. 23 pp.

Burr, Nelson R. (compiler). SAFEGUARDING OUR CULTURAL HERITAGE: A BIBLIOGRAPHY ON THE PROTECTION OF MUSEUMS, WORKS OF ART, MONUMENTS, ARCHIVES, AND LIBRARIES IN TIME OF WAR. Washington, DC: General Reference and Bibliography Division, Library of Congress. 1952. 117 pp.

Committee on Conservation of Cultural Resources. THE PROTECTION OF CULTURAL RESOURCES AGAINST THE HAZARDS OF WAR. Washington, DC: National Resources Planning Board. February 1942. 50 pp., biblio.

Coremans, Paul. LA PROTECTION SCIENTIFIQUE DES OEUVRES D'ART EN TEMPS DE GUERRE (The Scientific Protection of Works of Art in Time of War: The European Experience during the Years 1939 to 1945). Brussels: Laboratoire Central des Musées de Belgique. 1946. 30 pp. In French.

Fall, Frieda Kay. "New Industrial Packing Materials: Their Possible Uses for Museums." MUSEUM NEWS, Vol. 44, No. 4 (December 1965). Technical Supplement No. 10.

FitzSimmons, Neal. "Emergency Measures and Museums." MUSEUM NEWS, Vol. 43, No. 6 (February 1965), pp. 23–24, biblio.

Goetz, Arthur H. "Books in Peril: A History of Horrid Catastrophes." WILSON LIBRARY BULLETIN, Vol. 47, No. 5 (January 1973), pp. 428–439.

Howe, Thomas Carr. SALT MINES AND CASTLES: THE DISCOVERY AND RESTITUTION OF LOOTED EUROPEAN ART. Indianapolis: Bobbs-Merrill. 1946. 334 pp.

Intergovernmental Conference on the Protection of Cultural Property in the Event of Armed Conflict. FINAL ACT, CONVENTION AND PROTOCOL ADOPTED BY THE UNITED NATIONS CONFERENCE ON THE PROTECTION OF CULTURAL PROPERTY IN THE EVENT OF ARMED CONFLICT, TOGETHER WITH REGULATIONS FOR THE EXECUTION OF THE CONVENTION AND RESOLUTIONS ATTACHED TO THE FINAL ACT, The Hague, May 14, 1954. London: Her Majesty's Stationery Office. 1954. 49 pp.

Intergovernmental Conference on the Protection of Cultural Property in the Event of Armed Conflict. RECORDS OF THE CONFERENCE CONVENED BY THE UNITED NATIONS EDUCATIONAL, SCIENTIFIC, AND CULTURAL ORGANIZATION HELD AT THE HAGUE FROM 21 APRIL TO 14 MAY, 1954. The Hague, Netherlands: Government of the Netherlands. 1961. 452 pp.

Library Technology Project. PROTECTING THE LIBRARY AND ITS RESOURCES: A GUIDE TO PHYSICAL PROTECTION AND INSURANCE. Chicago: American Library Association. 1963. 322 pp., illus., biblio.

Liddy, John C. "Civil Defence Scheme for Art Galleries and Museums." KALORI (Melbourne), No. 34 (October 1968), pp. 31–34.

Myers, James N., and Denise D. Bedford. DISASTERS: PREVENTION AND COPING, Proceedings of the Conference, May 21–22, 1981, organized by Sally Buchanan. Palo Alto, CA: Stanford University Libraries. 1981. 177 pp., illus. Various authors.

Noblecourt, Andre F. PROTECTION OF CULTURAL PROPERTY IN THE EVENT OF ARMED CONFLICT. Museums and Monuments Series VIII. Paris: UNESCO. 1958. 346 pp., illus., biblio.

REPORT OF THE AMERICAN COMMISSION FOR THE PROTECTION AND SALVAGE OF ARTISTIC AND HISTORIC MONUMENTS IN WAR AREAS. Washington, DC: U.S. Government Printing Office. 1946. 238 pp.

Rorimer, James J. (in collaboration with Gilbert Rabin). SURVIVAL: THE SALVAGE AND PROTECTION OF ART IN WAR. New York: Abelard Press, Inc. 1950.

Schwartzbaum, Paul M., Constance Silver, and Carol A Grissom. "Earthquake Damage to Works of Art in the Ariculi Region of Italy." JOURNAL OF THE AMERICAN INSTITUTE FOR CONSERVATION, Vol. 17, No. 1 (1977), pp. 9–16.

Skilton, John D. DEFENSE DE L'ART EUROPÉEN: SOUVENIRS D'UN OFFICIER AMÉRICAIN "SPÉCIALISTE DES MONUMENTS" (Protection of European Art: Recollections of an American Officer "Specializing in Monuments"). Paris: Editions Internationales. 1948. 100 pp.

Sohl, Stanley D. "Tornado in My Museum." In PAPERS, 64th ANNUAL MEETING, AMERICAN ASSOCIATION OF MUSEUMS, San Francisco, 1969. pp. 56–59.

Upton, M. S., and C. Pearson. DISASTER PLANNING AND EMERGENCY TREATMENTS IN MUSEUMS, ART GALLERIES, LIBRARIES, ARCHIVES, AND ALLIED INSTITUTIONS. Belconnen, A.C.T., Australia: Institute for the Conservation of Cultural Materials, Canberra College of Advanced Education. 1978. 54 pp., 4 figs, biblio.

Williams, Sharon Anne. THE INTERNATIONAL AND NATIONAL PROTECTION OF MOVABLE CULTURAL PROPERTY: A COMPARATIVE STUDY. Dobbs Ferry, NY: Oceana Publications, Inc. 1978. 302 pp.

PART 28: NATURAL DISASTERS

A. General Works

Culver, Charles G., and others. NATURAL HAZARDS EVALUATION OF EXISTING BUILDINGS. Building Science Series No. 61. Washington, DC: National Bureau of Standards, U.S. Department of Commerce. 1975.

DIGEST OF FEDERAL DISASTER ASSISTANCE PROGRAMS. 2nd edition. Washington, DC: Federal Emergency Management Agency. October 1979.

DIRECTORY OF DISASTER-RELATED TECHNOLOGY. HUD Report No. 401-FDAA. Washington, DC: U.S. Department of Housing and Urban Development and the Federal Disaster Assistance Administration. August 1975.

"Emergency Service Communications Withstand Natural Disasters." From an interview with Robert W. Lassell and Charles R. McRedmond. SECURITY WORLD, Vol. 11, No. 6 (June 1974), pp. 32-33.

MULTI PROTECTION DESIGN MANUAL. Publication No. TR-20. Washington, DC: Defense Civil Preparedness Agency. 1975.

Stallings, Robert A. COMMUNICATIONS IN NATURAL DISASTERS. Columbus: The Disaster Research Center, Ohio State University. 1971.

Wright, Richard, and others. BUILDING PRACTICES FOR DISASTER MITIGATION. Building Science Series No. 46. Washington, DC: National Bureau of Standards, U.S. Department of Commerce. 1973.

B. Earthquakes

Botsai, Elmer E., and others. ARCHITECTS AND EARTHQUAKES. Washington, DC: AIA Research Corporation. 1978. 94 pp., illus., biblio. Available from U.S. Government Printing Office.

BUILDING CODE REQUIREMENTS FOR MINIMUM DESIGN LOADS IN BUILDINGS AND OTHER STRUCTURES. ANSI A 58.1. New York: American National Standards Institute.

DESIGNING FOR EARTHQUAKES. Proceedings from the 1978 Summer Seismic Institutes for Architectural Faculty. Washington, DC: AIA Research Corporation. September 1979. 316 pp.

Dowrick, D. J. EARTHQUAKE RESISTANT DESIGN: A MANUAL FOR ENGINEERS AND ARCHITECTS. New York: John Wiley and Sons. 1977.

Holman, G. "Water Systems — Earthquake Preparedness." Address delivered at the Earthquake Fire Seminar, Anaheim, California, June 5, 1973. Published by California Fire Chiefs Association and the Arizona Chapter of the Society of Fire Protection Engineers. SFPE No. 73-02.

McCue, Gerald M., and others. ARCHITECTURAL DESIGN OF BUILDING COMPONENTS FOR EARTHQUAKES. San Francisco: MBT Associates. 1978.

McCue, Gerald M., and Garrison Kost. THE INTERACTION OF BUILDING COMPONENTS DURING EARTHQUAKES. San Francisco: McCue, Boone and Tomsick Associates. 1976.

Pregnoff, Matheu, Beebe, Inc. and Saphite, Lerner, Schindler Environetics, Inc. EARTHQUAKE RESISTANCE OF BUILDINGS. Washington, DC: U.S. General Services Administration. 1976. 3 Vols.

REPORT OF THE FIRE AND RESCUE PROBLEM – EARTHQUAKE DISASTER, MANAGUA, NICARAGUA, DECEMBER 23, 1972. Sacramento: Office of Emergency Services, Fire and Rescue Division, State of California. February 20, 1973.

Simonson, T. R., and others. SEISMIC RESISTANT DESIGN OF MECHANICAL AND ELECTRICAL SYSTEMS. San Francisco: G. M. and T. R. Simonson, Engineers. 1976.

Weigel, Robert L. (ed.) SEISMIC DESIGN FOR BUILDINGS. Washington, DC: Department of Defense. 1973.

Weigel, Robert L., and others. EARTHQUAKE ENGINEERING. Englewood Cliffs, NJ: Prentice-Hall, 1969.

Yanev, Peter I. PEACE OF MIND IN EARTHQUAKE COUNTRY: HOW TO SAVE YOUR HOME AND LIFE. San Francisco: Chronicle Books. 1974.

C. Floods

AIA Research Corporation. ELEVATED RESIDENTIAL STRUCTURES: REDUCING FLOOD DAMAGE THROUGH BUILDING DESIGN: A GUIDE MANUAL. Washington, DC: Federal Insurance Administration. 1977.

FLASH FLOODS. NOAA/PA 73018. Washington, DC: National Weather Service, U.S. National Oceanic and Atmospheric Administration. 1973.

FLOOD DAMAGE PREVENTION. AIA Special Interest Bulletin No. 323. Washington, DC: American Institute of Architects. October 1970.

FLOOD EMERGENCY AND RESIDENTIAL REPAIR HANDBOOK. Washington, DC: Federal Emergency Management Agency. 1979.

FLOODPROOFING REGULATIONS. Washington, DC: Corps of Engineers, U.S. Department of the Army. 1972.

FLOODS, FLASH FLOODS AND WARNINGS. NOAA Publication No. 71009. Washington, DC: National Weather Service, U.S. National Oceanic and Atmospheric Administration. 1973. 6 pp.

D. Tornadoes, Hurricanes, and Other Wind Storms

Eagleman, J. R., and others. THUNDERSTORMS, TORNADOES AND BUILDING DAMAGE. Lexington, MA: D. C. Heath and Company. 1975.

Houghton, E. L., and N. B. Carruthers. WIND FORCES ON BUILDINGS AND STRUC-TURES. New York: John Wiley and Sons. 1976.

"How to Prepare for the Hurricane Season." SECURITY MANAGEMENT, Vol. 24, No. 9 (September 1980), p. 147.

HURRICANE: THE GREATEST STORM ON EARTH. Washington, DC: National Weather Service, U.S. National Oceanic and Atmospheric Administration. 1971.

INTERIM GUIDELINES FOR BUILDING OCCUPANT PROTECTION FROM TORNADOES AND EXTREME WINDS. Publication No. TR-83A. Washington, DC: Defense Civil Preparedness Agency. September 1975. 24 pp.

LIGHTNING. NOAA Publication No. PA 70005. Washington, DC: National Weather Service, U.S. National Oceanic and Atmospheric Administration. 1976. 6 pp.

Marshall, Richard D., and others. BUILDING TO RESIST THE EFFECT OF WINDS. 5 vols. Washington, DC: National Bureau of Standards, U.S. Department of Commerce. 1977.

Stone, Judy. "Hurricane Frederick: Protection in the Aftermath." SECURITY MANAGEMENT, Vol. 24, No. 2 (February 1980), pp. 22, 23, 26, 28.

THUNDERSTORMS. NOAA Publication No. PA 70017. Washington, DC: National Weather Service, U.S. National Oceanic and Atmospheric Administration. 1971. 6 pp.

TORNADO, NOAA Publication No. PA 70007. Washington, DC: National Weather Service, U.S. National Oceanic and Atmospheric Administration. 1973. 16 pp.

TORNADO PREPAREDNESS PLANNING: OPERATION SKYWARN. NOAA Publication No. 70009. Washington, DC: National Weather Service, U.S. National Oceanic and Atmospheric Administration. 1973. 28 pp.

TORNADO PROTECTION: SELECTING AND DESIGNING SAFE AREAS IN BUILDINGS. Publication No. TR-83B. Washington, DC: Defense Civil Preparedness Agency. April 1976.

Weigel, Edwin P. "Some New Ideas About Tornadoes." NOAA (the Quarterly Magazine of the National Oceanic and Atmospheric Administration), Vol. 5, No. 3 (July 1975), 7 pp. Illus.

WINTER STORMS. NOAA/PL 70018. Washington, DC: National Weather Service, U.S. National Oceanic and Atmospheric Administration. 1970. 8 pp.

PART 29: SALVAGE AND RECOVERY OF DAMAGED BUILDINGS AND COLLECTIONS

Agricultural Research Service. HOW TO PREVENT AND REMOVE MILDEW: HOME METHODS. Home and Garden Bulletin No. 68 (rev.). Washington, DC: U.S. Department of Agriculture. 1971. 12 pp.

Burns, Robert. "Space Age Drying Method Salvages Library Books." FIRE ENGINEERING, Vol. 126, No. 12 (December 1973), p. 52.

Cohen, William. "Halon 1301, Library Fires and Post-Fire Procedures." LIBRARY SECURITY NEWSLETTER (May 1975), pp. 5-7.

Crosby, E. "Cyclone Tracy and the Museum in Darwin." KALORI (Australia), No. 50 (June 1975), pp. 28-32.

Cunha, George Martin. CONSERVATION OF LIBRARY MATERIALS: A MANUAL AND BIBLIOGRAPHY ON THE CARE, REPAIR, AND RESTORATION OF LIBRARY MATERIALS. 2nd edition. Metuchen, NJ: Scarecrow Press. Vol. 1, 1971; Vol. 2, 1972.

– – –CONSERVING LOCAL ARCHIVAL MATERIALS ON A LIMITED BUDGET. Technical Leaflet No. 86. Nashville, TN: American Association for State and Local History. November 1975. 8 pp., biblio.

Cunha, George Martin and others (eds.) CONSERVATION ADMINISTRATION: THE 1973 SEMINAR ON THE THEORETICAL ASPECTS OF THE CONSERVATION OF LIBRARY AND ARCHIVAL MATERIALS AND THE ESTABLISHMENT OF CONSERVATION PROGRAMS. North Andover, MA: The New England Document Conservation Center. 1975. 351 pp.

Cunha, George Martin, and Norman Paul Tucker (eds.) LIBRARY AND ARCHIVES CON-
SERVATION: Proceedings of the Boston Athenaeum's 1971 Seminar on the Application of
Chemical and Physical Methods to the Conservation of Library and Archival Materials, May
17–21, 1971. Boston: The Library of the Boston Athenaeum. 1972. 255 pp.

Duckett, Kenneth W. MODERN MANUSCRIPTS: A PRACTICAL MANUAL FOR THEIR
MANAGEMENT. Nashville, TN: American Association for State and Local History. 1975. 375
pp.

Fikioris, Margaret. FIRST STEPS TO BE TAKEN FOR EMERGENCY TREATMENT OF
TEXTILES. Unpublished manuscript on deposit at the New York State Historical Association
Library, Cooperstown, N.Y. 1972. 2 pp.

FIRST AID FOR FLOODED HOMES AND FARMS. Agriculture Handbook No. 38. Washington, DC: U.S. Department of Agriculture. 1972. 31 pp., tables, recipes, checklist.

Fischer, David J. "Problems Encountered, Hurricane Agnes Flood, June 23, 1972 at Corning,
NY and the Corning Museum of Glass." CONSERVATION ADMINISTRATION by George M.
Cunha. (See previous citation.) pp. 170–187.

Fischer, David J., and Thomas Duncan. "Conservation Research: Flood-Damaged Library Materials." AIC BULLETIN, Vol. 15, No. 2 (Summer 1975), pp. 27–48.

Gallo, Fausta. "Recent Experiments in the Field of Disinfection of Book Materials." PROCEED-
INGS OF THE ICOM COMMITTEE FOR CONSERVATION, 4th TRIENNIAL MEETING,
VENICE, 1975.

Haas, J. Eugene, and others (eds.) RECONSTRUCTION FOLLOWING DISASTER. Cambridge,
MA: The MIT Press. 1977.

Hamblin, Dora Jane. "Science Finds Way to Restore the Art Damage in Florence." SMITH-
SONIAN, Vol. 4, No. 11 (February 1974), pp. 26–35.

Hirshleifer, Jack. DISASTER AND RECOVERY: A HISTORICAL SURVEY. Santa Monica,
CA: The Rand Corporation. 1963.

Horton, Carolyn. REPORT AND RECOMMENDATIONS ON THE RESCUE OF THE
WATER-DAMAGED BOOKS AND PRINTS AT THE CORNING GLASS CENTER,
CORNING, NEW YORK, JUNE 1972. Unpublished manuscript on deposit at the New York
State Historical Association Library, Cooperstown, N.Y. 1972. 4 pp.

– – – "Saving the Libraries of Florence." WILSON LIBRARY BULLETIN, No. 41 (June 1967),
pp. 1034–1043.

Keck, Caroline K. "On Conservation: Instructions for Emergency Treatment of Water Damage."
MUSEUM NEWS, Vol. 50, No. 10 (June 1972), p. 13.

Keck, Sheldon. EMERGENCY CARE OF MUSEUM ARTIFACTS AND LIBRARY MATER-
IALS AFFECTED BY THE FLOOD. Unpublished manuscript on deposit at the New York State
Historical Association Library, Cooperstown, N.Y. 1972. 3 pp.

Koesterer, Martin G., and John A. Getting. "Restoring Water-Soaked Papers and Textiles:
Applying Freeze-Drying Methods to Books and Art Objects." TECHNOLOGY AND CONSER-
VATION (Fall 1976), pp. 20–22.

Martin, John H. "Resuscitating a Waterlogged Library." WILSON LIBRARY BULLETIN
(November 1975), pp. 241–243.

Martin, John H. (ed.) THE CORNING FLOOD: MUSEUM UNDER WATER. Corning, NY:
Corning Museum of Glass. 1977. 60 pp., illus., biblio., checklist.

Martin, Mervin. EMERGENCY PROCEDURES FOR FURNITURE. Unpublished manuscript
of deposit at the New York State Historical Association Library, Cooperstown, N.Y. 1972. 2 pp.

McGregor, L., and J. Bruce. "Recovery of Flood Damaged Documents by the Queensland State Archives." ARCHIVES AND MANUSCRIPTS, Vol. 5, No. 8 (August 1974), pp. 193-199.

Minoque, Adelaide. "Treatment of Fire and Water Damaged Records." AMERICAN ARCHIVIST, Vol. 9, No. 1 (January 1946), pp. 17-25.

Montuori, Theodore. "Lesson Learned from Agnes." THE JOURNAL OF MICROGRAPHICS, Vol. 6, No. 3 (January-February 1973), pp. 133-136.

Organ, Robert M., and Eleanor McMillan. "Aid to a Hurricane-Damaged Museum." BULLETIN OF THE AMERICAN GROUP — IIC, Vol. 10, No. 1 (October 1969), pp. 31-39.

Petty, Geraldine, Lilita Dzirkals, and Margaret Krahenbuhl. ECONOMIC RECOVERY FOLLOWING DISASTER: A SELECTED, ANNOTATED BIBLIOGRAPHY. Santa Monica, CA: The Rand Corporation. 1977.

Rabin, Bernard. EMERGENCY PROCEDURES FOR MUSICAL INSTRUMENTS. Unpublished manuscript on deposit at the New York State Historical Association Library, Cooperstown, N.Y. 1966. 1 p.

SALVAGING AND RESTORING RECORDS DAMAGED BY FIRE AND WATER. Recommended Practices No. 2. Washington, DC: Federal Fire Council. 1963. 17 pp., illus.

Schmelzer, Menahem. "Fire and Water: Book Salvage in New York and in Florence." SPECIAL LIBRARIES, Vol. 59, No. 8 (October 1968), pp. 620-625.

Sellers, David Y., and Richard Strassberg. "Anatomy of a Library Emergency." LIBRARY JOURNAL, Vol. 98, No. 17 (October 1973), pp. 2824-2827.

Spawn, Wilman. "After the Water Comes." BULLETIN of the Pennsylvania Library Association, Vol. 28, No. 6 (November 1973), pp. 243-251.

Stender, Walter W., and Evans Walker. "The National Personnel Records Center Fire: A Study in Disaster." AMERICAN ARCHIVIST, Vol. 37, No. 4 (October 1974), pp. 521-550, illus.

Still, J. S. "Library Fires and Salvage Methods." AMERICAN ARCHIVIST, Vol. 16, No. 2 (1953), pp. 145-153.

Surrency, Erwin C. "Freeze-Dried Books." LIBRARY JOURNAL, Vol. 99, No. 16 (September 15, 1974), pp. 2108-2109.

— — — "Guarding Against Disaster." LAW LIBRARY JOURNAL, Vol. 66, No. 4 (November 1973), pp. 419-428.

Walker, Evans. "Records Recovery — Salvage of Wet Papers." FIRE JOURNAL, Vol. 68, No. 4 (July 1974), pp. 65-66.

Walston, S. "Emergency Conservation Following the Darwin Cyclone." ICCM BULLETIN, Vol. 2, No. 1 (March 1976), pp. 21-25.

Waters, Peter. "Does Freeze Drying Save Books or Doesn't It? Salvaging A Few Facts from a Flood of (Alleged) Information." AMERICAN LIBRARIES (July-August 1975), pp. 422-423.

— — — PROCEDURES FOR SALVAGE OF WATER-DAMAGED LIBRARY MATERIALS. Washington, DC: The Library of Congress. 1975. 30 pp.

Weidner, Marilyn Kemp. INSTRUCTIONS ON HOW TO UNFRAME WET PRINTS. Unpublished manuscript on deposit at the New York State Historical Association Library, Cooperstown, N.Y. 1973. 4 pp.

Whipkey, Harold E. AFTER AGNES: A REPORT ON FLOOD RECOVERY ASSISTANCE BY THE PENNSYLVANIA HISTORICAL AND MUSEUM COMMISSION. Harrisburg: Pennsylvania Historical and Museum Commission. 1973. 23 pp., illus.

PART 30: BOMBINGS AND TERRORISM

Boyd, Raymond G. "Bomb Call!!!" SECURITY WORLD, Vol. 14, No. 11 (November 1977), p. 29.

BOMB THREATS AND SEARCH TECHNIQUES. Washington, DC: Bureau of Alcohol, Tobacco, and Firearms, U.S. Department of the Treasury. 1976. 18 pp.

BOMB THREATS: SUGGESTED ACTION TO PROTECT EMPLOYEES AND PROPERTY. Chicago, IL: National Association of Manufacturers. 1970.

Boston, Guy D. TERRORISM: A SELECTED BIBLIOGRAPHY. Supplement to the second edition. Washington, DC: National Institute of Law Enforcement and Criminal Justice, U.S. Department of Justice. September 1977. 63 pp.

Boston, Guy D., Kevin O'Brien, and Joanne Palumbo. TERRORISM: A SELECTED BIBLIOGRAPHY. Second edition. Washington, DC: National Institute of Law Enforcement and Criminal Justice, U.S. Department of Justice. March 1977. 62 pp.

Chase, L. J. (ed.) BOMB THREATS, BOMBINGS, AND CIVIL DISTURBANCES — A GUIDE FOR FACILITY PROTECTION. Corvallis, OR: Continuing Education Publications. 1971. 105 pp.

Couch, Virgil L. "Bomb Threats and Disasters — A Guide to Corporate Planning." ENVIRONMENTAL CONTROL AND SAFETY MANAGEMENT (May 1971), pp. 14–19.

Cox, David L., and John M. DeMarco. "Bomb Threat Response: The Facility Self-Protection Plan." SECURITY MANAGEMENT. Vol. 20, No. 6 (January 1977), pp. 8–10.

Ellis, Ernest W. "The Bomb: Solid Risk Management = Assets Protected." ASSETS PROTECTION, Vol. 1, No. 4 (1976), pp. 27–28.

Hall, Tony. "Letter and Parcel Bomb Precautions." THE BOOKSELLER, December 7, 1974, p. 2834.

INDUSTRIAL DEFENSE AGAINST CIVIL DISTURBANCES, BOMBINGS AND SABOTAGE. Washington, DC: Office of the Provost Marshall General, U.S. Department of the Army. January 1971. 50 pp., biblio.

Kaiser, Martin L. "Bombs Away! Fail-Safe Institutional Protection." LAW ENFORCEMENT COMMUNICATIONS, Vol. 3, No. 6 (December 1976), pp. 9, 32–33.

Killam, Edward W. "What To Do Before the Bomb Squad Arrives." ASSETS PROTECTION, Vol. 6, No. 5 (September–October 1981), pp. 21–22.

Knowles, Graham. BOMB SECURITY GUIDE. Woburn, MA: Butterworth Publishers. 1976. 151 pp.

Lenz, Robert R. EXPLOSIVES AND BOMB DISPOSAL GUIDE. Springfield, IL: Charles C. Thomas. 1965. 303 pp., illus.

Linenberg, A. "Explosives Detectors." ASSETS PROTECTION, Vol. 5, No. 6 (November--December 1980), pp. 38–41.

Lipman, Ira A. PLANNING FOR THE BOMB THREAT. New York: Guardsmark, Inc. 1971.

Mahoney, H. T. "After A Terrorist Attack — Business as Usual." SECURITY MANAGEMENT, Vol. 19, No. 1 (March 1975), pp. 16, 18, 19.

Momboisse, Raymond M. INDUSTRIAL SECURITY FOR STRIKES, RIOTS AND DISASTERS. Springfield, IL: Charles C. Thomas. 1968. 496 pp.

MTI BOMBS FAMILIARIZATION AND BOMBS SCARE PLANNING WORKBOOK. Schiller Park, IL: Motorola Teleprograms, Inc. 1973.

Pike, Earl A. PROTECTION AGAINST BOMBS AND INCENDIARIES. Springfield, IL: Charles C. Thomas. 1972. 87 pp., illus.

Private Security Advisory Council. PREVENTION OF TERRORISTIC CRIMES — SECURITY GUIDELINES FOR BUSINESS, INDUSTRY AND OTHER ORGANIZATIONS. Washington, DC: Law Enforcement Assistance Administration, U.S. Department of Justice. 1976. 33 pp.

"Protection Against Terrorist Bombers." ASSETS PROTECTION, Vol. 1, No. 4 (1976), pp. 28–33.

Universal Teleprograms Co. and Universal Training Systems Co. "In Preparation for a Terrorist Attack." SECURITY INDUSTRY AND PRODUCT NEWS, Vol. 7, No. 8 (August 1978), pp. 28, 30.

PART 31: VANDALISM, VIOLENCE, AND CIVIL DISORDER

Note: Some works cited in Part 29 also contain information on this subject.

Burns, William A. "Vandalism and Other Museum Hazards." ENVIRONMENT SOUTHWEST (San Diego), No. 438 (1971).

CIVIL DISTURBANCES. Washington, DC: U.S. Department of the Army.

Colozzi, Carl A. "Lessons Learned from a Strike." SECURITY MANAGEMENT, Vol. 24, No. 2 (February 1980), p. 17.

Connors, Edward F., III (compiler). BIBLIOGRAPHY FOR PUBLIC SAFETY AND ENVIRONMENTAL PROTECTION FOR RECREATION AND PARK AREAS. McLean, VA: PRC Public Management Services, Inc. September 1974. 11 pp.

Deanne-Drummond, Anthony. RIOT CONTROL. Woburn, MA: Butterworth Publishers. 1975. 168 pp.

Godette, M., M. Post, and P. G. Campbell. GRAFFITI REMOVERS: EVALUATION AND PRELIMINARY SELECTION CRITERIA. NBSIR 75-914. Washington, DC: National Bureau of Standards, U.S. Department of Commerce. December 1975. 36 pp.

IF RIOTS HIT. San Francisco: Fireman's Fund American. 1968. 5 pp.

Keck, Caroline K. "On Conservation: Precautions to Prevent Vandalism." MUSEUM NEWS, Vol. 50, No. 9 (May 1972), p. 9.

PREPARING FOR CIVIL DISTURBANCE. Memphis, TN: Guardsmark, Inc. 15 pp.

VANDALISM. Washington, DC: International City Management Association.

VANDALISM AND VIOLENCE: An EDUCATION U.S.A. Special Report (No. 29). Washington, DC: National School Public Relations Association. 1971. 57 pp.

Waxman, Jerry J. CHANGES IN RESPONSE PATTERNS OF FIRE DEPARTMENTS IN CIVIL DISTURBANCES. Columbus: The Disaster Research Center, Ohio State University. 1972.

PART 32: USEFUL ADDRESSES

A. Sources for Useful Periodicals

This listing includes names and addresses of publishers, professional societies, and other organizations from which the reader can obtain periodicals that always or frequently contain information on the subjects covered in this bibliography. Many of them are cited in the bibliography. Some periodicals may be available only as a benefit of membership in an organization; however, most are available on subscription and as single copies. Sources for journals cited in the bibliography but not included in this listing can be obtained from the READER'S GUIDE TO PERIODICAL LITERATURE and similar references available in most libraries. The reader also should note that some listed sources also may publish books and monographs.

AIC BULLETIN
    American Institute for Conservation of
        Historic and Artistic Works
    Suite 725
    1511 K Street, NW
    Washington, DC 20005

ALARM SIGNAL (formerly SIGNAL)
    National Burglar and Fire Alarm
        Association
    1101 Connecticut Avenue, NW
    Washington, DC 20036

AMERICAN LIBRARIES
    American Library Association
    50 West Huron Street
    Chicago, IL 60611

ARCHITECTURAL RECORD
    McGraw Hill, Inc.
    1221 Avenue of the Americas
    New York, NY 10020

ARTS REVIEW
    16 St. James Gardens
    London W 11
    ENGLAND

ASSETS PROTECTION
    The Territorial Imperative, Inc.
    Suite 503
    500 Sutter Street
    San Francisco, CA 94102

THE BOOKSELLER
    J. Whitaker & Sons, Ltd.
    12 Pyott Street
    London WC1A 1DF
    ENGLAND

THE BUILDER
    Empire Life Insurance Co.
    Box 1000
    Kingston, Ontario K7L 4Y4
    CANADA

BUILDINGS
    Stamats Publishing Co.
    427 6th Avenue, SE
    Cedar Rapids, IA 52401

CANADIAN ARCHITECT
    1450 Don Mills Road
    Don Mills, Ontario M3B 2X7
    CANADA

THE COLLECTOR-INVESTOR
    Crain Communications, Inc.
    740 Rush Street
    Chicago, IL 60611

COLLEGE AND RESEARCH LIBRARIES
    American Library Association
    50 West Huron Street
    Chicago, IL 60611

CONSUMER REPORTS
    Consumer's Union
    P.O. Box 1111
    Mount Vernon, NY 10550

CURATOR
    American Museum of Natural History
    Central Park West at 79th Street
    New York, NY 10024

DUPONT MAGAZINE
    E. I. duPont de Nemours and Co.
    2539 Nemours Street
    Wilmington, DE 19898

ELECTRICAL REVIEW
    Electrical-Electronic Press Ltd.
    Dorset House
    Stamford Street
    London SE1 9LU
    ENGLAND

ENVIRONMENTAL DESIGN
    Industrial Publications, Inc.
    209 Dunn Avenue
    Stamford, CT. 06905

ERGONOMICS
    Taylor and Francis, Ltd.
    4 John Street
    London WC1N 2ET
    ENGLAND

FIRE JOURNAL, FIRE COMMAND, and
FIRE TECHNOLOGY and others
National Fire Protection Association
Batterymarch Park
Quincy, MA 02269

FIRE SURVEYOR
Victor Green Publications
44 Bedford Row
London WC1R 4LL
ENGLAND

GAZETTE
Canadian Museums Association
Suite 400
330 Cooper Street
Ottawa, Ontario K2P OG5
CANADA

ICOM NEWS
International Council of Museums
Maison de l'UNESCO
1, rue Miollis
75732 Paris CEDEX 15
FRANCE

JOURNAL OF RISK AND
INSURANCE
American Risk and Insurance
Association
297 Brooks Hall
University of Georgia
Athens, GA 30602

JOURNAL OF SYSTEMS
MANAGEMENT
24587 Bagley Road
Cleveland, OH 44138

LAW ENFORCEMENT COM-
MUNICATIONS
United Business Publications
475 Park Avenue, South
New York, NY 10016

LAW LIBRARY JOURNAL
American Association of Law Libraries
Room 1201
53 West Jackson
Chicago, IL 60604

LIBRARY AND ARCHIVAL
SECURITY NEWSLETTER
Haworth Press
149 5th Avenue
New York, NY 10010

LIBRARY ASSOCIATION RECORD
Library Association
7 Ridgemount Street
London WC1E 7AE
ENGLAND

LIBRARY JOURNAL
R. R. Bowker Co.
1180 Avenue of the Americas
New York, NY 10036

LIGHTING DESIGN AND
APPLICATION
Illuminating Engineering Society
345 East 47th Street
New York, NY 10017

LOCKSMITH LEDGER
Nickerson and Collins Co.
2720 Des Plaines Avenue
Des Plaines, IL 60018

KALORI
Royal South Australian Society of Arts
Institute Building
North Terrace
Adelaide, SA 5000
AUSTRALIA

MMC QUARTERLY
Midwest Museums Conference
MMC Treasurer
c/o Oshkosh Public Museum
1331 Algoma Boulevard
Oshkosh, WI 54901

MUSEUM (published by UNESCO)
UNIPUB, Inc.
345 Park Avenue, South
New York, NY 10010

MUSEUM NEWS and AVISO
American Association of Museums
Suite 428
1055 Thomas Jefferson Street, NW
Washington, DC 20007

MUSEUMS JOURNAL
British Museums Association
87 Charlotte Street
London W1P 2BX
ENGLAND

PLA BULLETIN
Pennsylvania Library Association
100 Woodland Road
Pittsburgh, PA 15232

POPULAR MECHANICS
Hearst Magazines
224 West 57th Street
New York, NY 10019

POPULAR SCIENCE
Times Mirror Magazines, Inc.
380 Madison Avenue
New York, NY 10017

PORTFOLIO
271 Madison Avenue
New York, NY 10016

PROFESSIONAL SAFETY
American Society of Safety Engineers
850 Busse Highway
Park Ridge, IL 60068

PROGRESSIVE ARCHITECTURE
Reinhold Publishing Co., Inc.
600 Summer Street
Stamford, CT 06904

RESTAURATOR
International Journal for the Preserva-
tion of Library and Archival
Material
Munksgaard
Noerre Soegade 35
DK-1370
Copenhagen K
DENMARK

SAFE AND SECURITY NEWS
S. E. G. Publications (Pty), Ltd.
Box 10122
Johannesburg
SOUTH AFRICA

SECURITY AGE MAGAZINE
Asher-Oppen Publishing Co.
9017 Reseda Boulevard
Northridge, CA 91324

SECURITY AND FIRE EQUIPMENT
SELECTOR
Batiste Publications, Ltd.
Pembroke House
Campsbourne Road
London N8 7BR
ENGLAND

SECURITY GAZETTE
Security Gazette Ltd.
109–119 Waterloo Road
London SE1
ENGLAND

SECURITY INDUSTRY AND PRODUCT
NEWS
PTB Publishing Corporation
250 Fulton Avenue
Hempstead, NY 11550

SECURITY LETTER
475 5th Avenue
New York, NY 10017

SECURITY MANAGEMENT
American Society for Industrial Security
Suite 651
2000 K Street, NW
Washington, DC 20006

SECURITY MANAGEMENT – PLANT
AND PROPERTY PROTECTION
National Foreman's Institute
24 Rope Ferry Road
Waterford, CT 06386

SECURITY POLICE DIGEST
Chief of Security Police
U.S. Air Force
Department of Defense
Washington, DC 20330

SECURITY AND PROTECTION
OF S.A.
South African Security Association
Thompson Publications S.A. (Pty), Ltd.
Box 8308
Johannesburg 2000
SOUTH AFRICA

SECURITY REPORT
Elsevier International Bulletins
Mayfield House
256 Banbury Road
Oxford OX2 7DH
ENGLAND

SECURITY SURVEYOR
Association of Burglary Insurance
Surveyors
Victor Green Publications, Ltd.
106 Hampstead Road
London NW1 2LS
ENGLAND

SECURITY SYSTEMS DIGEST
Washington Crime News Service
7620 Little River Turnpike
Annandale, VA 22003

SECURITY WORLD and SECURITY
DISTRIBUTING AND MARKETING
Cahners Publishing Co.
5 South Wabash Avenue
Chicago, IL 60603

SPECIFYING ENGINEER
Cahners Publishing Co.
5 South Wabash Avenue
Chicago, IL 60603

STOLEN ART ALERT
International Foundation for Art
Research
46 East 70th Street
New York, NY 10021

TECHNOLOGY AND CONSERVATION
The Technology Organization
One Emerson Place
Boston, MA 02114

U.S. GLASS, METAL AND GLAZING
Ext. Suite 401
2701 Union Avenue
Memphis, TN 38112

WILSON LIBRARY BULLETIN
H. W. Wilson Co.
950 University Avenue
Bronx, NY 10452

WISCONSIN LIBRARY BULLETIN
Department of Public Instruction
Division for Library Services
126 Langdon Street
Madison, WI 53702

B. Sources for Useful Books and Monographs

This listing includes names and addresses of publishers, professional societies, and other organizations whose works have been frequently cited in the bibliography. With some few exceptions, so-called "trade" publishers have not been included because their titles can be obtained from most booksellers and libraries. Some of the listed sources also may publish periodicals. They are listed here if their primary or best known product is books.

AIA Research Corporation
1735 New York Avenue, NW
Washington, DC 20006

American Association for State and Local
History
708 Berry Road
Nashville, TN 37204

American Institute of Architects
1735 New York Avenue, NW
Washington, DC 20006

American Management Association
135 West 50th Street
New York, NY 10020

American National Standards Institute
1430 Broadway
New York, NY 10018

Boston Athenaeum
10½ Beacon Street
Boston, MA 02108

Canadian Conservation Institute
1030 Innes Road
Ottawa, Ontario K1A ON8
CANADA

Center for Building Technology
see National Bureau of Standards

Chronicle Books
Suite 915
870 Market Street
San Francisco, CA 94102

College of Architecture
Clemson University
Clemson, SC 29631

Continuing Education Publications
Oregon State University
Corvallis, OR 97331

Defense Civil Preparedness Agency
see Federal Emergency Management Agency

Department of Agriculture
Office of Governmental and Public
Affairs
14th St. and Independence Avenue
Washington, DC 20250

Department of Energy
Assistant Director for Research and
Development
Safeguards and Security
Washington, DC 20545

Disaster Research Center
Ohio State University
128 Derby Hall
154 North Oval Mall
Columbus, OH 43210

Federal Disaster Assistance Administration
see Federal Emergency Management Agency

Federal Emergency Management Agency
1725 I Street
Washington, DC 20472

Federal Insurance Administration
see Federal Emergency Management Agency

Fireman's Fund American
Public Affairs Office
3333 California Street
San Francisco, CA 94119

General Adjustment Bureau
123 Williams
New York, NY 10004

General Services Administration
18th and F Streets, NW
Washington, DC 20405

Guardsmark
Box 45
Memphis, TN 38101

Industrial Press, Inc.
200 Madison Avenue
New York, NY 10016

Institute for the Conservation of Cultural
Material
Canberra College of Advanced Education
P.O. Box 1
Belconnen, A. C. T. 2616
AUSTRALIA

Institute for Disaster Research
Texas Tech University
P.O. Box 4089
Lubbock, TX 79409

International Association of Chiefs of Police
11 Firstfield Road
Gaithersburg, MD 20760

International City Management Assn.
1140 Connecticut Avenue, NW
Washington, DC 20036

Law Enforcement Assistance Administration
see U.S. Department of Justice

The Merritt Company
P.O. Box 1256
Santa Monica, CA 90406

MTI Teleprograms, Inc.
4824 North Scott Street
Suite 23
Schiller Park, IL 60176

National Association of Manufacturers
1776 F Street, NW
Washington, DC 20006

National Bureau of Standards
U.S. Department of Commerce
Washington, DC 20234

National Criminal Justice Reference Service
see U.S. Department of Justice

National Institute for Law Enforcement and
Criminal Justice
see National Institute of Justice

National Institute of Justice
see U.S. Department of Justice

National Oceanic and Atmospheric
Administration
U.S. Department of Commerce
Washington, DC 20230

National School Public Relations Association
1801 North Moore Street
Arlington, VA 22209

National Technical Information Service
U.S. Department of Commerce
5285 Port Royal Road
Springfield, VA 22161

New England Document Conservation Center
Abbot Hall
School Street
Andover, MA 01810

New York State Historical Association
Box 391
Cooperstown, NY 13326

Office of the Assistant Director for
  Preservation
Library of Congress
Washington, DC 20540

Office of Civil Defense
  see Federal Emergency Management
    Agency

Office of the Provost Marshall General, U.S.
  Department of the Army
  see Federal Emergency Management
    Agency

Office of Risk Management and Safety
University of California
Room 502
2111 Bancroft Way
Berkeley, CA 94720

Pennsylvania Historical and Museum
  Commission
P.. Box 1026
Harrisburg, PA 17120

PRC Public Management Services
7600 Old Springhouse Road
McLean, VA 22102

Preservation Services Division
National Archives
8th and Pennsylvania, NW
Washington, DC 20408

Rand Corporation
1700 Main Street
Santa Monica, CA 90401

Sandia Laboratories
  see U.S. Department of Energy

Society of American Archivists
Suite 810
330 South Wells Street
Chicago, IL 60606

Superintendent of Documents
  U.S. Government Printing Office
Washington, DC 20402

Charles C. Thomas, Publisher
301 East Lawrence Avenue
Springfield, IL 62717

Underwriters Laboratories, Inc.
  Publications Stock Department
333 Pfingsten Road
Northbrook, IL 60062

U.S. Army
  AG Publications Center
  HQDA (DAAG-PAD-I)
Washington, DC 20314

U.S. Department of Justice
  Office of Justice Assistance, Research,
    and Statistics
633 Indiana Avenue, NW
Washington, DC 20531

U.S. Fire Administration
  see Federal Emergency Management
    Agency

U.S. Fire Prevention and Control
  Administration
  see National Bureau of Standards

University of California Press
2223 Fulton Street
Berkeley, CA 94720

C. Other Useful Addresses

Many of the better known and more useful professional societies and other organizations are listed in the two preceding sections. However, there are others that either have no publications available or that are simply not cited in the bibliography. Therefore, this section lists these other potentially useful sources of information or assistance as a service to the reader.

American Red Cross
  National Headquarters
  18th and E Streets, NW
  Washington, DC 20006

Automatic Fire Alarm Association
  c/o Martin H. Reiss
  Gamewell Corporation
  7 Industrial Park Road
  Medway, MA 02053

Canadian Automatic Sprinkler Association
  Suite T2
  1 Sparks Avenue
  Willowdale, Ontario M2H 2W1
  CANADA

Central Station Electrical Protection
  Association
  1000 Vermont Avenue, NW
  Washington, DC 20005

Factory Mutual System
1151 Boston-Providence Turnpike
Norwood, MA 02062

Fire Equipment Manufacturers Association
2300 9th Street, South
Arlington, VA 22204

Fire Extinguisher Manufacturers Institute of
Canada
33 Laird Drive
Toronto, Ontario M4G 3S9
CANADA

Industrial Risk Insurers
85 Woodland Street
Hartford, CT 06102

International Association of Fire Chiefs
1329 18th Street, NW
Washington, DC 20036

International Centre for the Study of the
Preservation and Restoration of Cultural
Property
Via de San Michele, 13
Rome 00153
ITALY

International Committee for Museum Security
(of ICOM)
c/o Mr. Robert B. Burke
Office of Protection Services
Smithsonian Institution
Washington, DC 20560

International Council of Monuments and Sites
(ICOMOS/International)
Hotel St. Aignan
75 rue de Tample
Paris 3 éme
FRANCE

International Society of Fire Service Instructors
Box 88
1 Ash Street
Hopkinton, MA 01748

Museum Association Security Committee (of
the AAM)
c/o Mr. E. B. Brown
Kimbell Art Museum
P.O. Box 9440
Fort Worth, TX 76107

Museum Reference Center
Office of Museum Programs
Smithsonian Institution (A&I 2235)
Washington, DC 20560

National Association of Fire Equipment
Distributors
111 East Wacker Drive
Chicago, IL 60601

National Association of Fire Science and
Administration
Suite 1436N
101 Park Avenue
New York, NY 10017

National Automatic Sprinkler and Fire Control
Association
P.O. Box 719
Mount Kisco, NY 10549

National Crime Prevention Institute
University of Louisville
Shelby Campus
Louisville, KY 40222

National Rifle Association
1600 Rhode Island Avenue, NW
Washington, DC 20036

National Safety Council
444 North Michigan Avenue
Chicago, IL 60611

Office of Hazardous Materials Regulation
Materials Transportation Bureau
U.S. Department of Transportation
400 7th Street, SW
Washington, DC 20590

Society of Fire Protection Engineers
60 Batterymarch
Boston, MA 02110

Special Libraries Association
31 East 10th Street
New York, NY 10003

Training Consultants, Inc.
P.O. Box 81
Knoxville, TN 37901

Underwriters' Laboratories of Canada
7 Crouse Road
Scarborough, Ontario M1R 3A9
CANADA

Index

Absenteeism, 723
Absorption, 470
Access control, 27, 344, 395, 481,
  569
Accession number, 769
Accident prevention, 601-602
Acquisitions, 114
Active alarm system, 361
Added security, 288
Adjustable focus, 473
AGC (automatic gain control), 486
Alarm contractors, 382
Alarm control panel, 311
Alarming sequential switcher, 486
Alarming switcher, 447-448
Alarms
  cost effectiveness of, 342
  responding to, 657-658
  types of, 79, 570, 657
  use of, 21, 265
Alarms checklist
Alarms systems, 550-551
  administrator's role in selection of,
    342, 343, 350, 351
  crime data on, 511
  design of, 20, 341-371, 550, 551
  monitoring of, 78, 79
  and security education, 502
ALC (automatic light control), 486
"All risk" art insurance, 56
AM (amplitude modulation), 486
American Association for State and
  Local History, 14
American Association of Museums, 14
American Society for Industrial
  Security, 7, 14, 23, 375
Analog processing, 479

Annunciation, 350
Antenna detection units, 284
Antimony trisulfide target, 435
Antimony trisulfide (Sb2S) tube, 441
Antiques, 777
Aperture stop, 486
APSD (Autonomous Processor for
  Security Data), 294, 296
Archeological items, 777
Archivist, 101
Armed robbery, 345
Art
  in castles, 41
  classification of, 798-805
  descriptions of, 798-805
  forgery of, 39-40, 790
  fundamentals of, 798-805
  investment value of, 35, 46
  phenomenon of, 34-35, 43, 47
  security systems and, 41-42, 46-47
  taxation of, 41
Art and Antique Squad, 748
Art boom, 26
Art collections, 41
Art data bank, 39, 774
Art dealers, 776
Art Dealers Association of America
  (ADDA), 777-778, 789-790
Art descriptions, 798-799, 800-805
Art exhibitions, 44-46, 52-54
Art Facilities, 18, 177, 178, 193, 645,
  666
Art insurance, 33-64
  alternatives to, 45
  art theft and, 787
  claims incidence in, 45
  of collections, 41, 51-52

Art insurance (cont.)
cost of, 44-45, 54-57
fire risk and, 44, 45, 56
fraud in, 40
government regulations of, 41, 54, 55
identification of art works and, 774
legal aspects of, 36, 51-53
of loaned items, 44-46, 50, 52-55
loss rates in, 55
Probable Maximum Loss in, 51
replacement or restoration funds and, 54, 56
of state property, 36
types of, 36, 45-46, 50, 51, 56
valuation of art works and, 40, 41, 56
Art insurance policies, 36, 41, 44, 47, 50-56
Art insurance premiums, 44-46, 51-52, 55-56
Art insurers, 36, 42, 55, 775
Art inventory, 773
Artist's name, 769-770
Artist's proof (AP), 788, 801-803
Art market, 775, 779
Art medium, 770, 799-805
Art prints, 800-801
Art publications, 776-778
Art security institutes, 7
Art techniques, 800-805
Art theft
dissemination of information on, 767-768, 775-778, 789-790
during crises, 150, 649
in Europe, 36, 39, 41-44, 47, 768, 780
investigation of, 654-656, 767-806
motives for, 35-44, 647, 779, 788
protection against, 587, 654-656, 758, 767-778
recovery and, 39, 41, 43, 775, 805-806
reporting of, 767-778, 784-790
security guards and, 654-656
seriousness of, 17, 26, 780
in United States, 44, 54, 768, 775, 777-778, 780, 806
See also Evidence; Descriptions, artwork; Identification, art work
Art theft investigators, 585, 780-781
Art thieves, 25, 755
Art works
authenticity of, 39

handling of, by security guards, 656-657, 658
identification of, 38-39, 41, 43, 47, 508, 768
indexes to, 769-774
inventory of, 783
medium of, 799-805
reporting of stolen, 767-778
transportation of, 44, 52-55, 545-586, 579-590
value of, 775, 788-789
Associated Press (AP), 119
Audio alarm system, 353
Audio detection, 357-359, 405
Audio detection unit, 350
Austria, 39, 41-42, 45, 47
Authorized access switch, 394-395
Automatic caretaking, 286
Automatic iris, 436, 442, 443, 486
Automatic iris diaphragm, 475
Automatic iris pinhole lenses, 474-475
Automatic iris right angle lens, 458
Automatic light control (ALC), 441
Automatic optical attenuator, 436
Auxiliary devices and equipment, 414
A-wire, 119

Background checks, 27, 501
Balanced cable, 486
Balanced magnetic switches, 397
Band Pass, 486-487
Bank vaults, 546-548
Barbed wire, 497
Barriers, 519-522
Basic security, 283-285
Beam current, 431
Beeper number, 118, 119
Beit, Alfred, Sir, 42
Bells, 408
Bernstein, Alan Bart, 132-133, 137
Beta format, 487
Bi-focal lens, 487
Bifocal optical image-splitting lens, 462-463
Blackmail, 37, 42-44
Bleeding, 607-609
Blockbuster exhibits, 26
BNC connector, 49, 443
Body language, 794-795
Bombs
discovery of, 653-654
handling of, 604

Bombs (cont.)
  identification of, 651-652
  intelligence information on, 653
  searching for, 603-604, 653-654
Bomb threats, 602-605, 652-653
Books, rare, 94
Boston Museum of Fine Arts, 27
Breakwire, 398-399
Bridging sequential switcher, 446, 487
Broadcasting industry, 121
Brown, E.B., 23
Building design, 71-72, 165
Building security, 22, 344, 496
Burglar alarms, 415, 657-658
Burglary, 5, 284, 509-511
B-wire, 119

C mount, 487
C mount lens, 455
Camera, 428-29, 431, 441-443, 449, 483-485
Camera, newvicon target, 475
Camera, silicon target, 475
Camera, vidicon, 431-432
Camera bracket, 457
Camera format, 487
Camera housing, 457-459, 464
Camera identification number, 441
Camera system, 431-443
Camera tube, 432, 436, 487
Camera video signal, 431
Capacitance detection, 347
Capacitance (proximity) sensors, 400-401
Caretakers, live museum, 286
Cargo loss, 581
Cargo thefts, 585, 586
Carpets, 776
Casement windows, 167
Castles, 41
Casualties, 146, 149-150, 155
Cataloging, 11
Cathode ray tube (CRT), 487
CB radio, 580
CCTV (Closed circuit television), 344, 406,
  427-492, 571
  characteristics of scenes covered by, 439
  definition of, 487
  110 degrees FOV, 463-465
  success of, in the prevention of crimes,
  427-428
  wide FOV, 460-463
CCTV access control system, 480-483

CCTV camera installations, 457-459
CCTV camera system
  and camera field of view, 433-435
  essentials of, 430
  fixed, 460-463
  pan-tilt mechanisms for, 449-455
  and right angle lens, 456, 458
  and scene characteristics, 435-439
  and split image lenses, 455-456
  and tri-split lens, 457
  and 200m lenses, 435
  and vidicon camera size, 431-432
CCTV equipment, 439-441
CCTV intrusion detector, 477-479
CCTV monitoring system, 443-448
CCTV motion detectors, 477-479
CCTV systems
  covert, 465-477
  multiple camera, 460-465
  one camera/monitor, 428
  power for, 449-451, 460
Ceiling-mounted camera housing, 457
Centralization, 284
Centrally stationed guard, 344
Centrally supervised patrol tours, 344
Central supervision station, 284, 260-291
Chain-work fencing, 496
Charge couple device (CCD), 487
Charge couple device (CCD) camera, 442
Charge couple device (CCD) chip, 442-443
Charge injection device (CID), 487
Charge injection device (CID) camera, 442
Charge transfer device (CTD), 487
Charge transfer device (CTD) camera, 442
Checklist
  alarm, 550
  key-control and lock-security, 534-537
  library security, 553-555
  lighting, 528
  listening skills, 612
  perimeter security, 521-522
  safety, 601-602
Chicago Art Institute, 22, 27
Chief executive officer, (CEO), 18, 128,
  133-134, 140-142, 145-146, 155, 159
Children, 791
Churches, 39
Civil defense organization, 245
Civil Service Commission, 732
Classified document security, 560-564
Cleaning staff, 563, 564

Climate control, 26
Clipping service, 159-160
Cloakroom facilities, 13
Close-up lens, 487
Coaxial cable, 428, 429, 431, 449, 487-488
Code of Federal Regulations, 4
Code of Professional Standards for the
  Practice of Public Relations, 114
Coherent fiber optic bundles, 476
Coinsurance, 36
Color photo ID badge system, 483
Communication
  art of, 111, 112, 123
  coded, 580
  importance of, in personnel motivation,
    714, 715
  in museum public relations, 127, 128,
    131-161 See also Public relations
  within museum staff, 133-134
  and security, 21
  standards of, 562
Communications systems, 498
Community newspapers, 120
Complete security, 283
"Components for Interior Security Alarm
  Systems," Federal Specification,
  W-A-00450B (General Services
  Administration), 374-381
Composite video, 488
Computer data processing centers, 192
Computerized security command, 296
Computers, 783
Concealed wiring, 389-391
Condition, art work, 773
Conductive foil, 398
Conflicts, 67-70
Conservation, 26, 286
Conservator, 255, 582, 586
Contingency planning, 576
Continuously displayed television snapshot,
  455
Control cabinet, alarm system, 391-393
Controls, alarm system, 392
Copier, 197
Cords, 196
Council of Europe, 39
Counterfeiting (of art works), 38
Courier, 564, 582
Covert CCTV systems, 465-477
CPS, 488
Credentials, media, 143

Crime analysis, 506, 509-511
Crime analysis reports, 509
Crime data, 509-511
Crime investigation, 595
Crime prevention, 505-555, 643, 645-648
  definition of, 512
  and opportunity reduction, 6, 8, 9, 10, 508
    710-711
Crime prevention program, 510
Crime risk management, 505-507
Crime statistics, 509-511
Crime vulnerability, 506-507
Criminal record, 501
Crises
  facilities for visitors during, 154
  litigation and, 135, 146-147, 155
  and public relations, 115
  security officers, role of, 134, 143-144,
    150, 154-155
  special equipment for, 148, 154
  types of, 131, 139, 147, 149-151
Crisis guidelines, 151
Crisis information, 140
Crisis Information Center (CIC), 147, 150,
  154
Crisis management, 20, 131-161
Crisis news copy, 159-161
Crisis Public Relations Communications Plan
  (CPRCP), 132-133, 145-161
  benefits of, 133, 152-153
  components of, 153-155
  coverage of loaned items in, 147
  development of, 149-157
  distribution of, 155
  effect of geography on, 149
  effect of new construction on, 156
  evaluation of, 158-159
  personnel involvement in, 146-147,
    150-151, 155
  planning summary, 155-156
  responding to inquiries on, 156-157
  revision of, 155-156, 158-159
  scope of, 149, 152
  testing of, 148-153, 158
  and timing of crises, 133, 144-145, 151
Crisis reporting, media, 145, 157
Criticality rating scale, 245
CRM guidelines, 7
Crowd control, 20-21, 24, 25
Cultural organizations, 125
Cultural property, 741, 742

Cultural Resource Management Guidelines, 5
Culture, 121
Curator, 15, 101, 112, 187, 345, 351, 582
Curatorial files, 769
Curriculums, 706-707

Damage, 239
Dead-locking bolt, 497, 499
Deductible, 51
Delivery procedures, 503
Demonstrators, 663-664
Department of Defense, 374
Depth of field, 488
Descriptions, art work, 798-805
    artists' proof number in, 788
    components of, 769-773
    condition of the work in, 773
    dimensions in, 770-771
    edition number in, 771-772, 778
    identification of artist in, 769-770
    medium in, 770, 799-805
    mixed media and, 799
    museum registrar and, 784
    photographs in, 773-774, 784
    techniques in, 800-805
    title of work in, 770
    use of in identifying, 769-774, 776, 778
Desk attendants, 102
Detection, crime, 284, 350, 510-511
Detection instruments, 288
Detectors, 394-407
Digital communicators, 414
Digital dialer, (Communicator), 365-367
Digital processing, 479
Diopter, 488
Direct connect (leased-line) systems, 413
Director, 102, 127
Director of Public relations (DPR). See
    public relations directory
Disaster, 231, 237, 238, 240, 258
Disaster plan, 237, 258
Disorderly persons, 662-663
Display cases, 346-353
Documents, 574
Door jambs, 532
Doors, 167
Double locks, 496
Double market, 25
Drawings, 777
Drills, 508
Duplicator, 197

Dust, 198

Earthquake, 238
Edition number, 771, 772, 788, 801-802
Electrical hazard, 178, 187, 188
Electrical motor, 191
Electromagnetic interference (EMI), 383
Electronic focus, 488
Electronic ID card code reader, 483
Electronic protection systems, 350-351
Electronic screen splitter, 441
Electronic security system, 298, 300
Electronic splitter (combiner), 488
Electronic switch, 445
Elevator CCTV system, 463-465
Emergencies
    assessment of, in crisis public relations
        138-139
    definition of, 236
    as diversionary tactics, 644
    publicity from, 139-140, 159-161
    reporting of, 140-145
    security guards and, 644-645
Emergency and disaster control plan, 242
Emergency crisis telephone number, 147
Emergency lighting, 525
Emergency management, 228
Emergency medical assistance (EMA),
    606-610
Emergency planning, 237, 242, 244, 259, 264
Emergency repairs, 242-243
Emergency Services Officer, 242, 243, 258
Emergency Services Session, 704-705
Emergency supplies, 205
Employee evaluation process, 96, 715-721
Employee motivation, 714, 715
Employee relations
    criticism and, 615-616
    listening skills and, 611-612
    personal counseling and, 616-617
    photographic waiver forms and, 147
    security guards and, 614-615
    security supervisor and, 610-617
    training methods and, 597-598, 614
Employee screening, 21
    See also Hiring Standards
Employee theft, 97
Employment application, 500
Enforcement of rules, 665-666, 703-704
England, 44, 45, 47, 768
Engraving, 803

Entrance diameter, 469
Entrances, 521
  See also Access control
Entry methods, criminal, 510
Environmental alarm, 415
Equipment alarm, 416
Equipment maintenance, 282, 292-293
Espionage, 4
Esprit de corps, 21, 722
Etching, 803
Evacuation plan, 251
Evacuations, 648-651
Evaluation process, 719, 723-724
Evidence
  art theft and, 781-783, 789
  fingerprints, 782, 784, 789
  handling of, 782
  interrogations in, 790-795
  photography in, 784
  physical, 782-784, 789
  See also Art theft
Exclusives, 119
Exits, 172, 173, 174
Explosives, 604-605
Exposure rating, 159-160
Extension cords, 189-190
Exterior security, 519-522
External switch closure, 448
External synchronization as camera feature,
  442
External theft, 345

False alarms, 415-417
FBI, 25, 581, 587, 775, 777, 789, 797, 805,
  806
Federal Law Enforcement Training Center, 6
Fence line surveillance, 463
Fence posts, 497
Fences
  barbed wire, 497
  specifications for, 496, 520
  use of, in perimeter protection, 520-522
  See also barriers
Fiber optic bundle, 476, 477, 488
Fidelity exclusion, 343
Field of view (FOV)
  choice of lens and, 433-435
  definition of, 428, 488
  function of, 430, 431
  versus lens focal length, 434
  and pinhole lenses, 469
Files, 538-549

Fingerprints, 782, 784, 789
Fire
  art insurance and, 44-45
  classes of, 239, 650
  crime prevention of, 6
  elements of, 649-650
  hazards associated with, 187
  in industrial commercial and residential
    facilities, 181
  policies and procedures for, 648-650
  reporting of, 651
  and security director's tasks, 21
Fire alarms, 657-658
Fire contents rate, 56
Fire control program, 20
Fire department, 181, 183, 657-658
Fire detection, 287, 292
Fire detection devices, 7, 8
Fire detection system, 13, 206
Fire exits, 351
Fire extinguisher, 190, 650, 651
Fire hoses, 183
Fire loading material, 178
Firemen, 182
Fire prevention, 185, 204, 572, 606, 649-650
Fire prevention survey, 11
Fire protection, 106-108, 181, 605-606,
  648-651
Fire protection system, 181
Fire Research Center, 7
Fire suppressant system, 211, 213, 217
Fire suppression, 106, 211
Fixed camera system, 460-463
Fixed duress alarm initiating devices (hold-up
  alarms), 406-407
Fixed focus, 473
Fixed lens systems, 460-463
Flexible fiber optic bundle, 477
Flexible fiber optic pinhole lenses, 477
Floating property, 50
Flood control, 106
FM (frequency modulation), 488
FM wireless transmitter, 348
F number, 488
Focal length (F.L.), 433-435, 441, 469, 488
Focus, 431, 473
Foot candle (Ft Cd), 489
Forgery, art work, 39, 790
Fourth Estate, 116
Frame, 489
France, 36, 39, 42, 44
Fraud, art insurance, 40

Front surface mirror, 489

Galleries, 645-666
Gallium arsenide (GaAs) infrared laser
    transmission, 452-453
Gaseous lamps, 437
Gate houses, 497-498
General Services Administration, 374
Georges Pompidou Centre of Art and
    Culture, 19
Ghent Altar, 37, 38, 42
Gore, Allen, 23
Gradual Security, 283
Grounding, 391
Guard agency, 585
Guard force, 591-617
    liabilities and, 594-595
    security techniques of, 592-595, 602-610
    supervision of, 610-617
    training and preparation of, 596-602
    See also Security guards
Gunn diode, 356

Handcuffs, 666
Handshake signal, 366
Hardware, active, 170
Hard-wire alarm systems, 346-348
Harpers Ferry (center), 8
Harper's Weekly, 95
Hidden cameras, 465-477
Hidden lenses, 465-477
High light power pinhole camera, 470-471
Hijacking, 581
Hiring standards, 732, 733
    See also Employee screening
Historic Monuments, security theory and,
    288
Historic sites, protection of, 8
Homing sequential switcher, 445-446, 489
Horizontal resolution, 489
Household art insurance, 41, 47, 166
Housekeeping, outdoor, 204
Housing, camera for 110 degrees FOV
    CCTV, 464
Housing, camera, 457-459
Human relations session, in sample syllabus
    for security officers, 703
HZ (hertz), 489

Identification, art work
    forgery of documentation in, 43
    insurance and, 774

law enforcement officials and, 768
    techniques of, 38-47, 506-508, 769-774,
        778
Identification Card, 502
Identification system, 502
Images (Camera), 435, 439, 455-456, 469,
    479
Impedance, 489
Indemnity Act, United States, 54
Independent contractors, 503
Indoor corner housing, 457
Indoor hallway surveillance, 463
Inflation, of art object value, 25
Information control, 134-137, 146-147,
    642-643, 652
Information processing, 285
Infraction alarm, 415
Infrared motion detectors (passive), 401
Infrared photoelectric beam detectors, 401
Infrared (IR) radiation, 360, 437
In-house training, 699-701, 737-739
Injuries, 728
    See also casualties
Inspection, 496, 557-558, 576-577
Insurance services office (ISO), 543-544,
    546-547
Intaglio process, 803-804
Integrated security, 288
Intensified silicon intensified target (ISIT)
    camera, 442
    tube, 439, 442, 489
Interlace, 489
Internal theft, 22, 345
International Association of Chiefs of Police,
    14
International Committee for Museum
    Security, 14
International Confederation of Art Dealers
    (CINOA), 746
International Council of Museums (ICOM),
    14, 747
International Foundation for Art Research
    (IFAR), 777, 780, 790
Interpol, 25, 39-47, 741, 789, 806
Interrogation, 790-795
Intervention, 285, 289
Intoxicated persons, 662
Intrusion alarm systems, 421-424, 496
Intrusion alarm systems, standards
    See standards, intrusion, detection/alarm
        systems
Intrusion detection systems

Intrusion detection systems (cont.)
  kinds of, 353-362, 382-383, 423-424,
    452-453
  standards
    See standards, intrusion detection/alarm
    systems
  use of, 13, 297-301, 383-387, 421-424, 479
Inventory, 508, 769-774, 783
Investment, art as, 35, 46
Ireland, 42
Iris, automatic, 436, 442-443, 486
Iris diaphragm, 464, 475-476, 489
Italy, 42, 44

Joint human and machine service, 286
Juveniles, 660, 791

Kennedy, John F., 28
Key control, 21, 499, 502, 527-535, 568
Keying systems, 532-533
Keys, 68
Kimball Art Museum, 23

Lamps, 437
Laser, 479
Latches, 168
Law enforcement, 7, 594-595, 768
Leadership, 129-130, 724
Leased/dedicated phone line, 367-368
Lens, 439-441, 455-456, 474-477
  bifocal optical image splitting, 462-463
  characteristics of, 428-435
  definition of, 428, 487, 489-490
  right angle, 456, 458
  tri split, 457, 463
Liability, 51-53, 594-595, 665-666, 728-729,
  798
Liaison, police, 86-87
Librarian, 98, 101
Libraries, 552-555
Library of Congress, 105
Library security checklist, 553-555
Light beams, 346
Lighting
  and conservation, 26
  as an electrical hazard, 178
  laser-illumination as source of, 479
  of scene covered by CCTV system camera,
    435-439
  and security, 521-526, 571
  technical aspects of, 436-437, 498-499,
    524-526, 571-572

Lighting systems, 523-528
Lightning, 196-197
Light threshold motion detectors, 402
Line amplifier, 490
Lithographs, 802-803
Litigation, 595, 601, 642
Loading, 584
Loading dock surveillance, 463-464
Loan exhibits, 52, 147, 343
Lobby camera location, 431
Local alarm signaling devices, 408-409
Local alarm system, 362-363
Locks
  and key control system, 12, 499, 530-535
  kinds of, 7, 166, 528-530
  and security, 529-532
Log, 291, 500
Long-range security plan, 293-294
Looping bridging sequential systems, 446
Looping homing sequential systems, 446
Loss limit, 51
Louvre, 27, 36-37, 42

McCulloh Loop, 368-371
McShane, Thomas, 780
Magnetic contact, 302
Magnetic contact switches, 346
Magnetic switches, 396-397
Magnification, 433, 441, 490
Mammoth Cave National Park, 6
Management techniques
  and communication, 86-89, 611-613
  and leadership, 67-91, 171, 610-617
  technical aspects of, 71-81, 89-91
Management training, 706-707
Manual active switcher, 445
Manual iris pinhole lenses, 471-473
Manual passive switcher, 445
Manual switcher, 443, 490
Manuscript thieves, 96
Marketing, 103, 128
Marking, 104
Mat switches, 400
Mechanical focus (vidicon, position), 431
Mechanical hazards, 197
Mechanical switches, 397
Media, 121, 142-145, 148, 585, 789
Media formats, 117
Media interviews, 141-142, 147-148
Media relations, 134-148, 153-161, 642
Medical assistance, 606-610
Memory chip, 365-366

Mentally disturbed persons, 660-662
Mercantile vaults, 549
Mercury switches, 346, 398
Mercury tilt switch, 361
Metropolitan Museum of Art, 23
Microfilming, 104
Microprocessors, 294
Microwave alarm system, 353
Microwave cavity, 356
Microwave detection, 350, 355-358
Microwave motion detectors, 403-404
Microwave transmission, 452-455
Middlemas, Keith, 25
Minicomputer, 294
Miranda law, 22
Misdeed detection, 284
Mixed media, 799
"Model Burglar and Holdup Alarm Business
    and User Statute." (International
    Association of Chiefs of Police), 374
Modified alert, 656
Modus operandi, 744
Mona Lisa, 27, 36-37
Money safes, 540-543
Monitors, 411-413, 428-431, 443, 446, 449
Motivation, 725-726
Moving art, 582-583
Moving firms, 583
Multiple authority, 68-69
Multiple camera CCTV systems, 460
Multiple pin tumblers, 499
Multiplexing networks, 368-371
Murphy's law, 198
Museum, 342
Museum archives, 159-161
Museum Association Security Committee, 14
Museum credibility, 136-140, 149, 780
Museum disaster planning, 246-252
Museum employee relations, 136-138,
    146-147, 156-159, 660
Museum expansion, 26
Museum of Natural History, 15
Museum patrons, 171
Museum personnel, 783, 792
Museum-police relations, 134-135
Museum property records, 13
Museum registrar, 88, 784
Museum research materials, 98
Mutilation, 287

Narrow angle lens, 455
National borders, 345

National Bureau of Standards, 7, 375
National Burglar and Fire Alarm
    Association, 7, 14, 375
National Crime Prevention Institute, 7, 14, 375
National Electrical Code (NFPA), 381, 387
National Fire Protection Association, 650
National Institute for Law Enforcement and
    Criminal Justice (NILECJ; now National
    Institute of Justice), 175, 374
National Institute of Justice (NIJ; formerly
    National Institute for Law Enforcement
    and Criminal Justice), 374
National Park Service, 3-9, 14, 373-374, 378
National Research Council of Canada, 165
Natural disasters, 13, 21, 237-238
Negligence, 53, 730-731
News coverage, 113, 115-116, 118-122,
    125, 145
News worthiness, 139-140
Newvicon target camera, 475
Newvicon tubes, 437-439, 490
Newvteon, 436
New York Times Magazine, 26
NFPA, 194
Night supervisor, 21
Non-profit organization, 120-121
Nordstern, 36
notice, theft, 775-778
Notification, personnel, 133, 135, 146,
    151-152
NTSC standard format, 490

Object protection, 344-345
Observation, 97
Occupancy/management relations, 171
Official representation, 719-720
Official statement, 134-138, 141-142, 155
Oil, 199
One camera/monitor CCTV systems, 428-431
110 degrees FOV CCTV, 463-465
Open time, 283-285
Open wiring, 388-389
Operating manual, 501
Optical dead zone, 461-462
Optical speed, 469
Optical splitter, 490
Orders, 639-640
Organizational needs, 700
Organizational weakness, 715
Orientation session, 701-703
Outdoor environmental camera housing,
    457-459

Overpainting, 39, 43

Package inspection, 660
Packing, 204, 582
Padlocks, 531, 574
Paintings, 346-353, 355
PAL format, 490
Panic bar, magnetically controlled, 352
Pan-tilt systems, 441, 449-455, 460-463, 490
Paper, 202
Parking, 498
Parking lot surveillance, 463
Park management, 15
Park Service
    See National Park Service
Park Superintendent, 11
Partial security system, 293
Passive alarm system, 361
Passive infrared alarm system, 307, 350, 353, 359-361
Passive infrared detection, 360-361
Pass system, 22
Patrol vehicles, 7
Pedestals, 346-353
Performance standard, 7
Perimeter protection, 463, 519-522
Perimeter security checklist, 521-522
Permanent Collection, 51-52
Permits, 498
Personnel turnover, 155-156
Photoelectric light beam, 305, 361
Photographs
    art reproductions and, 37
    as deterrents to art theft, 39
    in museum archives, 137
    theft reports and, 784
    use of
        in evidence collection, 784
        in identification of art works, 508, 772-774, 784
        in physical security planning, 567
        in public relations, 136-137, 147-148
Photo ID-CCTV access control, 481
Physical security, 5-7, 9-10, 14
    concept of, 297, 567
    specialist, 6, 10, 11, 14
    standards, 495, 496
    survey report, 10
Pinhole camera system, 467, 470-471, 490
Pinhole lens
    definition of, 490

fiber optic specifications for, 478
geometry of, 469-470
manual iris of, 471-473
misconceptions about, 467-469
Picasso Exhibition, 53-54
Picture frames, 583
Plumbicon, 490-491
Police, 71, 657-658, 749, 797-798
Police connected and central station alarm units, 413-414
Police powers, 707
Policies and procedures, 635-677
"Pop" formula, 700
Portable detection and transmission units, 293
Portable duress alarm initiating devices, 407
Portable microcentralizer, 290
Possible Maximum Loss, 506
Power sources for alarm systems, 383-384, 386-387, 525, 573
Premiums, 51-52, 55-56
Preservation, 27, 579
Press advisory, 138
Press conference, 125, 147-148
Press kits, 136, 144, 148
Press room, 153
Pressure points, 608-609
Preventive planning, 6, 8
Prints, 777-801
Probability ratings, 245
Probable Maximum Loss (PML), 51, 56, 504
Problem solving, 67-68
Processing electronics, 479
Product quality, alarm system, 382
Products of combustion devices, 407
Proper detection sensitivity, 416
Protection lighting system
    See Lighting system
Protection of assets, 19-20, 93
Public communication, 125
Public donors, 114
Public employee liability, 729
Public information officer (PIO)
    See Public relations director
Publicity, 112-114, 121, 128, 159
Public Library Act, 99
Public relations
    broadcasting and, 123
    children and, 660
    fundamentals of, 114
    as a game, 115

management of, 126
of museums, 131-161
security department and, 112, 113, 115,
    642-644
training of non-professional in, 111
writing style in, 112
Public relations communication, 111-112
Public relations department, 127
Public relations director, 127-128, 134-135,
    138, 142-143, 145-148, 152, 154, 157
Public relation firms, 157
Public relations program, 120
Public Relations Society of America, 113-114
Public service programming, 121, 123

Questioning
    See Interrogation

Radar detection
    See Microwave detection
Radiation resistance detection
    See Microwave detection
Radio communications, 119, 121, 123-124,
    144, 153
Radio transmission, 368-371
Random interlace, 491
Ransom, art work, 43
Rare books, 94
Real time CCTV transmission, 453
Real time duplex television, 451
Receiver, 350, 365
Receiver codes, 366
Receiving, 562
Record safes, 537-538
Recovery, stolen art work, 253, 775-778,
    805-806
Reflection, 470
Reinsurance, 36, 45-46
Rekeying, 533
Replacement, stolen art work, 54, 56
Reporting practices, 117, 142-145, 157
Reports, art theft, 784-790
Report writing, 599-601
Repository, See Library
Required time, 283
Resolution, image, 435
Respondent superior, doctrine of, 728
Restoration, art work, 56
Restraining devices, 666
RF (radio frequency) detection. See
    Microwave detection.

RF modulator, 441-442
Right angle lens, 456, 458, 473
Right angle pinhole camera, 469
Rigid fiber optic pinhole lenses, 475-476
Risk, 76-77, 165, 506-507
Risk analysis, 73-74, 78, 507-508, 557-558
Risk factors, 502, 507
Room surveillance, 463-464

Sabotage, 4
Safes, money, 537-541
Safety checklist, 601-602
Safety codes, 381
Safety patrols, 645-648
Salvage covers, 183
Screening process, 143-144, 713
Sculpture, 777, 804-805
SECAM, 491
Security
    components of, 557
    cost of, 89
    definition of, 3
    management role in, 73, 510
    theory of, 70, 95, 283-296, 593
    types of, 72, 559
    value of 73, 559
Security car drivers, 580
Security chief, 18, 19
    See also Security director; Security
        manager; Security supervisor
Security consultant, 14
Security containers, 574
Security controls, minimum, 495
Security deficiencies, 512
Security department
    conduct of, 636-639, 642-644
    internal communication of, 637
    objective of, 635-636, 715
    orders and, 639-640
    property and equipment of, 640-641
    public relations and, 642-644
    relations of, with other departments,
        68-69
    responsibilities of, 635-641
    supervision of, 641-642
    See also Security guards
Security director
    efficacy of, 713-714
    and personnel relations, 714, 716
    responsibilities of, 14, 21, 70, 291, 582
    and technology, 23

Security director (cont.)
  See also Security chief; Security manager;
    Security supervisor
Security equipment, 640-641, 647
Security firms, 735
Security guard companies, 592
Security guards, 591-617
  contract, 591-592
  duties of, 20, 81-82, 592-594, 627, 630,
    632, 645-666
  in-house, 591-592
  liabilities and, 594-595, 665-666, 733-738
  mission of, 591-593, 713
  motivation of, 713, 722-723
  personal qualities of, 18, 636-639, 642-644,
    648, 719, 720-721
  qualifications of, 598, 627, 631, 637,
    714-715
  safety and, 601-602, 647-648
  security awareness of, 501, 598-599
  training of, 81, 83, 595-598, 614
Security hardware, 12, 170
Security improvements, 512-513
Security inspection, 557
Security management, 285-288
Security manager
  and art transportation problems, 579
  collateral public relations duties of,
    112-113, 115-117, 701
  and stroking, 725
  See also Security chief; Security director;
    Security supervisor
Security manual, 680, 684, 688
Security orientation, 566
Security patrols, 645-648
Security planners, 72-73
Security posts, 644-645
Security problems, 8, 344-345
Security reports, 599-601
Security representative, 581
Security requirement studies, 288-289
Security reviews, 20
Security rooms, special, 500
Security supervisor
  employee relations and, 614-615, 616-617
  professional and personal qualifications of,
    613-614, 619, 624-625
  responsibilities of, 610-617, 619, 623-624,
    626, 641-642, 655, 690-691
  See also Security chief; Security director;
    Security manager

Security survey, 505-555
  communication in, 512
  conducting of, 511-512
  definition of, 511-512
  effectiveness evaluation of, 512
  method of, 73, 74
  use of, 11, 14, 552-555
Security survey report, 513-518, 637
Security systems
  for art works, 41-42, 46-47
  designing of, 508
  development of, 42
  electronic, 298
  importance of, 96
  limitations of, 54-55
  perimeter protection and, 519-522
Security vehicles, 580
Senior citizens, 792
Sensors, 394-407
Serigraph, 804
Shirar, Gerard, 27
Shock sensors, 348
Shoplifting, 100
Shunt switch, 394-395
Signal to noise ratio, 491
Sign-in, visitor, 658-660
Silent alarm system, 362-363
Silicon intensified target (SIT) camera, 442
Silicon intensified target (SIT) tube, 439
Silicon target, 436
Silicon target camera, 475
Silicon tube, 439, 491
Silk screen, 804
Simultaneous wide field and narrow field
  coverage, 455
Single system, 416
Sirens, 350, 408-409
Site and operation analysis, 289
Sliding windows, 167
Slow scan television, 491
Smithsonian Institution, 21-22
Smoke alarms, 657-658
Smoke detectors, 202, 209
Society of Illuminating Engineers, 499
Sonic detectors, 354, 402
Sound, 354
Sound sensing detectors (passive audio),
  402
Souvenir collectors, 345
Space protection, 305
Special Collection Departments, 95

Spherical dome camera housing, 457
Splices, 388
Spokesperson, 117, 125
Sprinkler systems, 218-220
Stair-way, 168
"Standard for Audible Signal Appliances"
    (UL), 408-409
"Standard for Capacitance Sensing Units for
    Intrusion Alarm Systems" (NILECJ), 401
"Standard for Combustion Products Type
    Smoke Detectors for Fire Protective
    Signaling Systems" (UL), 407
"Standard for Connectors and Switches for
    Use With Burglar Alarm Systems"
    (Underwriters Laboratory), 394, 397
"Standard for Hold-Up Alarm Units and
    Systems" (UL), 407
"Standard for Infrared Motion Sensors for
    Intrusion Alarm Systems" (NILECJ), 401
"Standard for Infrared Photo-electric Sensors
    for Intrusion Alarm System" (NILECJ),
    401
"Standard for Installation and Classification
    of Mercantile and Bank Burglar Alarm
    Systems" (UL), 398, 399, 402, 405
"Standard for Intrusion Detection Units"
    (UL), 401, 402, 403, 404, 405, 407
"Standard for Local Burglar Alarm Units
    and Systems" (UL), 408
"Standard for Magnetic Switches for Burglar
    Alarm Systems" (NILECJ), 397
"Standard for Mechanically Activated
    Switches for Burglar Alarm Systems"
    (NILECJ), 397, 407
"Standard for Metallic Window Foil for
    Intrusion Alarm Systems" (NIJ), 398
"Standard for Microphone Vibration Sensors
    for Intrusion Alarm Systems" (NILECJ),
    405
"Standard for Microwave Motion Detectors
    for Intrusion Alarm Systems" (NILECJ),
    404
"Standard for Police Station Connected
    Burglar Alarm Units and Systems" (UL),
    409
"Standard for Sound Sensing Units for
    Intrusion Alarm Systems" (NILECJ), 402,
    405
"Standard for Ultrasonic-Motion Detectors
    for Burglar Alarm Systems" (NILECJ),
    403

Standard Products, 382
Standards Intrusion detection alarm systems
    general provisions of, 381-382
    general technical requirements, 385-386
    planning and layout, 386-387
    purpose of, 378-381
    system philosophy, 382-386
    See also under name of type of intrusion
        detection/alarm system
Star of India, 19
STARP (Systeme de Teletransmission
    d'Alerter a Recepteurs Portatifs), 288,
    293, 295-296
State property, 36
Statistics, 509
Stolen Art Alert, 790
Storage areas, 13, 500
Structural fire, 259
Subrogation, 53
Surveillance, 27, 78, 344, 463, 584
    equipment, 20
    technician, 288
Switchboard operator, 133, 146-147, 153
Switcher, 431
Switch housing, 394-395
System reliability, 415-417
System Tests, 417-421

Tailgating, 483
Tamper protection, 384-385
Tamper switches, 385
Tandem vehicle arrangement, 580
Tape dialers, as alarm transmission system,
    363-365
Target, 491
Target-hardening, 510
Target voltage, 431
Telephone dialing and reporting devices,
    409-411
Telephone equipment, 147, 153
Telephone line connections, 363-368, 411,
    452-453
Telephone switching station, 451
Telephoto lenses, 439
Television, real time duplex, 451
Television coverage, 121, 123-124, 145
Television ID camera system, 481-483
Television snapshot, 455
Television transmission, slow scan, 455
Temporary displays, 189
Termination procedures, 566

"Terms and Definitions for Intrusion Alarm Systems" LESL-RPT-0305.00, (National Institute of Law Enforcement and Criminal Justice), 375
Terrorism, 21, 26, 42-43, 345, 581, 651
Theft alert, 654-656
Theft Notice Service, 777-778
Thermistor, 360
Thermocouple, 360
Time lapse recorders, 448
Training
  government mandates and, 596, 598
  methods of, 596-598, 614
  prescrvice, vicarious liability and, 735
  refresher course in, 7
  of volunteers, in public relations, 111
Training manual, 701
Training program, security guard, 18, 81, 501-502, 595-598, 614, 679, 700, 713
Training syllabus, 701-706
Transducers, 359-361
Transformers, 191-192
Transmission, alarm signal, 350, 362-371
Transmitter, 365
Transportation company, 581-582
Trash cans, 202
Triage, 254
Tri split lens, 457, 463
Trucks, 583, 584
Tubes, camera, 437-439
Tungsten iodine lamps, 437
Tunneling, 469

UHF (ultra high frequency), 491
UHF connector, 443, 449
Ultrasonic alarm system, 353
Ultrasonic detection, 356, 357, 358
Ultrasonic motion detectors, standards for, 402-403
Ultrasonic transmitter, 348-350
Ultrasonic/ultrasound, 354
Ultrasonic/ultrasound detectors, 354-355
Ultrasonic waves, 350, 355
U-matic, 491
Unbalanced cable, 491-492
Undercover operations, 795-798
Underinsurance, 41
Underwriters Laboratory, Inc., 7, 374, 375, 381
  safe classifications of, 541-543
  vault classifications of, 544-545
UNESCO, 18, 23, 756

Uniforms, 501
United Press International (UPI), 119
United States
  art insurance in, 44
  art theft in, 44, 54, 780, 806
  investigation of art theft in, 768, 775, 777, 778, 780, 806
United States code, 4
United States Indemnity Act, 54
University of Delaware, 7, 14
University of Minnesota, 7, 14
Utilities, 573

Valid alarm, 415
Valuation, art work, 40, 56, 788-789
Value, art, 35, 36, 40, 248, 775
Vandalism, 3-4, 354, 457
Vaults, 543-549
Vault wall equivalency tables, 548-549
Vendors, 498
Vertical deflection coils, 455, 473
Vertical resolution, 492
VHF (very high frequency), 492
VHS (Victor Home System), 492
Vibration sensors, 404-405
Vibrators, 348
Vicarious liability
  of administrators, 727-738
  areas of, 729-733
  definition of, 728
  preemployment background investigation and, 733-734
  training and, 734-736
Vicarious liability suits, 738
Video recorders, 448, 492
Video signal transmission, 449-455
Vidicon, 435, 492
Vidicon tubes, 437-438
Vignetting, 492
Virginia Library Act, 99-100
Visitors, 345, 564, 658-660
Visual aids, 124
Visually indicating alarm devices, 409
Volcanoes, 238
Volumetric alarms systems, 353-361
Vulnerability, crime, 512

Wall-mounted camera housing, 457
Wall-mounted television access control system, 483
"Wall to wall" insurance, 44, 52-53

Waste, 575
Water sprinkler system, 107
Weapons, 501, 708
Wide angle lenses, 439, 455
Wide FOV CCTV, 460-463
Wilson, O.W., 643
Windows, 167, 303-304
Winslow, Homer, 94
Wireless alarm systems, 346, 348-353
Wireless RF transmission system, 348

Wire mesh, 496
Wires, dedicated, 451
Wiring, alarm system, 386-391
Wiring hazards, 188
Witnesses, 782
Wood cuts, 801-802
Written communication skills, 719

Zero fire hazards, 180
Zoom lens, 435, 440-441, 492